PRAISE FOR *FORGING AMERICA*

"By placing American events in a global context, Steven Hahn has written a remarkably inclusive narrative. It puts people first, not government systems. It places working people and others on the periphery at the center of the story. The result is a refreshing and new interpretation of American history."

> **—Justin Behrend,** *The State University of New York, Geneseo*

"In *Forging America* Steven Hahn weaves a remarkable variety of threads into a lively, engaging, and challenging history of North America. Masterfully recapturing a sense of contingency, Hahn raises thought-provoking questions, offers insightful explanations, and illuminates a complex and multi-faceted story."

> **—Cara Shelly,** *Oakland University*

"Steven Hahn's *Forging America* has the appealing double-benefit of communicating to students the necessary information to understand America's history, while also prompting students to think like historians in their own right."

> **—John William Nelson,** *Texas Tech University*

"Many of our students now get their information through podcasts instead of print. The *Forging America* audiobook, with its professional narration and music, will help draw students into the reading and give them two ways to remember the material."

> **—Mary Lyons-Carmona,** *Metropolitan Community College*

About the Cover

Left. In 1837 the New Orleans artist François Fleischbein painted an unidentified woman of color wearing an elegant *tignon*, a type of headwrap still worn by women of African descent in Louisiana today. Delicate earrings, an elaborate lace collar, and a golden bow over a black frock complete the sitter's costume.

Right. This 1840 painting by an unknown artist depicts a New England textile merchant in his office. He is dressed in professional attire, writing a letter at his desk. The bolts of silk behind him suggest the importance of the China trade to his business.

Forging America

Forging America

A CONTINENTAL HISTORY
OF THE UNITED STATES

VOLUME ONE: TO 1877

Steven Hahn
New York University

OXFORD
UNIVERSITY PRESS

OXFORD
UNIVERSITY PRESS

Oxford University Press is a department of the University of Oxford.
It furthers the University's objective of excellence in research, scholarship,
and education by publishing worldwide. Oxford is a registered trade mark
of Oxford University Press in the UK and in certain other countries.

Published in the United States of America by Oxford University Press
198 Madison Avenue, New York, NY 10016, United States of America.

© 2024 by Oxford University Press

Library of Congress Cataloging-in-Publication Data
Names: Hahn, Steven, 1951- author.
Title: Forging America : a continental history of the United States /
   Steven Hahn, New York University.
Other titles: Continental history of the United States
Identifiers: LCCN 2023017322 (print) | LCCN 2023017323 (ebook) | ISBN
   9780197540190 (v. 1 ; paperback) | ISBN 9780197540206 (v. 2 ; paperback)
   | ISBN 9780197540251 (v. 1 ; epub) | ISBN 9780197540268 (v. 2 ; epub)
Subjects: LCSH: United States—History—Textbooks.
Classification: LCC E178.1 .H15 2024 (print) | LCC E178.1 (ebook) | DDC
   973—dc23/eng/20230419
LC record available at https://lccn.loc.gov/2023017322
LC ebook record available at https://lccn.loc.gov/2023017323

Printed by Quad/Graphics, Inc., Mexico

To history's students, who know that forging a just and humane

future demands a serious and honest encounter with the past

Brief Contents

Contents

CHAPTER **4** **Colonial Convulsions and Rebellions, 1640–1700** *127*

WHAT IF the Anti-Federalists Blocked Ratification of the Constitution?   **289**

PART THREE   Unmaking a Slaveholders' Republic

CHAPTER   **9**   **Expansion and Its Discontents, 1815–1840**   *339*

CHAPTER 10 Social Reform and the New Politics of Slavery, 1820–1840   *387*

CHAPTER **13** **A Slaveholders' Rebellion, 1856–1861** *523*

WHAT IF Lincoln Hadn't Won in 1860 or, as President, Had Hesitated on Fort Sumter? 557

WHAT IF Enslaved People Had Stayed Put? 603

PART FOUR   Industrial Society and Its Discontents

WHAT IF the Confederate Rebels Had Been Punished as Traitors?   **683**

Maps, Tables, and Figures

Maps

Tables

Figures

Features

Perspectives

Mapping America

Sources for *Forging America, Volume One: To 1877*

Edited by Alexandra E. Stern and Stefan Lund

The primary sources listed below are found in this volume's e-book as well as in the print and e-book companion sourcebook, *Sources for Forging America*.

Preface

Not long after I began to teach, I went to see a special exhibition of the works of Pablo Picasso. Picasso's art always spoke to me in powerful ways, with his use of color and his edgy depictions of objects and people. As a college freshman, I had a poster of his *Three Musicians* on the wall in my dorm room, and it remained with me for years. But this time, I looked at his paintings with the new eyes of a historian, and suddenly I had a much deeper understanding of what he was offering us. It was not simply his interpretation of a world in the throes of change and turmoil. It was also his attempt to have us see the world from multiple perspectives *simultaneously*, from the inside out as well as the outside in. Picasso was doing on a canvas what historians struggle to do in their research

≡ **Pablo Picasso, *Three Musicians* (1921)**

and writing; he was trying to capture the world in its many dimensions, recognizing that no single one of them could represent the truth.

Artists like Pablo Picasso have great license to represent their subjects and to invite us to look at the world as they do. Historians have more constraints. We need to base our representations of the past on the words and signs that people at many different times produce. But, like artists, we also learn very quickly that historical events are many layered and that historical actors have different understandings of what is happening. This is a challenge because it leaves us with few hard truths however deep we dig in the sources. Yet it is also exciting because we realize that all sorts of people—rich and poor, prominent and obscure, female and male—play roles in historical change, and because we recognize that history is a continuous process of discovery: and that we can be the discoverers.

A history of the United States is a daunting undertaking for readers and writers alike. It covers well over 400 years and involves people and places from all over the globe. It also requires that we transport ourselves into worlds very different than our own and try to see those worlds through the eyes of the people we study. It requires that we acknowledge the "pastness" of the past and do what we can to reckon with it. At the same time, we must also acknowledge the "presentness of the past," that the past is always living within us, is being carried by us even if we're not aware of it. "The past is never dead," a famous novelist once wrote. "It's not even past." History is our companion and our teacher. History is a way of learning and thinking. History is something we cannot escape nor should we want to.

I wrote *Forging America: A Continental History of the United States* because, after many years of teaching and writing, I thought that there might be a way to envision US history that speaks both to the complexities of historical experience and to the meanings of the past for our present-day lives. And I've come to think that *perspectives* of many sorts can be the key. There can be perspectives on geography, social class or status, race and ethnicity, gender and sexuality. There can also be perspectives about power and how power is wielded, about how those who are empowered and those who are subject to power view their relationships. Perspectives are about the vantage points we choose to take and from which we make historical narratives. Should we, for example, approach the colonization of North America from the point of view of Europe and the settler-colonizers or should we approach it from the point of view of North America and the Indigenous peoples who already resided there? Or, Picasso-like, should we view colonization from both perspectives simultaneously? Should we accept the label of "Civil War" to capture the brutal conflagration that erupted between 1861 and 1865, suggesting as it does a struggle between parties with comparable perspectives and political standing; or, Picasso-like, should we speak of a "War of the Rebellion" because it captures, simultaneously, the view of the Lincoln administration, which regarded secession as a rebellion, and the view of rebel enslavers, who saw themselves rejecting the authority of the federal government in order to safeguard their slave system?

Perspectives are important springboards because they allow us to validate the ideas and experiences of many more people than usually find themselves in historical accounts. They remind us that people make history, and even if they do not get what they want or are defeated in their quests, we can see how they give shape to the outcomes. Perspectives are also important because they demand that we try to identify a very full range of human and social relationships—from household and home to the highest levels of the state—and explore how power operates within and between those relationships. In fact, perspectives do not simply permit us to gain a fuller and deeper sense of how social relationships and power operate: perspectives are relationships and forms of power. In the most basic sense, power is getting people to do what you want them to do whether they want to or not, and power reveals itself in who controls the wealth, who works for whom, who can enjoy life's opportunities. But power is also about whose ideas and values and interpretations gain support, about whose notion of the public good is validated, whose construction of gender and sexuality is privileged, whose vision of what is beautiful and ugly or of what are acceptable or unacceptable aspirations come to prevail. In short, power is about whose perspectives are privileged, consulted, and spread about and whose are not.

Forging America uses multiple and shifting perspectives to narrate the history of the United States and to focus the readers' attentions on those moments when historical change occurs. In effect, we tell the story from the inside out as well as the outside in, from the West to the East as well as the East to the West, from the South to the North as well as the North to the South, and from below to above as well as above to below. In order to do this, we use a number of distinctive methods and devices:

Geography

Histories of the United States generally move from Europe and the Atlantic westward. They usually begin with an Atlantic world taking shape in the fifteenth and sixteenth centuries as a context for the European colonization of North America and its eastern interior. The Pacific and its world appear much later in the story and as a product of American "expansion" and "conquest." *Forging America* does something different. We start from Asia and the Pacific, China in particular, and thereby make the Pacific world as much a part of United States history as the Atlantic world has been. After all, China was the globe's greatest empire during the fifteenth and sixteenth centuries, and both the Pacific and trans-Mississippi West produced formidable societies and empires in their own right. *Forging America* is the story of the collision of these powers and how the collision transformed everyone, sometimes in unexpected ways. Emphasizing the Pacific also helps explain why leaders of the early American republic saw the country's destiny as taking hold of the Pacific coast, why the question of slavery's fate in the American West proved so convulsive, why the search for foreign markets in the late nineteenth century looked to East Asia, why American entry into World War II was triggered by a Japanese attack on Pearl Harbor in the Hawaiian Islands, and why the United States became embroiled militarily in Vietnam during the 1960s. *Forging America*, logically, ends with the reemergence of China on the world stage as the new and leading rival of the United States.

The maps in *Forging America* support the book's multifocal approach to geography. Textbooks usually follow standard geographical conventions in their depiction of events and developments, and many of the maps in *Forging America* will be familiar to most readers. But *Forging America* breaks from convention by striving, whenever possible, to map continuity and change from the perspectives of the people who lived through them. Instead of relying exclusively on standard projections that show the United States with an east-west and north-south orientation, some maps in *Forging America* show events from a south-north or west-east perspective. For example, when discussing the borderlands of the Southwest, maps that show a south-north view better reflect the experiences of local peoples than ones that take a north-south orientation. In addition, each chapter includes a "Mapping America" feature that juxtaposes two different ways cartographers might document the same event or development. For instance, the "Mapping America" feature in Chapter 11 (which looks at the 1830s and 1840s) contrasts a standard view of westward expansion with one that offers a different spatial geography, namely, a view from a Comanche perspective.

Visuality

Perspectives can be presented in written form, but they also appear visually in paintings, displays, parades, demonstrations, protests, cartoons, and ceremonies. Eventually they appear in photographs and film. *Forging America* uses a variety of images to convey the substance and meaning of differing perspectives. Maps and charts are especially interesting because they help us understand how people envisioned the world around them: do they focus on changes in the land, on the flora and fauna? Do they focus on borders and boundaries that are imposed by those in power? Do they focus on the groups of people who populate the landscape? Do they focus on the ways that people gain their subsistence and engage in trade? These are the many ways in which we can attempt to capture different perspectives and suggest how those who are long gone *saw* themselves and their societies. To give students opportunities to engage visually with different perspectives, each chapter in *Forging America* offers a "Perspectives" feature that compares multiple images. For example, Chapter 15 pairs two images that contrast the different ways the Civil War was remembered by the North and South. By asking students to consider different ways of looking at the same event or place—as well as to consider the audience for, and purpose of, the arguments made by visual sources—the "Perspectives" features encourage visual literacy as well as historical thinking.

Contingency

Many people assume that history is pretty much preordained. They assume that what happened in the past was destined to have happened, that alternative outcomes were extremely unlikely to have occurred. Yet those who lived at times when important historical events took place did not themselves know what the outcome would be; after all, we don't know how the challenges we face will play out. One of the important themes of *Forging America* that relates to the issue of perspective is the contingency of history: the idea that at any one point several outcomes may be possible, and a confluence of events—some personal decisions, some impersonal forces—usually determines what happens in the end. This is not, of course, to say that anything is possible. Far from it. Contexts limit the range of possibilities and do make certain outcomes more likely than others. Yet highly unexpected developments such as a major storm, a chance encounter, or a small error of judgment can shift history's balances in one direction or another and, in some cases, have huge repercussions.

What If?

To bring added emphasis to the phenomenon of contingency, *Forging America* has another distinctive feature. Every chapter ends with a "What If?" section: an alternative outcome accompanied by original source materials that bear on the case for students to consider, discuss, and debate. The purpose is not to construct a parallel universe of history-making but rather to sharpen students' perspectives on the past and the questions they ask of it. The alternative outcomes are not far-fetched; they reflect the specific struggles and ideas of that moment, and they are the sort of things that observers at the time and scholars since have speculated about. In Volume One, the "What If?" feature for Chapter 8 looks at what the consequences might have been if the slave rebellion on Saint Domingue/Haiti had been defeated. In Volume Two, Chapter 29 explores the different trajectory that might have unfolded for the United States if 9/11 had never happened.

As Americans struggle over how to envision and construct their future, history is more than ever at the center of their discussions and concerns. History is continuously invoked to frame political debates, to fashion public policy, to consider the nature of American identity, and to decide what is taught in our schools. This has not made the process easier; if anything, it has shown that historical interpretation is no less contested than our politics. But the process also suggests that historical thinking and understanding are crucial resources for all of us. They not only offer critical perspectives on the relation of past and present; they are our best defenses against manipulation and repression. The ambition of this textbook is to promote the historical thinking and understanding we so desperately need.

Digital Learning Resources for *Forging America*

Oxford University Press offers instructors and students digital learning resources that increase student engagement and optimize the classroom teaching experience.

Enhanced E-book

The enhanced e-book delivers learning experiences that empower students to actively engage in course content. It includes an integrated audio book narrated by professional actors, "What If?" videos, "Check Your Understanding" assessments, and note-taking guides. The enhanced e-book also includes all of the primary sources from the two-volume sourcebook (see page xxxi for the list of sources), a significant savings for students. E-books are available for purchase directly at www.oup.com as well as at Vital Source, RedShelf, Perusall, and other vendors.

Oxford Learning Link (OLL)

The online resource center www.learninglink.oup.com is available to adopters of *Forging America*, and it offers a test-item file, a computerized test bank, an instructor's resource manual, quizzes, PowerPoint slides, videos, handouts, and primary sources. The digital learning resources for *Forging America* can be embedded directly in an LMS via a one-time course integration, or instructors may choose to assign the resources in OUP's user-friendly, cloud-based platform.

Acknowledgments

Writing a book such as this is a lengthy process that depends upon the help, comments, and criticisms of many people. Some are historians and instructors of history who have been asked for responses to many of the chapters, but who have submitted them in a way that remained anonymous to me. Therefore, since I can't thank them individually, I'd like to offer my thanks to them collectively for their insights, judgments, and sometimes dissatisfactions. These were not always easy to read, but together they improved the book in organization, style, and substance. Nonetheless, a number of friends who were not anonymous agreed to review sections of the book, and their reactions and ideas have been invaluable. My sincere thanks go to Greg Downs, Rachel Klein, Jonathan Prude, and Amy Dru Stanley.

I also benefitted from the extraordinary resources of the Huntington Library, where I was a Rogers Fellow for the 2016–2017 academic year, and where I wrote a great deal of the first draft. Special thanks to Steve Hindle and Roy Ritchie of the Huntington Library and fellows John Demos, Woody Holton, Scott Heerman, and Beth Sayler.

Charles Cavaliere of Oxford University Press has been a remarkable editor. A close student of American and European history in his own right, he has been insightful, encouraging, demanding when necessary, and committed to the project I was hoping to complete. I could not have asked for more wisdom or textbook sense. At Oxford, too, I was helped in important ways by Meg Botteon, Elizabeth M. Welch, Ann West, Sukwinder Kaur, Julia Wray, Nicholas Ashman, Stefan Lund, Sheryl Adams, and by fact-checker Hannah Craddock. Copyeditor Leslie Anglin polished my prose and Senior Production Editor Cheryl Loe juggled with great dexterity a schedule that was both compressed and complex. I also thank Samara Naeymi at Brick Shop Studio for coordinating the production of the audio book.

Forging America took shape over quite a number of years, more than I had initially expected, and the process necessarily takes a toll on loved ones surrounding you. I would like to offer a special thanks to my partner, Susan Wishingrad, and my—now grown—children, Declan and Saoirse, for putting up with my writing obsessions and, most important, for reading much of the book manuscript and discussing it with me. I know they share my pleasure in finally seeing it done.

The book's dedication is a measure of the crisis our society faces and the importance of history teaching, learning, and thinking to any positive resolutions that may be found. History has come to the forefront of contemporary political struggles, and their outcome will determine whose values will prevail, whose vision of the future will guide us, and who will wield power and how. History instructors at all educational levels are embattled if not outright threatened in their efforts to help us understand worlds very different than our own as well as recognize how the past resonates in our daily lives. Their determination is inspiring and we must do our best to stand with them.

Expert Reviewers

Justin Behrend	SUNY Geneseo
William Bolt	Francis Marion University
Kyle Bulthuis	Utah State University
Kevin D. Butler	University of Arkansas at Pine Bluff
Mylynka Cardona	Texas A&M University—Commerce
Brad Cartwright	University of Texas at El Paso
Colt Chaney	Tyler Junior College
Christopher Childers	Pittsburg State University
Dawn Ciofoletti	Florida Gulf Coast University
Michael Leonard Cox	San Diego Mesa College
Christine Dee	Fitchburg State University
Brian Dempsey	University of North Alabama
Gregory P. Downs	University of California, Davis
Jeff Ewen	Ivy Tech Community College
Joshua Farrington	Bluegrass Community and Technical College
Andre Fleche	Castleton State University
Jeffrey Fortney	Florida Gulf Coast University
Alison Gough	Hawaii Pacific University
Jennifer Grohol	Bakersfield College
Evan Haefeli	Texas A&M University
Ian Hartman	University of Alaska Anchorage
David Head	University of Central Florida
Kenneth Heineman	Angelo State University
Jennifer Heth	Tarrant County College
Karlos K. Hill	University of Oklahoma
Brady L. Holley	Middle Tennessee State University

Michael Holm	Boston University
Maya Lisa Holzman	Oregon State University–Cascades
James Hrdlicka	Arizona State University
Katherine Jenkins	College of Charleston
Benjamin Johnson	Loyola University Chicago
Katherine Johnson	Montana State University
Sarah Keyes	University of Nevada, Reno
Rachel Klein	UC San Diego
Gary Lee	Georgia State University–Perimeter College
Leslie Leighton	Georgia State University
Lawrence M. Lipin	Pacific University
George Lloyd Johnson	Campbell University
Camilo Lund-Montaño	Whitman College
Mary Lyons-Carmona	Metro Community College
Scott C. Martin	Bowling Green State University
Thomas Massey	Cape Fear Community College
Lindsay Maxwell	Florida International University
Daniel Murphree	University of Central Florida
Jennifer M. Murray	Oklahoma State University
Sarah Naramore	Northwest Missouri State University
Benjamin Park	Sam Houston State University
Robert Parkinson	Binghamton University
Brian Peterson	Shasta College
Christopher Pieczynski	Tidewater Community College
Jonathan Prude	Emory University
Ansley Quiros	University of North Alabama
Mervyn Roberts	Central Texas College
Sarah Robey	Idaho State University
Joseph A. Rodriguez	University of Wisconsin–Milwaukee
Cara Shelly	Oakland University
Suzanne E. Smith	George Mason University
Robert S. Smith	Marquette University

Marie Stango	Idaho State University
Amy Dru Stanley	University of Chicago
Rowan Steineker	Florida Gulf Coast University
Michael Stout	University of Texas at Arlington
Tom Summerhill	Michigan State University
Julie Anne Sweet	Baylor University
Matthijs Tieleman	Arizona State University
Evan Turiano	Queens College, CUNY
Felicity Turner	Georgia Southern University
Felicia Viator	San Francisco State University
Robert Voss	Northwest Missouri State University
William Wantland	Mount Vernon Nazarene University
Jamin Wells	University of West Florida
John William Nelson	Texas Tech University
Lee B. Wilson	Clemson University
Jonathan Wilson	Rowan University
Thomas Wirth	SUNY Cortland

About the Author

Steven Hahn earned his BA at the University of Rochester and his MA and PhD at Yale University. He is a specialist on the social and political history of the nineteenth-century United States, on the history of the American South, on slavery, emancipation, and race, and on the development of American empire on the North American continent, in the Western Hemisphere, and in the Pacific world. His books include the Pulitzer Prize–winning *A Nation Under Our Feet: Black Political Struggles in the Rural South from Slavery to the Great Migration* (2003); *The Political Worlds of Slavery and Freedom* (2009); *A Nation Without Borders: The United States and Its World in an Age of Civil Wars, 1830–1910* (2016); and most recently, *Illiberal America: A History* (2024).

Hahn has held fellowships from the John Simon Guggenheim Foundation, the National Endowment for the Humanities, the American Council of Learned Societies, the Center for Advanced Study in the Behavioral Sciences at Stanford, and the Cullman Center for Scholars and Writers of the New York Public Library. He has taught at the University of Delaware, the University of California San Diego, Northwestern University, and the University of Pennsylvania, and is currently Professor of History at New York University, where he is also actively involved in the NYU Prison Education Program.

Forging America

1

Beginnings
To 1519

Chapter Outline

≡ **Panther man**   Sometime between 700 and 1500 CE a Native American artist on Key Marco, an island off the southwest coast of Florida, carved this feline-human figurine using shell scrapers and a shark's tooth. Panthers are native to Florida, and the Indigenous people of southeastern North America include in their oral histories the concept of a world order kept in balance by Underwater Panthers, rulers of the watery Lower World. It is unknown who the inhabitants of Key Marco were in 700, but by 1500 the island was part of the domain of the Calusa peoples.

Where does a history of the United States begin? It's a good question and not an easy one to answer. Truth is, there is no *one* answer—certainly no *correct* answer—to the question, and that is because of the fundamental nature of history writing itself. History writing is about uncovering and making meaning of the past, about offering perspective on and order to events that themselves can resist ordering or move into and out of focus.

Think about the world in which you live. On any one day, an enormous number of things happen close to home and around the world. If you were writing a "history" of this one day, you would have to decide what to include and what not to include, what was significant and what was insignificant. Choices such as these are interpretive; they reflect your view of how the world works and what is important, who the important actors are, and where the important decisions are made. You would also have to decide who to listen to—which commentators, media sites, or observers offer the clearest

Timeline

30,000 BCE	20,000	10,000	1 CE	200	400	600	800	1000

23,000–11,000 BCE ▸ Traditional dates for the start of the migration of peoples from northeast Asia to North America

11,500–11,000 BCE ▸ Clovis people in current-day New Mexico establish a settlement

7000 BCE ▸ Northeastern Asian migrants reach southern tip of South America

1500 BCE ▸ Beginning of sedentary agriculture in the Western Hemisphere, with cultivation in central Mexico of corn, squash, and beans

250 CE ▸ Beginning of classic Maya era in present-day Mexico

700 CE ▸ Evidence of Cahokia civilization near present-day St. Louis

850 CE ▸ Evidence of Chaco Canyon culture in present-day Southwest

and most reliable information and analysis. And if someone else were also writing a history of this one day, you should not be surprised to learn that it would be very different from yours: that person would discuss events that you ignored, developments you found inconsequential, people you overlooked.

This is the stuff of history writing on a large, as well as a small, scale; this is what historians do. Because history writing and history learning are first and foremost interpretive undertakings. They are about perspective: the perspective of the material studied together with that of the historian. We reach back into the past, study it as fully as we can, try to understand the world as people at the time might have understood it, put together a story—a narrative—about how they lived, worked, and struggled, about what they dreamed and feared, and, of course, about how they did or did not change their societies and communities. But we also discover that there is a lot we cannot really "know." Everything we learn about the past comes to us from people who had

1250 CE	1300	1350	1400	1450	1500	1550	1600

1271 CE ▸ Founding of Yuan Dynasty in China

1300 CE ▸ Beginning of "Little Ice Age," which lasts until about 1850; founding of Oyo Empire in western Africa

1325 CE ▸ Founding of Tenochtitlan by Mexica peoples (Aztecs) near present-day Mexico City

1337–1453 CE ▸ Hundred Years' War scorches continental Europe

1346–1353 CE ▸ Bubonic plague (Black Death) ravages Eurasia

1368 CE ▸ Beginning of Ming Dynasty and Empire

1390 CE ▸ Founding of Kingdom of Kongo in west-central Africa

1492 CE ▸ First voyage of Christopher Columbus lands in what he calls "Espanola" (Hispaniola), later known as Santo Domingo and then the Dominican Republic

1519 CE ▸ Beginning of Spanish conquest of Central and South America

their own points of view, their own perspectives, and were making their own assessments of what was going on around them. They were letter writers, diarists, political figures, newspaper reporters, census takers, administrators, clerics, missionaries, police officers, judges, and artists of many sorts. For centuries, most were men. Some may have been well-to-do, educated, and worldly; some may have been poor or in humble circumstances, uneducated, and parochial. They will tell us different things. Who do we believe? What was really going on? What is the "truth?"

Historians evaluate as much evidence as they can and try to find the historical narrative that makes the most sense—one that is empirically valid (we know where the evidence comes from) and interpretively persuasive (the pieces fit together logically). Sometimes fellow historians are mostly persuaded and happily go along with the narrative. But more often than not, fellow historians are not fully persuaded, and they argue with one another over matters large and small. History writing and learning is about engagement and argument, and we hope that in the process of arguing—of disagreeing over what questions are asked, how a story is put together, and what conclusions are to be reached—we can discover more and more about and get closer and closer to the world we are examining.

1.1   Conceiving a History of the United States

||| Describe how the concept of historical interpretation shapes the writing of history.

Studying history is a bit like sitting on a jury in a courtroom. Let's say that two automobiles collide at an intersection and one driver sues the other. The case goes to trial. There are four witnesses, each of whom was standing on a different corner at the intersection. Each one is called to the witness stand, and each one tells a slightly different story about what "happened," about who did or didn't run the red light, about who was or wasn't driving too fast. As a juror, you have sworn to determine the truth just as each witness has sworn to tell the truth.

But what is the truth? What did happen? Conscientious as you are, you try to weigh all the evidence. Which of the witnesses was most believable and why? Does it have anything to do with their accents, their vocabularies, how they were dressed, their racial or ethnic features, or how they told their story? Perhaps one account is so clear that all members of the jury agree and easily reach a verdict. Perhaps jurors spend hours arguing before finally agreeing. Or perhaps they simply can't reach a unanimous agreement and the judge declares a mistrial.

Where and how a historian begins a history tells us important things about the interpretive direction of the work, about how to read and make sense of it. What does that mean? For a long time, histories of the United States began with European conquerors and settlers who arrived in the Americas sometime between the late fifteenth and early seventeenth centuries: with ambitious men like Christopher Columbus who found his way to the Caribbean Island that he called "Espanola" (Hispaniola, "Little Spain"), or with Spanish conquerors and explorers like Hernán Cortés, Hernando de Soto, and Francisco Vázquez de Coronado, or with the British men and women who settled Roanoke Island, Jamestown, and Plymouth. Such beginnings suggest that the Europeans were the most important actors, the movers and shakers, and that the peoples they encountered in the Americas did not count all that much in the unfolding story.

Eventually historians recognized—thanks largely to the work of archaeologists and anthropologists—that the Western Hemisphere was populated by millions of people who had lived there for thousands of years and who had built a wide variety of societies and civilizations, some developing into substantial empires. (An empire, defined broadly, is a political entity or unit composed of a number of different territories or states and peoples within them, usually the result of military conquest, in which there is a dominant center or state to which the territories or dominated states owe allegiance or tribute.) They recognized, in short, that Europeans didn't "discover" these lands but rather met up with Indigenous peoples who spoke

≡ **The Traces They Left**   Petroglyphs, or rock carvings, across the Western Hemisphere attest to the presence of thriving cultures thousands of years before the arrival of Europeans. At Mesa Verde National Park in Colorado (*left*), petroglyphs depict the clans of Ancestral Puebloans (Anasazi) as well as a *sipapu*, a double-spiral sign representing the place where Pueblo people believe they originally emerged from the earth. At Caurita, on the island of Trinidad, petroglyphs carved by the Taino (Arawak) people c. 1000–1500 CE (*right*) may also represent ancestors or spirits.

many different languages, subsisted in many different ways, practiced many different religions, and had a profound impact on what would happen when and after they all met. Indigenous peoples were also movers and shakers, and so these histories would sensibly begin with the first of them to cross over into the Western Hemisphere (from northeastern Asia we believe), migrate down through North, Central, and South America, and learn how to survive and thrive much as peoples who found their way to western Europe (after moving out of Africa and across the Mediterranean) had done.

Most recently, historians have devoted growing attention to a very broad "Atlantic world," encapsulating Europe, the Americas, and western Africa, that had been developing in similar and dissimilar ways before they came into "contact" and, as a result, changed everything and everybody. Such an approach—such a beginning—reflects a view that what became the United States was deeply influenced by a host of important actors, in a large number of places, often at great distances from one another, and composing social organizations of many types.

This is a view that is both challenging and satisfying. It envisions complex and often searing encounters, cultural and empirical battles, shifting political dynamics on large stages, and historical outcomes that were not preordained. And the book you are reading appreciates and takes account of such a perspective and approach. But for reasons that I hope will become apparent, we are beginning in a very different place with very different encounters and dynamics: we are beginning in China of the sixteenth century, far across another great ocean and a place that is usually left out of our history until nearly three centuries later.

1.2   Looking East Across the Pacific

‖‖‖ Recognize that societies in different parts of the globe were already in contact before Europeans reached the Western Hemisphere.

China is customarily portrayed by historians of Europe and the Americas as something of a sleepy and relatively backward giant, some of whose riches of silk, cloth, porcelain, spices, and tea were first encountered by European traders and missionaries as early as the thirteenth century. The famed Marco Polo, a merchant from Venice who wrote *The Travels of Marco Polo*, was one of them. But, by and large, the picture we get is of a rural, inward-looking society that remained pretty much outside the developing world economy until the nineteenth century—and only then was dragged in, chiefly by the British and the Americans (we'll get to that). As it turns out, this perspective is extremely inaccurate.

Ming China and Its Asian Empire

By the sixteenth century, China was the most formidable and unified empire in the world. Its powerful dynastic rulers were known as the Ming, and they had ruled since the latter half of the fourteenth century. Ming China boasted a wide-ranging and highly educated bureaucracy, very productive peasant agriculture, growing cities and towns, artisans and merchants whose wares and activities were known across the globe, a military able to ward off invasions from several different directions, and tributary clients (states that effectively paid the Ming for their protection and trade) extending around southeast Asia.

Especially remarkable was the extent and diversity of the **Ming Empire**, which covered a huge and multiethnic territory across much of Asia. To the west in Ming China, the physical terrain included great mountain ranges, high plateaus, and expansive deserts. To the south, lower mountain ranges and rolling hills predominated. And to the east, where most of the people lived, extensive alluvial plains and river deltas—both especially good for agriculture—prevailed. Indeed, Ming China could claim more than 1,500 rivers, including the Yangtze ("Long River"), which flowed east from the Tibetan Plateau nearly 4,000 miles to the Yangtze delta on the sea, taking its place as the world's third longest river after the Nile and the Amazon. What's more, Ming China held at least one-quarter of the world's population (somewhere between 160 and 200 million), greater than all of the empires, states, kingdoms, and principalities of Europe combined. It was the world's demographic powerhouse and would remain so to this day (see Map 1.1).

The Ming emperor was regarded as all powerful (the "Son of Heaven"), and he ruled with the aid of a large bureaucracy staffed by men who had performed well on civil service exams. The bureaucrats, in turn, oversaw a number of ministries responsible for collecting taxes, dispensing justice, engaging in public works projects, and waging war. Key to the emperor's success and to the empire's stability was his complex relationship with the local elites and officials who held power in China's provinces and counties. Many of them were landlords and jealous of their prerogatives, not to mention of the revenues they could harvest from taxes on the peasants who worked the lands under their control. Agriculture was the basis of Ming society—as it was of the early modern world generally—and of the market towns that grew up along the rivers and deltas of eastern China. Peasants raised crops in the colder and hard-scrabble north and northeast, as well as in the paddies of the wet and warmer south.

Then, after 1570, China's wealth and power increased even more. That was because the highly valued metal, silver, began to flow in large quantities into its ports, fill the Ming treasury, and spur greater trade. What had happened? The silver was not being mined in China or anywhere else nearby. It was being mined in central

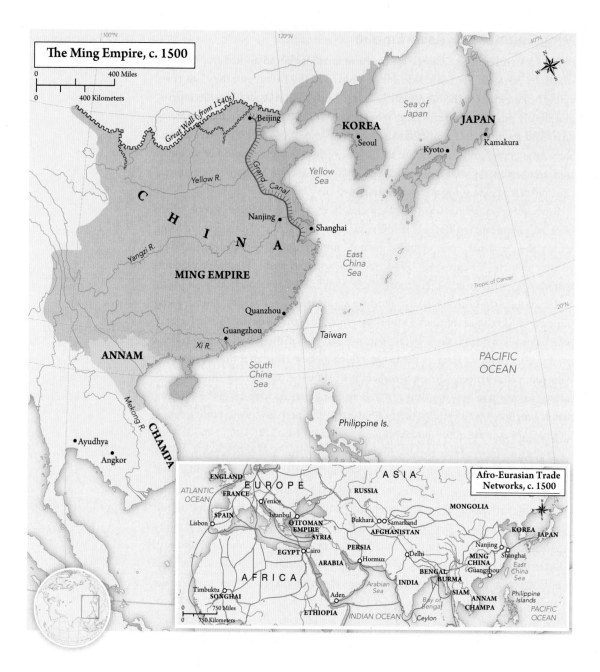

The Ming Empire, c. 1500

0   400 Miles

0   400 Kilometers

Great Wall (from 1540s)

Beijing

KOREA

Seoul

JAPAN

Kamakura

Sea of
Japan

Kyoto

Yellow R.

Grand Canal

Yellow
Sea

C H I N A

Nanjing

Shanghai

East
China
Sea

Yangzi R.

MING EMPIRE

Tropic of Cancer

Quanzhou

Guangzhou

Xi R.

Taiwan

PACIFIC
OCEAN

ANNAM

South
China
Sea

Mekong R.

CHAMPA

Philippine Is.

Ayudhya

Angkor

**Afro-Eurasian Trade
Networks, c. 1500**

ENGLAND

EUROPE

ASIA

ATLANTIC
OCEAN

FRANCE

RUSSIA

SPAIN

Venice

Istanbul

MONGOLIA

Lisbon

OTTOMAN
EMPIRE

Bukhara

Samarkand

KOREA

JAPAN

SYRIA

AFGHANISTAN

EGYPT

Cairo

PERSIA

Delhi

Nanjing

Shanghai

ARABIA

Hormuz

MING
CHINA

East
China
Sea

AFRICA

BENGAL

Guangzhou

BURMA

INDIA

Philippine
Islands

Timbuktu

SONGHAI

Arabian
Sea

SIAM

0   750 Miles

Aden

Bay of
Bengal

ANNAM

CHAMPA

PACIFIC
OCEAN

0   750 Kilometers

ETHIOPIA

INDIAN OCEAN

Ceylon

≡ **MAP 1.1   The Ming Empire, c. 1500**   Intensive agriculture and thriving trade made Ming China the world's
economic powerhouse.

Mexico (an area known as the Bajío) and in the South American Andes (especially
a place known as Potosí). From there, the silver was shipped across the Atlantic and
the Pacific, reaching China mainly through Manila, the chief city of the Philippines,
where Chinese merchants had been trading with the locals since the ninth century.

But the mines were not controlled either by the Chinese or any of the Indigenous peoples who lived in the Bajío or the Andes. The mines were controlled, instead, by *conquistadors*, or conquerors, who had come to the Western Hemisphere from Spain and had learned of the riches lying beneath the surface of the land and mountains. The Spanish conquest of Central and South America (discussed further in Chapter 2) began in 1519; by around 1570, the Spanish had taken control of Manila as well.

Spain Links the Pacific and Atlantic

The Spaniards originally traveled to the Western Hemisphere in search of the goods they could find in China and south Asia. They hoped that by sailing west across the Atlantic they could discover a sea route much shorter than the one to the east (down the coast of west Africa and around the Cape of Good Hope into the Indian Ocean) and certainly shorter than the overland routes that began in what we now call the Middle East and were mostly controlled by rival Muslims. They also were interested in converting Asians to Christianity, energized by the crusading spirit that had in 1492 pushed Muslims out of Spain, completing what is known as the *Reconquista* (Reconquest) of Spain. This same crusading spirit was still directed at Islamic rulers in the eastern Mediterranean (including Jerusalem), who had been under Christian attack since the eleventh century.

There can be no underestimating the force of religion for exploration and conquest; converting the "heathen" was regarded as a moral imperative for soldiers and sailors alike. But economic motives were certainly the other side of this imperial coin, and the Spanish were not new to the Atlantic. Since the fourteenth century they had been sailing west out of the Mediterranean and were soon establishing footholds on what are known as the Atlantic Islands: the Canaries, the Azores, and the Madeiras, where they would eventually set up colonies and grow wheat, grapes, and especially sugar. There, both the Spanish and the Portuguese (who were out in the Atlantic Islands, too, close as those islands were to Portugal) learned a great deal about colonial exploitation, outfitting ships, negotiating the ocean currents, deploying armed troops and their supplies, and carving out agricultural plantations meant to produce commodities for sale.

It was Christopher Columbus—an experienced mariner from the Italian port of Genoa, a student of Marco Polo's travels, and a fierce Catholic in faith—who managed to convince the recently united Spanish crown to support his journey farther west. He had already tried, without success, to interest the Portuguese, French, and English in the venture, and, as it turned out, he woefully underestimated the circumference of the world. But the Spanish monarchs, Ferdinand of Aragon and Isabella of Castile, knew well of the Atlantic Islands and figured Columbus would find something new like them. So, with the Reconquista just completed, they signed on and he sailed with three ships in 1492 (see Map 1.2).

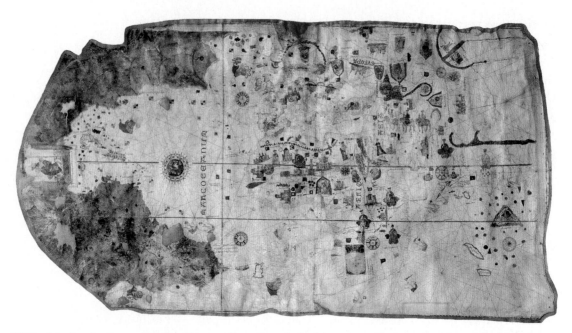

≡ **Envisioning the Known World** This portolan, or "port finder," chart created by Spanish explorer Juan de la Cosa in 1500 is typical of charts used by Spanish and Portuguese mariners beginning in the late fourteenth century.

After four months at sea, Columbus's expedition landed on the island he called Espanola (Hispaniola), but it wasn't in the East Indies as he had imagined. It was in the Caribbean Sea (named after the Indigenous people known as the Caribs, or Kalinago), and it would soon become both a site of Native exploitation and something of a springboard for further expeditions to the mainland of North, South, and Central America. Between 1519 and 1550, Spanish conquistadors subdued Native populations in what would become Mexico, Bolivia, and Peru, and after the discovery of gold and, especially, silver, they began large-scale mining operations in places they called Guanajuato, San Luis Potosí, Zacatecas, Parral, and Potosí. It was backbreaking and dangerous work, and for this the Spanish relied on the enslaved and otherwise coerced labor of the Indigenous peoples (see again Map 1.2).

1.3 Indigenous Peoples of the Western Hemisphere

‖‖‖ Explain the migrations that made possible the peopling of the Western Hemisphere, and identify the distinctive civilizations that arose in the Americas.

Who were these Indigenous peoples, and how were the Spanish able to enforce this type of submission? The Native or Indigenous populations (meaning populations who long occupied the Western Hemisphere) whom the Spanish encountered were among the most advanced people on the globe in the sixteenth century, although the societies they had built were relatively new at that time. Many readers may still have a sense of Native Americans as living in static, rather primitive communities—at least compared to Europeans. But this was hardly the case.

Asian Migrations

As best as we know—and admittedly we rely on fairly scattered, though fascinating, archaeological evidence—the first "Americans" arrived from northeastern Asia and Siberia perhaps as early as 23,000 years ago. Historians once believed that most, if not all, of them came across what is now the Bering Straits, a body of water, because much of the Northern Hemisphere was in an Ice Age that froze large sections of the Arctic oceans and allowed people to walk from what is now Asia to what is now Alaska. And, to be sure, this was an important route, aided eventually by a warming trend that began to melt the thick glaciers and open passageways through what is now western Canada. Little by little, some traveled farther south and east into the North American interior, and settled in what we now call the Southwest, most famously in "Clovis."

But it is now increasingly clear that there was an older, and possibly busier, route that hugged the Pacific coasts of North and South America and brought people along the shore in boats made of skins on what some have come to call a "kelp highway," rich in marine life that could sustain them in their travels. These coastal seafarers may have reached as far south as present-day Chile by 16,500 BCE, and, certainly by around 10,000 BCE (or 12,000 years ago), Indigenous peoples could be found from the northernmost reaches of North America to the southernmost tip of South America, a remarkable span of 8,000 miles.

Either way, for most of the next 5,000 or 6,000 years, Indigenous peoples throughout the Western Hemisphere relied mainly on hunting, fishing, and the gathering of fruits, nuts, and wild plants to subsist, which meant that they generally lived in small bands and were often on the move, though trading relations did develop among them. Then, sometime around 1500 BCE the Indigenous peoples of central Mexico—in part because of changes in climatic conditions that produced a warming trend—succeeded in growing three new and important food crops: maize (corn), squash, and beans. Together, these crops provided much of the nutrition that Indigenous peoples needed and many of the calories required for work and reproduction.

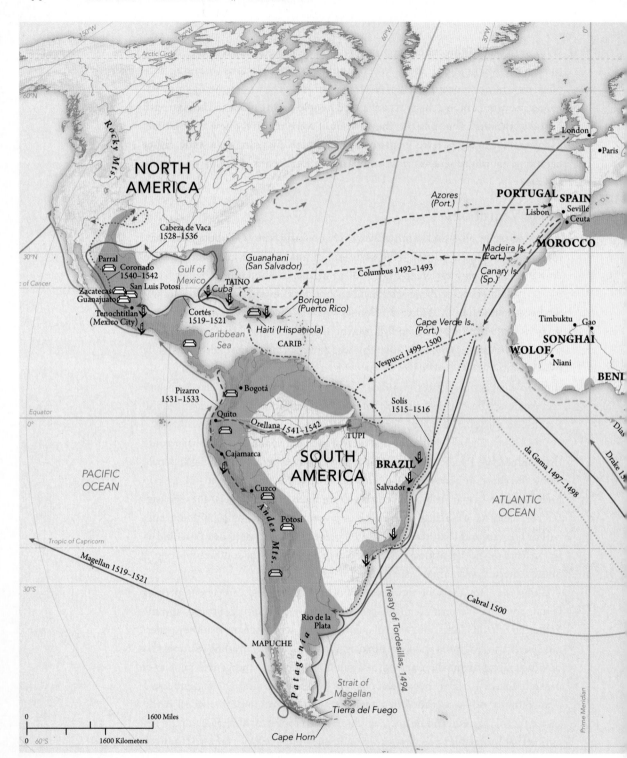

≡ **MAP 1.2   European Voyages of Discovery, c. 1420–1600**   In remarkably short time, the Portuguese and Spanish went from exploring the eastern Atlantic to circumnavigating the globe.

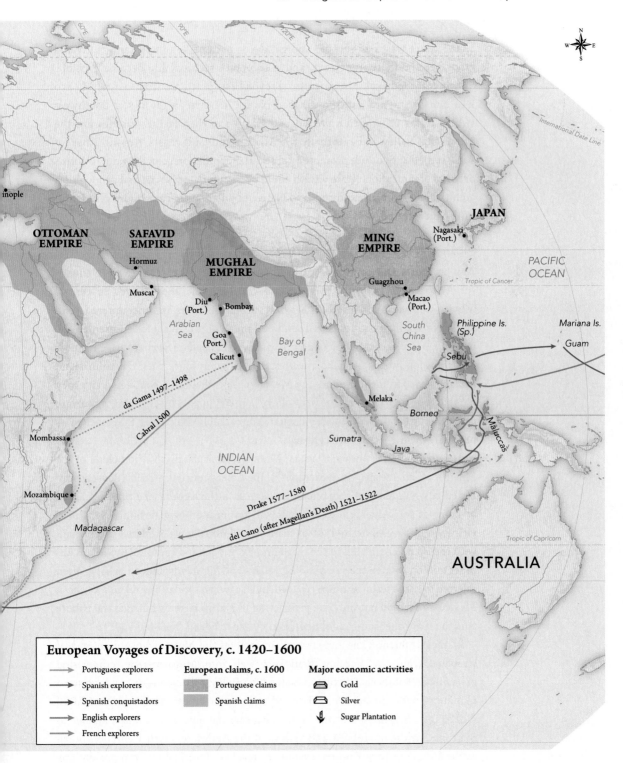

European Voyages of Discovery, c. 1420–1600

Portuguese explorers	European claims, c. 1600	Major economic activities
Spanish explorers	Portuguese claims	Gold
Spanish conquistadors	Spanish claims	Silver
English explorers		Sugar Plantation
French explorers		

The result was that hunting and gathering became less important, cultivated crops became more important, and a sedentary (settled) life became possible. Slowly, knowledge of this agricultural revolution spread out from central Mexico into North America and transformed Native life, first in the desert Southwest (where forms of irrigation proved necessary) and then farther east toward the Mississippi Valley and eventually the Atlantic and Gulf coasts. Among other results, settled agriculture promoted substantial population growth and new forms of social organization. More wealth could be accumulated, social and gender hierarchies grew more pronounced, and Native populations became more geographically concentrated.

Native Worlds of the Americas

Among those who continued to head south in the hemisphere were Nahuatl-speaking people known as **Mexicas** or Chichimecas. They arrived in central Mexico (the name derives from "Mexica") around 1325 CE and encountered a collection of small city-states that dominated much of the area and represented the descendants of earlier peoples and civilizations that had unraveled and re-formed. Searching for unoccupied land, the Mexicas ultimately found their way to an island in Lake Texcoco (near present-day Mexico City), where they founded a city they named **Tenochtitlan** ("cactus fruit place"). There, in part by engaging in warfare and building local alliances, they created a remarkable civilization that reached its height by the early sixteenth century.

The civilization is known to us as the Aztec, from the mythic homeland of the Mexicas called Aztlan ("place of cranes"). The Aztecs concentrated in a densely populated city—unquestionably one of the largest in the world at the time—marked by complex social hierarchies, hereditary elites, peasant-type farming in the near vicinity, and slave labor. By 1500 as many as 200,000 people lived in Tenochtitlan; with the island connected to the mainland by bridges and causeways, perhaps another million lived in the surrounding valleys and highlands. Indeed, what is often referred to as the **Aztec Empire** covered much of what is today central and southern Mexico and fed off not only the production of Native farmers but also the tribute paid them by other Indigenous peoples they had subdued (see Map 1.3).

In their influence, the Aztecs had superseded the **Maya**, whose domain had stretched from the Yucatan Peninsula well into Mesoamerica (comprising present-day southern Mexico, Guatemala, Belize, El Salvador, and western Honduras) between 250 and 900 CE and had boasted cities with as many as 50,000 inhabitants. But the era of the Aztec also saw the emergence, much farther to the south, in the mountains and valleys of the Andes, of another empire known as the Inca. The **Inca Empire** eventually reached, formidably, from present-day

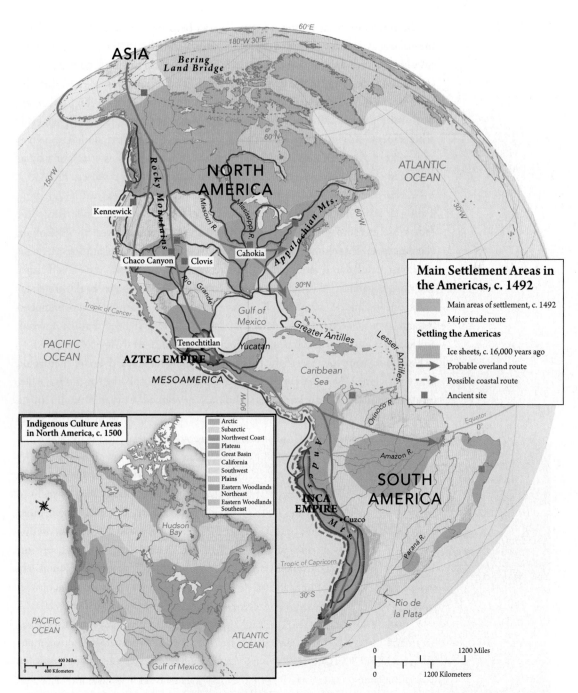

≡ **MAP 1.3   Main Settlement Areas in the Americas, c. 1492**   The most widely accepted theory about the peopling of the Western Hemisphere holds that migrants crossed into North America from northeastern Asia during the Ice Age.

southern Colombia to northern Chile—easily the largest geographically in all of the Americas—and used sophisticated political and administrative organization to hold sway militarily and to appropriate Native labor for raising food as well as for constructing roads, bridges, irrigation projects, and religious sites, especially difficult work given the steep altitudes (the peaks of the Andes rise as high as 23,000 feet). With their architectural sophistication, craft and artisanal skills, scientific achievements (including calendars, numeric systems, medicine, and astronomy), and military prowess, these Mesoamerican and Andean peoples were every bit as advanced—and likely more so—than their European contemporaries.

No Native civilization of North America ever compared—not in wealth, scale, population, or economic complexity—to those of Mesoamerica and the Andes. But some came close and bore resemblance. In the desert areas of the Southwest, the **Hohokam** and **Ancestral Puebloan** (Anasazi) peoples lived in villages and some larger towns and constructed dams, reservoirs, and canals to enable the production of food crops. They also began to build adobe row houses and "great" houses that could stretch for miles; one in Chaco Canyon may have had 650 rooms, an enormous feat of engineering and labor that likely required the use of slaves. Roads extended for miles around, and archaeological excavations suggest some trade with central Mexico.

Even more impressive were the Mississippian cultures along the river that would bear their name. The largest of them was a complex just across the Mississippi River from present-day St. Louis, known as **Cahokia**. It developed between 700 and 1100 CE and, at its height, as many as 20,000 people (about the population of New York City at the time of the American Revolution) may have lived there. But there were other substantial towns as well—mirroring the sort of "urban" impulses found in central Mexico—each with plazas and earthen pyramids, or "mounds," which served as ceremonial sites for religious rituals and were probably built with the aid of, if not entirely by, coerced labor. Conflict between Native groups was nearly constant,

≡ **The City on the Plains**   Cahokia in what is now Illinois was the largest Mississippian site and boasted over 100 earthen mounds. This aerial view shows the most massive of the surviving mounds.

and as in central Mexico, these towns were likely supplied with food by surrounding Native villages that may have been conquered or owed tribute (see again Map 1.3).

Although the Aztec and Inca empires were especially robust at the time of their contact with Spanish conquistadors, both the southwestern and Mississippian cultures of North America began to suffer major crises three centuries earlier—owing to environmental and climate changes, including earthquakes and serious droughts—and they unraveled during the thirteenth century, with the major centers of population and spirituality increasingly abandoned. The Hohokam and Ancestral Puebloan peoples seem to have reconstituted themselves as Hopi, Zuni, Acoma, and what would be called Pueblo peoples in the eastern parts of today's Arizona and New Mexico, while the Mississippians seem to have scattered farther to the southeast, where their towns would be organized on a much smaller scale.

Even so, agriculture remained central to Native sustenance across most of North America and gave shape to their social hierarchies, gender relations, and ideas about power and provenance. Wherever one looked, from the Southwest across to the Atlantic coast, a set of common cultural assumptions and concerns linked what was otherwise an enormous range of Native groups: ideas about the obligations of kinship (who worked or lived where,

≡ **A Palace in the Desert** A society of Ancestral Puebloans built entire villages in the sides of cliffs in southwestern Colorado. Today, many of the buildings, including this imposing cliff dwelling, are preserved in Mesa Verde National Park, Colorado.

who contributed to collective needs, who held influence), notions of a spirit world inhabiting everything in the earth and sky, communal imperatives as to the control of essential resources, the vitality of trade in goods, the waging of war and the taking of captives, and the forging of political alliances.

1.4 The Peoples of West Africa

||| Describe the peoples and societies of western Africa and their role in the making of an Atlantic world.

Histories of North America, especially those that move east to west, often begin with Europe and its people since they emerged first as the main explorers and then as the predominant colonizers. We look west from Europe and often conceive of the "Atlantic world" as principally encompassing Europe and the Western Hemisphere. Yet Africa, and particularly west and west-central Africa, proved to be equally important to that history both in terms of the peopling of the Americas and in terms of the robust trading relations that would link Africa to Europe and the Western Hemisphere. A full perspective requires that we look out from there and in from the Atlantic.

Complex Societies

Even before they found their way to the Western Hemisphere, the Spanish and the Portuguese had not only encountered the land and peoples of the Atlantic Islands but also were moving, rather haphazardly, down the west coast of the very large African continent. And in many ways, the societies of the sub-Saharan world had, by that time, come to resemble those of the Western Hemisphere—although they had been populated since near the dawn of humankind. There was, to be sure, enormous diversity as to the size of communities, the foundations of economic life, and the forms of political organization. Along the coast, stretching from what became known as Upper Guinea down to Angola, most Africans lived in relatively small societies and mini-states with distinct ethno-linguistic cultures. These were, in all likelihood, the geographical size of later US counties, with anywhere from a few thousand to 30,000 inhabitants (see Map 1.4).

Farther inland, population density generally grew, societies were increasingly complex, and political systems became more extensive, though most culture areas remained small. But in some cases, empires in the fashion of the Aztecs and Inca were forged. The most prominent of these included the Jolof Empire of northwestern Senegal, the Oyo Empire in present-day southwest Nigeria, the Songhai Empire of the western Sudan and Niger River valley, and the Kingdom of Kongo (modern Angola), reaching from the Atlantic coast well into the interior of central-west Africa, all dating from the late fourteenth and fifteenth centuries (as was true for the Aztec and Inca).

Despite their proximity to the Atlantic, most of these groups and states lived, as one historian put it, "with their backs to the sea": they depended chiefly on the resources of the land rather than the ocean and established their political or urban centers well into the interior. Productive activities across what was a very large territorial space ranged from hunting and gathering, livestock raising, and relatively simple crop cultivation to labor-intensive (involving irrigation, terracing, and fertilizing) agriculture, textile manufacture, gold mining, and iron making. Grain crops like rice, millet, and sorghum were raised together with yams and plantains. A lively trade in various goods brought these societies and states into contact with

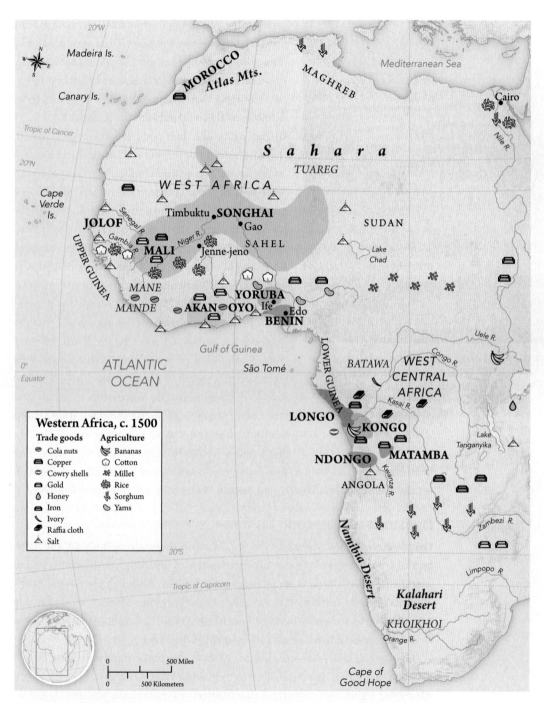

MAP 1.4 Western Africa, c. 1500   In 1500, the many dynamic states of Western Africa were sources of both luxury commodities and enslaved people.

☰ **The Power of the Oba**   The Oba, or king, of the Oyo people lived in a palace in what is now southwestern Nigeria. The palace was decorated with beautifully worked bronze plaques like this one, which shows the entrance to the palace and its guards.

one another, although trading relations were mainly localized. As best as we can tell, the combination of agricultural production, small-scale manufacturing, pastoral activities, and trade enabled most communities to supply their essential needs, and at a material level certainly comparable to the Americas.

But, again like their counterparts in the Western Hemisphere, the economic and political ambitions of states brought them into conflict. Warfare proved an ever-present feature of life in many areas, and while it contributed to the expansion of some states and the creation of empires, the chief goals seem to have been the extraction of tribute and the acquisition of slaves from neighboring peoples. Some of the enslaved were put to work in agriculture, mining, or manufacturing, where labor needs were considerable and methods of production intensive; some served wealthy households; others assumed political and military roles for the state. Almost all enslaved Africans were regarded as a significant form of wealth—there was no such thing as private ownership of land—and thus were symbols of social differentiation within communities and states. Wherever one looked in west and west-central Africa, there were elites and commoners, wealth-holders and poor people, skilled and unskilled workers, leaders and their followers. There were, in sum, clear social and political hierarchies.

Dynamics of Trade and Culture

Despite having their "backs to the sea," African states along the west and west-central coast often had vessels that were capable of repelling maritime attacks and supporting water-borne trade relations among them. Although the deeper ocean currents proved too difficult to navigate, the waters closer to shore were relatively easy to traverse and gave rise to centers of mercantile and military activity. These would be of great consequence and enduring importance.

But over the course of many centuries an increasingly important trade moved overland in another direction. It came to link the West African states with North Africa and Egypt by way of the Sahara Desert—a trade made possible by the introduction of camels as early as the third century CE. Gold extracted from areas of West Africa (especially Ghana and Mali) was central to this trade. It was exchanged for salt, essential for food preservation and largely unobtainable in West Africa, as well as for goods and currency available in the broad Mediterranean world. In fact, European traders undoubtedly learned of West Africa and its products because of the **trans-Saharan trade** (see Map 1.5).

Yet also significant to this was the trade in enslaved Africans, usually captives in interstate warfare, whose number between the mid-seventh century and the end of the nineteenth may have exceeded (somewhere between eleven and seventeen million) the entire volume of the Atlantic slave trade, which we will discuss in

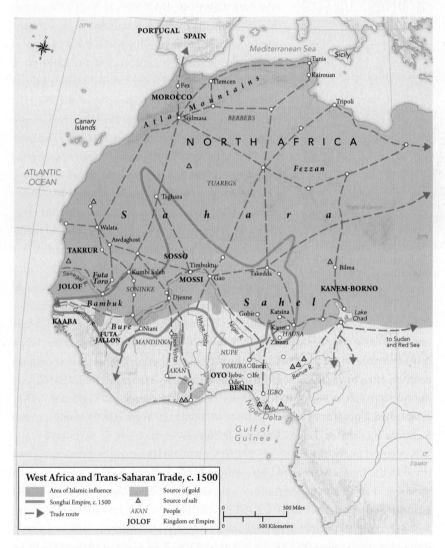

≡ **MAP 1.5   West Africa and Trans-Saharan Trade, c. 1500**   Muslim merchants pioneered trade routes across the Sahara Desert in pursuit of gold and other precious goods.

≡ **The Sankoré Mosque**   Built in the fifteenth–sixteenth centuries, the Sankoré mosque was one of many established across Africa when local rulers converted to Islam.

Chapter 2. The great majority of the enslaved in the trans-Saharan trade were women and children, destined to be domestic servants and concubines, while the males among them would be put to work in mines and fields, as court eunuchs, or in military units.

The Spread of Islam

The trans-Saharan trade carried a variety of influences in both directions, from West to North Africa and then back again. These were cultural as well as economic, and one of the most important was a religion: **Islam**. The spiritual practices and sensibilities of west and west-central Africans varied enormously, as they did among Indigenous peoples of the Western Hemisphere, although, as in the Americas, some ideas were broadly shared. There was, very widely, a sense of "this" and "other" worldliness, of powerful gods who bridged the two and might inhabit living and inanimate objects (animals, plants, soil, water), of souls who moved from one to the other, of revelations as sources of knowledge and action, of mediums who could offer direction and interpretation.

Islam shares many features of these spiritual sensibilities, but it is organized around the notions of a single, all-powerful God (and is therefore "monotheistic") and of revealed truths in the Qur'an, a text imparted to the prophet Muhammad in seventh-century Arabia. Thereafter, Islam spread north, east, and west, as far to the west as the Iberian Peninsula in the eighth century, often by means of Muslim armies, though its expansion across the Sahara into western Africa seems to have been the work of clerics and merchants. They established footholds in centers of trade and political authority, Timbuktu in the Sudan being perhaps the best known, which grew in the centuries to follow.

Not surprisingly, the Islamic faith first won converts among political elites and those in the long-distance trading communities, and a deepening set of cultural bonds, including language (Arabic), education, and marriage, came to link the Western Sudan with North Africa and Egypt. Islam would serve as the glue of important family alliances. Eventually, the knowledge and influence of Islam would become more widespread, in West and, especially, East Africa, and would have an enormously powerful impact in the Indian and Atlantic Ocean worlds.

1.5   Late Medieval Europeans

Discuss how the complex and small-scale societies of late medieval Europe responded to the crises that beset them.

The Western Hemisphere and western Africa were clearly worlds in motion during the fourteenth, fifteenth, and sixteenth centuries, witnessing great changes in their cultures, economies, and forms of political organization. They were also worlds in which conflict was widespread, indeed often central to their survival and advancement. Much the same could be said of the continent we call Europe, which would figure large on the world stage in the early modern period, especially in relation to West Africa and the Americas.

Europe in Motion and in Crisis

We have so commonly referred to the land mass west of the Ural Mountains as "Europe" that it might come as a surprise to discover that the inhabitants of the time would not have thought of themselves as "Europeans." Theirs was a world defined by small-scale states (known as principalities and kingdoms), vertical relations of allegiance and interdependence (known as knighthoods and nobilities), the coerced labor of peasants (known as serfdom or servitude), economies oriented to self-subsistence and local trade, and a religious life unified, though only to an extent, by the Catholic Church. This world began to take shape with the decline of the western Roman Empire in the fifth century CE, reached its height in the centuries 1000 to 1300, and lasted until the fifteenth century. It is the world that historians—regarding these many centuries of slow transformational change as distinct from the ancient and modern periods—named "medieval" or the "Middle Ages" (see Map 1.6).

The transformations had several important sources, as did those elsewhere around the globe. The fourteenth century experienced a cooling trend in the global climate known as the **Little Ice Age**, which persisted into the nineteenth century. Colder temperatures and shorter growing seasons challenged agricultural production and reduced the size of food harvests, especially in northern Europe. In and of itself, this would have presented problems for sustaining the population and securing the generational and cultural bonds of the era. But fourteenth-century Europe also suffered a demographic disaster caused by the **bubonic plague** (also known as the Black Death), which spread east to west—likely from northwestern China (Mongolia)—and south to north, from the Mediterranean to the Baltic, between the 1340s and the 1350s. A bacterial disease transmitted by fleas to rats

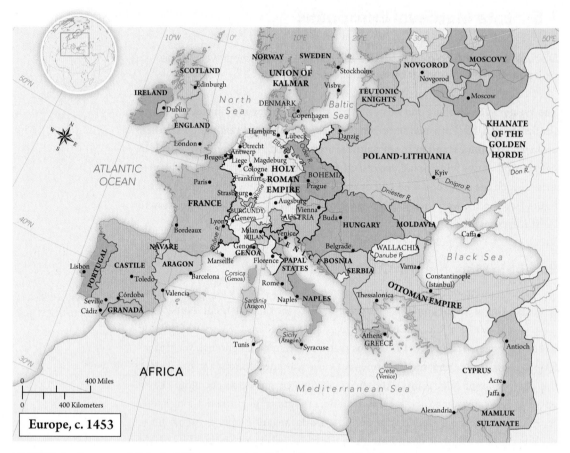

≡ **MAP 1.6**   **Europe, c. 1453**   In 1453, most people in Europe lived in small-scale societies.

and by infected rats to humans, the plague passed rapidly through communities, particularly towns and large villages. Before the Black Death had run its course, as many as twenty-five million people had died, somewhere between one-quarter and one-third of the entire population of Europe, and the continent was in the thralls of crisis.

The fourteenth century was hardly the first time that a lethal pandemic was unleashed, and it would hardly be the last. Nor was the fourteenth century the first time that bubonic plague spread among humans. Ancient Egypt, Greece, and Rome had epidemics of leprosy, tuberculosis, syphilis, measles, and especially smallpox. There is evidence of plague in Han China around 160 CE and in the Roman Empire soon after. Over the course of history, smallpox has proved a particularly deadly and destructive disease. Basic understandings of the nature and transmission of infectious diseases developed slowly; effective treatments developed even more slowly, although inoculation—exposing people to a pathogen in order to stimulate the production of antibodies—was practiced in China, Africa, and India well before, perhaps as early as the fifteenth century or roughly 300 years before, it was in Europe and the Americas.

Without question the transmission and virulence of infectious diseases have accompanied momentous changes in the human condition: the rise of sedentary agriculture and the cultivation of new crops; the raising of livestock for food, clothing, and work; long-distance migrations and explorations; the expansion of trade; and the growth of urban and other sites of high-density populations. Equally important, infectious disease epidemics have not only had devastating impacts on human societies but have also dramatically tipped the balances of power at crucial historical moments, as we will see.

Consequences of Crisis

The "fourteenth-century crisis," as some have called it, tore at the fabric of medieval societies, provoked warfare on an unprecedented scale, rearranged the sources and nature of power, and undermined some of the bases of religious faith. The demographic decline especially disrupted well-entrenched relations and expectations of life and work. In some places, the coercive chains of servitude may have been relaxed as peasants were now able to negotiate lighter obligations to their noble landowners or to commute cus-

Death in the Streets   As two gravediggers lower a plague victim into a mass grave in the city of Pavia, Italy, one of them (*left*) suddenly collapses as a "bubo," or plague sore, emerges on his neck. More corpses are being carried to the grave, and another lies unattended in the street. In the sky, the martyr St. Sebastian (shot through with arrows) pleads with God to end the plague. Josse Lieferinxe, *St. Sebastian Interceding for the Plague Stricken*, c. 1497–1499.

tomary payments in kind or labor into cash, concerned as the landed nobles were to have their fields cultivated. In other places, nobles responded to the crisis in just the opposite way: by tightening their reins on the peasantry, increasing the burdens of work and payment they imposed, and limiting peasant mobility. Small wonder that peasant rebellions swept through France, England, and the Low Countries during the second half of the fourteenth century, and, despite being suppressed, left a powerful legacy.

By all accounts, the crisis intensified both the conflict between nobles (who claimed control over relatively small areas) and aspiring monarchs (who hoped to centralize their power and authority over much larger areas) and between different monarchical regimes, such as in England and France. In what is known as the **Hundred Years' War**, England and France battled for power on the continent between 1337 and 1453. Ultimately the French defeated the English, but the war transformed both sides. If war-related casualties are added to those that resulted from the plague and a series of other smaller, more localized outbreaks of disease in the late fourteenth century, France may have lost 40 percent of its population and England may have lost 50 percent. By 1450 all of Europe may have lost two-thirds of the population it had in 1300.

The spoils, such as they were, would go to those among the powerful who could attract the most formidable allies and have access to the resources of wealth and might, all the more so as advances in military technology (gunpowder, metal crossbows, and artillery) gave the clear advantage to the players able to construct massive fortifications and pay for larger armies. The roving bands of armored ruffians—glorified as knights—who had terrorized the countryside and helped establish and sustain the ruling families of the medieval era would be of limited use in the face of this new weaponry.

For the next five centuries, the landscape of Europe would be scarred by these social and political conflicts, making for revolutions as well as continent-wide warfare. Indeed, the process of contestation may not have fully run its course until the end of World War II, but well before that the trend toward centralization was steadily gaining the upper hand and encouraging those who prevailed to engage in ambitious projects aimed at conquest and revenue. That the Spanish and Portuguese crowns brought their respective nobilities to heel by the last third of the fifteenth century helps explain why—together with their geographical proximity—they could have led the way into the Atlantic.

Spiritual Tensions

The destabilization of social and political life during the fourteenth century was accompanied by ruptures in religious life. This was surely the case with the Roman Catholic Church. Monotheistic like Islam, Christianity—effectively the Roman Catholic Church at this point—was nonetheless being pulled apart by rival claimants to the papacy (the central office of the church). This Great Schism roiled the waters of the institution and, equally important, began to lay the groundwork for the Protestant Reformation of the early sixteenth century (discussed in Chapter 2). Already in the fourteenth century dissident voices could be heard who challenged the privileges of the Pope and clergy and the inaccessibility of the Latin Bible to the laity, expressing popular discontent with the formal reign of the Catholic establishment. Always at risk, those regarded as nonbelievers or heretics would be increasingly vulnerable to persecution. They included members of renegade sects, practitioners of witchcraft, and especially those of the Jewish faith who were cast into social isolation, imagined as purveyors of lethal conspiracies against Christians and their children, and widely blamed for causing the death of Jesus Christ.

Even so, as was true among Indigenous peoples of the Western Hemisphere and Africa, spirituality and faith were fundamentally part of the daily lives of most ordinary folk in Europe. Cathedrals, like the sacred mounds, pyramids, and temples to the West and South, rose on ceremonial sites often centuries old and took many years, if not generations, to build. Like the crusading struggles against Islam on the Iberian Peninsula and in the eastern Mediterranean, they—together with a network of local parishes—created measures of cultural cohesion in a world of change.

Yet there is good reason to question the full extent of cultural cohesion that Christianity may have provided. Much as with Islam, Christianity took firmest hold in urban places and among more educated elites and merchants. Elsewhere it seems to have established a broad framework in which popular beliefs and practices—which bore resemblance to those of Indigenous peoples in the Americas and Africa, with their many deities, ideas of revelation, rituals, and sacrifices—could be assimilated. The clergy of many rural parishes had little if any formal education and usually needed to accommodate local ways, whose connection to Christianity were often dubious, if they wished to maintain the allegiance of the parishioners. The priests who pushed back or seemed too beholden to the wishes of clerical superiors courted popular resistance. Anticlericalism ran wide and deep across Christian Europe and suggested the tensions that were very near to the surface of religious life.

Societies in the Atlantic Before the Atlantic World

Indeed, the peoples, communities, and states on all sides of the Atlantic had, simultaneously, reached very similar levels of development by the late fifteenth century while showing a remarkably diverse character. Everywhere they cultivated important food crops and had intricate methods for making cloth, tools, ceramics, and metal objects. Everywhere they had fashioned both local and longer-distance trading networks that brought them into contact with different cultures. Everywhere they had constructed social and political hierarchies based on the unequal distribution of wealth and power. Everywhere they engaged in warfare aimed at expanding their domains of authority, finding new sources of enrichment, and enslaving captives. Everywhere they adhered to belief systems that mixed the secular and the sacred, the material and the spiritual world, providing a deep sense of what they

PERSPECTIVES

Looking Outward or Turning Inward? Fifteenth-Century Venice and the Courts of Ming China

The merchants, gondoliers, housekeepers, and traders of cosmopolitan Venice, shown here in a 1494 painting by Vittore Carpaccio, are too busy interacting with one another to pay attention to the "miracle" being performed by priests on the balcony in the upper-left-hand corner of the scene. (A boy possessed by a demon is instantly healed by the sight of the relic of the True Cross.) Two of the fourteen gondoliers are Black men; Turkish and Arabic merchants are recognizable by their turbans, while Armenians are distinguished by their tall black hats. Venice in the fifteenth century was a center for trade and commerce from as far away as Africa, China, and the East Indies. Carpaccio's painting was commissioned by a Venetian fraternal organization (a social organization whose members freely associate for a

≡ Vittore Carpaccio, *The Miracle of the Relic of the True Cross on the Rialto Bridge,* 1494 (oil on canvas), Galleria dell' Accademia, Venice, Italy

mutually beneficial purpose, with this one dedicated to Saint John the Evangelist) and displayed in its headquarters.

The extraordinary wealth and power of the Ming Dynasty is celebrated in a hand-scroll depicting the annual procession of the emperor and his court to the imperial tombs nearly 30 miles from the walled city of Beijing. Ceremonial guards keep watch along the banks of the route, while the emperor himself is shown seated in splendor on a ceremonial barge. This is just one section of a nearly 100-foot-long silk scroll, which took a team of anonymous court artists years to complete. As an idealized demonstration of imperial splendor and power, as well as a depiction of an ancient ritual, the work would have been for court eyes only.

☰ **Anonymous, "Return Clearing," Ming Dynasty (1368–1644)**

CONSIDER THIS

Both of these paintings reflect wealthy and powerful societies, each of which sought to explore and dominate distant places. What are some key differences you notice in the people and activities depicted in each painting? In what ways is either painting idealized or realistic? How would you describe the social and cultural priorities expressed by each image? For example, do the paintings emphasize tradition or innovation?

shared and what they feared. And everywhere they were highly vulnerable to the effects of disease and natural disaster.

But everywhere, too, the peoples, communities, and states of the Atlantic had their distinctive ways and dynamics, their own frameworks and representations, which could appear very strange to outsiders and jostle the sensibilities of those unaccustomed to them. Thus, in some places there was no such thing as "property," either private or public; in other places, the only property was controlled by states; and in still other places, forms of private property had begun to emerge, though usually in complex relation to multiple use rights. Conceptual barriers such as these could be very difficult to traverse. And nowhere did any people imagine themselves as Native Americans, Africans, or Europeans: that is, until well after they encountered one another.

1.6   China's Great Shadow

||| Give examples of the global reach of the Yuan and Ming Empires.

Distant as it was, China made at least two important contributions to Europe's fourteenth-century crisis. One was gunpowder, which Chinese alchemists, working with substances for medicinal purposes, may have discovered as early as the ninth century CE. The discovery made possible the use of new, explosive weaponry that Europeans would encounter firsthand in the mid-thirteenth century in battles against invading Mongols and then quickly put to their own purposes. The second contribution was the Black Death, which appears to have originated on the edge of northwestern China (Mongolia) before being transmitted by Mongols to Crimean (Black Sea) trading towns. Italian merchants operating there then seem to have carried it home. Much of Europe was very soon infected.

Chinese Worlds in Motion

Imperial China of the thirteenth, fourteenth, and fifteenth centuries was also a world in motion and one whose influence was spreading across much of the globe. First, the **Yuan Empire**, founded in 1271 by Mongol conqueror and Great Khan Khubilai, and then the Ming Empire, founded on the overthrow of the Yuan by Zhu Yuanzhang in 1368, helped to create an imposing state that not only ruled over more than 100 million people within its shifting boundaries but also extended its imperial reach east, south, and west across the Eurasian continent and the south Asian seas and territories. Centralized politically and geographically mostly around Beijing (the Ming moved their capital briefly to Nanjing to the south before returning it to Beijing), both the Yuan and Ming Empires established multilevel administrative units to unify their authority across thousands of miles. The units included provinces, prefectures, and more than 1,100 counties held together by complex kinship ties, dynastic rituals, a state bureaucracy, and remarkably effective communication networks, including postal and courier systems dependent mainly on horses.

Chinese Economic Life

Although the Mongols who established the Yuan Empire were nomadic pastoralists, both the Yuan and Ming Empires rested on the foundation of a settled agricultural economy. True, the towns and cities of China came to buzz with life and merchandise and featured impressive homes of artisans, merchants, and political officials. The largest of them, Suzhou, in the Yangtze River delta and linked closely to the port of Shanghai, may have had a million people around 1400; Nanjing may have had nearly three-quarters of a million; and Beijing more than half a million. No city in the world, not even Tenochtitlan, was nearly as large as any of them.

But the fortunes of even these extremely large cities, as was the case for the empire more generally, depended on the countryside. The overwhelming majority of those in Yuan and Ming China farmed the land, growing a variety of grain crops like millet, soy, and wheat in the north and rice in the south. Most of the cultivators either owned small plots or leased them from landlords who often lived in towns and villages; they focused on raising enough food for themselves and their families who worked alongside; and then they sold surpluses in networks of vibrant markets. They also needed to grow enough to pay the state's tax on grain production (perhaps as high as 9.1 percent), which was crucial to the revenues that the rulers had at their disposal and to the power that the rulers were able to wield over the empire as a whole.

For their part, the Yuan and Ming alike used those revenues to build an impressive infrastructure and complex of fortifications. The best known are the Great Wall, which guarded China's northern border in an east-west direction (much of it constructed by the Ming), and the Grand Canal, which starts near Beijing and heads south toward Shanghai (the longest canal in the world, dating from the seventh century though renovated by the Ming), but many other canals and irrigation projects crisscrossed the land, especially in the east, while thousands of government grain barges helped to keep imperial storehouses full (see again Map 1.1).

The increasing pulse of commercial activity together with the state's revenue needs promoted the use of official currencies in exchange transactions. These currencies included coppers on strings of a thousand, paper known as Great Ming Precious Scrip, and silver, which was especially valued by the government and by

MAPPING AMERICA

The Atlantic and the Pacific

Maps, and mapmaking, illustrate the stories that peoples tell about themselves and that explorers imagine about others. Maps can reinforce existing power structures, but they can also empower change. Think about the maps of the world you have seen in US classrooms: Where is North

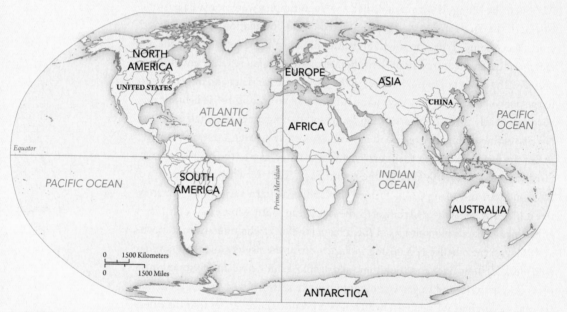

≡ **MAP 1**   Most maps of the world place Europe near the center. In this view, the Atlantic Ocean and the countries along its rim are portrayed as exerting the most influence on the United States, and US history progresses from east to west.

many coastal traders. Small wonder that even in the late thirteenth century Marco Polo could marvel at the goods and prosperity he claimed to see in his travels: merchandise in abundance, neatly tilled fields, and opulent palaces. In the Great Khan Khubilai, Polo found "the mightiest man."

The Imperial Reach

But there was an important overseas dimension as well. China's foreign relations of this time partly involved a tribute system that brought emissaries to the

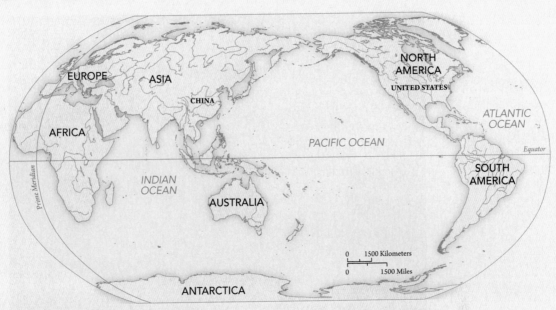

≡ **MAP 2**   World maps that are centered on the Pacific reorient the way we view the United States in relation to other countries. Europe is placed on the margin and China occupies a central position.

America positioned on such maps? How does your understanding of world history—and the place of the United States in that history—change if you do not see North America at the center of the world?

Thinking Geographically

1. How do these two maps encourage a different perspective on US history?
2. What does Map 1 suggest about the most important relationships and exchanges in the history of North America? What does Map 2 suggest about those relationships and exchanges?

imperial court from many distant places, including Champa and Annam (southern and northern Vietnam), Korea, Java, Borneo, Japan, Siam, Sumatra, Coromandel (southeast India), and Tibet. An early fifteenth-century state-sponsored maritime expedition to tributaries around what Chinese called the Western Sea (Indian Ocean) further familiarized Ming rulers with tributary and trading networks, and helped account for the knowledge that both the Yuan and Ming showed for a world extending as far west as the Black Sea, the Mediterranean, the east African coast, and the Arabian Peninsula (see again Map 1.1).

≡ **A Wild Gift as Tribute**   During the Ming Empire, trading relationships were established between China and Africa. In this Ming painting, an African Swahili merchant presents a lion as a gift to the Ming court.

Equally if not more important was the expanding trade in the South China Sea that had been under the control of Muslim merchants but that the Chinese began to challenge in the fifteenth century. Based in ports on the eastern coast of China (Suzhou and Quanzhou), this trade encompassed Japan and Taiwan on the northern end as well as the Philippines, Moluccas (Spice Islands), Borneo, Java, and Malacca on the southern, a large and interconnected zone in which Chinese grains and manufactured goods were of special importance in value and volume. The South China Sea was becoming a Ming lake, and Chinese merchants were establishing significant outposts all over south and southeast Asia.

Such was the world that the Spanish, Portuguese, and Dutch found when their own traders and explorers arrived at different points in the sixteenth century. And such was the world into which the silver mined by Andean Indigenous peoples and shipped by Spanish conquistadors arrived through the port of Manila, where the Spanish had found well-entrenched communities of Chinese and Muslim merchants. It was a world of Chinese political and economic power, on land and sea, within dynastic borders and beyond, a world that not only rivaled but may have surpassed any of those to be found in Europe, Africa, the Americas, or the Middle East.

Conclusion: Asia and the Pacific

History is an interpretive undertaking, and one of the most important signs of interpretation in history writing is where and when you begin a historical narrative. Here, unlike other American history books, which begin in Europe or the Atlantic, we begin in China and the Pacific both because of the enormous, and often underappreciated, significance of the Pacific world in our history and because it was from Asia and the Pacific that the first inhabitants of the Western Hemisphere arrived.

The worlds that these Asian migrants made in the Western Hemisphere in the many thousands of years before Europeans set eyes on them, were very diverse culturally, linguistically, and socioeconomically. And by the time of European contact, they—much like societies of the time in Europe and Africa—were very much in motion: growing, declining, changing their modes of life, exploring and migrating by land and sea, and in many respects making their sustenance, relating to one another, and understanding the world and its spiritual forces in similar ways. Already, contacts had been made over long distances as a result of the search for trade, and networks were connecting China, Mediterranean Europe, and northern Africa. And, indeed, when new and more extensive contacts began to be made during the fifteenth century, Ming China was clearly the most formidable state and empire on the globe.

WHAT IF Chinese Navigators Reached North America?

The Chinese had experience at sea for centuries before the Ming came to power, and it seems that Ming rulers, especially the Yongle emperor, Zhu Di (r. 1402–1424), had their eyes on the oceans. Zhu Di ordered what was known as a "treasure fleet," which included wooden sailing vessels (often made from teak) at least twice the size of anything to be found in Europe, and he sponsored seven voyages that took them around the South China Sea, across the Western (Indian) Ocean, and through what we know as the Straits of Hormuz.

So interested was Zhu Di in these massive voyages that some researchers have suggested yet another remarkable one: between 1421 and 1423, they say, large Chinese fleets actually crossed the Indian Ocean, rounded the southern tips of Africa and South America, and then sailed across the Pacific, making a raft of discoveries along the way. These included Australia, the Arctic and Antarctic, Greenland, and much of the Western Hemisphere.

DOCUMENT 1.1:   Reproduction of Waldseemüller Map of 1507

Created by German cartographer Martin Waldseemüller, this is the first known map to show both the Pacific and the Atlantic sides of the Western Hemisphere. Some regard it as evidence of Chinese oceanic exploration.

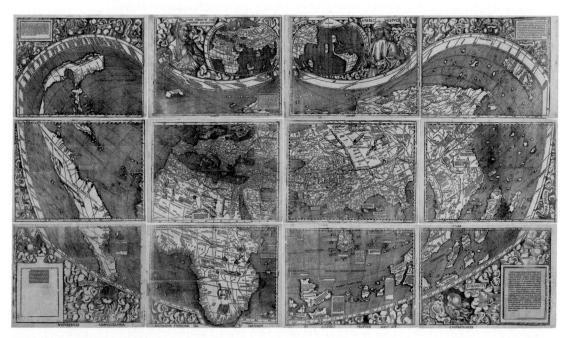

≡ **Waldseemüller Map of 1507**

How can these researchers say this? The researchers point to scattered evidence—maps of places drawn before Europeans ever arrived, materials from sunken ships, plants and animals that seem native to China, and perhaps DNA in local populations—which shows, they insist, not only that the Chinese made landings there but also may have established colonies along the Pacific coasts of North and South America. Which is to say that, if these claims are correct, the Chinese "discovered" the Americas well before Columbus landed in Hispaniola, and they circumnavigated the globe well before Ferdinand Magellan did (1519–1522).

There are no records of these "discoveries" in China because some of the vessels never returned and because the Ming apparently destroyed many accounts of sea voyages. And it should be said that academically trained historians have serious doubts about these conclusions. But what if at least some of them are credible? What if Chinese explorers, at the behest of the Ming state, did reach across the Pacific or did round the Cape of Good Hope and head across the Atlantic? What if Chinese fleets did sail along the coast of the Western Hemisphere even if they did not establish colonies? How might this change our view of the "beginnings" of US history?

DOCUMENT 1.2: Petroglyphs from New Mexico

Not long ago, a researcher from Illinois named John Ruskamp discovered unusual stone markings while walking in Petroglyph National Monument in New Mexico (petroglyphs are designs and symbols carved into volcanic rocks). He claims that the markings resemble very old styles of Chinese script, suggesting that explorers from China may have been in the Americas around 1300 BCE or nearly 2,800 years before Columbus arrived in Hispaniola. Archaeologists and other experts remain skeptical, but it is potentially a fascinating discovery.

≡ **Petroglyphs from New Mexico**

Thinking About Contingency

1. What type of evidence would you find most convincing for claims about China's "discovery" of the Western Hemisphere? What type of evidence would you regard as strong, and what type would you regard as weak?
2. We are used to written evidence, but what other types of evidence can be used effectively in historical analysis?
3. If the Chinese did find their way across the Pacific or across the Atlantic to the Western Hemisphere (and perhaps elsewhere) before Europeans, why might it have taken us so long to learn about this?

REVIEW QUESTIONS

1. How important a role does perspective play in historical writing? Can there be historical writing without perspective?

2. How were the Ming able to build such a formidable empire by the sixteenth century? What were its foundations?

3. Why were the Spanish interested in setting out across the Atlantic by the end of the fifteenth century?

4. From where did the early peoples of the Western Hemisphere come, and, as best as we know, when did they begin to arrive?

5. How varied were the societies that the Western Hemisphere's Indigenous peoples created, and where were these societies most densely populated?

6. Why were Europeans interested in trading with West and West Central Africans, and why were Africans interested in trading with Europeans? What were they trading?

7. How different were the societies of medieval Europe from those in the Western Hemisphere and Africa of the time? Were there more similarities or differences?

KEY TERMS

ancestral Puebloans (p. 18)

Aztec Empire (p. 16)

bubonic plague (p. 25)

Cahokia (p. 18)

Hohokam (p. 18)

Hundred Years' War (p. 28)

Inca Empire (p. 16)

Islam (p. 24)

Little Ice Age (p. 25)

Maya (p. 16)

Mexicas (p. 16)

Ming Empire (p. 9)

Tenochtitlan (p. 16)

trans-Saharan trade (p. 23)

Yuan Empire (p. 32)

RECOMMENDED READINGS

Inga Clendenin, *Aztecs: An Interpretation* (Cambridge University Press, 1991).

Pekka Hamalainen, *Indigenous Continent* (Liveright, 2022).

Linda Heywood and John Thornton, *Central Africans, Atlantic Creoles, and the Foundation of the Americas* (Cambridge University Press, 2007).

John Hunwick, *West Africa, Islam, and the Arab World* (2010).

Charles C. Mann, *1491: New Revelations of the Americas Before Columbus* (Vintage, 2011).

Klaus Muhlhahn, *Making China Modern: From the Great Qing to Xi Jinping* (Harvard University Press, 2019).

Hongping Annie Nie, *The Selden Map of China: A New Understanding of the Ming Dynasty* (2006).

Marco Polo, *Travels of Marco Polo.*

David Roberts, *The Lost World of the Old Ones: Discoveries in the Ancient Southwest* (Norton, 2016).

David M. Robinson, *Ming China and Its Allies: Imperial Rule in Eurasia* (Cambridge University Press, 2020).

Steve J. Stern, *Peru's Indian Peoples and the Challenge of Spanish Conquest* (University of Wisconsin Press, 1993).

Chris Wickham, *Medieval Europe* (Yale University Press, 2017).

Contact Zones
1450–1600

Chapter Outline

2.1 Why a "New World"?

||| Explain why the world in which Europeans, Africans, and Indigenous peoples of the Western
||| Hemisphere made contact was a "new" one for everybody.

2.2 Contact Zone: The West African Coast

||| Describe the meetings of Europeans and West Africans in the fifteenth century.

2.3 Contact Zone: The Caribbean Basin

||| Analyze the diverse contacts of Spanish and Indigenous peoples across the Caribbean
||| basin.

2.4 Contact Zone: Central and South America

||| Analyze the diverse contacts of European and Indigenous peoples across Central and South
||| America.

2.5 Contact Zone: Eastern North America

||| Appraise the consequences of contact on both European and Indigenous cultures.

≡ **Go-Between**   The Native American cultural mediator (or go-between) La Malinche translates for the Spanish
conquistador Hernán Cortés, as depicted in *The History of the Indies of New Spain* (c. 1579–1581), a Spanish work also
known as the Codex Duran.

Along the West African coast, beginning in the mid-fifteenth century, a series of trading posts began to emerge to facilitate the growing commerce between Africans and a host of Europeans. One of the African merchants who came to thrive during the seventeenth century was Abee Coffu Jantie Seniees, a name that suggests a possible Islamic connection. But if we consult the accounts and account books of the Europeans with whom he traded, he appears as Jan Snees, Jacque Senece, Johan Sinesen, and Jante Snees.

On the one hand, these different representations of Seniees's name suggest the range of Europeans who found their way to the West African coast during the sixteenth and seventeenth centuries. They were Danish and Dutch; they were English and Portuguese. Some may have been French. On the other hand, Seniees may well have been the embodiment of a historical figure created by the process of such contact itself: a cosmopolitan figure knowledgeable about the worlds of Africans and

Timeline

1000 CE	1200	1400	1425	1450	1475

1000 CE ▸ Norse explorers reach North America

1441 CE ▸ The first enslaved Africans transported by ship in Atlantic waters arrive in Portugal

Europeans, multilingual in speech, and flexible culturally, something of a **cultural mediator (go-between)** as well as an economic player bent on enriching himself.

2.1 Why a "New World"?

Explain why the world in which Europeans, Africans, and Indigenous peoples of the Western Hemisphere made contact was a "new" one for everybody.

Abee Coffu Jantie Seniees gives us a very different perspective on what was really "new" about the worlds being created in the Atlantic of the fifteenth, sixteenth, and seventeenth centuries. Most textbooks and historical accounts of the period refer to the Western Hemisphere as the "New World," effectively expressing a European perspective on encounters with land masses and societies that were

1500	1525	1550	1575	1600	1625

1482 ▸ Portuguese establish a *feitoria* (fortified trading post) at Elmina, in present-day Ghana

1492 ▸ Sailing for Spain, Christopher Columbus makes landfall in the Bahamas and then on Hispaniola

1497 ▸ Sailing for England, John Cabot reaches Newfoundland

1498 ▸ Portuguese explorer Vasco da Gama rounds Africa and reaches the Indian Ocean

1500 ▸ Portuguese explorer Pedro Alvares Cabral reaches northeastern Brazil

1503 ▸ Italian explorer Amerigo Vespucci first uses the term "New World" to describe the Western Hemisphere

1517 ▸ Martin Luther publishes his *Ninety-Five Theses*, sparking the Protestant Reformation

1519–1521 ▸ Hernán Cortés leads the Spanish conquest of the Aztec Empire

1524 ▸ In the service of France, Giovanni da Verrazzano sails up the eastern coast of North America

1528–1536 ▸ Spanish explorer Alvar Nunez Cabeza de Vaca travels across the Gulf coast of the present-day United States and Mexico

1532–1536 ▸ Francisco Pizarro leads the Spanish conquest of the Inca Empire

1534–1536 ▸ French navigator Jacques Cartier travels the St. Lawrence River

1540–1542 ▸ Spaniard Francisco Vázquez de Coronado becomes the first European to explore the southwestern areas of North America

1558–1603 ▸ Reign of Queen Elizabeth of England

1565 ▸ Spanish establish on the Florida peninsula a fort and outpost they call St. Augustine.

1585–1586 ▸ English privateer Francis Drake's "Great Expedition" to Spanish America

1585–1590 ▸ English efforts to settle Roanoke Island off present-day North Carolina fail

previously unknown to them and that they then claimed to "discover." As best as we know, the term "New World" was coined in 1503 by the Florentine navigator and explorer Amerigo Vespucci (from whose name "America" is derived), in part to dispute Christopher Columbus's claim that Hispaniola and the larger Caribbean were close to Asia.

Needless to say, the many millions of Indigenous people who had been living for thousands of years in the Western Hemisphere would have been puzzled, perhaps even amused, to learn that Europeans regarded their homelands as "new" and only recently "discovered." From the Native perspective, looking "east" from where they lived, the Europeans and the worlds they represented were what was "new" and effectively just "discovered" by them.

One solution to this problem would be to discard the term "New World" for making it difficult to see the whole story and from all sides. But perhaps we can use the term more creatively and more in tune with what was happening historically. Europeans, Africans, and Indigenous peoples brought very different things to their encounters in the Western Hemisphere. Although they may have attained comparable levels of social and political development, they were very different in how they ate and dressed, worshipped, organized their families and productive activities, related to their natural environments, and thought about their futures. They looked strange to one another, spoke incomprehensible languages, and could seem mutually threatening.

Yet, as the person of Jantie Seniees shows, once Europeans, Africans, and Native Americans met, things began to change and change quickly. Sometimes the changes were catastrophic and sometimes wondrous; sometimes they were a little of both. But, in a sense, the worlds they were creating as a result of their encounters were new and different for everybody. The Western Hemisphere, north to south, became a "New World"—as did Europe and Africa—not because Europeans discovered it but because what we can call "contact," the early encounters of these groups, transformed the hemisphere and everything that would touch it, or be touched by it, in profound ways, often beyond recognition.

2.2   Contact Zone: The West African Coast

‖‖‖ Describe the meetings of Europeans and West Africans in the fifteenth century.

Although, as we saw in Chapter 1, historians may speculate about early Chinese explorations of the Western Hemisphere, we have no reliable documentation for any of these explorations. But we do have documentation for a number of enormously important encounters that are relevant for a history of the United States.

The first of these involved Europeans (notably the Portuguese and Spanish) and peoples who resided along the coast of west and west-central Africa. And there are two keys to the story. One is the familiarity that Europeans and Africans had with each other's goods owing to the trans-Saharan trade that linked West Africa with the Mediterranean. The second is oceanic navigation.

Dynamics of Early Contact

For centuries, European merchants had been sailing along the north African coast, stopping off in Algiers, Tunis, Tripoli, and Alexandria to trade in cloth, metal products, ivory, pepper, gold, and slaves. Before long they were joined by pirates, some with the protection of European states, who preyed upon the lucrative shipping and found havens in some of the remote harbors of North Africa. West Africans, in turn, gained knowledge of European wares as caravans, often controlled by Muslim merchants, headed southwest over the Sahara toward Ghana, Mali, and the Sudan. Direct contacts between Europeans and Africans, that is, came in part as a product of indirect acquaintance.

The second key to what happened is navigation. The Europeans were interested in finding a shorter route to the West African markets and gold fields they had long known of as well as to the Asian sources of ceramics, teas, and spices they had learned of in the thirteenth century. It would make sense, especially for the Portuguese, to head out into the Atlantic and then turn south to follow the African coast and see where that led. The problem was that the eastern Atlantic was extremely treacherous to navigate. Vessels sailing out of the Mediterranean or out of Lisbon and Seville on the Iberian Peninsula quickly entered what was known as the **Canary Current** (after the Canary Islands), which swept them to the west, past the Canaries and out into the open Atlantic. And if navigators did manage to turn south and southeast, putting them in range of western and west-central Africa, they faced great challenges returning north.

Africans were themselves tested mariners who had been active in the waters for centuries, but because of the complex Atlantic currents they had their boats and other sailing vessels hug the coastline and move into the interior of the continent along river routes rather than head west. What made the difference for the Europeans—what gave them the opportunity to break out of this maritime box—was oceanic experience, not well into the Atlantic, but in a developing trade in grains that came to link the Mediterranean in the south with the Baltic Sea in the north during the thirteenth century. In order to reach the Baltic ports, as well as the French and English ports where the grain trade was lively, too, European merchants had to sail into the Atlantic and North Sea. Over the course of two centuries, which included shorter travels to the Atlantic Islands, where they became familiar with the Canary Current and began to grow crops, the Europeans acquired more and more knowledge about currents and winds that would eventually enable them to negotiate the seaborne journeys to West Africa. This is why the new European–West African **"contact zone"** would be in Africa rather than in Europe (see Map 2.1).

Yet it was a haphazard process made in leaps and lags. The Cape of Good Hope at the southern tip of Africa would not be rounded until Vasco da Gama of Portugal did so in 1498. Initially the leaders of the Portuguese expeditions were merchants looking for profits and younger members of the nobility looking to hone their military skills and make reputations for themselves. Before too long, by the mid-fifteenth century, the Portuguese crown became involved, interested as it was in both the commercial and political possibilities that western Africa—and a new route into the Indian Ocean—seemed to present. But the ambition was neither settlement nor conquest; the ambition was trade. The Portuguese recognized that the West African states and societies they encountered

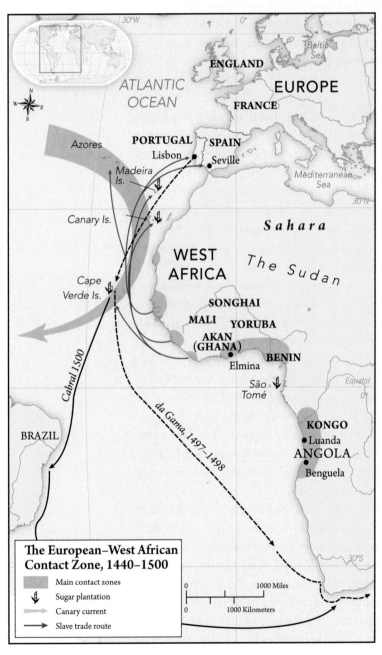

≡ **MAP 2.1** **The European–West African Contact Zone, 1440–1500**

had extensive networks of communication and were militarily formidable. Using forceful methods would only court disaster; instead, they relied on cooperation and diplomacy. They viewed African rulers much as they viewed European rulers: as people who had power and authority and had to be treated with respect.

Limits of European Power

Thus, rather than attempting to push their way inland and carve out their own zones of settlement, the Portuguese either established small fortified trading posts along the coast called *feitorias* (from "factor," a mercantile agent or representative), which served as rendezvous and transshipment points, or they engaged in shipboard trade from the decks of their own anchored vessels. In both cases, the trade effectively remained in the hands of the Africans, and the Portuguese did business at African forbearance.

The first of the feitorias, called **Elmina**, was founded off the coast of Ghana in 1482, not far from where gold was being mined. A fortress was soon built (called São Jorge da Mina), and a small town slowly grew around it. As the Portuguese

☰ **Elmina Castle, Ghana**   The site of the first Portuguese feitoria, begun in 1482 and expanded by later fortifications.

made their way farther down the African coast, they established additional feitorias, as did European competitors—initially the Dutch and then the Danes, French, English, and Swedes—when they arrived during the next two centuries. Indeed, Elmina served as a model for most of what followed. Only in the area of the Kingdom of Kongo (Angola) and later in southern Africa were settler colonies constructed, and even they required the help of African allies to be secure (see again Map 2.1).

It is not entirely clear how fully this fifteenth-century "contact" transformed African societies and states in the interior of west and west-central Africa. For the most part, European traders were selling goods that Africans were already producing, and Africans were buying European goods that served, more or less, as luxury items or to satisfy new aesthetic tastes. Quite simply, Europeans did not initially provide anything that Africans did not make for themselves, and Africans did not become "dependent" on the European trade. Organizationally, Euro-African trade appeared as mirror images: in both cases, traders operated under the administrative supervision of states, whether European monarchs or African rulers, who attempted to constrain the market parameters of their merchants and make sure they received political and economic benefits. As might be expected, tight control was very difficult to maintain though traders on each side saw the use for some of it.

These conditions, and the political balances more generally, may have been maintained by the epidemiological consequences of contact. West Africans, owing to the centuries-old trans-Saharan and Red Sea trades, were likely exposed to many of the pathogens that had ravaged Europe, Asia, and the Middle East and therefore had some immunity when the Portuguese and Spanish arrived in the fifteenth century. No disease-based demographic disaster spread across the African continent. If anything, the toll fell heaviest on the Europeans, who now had their initial exposure to the tropical diseases of sub-Saharan Africa, such as malaria, which sickened and killed them in great numbers and made their populations, small as they were, tough to sustain.

The significant transformations brought about by contact were of two sorts. For one thing, European feitorias became new cultural arenas. In the immediate vicinity of places like Elmina, African farmers, boatmen, food preparers, and petty traders provisioned and provided other services for the Europeans (Portuguese in this case) who resided there. Soon they intermingled sexually and, at times, intermarried. A racially and culturally mixed population therefore began to grow and took on distinctive features. They came to speak each other's languages, or create what are known as **pidgins**, simplified languages that combine elements of two or more; learn each other's ways; and serve as translators, guides, messengers, and other sorts of intermediaries, better acquainting Europeans and Africans.

Some scholars have called them **Atlantic creoles**, emphasizing both their mixed ancestry and the newness of the cultural and historical context in which they emerged. Relatively few in number, like Abee Coffu Jantie Seniees, they would nonetheless be of enormous consequence in the larger Atlantic world that was being made.

A New Slave Trade

Perhaps even more significant, a new trade in enslaved Africans came into being. Enslaving people and trading them was not new to western Africa. Most African societies accepted slavery as a fundamental part of their social orders and had enslaved captives for centuries. They also bought and sold slaves, sometimes over short distances and sometimes over very great ones, most notably the trans-Saharan region. Not surprisingly, once the Portuguese arrived, enslaved Africans were as much a part of the West African trading economy as were gold, cloth, ivory, and spices. The first enslaved Africans transported by ship in Atlantic waters arrived in Portugal sometime around 1441; by 1550 several thousand slaves could be

≡ **Contact Zones**   Enslaved and free Africans mingle with merchants and townspeople on the Lisbon waterfront in this c. 1570–1580 painting by an unknown Flemish artist.

found in Lisbon (composing as much as 10 percent of the total population there) and Seville. African merchants and political officials were primary actors in this trade. They were directly involved in enslaving Africans from the coast or interior, having them transported to the European enclaves, and arranging their sale. Indeed, these merchants and officials were often slave owners themselves, and thus just the sort of people the Europeans could rely upon.

Yet there was more afoot. The Portuguese and Spanish not only brought enslaved Africans back to the Iberian Peninsula to serve as domestics and symbols of wealth and prestige. They also shipped them to the Atlantic Islands—Madeira, the Azores, the Canaries, and Cape Verde, where settlements had been established in the fifteenth century—to work on landed estates cultivating grains, grapes, and especially sugar (sugarcane had long been cultivated in the Mediterranean).

At first, European participation in the African slave trade does not appear to have changed the political and demographic dynamics that were already in place. The overall demand for enslaved labor was not substantially altered; African states did not engage in more raiding or warfare in order to enslave more people; and the population of affected areas in western Africa did not seem to experience any notable declines. Some African states in fact saw to it that enslaved Africans would no longer be part of their trading mix.

But there was now in place a channel of supply, involving sources, personnel, political connections, and credit mechanisms, which could be tapped if the demand for enslaved labor grew. And because the Euro-African trade came to include guns and other gunpowder weaponry, African states could be more lethally equipped to conduct the wars and raids that expanded their power and increased the number of captives. It was a potentially perilous arc of change.

2.3   Contact Zone: The Caribbean Basin

‖‖‖ Analyze the diverse contacts of Spanish and Indigenous peoples across the Caribbean basin.

A decade after the Portuguese founded Elmina on the African coast, a new contact zone came into being far to the West. It was the work of Christopher Columbus, a native of Genoa sailing for Spain who, as we saw in Chapter 1, made landfall not near China, as he assumed, but first in the Bahamas and then on the Caribbean island of Hispaniola in the fall of 1492. Indeed, Columbus proved to be an important link between the two different sites—he had visited Elmina just after it was established and observed the brisk trade in goods and slaves. A deep impression was made.

Columbus and the Taino

As Columbus may have expected, he and his men were not alone on the island. Like western and west-central Africa, Hispaniola was populated by large numbers of Indigenous people (likely over, perhaps well over, 300,000) known, in this case, as the **Taino** (Arawak). They had been there for a very long time. The Taino had come across the Caribbean from the Orinoco River delta on the northwest coast of South America or from the Yucatan Peninsula and settled the island 2,000 or more years before (see Map 2.2). Their population grew into dense clusters, they made exquisite pottery, they became sophisticated boatmen, and they cultivated

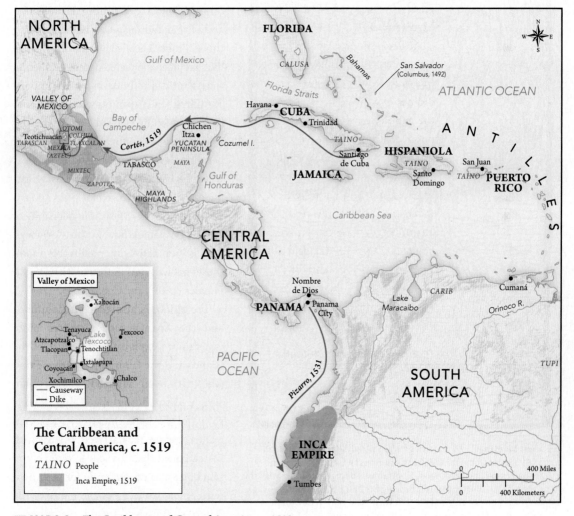

≡ **MAP 2.2**   **The Caribbean and Central America, c. 1519**

a variety of crops, including yucca, maize, beans, cotton, tobacco, and sweet pota-toes. They were also divided into small states or kingdoms, a political environment similar to what was to be found on the West African coast.

Like the Portuguese merchants in western Africa, Columbus was therefore inter-ested in trade he might find. And yet, unlike those merchants, he was also interested in conquest, conversion to Christianity, and precious metals. Along with these distinc-tive challenges, Columbus and his men were heavily outnumbered. But his ambitions were advanced by the political situation on Hispaniola. At the time of his arrival, some of the Taino states were in conflict, and Columbus saw an opportunity. He quickly forged alliances to help him gain protection and a firmer footing on the island. In doing this, Columbus availed himself of a practice that had been pioneered decades earlier on the Atlantic Islands. An especially import-ant alliance in Hispaniola was with a Taino *cacique* (chieftain) named Guaconari, who was impressed by Spanish weaponry and permitted Columbus to build a fort near where he landed. Despite some rough go-ing, the alliance endured for years and en-abled the Spanish to get the upper hand not only on Hispaniola but on other Caribbean islands populated by groups of Taino: those that we know as Puerto Rico (1508), Jamaica (1509), and Cuba (1511).

≣ **First Meetings** In this woodcut from an illustrated edition of a 1493 letter from Christopher Columbus to Gabriel Sanchez, treasurer to King Ferdinand, Columbus is depicted trading with the native Taino of Hispaniola following his first trans-Atlantic voyage in 1492. Convinced that he was at least "east of India," Columbus called all the Indigenous peoples he encountered "Indian."

The alliances also enabled Columbus and the Spanish conquistadors more generally to exploit the resources of the islands and the labor of the native Taino who had been subdued. Rather than simply dismantling the Taino leader-ship and the social hierarchies that had existed before they arrived, the Spanish instead used the alliances to build a sys-tem known as ***encomienda*** for their own enrichment and to enslave many of the Taino commoners to aid the process.

The encomienda system resembled medieval European feudalism: Indigenous people were required to offer tribute to their Spanish "lord," the encomendero, in exchange for military protection. Sometimes the tribute payments were in goods or gold (of which there was some in Hispaniola); sometimes they were in labor. And, perhaps reflecting what he had seen at Elmina, Columbus soon sent captive Indigenous people (550 of them in 1495) back to the slave markets of southern Spain, effectively initiating an Atlantic slave trade in the opposite direction from what we customarily imagine: this one from the New World to the Old.

Catastrophic Contact

As in western Africa, the alliances that Columbus and other Spaniards forged could make for new cultural mixes. Both the demographic balances (the Spanish were few in number and almost entirely male) and the encouragement of the crown promoted sexual relations with the Tainos and other Indigenous peoples as well as intermarriage between them. A *mestizo* (mixed race, European and Native) population thus early came into being, providing the Caribbean basin with its version of Atlantic creoles.

But unlike the experience of western Africa, creolization took shape in an environment of drastic depopulation. Within a decade of arrival, as many as two-thirds of the Spanish conquerors and colonists had died, though the impact on the Taino was far, far worse. During roughly the same period, the Taino population of Hispaniola dropped from about 300,000 to about 60,000, or by around 80 percent, and by 1510 the population was down to a mere 33,000. By 1550 the Taino would, for all intents and purposes, be gone.

Diseases unquestionably played a great part in this demographic catastrophe. Although Native populations across the Caribbean basin had long interacted with one another—the Caribs (basis of "Caribbean"), enemies of the Taino, were especially adept sailors—they had no exposure to European-borne pathogens, nor did they raise domesticated animals from which many of these pathogens originated. As a result, Indigenous peoples were quickly afflicted with measles, mumps, influenza, and smallpox, and, in many villages, suffered near total losses (see Map 2.3). Nothing like this had ever happened to the Taino or to other Indigenous peoples of the Caribbean; there had never been plagues among them such as those that swept through fourteenth-century Asia and Europe. Yet the near extinction of the Native population was not simply a product of European pathogens. It was also a product of the cruelty and brutality of the Spanish conquest. The enslavement and near enslavement of thousands of Indigenous people (probably well over 200,000 around the Caribbean between 1492 and 1550), the harsh work regimes they were forced to endure, and the tribute demands that the Spanish exacted further decimated the Taino. Highly vulnerable to disease and weak from exploitation, their communities collapsed.

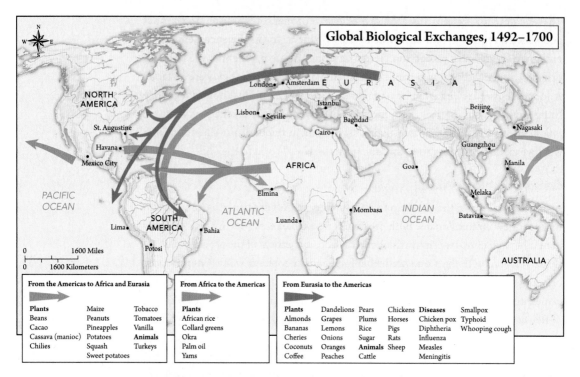

MAP 2.3   Global Biological Exchanges, 1492–1700

The system had its critics, even among the Spanish. One was Bartolome de Las Casas, a Hispaniola encomendero's son turned Dominican priest who became the leading defender of Native American rights in early modern times. Through pleading at court, and in university debates and publications, Las Casas helped to suppress the Indigenous slave trade and restrict the encomienda system of the early 1540s. Alarmed by the news of massive abuse and high death rates, the Spanish crown, too, called for an end to Native enslavement and an improvement in their material conditions. For the Taino, the reforms came too late.

2.4   Contact Zone: Central and South America

Analyze the diverse contacts of European and Indigenous peoples across Central and South America.

Hispaniola and other Caribbean islands served, for the Spanish, as important models for further contact and conquest. They had learned that Indigenous peoples had political divisions among themselves and were likely to be in some sort of military conflict; alliances could therefore be fashioned to Spanish benefit. They had learned that territories in and around the Caribbean basin might contain precious metals and other valuable resources, which could be obtained by enslaving the Indigenous people and extracting tribute from them. And they had learned that they didn't need to construct their own system of exploitation; they could effectively appropriate the mechanisms of domination and exploitation that the much more numerous Native societies already had developed.

Tenochtitlan

In these respects, the Spanish could have found no more alluring, or more formidable, Native society than the one that had arisen during the previous century in Tenochtitlan, the Aztec capital in the middle of Lake Texcoco in the valley of central Mexico (discussed in Chapter 1). By 1500 Tenochtitlan was connected to the mainland by bridges and causeways, supplied with fresh water by aqueducts,

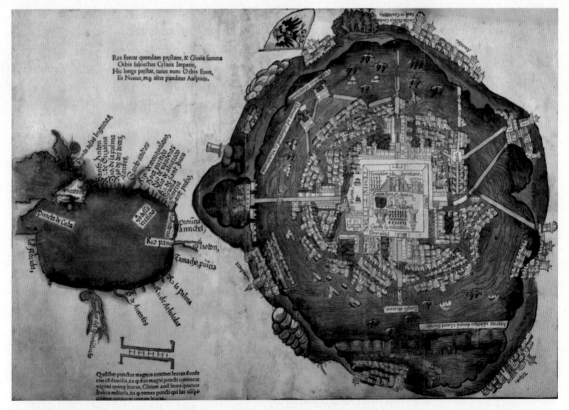

≡ **The City on the Lake**   The thriving and sophisticated large city of Tenochtitlan was also an extraordinary feat of urban planning, as it was built on an island in the middle of a lake. This 1524 map by a German cartographer illustrated the published letters of Hernán Cortés to Emperor Charles V. By then the Spanish had left Tenochtitlan in ruins.

and laced with canals; it also boasted a hereditary nobility, highly skilled crafts-men, and merchants who operated in the many local markets. In the adjacent coun-tryside, a large subordinated peasantry grew the crops that fed the city. Perhaps 5 percent of the population of more than 200,000 was enslaved, the result of warfare and tribute.

The religious life of Tenochtitlan was elaborate and polytheistic (with multiple gods), presided over by a powerful priesthood and deities such as Huitzilopochtli, the war god, who demanded human sacrifices—an incentive for conquest and captivity, owing to the need for sacrificial victims. Atop it all was the Aztec king (*Tlatoani*) who claimed descent from the Toltecs, a central Mexican civilization that had apparently flourished in the eleventh and twelfth centuries. Since 1502, that king was **Moctezuma II** ("Angry Lord the Younger"), the ninth ruler of Tenochtitlan, who brought the Aztecs to the pinnacle of their power and influence.

Surprising as it may sound, internal weaknesses marked the Aztec Empire at its height. Incessant captive wars and tribute demands had reached their limits, and chronic enemies such as the Tlaxcalans remained belligerent. New conquests were blocked by difficult terrain, declining tribute, and resistant locals. Given the tech-nologies available, there was no place else for the empire to grow, and even with complex water works in place, agricultural productivity barely kept the people fed. When several hundred strangers of Spanish descent appeared on Mexico's shores in 1519, points of vulnerability therefore abounded in the Aztec Empire.

The Spanish found out about the Aztecs inadvertently. Ever since Columbus had established a beachhead on Hispaniola, Spaniards had been taking the measure of the wider Caribbean basin and during the 1510s reached the Yucatan Peninsula on the mainland, where they encountered still-powerful remnants of the Maya civ-ilization (see Chapter 1). They also were busy raiding Native settlements to find slaves to replace the Taino, who were rapidly dying off. Word then came back to the Spanish bases in Hispaniola and Cuba of Native societies very different from those they had met on the islands and of the prospects for significant quantities of gold. There were tales of grand palaces and temples, of great riches and fierce warriors, and of pagan sacrifices, which together fired their greed and Christian fervor.

For their part, the Aztecs had learned that strange-looking, hairy men with leather shields and iron spears who snorted, bellowed, and sweated profusely were arriving in vessels miles to the east. Moctezuma consulted with his advisors and spiritual leaders to determine what might be afoot.

Cortés and Moctezuma

The Spanish colonial governor was determined to extend the realm of conquest and conversion. To lead the expedition, he chose the brash and ambitious Hernán Cortés, who had arrived in Hispaniola from Spain in 1504 and had been involved in the taking of Cuba. Along the way, Cortés was rewarded with an encomienda, which enabled him to prosper at the expense of the Taino, and he learned something about Spanish tactics of military domination. So, in February 1519, Cortés set out for the Yucatan with eleven ships, nearly 600 men, sixteen horses, and some artillery. He would clearly need help; the Native population of the Yucatan and central Mexico numbered well over one million (see Map 2.4).

Cortés got the help, as the Spanish had elsewhere, by forming alliances with Native groups and small states that had been subdued by the Aztecs and had become the Aztecs' sworn enemies. Although the Spaniards were relatively few, they often sealed the alliances by demonstrating their military might or by defeating Indigenous peoples in battle. The Tlaxcalans, who had thousands of soldiers, were sufficiently impressed to offer to "pay tribute [to Cortés] and serve him as subjects."

But significant help came as well from an unexpected source: a woman who has come to be known as La Malinche (meaning, variously, "translator" or "traitor") and who would act as an important interpreter and cultural go-between. To the best of our knowledge, she was born and grew up as the daughter

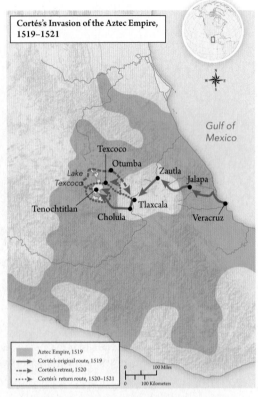

MAP 2.4 Cortés's Invasion of the Aztec Empire, 1519–1521 Cortés's campaigns in Mexico were facilitated by alliances with Indigenous peoples.

of an Aztec *cacique* and may have been named Malinal but was sold into slavery (perhaps by her mother) after her father's death. When Cortés arrived, Malinal's enslaver passed her along to Cortés, together with several other enslaved women. Educated and clever, Malinal quickly distinguished herself and was recognized not only as a go-between but as a guide to the people and territory Cortés planned to conquer. As a measure of their respect, the Spanish called her Doña (Lady) Marina. Cortés chose her as his consort, and she gave birth to one of his children, a mestizo son.

With La Malinche, the Tlaxcalans, and other Native groups now at his back, Cortés soon marched into Tenochtitlan and responded to the generous reception of Moctezuma (who viewed Cortés as possessing some great power, whether or not he was actually a deity) by taking the Aztec king hostage and beginning a campaign of brutal warfare that would eventually involve as many as 200,000 Tlaxcalans and their allies. Before long, smallpox added to the unfolding devastation. One Spanish soldier, Bernal Diaz del Castillo, who wrote a valuable account

Quitlauhtique

≡ **Offering Tributes**   Diego Muñoz Camargo (1529–1599), the mestizo son of a Spanish conquistador and a Tlaxcalan woman, was an earlier chronicler of Mexican history. In this illustration from his 1585 codex *History of Tlaxcala*, the Tlaxcalans offer gifts and provision to Cortés (seated) and his men. La Malinche, in her role as go-between, stands beside Cortés and translates.

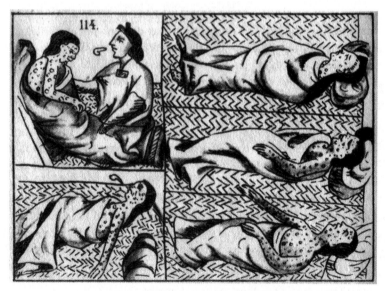

114.

≡ **A Devastating Disease**   This sixteenth-century image by an Aztec artist shows the ravages of different stages of smallpox.

of the campaign and had been dazzled by Tenochtitlan, soon saw "the street, the squares, the houses, and the courts . . . covered with dead bodies" and "all the causeways full, from one end to the other, of men, women, and children, so weak and sickly, squalid and dirty, and pestilential that it was a misery to behold them." By the time the Aztec submitted in 1521, Moctezuma was dead, Tenochtitlan was in rubble, and many thousands had perished.

Cortés was not finished, and neither were the other Spaniards on the mainland. Continuing to utilize alliances with Native states—including the now defeated Aztecs— Cortés brought thousands of soldiers to his side and managed to extend Spanish military hegemony first to the north and then to the southeast, where the Maya fell during the 1540s. By the time Cortés returned to Spain, where he died in 1547 as an immensely rich man, a smaller number of conquistadors (fewer than 200) under the command of Francisco Pizarro took advantage of warfare among the Inca—one side centered in Cuzco (in present-day Peru) and the other in

Quito (in present-day Ecuador)—to conquer that sprawling empire during the 1530s. The ensuing bloodbath claimed the lives of two of the most powerful Inca rulers as well as that of Pizarro himself.

Demographic Disaster

Spanish horses, swords, guns, and allies (shifting though they often were) proved critical to Spain's military success against what would seem to be enormous odds. But everywhere, too, the Spanish carried weapons that, while not visible to the eye, may have been the most devastating of all: pathogens. As on the Caribbean islands, the Native populations of the Central and South American mainland began to decline rapidly, which certainly suggested to them that the conquistadors had powers beyond anything they had ever seen. "There was then no sickness," a Mayan recalled of the times before the Spanish arrived. "They had no aching bones; they had then no high fever; they had then no smallpox; they had then no burning chest; they had then no abdominal pain; they had then no consumption; they had then no headache. At that time the course of humanity was orderly. The foreigners made it otherwise."

What to make of this disaster that befell them? There continues to be significant dispute over how large the precolonial population of Central and South America was and over how many Indigenous peoples may have died as a result of smallpox and other European-borne diseases.

But it is reasonable to say that between 1500 and 1650, the Native population of this very large area declined from somewhere between forty-five and fifty-five million (possibly more) to somewhere between eight and nine million, or by something over 80 percent. In the hardest hit areas, the decline might have been over 90 percent. Not even the Black Death in Europe had wrought human devastation such as this, and, over time, it encouraged adaptation—spiritual and political—among Indigenous peoples reeling from the experience.

Neither observers on the scene nor later scholars doubted the demographic disaster that Indigenous peoples experienced. They differed, however, over the explanation. For a long time, their perspectives focused on the cruelty and exploitation that the Spanish conquest inflicted. Some called it the **Black Legend**, a term suggesting that the Spanish alone were responsible. This view appealed to Indigenous peoples as well as to Europeans who despised the Spanish.

But more recent research of historians, archaeologists, and demographers suggests a deeper and more balanced understanding of what happened. What the researchers did was take a closer look both at the Native population before contact and at the reasons for its rapid and devastating decline thereafter. In the 1960s historians Woodrow Borah and Sherburne Cook estimated the size of the Native

PERSPECTIVES

Alliances and Betrayals

The *Lienzo (Canvas) de Tlaxcala*, which now survives only in a few fragmentary copies, was created by an anonymous Indigenous painter to document the defeat of the Aztec empire by the Mexican kingdom of Tlaxcala in alliance with Hernán Cortés. It is one of very few surviving examples of an Indigenous perspective on the conquest of Mexico. The original was created about twenty years after the key events of 1519. The text is in Nahuatl, the Indigenous language spoken by the Tlaxcalans. In this fragment, Cortés is shown in his Spanish armor seated between Xicoténcatl, a leader of the Tlaxcalan people, and La Malinche. Xicoténcatl is hosting them in his own house, and the ground before them is covered with presents given to the Spanish: corn, quail, turkeys, and tortillas. Both La Malinche and Xicoténcatl, clothed in the traditional red and white colors of the Tlaxcalans, are depicted by the Indigenous artist with their hands raised and fingers pointed. This gesture is a sign that both La Malinche and Xicoténcatl are speaking with authority. The Spanish conquistadors are at the left of the image, while Tlaxcalan leaders are at the right.

The eight paintings that make up the series known as the "Conquest of Mexico" were created in Mexico by anonymous artists some 150 years after the Spanish conquest of the Aztec Empire. They document the main events leading up to the defeat of Moctezuma II and the destruction of Tenochtitlan. We do not know who commissioned these paintings, or for what purpose, but the style in which they are painted

≡ **Fragment of the *Lienzo de Tlaxcala***

and details in the depictions of key figures show a view of the conquest that is very flattering to Spain and probably based on Spanish, not Indigenous, sources. The Spanish text (bottom left corner) explains what is happening: Moctezuma has left his city of Tenochtitlàn to greet Cortés and offers him a "a chain that he was wearing around his neck." Cortés moves to embrace Moctezuma, who raises his left hand to prevent Cortés from touching him, as that is not the custom among the Aztecs. La Malinche, behind Cortés, is dressed in elaborate Spanish clothes. Although European painters frequently depicted Indigenous peoples of the Americas in feathered skirts (see Perspectives in Chapter 6 for another example), neither Moctezuma nor the Aztec people are known to have ever worn such clothing.

≡ **Conquest of Mexico**

CONSIDER THIS

When future historians study the early twenty-first century, they will have an abundance of evidence and perspectives to examine (assuming that all of the digital media that record our lives today will still be accessible). For historians of the early modern Americas, however, the evidence is fragmentary, and the perspectives of subjugated peoples have been frequently neglected, lost, or erased. Which of these two images would you consider to be a more "authentic" depiction of the encounters between Cortés and Indigenous leaders? What does each image suggest about the role of La Malinche in these encounters? How does analysis of a visual image differ from analysis of a written document?

population in Mexico and the Caribbean basin and accounted for its decline by a combination of disease and Spanish exploitation.

Their research, still actively debated, caused a division among historians between what are called "low counters" (who estimate that the Native population of the Western Hemisphere in 1492 was about ten million, with one million of them in today's United States and Canada) and "high counters" (who at least double those estimates but occasionally argue that the Native population in 1492 may have been over 100 million). By the early 2000s, a scholarly consensus emerged that the Western Hemisphere had a population of about fifty million in 1492, about five million of whom were in present-day United States and Canada.

What of the decline? Historians would agree that disease struck Indigenous peoples the most devastating blows and likely accounts for their near extinction in some areas. But the most recent scholarship also reminds us of the impact that labor exploitation and enslavement had between the sixteenth and nineteenth centuries. We may never answer the big questions about the pre-contact Western Hemisphere or the relative impact of disease and exploitation, but we are getting closer and closer to an accurate picture. The Spanish, of course, had a different experience and a different perspective on what had happened. Many saw their military and political triumphs, as well as the collapse of Native states and societies, as the work of God's will, a testament to the righteousness of their exploits and the sinfulness and helplessness of their Native opponents. Conquest and colonization would thereafter join the forces of the sword and the Bible.

Encounters in Brazil

During most of the sixteenth century, the main contact zones involving Europeans (primarily the Spanish and Portuguese) and Indigenous peoples took shape in Central and South America. Indeed, as early as 1500, Portuguese sailors led by Pedro Álvares Cabral had encountered—by accident, as they were attempting to sail down the west coast of Africa and were taken many miles off course by currents and winds—the northeast corner of what we now call Brazil.

There Cabral and his expedition met up with Indigenous peoples who organized their lives very differently from the Aztecs and Incas but more like the Tainos and Caribs. Known as Tupi-speaking people and consisting of many small societies, they dominated the coastline from near the Amazon River delta in the north to the Rio de la Plata in the south, having emerged from long struggles with Tapuia (as the collection of non-Tupi rivals were called). They had not built great urban centers or constructed sprawling empires but were chiefly small-scale agriculturalists who supplemented their diets by hunting and gathering. Like the Spanish, the Portuguese benefitted from go-betweens and by forging alliances between warring groups, and although few Portuguese remained there for the first thirty years, they soon engaged in a lively trade in brazilwood (thus the name Brazil), a hardwood that was also used to make a highly valuable red dye. Like the Spanish, the Portuguese also benefitted from the coerced labor of some of the Tupi, particularly for work on the sugar plantations that accounted for Brazil's major cash crop. And like the contact zones of the Caribbean basin and the mainland of Central and South America, the Tupi soon suffered from deadly diseases that, by 1650, cut their numbers to near extinction.

2.5   Contact Zone: Eastern North America

||| Appraise the consequences of contact on both European and Indigenous cultures.

The Spanish would soon move farther into the north and west in Mexico and then, owing to an expedition led by Francisco Vázquez de Coronado in 1540–1542, into the North American southwest. They would also be the first Europeans to make their way through the Native country of the North American southeast and lower Mississippi Valley, under the lead of Hernando de Soto in 1539–1542, and of north-central Mexico, much of which we now call Texas, under the lead of Álvar Núñez Cabeza de Vaca in 1528–1536. But the absence of gold or other precious metals discouraged further forays, and although they had been sailing around the peninsula they called *La Florida* ("the flowery one") for some time, the Spanish were able to establish only one settlement, named St. Augustine, in 1565 to challenge the inroads of a small colony of French Protestants (known as Huguenots). Despised Protestants in Spanish eyes, and having fled harassment and persecution by the Catholic French crown, the Huguenots were quickly slaughtered. Mere outpost that it was, St. Augustine would stand as the longest continuously occupied European settlement in all of North America (see Map 2.5).

Farther north, from what are now the Carolinas up through Newfoundland, and from the Atlantic coast to the Mississippi River, lived as many as two million Indigenous people. They composed several major language groupings and a much larger number of villages, bands, and confederations. They were Algonquian, Iroquoian, and Siouan speakers, and they organized as chiefdoms, or **sachemships** (a term for chiefdom used in the Northeast), that we would come to know as Cherokee, Creek, Powhatan, Senecan, Mohawk, Chickasaw, Shawnee, Catawba,

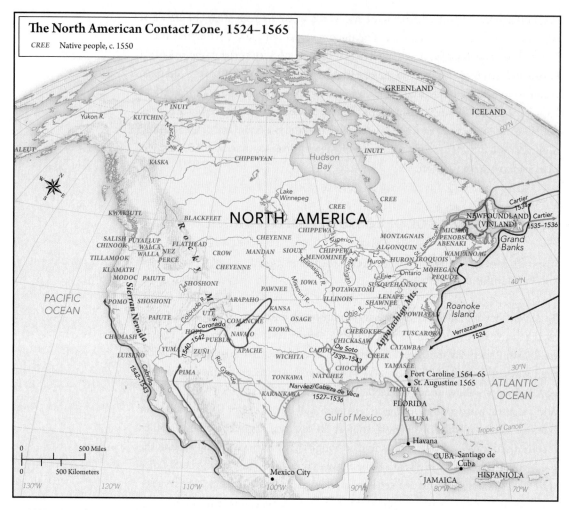

The North American Contact Zone, 1524–1565

CREE Native people, c. 1550

≡ **MAP 2.5** **The North American Contact Zone, 1524–1565** By the middle of the sixteenth century a North American contact zone brought Indigenous peoples increasingly in contact with European explorers, traders, and fishermen.

and Huron (Wendat), among many others. They mixed, in different ways, agricultural cultivation with hunting, fishing, and gathering, and in some cases were among the Indigenous peoples who reconstituted their groups and allegiances after the Mississippian cultures had collapsed in the thirteenth and fourteenth centuries (see again Map 2.5).

These were not egalitarian or undifferentiated societies. With rare exception, Native sachemships, almost by definition, were socially stratified with elites of various sorts among them. But some had distinctive features, certainly compared with societies in Europe at the time, with women wielding unusual power in decision-making and with kinship organized around the female line of descent (known as matrilineal; kinship and power among Europeans were organized along the male line of descent, known as patrilineal). Most everywhere, political and cultural power was also linked both to spirituality and to the accumulation and distribution of resources—we might call them "prestige goods"—that provided Native elites with influence over kin and non-kin alike. The key was not how much you *possessed* but rather how much you could *give away*, and so, for the most part, chiefdoms were mechanisms of social cohesion and wealth redistribution.

As a result, trade relations between different chiefdoms or confederations could extend over very large territories and proved crucial, less to the economic sustenance of Indigenous peoples than to the display of power that goods from afar—shells, beads, metals—could secure. Trade was not regarded as a source of "profit" or "enrichment," nor as an opportunity to drive hard bargains, but as a vehicle to develop alliances across space while building and consolidating followings at home. The greater the number of recipients of trade goods, the greater the authority of elite Indigenous peoples.

No surprise, therefore, that when Native Americans of eastern North America first encountered—first "discovered"—Europeans, what they imagined happening between them was trade. But there were some initial missteps. As best as we know, the earliest contact between Native North Americans and Europeans occurred around 1000 CE—500 years *before* Columbus. Norse explorers from western Scandinavia (present-day Denmark, Sweden, and Norway) had been sailing the northern Atlantic since at least the ninth century, in part owing to population and political pressures in their homelands. Often called Vikings, they established settlements on the British Isles and then headed north and west, making landfalls in what we now call Iceland and Greenland. From there, they eventually reached the far northeast coasts of North America, where they seem to have founded a colony (or colonies) they called **Vinland**, devoted to some farming, fishing, and livestock raising. Perhaps there was trade as well with Native inhabitants to whom they gave the derogatory name of "Skraelings," though their relations appear to have quickly degenerated into violence. Before too long, the Norse retreated to Greenland.

Five hundred years later, and only a few years after Columbus landed on Hispaniola, another Genoese mariner, this one named John Cabot, reignited European contact with North America (1497). Cabot was employed by the English, not the Spanish, crown and was commissioned to search for a northerly route across the Atlantic to Asia. Like his Genoese counterpart Columbus, Cabot failed in this project, but he did manage to find what the Norse had earlier called Vinland and what he called Newfoundland. (It appears Cabot knew nothing of the Norse ventures.) Over the following decades, mariners from England, France,

Portugal, and even the Basque country of northern Spain found their way to the waters off Newfoundland, which they had learned were immensely rich in codfish (we know this area as the Grand Banks).

The remainder of the sixteenth century would see a number of European journeys to North America, including two failed attempts by the English to establish a colony on the island of Roanoke off the coast of present-day North Carolina. All of these were, to a large extent, efforts by the English, French, and Dutch to raid Spanish shipping and contest Spanish power on both sides of the Atlantic. Lacking much in the way of formal navies, they issued licenses (letters of *marque*) to individuals, generally known as privateers, to do the work and share the spoils, though the line between privateers and pirates was hard to draw. The Spanish, after all, had established themselves as the dominant force in Europe and the Atlantic and were transporting gold and silver in growing quantities across the seas. The fastest route to wealth, as the Spanish had clearly demonstrated, was to seize someone else's.

Religious Turmoil in Europe and the Atlantic

But there was an increasingly important cultural push as well. During the second decade of the sixteenth century, tensions within the Catholic Church, first marked by the Great Schism of the late fourteenth and early fifteenth centuries, exploded into what is known as the Protestant Reformation. The leading voice was a German monk and theologian named Martin Luther who circulated his "Ninety-Five Theses," a set of propositions attacking the Catholic Church's practices and doctrines, in 1517. Luther and his followers argued that the Church had so far deviated from early Christian teachings that only radical reform could save it. Outraged Catholic officials branded them Protestant (or protesting) heretics; Luther was excommunicated, whereupon he formed his own "Lutheran" church. Other branches of Protestantism would follow.

What did the Protestant Reformation mean? For one thing, there was now an opening for monarchs like England's Henry VIII (r. 1509–1547) to grab power at the Catholic Church's expense, no small feat given the enormous wealth and authority that the Church held. In 1534, Henry orchestrated his own version of a Reformation and established the Protestant Church of England.

Even more important, Luther and his followers validated spiritual and doctrinal sensibilities that had been bubbling below the surface of Christian religion for some time and were at odds with Catholicism: discontent with papal indulgences (forms of absolution for sinful behavior) and church hierarchy, hostility to priests and their insistence on mediating parishioners' relationship with God, and the desire for the personal experience of God's grace. New ideas about faith, justification, conversion, sin, and salvation were embraced by Protestants. It was not simply a

☰ **From Pilgrimage to Pillaging**   During his reign, Henry VIII presided over the dissolution and sacking of Catholic monasteries across England, such as St. Mary's Abbey of York, shown here (founded in 1088, destroyed around 1539), enriching his coffers enormously in the process.

difference of opinion or practice; it was a potentially deadly divide, as Protestants and Catholics both saw it, between true believers and heretics.

Across the sixteenth century and well beyond, the Protestant Reformation would give enormous support to what was becoming an intense scramble among rival Europeans who not only aimed to enrich themselves but also hoped to punish their religious enemies and convert the heathen they met. Still, there was no discounting the lure of riches, and during the sixteenth century the French (mostly Catholics) joined the fray both to explore the territories of the "New World" and find a maritime passage to the markets of Asia. As early as 1524, an Italian-born navigator who had made his way to France, Giovanni da Verrazzano, crossed the Atlantic at the French crown's behest and sailed the North American coastline from Cape Fear in North Carolina to Newfoundland, making contact with different groups of Indigenous peoples along the way. Soon after (1534–1536), Frenchman Jacques Cartier followed in the sea steps of John Cabot, first sailing the waters around Newfoundland and, on a second voyage, moving down the St. Lawrence River to the Haudenosaunee (Iroquois) villages of Stadacona and Hochelaga, establishing small outposts named Québec and Montreal, mapping the area, and claiming what he called the "Country of Canadas" (from the Iroquoian) for France (see again Map 2.5).

English Colonizations

During the second half of the sixteenth century, the English came on the Atlantic scene and soon emerged as the leading maritime predators. Especially notorious and effective was their privateer Francis Drake. He had great success raiding Spanish shipping across the Caribbean basin and was soon sailing around Cape Horn (the southern tip of South America) into the Pacific, setting his sights on the Spanish silver trade to Manila. In the process, he became the second man to circumnavigate the globe (after Magellan) in 1577–1580 and was awarded a knighthood by Queen Elizabeth I for his various contributions to England's wealth, status, and power.

Almost simultaneously, the English were carrying out a different sort of project. The project was one of colonization, not in the Americas but in Ireland, which had formal allegiance to the crown (Ireland was regarded as a lordship) though was mostly Gaelic-speaking, culturally distinct, and governed by local Gaelic rulers and clans (large kinship groups) who claimed control of a great deal of land and insisted on doing things their own way. During the 1530s and 1540s, under the reign

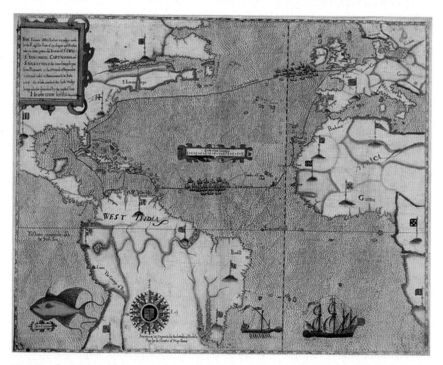

≡ **A Fearless Adventurer**   A map by Italian cartographer Giovanni Battista Boazio of Francis Drake's "Great Expedition" of 1585–1586, when at the behest of England's Queen Elizabeth Drake commanded a fleet of nearly thirty ships to attack Spanish possessions in the Americas.

of Henry VIII, the English attempted to reassert their authority and Anglicize the island; for the Protestant monarchy the Catholic Gaelic peasants who populated the Irish countryside were dangerous heathen and their leaders a threat to English power. Indeed, an unstable or hostile Ireland could bring the intervention of the Spanish or the French.

But when the English terms of incorporation were rejected and then provoked a series of local rebellions over the next several decades, the English crown, especially Henry's daughter Elizabeth I (r. 1558–1603), responded with a heavy fist: brutally suppressing the rebels and their peasant followers, confiscating their land, and sending English, Welsh, and Scottish Protestants to establish permanent settlements, known as **plantations**, to keep the Gaelic peasants in thrall and serve as symbols of an English "civilized" life. Much like the Spanish and Portuguese forays onto the Atlantic Islands of the fifteenth century, the English colonization of Ireland in the sixteenth century would be a "rehearsal" for North American ventures soon to follow, not to mention the beginning of five centuries of occupation and struggle.

One might suppose that the English, like the Portuguese, were destined to enter early the maritime competition for riches and power in the Americas, owing to their proximity to the Atlantic if nothing else, but this was hardly the case. During the fifteenth century, when the Spanish and Portuguese were heading into the Atlantic, England was embroiled in a convulsive conflict known as the War of the Roses (1455–1485) to determine which of two family lineages would claim the country's crown. Once the battle was finally settled, the victors, as might be expected, looked for any means available to refill their coffers and strengthen their hands. The Atlantic clearly beckoned.

Yet there were other developments in play as well. England, like the rest of Europe, had suffered terribly from outbreaks of bubonic plague during the fourteenth century. But the population began to recover and grow in the fifteenth and sixteenth centuries. More people meant more mouths to feed. In the countryside, larger landowners from the ranks of the gentry and nobility (meaning those who held landed estates or held wealth and power owing to hereditary title) began to experiment with new ways to increase crop yields (especially grains) and sheep herds (for their meat and wool). This involved the use of fertilizers to enrich the soil, the refining of crop rotations like the three-field system (in which a field is planted with one set of crops one year, a different set in the second year, and left fallow in the third year) to replenish worn-out fields, and the closing off of land that had been used by peasants and cottagers to cultivate crops and feed livestock in the interest of more efficient agricultural production.

As sensible as these experiments may sound, they spelled disaster for the overwhelming majority of English people in the countryside who—not unlike their Native counterparts in eastern North America—were small-scale agricultural cultivators dependent on customary practices of land use: on access to strips of land in different fields and on **common use rights** to forage, fish, hunt, and find firewood. The last of these experiments—the closing off of arable land—became known as **enclosure**, and over time it not only deprived smallholders and tenants of their common use rights but increasingly drove them off the land entirely. Growing numbers of the displaced and dispossessed began to wander through rural and village districts or head to towns and cities to find employment.

Poor, without work or prospects for it, and heavily male in composition—they were often referred to as "**masterless men**," their ties to the gentry and nobility having been severed—these internal refugees struck fear into the hearts of the established order. They were called beggars, thieves, idlers, vagabonds, and vagrants—able-bodied people who simply refused to work and, consequently, were likely to become fomenters of riot and unruliness. The official reaction, as with the Irish rebels, was merciless. Vagrancy was now legally defined to include an incredible range of activities regarded as forms of idleness, and over the course of the sixteenth century Parliament prescribed punishments for vagrants that spanned from whipping and branding to enslavement, banishment, and, for multiple offenses, even execution.

Yet the problems associated with wandering, masterless men had another possible solution that English observers and policymakers began to glimpse in the 1560s, 1570s, and 1580s: emigration and colonization. To be sure, interest in colonizing Ireland had much to do with the conquest and subjugation of a Gaelic population already deemed beastly and unruly; and interest in colonizing North America was nurtured by the lure of commercial gains and geopolitical advantage. But more than a few visionaries of the time, like geographer and minister Richard Hakluyt

≡ **Criminalizing Poverty**   English laws criminalized begging and vagrancy at the same time that enclosure laws forced rural people off the land. In this 1536 English woodcut, a vagrant (center) is led through the streets by his bound hands as a law enforcement official (right) whips him with a cat-o'-nine tails. In the distance, a man hangs from the gallows, perhaps as punishment for stealing.

(called "the younger," to distinguish him from his similarly eminent cousin), saw "the manifolde imployment of numbers of idle men" as a central part of the colonial logic. "Many men of excellent wittes and of divers singular gifts that are not able to live in England," Hakluyt wrote in 1584, "may there be raised againe, and doo their Contrie good service: and many nedefull uses there may require the saving of great nombers that for trifles may otherwise be devoured by the gallowes."

The English crown of the sixteenth century lacked the means—at least in terms of personnel, ships, and treasury—to get directly involved in distant and uncertain colonial ventures. As a result, the English, much like the Spanish and French before them, effectively subcontracted the job to private individuals and companies —known as "joint stock companies"—which would assume the risks in hopes of gaining the rewards. Among those most interested in the project were not well-established merchants in London (they preferred their safe investments and steady incomes) but rather ambitious and well-placed men from England's southwest who already had some experience in raiding Spanish shipping and colonizing Ireland: Sir Francis Drake, Sir Walter Ralegh, and Sir Humphrey Gilbert chief among them, all knighted by the crown. The two Richard Hakluyts, who both lived in London, would be their voices and interpreters.

The elder Hakluyt identified three "ends" of North American colonization: "to plant Christian religion," "to trafficke" (engage in trade), and "to conquer," though not necessarily in that order. "To plant Christian religion without conquest, will bee hard," he conceded, but "Trafficke easily followeth conquest." As Hakluyt's words suggest, the objectives of the investors had more in common with the medieval and early modern society in which they lived than in the market-driven world of the future. They hoped, that is, to establish large landed estates and enrich themselves chiefly through the extraction of rents and other forms of dues and tribute from an assortment of tenants and laborers—as the Spanish were already doing in Mexico and Peru and the English themselves were already doing in Ireland—rather than through the cultivation and sale of crops on the international market.

Indigenous and English Perspectives

What did Indigenous peoples see coming? Indigenous peoples in various parts of eastern North America responded to their "discovery" of these Europeans in different ways. For some of them, it was a frightening and unsettling experience from the initial sightings, with reports of ghostly apparitions, sea monsters, or rare fish. Some Algonquians apparently "tooke the first ship they saw for a walking Iland, the Mast to be a Tree, the Saile white Clouds, and the discharging of Ordinance for Lighting and Thunder." By contrast, along the St. Lawrence River Jacques Cartier found that the Indigenous peoples "came towards our boats in as friendly and

MAPPING AMERICA

Winds, Currents, and Transatlantic Exploration

Is there something particular about European culture that explains why Europeans rather than explorers from other cultures discovered the Atlantic oceanic routes that linked the "Old World" to the "New"? Until fairly recently, some historians argued just that—that Europeans were uniquely poised to achieve this milestone in world history. Such a contention, however, has been severely undermined by environmental historians who have demonstrated that for most of history winds and currents have played a huge part in conditioning, and even determining, who and what went where in the world.

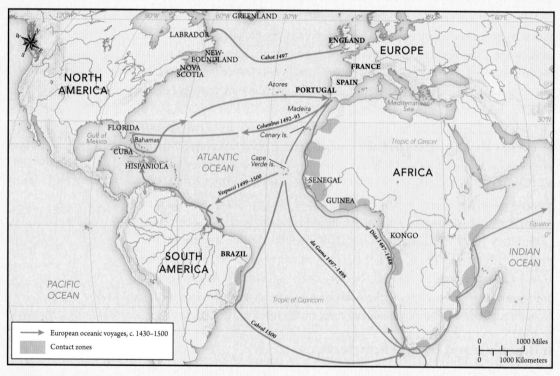

MAP 1   Maps such as this one, which charts European oceanic exploration of the fifteenth and early sixteenth centuries without showing winds and currents, can give the impression that these voyages were carefully planned and smoothly executed.

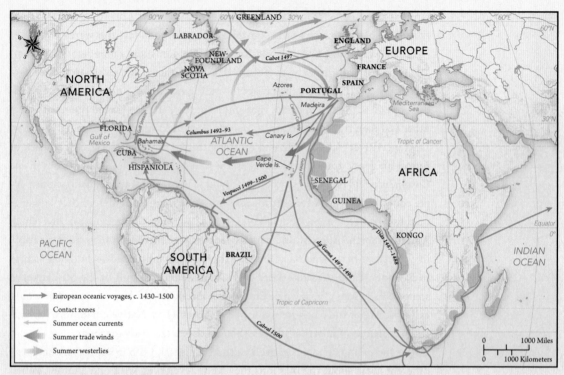

≡ **MAP 2**   In contrast, a map such as this one, which sets European ocean explorations in the context of the wind systems and currents of the Atlantic basin, show these voyages in a different light. Currents like the Canary Current and fixed-wind systems like the trade winds and westerlies largely determined where Spanish and Portuguese navigators would land. What distinguishes explorers like Christopher Columbus and Amerigo Vespucci is not that they set off with the right kind of culture, but that they set off from the right place.

Thinking Geographically

1. As a historian, what sorts of questions could you ask about climate and topography (the physical features of an area, such as mountains and rivers) that would lead to a better understanding of why key events unfolded in the way that they did?

2. If you were creating a map of the world at this exact moment to be placed in a time capsule for a historian to open in fifty years, what key information (geographical, topographical, and climatological) would your map include? What sorts of questions might that future historian ask about this moment, and what would be most essential for them to know?

familiar a manner as if we had been natives of the country, bringing us great store of fish and of whatever else they possessed, in order to obtain our wares."

Either way, Indigenous peoples in their chiefdoms and confederations generally viewed the Europeans as potential allies in their own rivalries and warfare and as potential partners in their own trading networks. The exchange of goods did not end at the site of trade; Indigenous peoples in turn traded them with each other and then traded them again. European goods originally exchanged in the St. Lawrence River Valley could end up along the Atlantic coast of the Northeast, or European goods traded in the area of the Chesapeake or the Outer Banks of the Carolinas could end up near the Great Lakes. The result was that Indigenous people could easily learn of the Europeans and their wares long before they laid eyes on these strange-looking people. As early as 1524, when Verrazzano reached North America's northeast coast, Indigenous peoples were there with furs in anticipation, likely because of the trade that French fishermen had cultivated around their camps in Newfoundland, Arcadia (later Nova Scotia), and the gulf of the St. Lawrence some years before. Thus, when English colonizers showed up at what they would call Roanoke or the Chesapeake or Massachusetts Bay, Native chiefdoms, perhaps with suspicions or mistrustful eyes, thought they were ready for them.

The Indigenous peoples as well as the English and other Europeans had very different ideas about the relations they were developing with one another. When contact occurred, Indigenous people generally expected to engage in trade for European goods—cloth and metals in particular—but they understood trade mainly in political terms. The exchange of goods, as they saw it, was a way of forming and strengthening alliances, of constructing hierarchies and supporting prevailing ones, of avoiding conflicts, and of expressing power and authority both within their communities and between different chiefdoms and confederations. Trade was also a way of conducting diplomacy. Nothing was more central to settling disputes or securing allies than the rituals of gift giving. Indeed, trade was an integral component of larger systems of gifting and redistribution that bound groups of Indigenous peoples together (see Map 2.6).

Europeans were not entirely unfamiliar with such systems of exchange. Outside of the larger cities and towns, and especially in the countryside on the continent and in England, trade was mostly local, usually involved barter of various types (material objects and food as well as labor), and often was tied to community rituals of redistribution and submission (notably in relation to the church or the nobility). But the Europeans who arrived in the Western Hemisphere during the sixteenth and seventeenth centuries were already part of a developing trade network that was increasingly global in scope and linked to the rise of centralized states—one that privileged economic gain, acquisitiveness, and domination.

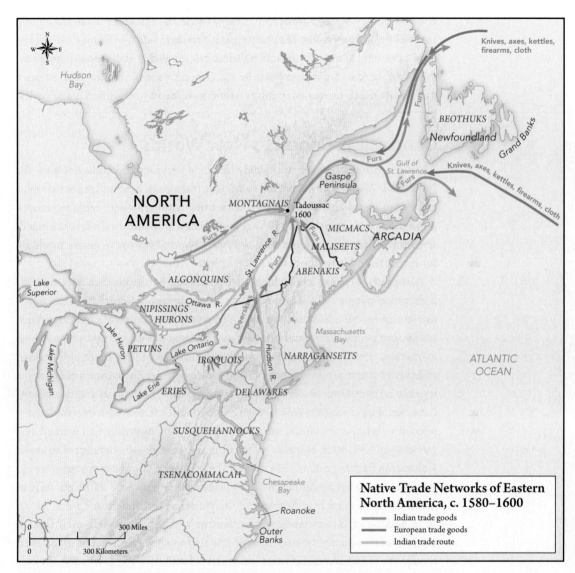

≡ **MAP 2.6**   Native Trade Networks of Eastern North America, 1580–1600

For a time, of course, particularly when Europeans were relatively few in number, they and Indigenous peoples could assimilate trade to their own understandings and practices. Indigenous peoples could refashion European goods to fill uses and needs they already had (rather than create new ones) and incorporate them into well-established networks and ceremonies. They could substitute copper pots for earthenware ones, metal for flint arrowheads fashioned from stone, and woolens for furs. And these new materials could simply be added to other prestige goods—as they were in western Africa—that were regularly exchanged among themselves or formed part of gifting rituals. On their side, the Europeans did not have to recognize the cultural and political meanings that Indigenous peoples ascribed to trade in order to collect the furs, deerskins, and tobacco that, in turn, flowed into the transoceanic trading systems governed by very different principles.

Conclusion: Contact's New Worlds

Although contact would ultimately lead to devastating consequences for Indigenous peoples, its impact led to transformations in how Indigenous peoples and Europeans alike came to live. These transformations for both Indigenous peoples and Europeans included how they ate, dressed, traveled, dwelled, worshipped, and formed families. In less than a century, imported European goods would be fundamental to Native life across eastern North America.

Europeans were no less influenced by contact. Far more than was true for Indigenous peoples, the European diet would be revolutionized by the introduction of new foods: corn, potatoes, squash, beans, tomatoes, and pumpkins. Indigenous peoples introduced Europeans to new goods that could be turned into marketable commodities, such as furs, skins, and tobacco. As a result of European and Native American sexual contact and intermarriage, Europeans were brought into Native communities. The mestizo offspring of their marriages and sexual contacts would be among the North American "Atlantic creoles" who operated as important political and cultural mediators, like the way Malinche had worked as a go-between for Cortés. Eventually the cultural exchange—often referred to as the Columbian Exchange, to note that it was the result of Columbus's voyage—would produce an entirely new mix, which would become emblematic of life not only in North America but across the whole of the Western Hemisphere.

Something of this dynamic was evident in West Africa as well, even though the Europeans did not seek to conquer or colonize the African interior and even though the most extended contact was with enslaved Africans. Over time, the cultural life of the Western Hemisphere was deeply influenced by African economic practices, languages, foodways, and spirituality. The West African coast felt the effects as well. Just think of Abee Coffu Jantie Seniees with whom the chapter began. This is what was "new" about the world being "discovered" by all parties and peoples.

WHAT IF North American Contacts with Europeans Were More Like West African Contacts?

Europeans and Indigenous peoples made contact with one another during the fifteenth and sixteenth centuries on three different continents many miles apart. They first met in west and west-central Africa in the mid-fifteenth century, then in the Caribbean basin in the late fifteenth and early sixteenth centuries, then in South America a bit later in the sixteenth century, and then in North America at various points in the sixteenth and early seventeenth centuries. There may also have been an even earlier meeting at the dawn of the eleventh century in what became Newfoundland.

Each of the meetings had different dynamics owing to the particular territory, the Native population there, and the ways in which Indigenous peoples may have been organized economically and politically. And yet there were certain similarities in all contact points regarding the importance of alliances, trade, and intermixing, which together made for a "new world" for everybody involved. But one of the great differences between Africa and the Western Hemisphere was the impact of disease: in Africa, Europeans did not bring pathogens for which Africans did not have immunities, while the disease environment for Europeans there proved to be harsh and often deadly; in the Western Hemisphere, Europeans brought diseases against

which Indigenous peoples had no immunities, while Europeans did not in turn suffer devastating consequences from the diseases they encountered there. The Western Hemisphere saw Native populations and communities unravel fairly quickly due to disease and exploitation, while the African continent would not experience a major depopulation for at least another century (as we will see, for different reasons).

What if the circumstances of contact in the Western Hemisphere turned out to be much more like Africa, where the societies remained robust and militarily formidable and the Europeans met them from a position of relative weakness? What if the Indigenous peoples of the Americas were able to conduct trading and political relations more on terms that were favorable to them? Would the Spanish, Portuguese, French, and English have been able to exploit the Indigenous peoples as much as they did and slowly destroy the societies that Indigenous peoples had built? And what might the hemisphere have looked like in the longer run if there was more of a standoff between contending parties? Or what if, especially in Central and South America, the Spanish had suffered a massive military defeat at Native hands? How might the course of history have been changed?

DOCUMENT 2.1: A Spanish Conquistador's Description of Tenochtitlan, 1568

Bernal Diaz del Castillo was a soldier in Cortés's army, and he later wrote an important history of the conquest of the Aztec Empire. Here he describes the capital city of Tenochtitlan and the Spaniards' first encounter with Moctezuma II.

During the morning, we arrived at a broad Causeway and continued our march towards Iztapalapa [Tenochtitlan], and when we saw so many cities and villages built in the water and other towns on dry land and that straight and level Causeway going towards Mexico, we were amazed and said that it was like the enchantments they tell us in the legend of Amadis. . . . And some of our soldiers even asked whether the things that we saw were not a dream. . . . We arrived near Iztapalapa, to behold the splendor of the other Caciques who came out to meet us, who were the Lord of the town named Cuitlahuac, and the Lord of Culuacan, both of them near relations of Moctezuma. And then when we entered the city of Iztapalapa, the appearances of the palaces in which they lodged us! How spacious and well built they were, of beautiful stonework and cedar wood, and the wood of other sweet-scented trees, with great rooms and courts, wonderful to behold, covered with awnings of cotton cloth. . . . Early the next day we left Iztapalapa [and] proceeded along the Causeway which is here eight paces in width and runs so straight to the City of Mexico that it does not seem to me to turn either much or little, but, broad as it is, it was so crowded with people that there was hardly room for them all . . . so that we were hardly able to pass by the crowds of them that came; and the towers and the cues were full of people as well as the canoes from all parts of the lake. . . . They took us to lodge in some large houses, where there were apartments for all of us, for they had belonged to the father of the Great Moctezuma, who was named Axayaca, and at that time Moctezuma kept there the great oratories for his idols, and a secret chamber where he kept bars and jewels of gold. . . . The Great Moctezuma was about forty years old, of good height and well proportioned, slender and spare of flesh, not very swarthy, but of the natural color and shade of an Indian. . . . He had many women as mistresses, daughters of Chieftains, and he had two great Cacicas as his legitimate wives. He was free from unnatural offences. The clothes that he wore one day, he did not put on again until four days later. He had over two hundred Chieftains in his guard, in other rooms close to his own, not that all were meant to converse with him, but only one another, and when they went to speak with him they were obliged to take off their rich mantles and put on others of little worth, but they had to be clean, and they had to enter barefoot with their eyes lowered to the ground, and not to look up in his face.

Source: Bernal Diaz del Castillo, *True History of the Conquest of New Spain, from* David Carrasco, ed., *The History of the Conquest of New Spain* (Albuquerque: University of New Mexico Press, 2008), 156–166.

DOCUMENT 2.2:   An English Explorer's View of Indigenous People on Roanoke Island, 1588

In this excerpt from his account of the first attempted English settlement in North America on Roanoke Island, explorer and scientist Thomas Hariot writes about the Native inhabitants he met.

It remains to speak a word or two about the native inhabitants, their nature and manners, leaving detailed discourse about them until a later, more convenient time. Now it is only necessary to reassure you that they are not to be feared. I do not think they will trouble our living there or obstruct our farming. I rather believe that they will have cause both to fear and to love us.

The clothing of the natives consists of loose deerskin mantles and aprons of the same fur which they wear around their waists; they wear nothing else. In stature they differ one from another, much as we do in England. They have no edged tools or weapons of iron or steel to attack us with, nor do they know how to make them. The only weapons they possess are bows made of witch hazel, arrows made of reeds, and flat-edged wooden truncheons, which are about a yard long. For defense they wear armour made of sticks wickered together with thread, and they carry shields made of bark.

Their towns are small and few, especially near the seacoast, where a village may contain but ten or twelve houses—some perhaps as many as twenty. The largest town we saw had thirty houses. In many cases the villages are walled with stakes covered with the bark of trees or with poles set close together.

The houses are built of small poles attached at the top to make them round in shape, much like the arbors in our English gardens. The poles are covered from top to bottom either with bark or with mats woven of long rushes. The dwellings are usually twice as long as they are wide; sometimes they are only twelve or sixteen yards long, but we have seen them as much as twenty-four yards in length.

In one part of the country a *Weroans*, or chief, may govern a single town, but in other parts the number of towns under one chief may vary to two, three, six, and even to eight or more. The greatest *Weroans* we met governed eighteen towns, and he could muster seven or eight hundred warriors. The language of each chief's territory differs from that of the others, and the farther apart they are, the greater the differences.

Compared with us, the natives are poor. They lack skill and judgment in using the materials we have and esteem trifles above things of greater value. But if we consider that they lack our means, they are certainly very ingenious. Although they do not possess any of our tools, or crafts, or sciences, or art, yet in their own way they show excellent sense.

They have already a religion of their own, which is far from the truth, yet for that reason there is hope that it may sooner and more easily be reformed.

They believe in many gods, which they call *Mantoac*. These gods are of different kinds and degrees. Their chief god has existed from all eternity. They affirm that when he created the world, he first made the other principal gods, in order to use them in the creation and government to follow. Then he made the sun, the moon, and the stars. The petty gods act as instruments of the more important ones.

It happened that within a few days of our departure the people began to die very fast. In some towns twenty people died, in some forty, in some sixty, and in one six score; this was a large portion of the inhabitants. And the strange thing was that this occurred only in towns where we had been and where they had done some mischief against us, and it happened always after we had left. The disease with which they were stricken was so strange a one that they did not know anything about it or how to cure it. Even their elders could not remember the like ever having happened before. After this disease had struck in four or five places, some of our native friends, especially Chief Wingina, were persuaded that it was we who brought it about, helped by our God. They thought that through Him we were able to slay anyone at any place and without the use of weapons.

Source: Thomas Hariot, A Brief and True Report of the New Found Land of Virginia (1588).

Thinking About Contingency

1. What strikes you most about Diaz del Castillo's description of the Aztec city and the people he saw there?
2. What are the similarities and differences between what Diaz del Castillo saw and what Hariot saw in their first encounters with Native Americans?
3. What might the hemisphere have looked like in the longer run if Spanish and English encounters were more like what Europeans experienced in West Africa?

REVIEW QUESTIONS

1. What challenges did the Portuguese, Spanish, and West Africans face in trying to sail the Atlantic Ocean? Why did the Portuguese and Spanish succeed in moving west across the Atlantic and south down the African coast while Africans remained much closer to shore?

2. How important were political alliances when different groups made first contact with each other? Were they more important in some places than others?

3. How different were Africans, Europeans, and Native Americans from one another in their forms of political and economic organization and in their cultural practices?

4. How did a small number of Spanish conquistadors manage to subdue both the Aztecs and the Incas, who had each built a formidable empire?

5. What role did Europeans monarchies play in the expeditions that resulted in early contact?

6. What was the relative role of disease in Africa and the Western Hemisphere? Why did some groups fare much better than others?

KEY TERMS

Atlantic creoles (p. 51)

Black Legend (p. 61)

Canary Current (p. 47)

common use rights (p. 72)

contact zone (p. 48)

cultural mediator (go-between)
  (p. 45)

Elmina (p. 49)

enclosure (p. 72)

encomienda (p. 54)

feitoria (p. 49)

masterless men (p. 72)

Moctezuma II (p. 58)

mestizo (p. 55)

pidgins (p. 50)

plantations (p. 71)

sachemships (p. 65)

Taino (p. 53)

Vinland (p. 67)

RECOMMENDED READINGS

Christopher Columbus, *The Four Voyages* (Penguin Classics edition, 1992).

Finn Fuglestad, *Slave Traders by Invitation: West Africa's Slave Coast in the Pre-Colonial Era* (Oxford University Press, 2018).

Charles Mann, *1493: Uncovering the New World Columbus Created* (Vintage, 2012).

Daniel Richter, *Facing East from Indian Country* (Harvard University Press, 2003).

Jose Luis de Rojas, *Tenochtitlan: Capital of the Aztec Empire* (University Press of Florida, 2012).

Kevin Siepel, ed., *Conquistador Voices* (Spruce Tree Press, 2015).

John K. Thornton, *Africa and Africans in the Making of the Atlantic World, 1400–1800* (Cambridge University Press, 1998).

Camilla Townsend, *Fifth Sun: A New History of the Aztecs* (Oxford University Press, 2019).

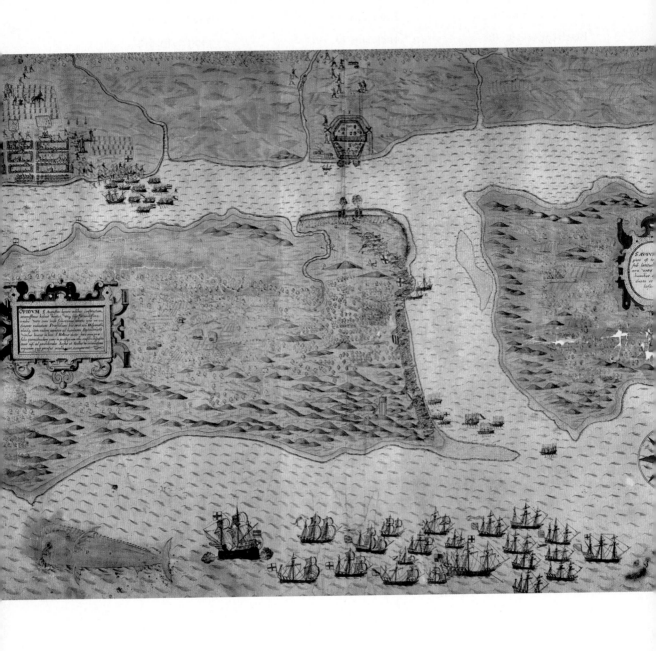

Settler Colonies and Imperial Rivalries
1565–1681

Chapter Outline

3.1 Spain's Empire

Explain why the Spanish pushed into North America, and describe the type of colonies they established in Florida and New Mexico.

3.2 An English Colony on the Chesapeake

Analyze the tenuous nature of English colonization in the Chesapeake and the role of tobacco and forced labor in transforming Virginia.

3.3 New England

Outline the different objectives that led to the colonization of New England and the conflicts that were generated.

3.4 The Middle Colonies and the Caribbean

Identify the distinctive features of both the Middle Colonies and the Caribbean, and explain why the Caribbean quickly became the center of attention for Parliament and the crown.

≡ **English Attack on St. Augustine**   This engraved, hand-colored map, created by Italian cartographer Baptista Boazio in 1589, depicts the attack by the English privateer Sir Francis Drake on the Spanish colony of St. Augustine, Florida, in 1586. Boazio's map is the earliest depiction of any city or territory now part of the United States.

Around Christmastime in 1606, an expedition of three ships set out from London, destined for Chesapeake Bay along the east coast of North America. The expedition was commanded by an experienced mariner named Christopher Newport and was financed by the Virginia Company of London, a group of merchant investors chartered by England's King James I. The ships carried 144 passengers and crew, all adult males, and their plan was to establish a base from which they could explore the terrain, perhaps locate a waterway to the East Indies, and hopefully find some gold or silver. With luck, they could return to England in a year or two.

This was already recognized as a precarious endeavor, and it must have taken no small amount of courage and greed to join this expedition. Two earlier efforts by the English to establish colonies on Roanoke Island, off the coast of present-day North Carolina in 1585 and 1587, ended first in failure and then in disaster as more 100 English settlers disappeared from what has come to be called the "Lost Colony." To this day, we don't know exactly what happened to them (our best guess is that they fled to the mainland

Timeline

1555	1565	1575	1585	1595	1605	1615

1565 > Spanish establish a settlement at St. Augustine

1585 > First English colony on Roanoke Island established but evacuated the next year

1587 > Second English colony on Roanoke Island established

1598 > Spanish establish the colony of Santa Fe in what they call Nuevo (New) Mexico

1607 > English begin colonization of Virginia with settlement at Jamestown

1609 > English explorer Henry Hudson sails up what is later renamed the Hudson River

1612 > Tobacco palatable for European tastes first grown in Virginia

and were killed by hostile Indigenous people), and they left no evidence of precious metal to be found. Why then keep at it? Why establish colonies in such a new and barely known place?

Although from a present-day perspective the colonization of what would become the United States by various groups of Europeans may seem to be an almost inevitable process, this was hardly the case at the time. The Europeans who made contact with Indigenous peoples across the Western Hemisphere were mainly interested in riches, plunder, trade, a faster route to Asia, and perhaps Christian conversion; they were not necessarily interested in establishing formal colonies in very far-off places, and their early experiences in western Africa suggested that colonization would not be easy to accomplish.

A project of colonization would in fact have been very new to the Europeans. Spain, Portugal, France, England, and the Netherlands were themselves in the process of

1625	1635	1645	1655	1665	1675	1685

1619 › First enslaved Africans sold in Virginia

1620 › English colony of Plymouth established under the leadership of William Bradford

1624 › Dutch establish colony of New Netherland

1627 › First English settlement on the Caribbean island of Barbados

1630 › English establish Massachusetts Bay Colony under the leadership of John Winthrop

1636 › Roger Williams, fleeing repression in Massachusetts Bay, settles Providence, Rhode Island

1637 › Sugarcane introduced to Barbados by the Dutch

1638 › Anne Hutchinson, banished from Massachusetts Bay, joins Roger Williams in Providence

1664 › English take New Netherland from the Dutch and call it New York

1681 › William Penn gets a royal English charter for the colony of Pennsylvania

attempting to bring various regions in their own countries under central control. Spain and Portugal took the lead during the fifteenth century; England, France, and the Netherlands followed during the sixteenth and seventeenth. Indeed, the European making of an Atlantic world was propelled in good part by the needs of centralizing states for the means to secure their power at home.

So long as it was possible to ship precious metals and valuable trade goods through small outposts in distant territories—like Elmina on the West African coast—the Europeans were content to do just that. But as the Atlantic became the site of increasingly intense rivalries among emerging European states, colonies became vehicles for expanding those outposts and preventing rivals from enlarging their own spheres of influence and power. These colonies were often very different from one another, yet they also symbolized the territorial claims of European states while effectively making those states into empires.

3.1   Spain's Empire

Explain why the Spanish pushed into North America and describe the type of colonies they established in Florida and New Mexico.

First, as we know, came the Spanish. During the 1490s, they had established important beachheads in the Caribbean. By the late 1530s, they had conquered the Western Hemisphere's two most formidable empires—the Aztec and Inca—and had been exploring the Gulf and Atlantic coasts of North America in search of slaves and precious metals. And by 1550, they had sent expeditions into the North American interior from the southeast to the southwest. Spain had not only become the major power on the European continent but over the course of less than a century had built an empire that extended from the Atlantic Islands off the coast of northwest Africa across the Atlantic Ocean to the Andes, Central Mexico and the Caribbean basin, and the southern tier of North America. Before the sixteenth century was out, it would also include the Philippines, way out in the western Pacific.

Spanish sovereignty in the Americas required legal support, however. Even before the voyages of Columbus, Portugal's overseas interests had clashed with Spain's. With the pope's mediation, in 1494 Spain and Portugal signed the **Treaty of Tordesillas**, dividing the globe between those two countries and giving the

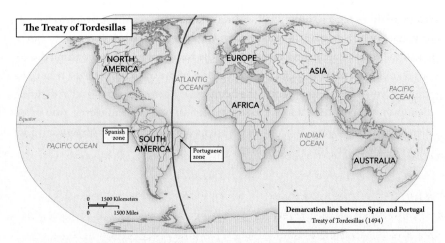

≡ **Map 3.1 The Treaty of Tordesillas, 1494** The boundary dividing the globe between Spain and Portugal was largely diplomatic and mostly unenforceable.

Spanish control of the entire Western Hemisphere, save for the northeast portion of South America (see Map 3.1).

Why was the Roman Catholic pope involved in an agreement of this kind? First, fifteenth-century Europeans regarded his authority as above that of secular rulers. More important, however, was the matter of spreading the Christian gospel. Iberian monarchs, as pious Catholics, promised to sponsor the conversion of everyone their subjects encountered abroad and also to continue the medieval fight against "infidels." Commerce may have supplied the initial and most powerful motive for overseas expansion, but a drive for religious and cultural hegemony soon played an important part in European colonization.

The Nature of Spanish Colonies

Spain's empire-building initially rested on the work of private contractors known as *adelantados*. Like Columbus, Cortés, and Pizarro, they received licenses from the Spanish crown to finance and carry out expeditions of plunder and conquest for which the crown would receive a portion of the take as well as political authority over any lands that were conquered. Most of the adelantados came from the ranks of the lesser gentry whose prospects in Spain were limited but who could make names for themselves militarily and strike it rich in the "New World." Some surely did and, in the process, laid the foundation of Spanish power.

But the Spanish crown also saw potential trouble in the making. If too much authority was left to the adelantados and their conquistadors, then before long the crown could watch a wealthy, landholding aristocracy take shape overseas with its own ideas of how to govern, who to obey, and how much silver and gold to claim. And if the enslavement and exploitation of the Native populations continued, a rebellion might be provoked that would push the empire into retreat. As a result, the Spanish crown began to organize the hemispheric conquests politically, dividing them into **viceroyalties** under the supervision of officials and clerics who owed allegiance to the crown. The first viceroyalty established was New Spain in 1535; the second was Peru in 1542 (see Map 3.2).

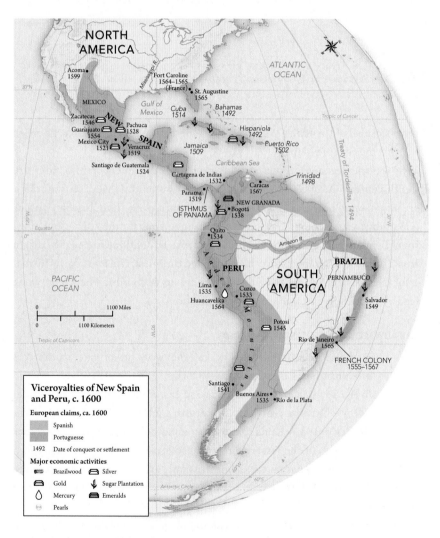

≡ **Map 3.2   Viceroyalties of New Spain and Peru, c. 1600**

The Spanish focused their main attention on the mining areas from Potosí in the Andes to Zacatecas north of what is now called Mexico City. This was where most of the silver was being extracted and shipped, and this was where the densest populations of Indigenous people, who could pay tribute and be forced to work the mines and the lands, were to be found. Not surprisingly, as word of the great riches spread through Spain, more Spaniards thought about taking their chances and heading across the Atlantic. Over the course of the sixteenth century, about 250,000 Spaniards did just that.

This was how Spanish colonization took place. The crown subcontracted with private individuals to explore the oceans and new territories and lay claim to any lands for Spain. The lands themselves would be controlled by the adelantados, who, in turn, attempted to subdue the Native population, demand tribute, exploit Native labor, and seek gold and silver. They would be joined by Catholic missionaries (friars), mostly of the Jesuit and Franciscan orders, who would carry out what the crown called its "principal purpose for which we order new discoveries and settlements to be made . . . preaching the holy gospel" and converting the Indigenous peoples to Christianity. As the Spanish population grew and the Native population declined, the crown took a larger hand in governance and, through their representatives and the friars, attempted to trim the sails of adelantados turned encomenderos. Royal Orders issued in 1573, in fact, forbade violence or unauthorized conquests against

≡ **Brutality Against Indigenous Peoples.**   This image, from the sixteenth-century *Codex Tepetlaoztoc*, depicts the brutality of many encomenderos toward Indigenous peoples. The *Codex* was evidence in a lawsuit by the Indigenous people of Tepetlaoztoc in Mexico against the encomenderos.

Indigenous peoples (the term "pacification" was used instead), though the Orders, like similar royal edicts across the centuries, were most often observed in the breach (that is to say, they were ignored—"obedezco pero no complo" was the familiar response, or "I obey but do not comply"). Some of these colonies remained small bases and transshipment points; some became larger settlements and administrative units; some developed into sizable towns and mining centers. Together they made up the viceroyalties of the Spanish crown; they were not "in" Spain but were possessions "of" Spain. This is what colonization and empire came to mean.

St. Augustine

Empires and their colonial outposts were always moving targets. They never had fixed borders and generally sought to extend their reach in search of riches, tribute, and converts. For the Spanish, the "action," so to speak, was and would remain in the Caribbean basin and Central and South America. But, already in the early decades of the sixteenth century, rumors spread of more fabulous Native civilizations to the north, with cities as grand as Tenochtitlan beckoning conquistadors. As a result, in the 1530s and 1540s new expeditions under adelantados Hernando de Soto and Francisco Vázquez de Coronado headed to North America's southeast and southwest, respectively. With large numbers of soldiers, Native allies, and livestock in their entourages, they managed to create havoc, spread disease, and alienate the Indigenous peoples in their path without finding anything that resembled Tenochtitlan or lesser cities of Mesoamerica. But they did encourage Spanish officials in Mexico City to recognize that northern colonies might be necessary to ward off other European interlopers in the Western Hemisphere, protect Spanish silver shipments, and give Spain a real hold on the developing trade in the Pacific.

Thus, by the late sixteenth century, the Spanish tried to establish colonies in two broad areas of North America. One was along the Atlantic coast, first in St. Augustine and then much farther to the north on Chesapeake Bay (see Map 3.3). The Chesapeake colony (1570) called Ajacan was really a small settlement of Jesuit missionaries who hoped to begin converting the Indigenous people there, though very quickly the Indigenous people determined to have none of it and killed most of them. St. Augustine, settled in 1565, was more strategic, owing to its location near Spanish shipping routes. It became something of a hub around which fortified outposts and Catholic (in this case Franciscan) missions grew up. The outposts included St. Elena on what would later be called Port Royal Sound, and the missions spread northward along what would be the Georgia coast and westward into the Florida panhandle. French predators and other pirates were the main concern, valuable as those silver shipments were, but Native souls were targets as well. The Franciscans generally established their missions next to larger Native villages, exploited Native labor and resources to build and sustain them, and used a heavy hand to wrench Indigenous peoples away from their spiritual practices. For their part, Indigenous peoples had interest in Spanish metal and cloth goods and, in some cases, given the devastating results of disease, were willing to convert to Christianity (though mostly put to their own uses). But Spanish–Native relations would be a tense mix, brimming with misunderstandings and coercions.

New Mexico and Santa Fe

The mix was even more tense in the second Spanish colonial undertaking, this time in the southwest. The Spanish adelantado Coronado first entered the region in the mid-sixteenth century when he took his expedition up the Rio Grande Valley in search of the mythic city of Cibola and the riches rumored to be found there (see again Map 3.3). As it turned out, he encountered not another Tenochtitlan

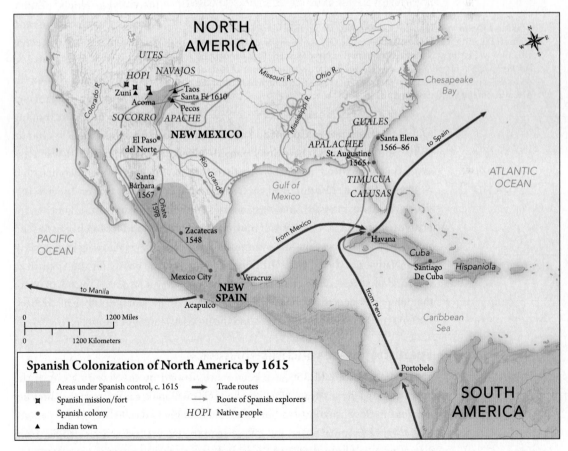

≡ **Map 3.3 Spanish Colonization of North America by 1615** Spanish attempts to colonize the Chesapeake failed, but in both Florida (St. Augustine) and New Mexico (Santa Fe) they established permanent settlements.

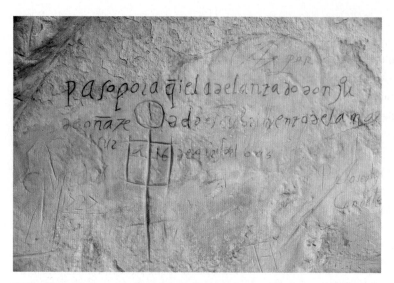

≡ **Staking a Claim** As Juan de Oñate and his men returned to Nuevo Mexico from an expedition as far west as the Pacific Ocean, he engraved this rock in what is now El Morro National Monument in New Mexico: *Pasó por aquí El Adelantado, don Juan de Oñate, del descubrimiento de la mar del sur al 16 de abril de 1605* ("The Adelantado Don Juan de Oñate passed through here from the discovery of the South Sea on April 16, 1605").

but Indigenous people living in adobe and brick dwellings and practicing sedentary agriculture. Coronado likened these villages to towns, and so he called all of the Indigenous peoples "Pueblos" (from the Spanish term for "town"), even though they numbered in the many thousands, spoke from at least four different language families, and called themselves Hopis, Zunis, Acomas, Pecos, Chililis, and Piro (among many other groups).

A half century later, in 1598, another adelantado, Don Juan de Oñate, hoping to find the silver mines Coronado had missed, headed back into the Rio Grande Valley and established the colony named "Nuevo (New) Mexico." It was a disaster for all involved, none more so than for the "Pueblos"—men, women, and children—who were brutalized by Oñate and his soldier-colonists. Indeed, soldiers, viceroyal officials, and missionaries all competed with one another for Native tribute and labor. They not only enslaved Native captives but began to send some of them south to the silver mines of Zacatecas in a developing Indian slave trade. Native resistance and rebellion made the venture costly for the Spanish as well, and once it became clear that precious metals would not be found, many of the prospective colonists headed south, too, leaving a small number of soldiers, settlers, and Franciscans in and around the new settlement of Santa Fe.

Spanish Missions and Missionaries

The Franciscans could not have been more pleased by the thinning out of the Spanish settler population, which made their own goals easier to attain. They set missions in close proximity to Native pueblos, sought to dazzle Indigenous peoples with their ceremonial attire and gifts, began to convert Indigenous peoples from groups who had been drawn to them, and then sought to relocate converts to the missions where they could live a "civilized" Christian life. The Franciscans were especially interested in Native *caciques* (chiefs) who could influence their followers to embrace Christianity, and they made important contributions as linguists and ethnographers. To this day, the work of Franciscan missionaries is vital to the research of historians and other scholars of the period. They left some of the most important written sources we have.

From their perspective, Indigenous peoples had a variety of incentives to accept the missionaries who came among them. They might benefit from trade goods that the missionaries could get, find allies in their struggles with rival Indigenous peoples as well as with Spanish encomenderos, and gain access to the spiritual powers that the missionaries and friars seemed to have. Yet there was a price, and the price was high because the missionaries had their own perspectives and objectives. They expected the Indigenous peoples to do the hard labor that built the missions and to work in the fields and pastures to sustain them, planting crops and raising sheep and cattle; many of the Native laborers were held in conditions akin to slavery. The missionaries did not regard Native shamans and other spiritual leaders as allies in their cause but as enemies who had to be marginalized, defeated, or destroyed. Coercion—persuasion through force or threats—was, in fact, an important instrument in the Franciscan repertoire of Christianization, which cast a wide net among Pueblo peoples. Only nomadic and seminomadic Indigenous peoples, like the Apaches, who could easily move beyond the Spanish reach, were able to maintain their independence.

Even so, the Franciscans and the Spanish settlers and officials who joined them in New Mexico achieved limited results. One Spaniard groused that few of the Indigenous people had "forsaken idolatry, and they appear to be Christians more by force than" by "Holy Faith." Some of the Indigenous people continued to worship secretly, keeping their religious practices and sensibilities alive beyond the gaze of the missionaries; many others simply adapted the forms and elements of Christianity to their own spiritual ways without fundamentally altering them.

≡ **Spreading Christianity** A page from a pictorial catechism created by the Franciscan missionary Pedro de Gante (1486?–1572) for teaching the basics of Christianity to Indigenous peoples in New Spain. Pedro de Gante learned Nahuatl and established a school for both children and adults in Mexico City that taught both Christian doctrine and Native arts and crafts. His catechism, completely free of text, was reprinted numerous times during the sixteenth century. We may find his brightly colored images puzzling, but they were easily grasped by his Indigenous audience.

MAPPING AMERICA

Comparing Eastern Seaboard and Continental Perspectives

Historians of early American history continually grapple with a basic problem. Should early American history focus mainly on the growth and

expansion of European colonies, particularly those English-speaking ones that combined to form the United States and then pushed westward across

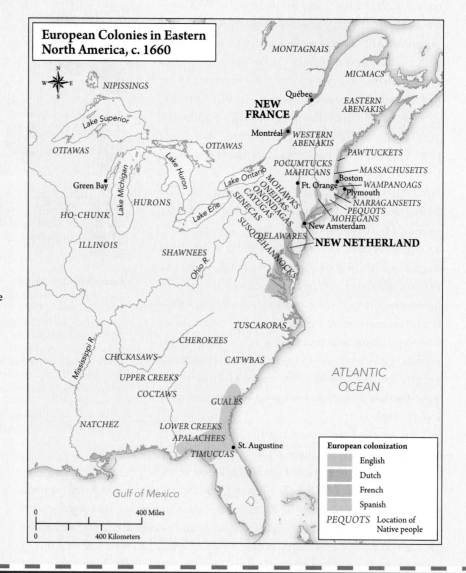

European Colonies in Eastern North America, c. 1660

MONTAGNAIS

MICMACS

NIPISSINGS

Québec

NEW FRANCE

EASTERN ABENAKIS

Lake Superior

Montréal   WESTERN ABENAKIS

OTTAWAS

Lake Huron

OTTAWAS

PAWTUCKETS

POCUMTUCKS

MAHICANS   MASSACHUSETTS

Green Bay

Lake Michigan

HURONS

Lake Ontario

MOHAWKS
ONEIDAS
ONONDAGAS
CAYUGAS
SENECAS

Boston

Ft. Orange   WAMPANOAGS

Plymouth

NARRAGANSETTS

PEQUOTS

MOHEGANS

HO-CHUNK

Lake Erie

New Amsterdam

ILLINOIS

SHAWNEES

SUSQUEHANNOCKS

DELAWARES   NEW NETHERLAND

Ohio R.

TUSCARORAS

CHEROKEES

Mississippi R.

CHICKASAWS   CATWBAS

UPPER CREEKS

COCTAWS

GUALES

NATCHEZ   LOWER CREEKS

APALACHEES

TIMUCUAS   St. Augustine

ATLANTIC OCEAN

Gulf of Mexico

0   400 Miles

0   400 Kilometers

European colonization

English

Dutch

French

Spanish

PEQUOTS   Location of Native people

≡ **Map 1**

Eastern Seaboard Perspective The conventional picture of North America in the second half of the seventeenth century takes an Eastern seaboard view. Maps such as this one show European settler colonies strung along the Atlantic coast, from Maine to Florida. Large blank spaces fill the western areas of the map, and regions beyond the Mississippi are not shown.

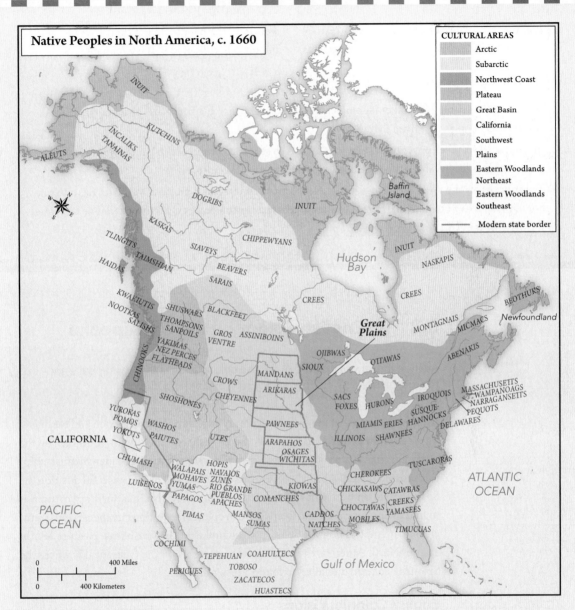

Native Peoples in North America, c. 1660

CULTURAL AREAS
- Arctic
- Subarctic
- Northwest Coast
- Plateau
- Great Basin
- California
- Southwest
- Plains
- Eastern Woodlands Northeast
- Eastern Woodlands Southeast
- —— Modern state border

INUIT
INCALIKS
TANAINAS
ALEUTS
KUTCHINS
INUIT
Baffin Island
DOGRIBS
INUIT
TLINGITS
HAIDAS
TSIMSHIAN
KASKAS
SLAVEYS
CHIPPEWYANS
BEAVERS
NASKAPIS
Hudson Bay
INUIT
CREES
CREES
BEOTHUKS
Newfoundland
KWAKIUTIS
NOOTKAS
SALISHS
SHUSWAPS
THOMPSONS
SANPOILS
BLACKFEET
MONTAGNAIS
MICMACS
CHINOOKS
YAKIMAS
NEZ PERCES
FLATHEADS
GROS
VENTRE
ASSINIBOINS
Great Plains
ABENAKIS
CROWS
CHEYENNES
MANDANS
ARIKARAS
OJIBWAS
SIOUX
OTTAWAS
IROQUOIS
MASSACHUSETTS
WAMPANOAGS
NARRAGANSETTS
SHOSHONES
SACS
FOXES
HURONS
SUSQUE-
HANNOCKS
PEQUOTS
YUROKS
POMOS
YOKUTS
WASHOS
PAIUTES
UTES
PAWNEES
MIAMIS
ERIES
DELAWARES
ILLINOIS
SHAWNEES
CALIFORNIA
CHUMASH
ARAPAHOS
OSAGES
WICHITAS
CHEROKEES
TUSCARORAS
ATLANTIC OCEAN
HOPIS
WALAPAIS
NAVAJOS
MOHAVES
ZUNIS
LUISEÑOS
YUMAS
PAPAGOS
RIO GRANDE
PUEBLOS
APACHES
COMANCHES
KIOWAS
CHICKASAWS
CATAWBAS
CREEKS
CHOCTAWAS
YAMASEES
MOBILES
PACIFIC OCEAN
PIMAS
MANSOS
SUMAS
CADDOS
NATCHES
TIMUCUAS
COCHIMI
TEPEHUAN
COAHULTECS
PERICUES
TOBOSO
ZACATECOS
HUASTECS
Gulf of Mexico

0   400 Miles
0   400 Kilometers

≡ **Map 2 Continental Perspective**   A continental perspective brings into the picture lands and people left out of the Eastern seaboard view. Instead of blank spaces, a map that takes a continental perspective includes societies and cultures that were flourishing by 1700 across North America, from the Arctic to the Caribbean. Such a map reflects, for example, that in 1700 more than twice as many people inhabited the Great Plains (189,000) than New England (92,000), and four times as many people resided in California (221,000) than in the colonies of New York, New Jersey, and Pennsylvania combined (53,000).

the continent? Or should early American history encompass the entire North American continent as well as all the peoples living there? We can see this dilemma highlighted in the two maps.

Thinking Geographically

1. What might be some political or ideological reasons for leaving "blank spaces" on a map instead of naming the peoples who lived there?

2. In what ways has the conventional view of an Eastern seaboard origin of the United States influenced stories and traditions about the American founding in popular culture?

3. The concept of "the West" has long captured the American imagination. How would an Eastern seaboard perspective imagine the West? How does taking a continental perspective challenge or change the myth of the American West?

3.2   An English Colony on the Chesapeake

||| Analyze the tenuous nature of English colonization in the Chesapeake and the role of tobacco and forced labor in transforming Virginia.

Around the time that the Spanish were laying claim to New Mexico and establishing a colony in and around Santa Fe, the English were looking for footholds on the other side of the continent. They were well aware of the silver-laden Spanish ships that crossed the Caribbean before returning home and of the powerful position the Spanish held on both sides of the Atlantic. But they also imagined opportunities to find their own riches and keep Spanish colonial ambitions in check. Thus, rather than attempt to contest Spanish strongholds in the Caribbean basin or southeastern North America, the English set their sights on the Chesapeake, where the Spanish had tried but failed to found a Jesuit mission.

English Colonial Visions

During the 1580s, the promoter Sir Walter Ralegh financed two efforts to settle Roanoke Island, off the coast just to the south of Chesapeake Bay. Both efforts failed: the first, when the colonists quickly pulled up stakes and headed back home; the second, when another group appeared to have abandoned the island for the mainland and then disappeared (likely killed by Indigenous people). Twenty years later, in 1606, the new English King James I granted London investors a charter to give the Chesapeake another try. They were incorporated as the Virginia Company of London—after the "virgin" Queen Elizabeth—a commercial venture known as a joint-stock company, with a royal charter but also private investors (shareholders). In December of that year, as we saw at the start of the chapter, three of the Company's vessels set sail across the Atlantic.

The area around Chesapeake Bay was then populated by more than 20,000 Algonquian-speaking Indigenous people who were organized into thirty chiefdoms and who farmed, fished, hunted, and foraged to make their subsistence. They generally lived in small villages of 100 to 200 and traded small surpluses of maize (corn) or shells with Indigenous people residing near the many rivers that ran well into the continental interior. In various ways, they owed allegiance to the paramount chief, known as Powhatan, whose entourage of servants, bodyguards, and many wives (perhaps 100) reflected an elaborate kinship network sustained by tribute payments in food, skins, and other goods offered up by subordinate villages and chiefdoms. So powerful was Powhatan that the bands and chiefdoms under his control were often referred to as Powhatans. *Tsenacomoco* ("the densely peopled land") was the name they gave to the lands they occupied (see Map 3.4).

How did the English think they would fare in such an environment, one they would name Virginia (again, after "virgin" Queen Elizabeth)? They certainly knew that there were large numbers of Indigenous people. They were also aware of the killing of Spanish Jesuits about thirty years earlier, in 1571. But their experience in Ireland during the sixteenth century (discussed in Chapter 2) encouraged them to feel militarily and culturally superior, to view the Indigenous people (as they viewed the Gaelic people of Ireland) as backward and degraded heathen, and to imagine that they would be greeted with submission rather than hostility. Indeed, they believed the Indigenous people would help supply them with food, trade with them for other necessaries, happily adopt "civilized" English ways, and be made to serve as menials. Otherwise, as in Ireland, they would crush any opposition mercilessly.

Jamestown

As it happened, the English would need all the help they could get. The 104 colonists who sailed for the Chesapeake under Captain John Smith were a motley assortment of gentlemen, adventurers, and vagrants whose main interest was in finding gold; few had any useful skills or were prepared to work in the fields and cultivate crops. "A more damned crew hell never vomited," the head of the Virginia Company scoffed. They arrived in the Chesapeake in April 1607, sailed up what they called the James River, and established a settlement they named Jamestown (both after the English king). Unfortunately, they picked a less-than-ideal spot. Jamestown sat next to a swampy area that bred disease (mosquitos and

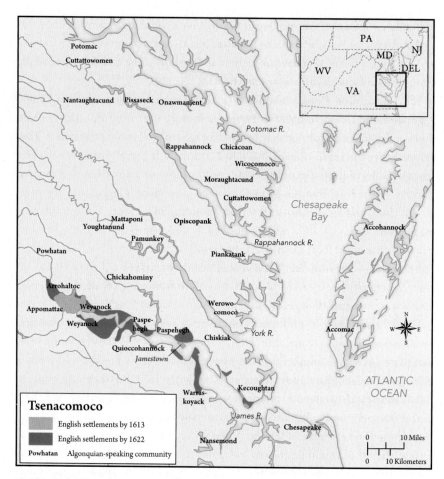

≡ **Map 3.4 Tsenacomoco**   Powhatan's chiefdom incorporated about thirty communities in the Chesapeake region, but by 1622 English colonists had established numerous small settlements.

tainted water in warm months), and the Indigenous people nearby raised barely enough food for themselves; they had little to trade or give away. So, when the colonists were not busily looking for gold, they were looking to take food from the Indigenous people. As might be expected, by the end of the year more than half of the English colonists were dead from disease or starvation, and relations with Powhatan's followers had quickly deteriorated.

Powhatan (his name at this time was Wahunsunacock) was not a man to be trifled with. He had been wielding and consolidating power for years, waging intermittent warfare with Native rivals to the north and west and exacting submission from his Native tributaries. Wary of falling into English hands, Powhatan regarded the English with suspicion, but he also thought he could either reduce them to tributaries or use them as allies against Native adversaries. At the very least, Powhatan expected to be treated with proper respect. "I also am a king, and this is my land," he told some of the English he encountered, and he refused to kneel to English visitors.

A deadly clash of perspectives was possibly in play, and the dynamics are well revealed by a much romanticized story—that of John Smith and Pocahontas—and the truths we can tease out of it. As the story is often told, Smith, captain of the expedition, was captured by Powhatan and threatened with execution; he was saved by the intervention of Pocahontas (one of Powhatan's many children), who then began a helpful relationship with the Jamestown colony that ended with her marriage to colonist John Rolfe. But the true story, as best as we can figure it, was far more complex.

Smith ended up as Powhatan's captive only after his own plan to capture Powhatan and assert the Jamestown colony's dominance had been sensed by Powhatan, who demanded that Smith come see him. Powhatan then constructed a ceremonial execution that was meant, not to take Smith's life, but rather to incorporate—perhaps ritually adopt—Smith into Powhatan's community as a subordinate and tributary who owed the Native leader allegiance. Life-and-death, or death-and-rebirth, ceremonies are common to many cultures, and Powhatan was performing one that was very familiar to his followers.

The Powhatan Economy   Native Americans fishing off the coast of North Carolina, as depicted by John White (c. 1585–1593). White was among those who sailed in the first attempt to colonize Roanoke Island in 1585, acting as artist and mapmaker to the expedition. The Secotan and Pomeiooc people he illustrates here had been fishing with dugout canoes and spears for thousands of years. Note, too, the extensive weir, built to control the flow of water.

It's not at all clear that Pocahontas intervened to save Smith's life (there are conflicting accounts) or if she played any role whatsoever in Powhatan's ceremony. If she did, Powhatan may have included her as a way of designating her an intermediary—a "go-between"—between his people and the English, which Pocahontas did in fact become. And when Smith expressed his gratitude when no execution took place, Powhatan understood it as Smith's acceptance of subordination. But from Smith's perspective, he escaped death because of Pocahontas's pleading and therefore owed Powhatan neither subordination nor allegiance.

Had the circuits of communication and perception been working better, some sort of accord might have been reached between Powhatan and the English.

PERSPECTIVES

Comparing John White's Watercolors with Theodore de Bry's Engravings

In 1585, the artist John White accompanied a group of English colonists sent by Sir Walter Ralegh to found a settlement along the tidewaters of what is today coastal North Carolina. White's instructions were to "draw to life all strange birds, beasts, fishes, plants, herbs," as well as "the figures and shapes of men and women in their apparel." White's watercolors provided England with its first view of America. Though White's visual documentation of Algonquin people were not exhibited until the twentieth century, Theodore de Bry, a Flemish printer, produced engravings based on White's illustrations, and these were published widely. Comparing White's representations of the Algonquin people he encountered with de Bry's interpretations offers an opportunity to see how a visual convention of America was constructed.

The first group of paired images shows a religious ceremony, most likely a Green Corn Festival, in the village of Secotan. White's watercolor (*left*) feels ethnographic. The circle on which the Algonquin dance appears worn and natural—the result of feet kicking up dust over the course of many years. In contrast, de Bry shows a perfect circle. At the center of the ceremony, White depicts a simple wooden column, but de Bry places a face at the top of the totem, to emphasize its status as an idol. In comparing the figures embracing near the base of the column, de Bry's version poses them in a highly stylized way so they look like the three graces of classical antiquity; in contrast, White shows the individual characteristics of each person. De Bry also has many of the dancers clutch stalks of wheat, which are absent in White's original. Perhaps de Bry wished to make them appear more pagan to European viewers.

≡ **A festive dance**

Similar differences can be seen in the second group of paired images. Both show the village of Secotan, and at first glance, they appear nearly identical. Closer examination, however, reveals some important distinctions. In addition to the houses and other structures, and the activities of the villagers, de Bry has added a hunting scene and plots of tobacco, pumpkins, and sunflowers not shown in White's original. In de Bry's version, the path in the center of the village is neatly bordered and looks like a street. The overall effect of de Bry's engraving is to portray Algonquin culture as peaceable and "European."

≡ The village of Secotan

CONSIDER THIS

De Bry's engravings appeared in 1590 in *A Brief and True Report of the Newfoundland of Virginia* by Thomas Hariot. Hariot's influential publication, with the engravings by de Bry, helped forge the European concept of America and its Indigenous peoples. But if de Bry (who never visited America) made a bigger impact than White, his depictions of Algonquin people and their culture were far less accurate. In considering the course of American history over the last 500 years, why has this gap between truth and fiction been so consequential for Indigenous peoples?

The Country wee now call **Virginia** beginneth at **Cape Henry** distant from **Roanoack** 60 miles, where was Sr. **Walter Raleigh's** plantation: and because the people differ very little from them of **Powhatan** in any thing, I have inserted those figures in this place because of the conveniency.

King Powhatan comands Cr Smith to be slaine, his daughter Pokahontas beggs his life his thankfullnes and how he subiected 39 of their kings. read o history.

printed by Iames Reeve

≡ Pocahontas Saves John Smith's Life   This engraving in John Smith's own narrative, *The Generall Historie of Virginia, New-England, and the Summer Isles* (1624), illustrates the moment when Pocahontas (far right, standing) "beggs his life" from her father, Powhatan.

But then again maybe not. The English, after all, were interested in conquest, not submission; they planned to make the Indigenous people their subjects, not the other way around. So, after Smith's return to Jamestown, the English continued to harass Powhatan and his followers about food and other resources and acted to inspire fear in them as they had done with the Gaelic in Ireland. Violence continued to erupt sporadically until 1614, when the marriage between Pocahontas and Englishman John Rolfe ushered in a period of peace.

The peace was short-lived. Before her marriage Pocahontas had converted to Christianity and was baptized as "Rebecca." She and Rolfe soon headed off to England where the Virginia Company hoped to use the couple to attract new investments and political support. But Pocahontas sickened and died in 1617 while still in England, and the next year Powhatan died as well. Now the power Powhatan held passed to his half-brother Opechancanough, whose patience for the English had worn even thinner than Powhatan's. Four years later (1622), as the English continuously trod on Native lands and then murdered an esteemed warrior, Opechancanough launched an attack on Jamestown that left one-quarter (347) of the colony's population dead and, in turn, sparked more than a decade of brutal English reprisals.

Salvaging Virginia with Tobacco and Servitude

To say the least, the Virginia colony appeared to be a thorough disaster. Between 1607 and 1622, roughly 10,000 people had come to Jamestown under the auspices of the Virginia Company, but fewer than 2,000 were left. Disease, hunger, and conflicts with the Indigenous people had turned a "plantacion" into a "slaughterhouse," as one observer put it. Small wonder that in 1624 the English crown dissolved the Virginia Company and took charge of the colony in its own right. But there were already brighter prospects on the horizon, and they came by way of the crop tobacco.

Tobacco was indigenous to the Western Hemisphere, especially to the Caribbean islands. Europeans had learned of it when they arrived in the late fifteenth and early sixteenth centuries. By the time Jamestown was first settled, the English and other Europeans had acquired a taste for tobacco, and a substantial market had been developing. But it was not until 1612 that English colonists in Virginia— led by none other than John Rolfe, who had obtained seeds from the Spanish—discovered that they could grow the crop. For all intents and purposes, it wasn't a minute too soon. The Virginia Company began to lure members of the gentry with the prospect of own-

≡ **Pocahontas** This portrait of Pocahontas, which hangs in the National Portrait Gallery in London, is based on an engraving made shortly after Pocahontas and her husband, John Rolfe, arrived in England in 1616. The portrait captures the dual novelty of England for Pocahontas and of Pocahontas for the English. Attire worthy of a princess signified to English observers that Pocahontas was royalty and to Pocahontas that the English viewed her as the "Emperor" Powhatan's daughter.

ing large estates and smaller planters with "headrights" (grants) to 50 acres for themselves and for each additional family member and laborer they brought along. All could hope to sell tobacco for many times the cost of producing it. In 1615, Virginia exported more than 2,000 pounds of tobacco to England; a decade later Virginia may have exported more than a million pounds. One historian has called this the "first American boom."

How did Virginia colonists turn tobacco into a successful cash crop? If those who received land grants relied solely on their own labor and that of family members, there was only so much that they could grow. Tobacco was a labor-intensive crop. It had to be planted, weeded, tended, harvested, dried, packed, and shipped. There were no machines; tobacco required many hands and hard work. The colonists needed more hands.

At first, the colonists looked to the Indigenous people, but the Indigenous people refused to be coerced into the fields. They avoided the labor or fled at the first opportunity. The colonists then turned to a more familiar solution: English servants. As we saw in Chapter 2, over the course of the previous century, as the English population grew and enclosures threw thousands off the land, "masterless men" had been wandering the English countryside and heading to cities and towns in search of work. The early advocates of colonization had in fact argued that over-seas settlements might help rid England of these poor and potentially dangerous people while expanding the power and wealth of the country.

Servitude had a long and significant history in England. Although formal slavery and serfdom had withered away well before the seventeenth century, most workers continued to labor—whether in urban or rural areas—under the supervision and personal domination of an employer or master. Some of these workers were apprentices, learning a trade; some were household servants, tending to kitchens and children; some were farm tenants, cultivating crops and herding livestock; some were orphans and paupers "bound out" to keep them under control. All bowed to the direction of the master and were subjected to harsh discipline—including corporal punishment—for insubordination. More than a few effectively belonged to their masters during the terms of their service. Modern ideas about "free labor" were neither current nor enforced by the courts. Landowners and other employers assumed that the only way you could get someone to work for you and keep them at it was by coercion.

Among the servants recruited for the Virginia tobacco fields were orphans or felons who were forcibly shipped out. But over time, most of them were humble laborers, young in age, likely unmarried, usually male, with little or no personal property, who signed what were known as **indentures**. An indenture was a legal agreement or contract: in return for the cost of transportation to the colony and of upkeep there, the servant agreed to work without pay for a term of normally four to seven years. During that time, the indentured servant was expected to perform whatever tasks the master demanded. Refusal to obey the master or the attempt to run away would be punished by whipping, branding, or extending the term of service. By most accounts, the conditions of life for English servants in Virginia were considerably worse than they were back in England. Not only did they work harder and longer and endure harsher punishments, but like the masters and other colonists, they died in great numbers owing to disease, overwork, and Native raids.

Still, they came in large numbers. Between 1620 and 1650, nearly 17,000 arrived in the Chesapeake, about three-quarters of all English immigrants to the colony, and before the seventeenth century was out, that number grew to near 90,000. But, if conditions were so dreadful, why did so many come? The answer is that prospects for any sort of work in England were very limited, while the possibilities for servants in the colonies had some appeal. Once a servant completed his term, he was entitled to "freedom dues," which included a new suit of clothes, several bushels of corn, a few farming tools, and—for some servants, though many needed to purchase land on their own after they became free—as many as 50 acres of land (female servants were not entitled to land but might marry someone who owned land). Which is to say that an English servant who managed to survive his term could become a man of inde-

≡ **Tobacco Harvest**   It was not just men who toiled in the fields. Thousands of Englishwomen were also forced as indentured servants into the tobacco fields of Virginia, as depicted in this c. 1722 engraving of a tobacco harvest.

pendence, a landholder and household head. Few did survive their terms, however; most died within three or four years.

1619: The First Enslaved Africans

There was another option for labor-hungry Virginia planters. In August 1619, as the tobacco economy was expanding, a Dutch ship arrived carrying "twenty Negars" who were up for sale. The "Negars" were not servants but enslaved people of African descent. They had been carried across the Atlantic from West Africa (present-day Angola in this case) and likely had spent some time in the West Indies. They may also have been taken by the Dutch from Portuguese slavers, and it is possible that some others may have arrived even earlier that year. John Rolfe bought the ones up for sale in August and put them to work, among the first enslaved Africans in the English North American colonies.

But they remained few in number. In part, English planters preferred the indentured servants, whose language they understood and whose ways were familiar. Equally if not more important, the servants made more economic sense as a labor force. They cost less than half of what enslaved Africans cost to buy, and even though servants could become free, between disease and exploitation it was unlikely either that indentured servants would live out their terms or that enslaved

Africans would survive any longer. By the mid-seventeenth century, Virginia could count only 300 enslaved Africans, about 2 percent of the colony's overall population.

Enslaved Africans in Virginia entered a world in which coerced labor was the norm but also in which there were no clear laws to govern their status. There was not yet a "slave code" (discussed in Chapter 5) or rules about how the condition of enslavement might be transmitted generationally. Nor were there special punishments for insubordination or flight based on enslavement or race. It does appear that Africans were purchased in Virginia with the expectation that, unlike servants, they would be enslaved for life, though it also appears that the material conditions of the enslaved resembled those of servants and that some of the enslaved managed to obtain their freedom and live as freed men and women. Because labor was in short supply, some servants and slaves were able to negotiate improvements in their living standards, perhaps getting extra free time or the opportunity to cultivate small plots of land where they could grow food crops or even a little tobacco (this would, of course, relieve owners of some of the responsibility for providing subsistence). In this period, moreover, many of the enslaved had been "re-exported" from the West Indies or Brazil (meaning that they first arrived there before being shipped to Virginia rather than arriving in Virginia directly from West Africa), and some may already have learned some European languages or taken

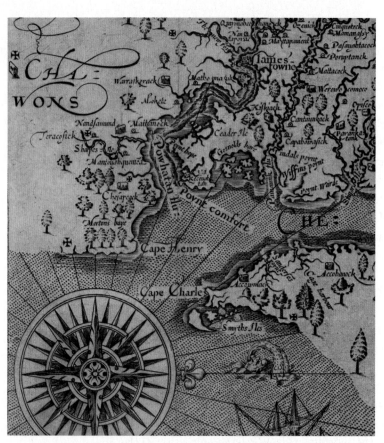

≡ **The Origins of American Slavery**   In 1619, the Dutch ship the *White Lion* arrived at Point Comfort, Virginia, shown near the center of this 1624 map of Virginia. On board were around twenty enslaved African people.

Europeanized names. Which is to say that they had already become a type of Atlantic creole (see Chapter 2).

To compare the circumstances of indentured servants and enslaved Africans in this way is not to suggest that both groups were treated relatively well. On the contrary, it is to suggest that servants and enslaved alike faced extreme exploitation, personal and sexual abuse, overwork, malnourishment, and brutal discipline. Few managed to survive more than three or four years in Virginia, whatever their status. Beginning in the 1620s, the colony of Virginia thus developed on a foundation of unfree labor, on the backs of a large and growing body of workers who were white and Black, English and African, and controlled by a minority of white Virginians who would ride the ups and downs of the international tobacco market. It was a potentially explosive situation, and it was entirely unclear if and how long this social structure would endure.

By the 1630s the tobacco market—and tobacco prices—had entered a slump, and as tensions with the Powhatans diminished, a new dynamic of trade between colonists and Native Americans developed. This involved not the Powhatans but the Iroquoian-speaking Susquehannocks to the north. The Susquehannocks were known as fierce warriors yet were also interested in European goods (cloth, axes, knives, beads) and were deeply involved in the rapidly expanding fur trade—especially in beaver pelts. The trade came to be centered on Kent Island in Chesapeake Bay, which Jamestown surveyor William Claiborne had purchased from the Susquehannocks in 1631. Here was an alternative course of economic activity, one dependent on interethnic (English-Native) alliances and exchange rather than on forced labor and the spread of English landholdings into Native territory. Could both survive, or would one achieve dominance?

3.3 New England

Outline the different objectives that led to the colonization of New England and the conflicts that were generated.

Whatever distinguished them, the Spanish and English colonies of New Mexico and the Chesapeake were driven by dreams of domination. The colonists dreamed of dominating the landscape and its resources and of dominating the Indigenous people who lived there by forcing economic or spiritual submission (or both). But a bit farther to the northeast, in colonies that would be named Plymouth and Massachusetts Bay, it appeared that things might be different, that colonists were

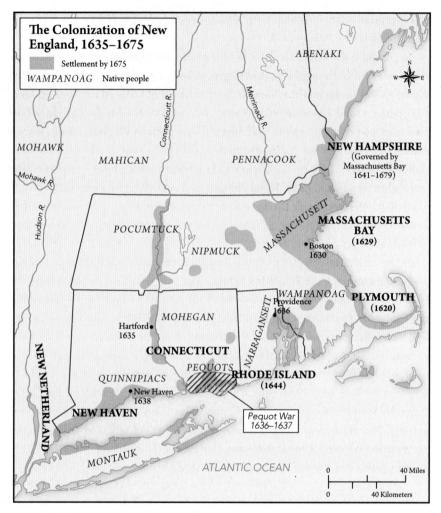

≡ Map 3.5   The Colonization of New England, 1635–1675   Like Jamestown to the south, Plymouth and Massachusetts Bay were planted in terrain already occupied by thousands of Indigenous people.

driven more by a dream of escaping domination in England than by one of enacting it in North America (see Map 3.5).

Puritans and Their Faith

Like their Virginian counterparts, the colonists who hoped to settle what had been named "New England" (by none other than John Smith, who on an exploring expedition in 1614 was struck by how similar the land seemed to England) obtained royal charters. Unlike the Virginians, however, they were motivated mainly by religious purposes. All were known as **Puritans** (though they called themselves the "godly"), a name given to those English people who embraced the Protestant Reformation but were deeply disturbed by the practices and hierarchies of the Anglican Church that Henry VIII had ushered in with his break from Roman Catholicism (see Chapter 2). Although a diverse lot, Puritans tended to come from the more commercialized areas of southern and southeastern England (not far from London) and tended to be of middling wealth and resources. They were neither from the gentry nor from the ranks of the "masterless" poor, as in Virginia; they were, in the main, farmers, artisans, and shopkeepers.

Why were they making a fuss? Like other Protestants who had rebelled against the Catholic Church, the Puritans sought to establish a direct relationship with God, one not mediated by priests or ministers, ceremonies or rituals. But Puritans were especially intent on reviving what they saw as a simpler and purer church of Jesus Christ in which congregants could experience God's saving grace (the alternative was being sent into the fires of hell and damnation). They saw the congregation as the basic unit of the church and the sermon, with its preaching of the Bible, as the heart of their religious services. They insisted that congregations choose their own ministers and engaged in an intense commitment to the faith by meeting for prayer, studying the Bible, discussing the meaning of God's word, and behaving in what they deemed godly ways.

But the Puritans did not believe that leading a good and moral life would gain them God's grace and heavenly salvation. Far from it. Rather, they followed the teachings of John Calvin, one of the foremost theologians of the Protestant Reformation. A central tenet of Calvin was **predestination**: he instructed that God alone determined who would and would not receive salvation and, most important, that this determination was made before individuals were born. One's fate, therefore, was predestined. At best, righteous living could be seen as a manifestation of God's grace, although the most important event in the life of a Puritan was conversion: a new member of the congregation had to persuade existing members that she or he had fully experienced conversion, an intense emotional and spiritual experience often enacted before the entire congregation.

The stakes were clearly very high. On the one hand, only God knew who would receive salvation, who would be among the "elect." On the other hand, Puritans believed that if one were among the elect, then one would surely act like it—be, that is, a **visible saint.** In Puritan thought, however, the connection between sainthood and saintly behavior was far from firm. Some members of the elect, for example, had never heard God's Word and did not know how to manifest their sainthood in their behavior. One reason the Puritans required church attendance was to enlighten visible saints who remained ignorant of God's truth. Other people might act as if they were saints, yet in fact not be among the chosen. But the Puritans thought that passing the demanding test of membership in one of their churches—demonstration of conversion—was a promising clue that one was in fact among God's elect. The involvement of priests, rituals, and other ceremonies would only interfere with the individual process of conversion and so, in the Puritan view, the Church of England could not be a halfway house out of Catholicism; the Church of England had to be fully reformed, or it would remain a relic of Catholicism and popery.

Most of the Puritans thought that this was possible, that they could remain within the Church of England and complete the Protestant Reformation that had been underway for nearly a century. But there were some among them who thought otherwise, who believed that the Church of England was beyond repair and that they had to withdraw, or "separate," from it and form their own discrete congregations. These Puritans, a tiny minority, were known as **Separatists**, and they put themselves into a very dangerous position. Separating from the Church of England violated the laws of the realm and amounted to a treasonous offense, punishable by long imprisonment or death. Small wonder that, facing more and more harassment, it was the Separatists—much later known as the **Pilgrims**—who first left for New England.

Landing in Plymouth

New England wasn't their first stop, however. In 1608, some of them headed to the Netherlands in hopes of establishing a safe community. They received a welcoming hand from the Dutch and settled in the town of Leiden. Unfortunately, before too long they grew uncomfortable with Dutch ways, preferred rural to urban life, and worried about their children's future. Thus, in 1620, with a patent from London's Virginia Company and financing from a group of merchants, 102 men, women, and children boarded a ship called the *Mayflower* and headed across the Atlantic.

The *Mayflower*'s destination was the mouth of the Hudson River, around present-day New York City though the English charter claimed it as the northern part of Virginia. But storms blew the vessel off course, and in early November, after two rough months at sea, the *Mayflower* and its passengers landed on today's Cape Cod, Massachusetts, for a month or so. These prospective colonists struggled to secure a suitable spot to debark and settle before they moved on to a site that John Smith had earlier found and called New Plymouth. Led by William Bradford, they took the name **Plymouth** for their own, in part after their final departure port of Plymouth, England.

Because they lacked a legal grant to Plymouth, forty-one of the men on the *Mayflower* quickly drew up a "Compact" organizing the settlement as a "Civil Body Politic" and pledging to enact "just and equal laws." For all the fame that the

Mayflower Compact later received (as the first such document of English colonization), it did little to save the Plymouth colonists over the next months. Indeed, by the spring of 1621, half of them were dead from hunger, exposure, and disease. Were it not for the help of local Indigenous people—Samoset, Tisquantum (Squanto), and Massasoit are the best known of them, from villages of Abenakis and Wampanoags—they may all have perished. No wonder that the surviving colonists, along with as many as ninety Wampanoags, celebrated their first harvest later that fall (probably in October). Eventually the occasion would be commemorated in the United States as Thanksgiving.

Massachusetts Bay

Plymouth would remain a small colony (estimates are between 400 and 1,500 settlers by the end of the decade), but its very establishment and survival helped initiate what would come to be called the "great migration" of Puritans in the 1630s. The migration's leader was a Puritan lawyer, from a large landowning family in England, named John Winthrop. The Massachusetts Bay Company, chartered by the crown, had enlisted Winthrop for the colonization project, and although he was not a minister, Winthrop had a religious vision. In a sermon likely delivered before he boarded the *Arbella*, one of the ships that headed out in 1630, Winthrop spoke of a "covenant" that the colonists had made with God, of the need to "knit [themselves] together, . . . to delight in each other; make others' conditions our own; rejoice together, mourn together, labor and suffer together" as "members of the same body." Addressing the importance of the mission, Winthrop told his shipmates, "we must consider that we shall be as a city upon a Hill" with "the eyes of all people . . . upon us."

During the decade of the 1630s, perhaps as many as 20,000 Puritans left England for Massachusetts Bay—and soon adjacent colonies—and they did create a distinctive sort of society. Politically they established representative institutions subject to the election of male voters—including the governor and an assembly known as the General Court—that were not directly tied to the Puritan (also known as Congregational) church. The General Court, in turn, could grant tracts of land to aspiring congregations that would be governed by their own town meetings and the "selectmen" they would choose. These "towns" would then distribute land to individual families so that each would receive a town lot (for the dwelling house) as well as parcels in the surrounding fields for cultivation and forage (maybe 50–100 acres in all). It was considerably more than ordinary rural folk could expect to farm in England and more equitably distributed than was the case in the Chesapeake. The land was also to be held as freeholds (full ownership) rather than leaseholds (use rights for a given length of time) as in England.

But if Massachusetts Bay appeared to be a budding egalitarian order, the appearances were deceiving. Although Puritans tended to be more of the "middling sort," there were differences in social status among them, and these differences were accepted as part of the natural order. Winthrop in fact began his sermon of 1630 (the sermon was called "A Modell of Christian Charity") by explaining why "some must be rich, some poor, some high and eminent in power and dignity, others mean and in submission." Indeed, as Puritans like Winthrop saw it, the world was organized around social hierarchies of high and low, superior and inferior, whether rich and poor, husband and wife, parent and child, master and servants. It was all part of God's design. What bound Puritans together was their **covenant**, their sacred agreement of faith with God, and their experience of grace and conversion, which made them "visible saints."

What then of the church? Although the Puritan church was not the governing political body in Massachusetts Bay or any other Puritan towns of New England, participation in political affairs—whether voting or officeholding—was restricted to male church members. This meant that church and state, though officially disconnected (ministers were not permitted to hold political office), were in fact intricately linked. Men from relatively wealthy and prominent backgrounds usually received larger distributions of land in New England; they also became leaders of the church and representatives in political life. They had great influence on the choice of ministers, on the activities of congregations, and on making and enforcing civil laws.

≡ **Puritan House of Worship** The interior of the Old Ship Church, built in 1681 in Hingham, Massachusetts. Its Puritan congregation first gathered in 1635, and the church itself is the oldest continuously operating church in the United States.

Turmoil: Roger Williams and Anne Hutchinson

Yet, however linked religious and civil society were, and however much Puritans were bound together by covenants of faith, there was considerable room for conflict among them. As the Separatists had already shown, Puritanism could be a very radical faith: suspicious of earthly authority, anti-institutional, and highly individualistic. If God's grace was freely given, if moral bearing and social behavior were inconsequential to receiving it, if conversion did not require any ministerial assistance, and if visible sainthood was a guarantee of salvation, individual Puritans, at least in theory, only had to obey their own impulses. Puritanism, that is, could promote anarchy.

The potential fallout quickly became clear in the form of a Puritan named Roger Williams. Williams was a well-educated lawyer and committed Separatist who arrived in Boston, the leading town of the Massachusetts Bay Colony, in 1631. He was invited to become minister of the Boston church but refused because that church was, in his eyes, fatally tainted. Williams held himself, as well as fellow Puritans, to an extreme standard of religious purity that he called "soul liberty." By this Williams meant that visible saints should follow the dictates of God's grace regardless of what earthly authorities had to say, that they should not worship with those who had not been converted, and that political officials and institutions had no place in religious affairs.

To make matters more complicated, Roger Williams also criticized Puritans who, from his perspective, encroached on Native lands as their population and towns expanded into the interior of New England. Although John Winthrop initially welcomed Williams to Boston with open arms, by the mid-1630s, he and other Puritan leaders found Williams's views and defiance unacceptable. Winthrop labeled Williams and his followers "Antinomians," that is, opponents of the law when it conflicted with faith in God's grace, and the General Court accused him of spreading "diverse, new, and dangerous opinions," then convicted him in 1635 of sedition and heresy: charges of utmost seriousness. To avoid the consequences of the conviction, Williams fled southwest about 50 miles, where he took up land offered him by sympathetic Narragansetts who knew of Williams's efforts on their behalf. There, Williams established the town of Providence and set the foundation for what became (in 1644) the new colony of Rhode Island and Providence Plantations.

Perhaps even more dangerous and disturbing to the Puritan leadership was a woman of deep and abiding faith named Anne Hutchinson, who showed up in Boston with her husband and many children in 1634, shortly after Williams did. Well-versed in theology (her father was a clergyman in England), Hutchinson shared Williams's beliefs about the singular power of God's grace and the hypocrisy of local ministers who seemed to think that congregants could prepare themselves for it and bow to the rules that they made. Most threatening of all, Hutchinson held meetings in her home, attended by women as well as men, where she led discussions of weekly sermons. This, as John Winthrop saw it, was neither "tolerable nor comely in the sight of God nor fitting for your sex." "You have stepped out of your place," Winthrop chided, "you have rather been a Husband than a Wife, and a preacher than a hearer, and a magistrate than a subject." In other words, she threatened to turn the Puritan world upside down around its most sensitive and intimate axis: gender. Banishment therefore seemed the appropriate punishment, and in 1637 Hutchinson left for Rhode Island, joining Roger Williams and others regarded as heretics in what the Massachusetts leadership called the "cesspool of New England."

Turmoil: Indigenous Peoples, Land, and Slaughter

Roger Williams's defense of Native land claims against the English suggests further sources of conflict that the Puritans quickly stirred. Like Jamestown to the south, Plymouth and Massachusetts Bay were planted in terrain already occupied by thousands of Indigenous people—probably more than 100,000 before European diseases began to take their toll—but unlike Jamestown there was no large confederation (such as Powhatan's) in New England. Instead, there were constellations of small villages connected with groups known as Wampanoags, Pequots, Mohegans, Nipmucks, Niantics, and Narragansetts who had complex rivalries and alliances with one another. And although the Puritans established the first substantial colonial settlements in New England, many of the Indigenous people there had made contact with French, Dutch, and English traders and fisherman in the years before. Some had been kidnapped by the English, taken to Europe, and put up for sale as slaves in Spain; Tisquantum (Squanto) had in fact been among them before finding his way back to New England (learning English along the way—another Atlantic creole) and then striding into the Plymouth colony.

As in most encounters between Indigenous people and Europeans, mutual interest in trade and political support was soon compromised by very different objectives and understandings of the rules. The Puritans were particularly troublesome. While they fled the domineering hand of the Church of England to construct their "city upon a hill," the Puritans had their own domineering impulses. They hoped to turn the New England landscape into something approximating what they knew in England; they regarded Christians who did not share their ways as unredeemed sinners; and they saw the Indigenous people as, in the words of Plymouth's governor William Bradford, "savage people, who are cruel, barbarous, and most treacherous," as "wild beasts" and heathens.

Rather than missionizing as the Franciscans and Jesuits did in New Spain and New Mexico, the Puritans looked chiefly to extract tribute payments that could then be used to purchase beaver pelts from Indigenous people farther north, an important item of transatlantic trade, and to pressure Native sachems nearby to sell lands that could be used for Puritan settlements. So far as the Puritans were concerned, the Indigenous people did not make proper use of the land: "they inclose noe Land, neither have any settled habitation, nor any tame Cattle to improve the Land by," according to Winthrop. As a result, they "have noe other but a Naturall Right to those Countries, soe as if we leave them sufficient for their use, we may lawfully take the rest."

The truth is that Indigenous people not only used the land to hunt and gather food but also to grow crops of maize, squash, pumpkins, and beans. They had developed patterns of land use that did not fit neatly into the English vision of arable fields, pastures, and woodlands, and, most of all, that did not involve ownership claims that English recognized. When, therefore, the Puritans had Indigenous people sign agreements to "sell" their lands (usually for trade goods), the Puritans believed that they had gained exclusive rights to the lands while the Indigenous people believed they had agreed merely to share in their use: two very different perspectives on land and land usage.

The seeds of conflict were thereby close to the surface, and they grew into outright violence as the tide of the great Puritan migration flowed through the 1630s. The largest explosion came in 1636 when Puritan and other English colonists tried to force Pequots south of Plymouth into submission and responded to their rebuff by launching a war against them, aided by some of the Pequots' Native rivals. Known as the **Pequot War**, it was in fact a Puritan-directed slaughter that left many of the Pequots (women and children as well as men) dead or enslaved, some shipped off to colonies in the Caribbean. Even the Puritans' Native allies were shocked by the murderous attack.

So it was that the Puritan colonists of New England had their own dreams of domination,

≡ **Encirclement**   A 1638 illustration of the brutal 1637 destruction of a Pequot village by Puritan settlers and their Narragansett allies. The village, near the present-day city of Mystic, Connecticut, was burned to the ground, and about 400 Pequot died.

very much fortified by a belief in the godliness of their endeavors. In this they joined the colonists of the Chesapeake and New Mexico, however distinctive some of their goals may have been. And in this they presented those who stood in their way or fell under their command an especially trying predicament—faced by not only the Indigenous people of New England but also the enslaved Africans who arrived shortly after the Pequot War came to its bloody end.

3.4   The Middle Colonies and the Caribbean

Identify the distinctive features of both the Middle Colonies and the Caribbean, and explain why the Caribbean quickly became the center of attention for Parliament and the crown.

Although the English laid claim to the lands of the Chesapeake and Massachusetts Bay, they were also actively involved in colonizing elsewhere on the east coast of North America as well as in the Caribbean, where the Spanish had first established their project of colonialism. The challenges and prospects of these colonies varied widely, reflecting the complex goals of the English colonizers. Their subsequent political histories also diverged, often dramatically.

From New Netherland to New York

Compared to Massachusetts Bay and the Chesapeake, the English devoted relatively little attention to a substantial area of North America's east coast during the first half of the seventeenth century. That area stretched from Delaware Bay north to Long Island Sound, making up what we would eventually call the Middle Atlantic. Here it was possible for European rivals to challenge the English hold and perhaps to establish formidable colonies of their own. None stepped in more eagerly than the Dutch.

In many respects, the Dutch were unlikely imperial rivals. The Netherlands had only recently been united politically after a lengthy and bitter struggle with Spain. It was a decentralized state with a small population of about 1.5 million (England already had 5 million). But the Netherlands was strategically located in the European trade linking the Mediterranean and the Baltic. It had an experienced and wealthy maritime sector, and it also attracted a great diversity of inhabitants (think of the Separatists) because of its relative openness and cultural toleration. As a result, during the first half of the seventeenth century, the Dutch constructed a remarkably far-flung empire, taking in the East Indies (a group of islands in the Pacific and Indian Oceans between Asia and Australia), the west coast and southern tip of Africa, and northeast Brazil. Added to these was a North American colony called New Netherland (see Map 3.6).

The Dutch foray in North America began in 1609 with a voyage by the English navigator Henry Hudson, who had been employed by the Dutch East India Company (an outfit much like the Virginia Company) to find a western sea route to Asia. Like everyone else who tried it at the time, Hudson failed to find the route. But, stopping at Cape Cod, the Chesapeake, and Delaware Bay beforehand, Hudson did find something else. He found a river, known today as the Hudson, that was navigable for 150 miles inland and sailed up the river to the point where it met what would later be called the Mohawk River. There, he engaged in fur trading with Indigenous people. Not long after, the Dutch established some outposts on the upper end of the river, meant to facilitate the fur trade. In 1625, the Dutch founded New Amsterdam to the south, where the river flowed into the Atlantic. It would all be part of the Dutch-proclaimed colony of New Netherland (see again Map 3.6).

Try as they might, however, the Dutch had a difficult time populating the colony with Netherlanders or any other Europeans. It was not because the environment was hostile; in fact, comparably temperate New Netherland was in many ways more appealing than either the swampy Chesapeake or, with its often frigid winters,

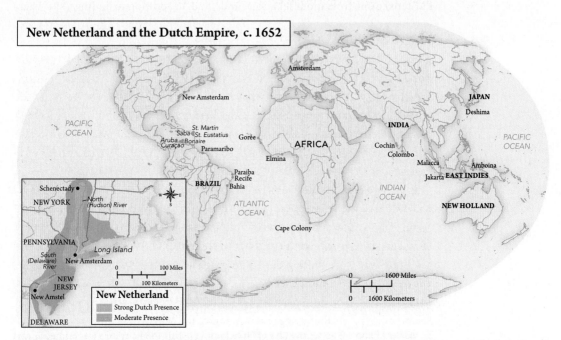

≡ **Map 3.6   New Netherland and the Dutch Empire, c. 1652**   New Amsterdam was an outpost in a far-flung Dutch Empire.

New England. Nor was it because of diseases, mortality, or Native resistance. It was because the Dutch had relatively few prospective colonists and because those who were interested in improving their fortunes could also try their luck in other parts of the Dutch world, especially the Caribbean basin and northeast Brazil, where raiding Spanish silver ships, growing sugar, and selling slaves were far more lucrative. By the 1660s, the Dutch were in no position to contest invigorated English designs in an imperial rivalry that was playing out across the Atlantic and Caribbean. And so Dutch New Netherland became English New York, and New Amsterdam became the town of New York.

Pennsylvania and the Jerseys

Before too much longer, the English established additional colonies in the Middle Atlantic, each marked by distinctiveness and contradictions. One was Pennsylvania, meant to be something of a refuge for **Quakers**, whose radical religious beliefs, like those of the Puritans, had run afoul of authorities in England. Quakers—or members of the Society of Friends, as they called themselves—frowned on worldly vanities, the educated ministry, and the established Church of England, and they believed that the "Inner Light" of God's grace burned in everyone, not only the few who were predestined for salvation. Most of them (like the Puritans) came from modest backgrounds, and, in addition to finding a site where

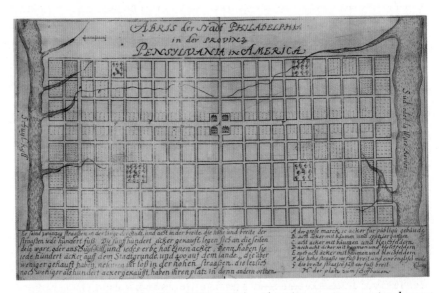

≡ **William Penn's Plan for the City of Philadelphia**   This 1684 city map was printed as part of a promotional campaign by Penn to develop the fur trade and industry in Pennsylvania. Philadelphia's historic section still preserves much of the street grid shown here.

they could worship freely, they also hoped to establish an example of fairness to the Indigenous people.

Their transatlantic leader was William Penn, a convert to Quakerism, who grew up in a wealthy and eminent gentry family. Despite his many run-ins with the government, Penn remained on good terms with Charles II, and in 1681 he secured a royal land grant of 45,000 square miles to be called Pennsylvania (or Penn's Woods, after Penn's father, who had served Charles). Although Penn set out to build a haven for Quakers and Protestants more generally, the charter for Pennsylvania seemed more a throwback to the Middle Ages. Penn deemed himself the absolute proprietor, expected Pennsylvania to be divided into "manors," and sold off much of the land in huge tracts, extending to the purchasers the power to set up "baronies" and hold court. As was true for the Puritans, Penn thought that "subordination" and "dependency" were both natural and inevitable, and he counseled "obedience to superiors, love to equals, and help and countenance to inferiors." Not surprisingly, indentured servants were on the scene from the outset—perhaps a third of all the arrivals—encouraged much as they were in Virginia. Before long, enslaved Africans were also at work, and, over time, their numbers would grow in the countryside as well as in the new port town of Philadelphia.

As for neighboring New Jersey (1664), originally part of a large grant to the Duke of York, the little interest there was in providing a religious refuge was vetoed by the English crown. Instead, there was more of a Penn-oriented effort to establish aristocratic estates and lordships, especially in East Jersey. Smallholders were more common in West Jersey, and in 1676 they would come to blows with their haughty neighbors to the East. In the meantime, both Pennsylvania and the Jerseys—unlike either the Chesapeake or Massachusetts Bay—attracted an ethnic polyglot of settlers, perhaps more of a cultural mix than anyplace on the planet: Swedes, Norwegians, Scots-Irish, Welsh, Dutch, Irish, German, French, Flemish, and Walloons. To the ears of one colonist, it was a "complete Babel."

Prospects in the Caribbean

Yet, in many ways, the most significant of the English colonial projects began unfolding much farther to the south, in the deeply contested Caribbean. For decades, English, along with French and Dutch, privateers and pirates had been coursing the Caribbean looking to plunder Spanish shipping and find convenient hideaways in the remote harbors of the islands. By the 1620s and 1630s, the English hideaways were increasingly turned into settler colonies and, learning the techniques from the Dutch who had been in Brazil, the settlers started to cultivate sugarcane. St. Christopher, Nevis, Antigua, and Montserrat began to emerge as sugar-producing islands, but none were more important in the seventeenth century than Barbados.

The rise of the English sugar complex had some of the features of Virginia's embrace of tobacco. Sugar was an especially labor- and capital-intensive crop. Sugarcane not only had to be planted, tended, and harvested, but it also had to be ground and prepared for shipment very quickly or the sugar would spoil. Where to find the labor? Like the Virginians, English planters in Barbados initially turned to white indentured servants who were both plentiful and exploitable. By the 1650s, however, the servants began to be replaced by enslaved Africans who were being transported and sold by Portuguese, Dutch, and eventually English slave traders.

Conclusion: The Lure of the West Indies

Beginning in the late sixteenth century and especially through the seventeenth, European powers organized settler colonies across the North American continent, from the Southwest out to the Atlantic coast. In various forms, these colonies shifted the goals from simply engaging in trade and plunder to establishing settlements that would give each of them bases of political and economic activity and would need to be defended. But although we tend to focus our attention on the great continental land mass, the English powers, whether the English, Spanish, French, or Dutch focused theirs on the Caribbean basin. And for good reason.

Sugar, not tobacco or furs, was the great money maker, and the Caribbean, not the mainland of North America, would become the great magnet of migration. By 1650 there were more English colonists in the Caribbean islands (mainly Barbados) than in the Chesapeake and New England combined, and what was increasingly called the West Indies quickly became the center of political and economic attention for the English crown and parliament as well as for the French, Spanish, and Dutch. Barbados, the Leeward Islands, and soon (in 1655) Jamaica would be the core of English colonial settlement and exploitation. The French would take Martinique, Guadeloupe, and Saint Domingue. The Dutch settled Aruba, Curaçao, and the Windward Islands. And the Spanish held Hispaniola, Cuba, Puerto Rico, Florida, and the mainland of Mexico and Central America.

The North American mainland, by and large, was at the colonial periphery, with all sorts of consequences for the Native, European, and African peoples living there.

WHAT IF the Separatists Had Arrived at Their Hudson Valley Destination?

While the Puritan Separatists were in the Netherlands in the very early part of the seventeenth century, they heard positive things about the lower Hudson Valley where a Dutch expedition had arrived in 1609 under the command of Henry Hudson. And so, when they decided that the Netherlands was not hospitable to the world they wished to make for themselves, they set their sights across the Atlantic and on the mouth of what was now the Hudson River as a destination. Had it not been for the fierce storms they encountered on their voyage, which blew the *Mayflower* more than 200 miles to the north, there they would have landed.

The lower Hudson Valley was attractive and increasingly complex in many ways. Networks of Native societies, especially of the Algonquian-speaking Lenapes and Mahicans laced the area, and further up the valley were the Mohawks and Haudenosaunee. Before too long, not only Dutch but Germans, Welsh, Scots-Irish, Norwegian, and Swedish settlers and traders settled in the area, while the English established new colonies in New Jersey and Pennsylvania.

DOCUMENT 3.1:   Two-Row Wampum Treaty, 1613

The 1613 Teioháte Kaswenta (Two Row Wampum Belt), similar to the one shown here, records an agreement between the Dutch and the Haudenosaunee. The two parties met south of present-day Albany, New York. The alternating rows of purple and white shell beads represent the two parties to the treaty moving forward together in parallel, but never merging, signifying respect for each other's rights. Haudenosaunee today consider the agreement to be the basis of all of their subsequent treaties with European and North American governments.

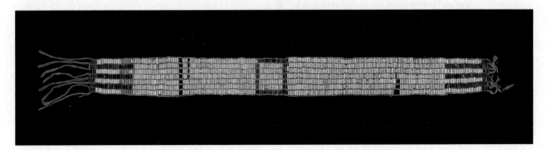

≡ **Wampum Belt**

DOCUMENT 3.2: Excerpts from "Articles, Whereupon the Citty and Fort Amsterdam and the Province of the New Netherlands Were Surrendered," 1664

Here is an excerpt of the terms of the transfer of the Province of New Netherland from the Dutch to the English in 1664.

Wee consent that the States General, or the West India Company shall freely enjoy all farms & Houses (except such as are in the fforts) and that within six months they shall have free Liberty to transport, all such arms and ammunition as now do belong to them, or else they shall be paid for them

* All people shall continue free Denizens and enjoy their Lands, Houses, Goods, Ships, wherever they are within this Country, and dispose of them as they please.
* If any Inhabitant have a mind to remove himself he shall have a year and six weeks from this day to remove himself, Wife, Children, Servants, Goods and to dispose of his Land here.
* It is consented to, that any people may freely come from the Netherlands and plant in this Country; and that Dutch Vessells may freely come hither, and any of the Dutch may freely return home, or send any sort of Merchandises home in Vessells of their own Country.
* All ships from the Netherlands or any other places, and goods therin, shall be received here & sent hence, after the manner, which. formerly they were before our coming hither for six months next ensuing.
* The Dutch here shall enjoy their Liberty of their Consciences in Divine Worship and Church Discipline.
* That the Townsmen of the Manhattan shall not have any Soldiers quartered upon them without being satisfied and paid for them, by their officers, and that at this present, if the effort be not capable of lodging all the Soldiers, then the Burge Master by His officers shall appoint some House capable to re[illegible]e them.
* The Dutch here shall enjoy their own Customs concerning their Inheritances. . . .

Source: www.Gilderlehrman.org

Thinking About Contingency

1. What would a landing in the lower Hudson Valley have meant for the Separatist and subsequent Puritan colonists?
2. How might the history of what John Smith called New England have been different?

REVIEW QUESTIONS

1. Why did Europeans become interested in establishing settler colonies as opposed to simply exploiting the mineral and other resources of the Western Hemisphere?

2. How did the Spanish go about establishing colonies and their structures of authority in Central and South America, and in what ways did these colonies differ from Spanish colonies to the North?

3. What challenges did English colonists to Virginia face, and how did they attempt to resolve them?

4. What were the motivations of English settlers at Plymouth and Massachusetts Bay as compared to those in Virginia? Did similarities outweigh the differences?

5. Why did the Middle Colonies become more ethnically and culturally complex than those to the south and north?

6. Why did England's Caribbean colonies attain a special status in the perspective of the metropolis?

KEY TERMS

adelantados (p. 89)

covenant (p. 114)

indentures (p. 106)

Mayflower Compact (p. 113)

Pequot War (p. 117)

Pilgrims (p. 112)

Plymouth (p. 112)

predestination (p. 111)

Puritans (p. 110)

Quakers (p. 120)

Separatists (p. 112)

Treaty of Tordesillas (p. 88)

Tsenacomoco (p. 99)

viceroyalties (p. 90)

visible saint (p. 111)

RECOMMENDED READINGS

Kristen Block, *Ordinary Lives in the Early Caribbean: Religion, Colonial Competition, and the Politics of Profit* (University of Georgia Press, 2012).

Kathleen Brown, *Good Wives, Nasty Wenches, and Anxious Patriarchs: Gender, Race, and Power in Colonial Virginia* (University of North Carolina Press, 1996).

Rebecca Goetz, *The Baptism of Early Virginia: How Christianity Created Race* (Johns Hopkins University Press, 2016).

Karen Ordahl Kupperman, *Pocahontas and the English Boys: Caught Between Cultures in Early Virginia* (New York University Press, 2021).

C. S. Manegold, *Ten Hills Farm: The Forgotten History of Slavery in the North* (Princeton University Press, 2010).

Edmund S. Morgan, *The Puritan Family: Religion and Domestic Relations in Seventeenth Century New England* (1966).

Andres Resendez, *A Land So Strange: The Epic Journey of Cabeza de Vaca* (Hachette, 2009).

Peter Silver, *Our Savage Neighbors: How Indian War Transformed Early America* (W.W. Norton, 2009).

David Weber, *The Spanish Frontier in North America* (Yale University Press, 1992).

Michael Winship, *Hot Protestants* (University of Pennsylvania Press, 2013).

Colonial Convulsions and Rebellions
1640–1700

≡ **Philip, King of Mount Hope**   The Wampanoag sachem (chief) Metacom, also known as "King Philip," as imagined decades after King Philip's War (1675–1676) in an engraving by Paul Revere, one of the Patriot leaders of the American Revolution.

127

In June 1675, the Wampanoag leader Metacom was preparing to rebel violently against neighboring colonists in New England. His determination to do so was the result of a lengthy and complex relationship between his people and the New England Puritans, which first took shape in 1621 when Metacom's father, Massasoit, formed an alliance with the newly arrived English Separatists (later known as Pilgrims) in Plymouth. The alliance involved trade, cultural exchanges, diplomatic means to resolve conflicts, and military support against mutual rivals. But, as with other contacts between Europeans and Indigenous people in North America, it was always beset by different objectives and understandings.

Born in 1640, Metacom knew only a world inhabited by Europeans as well as Indigenous people; indeed, Puritans already outnumbered the Wampanoags and other Indigenous people in New England, owing to immigration and the devastating effects of disease. He recognized that the New England Puritans had designs on Wampanoag land, as they did on the land of other Indigenous people nearby. Initially Metacom and his brother Wamsutta attempted to maintain peaceable connections.

Timeline

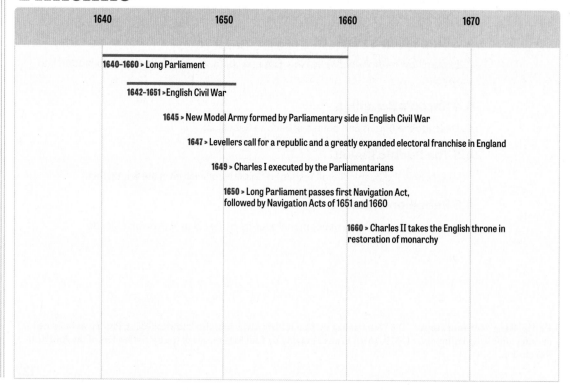

1640	1650	1660	1670

1640–1660 > Long Parliament

1642–1651 > English Civil War

1645 > New Model Army formed by Parliamentary side in English Civil War

1647 > Levellers call for a republic and a greatly expanded electoral franchise in England

1649 > Charles I executed by the Parliamentarians

1650 > Long Parliament passes first Navigation Act, followed by Navigation Acts of 1651 and 1660

1660 > Charles II takes the English throne in restoration of monarchy

But a series of humiliations inflicted by the Puritans, which left Wamsutta dead and three Wampanoags executed, taught a lesson to the anguished sachem. There was to be no future for the alliance, and what little land the Wampanoag had left for themselves would soon be grabbed by the Puritans. So, in June 1675, Metacom and the Wampanoags, aided by many other Indigenous groups, launched a massive attack against the Puritans that, before it was through, would become—proportionately— the single bloodiest episode of warfare in all of American history.

Rebellions, revolts, and uprisings are among history's most dramatic incidents. And they occur relatively infrequently. For the most part, people accept the circumstances into which they are born even if they believe them to be wrong, exploitive, or unjust. Sometimes they simply grumble, complain, or engage in individual and small-scale acts of noncooperation. Sometimes they create alternative authority figures of their own choosing, set goals and values for themselves, worship their own gods, or simply flee. And sometimes they display their discontent in public ways by demonstrating, petitioning, and organizing their ranks. Yet, once in a while, as in the world of

1680	1690	1700	1710

1675–1676 ▸ Metacom's, or King Philip's, War in New England

1676 ▸ Bacon's Rebellion in Virginia

1680 ▸ Pueblo (Po'pay's) Revolt in New Mexico

1688–1689 ▸ Glorious Revolution puts William of Orange and his wife, Mary, on the English throne

1692–1693 ▸ Salem witchcraft accusations and trials

Metacom and the Puritans, resistance turns into rebellion, and because rebellions can threaten the entire social order, they usually require and are met with force of arms.

During the first half of the seventeenth century, the Dutch, the French, and—especially—the Spanish and the English established or extended on the North American continent the reach of **settler colonialism**, the process by which Indigenous peoples of a region are displaced by settlers intent on forming their own society there. They did so in an ongoing search for precious metals or a faster route to Asia, and as they attempted to contest the claims of imperial rivals in the Western Hemisphere. Political and military power on the eastern side of the Atlantic was increasingly tied up with power on the western side.

For their part, colonists generally looked to carry out the objectives of their home governments or to grab opportunity for themselves (or both), though at times—as in New England—they were more interested in escaping the rule of the home country. In all cases, however, the colonists not only came into contact with Indigenous people but tried to subdue them. It made for tension, conflict, and misunderstanding, because the Indigenous people had their own ideas and intentions, which included making the Europeans submit in some ways.

During most of the seventeenth century, as Europeans and Indigenous people were dying in considerable numbers owing to disease and deprivation, there was also jockeying, skirmishing, and bloodletting: encroachments here, attacks there, acts of vengeance most everywhere. But late in the century, these tensions and conflicts exploded into a series of rebellions in very different places on the North American continent though within a very few years of one another. The rebellions were carried out with great brutality, and they were met with great brutality. They shocked European officials as well as settlers, and, as we will see in Chapter 5, they transformed the colonial world in significant ways. What happened and why?

4.1 The Turbulent Atlantic

||| Recognize the broad Atlantic context for the rebellions of the second half of the seventeenth century.

Rebellion, revolution, and warfare were facts of life for Europe, the Atlantic world, and the North American continent during the seventeenth century. By one estimate, there were only three years between 1600 and 1700 when peace prevailed; otherwise, warfare, especially among European powers, proved endemic. To these we may add civil wars—wars and rebellions that exploded *within* the borders of different countries—that were remarkable in their number and extremely consequential in their effects. They occurred in Russia and France, in Italy and the Netherlands, in Ireland and Catalonia, in Portugal and the Ottoman Empire, in Denmark and the Swiss Confederation. Perhaps the greatest and most consequential of all occurred in England. The rebellions were of many different sorts, involving peasants against their lords and landlords, members of the gentry against the aristocracy, noble landowners against the crown, and parliaments against the monarchs.

Sources of Conflict

There were several important reasons for all this warfare and civil violence. For one, the seventeenth century saw the entrance of new and important actors on the stage of imperial projects and colonization. During the fifteenth and sixteenth centuries, the Spanish and the Portuguese were the main players, and while they established significant colonial settlements in the Western Hemisphere, they were rarely direct rivals. The Portuguese were strongly situated along the West African coast as well as in the Brazilian northeast; the Spanish were dominant in the Caribbean, the Andes, and Mexico, and, to a lesser extent, in southern sections of North America. They had also signed the Treaty of Tordesillas, effectively dividing the world up between them (see again Map 3.1).

But by the late sixteenth century, both the Portuguese and Spanish were being challenged by the English and French; and by the early seventeenth century, the Dutch (who had once been controlled by Spain) entered the fray. Over the next decades, the English fought with the Spanish, French, and Dutch; the French fought with the English and Spanish; the Dutch fought with the Spanish, Portuguese, English, and French; and the Spanish, who fought almost continuously, battled with everybody, including the Portuguese. The immensely destructive religious conflagration known as the Thirty Years' War (1618–1648) spread from Germany across much of continental Europe and resulted in as many as eight million casualties. At war's end at least a third of the population of Germany had died.

At the same time, the seventeenth century also saw intensifying conflicts between absolute monarchs (who claimed sole, "absolute" power over their subjects) in England, Spain, and France and regional nobilities who were jealous of surrendering their power and prerogatives. To strengthen their respective hands, the nobles and the monarchs then sought the support of loyal peasants. The Fronde in France (1648–1653), the Catalan Revolt in Spain (1640–1659), the Scottish Revolution (1637–1651), the revolts of Naples and Sicily (1647–1648), the Irish

≡ **Little Ice Age**   In 1683–1684, Dutch painter Abraham Hondius depicted a *Frost Fair on the Thames at Temple Stairs.* During the Little Ice Age, rivers and canals across Europe froze so solidly that crowds of people, horses and carriages, and even shops could all be supported by the thick ice. Despite the liveliness and vitality suggested by this painting, the prolonged climate shift was devastating to Europe's economy and especially to its poor.

rebellion (1641–1653), and the English Civil War (1642–1660) were examples of conflicts such as these.

There were, as well, environmental factors. The seventeenth century experienced climate change that has come to be called a **Little Ice Age**. It saw extreme weather in many parts of the globe, including Europe and elsewhere in the Northern Hemisphere. Droughts, floods, and a general cooling trend—bringing unusually cold temperatures in some years—compromised growing seasons and crop harvests, adversely affecting rural and urban districts alike. Together these developments placed stress up and down the line: on centralizing governments seeking power and revenue; on landed elites who wanted their influence recognized while worrying about extracting rents and other services from the people who worked their lands; and on peasants in various conditions of subordination, who not only faced greater exploitation but also risked starvation if the harvests failed. Indeed, Russia and much of eastern Europe witnessed what has been called a "second serfdom" during this period, as noble landowners with the aid of the Tsar (the Russian monarch) reduced peasants to the status of enslaved people, bound to their estates and able to be bought and sold.

4.2 Revolution in England

‖‖‖ Characterize the impact of the English Civil War on the colonies.

For the larger history of North America, conflicts in seventeenth-century England stand out because of the wide-ranging impact they had. They began to transform the terms of governance, the principles of power and rule, and the institutions that would remain in place to this day. They also brought to the surface new ideals and political visions held by men and women who had largely been excluded from formal political life: ideals and visions that would continue to resonate in England and in the empire that the English were constructing.

Parliament and the Crown

The conflict in England initially set the king, Charles I (r. 1625–1649), against the Parliament, the legislative body, which was supposed to represent the interests of the burgesses (wealthy townspeople), landed gentry, and hereditary nobility. Charles, like his predecessors on the English throne, imagined himself as all-powerful, a virtual god on earth in place by divine right, and he saw the Parliament only as an advisory body. That was his perspective.

Those who sat in Parliament, either in the House of Lords (nobles not subject to election) or the House of Commons (burgesses and gentry subject to election by other burgesses and gentry), had a different perspective, especially because they played a role in imposing and collecting the taxes that the king needed to exercise his power. Charles I disturbed many Protestants, both in Parliament and the country as a whole, by his favoring of highly centralized and ceremonial religious practices and his marriage to a French Catholic. Charles refused to call Parliament into session throughout the 1630s, but a rebellion in Scotland forced his hand. Strapped for cash, he called Parliament into session in November 1640. By then, many of the members had had enough. They issued demands for regular sessions and more formal power. Charles promptly rejected them. Parliament dug in (it would remain in session for the next two decades, thereby called the "Long Parliament"), passed new laws, and executed one of the king's advisors for high treason. Charles fled London, marshaled his forces, and a civil war was soon underway.

The **English Civil War** of 1642–1651 proved to be lengthy, complex, and extremely destructive. From Scotland and England it spread into Ireland and Wales, devastated over 200 towns and villages, and killed about 7 percent (around 250,000 people) of the population. This was more than triple the proportion of the British who would die in World War I (1914–1918). And the political fractures of civil war kept spreading. Initially, the parliamentary side was strongest in the urban and manufacturing areas and the royalist side was strongest in the countryside. But the parliamentary side soon split between those who wanted to work out a compromise with the king and the so-called Independents, those who wanted to establish the supremacy of Parliament even if the monarch remained. Before too much longer, the Independents gave rise to a more radical faction, known as the **Levellers**, who hoped to end the monarchy and the House of Lords, expand the right to vote and hold office, and proclaim a republic. The Levellers, in turn, helped give birth to even more radical groups, such as the **Diggers**, who questioned the very sanctity of private property.

≣ **Intolerance and Propaganda**   Mistrust of Anglicans and Catholics rose during this period, as reflected in this English woodcut from the 1640s. The clergyman on the left, labeled "Of God," is depicted in simple, somber robes befitting a Protestant minister and holds a Bible. The Anglican clergyman in the center ("Of Man") and the Catholic clergyman on the right ("Of the Divell")—nearly identical and likely representations of Archbishop Laud—are in sumptuous clothes and hold books labeled "sermons" and "superstitions," reflecting anti-Anglican and anti-Catholic prejudice.

These rapidly changing divisions were intensified by issues of faith. As we have seen, the Protestant Reformation of the early sixteenth century led to a break between England and the Catholic papacy. But the Anglican Church, which replaced the Catholic Church as the country's official religious institution, bore many of the marks of Catholicism, including its hierarchies, rituals, and mediations between worshippers and God. As dissenting Protestant sects, such as the Puritans (who believed that Anglicanism was simply Catholicism in another guise), began to emerge, religious tensions were added to the economic and political. It was one thing to accuse the king of overstepping his bounds; it was quite another to accuse him of "popery" and religious persecution. Small wonder that one of the first to fall was William Laud, appointed Archbishop of Canterbury by Charles I, who was intent on consolidating the power and ways of Anglicanism and punishing his opponents mercilessly. In 1640, Parliament had Laud arrested and charged with treason; before long he was executed.

Who Is to Rule and How?

In an important sense, the English Civil War—as civil wars and rebellions often do—opened up questions about how society was organized and who would rule it. Once the power of the king was challenged, the power of other institutions and relationships came up for discussion, and social groups who had been outside the arenas of formal politics—peasants, artisans, laborers, people of small means—hoped to come inside. By the mid-1640s, the Independents seemed to have the upper hand, but responding to pressure from the Levellers, they began to move in more radical directions. They created a **New Model Army** led by Thomas Fairfax (later by Oliver Cromwell), invaded Ireland and Scotland as well as Royalist strongholds in England, debated a dramatic expansion of the franchise, and in 1649 beheaded Charles I for high crimes and treason. The civil war appeared to be turning into a revolution.

The King Loses His Head   A gruesome depiction of the execution of Charles I by an anonymous Dutch artist c. 1649, who likely worked from eyewitness accounts. In the front, a woman faints; one eyewitness said that when the axe fell, "There was such a groan by the thousands then present as I never heard before and desire I may never hear again."

How ready were the English for a revolution, and who among them might have been most ready? The Civil War was mainly a battle between different sections of the English elite: between nobles, gentry, and burgesses who were loyal to the monarchical order and those who wanted to limit the monarch's power and boost the power of Parliament. Not surprisingly, the parliamentary side tended to be most involved in commercial affairs, in regional and overseas trade, and in producing crops for market. They wanted a freer hand to make policy and take advantage of a new era of globalization. But most of them were substantial property owners. They owned landed estates, townhouses, and mercantile establishments. They wanted political change and reform, not an attack on the system as a whole or on the overall structure of power. Yet in contesting the authority of the king they also tried to rally the support of ordinary folk, the majority of English people, those who worked with their hands, owned little if any property, and could do the hard fighting: folk who were far less invested in the power structure.

Levellers and Diggers were ready for something like a revolution; the Independents, who had great resources and control in the army, were not. And by the late 1640s, the Independents made clear that they, not the Levellers or Diggers, would direct the politics of the civil war. But Cromwell, who styled himself "Lord Protector," proved instead to be a military dictator. During the so-called Protectorate, dissenters were killed or oppressed, and Cromwellian forces subjugated Scotland and Ireland through terror and mass displacement. Overseas conflicts with the Dutch and French resulted in scant victories and expanded taxes. When Cromwell died in 1658, few English subjects mourned his passing. Instead, the reaction was a sweeping revival of Anglicanism and restoration of the monarchy in 1660 under Charles II, son of the executed king.

In the meantime, the Long Parliament enacted the **Navigation Acts** of 1650, 1651, and 1660 requiring that colonial-produced goods be shipped in English vessels to English ports. The Navigation Acts were intended to divert the colonies' trade from England's enemies, the Dutch and the French, as well as to yield custom revenues for the monarchy and profitable business for English merchants and shippers. They were a clear victory for mercantile interests in the port towns.

Unfortunately, the large question of where power and authority ultimately rested was not yet decided, and the king and Parliament soon resumed their conflicts. After coming to power in 1685 (following the death of his brother Charles II, who left no heir), James II ran afoul of Parliament with his absolutist tendencies and apparent desire to impose his and his wife's Catholicism on English subjects. In 1688, Parliament deposed James, an act that proved far less bloody than the removal of Charles I, and invited James's Protestant daughter Mary (r. 1689–1694) and her Dutch husband, William of Orange (r. 1689–1702), to assume the throne. William and Mary's supporters called their accession a **Glorious Revolution**.

Was anything finally settled? Yes and no. William (now King William III) and Mary (Queen Mary II) may have been elevated to the throne, securing the monarchy and the Protestant Reformation. But they recognized it would be necessary to bow to Parliament if they expected to hold on. Indeed, William and Mary agreed to a **Declaration of Rights** that catalogued parliamentary grievances against previous monarchs, assured parliamentary supremacy in the important areas of governance and lawmaking, and provided for rights of expression, justice, arms bearing, and election. It was the precursor to the **Parliamentary Bill of Rights** formally adopted in 1689.

The five decades encompassing the Civil War, Cromwell's Protectorate, the restoration of the monarchy, and the Glorious Revolution helped consolidate the power of the increasingly commercially minded gentry and their merchant allies, who wished to break down barriers to agricultural innovation and the development of manufacturing while strengthening their hands in colonial trade. There was, that is, an important shift in the balance of power away from the crown and its aristocratic allies, who represented a world of entrenched hierarchies and vertical allegiances, and toward newer commercializing elites, who represented a world of more fluid hierarchies and market practices. Yet still bubbling below the surface were the more democratic demands of the Levellers and Diggers, and still to be determined were the full consequences for the colonies in the Western Hemisphere.

4.3   King Philip's War

III Explain how tensions between New England colonists and Wampanoags exploded into warfare.

Without question, the social and political tensions that erupted in mid- to late seventeenth-century England had important echoes in North America, and at the center of tension and conflict were the issues of land and political authority. In New England the tiny settlements of Plymouth and Massachusetts Bay, surrounded by a much larger number of Indigenous people, grew rapidly between the 1630s and the 1670s. Waves of English immigrants first pressed on the boundaries and resources of the early towns, and then moved north and west to found newer towns and the colonies of Rhode Island, Connecticut, and New Hampshire. As of 1670, New England settlers numbered more than 50,000 and, whether Puritan or not, had little regard for Indigenous claims to land or sovereignty (see Figure 4.1).

Settler Pressure on New England Indigenous Peoples

Settler ambitions were emboldened by Native weaknesses. As we saw in Chapter 3, the Native population of eastern New England had declined dramatically in recent decades. Warfare, but especially disease, reduced their numbers to fewer than 20,000 people scattered among many villages. The Narragansett and Wampanoag were the largest of the confederations; most of the others—Nipmuck, Pokanoket, Mohegan, and Pennacook—were much smaller. For a time, settlers and Indigenous people tried to balance a shared interest in trade with conflicts over resources, and Puritans established some "praying towns" for Indigenous people willing to convert to Christianity and submit directly to Puritan authority. But the balances proved hard to maintain, and Indigenous people came under constant pressure to surrender their lands and their weapons.

Metacom, sachem of the Wampanoag people, may have seemed an unlikely antagonist. He was the son of Massasoit, who had lent a helping hand to the Plymouth colonists and then formed an alliance with them organized around trade and military support. Indeed, in 1660, Metacom and his brother Wamsutta had gone before the leaders of the Plymouth colony hoping to be granted English names: recognition of diplomatic relations and political parity from the Wampanoags' perspective. The names then conferred, "Alexander" for

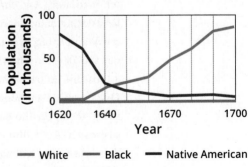

≡ **FIGURE 4.1**   **Population of New England Colonies, 1620–1700.**

Wamsutta and "Philip" for Metacom ("King" Philip to acknowledge his sachemship), harked back to ancient Macedonia, homeland of Philip II of Macedon and his son Alexander the Great. From the perspective of the colonists, who regarded the ancient leaders as uncivilized heathens, the names were derogatory, though neither Wamsutta nor Metacom would have grasped this meaning.

Over the next decade, tensions mounted. Wamsutta died after the colonists had forcibly interrogated him about an alleged Native conspiracy, and the trade that had tied the Wampanoag to Plymouth began to flounder. Metacom himself faced a legal dressing down in Plymouth after he refused to hand over all his weapons, as the English had ordered. It now required little more than a spark for the relationship to explode, and that spark was finally lit in June 1675. A Christianized Native, John Sassamon, who had assisted Metacom while also informing the colonists about a "war" Metacom was said to be planning, suddenly turned up dead. Colonial officials quickly seized three Wampanoag who were advisers to Metacom, tried them for murder, and had them executed. Outraged, Metacom and the Wampanoags responded by launching brutal attacks on the colonists and their towns. In short order, they were joined by most other Algonquian-speaking peoples in the region—Narragansetts, Nipmucks, Pocumtucks, and Abenakis who fought under their own leaders and had grievances of their own (usually involving land and violence) they wished to settle. Only the Mohegans and Pequots (themselves previous victims of colonist violence) chose the English side of **King Philip's (or Metacom's) War**.

Death to the Settlers or the Indigenous People?

The fighting turned massively brutal and destructive. For months it appeared that the New England colonies might well be dismantled and the colonists driven off. More than half of all English towns occupying the landscape from the Atlantic coast to the Connecticut River Valley came under attack, and at least thirteen were destroyed (see Map 4.1). Women and children as well as men were killed and often mutilated. And through a variety of tactics, the Indigenous people inflicted devastating damage on the colonists who set out to tame them. It appeared that the Wampanoag and their Native allies aimed not simply to defeat and chase out the English settlers but to remove as much of the English cultural imprint as possible, to burn and desecrate dwellings and churches and fields and fences. One Narragansett boasted, according to an apoplectic Roger Williams, "God was [with] them [the Indigenous people] and had forsaken us [the settlers] for they had so prospered in Killing and Burning us far beyond What we did against them."

In truth, the "Killing and Burning" went both ways and, before it was all done, the Indigenous people suffered by far the worst of it. In part, this was because colonists turned their vengeance on any Indigenous people they could find, including those of the praying towns who were unprepared to fight them. And in part this

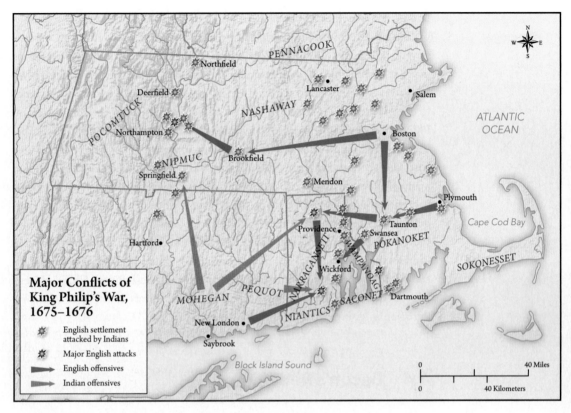

Major Conflicts of King Philip's War, 1675–1676

- ✹ English settlement attacked by Indians
- ✹ Major English attacks
- ➜ English offensives
- ➜ Indian offensives

≡ **MAP 4.1   Major Conflicts of King Philip's War, 1675–1676**

was because the Puritan colonists, too, were fired by a sense of spiritual conquest, of destroying what they regarded as Satan's evil savages and reclaiming their worthiness in God's eyes. As Williams put it, "God had prospered *us* so that we had driven the Wampanoags with Philip out of his Countrie and the Narragansetts out of their Countrie, and had destroyed Multitudes of them in Fighting and Flying, in Hunger and Cold . . . and that God would help us Consume them."

Metacom was indeed soon on the defensive. The colonists had enlisted the aid not only of Mohegans and Pequots but also of Mohawks west of the Connecticut Valley, who had long been enemies of the Algonquian peoples. The territory of the Wampanoag and their allies steadily shrank, and by the spring of 1676 they were running out of food and ammunition as well as space. During the late summer, in one pitched battle, Metacom himself fell—shot down (apparently by a Native ally of the English), mutilated, and beheaded, his skull then set atop a Plymouth tower for all to see. What remained of King Philip's War quickly unraveled and other leaders were captured and killed.

What for a time seemed an uprising nearing success turned into a complete disaster for the Indigenous people of New England. Two thousand of them were killed or executed. Another 3,000 perished from hunger, disease, and the consequences of dislocations. One thousand (including Metacom's wife and young son) were enslaved and shipped off to the West Indies. And perhaps 2,000 became refugees, many driven northward to settle among the Abenaki. In all, roughly half the population was lost. Those who survived and managed to remain were either remanded to one of four praying towns or were forced into servitude for the colonists. King Philip's War began to erase the Native presence from the New England landscape.

Yet, if the English colonists "won" the war, it proved to be victory at immense cost. One thousand of them (about 2 percent of the population) had been killed, many of their towns were abandoned if not destroyed, and the costs of the conflagration would weigh heavily on the colonists who survived and wished to rebuild. King Philip's War left the New England colonists with an enduring hatred of Indigenous people, a large war debt, and a devastated frontier. It was one of a series of crises that Puritans and other New England colonists began to face toward the end of the seventeenth century, not least as the Long Parliament, Charles II, and James II decided to regulate more of the colonial economy and centralize more of the colonies' governance.

4.4   Bacon's Rebellion

‖‖‖ Describe the origins and course of Bacon's Rebellion.

Tensions over land and authority between Indigenous people and settlers rocked the Virginia colony at the same time, though the dynamic was more like the Civil War back in England. What was going on? As we saw in Chapter 3, after a very difficult decade and a half when early colonists starved in failed searches for riches, Virginia achieved some stability and then, by 1625, prosperity by raising a valuable crop for export—tobacco—and engaging in a lucrative trade in deerskins with the Indigenous people to the west. The tobacco economy came to be based on large landholdings and mainly the labor of white indentured servants. In the tobacco fields, as well, however, were a small number of enslaved Africans, who first arrived in 1619, labored much as the servants did, occasionally gained their freedom, and effectively supplemented the predominately white workforce.

Growing Tensions

Although indentured servants might have been attracted to Virginia by the prospect of becoming landholders, relatively few of them lived out their terms, owing mostly to disease and overwork. As we saw in Chapter 3, enslaved Africans were more expensive to buy than servants were (and also had limited life spans), so it made most sense for the Virginia planters to rely mainly on white servants to grow the tobacco. It was also easy for Virginia's governors to hand out big land grants to their friends because with many servants dying before they received freedom dues, the pressure on available land within the colony was not all that great.

Everything began to change in the middle of the seventeenth century, and the consequences would be momentous. In a major development, the disease environment began to improve; white settlers, whether freemen or servants, could expect to live longer. As more servants completed their terms, they could hope to farm and create households; a disproportionate number of males in the colony gave way to family formation. The pace of population growth quickened—it more than quadrupled between 1640 and 1680, from about 10,000 to over 40,000 (see Map 4.2).

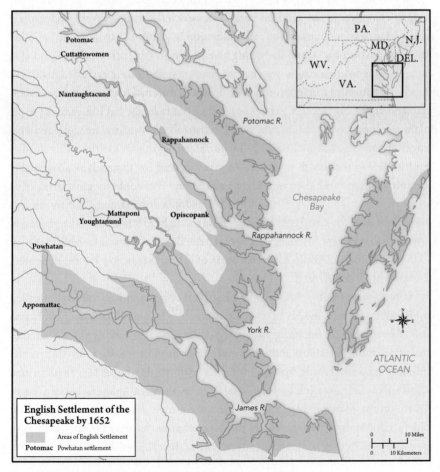

Potomac
Cuttattowomen
Nantaughtacund
Potomac R.
Rappahannock
PA.
MD. N.J.
WV. DEL.
VA.
Chesapeake
Bay
Mattaponi Opiscopank
Youghtanund
Powhatan
Rappahannock R.
Appomattac
York R.
ATLANTIC
OCEAN
James R.

English Settlement of the Chesapeake by 1652

Areas of English Settlement
Potomac Powhatan settlement

0   10 Miles
0   10 Kilometers

≡ **MAP 4.2** **English Settlement of the Chesapeake by 1652**

Also, a new governor named William Berkeley was installed in 1641 by the soon-to-be-executed Charles I. Berkeley imagined something of an aristocratic society for himself and his elite supporters. He appointed wealthy planters to public office, granted them land and licenses to trade in deerskins with Indigenous people to the west, and had little but contempt for indentured servants and smallholders, whom he excluded from governance and burdened with taxes to support his regime. "I thank God, there are no free schools nor printing [in Virginia]," Berkeley sneered, "and I hope we shall not have these for a hundred years; for learning has brought disobedience and heresy into the world." Indeed, Berkeley invited royalist refugees from the Civil War in England to come to Virginia, a move that caused Parliament to force him out of the governorship. Once the monarchy was restored and Charles II was given the throne, however, Berkeley was put back in place.

Whatever smallholders and indentured servants might have hoped for out of the Civil War in England, Berkeley's return did them no good. More and more of the colony's land was in the hands of Berkeley's wealthy cronies; Berkeley indefinitely suspended new elections for the colonial assembly (the one that sat would be called the "Long Assembly"); and the sitting assembly not only increased taxes but also squeezed the white servants even harder. Servants' terms were extended for acts of insubordination, and on obtaining their freedom they had to choose between renting land on the big planters' estates or heading out to lands that Indigenous people claimed. The growing numbers of poor English folk, servant and free, seethed with anger against the colonial officials—who referred to them as "the giddy-headed multitude"—while those who tried to take up land for themselves unavoidably got into conflicts with their new Native neighbors. "We confess a great many of us came in servants to others," one of these freedmen complained, "but we [indentured] our lives for it and got our poore living with hard labor out of the ground in a terrible Wilderness." Berkeley recognized the danger: "How miserable that man is that Governes a People where six parts of seven at least are Poore, Endebted, Discontented, and Armed."

As settlers and Indigenous people lashed out at one another, the settlers called on Berkeley for help, mostly in the form of troops who would have their backs and inflict vengeance on the Indigenous people. But Berkeley and his allies wanted to maintain trading relations and avoid escalating the violence. He refused them the military support. Taking matters into their own hands, the settlers then formed a militia of their own led by John Washington (the great-grandfather of George Washington), marched into Susquehannock country, and murdered five of their chiefs. Like Metacom to the north, the Susquehannocks would make the English pay, and in 1675 they launched an all-out war against the settlers and planters.

Virginia's Civil War

Into this increasingly bloody mess stepped Nathaniel Bacon. Born into a gentry family in England, Bacon was well connected to the Berkeley regime in Virginia when he arrived in 1674. Indeed, Bacon was the nephew of Berkeley's wife. He quickly received a seat on the governor's council, and he got himself a large plantation about 40 miles up the James River from the colonial capital of Jamestown. Not a bad start—but one that put Bacon in the middle of hostilities with the Susquehannocks. In violation of Berkeley's instructions, he was soon leading expeditions of disgruntled settlers against them: in fact, against any Indigenous people in their way, all of whom he regarded as their "Enemies." Berkeley would not put up with this insubordination, whatever Bacon's status and influence. He declared Bacon a traitor and demanded his arrest.

Now Bacon had a new and more powerful enemy, and the stakes couldn't be higher. Treason was a capital offense, punishable by death. So instead of continuing his pursuit of the Indigenous people, in 1676 Bacon rallied his supporters and turned them toward Jamestown, where Berkeley and his allies had their base. Along the way, Bacon called upon smallholders and servants to join his ranks, overthrow Berkeley, and seize better opportunities for themselves. "The poverty of the Country is such that all the power and sway is got into the hands of the rich, who . . . having the common people in their debt, have always curbed and oppressed them," Bacon thundered. Many of the "common people," servants and even enslaved captives among them, came on board.

The English Civil War may have ended, but one was now engulfing Virginia. As in England,

≡ Simplicity and Splendor   Standards of living were vastly different for those in a typical seventeenth-century Chesapeake planter's house (*top*, modern reconstruction) compared with the household of Governor Berkeley's mansion he named "Green Spring" (*bottom*), located near present-day Williamsburg, Virginia.

Bacon's Rebellion began with a revolt against the official authorities and their landed elite supporters led by other members of the landed elite. As in England, it saw appeals to those at the bottom of the social and economic ladder. And as in England, it resulted in death and destruction on a massive scale. Plantations and farms were plundered on both sides, Jamestown was burned to the ground, and the Berkeley government was forced to flee across the Chesapeake—though unlike Charles I, Berkeley kept his head.

Bacon and his troops seemed poised to take control of the Virginia colony when he suddenly died, either of dysentery (known at the time as the "bloody flux") or typhus fever. No one else on his side appeared able or willing to keep the fire of rebellion burning. As a result, Bacon's ranks quickly unraveled, and now it was Berkeley who was poised to take control. "Bacon is Dead I am sorry at my hart / that Lice and flux should take the hangman's part." Berkeley proceeded to return to Jamestown and round up the rebels, eventually hanging twenty-three of them.

Berkeley's brutality in crushing Bacon's Rebellion may have given him and his supporters the temporary upper hand in Virginia, but it did not impress his superiors back in England. Charles II sent troops to reestablish order in both Virginia and New England, and a royal commission, very critical of Berkeley's actions, sent him back to England, where he soon died. The commissioners then reached an agreement with the remnants of Powhatan's chiefdom in the vicinity of Jamestown in which the Indigenous people accepted the "King of England" as their "Soveraigne" and the ultimate holder of their lands in return for protection against aggressive English settlers. For their part, the Susquehannocks moved northward. It was all an expression of a new regime that the post–Civil War English crown sought to impose on the fractious colonies, and one that survived the Glorious Revolution of William and Mary.

4.5   The Pueblo Revolt

||| Assess how the Pueblo Revolt reshaped Spanish colonialism in the Southwest.

The many rebellions of the seventeenth century —and certainly the English Civil War, King Philip's War, and Bacon's Rebellion—showed that there were always several important factors at play. Grievances against the powerful certainly helped unite people who might otherwise be divided. But grievances alone were not enough for a rebellion to take place. Prospective rebels needed to sense that the powerful were divided among themselves and that therefore they could have allies from those ranks.

Triggering events were also crucial: droughts and famines that placed great stress on the social order and raised questions about the powers of the elite; the violation of social and political norms that suggested new forms of domination and exploitation; and personal injustices committed against popular leaders.

A Tense Alliance

No rebellion on the North American continent during the seventeenth century was larger or more successful than the one that occurred in New Mexico in 1680, and it showed how a combination of developments made rebellion possible. How did it happen? As we saw in Chapter 3, the Spanish had established footholds in New Mexico at the end of the sixteenth century, with Santa Fe as a political center and numbers of Franciscan missions scattered across the hinterlands as sites for the Christian conversion of the Pueblo people. All of the Spanish—the political officials, the colonists, and the Franciscans—competed for the use of Pueblo labor, leading to rivalries and tensions among the Spanish. As for the Pueblos, alliance with the Spaniards offered them support in battles against hostile Apaches, Navajos, Utes, and Comanches, who were nomadic rather than sedentary, and together they launched slaving raids against the nomads when labor shortages occurred. Pueblo agriculturalists might have been drawn to the missions because they believed the Franciscans had extraordinary powers that could benefit them without necessarily changing their spiritual practices.

It was an uneasy set of relationships, and the first half of the seventeenth century witnessed small-scale Pueblo uprisings against the Spanish in some mission towns as well as in several of their own villages. But tensions mounted in the 1660s and 1670s. Although the Little Ice Age continued to grip much of the Northern Hemisphere, climate change in the Southwest manifested itself in higher temperatures and serious drought conditions. So severe was the drought that starvation increasingly haunted Indigenous people and Spaniards alike (the Indigenous people already had their ranks decimated by disease) and intensified the raiding of the Apaches and other nomads. After all, the Pueblos had nothing to offer in trade. What's more, the apparent inability of the Franciscans to use their Christian religion to end the drought raised questions among the mission Pueblos about how powerful the Franciscans really were. Not surprisingly, they turned again to their spiritual leaders (shamans) and ceremonies and recognized the Spaniards' vulnerabilities.

A Successful Rebellion

The Franciscans were alarmed by the Pueblos' spiritual rejection, but they soon received help from a new royal governor, Juan Francisco Treviño, who arrived in 1675 and quickly determined to crack down. He rounded up more than forty

Pueblo holy men. He subjected most of them to whippings, imprisonment, and the threat of enslavement, and he had three of them executed; a fourth committed suicide. Outraged Pueblo village leaders confronted Treviño and forced him to release some of the captives. One was a man known as "Po'pay" (the Spanish called him "Pope").

Po'pay headed north to Taos, a good distance (about 70 miles) from the Spanish officials in Santa Fe, and there began to plot a rebellion. It would not be easy to do. Pueblo villages engaged in their own rivalries, spoke numerous languages, and were spread out across a few hundred miles of desert and mountains. These were divides that would have to be overcome. But the Pueblo also had nearly a century of experience with the Spanish, claimed leaders who could speak Spanish and thus communicate with one another, and suffered more than their share of abuse and exploitation. Po'pay also deployed Native runners who could bring messages to different villages. By August 1680, with Po'pay's important organizing (there were other organizers as well) and message of destroying the Spanish and worshipping in their own way, they were ready to revolt (see Map 4.3).

Po'pay's rebellion—often known as the **Pueblo Revolt**—was remarkable for its scope and intensity. Despite the challenges of communication and potential disunity, many of the roughly 17,000 Pueblos rose against the Spanish, first in their towns and villages and then converging on Santa Fe. They not only killed the Spanish and the Franciscans, but, like the Wampanoag in New England, they also sought to rid the landscape of any vestige of Spanish or Christian rule. With Po'pay's encouragement, in the words of one of his followers, they "break up and burn the images of the holy Christ, the Virgin Mary and the other saints, the crosses, and everything pertaining to Christianity, and that they burn the temples and break up the bells [and] in order to take away their baptismal names, the water, and the holy oils, they were to plunge into the rivers and wash themselves." The Pueblo rebels also burned Spanish estates and government buildings and executed more than twenty Franciscan priests, often accompanied by torture and mutilation.

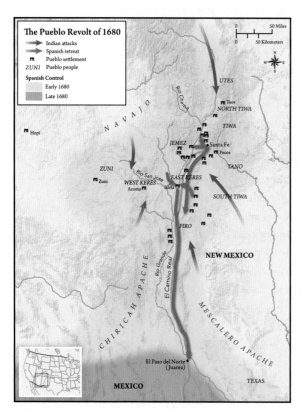

≡ **MAP 4.3**   **The Pueblo Revolt of 1680**

One of the Franciscans, in a ritual of public shaming, was forced to ride naked on the back of a hog before he was killed.

The Pueblo Revolt was the greatest Native blow to European colonialism ever struck in the Western Hemisphere. About 400 of the Spanish (more than 10 percent of them) were killed, and the survivors fled Santa Fe for the Spanish outpost at El Paso, 300 miles to the south. There they remained for well over a decade. When the Spanish finally succeeded in 1692 in retaking Santa Fe and their colony of New Mexico, owing in part to Pop'ay's death and

≡ **Pueblo Revolt**   In the foreground of this 1976 painting by artist Fred Kabotie, Hopi people string up and prepare to burn a Franciscan priest. In the background, other Hopis disassemble the church he had forced them to build.

deepening divisions among the Pueblo, a new regime was soon installed: one lighter on the exploitation of Native labor and much less zealous in warring against Pueblo spiritualism. Indeed, the Spanish and Pueblo people became allies of sorts—unequal allies to be sure—to protect New Spain's far northern boundary from the incursions of rival European powers and especially from the withering raids of hostile Apaches, Utes, Navajos, and Comanches.

4.6   Rebellion in Salem

Analyze the gender and generational aspects of the Salem witchcraft episode.

The seventeenth century was clearly a time of great convulsion on both sides of the Atlantic, as imperial warfare, civil wars, and more localized rebellions roiled England, continental Europe, the high seas, and parts of North America. But the convulsions could also take form beyond political unrest and upheaval, turning stresses and conflicts in more supernatural directions and reminding us that the seventeenth century was still very much premodern in its cultural and religious sensibilities. They could also emanate from sources rarely recognized as consequential, drawing our attention to pains and resentments often glossed over. Such was the case in Salem, Massachusetts, in 1692, when accusations of witchcraft against some of the most disempowered community members nearly tore the entire colony apart.

Witchcraft accusations were by no means peculiar to Salem, Massachusetts, or to New England more generally. Across the seventeenth century there were nearly 100 cases in the colonies of Massachusetts and Connecticut, along with more than twenty-five civil suits involving witchcraft allegations that touched Rhode Island as well as Connecticut and Massachusetts. Across the Atlantic, by the late seventeenth century witchcraft accusations were becoming less and less common in England, but in the two centuries prior, well over 300 people there were convicted and executed. On the European continent, moreover, witch-hunting was even more widespread and lethal in the German states, the Swiss Confederation, and France, though less so in Italy, Spain, and the Netherlands. Salem, in sum, was an example of a far broader phenomenon. But it was also especially convulsive and deadly.

Accusations of Witchcraft

People at the time claimed that it all started in 1691 when several young girls in rural Salem Village began meeting among themselves to talk about their futures. To help them, one of the girls devised a sort of crystal ball. But in the ball they apparently saw a specter that frightened them, and by February 1692, they seemed to the adults of the village to be behaving strangely, with "foolish, ridiculous speeches" along with "distempers" and "fits." A physician who examined them thought that an "evil hand" was at work as the affliction spread to seven or eight other girls of their age as well as to a few young married women. Finally, under intense questioning, the girls named three local women as their tormentors, two of whom denied any guilt. But the third confessed, and all three were accused of being witches and jailed in nearby Boston to await trial.

What did it mean to be a witch? New England Puritans understood the world as involving an intense, never-ending struggle between good and evil, between God and the devil. They also saw many spirits at work around them and often interpreted important events—joyous and catastrophic alike—as spiritual manifestations. They looked for ways to celebrate the presence of God or condemn the presence of the devil. After all, living in the midst of repeated epidemics, Native raids and conflicts, droughts, floods, poor harvests, solar eclipses, and birth-related deformities raised questions about what and who might be responsible.

As we saw in Chapter 3, those who had conversion experiences became visible saints, church members regarded as among God's chosen. But what of the others? A witch in their view was someone who not only was not among God's chosen but had also made a pact with the ever-present devil; who was the devil's embodiment in the world intent on inflicting harm. No accusation could be more serious in this world. It was like a political charge of treason, and like treason potentially punishable by death.

Among the English colonies of North America, those of New England were most prone to witness witchcraft accusations and trials even after midcentury when they became extremely rare in England itself. Over the course of the seventeenth century, the colonies of Massachusetts and Connecticut had just over ninety witchcraft cases between them, though each of the episodes was mostly brief in duration and limited in the number of accusations. They resulted in a total of sixteen executions.

Salem was different. Witchcraft accusations were made for months and the accusations escalated in number until they reached over 300 people, mostly women. Before the episode was over, twenty accused witches (including one man) had been put to death.

Why Salem?

It's almost impossible to explain just why the **Salem witchcraft episode** occurred where and when it did. Historians have argued about it for years. In part, this is because the episode places early American history—and the Puritans of New England—in a rather ugly light, and in part because it reminds us that even decent people and well-ordered societies can persecute those they fear. In the 1950s, during the period of McCarthyism (Chapter 25), when thousands of Americans were persecuted for their political convictions, the great playwright Arthur Miller wrote *The Crucible* (1953) as a way of linking what happened in Salem to what was happening around him.

Perhaps we can get some clarity by trying to understand the larger context, and the perspectives the context reveals. By the late seventeenth century, New England settlements—and especially Puritan settlements—had experienced a great deal of change and stress. They were established in an environment of great uncertainty and danger but also with very clear rules about conducting themselves. Community life revolved around the town and the church. Land was distributed under the supervision of town officials, and it would be passed on generationally by family patriarchs. Political decisions were made by town meetings in which all male church members participated. And it was expected that children of visible saints would themselves have conversion experiences and thereby become members of the church in their own rights.

The Age of Homespun in a Larger Atlantic World

By the middle of the seventeenth century, cloth making had become an integral part of New England life. Colonial legislators encouraged the sowing of flax to make linen and the raising of sheep to manufacture wool. But cotton more than any other fiber characterized New England's textile production.

The romantic image of New England "goodwives" spinning cotton in front of cozy hearths should not obscure the fact that the cotton came from the West Indies, grown and harvested by enslaved Africans. Each year, New England mariners sailed to Barbados and other English colonies in the Caribbean, their holds filled with fish and lumber. They returned laden with sugar, cotton, and other commodities produced by

≡ **Cloth Making: Household Production**

slave labor. As the great historian Laurel Thatcher Ulrich reminds us, New England's "cloth making was implicated in the expansion of New World slavery."[1]

This sculpture from 1885 casts a warm glow on an imagined "Age of Homespun" among the Puritans of Massachusetts. It illustrates a famous scene from a poem by Henry Wadsworth Longfellow when John Alden declares his love to Priscilla Mullins. The sculptor has placed a spinning wheel at the very center of the action, symbolizing the domestic tranquility that will characterize their eventual marriage.

In *Linen Day, Roseau, Dominica—A Market Scene* (1770) the painter Agostino Brunias puts the Atlantic trade in cotton on vivid display. Free people of color, well-to-do whites, and enslaved people mingle in a weekly textile market on the island of Dominica, an English colony in the West Indies. Throughout the Caribbean, markets such as this one were dynamic sites of economic and social exchange. They operated within imperial networks that spanned oceans and continents.

☰ **Cloth Making: Atlantic Trade Networks**

CONSIDER THIS

By 1700, about half the households in Massachusetts owned spinning wheels. What does this say about the place of homespun cloth in a wider Atlantic economy? Do you think the spinners were aware of their connection to slavery?

[1] Laurel Thatcher Ulrich, *The Age of Homespun: Objects and Stories in the Creation of an American Myth* (New York: Random House, 2001), 38.

Under the best of circumstances, this sort of stability would have been hard to maintain, yet it proved all the more difficult as the population grew (owing to births and immigration) and the early towns no longer had the lands to distribute either to new settlers or to the children of those who lived there. What's more, as church members had children and the number of young Puritans increased, it appeared that fewer were having conversion experiences at all. Worried about the consequences for their communities, about what they called "declension" (a decline in religious orthodoxy), Puritan leaders then devised what was known as the **half-way covenant**: partial church membership for the children and grandchildren of visible saints who did not themselves have conversion experiences.

Little by little, the authority of the towns, of the churches, and of Puritan fathers could be seen as weakening. Settlers had to look farther inland to establish new towns or to find land in new towns that had been established. The children of visible saints could no longer count on receiving an adequate inheritance from their families and so were less happy about submitting to patriarchal demands. But submission was still demanded of them, part of a larger regime of harsh discipline, corporal punishment, and labor exploitation that was still very much in place. Childhood and adolescence, for boys and girls, could be a dispiriting experience of apprenticeships, servitude in other households (also known as "binding out"), and intense community surveillance. To make matters worse, as the population of New England moved farther away from the coast, Indigenous land and use claims were challenged, undermining trading relations and regularly inciting warfare.

Salem seemed a microcosm of all these changes and problems. It was divided into a seaport Town (present-day Salem) and a rural Village (present-day Danvers). Salem Town thrived with commercial and fishing activity and had become relatively prosperous over the course of the seventeenth century. The Town was also the center of governance (it had the meetinghouse) and religious life (it had the church). Salem Village, by contrast, was less commercial and less well-off, and it lacked both a meetinghouse and a church. Village residents had to travel to the Town for church services and political meetings. Further, over time, newer communities were established near the Village's borders, so that as the population grew there was little room to expand.

Eventually the Village managed to get its own church and meetinghouse, but conflicts among Village members made it difficult to find and keep a minister. When a new minister named Samuel Parris arrived in 1689, he soon provoked further contention in the Village while constantly invoking the figure of the devil in his sermons. At the same time, the Massachusetts colony was drawn into extended Native warfare (called King William's War) in northern New England, which took a heavy toll on the Village in manpower and refugees.

Social and Cultural Dynamics

As it turned out, the circle of girls who leveled the first accusations of witchcraft included Parris's daughter and his niece. They singled out an enslaved woman in Parris's household of Native or African descent—Tituba—who likely had been sold to New England from a Spanish colony to the south, and two outcast women who lived closer to Salem Town. By the time the first trials began in June, more than sixty additional accusations had been made, and although early on the accused witches fit the mold of women who were poor, lived alone, and had cantankerous reputations, as time went on, the targets moved up the social scale and were associated with Salem's opposition to Minister Parris. By summer's end, even the colonial governor's wife stood accused, at which point the religious and legal authorities (including the governor) stepped in and put a halt to the proceedings. It would be the last such outbreak of alleged witchcraft in the English colonies.

The Salem witchcraft accusations, trials, and executions were deeply troubling. They showed that, especially in a very strong religious environment, secular issues could easily be infused with the sacred and the satanic. The tensions between Salem Town and Salem Village would appear, on the surface, to be social and political, resonant with those coming to the surface in other New England communities. But in Salem, the new Village minister became a lightning rod of controversy.

Equally troubling, the witchcraft episode showed how gender could be a hub around which community stress and conflict revolved. Indeed, this was a society in which women walked a very perilous line, one that tipped quickly between good and evil. And those who tried to fend for themselves, who stood up against established authorities and institutions, or who refused to play by an assortment of rules, invited retribution. Beaten by Parris into confession, the enslaved Tituba described the devil as "a thing all over hairy, all the face hairy, and a long nose." But in Salem and elsewhere in the Anglo-Atlantic world, the devil truly appeared to

≡ **Trial by Water** The persecution of marginalized women for perceived "witchcraft" spread from England to the colonies. This 1613 English pamphlet illustrates the trial by dunking of Mary Sutton in Bedford, England, in 1612. Mary Sutton as well as her mother, who had tended the village's livestock, came under suspicion when pigs and horses died suddenly. After Mary's son Henry was caught and punished by a local landowner, Master Enger, for throwing stones into the Mill Dam (shown in this woodcut), both Sutton women vowed vengeance on Enger. After Enger's own young son mysteriously died, Enger and other villagers accused the Sutton women of witchcraft. Mary Sutton was bound, beaten, and dragged into the mill stream to see if she sunk or stayed afloat. This is believed to be the first recorded instance of a trial by water of an accused witch in England. Both Sutton women were arrested, tried, and found guilty of witchcraft. They were hanged on April 7, 1612.

MAPPING AMERICA

Placing Colonial Convulsions in a Wider Context

The warfare prompted by rebellion and revolution was a devastating fact of life for ordinary people—not just soldiers, politicians, and royalty—in many areas of the world during the seventeenth century. China exploded into a civil war that ended in 1644 with the fall of the Ming Dynasty.

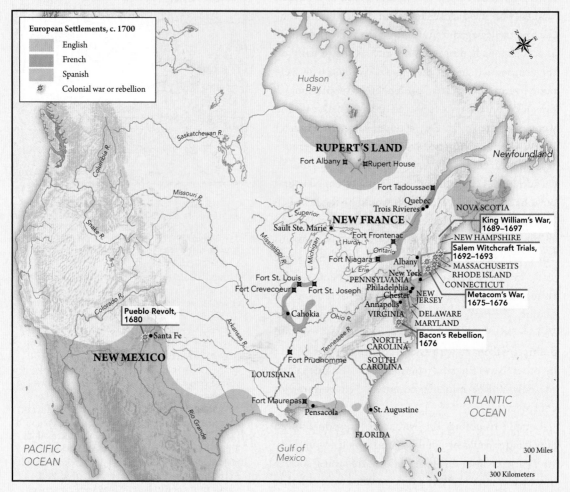

European Settlements, c. 1700
- English
- French
- Spanish
- ⚜ Colonial war or rebellion

King William's War, 1689–1697

Salem Witchcraft Trials, 1692–1693

Metacom's War, 1675–1676

Bacon's Rebellion, 1676

Pueblo Revolt, 1680

≡ **MAP 1**   Examining these crises from a North American perspective shows the distribution of these deadly disturbances from New England to New Mexico. This perspective is useful for identifying the conflicts within and between European colonial settlements within North America. But it only tells us part of the story.

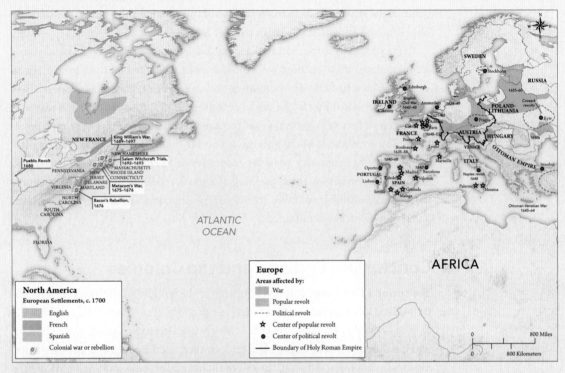

≡ **MAP 2**   Broadening our lens so it brings into view both sides of the Atlantic allows us to understand these upheavals as part of a wider pattern of conflict and struggle. The effects of these revolts and revolutions in Europe rippled back and forth across the ocean.

Russia endured a "Time of Troubles" from 1598 to 1613 and persistent instability throughout the seventeenth century. Intermittent revolts wracked the Ottoman Empire during much of this same period. Cartography (the science of mapmaking) can help us to better understand both the sheer scale and the intimate impact of these conflicts.

Thinking Geographically

1. What factors or conditions might account for so much instability on a global level during the seventeenth century? Consider, for example, the availability of new technologies, the discoveries made by scientists, or changes in climate.

2. In disciplines ranging from meteorology to mathematics, the concept of the "butterfly effect" suggests that a tiny event in one part of the world can have a major impact thousands of miles away. Consider what you have learned so far in this course. What kinds of connections can you suggest between areas of conflict on these two maps?

come in the shape of a woman. What would this mean for the future of women in New England and other Christian parts of North America?

There was, as well, the matter of generations. The accusers were girls and young women; many of the accused were older women who lived on their own, claimed some property, had few if any children, and were often regarded as abrasive. They were women who didn't fit the model of the female in Puritan society and may well have been victimized chiefly on that account. Yet there is another or related possibility. The accusations of the girls moved rapidly up the social scale, in effect placing the entire community, even the exemplars of Puritan propriety at lethal risk. May we then be witnessing something of a youth rebellion that followed a course most readily available to them, an outburst of generational hostility that Puritans had struggled to keep contained?

Conclusion: England and the Colonies

The turmoil that swept through England in the middle of the seventeenth century raised large questions about what the English empire would be and how the empire's colonies would be governed: how much latitude colonists would have in making their own rules, engaging in trade, traversing the continent, and constructing local economies. After all, they were thousands of miles away at a time of very slow means of transportation and communication. The restoration that brought Charles II and James II to the throne suggested that there would be a cracking down, an effort to bring the North American colonies under firmer control.

But the dissatisfactions that James II provoked in England were soon matched by colonial oppositions to the regime he was attempting to implant in North America. And so, the Glorious Revolution, which forced James II into exile, ushered in a lengthy era of compromise on both sides of the Atlantic: one in which Parliament and the monarchy reached a truce and in which home rule would include substantial room for colonial initiative. The stage was thereby set for massive imperial struggles that would decide the future of the North American continent.

WHAT IF King Philip's War Had Succeeded?

Of the four convulsions that erupted in late seventeenth-century North America, two involved Indigenous rebellions against European colonizers. One, in New Mexico, pushed the Spanish out of Santa Fe and down toward El Paso, 300 miles away, enabling Pueblo people to reclaim territory they had long occupied and forcing the Spanish to tread more carefully in their ways when they ultimately returned. The other, in New England, saw Metacom (King Philip), the Wampanoags, and their allies nearly inflict the same sort of defeat on the English before their fortunes were reversed and the English settlers prevailed.

But what if King Philip's War had succeeded something in the manner of the Pueblo Revolt in New Mexico? What if the Wampanoag alliance had pushed the English out of the towns they had settled away from the coast, cleared the landscape of English and Puritan symbols and structures, and managed to

hold their ground at least for an extended period of time? Would such a turn of events have allowed the Indigenous people of the region to reestablish their land claims and rebuild the villages that had been destroyed or surrendered? Would the English have been forced to abandon much of what they called New England or perhaps maintain their footholds by seeking different relationships with the Indigenous people, as the Spanish had been forced to do? Could this have been the basis of a different history for northeastern North America and the Indigenous populations who had long resided there?

The following two documents offer contrasting accounts of the causes of King Philip's War. The first, written by the son of a New England colonist, presents the perspective of many English Puritans at the time. The second is the transcription of a speech by Metacom or one of his spokesmen offering the Wampanoag perspective.

DOCUMENT 4.1: Thomas Church's View of King Philip's War, 1716

The Pilgrim colony of Plymouth had lived in harmony with its Indian neighbors since the time of the First Thanksgiving in 1621. The wise policies of the Wampanoag chief Massasoit combined with the justice of the Puritan founders to keep the peace. As was the practice among New England Indians, after Massasoit's death his office descended to his sons, first "King Alexander" (Wamsutta) and then "King Philip" (Metacom or Metacomet). Unlike his father, Philip harbored inexplicably deep resentments against the English. Almost immediately, he began plotting a bloody design and sending his messengers to all the neighboring sachems, to engage them in a confederacy with him in the war. He bullied such peaceful Indians who tried to resist his recruiting efforts . . . by threatening to send his men over privately, to kill the English cattle, and burn their houses which would provoke the

English to fall upon [them]. Philip's minions soon began their hostilities with plundering and destroying cattle, but did not long content themselves with that game, because they thirsted for English blood. Between the summer of 1675 and the spring of 1676, a dozen or more English towns fell to his fury, forcing the colonists to abandon most of what is now western Massachusetts and northwestern Connecticut.

Source: Thomas Church, "Entertaining Passages Relating to King Philip's War" (1716), quoted in Daniel Richter, *Looking East from Indian Country: A Native History of Early America* (Cambridge MA: Harvard University Press, 2001), 90–91.

DOCUMENT 4.2: Speech by Metacom or One of His Spokesmen, 1675

[The Wampanoags] said they had been the first in doing good to the English, and the English in doing wrong, [and they] said, when the English first came, their king's father [Massasoit] was a great man and the English was a little child. He constrained other Indians from wrongdoing the English and gave them corn and showed them how to plant and was free to do them any good and had let them have 100 times more land, than now the king had for his own people, but their king's brother [Wamsutta], when he was king, came miserably to die by being forced to Court as the judged poisoned, and another grievance was [that] if 20 of their honest Indians testified that an Englishman had done them wrong, it was as nothing, and if but one of their worst Indians testified against any Indian or their king when it pleased the English that was sufficient. Another grievance was that their kings sold land the English would say it was more than they agreed to and a writing must be proof against all them, and some of their kings had done wrong to sell so much [that] he left his people none and some being given to drunkenness the English made them drunk and then cheated them in bargains. . . . Now the English [would] make another king that would give or sell them their land, that now they had no hopes left to keep any land.

Source: Transcribed by John Easton, "A Relacion of the Indyan Warrr," 1675; quoted in Richter, *Looking East from Indian Country,* 103–104.

Thinking About Contingency

1. In what ways does Thomas Church blame Metacom and the Wampanoags for the war?
2. What does Metacom believe is at stake for the Wampanoags in the face of English aggression?
3. Can one of the accounts be seen as more credible than the other? Why or why not?

REVIEW QUESTIONS

1. What was the nature of the conflict that resulted in the English Civil War of the 1640s, and how did the conflict give rise to radical groups like the Levellers?

2. Were there clear winners and losers at the end of the English Civil War, and if so, who were they?

3. What was the perspective of Wampanoags and the Indigenous people allied to them on King Philip's war, and how did it differ from the perspective of the English colonists?

4. How threatening to the social order of Virginia was Bacon's Rebellion, and why did Governor Berkeley repress it so brutally?

5. Why did Po'pay and his followers wish to drive off the Spanish colonizers and Franciscan missionaries in New Mexico, and how were they able to succeed?

6. What were the circumstances that surrounded the witchcraft episode in Salem, Massachusetts, and what were the gender and generational aspects of it? What sort of people were first accused, and why?

KEY TERMS

Bacon's Rebellion (p. 144)

Declaration of Rights (p. 136)

Diggers (p. 133)

English Civil War (p. 133)

Glorious Revolution (p. 136)

half-way covenant (p. 152)

King Philip's (or Metacom's) War (p. 138)

Levellers (p. 133)

Little Ice Age (p. 132)

Navigation Acts (p. 136)

New Model Army (p. 135)

Parliamentary Bill of Rights (p. 136)

Po'pay's Rebellion (Pueblo Revolt) (p. 146)

Salem witchcraft episode (p. 149)

settler colonialism (p. 130)

RECOMMENDED READINGS

Lisa Brooks, *Our Beloved Kin: A New History of King Philip's War* (Yale University Press, 2019).

Christopher Hill, *The World Turned Upside Down: Radical Ideas during the English Revolution* (Viking, 1972).

Carol Karlsen, *The Devil in the Shape of a Woman: Witchcraft in Colonial New England* (W. W. Norton, 1987).

Andrew Knaut, *The Pueblo Revolt: Conquest and Resistance in Seventeenth Century New Mexico* (University of Oklahoma Press, 1995).

Matthew Kruer, *Time of Anarchy: Indigenous Power and the Crisis of Colonialism in Early America* (Harvard University Press, 2022).

Edmund Morgan, *American Slavery, American Freedom: The Ordeal of Colonial Virginia* (W. W Norton, 1975).

Mary Beth Norton, *In the Devil's Snare: The Witchcraft Crisis of 1692* (Vintage, 2003).

Geoffrey Parker, *Global Crisis: War, Climate Change and Catastrophe in the Seventeenth Century* (Yale University Press, 2013).

Steven Pincus, *England's Glorious Revolution, 1688–89* (Yale University Press, 2009).

5

Colonial Societies and Contentious Empires
1625–1786

Chapter Outline

5.1 The Rise of Slave Societies: The Caribbean

‖ Describe the process by which slave societies based on the production of sugar turned the
‖ English Caribbean into significant economic colonies.

5.2 The Rise of Slave Societies: The Chesapeake

‖ Explain how the Virginia colony became a slave society over the course of the seventeenth
‖ century.

5.3 The Rise of Slave Societies: Carolina

‖ Enumerate the similarities and differences between the Chesapeake and Carolina paths to
‖ slavery.

5.4 The Rise of Slave Societies: The Lower Mississippi Valley

‖ Describe the different dynamics involving the French that went into the making of a slave
‖ society in the lower Mississippi Valley.

≡ **Enslaver and Enslaved** A 1710 portrait of Henry Darnall III, scion of one of the wealthiest families in colonial
Maryland, who would grow up to become the deputy governor and naval officer of the colony. The painter, Justus
Engelhardt Kuhn, born in Germany and the first professional artist to work in the Chesapeake and Middle Colonies,
shows the boy proudly holding a bow and arrow, which he may have used to kill the bird held by the enslaved child beside
him. The enslaved boy, whose name is likely engraved on the silver collar around his neck, was Darnall's personal valet.
As an adult, Darnall was accused of embezzlement and fled the colonies in disgrace. Nothing further is known about the
fate of the enslaved boy.

5.5 The Rise of Mission-Presidio Societies: The Southwest

‖ Define the purpose of mission-presidio societies and distinguish between those of
‖ New Mexico and California.

5.6 The Rise of Farming Societies: New England and the Middle Atlantic

‖ Identify differences between farming societies in the Northeast and Middle Atlantic
‖ and the developing plantation systems of the South.

5.7 The Rise of Equestrian-Based Indigenous Societies: Peoples of the Great Plains

‖ Explain the complex societies and polities that Indigenous peoples of the Plains
‖ constructed.

During the early years of the eighteenth century, the one place that brought
rural Virginians together was the Anglican Church. On Sundays, as well as on
special religious occasions, many of them took their places in the pews.

Timeline

1620	1630	1640	1650	1660	1670	1680	1690	1700

1627 > English establish settlements on Barbados and the Leeward Islands

1627–1635 > French establish settlements on Dominica, Guadeloupe, and Martinique

1640 > First laws regulating slavery in the Chesapeake

1655 > English take control of Jamaica from the Spanish

1663 > Royal African Company chartered by Charles II of England

1670 > English colonists from Barbados establish first settlement in South Carolina

1676 > Bacon's Rebellion in Virginia

1680 > Pueblo (Po'pay's) Revolt in New Mexico

1682 > French explorer Robert de La Salle claims Louisiana for Louis XIV of France

But it wasn't simply God's grace that they were seeking; they also bore witness to an enactment of their community's social structure. Wealthy church members had purchased pews at the front of the church, near where the minister preached and led prayers; more humble white members sat on benches toward the rear. Enslaved people may have stood at the back of the church but were more likely outside, under watch. Then a powerful ritual began. As a plantation tutor recorded, it was "not the custom for Gentlemen to go into Church till Service is beginning, when they enter in a body, in the same manner as they come out." On holidays such as Easter, "all the Parish seemed to meet together, High, Low, black, White," together participating in an expression of faith and a performance of social and racial distinctions. In effect, the brutal social hierarchy of colonial Virginia was on display.

Virginia was not alone. By the late seventeenth and early eighteenth centuries, settlements established by European empires and colonizers were undergoing

1710	1720	1730	1740	1750	1760	1770	1780	1790

1705 > Enactment of Virginia's Slave Code

1729 > Natchez Revolt in the Lower Mississippi Valley

1739 > Stono Rebellion in South Carolina

1769 > Spanish establish first mission in California, known as Mission San Diego de Alcala

1786 > Ute-Comanche Treaty ushers in lengthy peace between the Comanches and the Spanish

transformations. After several decades of instability and vulnerability owing to disease, starvation, and attack, they were embarking on new and, in some cases, unexpected paths. What had been colonial outposts and settlements became full-fledged colonial societies. They grew in size, were marked by old and new forms of social differentiation, gave rise to economic and political elites, forged balances of power with surrounding Indigenous peoples, and were governed by institutions that home countries had prescribed but that colonials mostly staffed.

Colonial settlements did not turn into societies overnight, and the process was never a smooth one. It involved disease, military conflict, depopulation, failed experimentation, and rebellions. Yet, as colonial societies came into being, they also presented challenges for their empires. On the one hand, they were the sources of imperial wealth, power, and design, and were the frontiers of imperial expansion and combat. On the other hand, they developed interests and ways of doing things that could conflict with the demands and goals of imperial rulers themselves. In short, the perspectives of the colonies and of the home countries could differ, especially over time. Colonial societies were simultaneously symbols of and problems for the empires of which they were a part, as Virginia's own history would demonstrate.

5.1   The Rise of Slave Societies: The Caribbean

||| Describe the process by which slave societies based on the production of sugar turned the English Caribbean into significant economic colonies.

Over the course of the seventeenth century, despite England's growing involvement in the African slave trade, most of the enslaved people who arrived in the Chesapeake did not come directly from Africa. Instead, they came from the islands of the Caribbean, where they had first been brought and perhaps sold. Why was this?

As we saw in Chapter 3, while the Virginia Company of London focused on establishing a settlement along the coast of North America and the Puritans sought an escape from the persecution they suffered in England, other English merchants and adventurers were eyeing the Caribbean basin. They knew that the Spanish had taken control of some of the islands there, that Spanish ships loaded with silver and gold passed through the Caribbean on their way to Spain, and that the Caribbean islands were good bases for expeditions to the mainland of the Western Hemisphere. During the 1620s and 1630s, English vessels made landfall in the far eastern Caribbean, on what would become known as the Lesser Antilles (the islands they named St. Christopher, Montserrat, Nevis, and Antigua), including what they called Barbados. By the mid-1650s, emboldened by the English Civil War, they moved directly against Spanish holdings farther to the west—part of a general attack on the Spanish—none more significant than Jamaica, very near to Hispaniola (see Map 5.1).

An Emerging Sugar Economy

The Caribbean islands initially offered the English havens for raids on Spanish shipping. Before too long, however, the English began to make more permanent settlements. The well-to-do among them received grants of land from the crown, and at first planted tobacco (already known in the Caribbean and already being

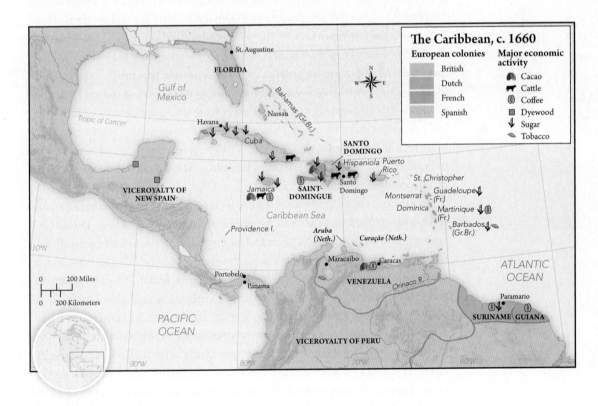

≡ **MAP 5.1   The Caribbean, c. 1660**   After initially using Caribbean islands as havens for raiding on Spanish shipping, the English transformed them into places whose economies centered on sugar production.

grown and marketed in the Chesapeake) and cotton as well as subsistence crops. But in the 1630s and 1640s, in good part from Dutch travelers and traders who had been in Brazil, the English learned about growing sugar. Sugar plantation economies soon began to take off most everywhere the English had settled.

In recruiting a labor force for the tobacco, cotton, and sugarcane fields, the planters of the Caribbean followed the course that had previously been charted out in Brazil. Where Native populations could still be found in some number, they looked to subdue and coerce them or to purchase enslaved Indigenous people who had been made captive in the Chesapeake and New England and then sent to new markets in the Caribbean. Far more significantly, however, they turned to white indentured servants, who, as we saw in Chapter 3, could be bought for terms of four to seven years and set to work under a discipline to which English property holders had long been accustomed. Indeed, many English people, whether free or indentured, headed to the Caribbean rather than to either the Chesapeake or New England: about 44,000 were there in midcentury compared to about 35,000 in all of North America. The Caribbean, not North America, was now and would remain the center of colonial development and imperial interest—the real center of action.

Yet, as in the Chesapeake, indentured servants would prove to be a troublesome lot. The "freedom dues" they were promised if they served out their terms initially included land or at least the promise of it. But as in the Chesapeake, land was soon in short supply, and the servants were increasingly disappointed and angry. Adding to a nasty mix were growing numbers of servants who had been convicts or political prisoners (many from Scotland and Ireland) taken during the English Civil War and subject to brutal exploitation. "Truly, I have seen such cruelty there done to Servants," an observer in Barbados recorded, "as I did not think one Christian could have done to another."

Faced with a combustible labor force of white servants, planters in Barbados and the Antilles looked to an alternative increasingly made available by Dutch traders: enslaved Africans. The Dutch had been supplying northeastern Brazil with enslaved people since late in the sixteenth century, and the West Indies was relatively close to West Africa and the Brazilian northeast, making the voyages shorter and the prices for enslaved people lower. Well before the emergence of the Royal African Company (charted by Charles II in 1660), thousands of enslaved Africans arrived in Barbados: by 1660 they not only outnumbered white servants there, but they also outnumbered all white people, free and in servitude. Barbados now had an enslaved Black majority (27,000 Black people to 26,000 white people), the first of the English colonies to have that demographic character, and it would be followed by most of the other Caribbean colonies being settled.

Terror on the Middle Passage

Most of the enslaved people shipped to Barbados and elsewhere in the West Indies came from a portion of the West African coast stretching south from Senegambia or Upper Guinea to the Bight of Benin and the Bight of Biafra, but especially from what was known as the **Gold Coast** (around present-day Ghana). These were multiethnic and multilingual agricultural societies that had been involved in Atlantic trade since the fifteenth century and in the trans-African trade for centuries before that. The enslaved Africans who were sold to Europeans—to the Spanish, Portuguese, Dutch, and English—most often had been captured as a result of warfare between African states, though some had been kidnapped by slave raiders hoping to find eager buyers. The enslaved may have been taken captive near the coast or well into the interior by Africans engaged in the trade, who then brought them to the European feitorias (fortified trading posts) for transport overseas (see Map 5.2).

The slave ships varied in size, though they often made only one or two stops in West Africa before heading, with their cargoes, across the Atlantic. Depending on how long they waited in the African pens, enslaved people may have begun to communicate with one another—developing pidgin languages if they came from different linguistic areas—before boarding began. Then, the captives would be crowded onto the vessels, most often below deck in the holds, where they would endure the **Middle Passage**, the trans-Atlantic voyage from what was once their homeland on the African continent to the plantation colonies of the Western Hemisphere. Their fates on these voyages would depend on how long they were on the ships and on whether the limited supplies of food and water ran out. It was not just a matter of nautical miles; it was also a matter of winds and ocean currents. These were sailing vessels, so it was impossible to know how long the Middle Passage would take. But the longer the Middle Passage, the more the enslaved sickened and died. The mortality rates on the slave ships ranged from about 15 percent to 25 percent (sometimes even more if a virulent disease broke out), which meant that, on average, a substantial number of the enslaved people who were purchased in West Africa did not survive to be resold.

But their fates also depended upon the sheer terror of captivity and the Middle Passage. Few of the enslaved Africans had ever seen the ocean; of those, even fewer who had would ever have sailed in ocean waters or experienced being at sea and losing sight of land. All were agonized about being separated from their families, communities, and familiar environments and distraught at the illness and death that they witnessed around them. And all were terrified by what might await them when their slaving vessels reached their destinations.

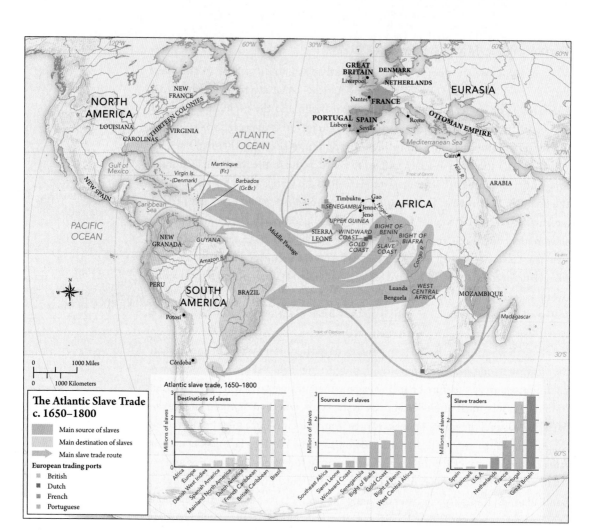

≡ **MAP 5.2**   **The Atlantic Slave Trade, c. 1650–1800**   The Atlantic slave trade grew dramatically after 1650 with the rise of plantation-based economies in the Caribbean, Brazil, and the North American mainland.

Booming Barbados

Most enslaved Africans managed to survive the Middle Passage. Once they reached the Caribbean, prospective buyers would come aboard the slave ship, inspect the enslaved people in the most intrusive and intimate ways, and decide which ones to buy. If they were starting up plantations, the buyers would prefer enslaved men, who could do the heaviest and most backbreaking work. Indeed, overall the gender balances of the slave trade brought many more men than women across the Atlantic—at least until well into the eighteenth century. Some of the buyers also favored some ethnic groups over others, as word began to circulate (of questionable reliability) about which ethnic groups were more submissive and which more rebellious. But this was a seller's market: buyers had to purchase whatever enslaved Africans were available. So great was the demand as Barbados, Jamaica, and other English islands turned to sugar production that slaving ships rarely went much farther to make their sales. Throughout the entire history of the Atlantic slave trade—from the late fifteenth century to the mid-nineteenth—the overwhelming number of enslaved Africans went either to the Caribbean or Brazil.

Planters in the seventeenth-century Chesapeake generally had to wait to receive enslaved people who were not immediately purchased in Barbados or in the Antilles or who had been resold by Caribbean enslavers. In fact, most of the enslaved people who ended up in the Chesapeake during the seventeenth century had spent time in the Caribbean, perhaps on developing sugar or tobacco plantations, and likely had learned some English, Dutch, or Portuguese; maybe all three. They may also have gained some knowledge of English ways. They were a version of the "creoles" who were populating much of the Atlantic rim by the end of the seventeenth century. Not until the 1680s and 1690s would the balances in the Chesapeake shift to enslaved people coming directly from West Africa rather than from the West Indies.

So rapid was the rise of plantations in English Barbados that something of a crisis was soon in the making. Many of the Caribbean islands are geographically and geologically diverse. They have relatively flat, cultivable land near the coast and often hilly and mountainous terrain farther into the interior. Barbados, by contrast, is not only small in size (21 miles in length and no more than 14 miles in width) but is mostly flat and suitable to plantation agriculture. As a result, the land

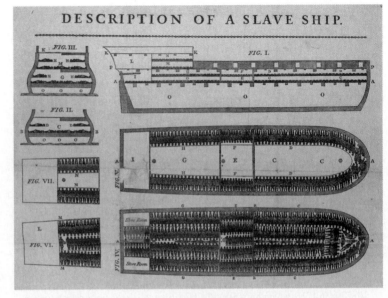

The Middle Passage   The English Royal Navy captured the French slaving ship *Vigilante* on April 15, 1822, in the Bonny River near the coast of what is now Nigeria. On board, as shown in this plan, were 345 enslaved people. The map's caption reads: "The slaves were found lying on their backs on the lower deck . . . those in the centre were sitting some in the posture in which they are shown and others with their legs bent under them, resting upon the soles of their feet." This document also shows the padlocked iron collars and fetters used around the necks, arms, and legs of the captives.

≡ **Mapping Barbados**   In this detail from a 1722 map of Barbados, based on the surveys of English cartographer William Mayo between 1717 and 1721, enslaved people assist a surveyor in making his measurements. The windmills were used for the processing of sugar. Mayo and his family emigrated to Virginia in 1723, where his surveys helped to establish the boundary between the colonies of Virginia and North Carolina.

in Barbados was quickly organized into sugar plantations, and the island attracted the attention of many Englishmen who were looking to make their fortunes. One was the son of John Winthrop, the leader of the Massachusetts Bay colony we met in Chapter 3 and himself familiar with the enslavement of Indigenous peoples and Africans. By the 1660s there was little land left for either emancipated servants or aspiring plantation owners in what had emerged as the first English Caribbean slave society.

5.2   The Rise of Slave Societies: The Chesapeake

||| Explain how the Virginia colony became a slave society over the course of the seventeenth century.

The first African enslaved people to reach North America may have come with Spanish expeditions to Florida and other spots up the Atlantic coast in the late sixteenth century, but, as we know, they came to Virginia in 1619 aboard a Dutch slaving ship. There they went to work in the tobacco fields, joining a labor force composed mainly of indentured servants, and could be found only in small numbers for several decades; cost and cultural affinity inclined tobacco planters to prefer white servants. That is, until later in the seventeenth century when a society that *included* enslaved Africans became a society *based on* their labor. How did that happen?

From White Servants to Black Slaves

As the population of white servants grew and their prospects for eventually finding land and economic independence began to dim, the Virginia colony was rocked by multiple forms of conflict and unrest. The servants blamed the planters and colonial officials for their plight and became more unruly. Some ran away, at times in the company of enslaved persons, and some resisted the labor demands that planters put upon them. A few staged small uprisings that were brutally suppressed. When former servants then headed west to find land of their own—land that had not already been bought up by wealthy Virginians, many of whom were friends of Governor Berkeley—they provoked warfare with aggrieved Indigenous people like the Susquehannocks. All they needed was a leader, and once Nathaniel Bacon showed up and happily played that role, the fuse was lit.

Bacon's Rebellion of 1676 shook the colony of Virginia to its core, as we saw in Chapter 4. But it also demonstrated the political dangers of a restless white, largely English, labor force. Indentured servants and those who survived their servitude—inspired in large part by the English Civil War—claimed the rights of Englishmen, and most were armed with guns and other weapons. It seemed that they could be pushed or squeezed only so far. Moreover, by the last third of the seventeenth century, economic conditions had improved in England, so fewer English poor folk looked to the colonies and servitude there as a means of livelihood. The flow of servants across the Atlantic began to slow, and the number of white servants in the Virginia tobacco fields began to decline (see Figure 5.1).

Who would take their place? The answer was enslaved people of African descent, though major adjustments occurred before the transition from servant to enslaved labor was completed. One development of importance was the direct involvement of the English in the African slave trade. During most of the seventeenth century, English planters who wanted enslaved people had to purchase them from the Spanish and the Dutch, who dominated the Atlantic and especially the waters off the coast of West Africa. Then, as the military and naval balances in the Atlantic shifted and the English Civil War ended, Charles II, the restored king, chartered the **Royal African Company** in 1663. With that, England entered

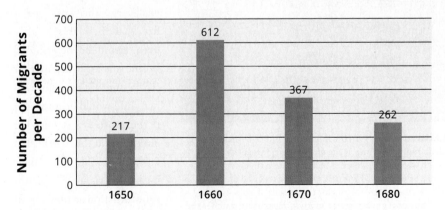

FIGURE 5.1   **Migration of Indentured Servants to Virginia, 1654–1686.**

the slave trade directly. Now more enslaved Africans would be available at lower cost. Whereas a mere 300 enslaved people could be found in the Chesapeake in 1650, more than 16,000 (just over 20 percent of the total population) could be found there by 1700.

But the challenges of building a plantation economy based on enslaved labor went well beyond the size of the labor force. Although enslaved Africans were regarded as enslaved for life, neither Virginia nor Maryland nor any other English colony had a code of laws to determine their legal status or treatment. How much power would the enslavers have? Did the enslaved have any rights or standing? How would enslaved people be punished if they disobeyed their enslavers' commands? If enslaved women had children, would the children be enslaved as well? And if a slave had a child with a person who was free, what would that mean for the status of the child?

Marking Enslavement and Race

Beginning in the 1640s and especially between 1660 and 1690, the Virginia colonial assembly answered these questions by passing a series of laws that, by 1705, would compose a colonial **slave code**. Those laws clarified a number of issues regarding African slaves and their descendants (Table 5.1). They specified that Africans would be enslaved for life and, legally, would be "chattel," tangible property—like chairs, horses, or other goods to be owned, bought, and sold at the whim of the enslavers. The laws specified that the status of children would be determined by the status of the mother (if the mother was enslaved her child would be enslaved; if the mother was free, her child would be free); that enslavers could punish their human "property" for insubordination as they saw fit and not be held responsible

≡ **A Colony Built on Enslaved Labor**   As the English architect Benjamin Henry Latrobe traveled around Virginia at the end of the eighteenth century, he filled his journals with watercolor sketches of local life. In this scene near Fredericksburg, Virginia, two enslaved women, with bare feet and uncovered heads, use hoes and fire to clear native forests for the benefit of a plantation owner. An overseer, in fine boots and a top hat, enjoys a cigar as he watches the women labor. Latrobe would go on to design the US Capitol building.

Table 5.1   Codifying Race and Slavery in Colonial Virginia
1640—Slave owners are required to arm everyone in their households except Africans (Virginia)
1643—All adult men and African women are taxable, on the assumption that they were working in the fields (Virginia)
1662—Children follow the condition of their mother (Virginia)
1662—Double fine charged for any Christian who commits fornication with an African (Virginia)
1664—All enslaved people serve for life; that is, slavery is defined as a lifelong condition (Maryland)
1664—Interracial marriage banned; any free woman who marries an enslaved man will serve that slave's owner until her husband dies, and their children will be enslaved (Maryland)
1667—Baptism as a Christian does not make a slave free (Virginia)
1669—No punishment is given if a punished slave dies (Virginia)
1670—Free Black people and Indigenous people are not allowed to purchase Christian indentured servants (Virginia)
1670—Indigenous people captured elsewhere and sold as slaves to Virginia are to serve for life; those captured in Virginia, until the age of thirty, if children, or for twelve years, if grown (Virginia)
1680—In order to prevent "Negroes Insurrections": no slave may carry arms or weapons; no slave may leave his or her owner without written permission; any slave who "lifts up his hand" against a Christian will receive thirty lashes; any slave who runs away and resists arrest may be killed lawfully (Virginia)
1682—Enslaved people may not gather for more than four hours at other than their owner's plantation (Virginia)
1682—All servants who were "Negroes, Moors, Mollattoes or Indians" were to be considered enslaved people at the time of their purchase if neither their parents nor country were Christian (Virginia)
1691—Owners are to be compensated if "negroes, mulattoes or other slaves" are killed while resisting arrest (Virginia)
1691—Forbidden is all miscegenation as "that abominable mixture"; any English or "other white man or woman" who marries a "negroe, mulatto, or Indian" is to be banished; any free English woman who bears a "bastard child by any negro or mulatto" will be fined, and if she can't pay the fine, she will be indentured for five years and the child will be indentured until the age of thirty (Virginia)
1691—All enslaved people who are freed by their owners must be transported out of the state (Virginia)
1692—Special courts of "oyer and terminer" are established for trying enslaved people accused of crimes, creating a separate system of justice (Virginia)
1705—Mulatto is defined as "the child of an Indian, the child, grandchild, or great grandchild of a negro" (Virginia)
1705—Africans, mulattoes, and Indigenous peoples are prohibited from holding office or giving grand jury testimony (Virginia)
1705—Enslaved people are forbidden to own livestock (Virginia)
1705—"Christian white" servants cannot be whipped naked (Virginia)
1723—Free Black people explicitly excluded from militia (Virginia)
1723—Free Black people explicitly denied the right to vote (Virginia)

if the enslaved died; that the enslaved could not become free by converting to Christianity, thus joining the enslaver's spiritual community; that they could not leave their plantations or farms without written passes; that they could not carry firearms or other weapons or meet together for any purposes, including funerals;

and that any white person married to a Black or person of mixed race would be banished from the colony and the minister who married them severely punished.

In short, by 1705 chattel slavery was established in Virginia. Not surprisingly, by the time the Virginia Slave Code was enacted, the colonial assembly was also reducing tax burdens on poor whites, easing their participation in the colony's politics, and guaranteeing land for former indentured servants who had gained their freedom. An early form of racial distinction was being established, and an early basis for an alliance between rich and poor white people was being created. The Chesapeake was becoming a society built around the enslavement of people of African descent and the crops and other goods that they would produce. Wealth, power, and influence—the social structure, the organization of social and economic life, the ideas of belonging—were directly related to the ownership of human beings regarded as personal property, as chattel. That is what it means to have a slave society.

5.3   The Rise of Slave Societies: Carolina

||| Enumerate the similarities and differences between the Chesapeake and Carolina paths to slavery.

As land ran out in the Caribbean for prospective English planters, they began to turn to the North American mainland, and particularly to the stretch of coast to the north of Florida and to the south of the Chesapeake, where settlement might be made and Spanish power contested. The advantage fell to the friends and allies of newly enthroned Charles II, who rewarded some of them in 1663 and 1665 with control of a colony to be known as "Carolina . . . in honour of His Sacred Majesty." Called Lords Proprietors, these beneficiaries hoped to set up an aristocratic society "most agreeable to the Monarchy" and as far as possible in character from "a numerous Democracy." Indeed, they proposed to divide the colony's land up into "baronies" to support their rule and to turn humbler white immigrants into hereditary servants, such as those who had lived on older English manors. Somewhat shockingly, the plan—"The Fundamental Constitutions of Carolina"—was drawn up in part by none other than John Locke, the English philosopher generally regarded as one of the progenitors of modern liberal thought.

The Carolina Road to a Slave Society

Substantial land grants lured some of the Barbadian planters, especially the sons of planters for whom prospects on the island were limited. Early on, however, most of

the migrants were small farmers, artisans, and indentured
servants who were effectively
being pushed out of Barbados.
Although Carolina could be
regarded as an extension of
the Caribbean—the "colony
of a colony," as one historian
put it—it was not entirely clear
how the colony would prosper.
Carolina summers were hot
and humid, but winters were
cooler than in the Caribbean
and not optimal for grow-
ing sugarcane, which has a
thirteen-month cycle from
planting to harvest. Tobacco,
the Chesapeake crop, did not
fare well either, and various experiments with cotton, olives,
and grapes proved no more
promising.

≣ **A Gift from a Grateful King**   Charles II gazes imperiously from the first
page of the 1663 Carolina Charter, granting the province of Carolina (named
for himself) to eight Lords Proprietors. The birds and flowers that decorate
the document, including the belted kingfisher shown here, are native to the
Carolinas. (In 1712 North and South Carolina became distinct colonies.)

For the most part, white
Carolina settlers raised an assortment of subsistence crops, herded livestock,
tapped trees for shipbuilding supplies (tar, pitch, turpentine, and rosin), and engaged in trade with Indigenous people, which included those who were enslaved,
as well as furs and deerskins. The slave trade in Indigenous people turned out to
be especially lucrative since the Native Westos (having migrated down from the
Great Lakes region) were at war with the local Cusabos at the time the Barbadians
arrived around 1670. Before then, Virginians were busily buying up the Native
captives to supplement the enslaved and servant labor force in their fields; now
most of the captives were bought by the Carolinians. Although it is difficult to get
precise numbers, over the next four decades anywhere between 30,000 and 50,000
Native men, women, and children (perhaps including Salem's Tituba) would be
purchased and transported to Barbados, New England, and the Middle Atlantic—
not to mention exploited in Carolina—to work on English plantations and farms
and in English households. The Native victims would come to include Westos
themselves (as the war with the Cusabos turned against them) as well as Shawnees
and Tuscaroras.

PERSPECTIVES

The African Origins of Rice Cultivation in Carolina

Africans captured and forcibly transported to the Americas brought complex social, political, and religious systems with them across the Atlantic. As the anthropologist Sidney Mintz has written, they "were not blank slates upon which European civilizations would write at will."[1] Nowhere is this truer than in the Carolina colony, where the success of its rice industry depended on the agricultural and technical knowledge of enslaved Africans, in particular women, who brought with them a long tradition of rice cultivation from West Africa.

In *Black Rice: The African Origins of Rice Cultivation in the Americas*, Judith Carney demonstrates that the enslaved Africans who carried the know-how of rice cultivation with them across the ocean did more than simply facilitate the movement of an important crop across the Atlantic. They also relocated a distinct culture from West Africa to North America.[2] Their descendants in the low country of South Carolina and Georgia continued to practice these rice-growing techniques into the twentieth century, as shown in these photographs.

≡ **Rice Cultivation** Men and women in the West African country of Sierra Leone demonstrate the husking of rice using a mortar and pestle, c. 1900 (*left*). Two women on Sapelo Island, in the low country of Georgia, husk rice using a mortar and pestle, c. 1910 (*right*).

176

≡ **Rice Cultivation**   Two women winnow rice with fanner baskets in the Sudan in 1963 (*left*). A woman in Santee, South Carolina, winnows rice with a fanner basket in 1923 (*right*).

CONSIDER THIS

Scholars like Judith Carney have documented that a greater percentage of enslaved females were transported to Carolina than to the Caribbean. What does this suggest about white planters' awareness of the crucial role of enslaved women in the creation of the Carolina economy? Can we make a case that Carolina's economy and culture would have been markedly different without the specialized knowledge systems of enslaved African women? How does the transfer of rice cultivation techniques from West Africa to Carolina low country put connections between West Africa and the Americas in a different light compared to one that focuses exclusively on the transatlantic slave trade?

[1] Sidney W. Mintz, introduction to the 1990 edition of *The Myth of the Negro Past* by Melville Herskovits.

[2] Judith A. Carney, *Black Rice: The African Origins of Rice Cultivation in the Americas* (Cambridge, MA: Harvard University Press, 2001).

The slavery taking shape in Carolina thus encompassed large numbers of captive Indigenous people as well as people of African descent, but a transition was emerging. At the outset, enslaved African and African-descended people brought to Carolina were put to work in a wide range of activities. Enslaved people could be found clearing fields, hunting and fishing, tending livestock, cutting timber, serving as intermediaries in the Indian trade, and taking part in exploring expeditions along the rivers, streams, and woods. After all, there was as yet no staple crop to plant and harvest. But those enslaved people from parts of West Africa where rice was grown began to cultivate the grain on the small provision grounds allotted them to supplement their diets. Before 1700, slaveholders began to glimpse the potential of large-scale rice cultivation, as rice had long been an important item of consumption around the Mediterranean. Enslaved labor was soon turned toward the construction of dikes and gates to flood and drain the fields with fresh water, successfully turning rice into a plantation crop.

As was true elsewhere, Carolina planters experimented with several different sources of labor to grow rice: indentured servants as well as enslaved Indigenous people. Yet by 1700, they were quite familiar with enslaved Africans, both on the sugar estates of Barbados and in the slave trade being organized by the Royal African Company. And it was to African and African-descended enslaved people that they turned. In 1690 the Carolina colony had about 1,500 enslaved Black people; twenty years later there were more than 4,000, and they made up a majority of the Carolina population.

Slaveholders would always defend the enslavement of Africans by depicting them as ignorant, backward, and heathen; as people in need of discipline, direction, and uplift; as people whose lack of skills made them appropriate candidates for forced labor in the fields. The tragic irony, however, is that enslaved Africans were of such great use to the Carolina planters precisely *because* they were very knowledgeable, especially about agriculture and cultivating crops like rice. In Carolina and elsewhere, it was often the European enslavers who learned key lessons from the enslaved Africans, not the other way around, and then prospered from what they learned while the enslaved were degraded.

There was yet another tragically ironic twist to the Carolina slavery story. Carolina and the Caribbean were potentially lethal disease environments for the new European arrivals of the seventeenth century. Malaria—called "fever and ague" by contemporaries—was especially widespread and debilitating, and it contributed to high mortality rates among Europeans. For this reason, the Caribbean quickly came to be known as a "white man's grave" for the many Europeans who sickened and died soon after they landed.

But Africans had special protections. In part, it was their prior exposure to some infectious diseases, such as smallpox, because of long-term contact with Europeans owing to trade and because they raised livestock, common transmitters of viruses and bacteria (neither of which was part of the Native experience in the Western Hemisphere). Even more significantly, they carried a genetic marker known as the sickle-cell trait, which offered immunity to malaria as well as yellow fever. The trait is to be found in different populations who inhabited malarial environments (like Sicily) over a very long term, and it enabled Africans to work in mosquito-infested rice fields when Europeans would have perished; the whites preferred to live in Charles Town, the main town (now Charleston, South Carolina), or in uplands away from the swampy rice districts. The sad news is that while the sickle-cell trait offered immunity from malaria, it could also—if both parents carried it—give rise to sickle-cell anemia in their children, a chronic and debilitating blood disease.

Carolina and the Chesapeake

Thus, just as a plantation economy and slave-based society was emerging in the Chesapeake in the late seventeenth and early eighteenth centuries, so, too, was one emerging in Carolina. By 1710 Carolina had a Black-majority population and an export economy organized around the production and sale of rice to European markets. As in the Chesapeake, this also meant an influx of the enslaved coming directly from West Africa, the intensification of their exploitation as planters looked to increase the size of the crop and reap the rewards, and the tightening of surveillance and other forms of control. That is, the development of the slave plantation, whether in Carolina or the Chesapeake, always involved the dramatic deterioration in the treatment and material conditions of enslaved Black laborers: it reduced their life expectancy (though few died of malaria, many died as a result of brutal treatment and of other ailments related to work in the rice swamps), exposed them to much longer and harder hours in the fields, subjected them to corporal and other forms of punishment, tied them closer to the plantations, and undermined their ability to form families.

The explosion would come in 1739, when a slave rebellion occurred near Carolina's Stono River. It would be called the Stono Rebellion. Before dawn on a September Sunday, a group of about twenty enslaved Africans attacked a country store, killed the two storekeepers, confiscated the store's guns and ammunition, and set out toward Spanish Florida, which guaranteed freedom from slavery. Enticing other rebels to join their march south, the group plundered and burned over a half dozen plantations and killed more than twenty white men, women, and children. A mounted force of white colonists attacked the rebels and killed most of them; Black survivors were sold into slavery in the West Indies. In response to the uprising, Carolina legislators passed the 1740 "Negro Act," a set of repressive laws designed to guarantee that whites would always have the upper hand. No other similar uprising occurred during the colonial period.

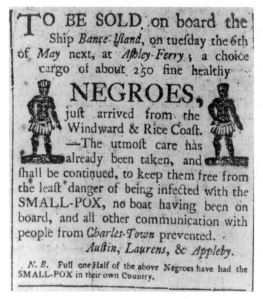

Building the Rice Economy on Enslaved Labor This 1760 advertisement for enslaved people from the "Rice Coast" of Africa, to be auctioned at Ashley Ferry near Charles Town (present-day Charleston, South Carolina), would have appealed to planters looking for expert rice cultivators who were also resistant to smallpox. Women were especially desirable as they often possessed detailed technical knowledge. Enslaved Africans, like the 250 advertised here, were essential to the creation of extraordinary wealth in the Carolina colonies—even as they would themselves live brutal lives of poverty and exploitation.

There were differences between Carolina and the Chesapeake as well as similarities. Africans and African-descended enslaved people never formed a majority in the Chesapeake, whether in Virginia or Maryland, and as greater numbers of enslaved people arrived, they were often dispersed on scattered units (known as "quarters") in the hinterlands. There they came to know one another, began to learn English, grew wheat and other food crops as well as tobacco, and, over time, saw the cultural distance between them and their enslavers narrow. The gender ratio among them would change, too, and by the middle of the eighteenth century they were forming families and raising children. The slave population of the Chesapeake, highly exploited though it was, could nonetheless grow by natural reproduction as well as by slave imports.

In Carolina, the early years of the eighteenth century saw a large influx of enslaved Africans who came to reside on plantations with large numbers of other enslaved people. Producing rice involved significant investments in equipment to regulate the flow of water in the rice fields, and this gave the advantage to wealthy planters who owned big tracts of land and many enslaved Black people. It also worsened the lives of the enslaved, who were driven mercilessly to build the rice plantations and bring in the valuable crop. Their mortality rates soared. To maintain enough labor for the arduous work, imports of enslaved men far exceeded those of enslaved women.

But the enslaved people also carved out a unique environment for themselves. Because they resided on large units and their owners preferred to live in nearby Charles Town for reasons of health, they could preserve many of their African ways, construct communities without as much white supervision (though plantation overseers were ever present), and tend more to their own affairs. Since healthy enslaved people were in the planters' best interest to grow as much rice as possible, enslaved people were allowed to cultivate their own small **provision grounds**, where they raised food crops to feed themselves. Eventually, the enslaved would bring these provision crops to local markets and earn small amounts of cash. As a result, the enslaved people of coastal Carolina helped to make a distinctive society on the North American continent, one more closely resembling the Caribbean to the south and east than the Chesapeake to the north. This unique culture, both the Gullah and Geechee, still survives today along the southeastern coast from Florida to North Carolina.

5.4   The Rise of Slave Societies: The Lower Mississippi Valley

Describe the different dynamics involving the French that went into the making of a slave society in the lower Mississippi Valley.

Although accounts of early American history tend to focus on the Atlantic coast and the southwest, and on the projects of the English, Spanish, and Dutch, the Gulf Coast—the southern region with a shoreline on the Gulf of Mexico—became a center of contest and conflict and the foundation of a substantial slave society. Like Carolina, the Gulf Coast and especially the Lower Mississippi River Valley were deeply connected to the Caribbean and Caribbean colonies—it was part of the broad Caribbean basin—but unlike Carolina, their colonizers were the Spanish and, even more so, the French. The development of a slave society in the lower Mississippi Valley, which would be a lengthy process, both shared a great deal with the Chesapeake, Carolina, and the Caribbean while marking out distinctive social and cultural patterns.

From New France to Louisiana

The French had established footholds on the North American continent during the sixteenth century, although their settlements in what they called New France remained thinly populated. Most of them could be found along the fertile St. Lawrence River Valley, and especially around Quebec (New France's capital) and Montreal; others were scattered across a large area around the Great Lakes, known to the French as the "upper country," and were devoted to a thriving fur and deer-skin trade with Indigenous people. Indeed, in New France, unlike in New England or the Chesapeake, the Indigenous peoples—Iroquois, Ottawa, Potawatomi, Sauk, and Fox among them—maintained a strong, if not dominant, position in the face of French traders and settlers, in part because French immigration was far more limited than was true for the English and the Spanish. During the seventeenth century, the French crown tried to encourage the further settlement of New France by distributing large land grants (known as *seigneuries*) to men of means as well as to army officers who, in turn, leased the lands out to French farming families called *habitants*. In effect, as in Carolina, a society with semifeudal trappings was imagined.

At the same time, some of the French were looking farther west and south. Robert de La Salle, who had arrived in New France in the late 1660s and explored some of the Great Lakes, learned that rivers like the Ohio connected with the great Mississippi. In 1682 he led an expedition of French and Native allies in hopes of finding (yet again) a route to Asia. Instead, the La Salle expedition made it down to the Gulf Coast and, to honor King Louis XIV of France, named the territory *La Louisiane* (Louisiana) and claimed it for the French (see Map 5.3).

For the next three decades, Louisiana was little more than a French outpost on the edge of the thriving Caribbean. Like the English, the French had begun to traverse the waters of the Caribbean largely to prey upon Spanish shipping, and in the process they established beachheads during the seventeenth century on islands they would call Martinique and Guadeloupe as well as on the western side of Spanish Hispaniola, which they named Saint Domingue. Before the century was out, these French islands would follow the path laid out in Barbados and Jamaica and turn their attention to producing large quantities of sugar with enslaved

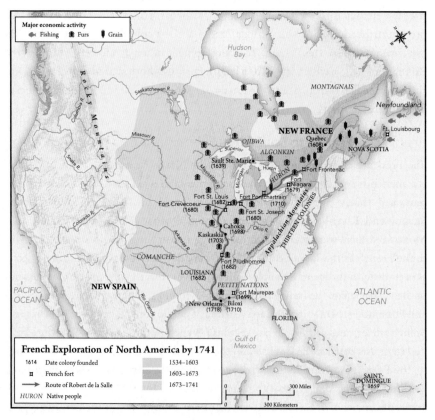

≡ **MAP 5.3**   **French Exploration of North America by 1741**

African labor. As for Louisiana, it seemed most valuable as a hedge against the expansion of the English and Spanish and their Native trading networks. So, for quite some time, Louisiana was populated mainly by French soldiers and an assortment of indentured servants, peasant farmers, and traders, not to mention some convicted criminals and political prisoners. Occupying fortified settlements at Mobile Bay and Biloxi Bay, they survived by trading for food, furs, and deerskins with small Indigenous bands in the vicinity—the French called them *Petite Nations*, though they called themselves Acolapissas, Bayagoulas, Biloxis, Chitimachas, Houmas, Opelousas, Pascagoulas, and Tohomes—while looking to form alliances with the more formidable Choctaws and Chickasaws of the interior.

Things began to change during the 1710s. The French crown chartered the Company of the Indies (something like the Virginia Company) to take charge of Louisiana, and in relatively short order the Company was bringing in Europeans as well as enslaved Africans with the idea of creating a plantation economy. To that end, they founded a new settlement site upriver named Nouvelle Orleans (New Orleans) and distributed lands along the nearby Mississippi to the Europeans, most of whom were French but some of whom were German. By the late 1720s, a majority of the inhabitants were enslaved African people—joined by a few hundred indentured servants and enslaved Indigenous people—and it appeared that Louisiana was headed down the road of Carolina and the Chesapeake.

A Distinctive Trajectory

Not quite. Aspiring planters had a tough time of it. The surrounding landscape was swampy, dense with vegetation, and teeming with mosquitos. The heavy rains and occasional hurricanes that swept through the Gulf added to the challenges, even with the benefit of enslaved labor. Cultivating sugar seemed well beyond the resources of the landholders, who not only had to have the fields cleared but also sugar mills constructed to grind the cane and ships ready

≡ **Alexandre de Batz, *Drawing of Indians of Several Nations* (1735)**
Alexandre de Batz was an architect, artist, and engineer charged with surveying the French territory of Louisiana. His sketches and watercolors of the Indigenous people of the lower Mississippi Valley are the earliest known recorded images of their extraordinary cultural diversity.

to sail up the river, pick up the sugar, and transport it across the Atlantic in a timely fashion. Experiments with tobacco and indigo were no more encouraging, and as planters attempted to expand their land claims into Native territories they provoked violent resistance. Thus, in 1729, the Natchez people to the north rose in revolt and, like the Wampanoags, Susquehannocks, and Pueblos elsewhere, killed large numbers of settlers, disrupted the slave system, and nearly destroyed the entire French colonial operation.

For the next few decades, Louisiana remained pretty much an appendage of the plantation economies of the Caribbean. Although enslaved people made up about half of the colonial population, they were involved as much with Native trading relations and with hunting, fishing, and herding (something like in early Carolina) as they were with growing crops. Louisiana gave the French a substantial footing on the Gulf Coast and, owing to alliances with various Indigenous people, served to obstruct English ambitions in the southeast and lower Mississippi Valley. But the foundations of a slave plantation society were in place if conditions and opportunities changed.

5.5   The Rise of Mission-Presidio Societies: The Southwest

‖‖ Define the purpose of mission-presidio societies and distinguish between those of New Mexico and California.

The Pueblo (Po'pay's) Revolt in New Mexico in 1680 (discussed in Chapter 4) exposed the enormous vulnerabilities that Spanish colonialism met in the northern reaches of New Spain. Hundreds of miles from both the political center of Mexico City as well as from the rich silver mines of Zacatecas, Guanajuato, and San Luis Potosí, Spanish settlement there was organized around thinly populated missions and towns (like Santa Fe) set in the midst of relatively dense communities of Indigenous people. In fact, it might have made sense after 1680 for the Spanish to retreat to safer and more defensible ground, were it not for the English and especially the French, who were pressing in on them from the southeastern and south central parts of North America, anchored by the new colony of Louisiana. The contest for dominance of the North American continent was of central importance to all of the imperial powers.

Presidios

To some extent, Spain attempted to encourage a process of settler colonialism by sponsoring the immigration of families from the Canary Islands, some of whom arrived in what the Spanish called Tejas (Texas) early in the eighteenth century. Overall, however, the interest of the Canary Islanders—or of Hispanicized Indigenous people—was limited and their impact paltry. As a result, the developing emphasis of Spanish officials was less on missions, which could and did stir Native resistance, as the 1680 revolt showed, and more on military bases known as **presidios**. Indeed, by 1750 it would have been hard to find a Spanish mission in northern New Spain that was not in very close proximity to a presidio; the presidio, not the mission, emerged as the dominant institution of Spanish colonial design.

The increasing importance of the presidio in Spanish North America reflected a shift in colonial policy. Earlier, the Spanish were mainly concerned with pacifying Native populations and converting them to Christianity, encouraging (or forcing) Indigenous people to settle near the **missions**, work for the missions' benefit, and accept Jesus Christ. Jesuit and Franciscan friars were therefore the main agents of colonialism, even though pacification and conversion were coercive and repressive projects in their own rights. The Indigenous people were often reduced to slavery and their own spiritual leaders brutally suppressed. But the friars' gains were not very impressive, and they fared poorly when Native discontent turned into outright rebellion, as was the case across northern New Spain (not only in New Mexico) toward the end of the seventeenth century.

Consequently, pacification took a back seat and military defense along with trade came to the fore. The whole area stretching from Louisiana in the east to New Mexico in the west proved to be a cauldron of Native warfare and raiding, all the more so as *Gran Apacheria* took shape in southern New Mexico, western Texas, Sonora, and New Biscay during the second half of the eighteenth century (see Map 5.4). Here, the Apache people, having moved south from the central Great Plains (pushed out, as we will see, by the Comanches), established an extended perimeter of control and set their sights on Spanish haciendas, ranches, and mines as well as on horses and other livestock the Spanish raised. Where the Spanish managed to form alliances with enemies of the Apaches, new avenues of trade in goods and enslaved Indigenous people sometimes opened. Otherwise, their fortified presidios offered the best means of maintaining a political footing.

Mission Societies on the Pacific

It was in California, and southern California in particular, where mission society experienced something of a rebirth. The Spanish had laid eyes on the Pacific coast of North America in the middle of the sixteenth century but were not impressed by its prospects for colonization. It seemed neither fertile enough for agriculture nor mountainous enough for the mining of gold and silver. Only when the Russians, English, and French took interest in the area during the eighteenth century—and

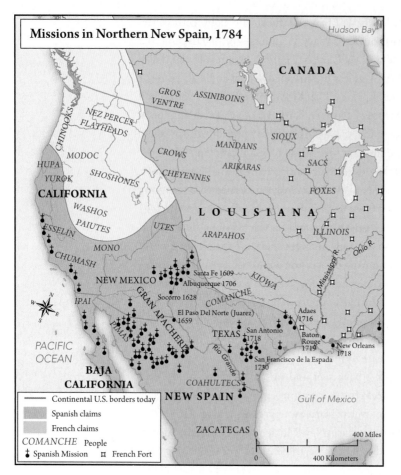

Missions in Northern New Spain, 1784

MAP 5.4   Missions in Northern New Spain, 1784.

potentially threatened to move toward the silver mines of Mexico from the northwest—did the Spanish decide to extend their reach into what was an even more distant territory.

However barren the Spanish may have thought the Pacific coast to be in the sixteenth century, it was in fact home to the densest population of human beings and the greatest cultural diversity to be found anywhere on the North American continent. By the early eighteenth century there may have been 300,000 or more Indigenous people who organized themselves into hundreds of bands and tribes. They called themselves Hupa, Yurok, Karok, Modoc, Shasta, Pomo, Esselin, Miwak, Konkowa, Paiute, Mono, and Ipai (among many others), lived in small communities, and spoke as many as ninety different languages. Rather than practice agriculture, they mostly thrived on the enormous supply of herbs and wildlife that California had to offer: they hunted elk, deer, rabbits, and antelope; caught salmon and marine mammals like seals and otters; and gathered berries, mushrooms, and other edible seeds and fruits.

For their part, the Spanish established a base in San Diego in 1769. Over the next decade and a half, they moved north along the coast, building missions, presidios, and agricultural settlements to sustain the small number of colonists and military officers who followed (see again Map 5.4). Indeed, utterly ignoring any Indigenous land claims, Spanish officials began distributing immense tracts of land called **ranchos** to the favored few. Most of the land grants and ranchos surrounded the missions and presidios of Los Angeles and Monterey, and they set the foundation for a rising group of landowners known as the ***Californios***, who would eventually compete with the missions for Indigenous labor.

But what of the missions themselves? The leader in establishing California missions was a Franciscan friar named Junipero Serra. Born on the Spanish island of Mallorca in the early eighteenth century, Serra came to Mexico in midcentury and was quickly involved in mission work around Mexico City and then in Baja California (a peninsula in northwestern Mexico). He helped plant the first mission in San Diego and then was active in extending the line of coastal missions north to San Francisco Bay until his death in 1784. Missions were established in San Juan Capistrano, Los Angeles, San Gabriel, Santa Barbara, San Luis Obispo, Monterey, and San Jose as well as San Francisco, and together they came to have nearly 5,000 Indigenous people within them.

As in seventeenth-century New Mexico, the Franciscans were interested in converting and "civilizing" the Indigenous people in their orbits. They lured Indigenous people with ceremonial displays of cultural and spiritual power together with trade goods, livestock, and new crops. And, for a time, some of the Indigenous people responded to what they imagined as a richer and possibly more secure life or to the power and authority that the friars appeared to hold.

But the missions also had very demanding regimens. The Indigenous people (called "neophytes" by the friars) were not only expected to embrace the Christian faith; they were also required to adopt Spanish ways of speech, dress, and family life and to work for the support of the missions. Native labor constructed mission buildings, cultivated the surrounding fields, tended the herds of livestock, and dug

≡ *The Destruction of Mission San Sabá in the Province of Texas and the Martyrdom of the Fathers Alonso de Terreros, Joseph Santiesteban*
The Mission of Santa Cruz de San Sabá, along with a nearby presidio, was established in 1757 in central Texas to convert members of the Lipan Apache tribe. The mission was completely destroyed just a year later by Comanche tribes and their allies, and although the presidio was never attacked by Indigenous people, Spanish soldiers abandoned it in 1770. This painting, by Mexican artist José de Páez, was commissioned in Mexico City a few years after the attack by a cousin of one of the martyred priests. The presidio is in the upper left corner of the painting; the mission, surrounded by a wooden stockade, features a church at its center. Ruins of the Mission San Sabá were rediscovered by archaeologists from Texas Tech University in 1993.

≡ **Missions and the Intersection of Cultures**   The Russian explorer Ludwig Choris sketched this image of Indigenous people dancing at the San Francisco de Assis Mission in California around 1816. Parts of the mission are still standing in San Francisco today.

the ditches used for irrigation. Indeed, the friars regarded long hours of physical labor, often backbreaking in nature, as essential to the civilizing process. For all intents and purposes, mission Indigenous people were held captive. They were not permitted to leave the mission community and were subject to harsh corporal punishments for running away or other forms of disobedience. The friars saw themselves ruling in the name of God, but they often did so with iron fists.

California Fault Lines

The California mission-presidio complexes of the eighteenth century did serve to secure Spanish imperial claims to the Pacific coast from San Francisco Bay south. The Spanish would not face attack from the Russians or English or French there, even as a result of the imperial warfare that roiled much of the globe during the last half of the century. Nor would they face serious resistance from Indigenous people, who were politically divided into very small units and never formidable militarily.

But the Spanish conquest of coastal California was disastrous for the Indigenous people who came within their orbit of exploitation and microbes. "They live well free," one of the friars wrote of the mission neophytes, "but as soon as we reduce them to a Christian and community life . . . they fatten, sicken, and die." Although the population of mission Indigenous people continued to increase during the eighteenth century, reaching 13,500 by 1800, the coastal Native population fell by half (from about 60,000 to 35,000) and the overall Native population of California dropped by one-third (from about 300,000 to about 200,000) during the same period.

As for the Spanish settlers, *Californios*, merchants, and military personnel among them, the California colony—distant from the political authority of Mexico City and from the trading networks of northern New Spain—proved to be a very isolating experience. Trouble was brewing, and before too very long, rebellion would come, not from the decimated Indigenous people but from the *Californios* and their allies.

5.6 The Rise of Farming Societies: New England and the Middle Atlantic

||| Identify differences between farming societies in the Northeast and Middle Atlantic and the developing plantation systems of the South.

In many respects, the most unusual societies emerging on the North American continent in the seventeenth and eighteenth centuries were in the Northeast. These societies, of course, had growing towns along the coast—Boston, Newport, New York, and Philadelphia—whose economies were oriented to the Atlantic. They were the seaports to which sailing and slaving vessels came with goods from England or the West Indies and from which they departed to both of those destinations. An emerging **triangular trade system**, linking English North America, England, and the English Caribbean provided the energy and direction (see Map 5.5). Many of the inhabitants of these port towns were therefore involved in the maritime trade or in the related fisheries that extended well out into the ocean and hauled in huge quantities of cod and other catches; other town dwellers were craftsman—carpenters, coopers, shoemakers—who plied their skills for a seaborne economy. Over the course of the eighteenth century, perhaps half of these town dwellers, especially the well-to-do merchants and political officials, would own slaves.

But most of the Europeans who lived in New England and the Middle Atlantic did not reside in these bustling towns. They resided, instead, in the countryside and participated in a farming economy that was as different from colonies to the south and west as it was to rural England and continental Europe—and different, too, from the towns nearby. Unlike England and the continent, the farming households of the Northeast mostly claimed ownership of the land they tilled, and unlike the southern and western colonies, they mostly depended on the labor of household members rather than enslaved people or captives. And unlike the seaport towns, the northeastern countryside had relatively little to do with the Atlantic trade and gave rise to societies that had a very distinctive character.

Rural Household Economies

How so? The rural villages of New England and the Middle Atlantic were covered by farms that were generally small in scale and given over to the cultivation of grain and orchard crops that were consumed either by the households cultivating them or by other farming households nearby. The division of farm labor saw adult and teenage males do the heavy fieldwork as well as the hunting and fishing, and

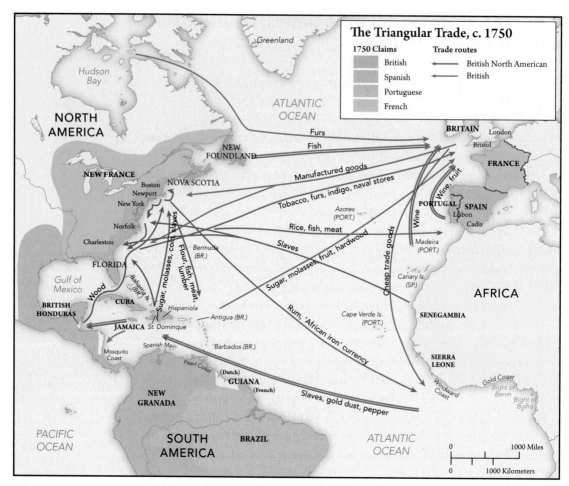

≡ **MAP 5.5 The Triangular Trade, c. 1750**   A triangular-trade system linked Britain, West Africa, the Caribbean, and British North America into a shared Atlantic world.

saw adult and teenage females prepare food, tend vegetable gardens and livestock, and manufacture textiles and clothing with spinning wheels and looms. Planting and harvesting, which required intensive labor, brought everyone into the fields; neighboring households often worked cooperatively in order to get the harvest in before it spoiled. Surplus grains, fruit, or dairy products were either sold locally or brought into a bigger town close enough to be reached by wagons. Some of these surpluses might eventually find their way to the West Indies, where New England timbers and other forest products were particularly valued. But, for the most part, these rural villages faced inward, their perspective landward, rather than toward the sea (see Figure 5.2).

This was a far from an idyllic world. The land that farming households cultivated had been seized from Indigenous people, whose numbers were rapidly declining and whose political power had been dramatically weakened by the end of the seventeenth century. What's more, the rural household economies of the Northeast and Middle Atlantic had their own social hierarchies. At the very top of this patriarchal system were husbands and fathers who legally owned the land and wielded power—enforced by custom and law—over their wives and children. This meant that wives and children were expected to obey the commands of the male household heads, which could mean long hours of labor and possibly rough treatment. Wives were economically dependent and had very little chance to seek a divorce if they were abused. For their part, male children needed their father's support to inherit or purchase land.

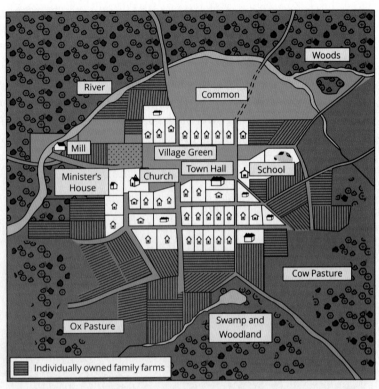

≡ **FIGURE 5.2 A Typical New England Rural Town** Many small rural towns in New England and the Middle Atlantic had a church and a common green at their center, and were surrounded by small farms, orchards, and grazing lands.

Social Stratification in the Northeast

The social hierarchies of the Northeast moved outward from the household as well. Land ownership, which derived from earlier settlement, was never equitably distributed. Prominent families who were connected to charter companies and the church received larger shares to start with, and those shares usually grew over time. The wealthiest farm owners could come to own many hundreds of acres, spread out over fields and woodlands, and they were most likely to raise surpluses for sale. While most farm households could only raise as much as the work of family members could produce, bigger farmers had the resources to get access to more labor.

MAPPING AMERICA

Center and Periphery

In the middle of the eighteenth century, Great Britain and its capital, London, was the undisputed center of the British Atlantic World. But not all of the places on the margins of the British Atlantic were equally peripheral. The economic network that connected the periphery to the center was "lumpy," as the historian Frederick Cooper memorably describes it, with some places on the margin exerting

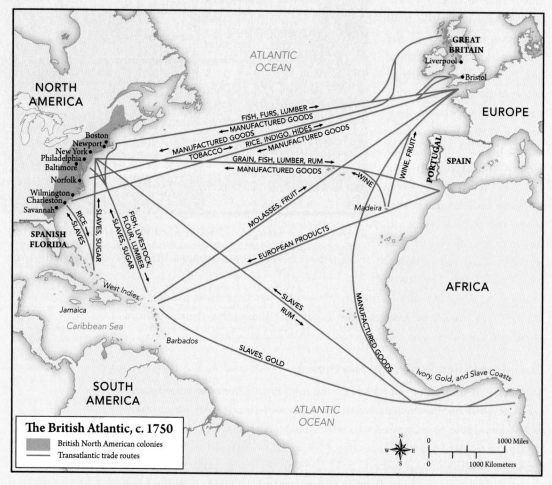

≡ **MAP 1 Center and Periphery: A Balanced View** The trade network of the British Atlantic in the first half of the eighteenth century is often shown as a triangle. In this view, the geographic zones in the transatlantic economy appear equally productive and important.

more influence than other places. Barbados, for example, is almost a thousand miles farther away from London than Boston, but it was far more central to the British transatlantic economy than was Boston.

Thinking Geographically

1. Consider this chapter's descriptions of the movement of people back and forth across the Atlantic at this time period. What stories does the "balanced" view of center and periphery overlook or ignore? What stories does the "lumpy" view reveal?

2. Given the economic importance of the West Indies to England between 1700 and 1750, what would you predict England's military and political priorities to have been at that time?

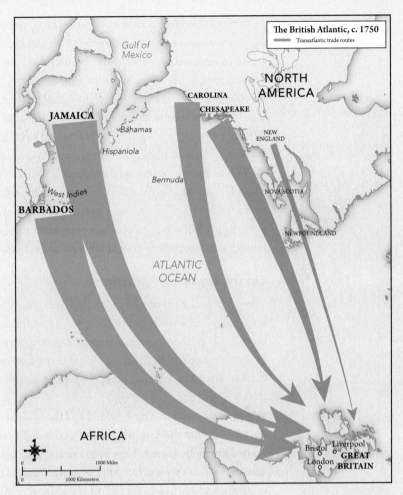

☰ **MAP 2 Center and Periphery: A "Lumpy" View**   Viewed from the perspective of the English crown and Parliament, however, the most important zones were the sugar, rice, and tobacco colonies of the West Indies, and only secondarily the Chesapeake and Carolina. The colonies of New England and the Middle Atlantic were outliers—their economies produced little that the English needed, and they bought relatively little that the English wished to sell.

Some of that labor was in a condition of servitude. Although the New England agricultural economy never depended on slave labor, enslaved Black people and white indentured servants could be found in the countryside as they could in seaport towns. The Winthrops of Massachusetts, among the most powerful of seventeenth- and eighteenth-century English families, not only had landholdings in Massachusetts and the West Indies but also owned and traded in enslaved Africans. Slavery was legal in all of England's colonies—to the north as well as to the south—and its importance continued to grow as the eighteenth century wore on. White European servants also kept arriving in New England and the Middle Atlantic, and as was true in the seventeenth-century Chesapeake, they worked in the fields as well as around the farmhouses. If anything, over time there was a growing pool of white colonists, young adult males, who lacked the resources to buy land and worked instead as laborers and tenants on farms large and small.

On the Imperial Periphery

Viewed from the perspective of the English crown and Parliament, the colonies of interest in the Western Hemisphere were first and foremost in the West Indies and secondarily in the Chesapeake and Carolina. Here the valuable plantation properties were to be found and the valuable staple crops were grown and brought to market. Here the shipping lanes were most heavily trafficked and the port towns alive with activity.

It was otherwise in New England and the Middle Atlantic. Their economies produced little that the English needed and bought relatively little that the English wished to sell. In a sense, New England and the Middle Atlantic were oddities in a colonial world in which the imperial powers looked to enrich themselves and ward off rivals, and so they could fall off the radar screens of English officials who were more concerned about the sugar, rice, and tobacco colonies and their enslaved-labor economies. But New England and the Middle Atlantic had growing populations with ambitions of their own: ambitions that would be capable of turning the imperial system into disarray.

5.7   The Rise of Equestrian-Based Indigenous Societies: Peoples of the Great Plains

┃┃┃ Explain the complex societies and polities that the Indigenous peoples of the Plains constructed.

Among the most formidable players in eighteenth-century North America were the Indigenous societies of the continent's interior, particularly of the Great Plains:

a region stretching north from the Rio Grande, east from the Rocky Mountains, and west from the Mississippi. There equestrian-based societies constructed long-distance trading and raiding networks, complex military alliances, and captive economies that dominated lesser Indigenous people and often forced Europeans to do their bidding. Together they would give decisive shape to the continent's political future.

Migrations and Contacts

This was, however, a relatively recent development. Until the ninth century CE, the Great Plains were peopled by small and culturally diverse Indigenous bands who were mainly hunter-gatherers and therefore nomadic in character. More than anything else, they followed the vast herds of bison that literally blackened the plains with their numbers (many millions of them) and served to sustain their diets and ways of life. A warming trend thereafter made agriculture possible in many areas that had previously been too dry, and spinoffs from the Mississippian cultures (discussed in Chapter 1) moved west along the many river valleys that fed into the Mississippi. They were river valleys we would later call the Red, the Arkansas, the Canadian, the Platte, and the Missouri. The climate changes of the thirteenth and fourteenth centuries (part of the Little Ice Age) helped reconfigure possibilities once again, leading to the dramatic decline of the Mississippian cultures and limiting the agricultural prospects of the Great Plains.

The Indigenous societies of the eighteenth century took shape as a result of population movements and increasing contact with Europeans (see Map 5.6). During the fifteenth century, new groups of Indigenous people moved onto the Great Plains from the mountains to the west and began to engage in struggles with the Sioux peoples (also known as Lakotas or Dakotas) to the north. Some—including those who would be known as Apaches and Comanches—moved farther south. They formed alliances or engaged in warfare

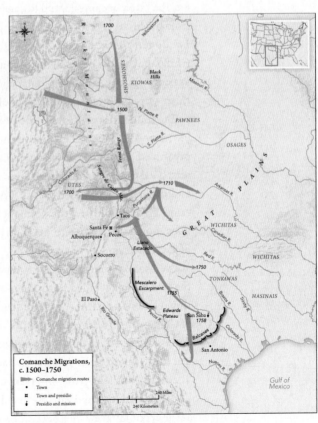

≡ **MAP 5.6 Comanche Migrations, c. 1500–1750** A need to expand their economy drove the Comanche east to the Great Plains; by 1750 they had pushed south into the Texas plains.

with Great Basin people like the Utes, and they attempted to pierce the trading networks developing around Santa Fe that involved Indigenous captives and Spanish goods and brought about contact with Navajos and Pueblos.

Although the balances of economic and military power on the Plains were ever shifting, over the course of the eighteenth century the Comanche people became dominant. The key to their rise was the horse. Not an animal native to the Plains, horses arrived by way of the Spanish who brought them across the Atlantic as part of their projects of conquest and colonialism. They then rode them north as New Spain extended into New Mexico and Texas. Before long, Comanches as well as Apaches and other Plains peoples began raiding both Spanish settlements and Native villages to acquire horses or trade for horses with the goods and captives they had taken in other raids.

La Comancheria

Now everything began to change. The Comanches became enormously skilled riders, the bison became central to their lifeways, and the horse enabled them to control a much larger territory for hunting and raiding. Eventually what would be called *La Comancheria* stretched from southeastern New Mexico and northeastern Chihuahua across Texas to the Arkansas River Valley. It was a territory bigger than Western Europe, and the Comanche, like the Europeans and the Aztecs before them, were building the equivalent of an empire.

The foundation of Comanche power—and the power of all Indigenous people who would seek to challenge them—was an economic and political system organized around the hunting of bison. The system would include trading centers, a vast raiding zone (mainly to the south), growing contacts with Spanish and other European merchants, and a complex of inter-Native alliances. The raiding zones allowed the Comanches to accumulate horses and human captives, both of which were necessary to hunting, trading, and the achievement of social status.

Even so, La Comancheria was very much of a decentered society. Its basic unit, the *rancheria*, included up to 250 people, most of whom were tied together by kinship relations, and it encompassed most of the important activities and hierarchies of Comanche life. As was true in many other Native societies of the Plains, gender and age served the Comanches as markers for the organization of economic, political, and social affairs. Adult men had the responsibility for hunting and raiding. Teenage boys took up the hard tasks of herding and breaking the horses. Women of all ages raised the children, processed the bison meat, and cooked the food, though as the economy grew they became more involved with horse herds and bison hides.

≡ *Comanche Feats of Horsemanship*   Pennsylvania-born painter George Catlin accompanied a US military expedition to Indian Territory in the 1830s, where he witnessed and recorded the skill of Comanche riders: "Amongst their feats of riding [is] a stratagem of war, learned and practiced by every young man in the tribe, by which he is able to drop his body upon the side of his horse [and] hang whilst his horse is at fullest speed, carrying with him his bow and his shield, and also his long lance . . . all or either of which he will wield upon his enemy as he passes."

In fact, the growing scale of economic activity increased the demand for labor and thereby made polygyny (the form of polygamy in which one man takes multiple wives) and enslavement (mainly of captive women and children) increasingly important to Comanche communities.

Comanches and other Indigenous people of the Great Plains and Great Basin had enslaved one another for a very long time. As in West Africa, enslavement was the result of raiding and warfare, and while some adult men were taken into captivity, most of the captives were Spanish or Native women and children; most of the men, regarded as unsuitable for enslavement, were killed instead. Some of the captives were then brought to slave markets and traded, but at least among the Comanche, most of them were kept to work in the booming horse and bison economy.

Like enslaved captives elsewhere in the world, these were immediately stripped of their familial and tribal associations and provided with new names—in a sense, this was a ritual of "social death" and "rebirth." And although they never had the same social status as those "born of Comanche," they could be assimilated into Comanche families as wives, sons, and daughters and could play key roles as cultural intermediaries, as go-betweens. Some of the males could even become mounted warriors and raiders. It was highly exploitive and traumatic but still very different from the chattel slavery that befell African captives in the Americas.

Relations of Comanche Life

The logic of this economic and political system grew out of the demands of equestrian-based bison hunting, ideas about land and wealth, and the pursuit of social prestige and manhood. They grew out of Comanche perspectives on the basic elements of their lives: perspectives often very different from those of Europeans. Comanches sought territorial expansion neither to define clear borders or titles to land nor to assert cultural superiority (as was true for the Europeans) but to gain access to the land's resources and to sources of wealth in the form of horses and captives. Horses were needed for hunting, and to be adequately nourished, the horses required extensive pasture lands. Along with captives, horses were also a recognized form of private property and personal wealth in Comanche society; there was no such thing as private property in land among the Comanches, however. Raiding was a central means for the acquisition of horses and captives, but it was, as well, the main way for males to achieve social acceptance and improve their social standing. Rancherias had to find new pastures for their horses, and trading networks enabled Comanches to exchange surplus livestock and the booty from raids for other needed goods. These exchanges and networks linked Comanches to other Indigenous people far to the north, west, and east, and opened them to economic relations with Europeans in towns like Santa Fe.

Yet, although rancherias were the basic units of Comanche society, they formed part of a larger confederation. Each rancheria was aligned with one of four larger Comanche divisions, which gathered annually to strengthen the bonds among them and hold political councils to settle conflicts and set goals as to warfare and diplomacy. Together, at these big encampments, decentered rancherias could turn into a powerful army capable of inflicting massive damages on those seen as enemies.

As a result of these developments, the Comanches emerged by 1775 as the dominant power on the Plains. Their numbers may have exceeded 40,000 (more than the Spanish and mestizo populations of Texas and New Mexico combined). They had pushed the Apaches south to what would be known as *Gran Apacheria*, opened trading relations with Pawnees, Kiowas, and Cheyennes to the north, reduced Indigenous bands to the east into tributary clients, and turned the northern reaches of New Spain into raiding domains. Small wonder that in 1786, the Spanish entered into a lengthy peace with the Comanches by signing the Ute-Comanche Treaty—a peace that would involve the Navajos and Utes, establish an integrated trading zone over a very large area, and secure their power when other Europeans pushed in from the east with visions of conquest and trade. In effect, the Spanish joined other Indigenous people in acknowledging the great power of the Comanches.

Conclusion: Toward Global Warfare

Between the last three-quarters of the seventeenth century and the fourth quarter of the eighteenth, a collection of new societies began to emerge on the North American continent and around the Caribbean basin. They stretched from the waters of the Caribbean up along the Atlantic coast and immediate hinterlands, around the Great Lakes and down the Mississippi Valley, across the Southwest and along the Pacific coast, and in the midsection of the continent. All were distinctive in their forms of social and economic organization (even if in many cases they were slaveholding), their political makeup, and in the ways that power was wielded from households and villages to colonial and imperial institutions.

As a result, this lengthy period saw intensifying rivalries and almost continuous warfare between European powers which had sponsored North American settlements, Indigenous people and settler societies wherever they grew, enslaved people and their enslavers, and Native confederations that were struggling with one another over resources and captives. By the second half of the eighteenth century, these conflicts set the stage not just for explosions on the North American continent, from Canada to the Gulf Coast and northern Mexico, but on a scale that could reasonably described as the first fully global war.

WHAT IF   We Looked Out from Comancheria?

The rise of Comanche power at the center of the North American continent poses interesting questions of perspective. For the most part, historians of North America and the United States move their stories from the coasts of the Atlantic, Gulf, and Pacific inward so it appears that the most important developments occurred along the Atlantic, Caribbean, or Pacific basins. Native Americans thereby seem in almost inevitable retreat in the face of European military might and the diseases the Europeans brought with them.

But what if our focus shifted from the coasts into the interior? What if we looked out from the Great Plains and from the forms of economic and political power that Comanches and other Indigenous people were constructing and that made European interlopers more the Comanches' equals or clients than their superiors? Among other things, we would see Indigenous people late into the eighteenth century and well into the nineteenth as formidable participants in the international struggle for dominance on the North American continent. We would see how Indigenous political economies differed from but also gave important shape to the commercial networks of the Spanish, French, and English, and how markets emerged from the encounters of a wide variety of economic actors and showed the marks of all of them. We would also recognize that the process of "conquest" of Native Americans was long and drawn out rather than swift and inevitable, that European alliances with Indigenous people resembled European alliances with other Europeans, that Indigenous people were political players every bit as significant as those who came to North America from Europe. If we shifted our perspective, that is, our interpretation of the history of North America would also shift and require that we take much more significant notice of the societies that Indigenous people were long building.

DOCUMENT 5.1:   The Comanche-Spanish Treaty of 1786

In 1786, the Comanche Captain, Ecuercapa, reached an agreement with Colonel Don Juan Bautista de Anza, governor of the Province of New Mexico. The treaty affirmed agreement on four points presented by Ecuercapa: (1) a new and lasting peace; (2) permission for the Comanches to move closer to New Mexico; (3) access to free trade; and (4) an alliance and renewed war against the Apache. The treaty marks a turning point in the history of the Southern Plains. Instead of warfare, Spain's relations with the Comanche would now be guided by diplomacy and commercial relations. The excerpt below lists the articles proposed by Ecuercapa.

Articles of Peace Agreed Upon and Arranged in the Villa of Santa Fe and the Pueblo of Pecos Between Colonel Don Juan Bautista de Anza, Governor of the Province of New Mexico, and the Comanche Captain, Ecuercapa, Commisioner-General of This Nation on the Days, 25th and 28th of February of 1786

Articles proposed by Ecueracapa:

1. That in the name of all his nation, he was soliciting a new and better established peace with the Spaniards, understanding that it would not be infringed on their part by ay word nor at any time, particularly with the advice of the captains and principal men.
2. That the nation is admitted under the protection of the king, and allowed to establish itself not far from distant settlements.
3. That for the best cultivation of friendship of both parties free and safe passage to the Commissioner-General himself through Pecos to the capital to repeat his trips, always provided that it is convenient; and to the community of the nation, the establishment of fairs and free trade with the cited pueblo.
4. That desirous of returning the favors he has received and hoping to enjoy the favors of the Spaniards, he binds himself to declare more offensively than ever against the common Apache enemies, offering at the same time to join expeditions of troops provided they take a direction and range which they [the Comanches] can follow.
5. That the reply to the points referred to be reserved to be placed before the other captains and ones authorized who were following and would arrive at Pecos; that he be given a token or credential so that with those as additional witnesses he could give evidence to the scattered *rancherías* that the entire nation was at peace so that none of the captains with the pretext of ignorance could avoid fulfilling what was obligated to them.

Source: Alfred Barnaby Thomas, *Forgotten Frontiers: A Study of the Spanish Indian Policy of Don Juan Bautista de Anza. Governor of New Mexico, 1777–1787* (Norman: University of Oklahoma Press, 1932), 328–329.

DOCUMENT 5.2:   Raiding and Trade Networks of *La Comancheria*

During the eighteenth century, the Comanche moved into the lower plains and began to construct networks of raiding and trading. This map depicts this world of commerce and warfare, a very different perspective on the development of the continent.

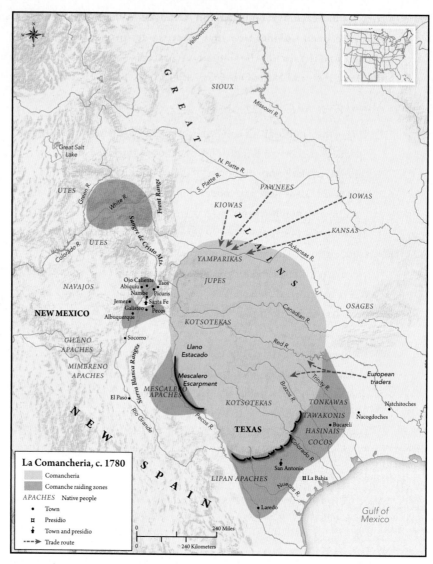

≡ **La Comancheria, c. 1780**

Thinking About Contingency

1. What would it mean to have a "Native-centric" rather than "Euro-centric" perspective on the development of the North American continent?

2. How could Comanches and other Indigenous peoples of the interior be seen as imperial rivals of the Europeans who were set upon colonization and conquest?

3. What would an eighteenth-century map of North America look like if the political and economic power of Comanches and other Indigenous peoples was accurately represented?

REVIEW QUESTIONS

1. How did slavery develop in the West Indies, and what crop was central to slavery's emergence as the basis of a plantation system?

2. What is the meaning of a "slave society," and how did the Chesapeake make the transition from a society with enslaved people and indentured servants during the seventeenth century to a slave society by the early eighteenth?

3. How did the development of slavery in Carolina compare with its development in the Chesapeake and the West Indies, and what crop came to be of central importance in Carolina?

4. Who were the main actors in the developing colonial societies of the lower Mississippi Valley, and

how did the slave system there in the eighteenth century compare to the slave system in the Chesapeake, Carolina, and the West Indies?

5. The Pueblo (Po'pay's) Revolt of 1680 established a new playing field in the North American southwest for the Spanish and Indigenous peoples. How did it differ from what had been in place before?

6. What were the key differences between New England farming societies and Southern slave societies? Were there similarities as well?

7. The Comanches developed a far-flung society in the North American interior. How would you characterize its political and economic features, and were any similar to what the Europeans had developed?

KEY TERMS

Californios (p. 187)

Gold Coast (p. 167)

Gran Apacheria (p. 185)

La Comancheria (p. 196)

Middle Passage (p. 167)

missions (p. 185)

presidios (p. 185)

provision grounds (p. 180)

rancheria (p. 196)

ranchos (p. 186)

Royal African Company (p. 171)

Slave Code (p. 172)

triangular trade system (p. 189)

RECOMMENDED READINGS

Ira Berlin, *Many Thousands Gone: The First Two Centuries of Slavery in North America* (Harvard University Press, 1998).

Kathleen Brown, *Good Wives, Nasty Wenches, and Anxious Patriarchs: Gender, Race, and Power in Colonial Virginia* (University of North Carolina Press, 1996).

Richard Dunn, *Sugar and Slaves: The Rise of the Planter Class in the English West Indies, 1624–1713* (University of North Carolina Press, 1972).

Pekka Hamalainen, *The Comanche Empire* (Yale University Press, 2009).

Philip Morgan, *Slave Counterpoint: Black Culture in the Eighteenth Century Chesapeake and Lowcountry* (University of North Carolina Press, 1998).

Lawrence Powell, *The Accidental City: Improvising New Orleans* (Harvard University Press, 2013).

John Thornton, *Africa and Africans in the Making of the Atlantic World, 1400–1800* (Cambridge University Press, 1998).

Daniel Usner, *Indians, Settlers and Slaves in a Frontier Exchange Economy: The Lower Mississippi Valley Before 1783* (University of North Carolina Press, 1992).

David Weber, *The Spanish Frontier in North America* (Yale University Press, 1992).

Peter Wood, *Black Majority: Negroes in Colonial South Carolina from 1670 Through the Stono Rebellion* (W.W. Norton, 1975).

Global War and American Independence

1730–1776

Chapter Outline

≡ **George Washington as Colonel in the Virginia Regiment**   This 1772 painting by Charles Wilson Peale is the earliest known portrait of the future president. Washington was by the time of this painting an established planter but chose here to wear the uniform of the Virginia Regiment, which he had commanded earlier during the Seven Years' War.

In the late fall of 1762, the British Parliament was wracked by controversy over a peace treaty that had been preliminarily signed in Paris, apparently ending a war that had erupted in North America in 1754 and then spread around the world. Along the way, the rival European empires of Britain, France, and Spain had clashed from the Pacific to the Caribbean to the shores of West Africa, as well as in North America, and something of a chess game followed, shifting colonies and colonial outposts around like rooks and pawns. Some British leaders like William Pitt believed that too much had been given up in Paris; he was taken from his sickbed to make that case before members of Parliament as they prepared to vote on the treaty's ratification. But, in truth, the treaty signaled Britain's triumph most everywhere, especially in North America, where the French had been forced to surrender their claims in Canada and in the lower Mississippi Valley, including the hub of New Orleans.

Timeline

1730	1733	1736	1739	1742	1745	1748	1751	1754

1730s › Jonathan Edwards leads a religious revival in New England known as the First Great Awakening

1740s › George Whitefield preaches revival of religion throughout the colonies

1747 › Ohio Company of Virginia formed

1754 › Hostilities between British and French troops erupt near Fort Duquesne; Albany Plan of Union between Iroquois and British colonists

British military success in North America owed in no small measure to Jeffery Amherst, the appointed Governor-General there, who (with Royal Navy Admiral Edward Boscawen) had captured the French fortress of Louisbourg on the St. Lawrence River in 1758, effectively ending the fortunes of New France (present-day Canada). Yet he and other British officials on the scene were already complaining about the dispositions and activities of their own North American colonists. Not only were they engaged in smuggling with the French; they were also reluctant to serve in expeditionary forces to be sent elsewhere, especially once "the immediate danger is removed from their own Doors." The British victory in what might be regarded as the first "world war," that is, simultaneously revealed political problems that an expanded empire brought with it.

1757	1760	1763	1766	1769	1772	1775	1778	1781

1756 > War is formally declared between Britain and France

1763 > Treaty of Paris ends Seven Years' War; George III issues the Royal Proclamation of 1763, which limits western settlement; Pontiac's War in the trans-Appalachian West

1765 > British Parliament passes the Stamp Act

1767 > Parliament passes the Townshend Acts

1770 > Boston Massacre; Townshend Acts repealed

1772–1773 > Committees of correspondence formed

1773 > Parliament passes the Tea Act; Boston Tea Party; first African Baptist Church founded in Savannah, Georgia

1774 > Parliament enacts the Coercive Acts and the Quebec Act; meeting of the First Continental Congress

1775 > Fighting breaks out between British troops and colonial militias at Lexington and Concord, Massachusetts; meeting of the Second Continental Congress

1776> Thomas Paine publishes *Common Sense;* Declaration of Independence is drafted and signed

What we have come to call the Seven Years' War (1756–1763) marked a significant historical turning point. Until then, warfare had generally been small in scale and geographically limited even if lengthy in duration—think of the Hundred Years' War of the fourteenth and fifteenth centuries—without having much of an impact on other parts of the world. By contrast, the Seven Years' War broke out between the major powers on the European continent and, before it was over, had spread to four other continents (all of them except for Australia and Antarctica). Not only was control over the European landmass at stake, but control over colonies in the Western Hemisphere, West Africa, and South Asia was at issue as well. Participants in the political jockeying and fighting included Indigenous people east of the Mississippi River and enslaved Africans in the Caribbean, along with European colonists and a variety of European armies and navies. Once the smoke began to clear and a new global map was taking shape, the rumblings of a rebellion in British North America—one that would have been inconceivable without the global warfare—could, as Jeffery Amherst warned, be detected.

6.1 Small Beginnings of a Global War

||| Outline the small-scale origins of a large, eventually global war.

Global warfare in the eighteenth century began, not on the European continent or on the waters of the Atlantic or along the increasingly populated east coast of North America, but rather well to the west, over the Appalachian Mountains, in the Ohio River Valley. There, in the late spring of 1754 an expedition of Virginia militiamen led by a young George Washington and aided by a small number of Native allies, encountered French soldiers in a small encampment not far from the French Fort Duquesne (near present-day Pittsburgh). They had been ordered there by Virginia's colonial governor, Robert Dinwiddie, a major shareholder in the **Ohio Company**, a land speculation outfit founded in 1748 by relatives of Washington, among others, for the settlement by Virginians of the Ohio country (approximately present-day Ohio). The company had a land grant from Britain and a treaty with local Indigenous people, but France also claimed the area.

As soon as Washington's detachment arrived, shots were fired. Some of the wounded French soldiers, including their commander, Joseph Coulon de Villiers de Jumonville, were summarily executed by Native allies of the British. Learning of the bloody encounter, the French at the fort sent out a much larger force of troops with their own Native allies to bring Washington to terms. Heavily outnumbered, Washington had no choice but to surrender, which he did on July 4, 1754, admitting in writing that he had ordered the killings before being permitted to return to Virginia. The episode could have gone down as little more than a skirmish on the frontier, one of many that erupted on the North American continent between rival imperial powers. But in this case, it proved to be a spark that ignited an imperial war, the likes of which had not been seen before.

Contours of Imperial Conflict

By the middle of the eighteenth century, France and England had emerged as the dominant powers in Europe, with the British holding the upper hand on the seas (it had the largest navy) and the French holding the upper hand on the land (it had the largest army). Both had been embroiled in warfare across the seventeenth century, and although a peace had been established after 1713 (which ended what was known as the War of the Spanish Succession in Europe and as Queen Anne's War in North America), it was expected that conflict between the rivals would soon resume.

British and French interests focused on the overall balance of power on the European continent: on access to trade, especially in slaves, along the west coast of Africa; on securing footholds in India's Mughal Empire and in eastern Bengal, and thus in the Indian Ocean; and on the booming sugar plantations of the West Indies, where enslaved labor brought great wealth. But continental North America increasingly beckoned as well. As the population of the British colonists there grew from about 50,000 in 1650 (including enslaved people) to about 1,200,000 a century later (also including the enslaved), the potential market for British manufactured goods grew along with it. British officials therefore wished to encourage expanded settlement to the west, even in the form of speculative undertakings such as the Ohio Company envisioned (see Map 6.1).

Such ambitions worried the French. Although French colonists in North America were far fewer in number and were spread thinly across an extended territory, they had engaged in a lucrative trade in furs and had forged significant alliances with Indigenous people, especially in the Great Lakes area that they called the *pays d'en haut* (or upper country). Indeed, the relative paucity of French merchants, settlers, and missionaries made them more dependent on Native traders and intermediaries in the fur trade than the British were, while representing a far less lethal and military threat than the British had clearly come to be. By some accounts, a vibrant cultural "middle ground" had formed between the French and their Native allies that promoted peaceful exchanges and discouraged resorts to war.

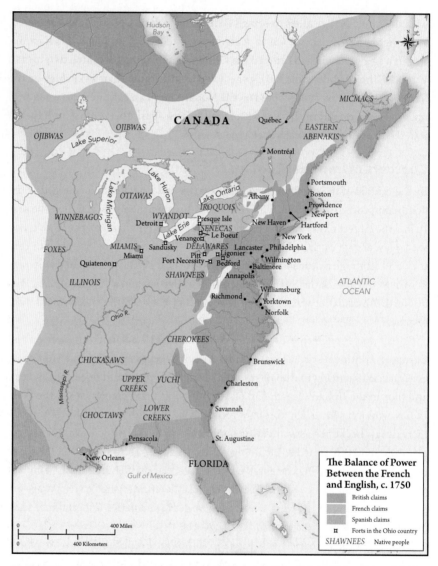

≡ **MAP 6.1   The Balance of Power Between the French and English, c. 1750**   Britain's desire to expand westward clashed with the French, whose claims extended across a vast territory.

Along with Quebec and the Great Lakes region, the French also claimed (as we saw in the previous chapter) the Mississippi River Valley, whose waters spilled into the Caribbean Sea. Thus, as the French saw it, British expansion threatened not only trading relations with France's Native allies but also the security of their Caribbean sugar plantations. "If we do not halt the rapid progress of the English colonies of the Continent," a royal advisor told the French king, "they will have, in a short time, such great facilities that they can make formidable armaments [sic] on the

Continent of America, and it will take them so little time to carry large forces either to Saint-Domingue or to the island of Cuba, or to our Windward islands, that there will be no hope of keeping them except at enormous expense." Such "progress," the advisor believed, would eventually give the British "superiority in Europe."

There were other important actors, too. As we have seen, during the seventeenth century, European—and especially British—colonial settlement was a source of al-most continual conflict and warfare with Indigenous people. Some of this was partic-ularly explosive, and in the course of the Pequot War and King Philip's (Metacom's) War in New England and, later, the Yamasee War (1715–1717) in South Carolina, co-alitions among Indigenous people inflicted massive damage on the colonists before succumbing to defeat. At the same time, Native groups struggled among themselves over access to game and other food supplies as well as over trading relations with Europeans. In the northeast, the **League of the Iroquois** (composed of Mohawks, Senecas, Cayugas, Onondagas, and Oneidas) battled their way to dominance over other Indigenous people while entering into an alliance, first with the Dutch and then with the British, known as the **Covenant Chain**. Farther to the west, around the Great Lakes, Algonquian-speaking peoples had forged trading and political alli-ances with the French, sometimes against the aggressive Iroquois, though in all cases the Indigenous people were at-tuned to playing the Europeans off against one another (see Map 6.1).

By the middle of the eigh-teenth century, much of the North American continent east of the Mississippi River, stretch-ing from the Great Lakes to the Gulf coast, was composed of Native villages and confedera-tions that had been reconfigured as a result of military defeat and disease. Some had been pushed out of the Northeast by the Iroquois and the British or out of the Southeast by the Cherokee and the British. Some had been dislocated because of intra-Native struggles. Those who iden-tified as Delawares and Shawnees,

≡ **Yuchi Native Prepared for a Hunt**   German explorer Philip Georg Friedrich von Reck traveled to Georgia in 1730. His journals are full of closely observed drawings and watercolors of Indigenous peoples, such as the Yuchi. The striped blanket and long gun carried by the central figure would have been procured through trade with the English.

≡ **Theyanoguin, or King Hendrick, a Mohawk Chief** This great Mohawk *sachem*, or chief, negotiated between the Iroquois Confederacy and Great Britain at the Albany Congress. After his death in 1755, this print of his portrait was widely distributed.

Seneca-Cayuga and Miamis, Creeks and Choctaws often came to live in small clusters of multiethnic villages, decentralized politically, which nonetheless shared the experience of dislocation and cultural redefinition. Indigenous people such as these had been repopulating the increasingly strategic Ohio country, and they were forces to be reckoned with on the imperial stage.

Indeed, to succeed in even a limited war, the British needed help from the colonists and some prospect of Indian support, or at least neutrality. Thus, in the early summer of 1754, representatives from seven colonies north of Virginia met to discuss alliances with Indigenous people—especially the Iroquoian Mohawks—and the need for military defense against the French as warfare brewed. But two of the delegates to the **Albany Congress**, Benjamin Franklin of Pennsylvania and Thomas Hutchinson of Massachusetts, went so far as to propose a **Plan for Union** involving all of the British colonies. Such a union, of special interest to Franklin, would attend to Native affairs, territorial issues between colonies, and perhaps taxation, and would be under the control of a president-general appointed by the king and an elective grand council. A bold idea it was, though apparently far too ambitious; none of the colonies showed interest.

Early Fighting

Although war had not been officially declared between them, both Britain and France recognized the stakes involved. The French sent a fleet with six regiments of soldiers to New France in 1755. The British sent two regiments to Virginia. Of special interest to the British were a series of forts the French, hoping to create a western barrier to British colonial expansion, had been building along a corridor from Lake Ontario south into the Ohio Valley as well as the large French settlements of Quebec and Montreal in the St. Lawrence River Valley. But they moved first against Fort Duquesne, the site of the skirmishes involving George Washington's troops, putting an experienced officer, Major General Edward Braddock, in command.

It turned out to be a big mistake. Braddock was very familiar with the European brand of open-field warfare but knew nothing about how to fight in the North American woodlands, where guerilla-type tactics thrived and soldiers marching in columns proved to be easy targets. Nor did Braddock, who regarded the French as inferior and their Native allies as "savages," have more than a few Native scouts to help him. On July 9, 1755, Braddock's army was ambushed by a combined French and Native force; Braddock perished along with more than 800 of his men and more than sixty of his officers. It was a disaster, and for the next couple of years the British were unable to reverse their military fortunes. In part, they were thrown on the defensive by the Delaware and Shawnee who, having learned of the British defeat, launched attacks on their colonial settlements in Virginia, Maryland, and Pennsylvania; and in part, they faced an effective French offensive under the leadership of General Louis-Joseph Montcalm that benefitted from Native support and Iroquois neutrality (the Iroquois were thought to be British allies) and that captured British forts in northern and western New York (see Map 6.2).

6.2   Expanding the Geography of Warfare

||| Analyze how the geography of warfare can expand quickly.

Still, there was no formal declaration of war. That didn't happen until the late spring of 1756 when the French attacked British-occupied Minorca, in the Mediterranean Sea, off the east coast of Spain. Seeing the opening, Britain's new Prussian ally, led by monarch Frederick II, quickly mounted an invasion of neighboring Saxony, which was closely tied to Austria, and Austria looked to France, its new ally, for a joint response. The French agreed to lend Austria military support, and so the conflict and bloodshed that had begun in eastern North America expanded onto another continental landscape (see again Map 6.2).

Also expanding across the Atlantic were the woes that the British had been enduring in North America. They lost Minorca, the Prussians were soon on the defensive, and King George II's son, put in charge of an allied army, was routed by the French and Austrians. It seemed a reflection of the rather half-hearted way that the British appeared to engage, holding their considerable resources close at home rather than expending them.

Ramping Up

This changed in 1757 when political backlash in Britain's Parliament empowered Secretary of State William Pitt to be architect of the warfare. Believing haughtily that he alone could "save the nation," Pitt moved aggressively to turn the tide. He sent thousands of troops to North America, directed the navy to attack French outposts in West Africa as well as their plantation colonies in the Caribbean, and determined to push the French out of India, securing a beachhead on the subcontinent that would be staffed mainly by the British East India Company.

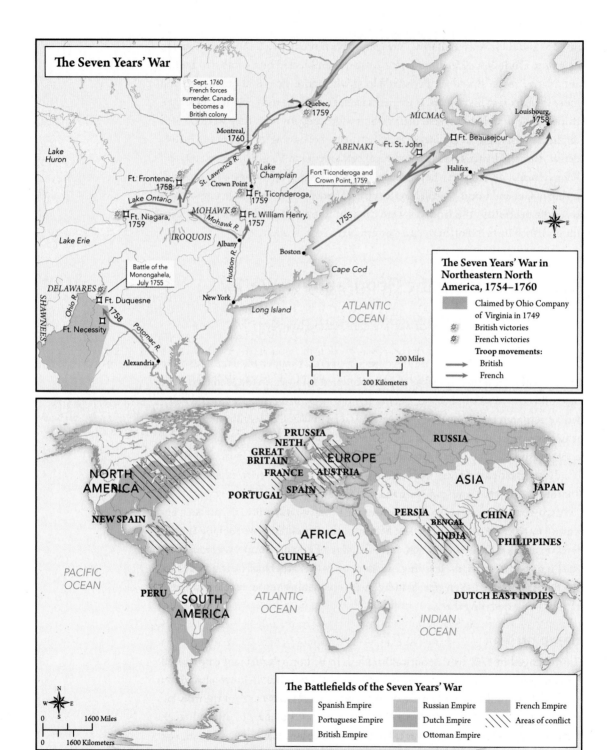

The Seven Years' War

Sept. 1760 French forces surrender. Canada becomes a British colony

The Seven Years' War in Northeastern North America, 1754–1760

Claimed by Ohio Company of Virginia in 1749
British victories
French victories
Troop movements:
British
French

The Battlefields of the Seven Years' War

Spanish Empire
Portuguese Empire
British Empire
Russian Empire
Dutch Empire
Ottoman Empire
French Empire
Areas of conflict

≡ **MAP 6.2   The Seven Years' War**   The conflict that began in eastern North America expanded until it encompassed the Caribbean, West Africa, Europe, and South Asia.

It proved to be a remarkable turnaround, thanks largely to the supremacy of the British navy. Pitt had squadrons in Antigua and Jamaica fortified and then sent a large fleet to attack Martinique and Guadeloupe, the French sugar colonies in the eastern Caribbean. Guadeloupe, the largest of the two, fell in the spring of 1759; Martinique, along with the smaller French islands of Dominica, St. Lucia, Grenada, and St. Vincent, would fall two years later. And when the Spanish decided to enter the war on the side of France in 1762, the British promptly moved to occupy Havana, Cuba, the great Spanish colonial port city that held much of the silver and gold being shipped out of their

≡ **José Martín Rufo,** *Asalto Ingles Al Castillo Del Morro De La Habana* (***British Attack on Morro Castle, Havana***) The Morro Castle was a Spanish fortification guarding the strategically important harbor at Havana, Cuba. A key stopping point for Spanish treasure ships traveling between South America and Spain, Havana was the home of the largest Spanish shipyard in the Americas, and by 1750 had a larger population than either Boston or New York. During the 1762 Siege of Havana, British forces captured Morro Castle, defeated the Spanish, and took possession of the city.

mines in Mexico and Peru. They moved, as well, to occupy Manila, way out in the South Pacific, which also served as a way station for Spanish precious metals.

Somewhat closer to home, the British fleet struck the French and Spanish heavy blows in sea battles off the coasts of France and Portugal, disrupting French plans to invade England and Scotland. In the meantime, British warships sailed farther south and attacked French bases along the coast of Senegal—where the trade in enslaved Africans and gum (used in silk manufacturing) was centered—and quickly managed to dislodge the French there and in neighboring Gambia. Warfare in India spread over time and space, beginning to the north and east in Bengal, where the British ousted the French version of their East India Company while retaking Kolkata, and moving south and west, where the British held onto their post in Madras and then forced the French to surrender their last significant hold in Pondicherry along what was known as the Coromandel Coast. From the Pacific and the Indian Ocean to the south Atlantic and the West Indies—truly planet-wide—the war raged, with the British now registering notable victories.

≡ **Benjamin West, *The Death of General Wolfe* (1770)**   Painted nearly twelve years after his death, this dramatic (and largely imaginary) depiction of a heroic Wolfe dying in the arms of his fellow soldiers became enormously popular among British people, who saw in it an allegory of the British victory in the Seven Years' War. Entirely self-taught, British-American artist Benjamin West so impressed George III that he was appointed historical painter to the court and overseer of the royal collection of pictures.

The North American Theater

But the struggle in North America proved particularly significant. Indeed, Pitt was especially focused on the war there and devoted massive resources to shifting the dynamic and defeating the French and their Native allies. On the one hand, Pitt was determined to take the Ohio country and, in the summer of 1758, ordered another march against Fort Duquesne, though this time with a larger force and a substantial number of Cherokees in support. The French simply fled, leaving the fort a shambles. The British responded by building a far larger fortification that they named Fort Pitt, homage to the prime minister and a clear indication that they intended to stay.

On the other hand, the British looked farther north, to New France, and launched a massive attack against Louisbourg, at the mouth of the St. Lawrence River, also in the summer of 1758, which they had failed to take a year earlier. This time, after a six-week siege, Louisbourg fell, opening the St. Lawrence Valley to British invasion while cutting off supplies to French troops and traders. Led by General James Wolfe, the British managed in September 1759 to take the capital of Quebec, defended by French troops under General Montcalm, though at the cost of both Wolfe's and Montcalm's lives. A year later, attacking from three sides, the British took Montreal, and the French—watching Native allies turn to the English, who could offer the goods the French now lacked—had little choice but to surrender all of New France. So important was the North American theater of the **Seven Years' War** to the British and their colonists alike that it came to be known as the **French and Indian War** (1754–1763), the name best recognized by historians and students of the United States.

Rewards of Victory

Although combat on land and sea continued a little while longer on the European continent, in the West Indies, and in West Africa, diplomats from the main warring parties gathered in Paris in 1761 to hammer out a peace. It took another two years to complete the process, yet when the **Treaty of Paris** was signed in 1763, the British were plainly the victors and, as might be expected, they reaped the greatest portion of the spoils. The French managed to recover the Caribbean islands of Guadeloupe, Martinique, and St. Lucia, along with their slaving outpost along the coast of Senegal and their trading posts in India. The Spanish succeeded in regaining Cuba and Manila from the British as well as receiving Louisiana from the French. But the British not only kept Senegal, strengthened their hold in Bengal, and won possession of Dominica, St. Vincent, Tobago, and Grenada in the West Indies. They also took Florida from Spain and,

Propaganda of the First Global War This English allegorical print, celebrating the English victory over the French at Louisbourg in 1758, reflects both pride in Britain's military triumphs and enduring political strife between Britain and France. The female figure of Britannia, representing England, extends her protection to representatives of Indigenous people of North America while Mars (god of war) and Neptune (god of the sea) shake hands under the British flag. A lion, also representing Britain, places a protective paw on a map showing Virginia, Nova Scotia, and Quebec. To the right, a gleeful British soldier points to the British coat of arms shining in the sky as it eclipses the French arms; beside him, as a French politician gasps in horror. French troops tumble over the Niagara Falls, and a pyramid-shaped monument at the center commemorates Britain's victory.

with the exception of a few islands off the coast of Newfoundland, fully dislodged the French from all of North America east of the Mississippi River: Canada and the Ohio country, most importantly. Thus, it appeared that the global Seven Years' War (which was longer than seven years, having begun unofficially in 1754) had come to an end.

6.3 Religious and Political Awakenings

||| Compare religious awakenings among colonists, free and enslaved Black people, and Indigenous peoples.

The British were now king of the imperial hill in eastern North America. They had defeated the French militarily and struck them a blow from which they would never fully recover. They had defeated the Spanish, showing how vulnerable Spanish

≡ **Pretensions of Gentility**   Around 1740, the wealthy
Rhode Island planter John Potter commissioned an
unknown artist to paint a portrait of himself with
his family to hang over one of the fireplaces in his
splendid home. Although he presented himself as
an upstanding gentleman, John Potter actually ran a
lucrative counterfeiting operation. He was arrested in
1742 and convicted. To avoid being pilloried (set into a
wooden framework with holes for the head and hands)
and having his ears cut off, he paid the exorbitant fine
of £10,000; several of his co-conspirators were not so
lucky. The porcelain tea set and silver tea pot, the tea and
sugar themselves, and the enslaved Black child reflect the
entangled networks of trade and slavery that wove the
Atlantic world together.

colonies had become both in the Western
Hemisphere and in the Pacific. And they now
seemed intent on paying much closer attention to
the North American world they had maintained
and inherited, in part because it was so costly
to wage war there. What sort of world had this
become?

In social and economic terms, the developments that were evident by the early eighteenth
century had only become more deeply entrenched. Port cities from Boston in the north
down to Charleston in the south were more
and more involved in an Atlantic economy that
linked Britain and the European continent
with the West Indies and North America. The
New England and Middle Atlantic colonies
were becoming more populated and expanding geographically, though their family-farming
economies were still oriented to subsistence agriculture and local trade. The slave plantation
system intensified in the Chesapeake and the
Carolinas—also in Georgia, a relatively new colony that had begun as a refuge for
British debtors in the 1730s and was legally off-limits to slavery and slaveholders
until the 1750s, though the law was frequently broken, with the smuggling of enslaved people into Georgia a common practice. In the South arose a very wealthy
planter class and an enslaved population that numbered in the many thousands
and was increasingly native-born. And colonial land claims that stretched from
the Atlantic coast to the Mississippi River lured money-hungry speculators who
hoped to buy up as much land as they could in hopes of selling it to land-hungry
British settlers at handsome profits. In religious and political terms, however, important transformations were taking place.

The Great Awakening

Across the British North American colonies, certain churches held sway. In New
England, the Puritan or Congregational church was dominant. In the Chesapeake
and the Carolinas, the Anglican church was foremost. And although there was more
cultural and religious diversity in the Middle Colonies, Pennsylvania was clearly
Quaker territory. What all of these colonies and churches had in common were fundamental links to the Protestant faith, challenges of spirituality and membership,

and divisions between ministers who believed that salvation could be achieved through reason and proper
behavior and those who believed that only the personal
experience of God and conversion sufficed.

These divisions would have been of limited significance were it not for shifting religious trends in the
colonies. Many of the colonial church leaders found
that while the church generally remained at the center
of community life, regular attendance was declining
and fewer colonists had become full-fledged members.
Even in New England, as we saw in Chapter 4, it was
necessary for the Puritan church to devise a "halfway
covenant" so that children and grandchildren of church
members who did not have conversion experiences
could participate in religious life. Increasingly, it was
the word of ministers rather than the word of God that
was being heard.

There had always been "revivals" of religious faith
among church communities, most of which were short
in duration and limited in reach. Revivals were events
meant to inspire spiritual fervor and draw new, often young, members into the fold. The sparks might
burn for a time, though in a little while they would die

≡ **John Wollaston,** *George Whitefield* **(c. 1742)**
George Whitefield was famous for his crossed eyes,
deep voice, and charismatic preaching style marked
by gestures. The woman gazing up at him here may
be Elizabeth James, a widow whom Whitefield
married in 1741.

down. But something different began happening in the 1730s and 1740s. Then,
the revivals that occurred in several locations and among a number of different
Protestant denominations—Dutch Reformed, Anglican, and Presbyterian as well
as Congregational—spread very rapidly from Great Britain and Protestant Europe
and soon encompassed much of British North America. Called a "great and general
awakening" at the time, it has come to be known as the **First Great Awakening**.

One of the most important early revivals occurred in Northampton,
Massachusetts, in 1734, inspired by the preaching of a fiery Congregational minister named Jonathan Edwards. Sensing the hunger for spiritual fulfillment among
"old and young, and from the highest to the lowest," Edwards emphasized the direct experience of God's grace and the necessity for personal conversion, of having
the heart "touched" rather than the head "stored." Congregants responded with a
powerful emotionalism, moaning and crying and shrieking, desperate for Christ's
saving hand. Within a short time, Edwards's church had many new members.
Before too long, much of the Connecticut River Valley was ablaze with revivalism
as was eastern New Jersey, and revivalist ministers began to contact one another.

Perhaps even more important was the arrival of an English Anglican minister named George Whitefield. Whitefield had learned of Edwards while still in England and, inspired by him, began to preach out of doors—in open fields, parks, and town squares—to large numbers of worshippers in various parts of England and Wales. Unlike Edwards, Whitefield was especially interested in men and women of humble origin who felt marginalized by the hierarchical Anglican Church but seemed desperate for the type of intense spiritual connection that Whitefield could offer. Whitefield was born to the role: a dynamic, charismatic orator with a powerful voice and a compelling message of salvation and self-worth.

Whitefield left England for Savannah, Georgia, in 1739, and he was soon working his way north, through colony after colony, holding his revivals. Some ministers opened their pulpits to him; others refused him. But the religious enthusiasm his arrival provoked usually required a large space out of doors where poor and rich rubbed shoulders with one another, sometimes in the many thousands. Indeed, one of his revivals on the outskirts of Philadelphia may have drawn as many worshippers as inhabitants of the city itself.

In Whitefield's wake came other revivalists like Presbyterian Gilbert Tennent of New Jersey, who sermonized about the "Danger of an Unconverted Ministry" (suggesting that established ministers themselves had not had conversion experiences), and the wilder James Davenport of Connecticut, a revivalist who called established ministers "dead husks" and "deceivers" and went so far as to set bonfires to burn their books and the worldly vanities of the colonial elite. Together these revivalists and itinerants (traveling preachers) challenged the established hierarchies in British North America and raised moral questions about the accumulation of wealth. They suggested that, whatever their earthly station, all people were equal in the eyes of God. Edwards, Whitefield, Tennent, and Davenport would be called "New Lights," and their ideas would have special resonance among the new Baptist and Methodist denominations. Their ministerial critics, who denounced their revivalism and evangelical style—and who were frightened by their popular appeal—were known as "Old Lights."

Spirituality's Expanse

The repercussions of the Awakening moved in unexpected directions, especially among the enslaved of African descent. Up through the first decades of the eighteenth century, few white Christians showed much interest in proselytizing among the enslaved, and few of the enslaved—most of whom were still African-born—showed much interest in the religion of their enslavers. Instead, the spiritual lives of the enslaved took shape mostly beyond their enslavers' reach and notice, and they consisted of those traditions that could be maintained in the face of forced separations or rearranged among Africans from different ethnic groups. The process was made possible by the sensibilities that West and West Central Africans broadly shared, not simply among themselves but also with Europeans of humble origins with whom the enslaved had most contact on slave ships or in the fields.

The itinerants who helped spark the awakenings preached a harsh Calvinism that had little resemblance to the worldviews of West Africans. But the itinerants themselves came from modest backgrounds and invited all ranks and races to hear their message: a message that emphasized the experience of spiritual rebirth and personal communion with Christ, that challenged the ways of the landed elite, at times questioned the morality of enslavement, and welcomed Black people as members.

The Awakening moved with particular influence through those areas of the southern colonies where whites and Black people had been in most intensive contact, and they allowed Black people—enslaved and free—exceptional initiative and participation. Indeed, in some places (Savannah and the surrounding rural areas most notably) Black evangelicals like George Liele converted their enslavers, established Methodist and Baptist churches before the whites did, and preached to both mixed and predominately white congregations. In the process, they introduced enslaved and free Black people to the Christian faith as they understood it, doubtless filtering it through an African cosmology, or spiritual perspective, which in one form or another still held sway.

The spiritual awakenings that swept through the British North American colonies, touching Black and white, had counterparts among Indigenous people during the 1760s. Responding to the defeat of their French allies and watching the British victors building new forts and moving into territory they claimed for themselves, a number of Native prophets—the most important of whom was known as Neolin, a Delaware who may have lived in a village near Lake Erie—fashioned new visions of

A

P O E M,

By PHILLIS, a *Negro* Girl, in BOSTON.

ON THE DEATH OF THE REVEREND

GEORGE WHITEFIELD,

≡ **A Young Enslaved Woman Mourns for Whitefield** The extraordinary Black poet Phillis Wheatley (c. 1753–1784) was still a teenager—and still enslaved—when her elegy commemorating the 1770 death of George Whitefield was published to great acclaim. In her poem, Wheatley imagined the preacher speaking to free Americans and enslaved people alike:

"Take him my dear *Americans*," he said,
Be your complaints on his kind bosom laid:
Take him, ye *Africans*, he longs for you,
Impartial Saviour is his title due:
Wash'd in the fountain of redeeming blood,
You shall be sons, and kings, and priests to God.

worldly domains and the hereafter. Drawing upon longstanding Native cosmologies though showing the influence of Christian beliefs and myths, Neolin in particular spoke of a Master of Life who created Indigenous people and Europeans separately, disapproved of Native practices of polygamy and dependence on European goods (especially alcohol), and ordered Indigenous people not to "suffer the English" to live with them. Indeed, according to Neolin's preaching, the Master of Life wished for Indigenous people to mend their ways, seize control of their spiritual destinies, and fight against "this bad meat [the English] that would come to infest" their lands. "This land where ye dwell I have made for you and not for others," the Master was said to have told Neolin. "Whence comes it that you permit the Whites upon your lands? Drive them out, make war upon them."

Pontiac's War

Neolin traveled many miles to spread his message, but the geographical reach of the Seven Years' War in North America also made it easier for Indigenous people to find one another and learn of what Neolin had prophesized even if they didn't hear him directly. The French alliance had brought many of them into contact, especially in New France and the Ohio country, but also as far off as the southeast and the lower Mississippi Valley. Native villagers were on the move almost everywhere, and then were reorganizing themselves along lines that mixed ethnic groups. Their cultural horizons and perspectives were consequently expanding and shifting. Some imagined the French returning to reconquer the lands they had been driven from and reconstituting their Native alliances. Others came to recognize that they were now likely on their own and had to orient themselves accordingly. There were signs of a **pan-Indian identity** emerging, a sense of "Indianness" transcending their particular Native identities. And one of Neolin's most devoted followers, Pontiac, an Ottawa chief, determined to turn prophecy into action.

What has come to be called **Pontiac's War** began in the spring of 1763, when Pontiac organized a coalition of Algonquian-speaking Indigenous people numbering several hundred to attack the British-held Fort Detroit. The rebellion spread quickly across the Great Lakes, the Ohio country, and into western Pennsylvania, Maryland, and Virginia. Not only the Ottawa and their allies but also Potawatomi, Illinois, Chippewa, Shawnee, Delaware, Kickapoo, and Iroquoian Seneca— inspired by Neolin's teachings and news of Pontiac's attack—launched brutal attacks on British forts and colonial settlements. In effect, they were carrying forward the French and Indian War in hopes of now pushing the British out and bringing the French back. Before their momentum slowed, Native warriors had taken nine of the British forts in the large area of the Great Lakes and Ohio country and laid siege to the remaining three, including Fort Pitt and Detroit (see Map 6.3).

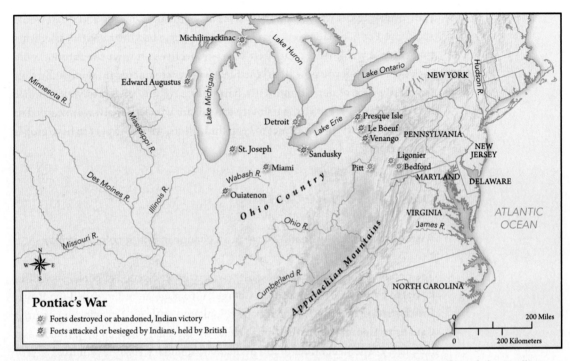

≡ **MAP 6.3   Pontiac's War**   The costly war made clear that Indigenous people had their own ideas of what an alliance with the British would mean and their own perspectives on what the future should look like.

The Native attacks provoked a brutal and bloody backlash, especially in those areas where British colonists had settled in significant numbers and felt the Indigenous people's wrath. The most notorious were Pennsylvania vigilantes known as the Paxton Boys, who hailed from the village of Paxtang in the Susquehanna River valley and took to massacring Indigenous people nearby: not those who had wrought havoc to their west but those who had tried to live peacefully among them (something like the end stages of King Philip's War, discussed in Chapter 4). They then brazenly marched on Philadelphia to slaughter Indigenous people gathered there for protection and came upon colonial officials, including Benjamin Franklin, who persuaded them to turn around in exchange for presenting their grievances to the colonial assembly and granting them immunity from prosecution. That is to say, the Paxton Boys were rewarded rather than punished for what they had done.

For the most part, however, Pontiac's War had a less explosive and more economic and political conclusion. Learning about the signing of the Treaty of Paris (the French weren't coming back) and running short on gunpowder, Pontiac and other Native warriors permitted the British to reoccupy their forts and gradually made peace with British military authorities, who were eager to bring the bloodletting to an end and secure their newly expanded North American empire with

Native alliances. It was a good idea, as events of the next decade and a half would show. But Pontiac made clear that Indigenous people had their own ideas of what that alliance would mean and their own perspectives on what the future should look like. "We tell you now [that] the French never conquered us, neither did they purchase a foot of our Country, nor have they a right to give it to you," Pontiac told the British. "We gave them liberty to settle for which they always rewarded us with great Civility. If you expect to keep these Posts, we will expect to have proper returns from you."

6.4 A New Reckoning

||| Assess how the Seven Years' War led to a change in British colonial policy.

The potential for continued and costly wars with Indigenous people, so well illustrated by Pontiac's War, caused George III to issue an order, called the **Royal Proclamation of 1763**, which forbade colonists to settle west of a line drawn from Canada to Georgia along the Appalachian Mountains (see Map 6.4). Meant as a temporary expedient rather than a permanent boundary, the line promised to protect not only the 150,000 Indigenous people who lived in the trans-Appalachian West but also the lucrative fur trade, now in British rather than French hands. But the pressure of population growth meant that the proclamation line would be difficult to enforce. Settlers had already moved west of the line, as had land speculators, such as those of Virginia's Ohio Company, who stood to lose opportunities for profitable resale of their claims.

Not surprisingly, then, the Proclamation angered a great many British colonists, especially members of the landed elite, who imagined that their victory against the French would enable them to move into territory that the French had claimed, force the Native inhabitants out, and avail themselves of the speculative windfall. But it turned out to be the beginning of a larger reckoning within the expanding British Empire that would turn growing numbers of colonists against imperial authorities in London.

The Price of Victory

The Seven Years' War brought Britain vast new imperial holdings and far more global power, but waging war on multiple continents also doubled Britain's debt, and administering the territorial spoils promised greater and greater expenditures. How would this be paid for? What's more, now that many more troops and officials were in North America, British leaders discovered that colonial subjects had become

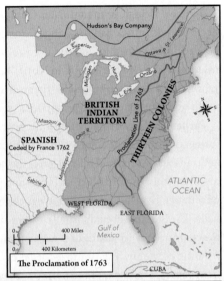

The Proclamation of 1763

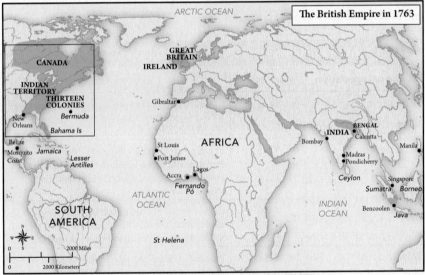

The Proclamation of 1763 and the Global Extent of the British Empire

≡ **MAP 6.4**   The Proclamation of 1763 and the Global Extent of the British Empire

accustomed to running things pretty much their own way. Especially galling were the many violations of the Navigation Acts, meant to control Atlantic trade to the benefit of Britain. Colonial merchants and shippers, it seemed, were brazenly trading with other countries and empires, especially in the Caribbean, thereby depriving British traders of their profits and the imperial treasury of its revenues.

The new British prime minister George Grenville and his allies in Parliament decided that things had to change. From their perspective, the colonial subjects needed to be reined in and required to pay new taxes to support their imperial rulers at home and the empire in North America. After all, the white colonists appeared to be doing quite well for themselves, and it was time that they paid tribute for their many benefits and protections (see Table 6.1).

Parliament began by enacting a Currency Act and a Sugar Act, both in 1764. The former prohibited the colonies from printing their own paper money, limiting market transactions beyond official gaze; the latter taxed the importation of sugar and molasses from the British West Indies and prohibited the importation of rum from outside the British Empire. But it was the **Stamp Act** (1765) that set off the alarm bells. The Stamp Act established a direct tax on a great deal of paper circulating in the colonies and especially in the dynamic coastal areas already integrated into the Atlantic economy. The Act taxed legal documents (court records and contracts), newspapers, other printed material, and even playing cards—and required that a

Table 6.1 British Taxes Levied on the Colonies, 1732–1765		
Name of Legislation	**Year Passed**	**Key Provisions**
Hat Act	1732	Barred colonists from producing beaver felt hats for export to other British colonies to protect British manufacturers
Molasses Act	1733	Imposed prohibitively high duty on sugar and molasses imported to British North America from French and Dutch Caribbean to protect British West Indian planters
Iron Act	1750	Barred colonists from building more rolling or slitting mills, which made hoops, tire iron, and nails that colonists usually imported from Britain
Currency Act	1751	Prohibited colonial governments from issuing more paper money, except in cases of emergency
Sugar Act	1764	Modified regulations issued under Molasses Act and bolstered their enforcement First overt tax raised by Parliament in British America Yielded more revenue than any imperial tax levied on British America prior to American Revolution
Currency Act	1764	Outlawed printing of paper money in colonies
Stamp Act	1765	Required colonists to purchase a stamp for any printed item (newspapers, legal documents, etc.)

special stamp be affixed to the paper proving that the tax had been paid. Although the tax was not very high, it generated a fierce backlash while revealing political divisions within the colonies themselves.

Why the protest? The period immediately following the Seven Years' War saw considerable social and economic dislocation in British North America as soldiers came home from the battlefields and Atlantic trade slowed in a time of political readjustment. Taxes, even small ones, could seem to be onerous and unnecessary burdens. But for protest leaders, who were mainly merchants, landowners, and lawyers not favored by imperial officials, the taxes—and the Stamp Tax in particular—seemed an infringement on their rights of self-governance. They appeared willing (or so they said) to accept taxes imposed by colonial assemblies. After all, the members of those assemblies were chosen by people like them. Parliament, on the other hand, was not only geographically remote but colonial representation in it was, at best, indirect. Indeed, from the perspective of the colonial protestors, they believed they were subject to the authority of the king, not the Parliament. For many, the king was imagined as their ally and Parliament increasingly as their enemy. Parliament's power, some insisted, ended at the British shoreline; beyond that was the king's domain.

Needless to say, members of Parliament (MPs as they were known) generally had a different view. During the previous century's political upheavals and civil wars, they had wrested much of the power that the king had wielded unilaterally. It was now they, with the king's assent, who ruled at home and abroad, not only up to Britain's shoreline but across Britain's sprawling empire, including the colonies in North America. Although submission to the authority of the king continued to be widely accepted, submission to the will of Parliament was now being rejected. And the room to accommodate these very different political perspectives was rapidly dwindling.

Colonists Resist

Popular anger proved easy to fan, and in the months after the Stamp Act was enacted, riots against tax collectors exploded in Newport (Rhode Island), Annapolis (Maryland), and New York City. The largest riot was in Boston, where a crowd of several thousand wreaked vengeance on tax collector Andrew Oliver's office and home. Oliver quickly resigned his post, as did other colonial officials who suffered harassment and violence. But of equal significance, leaders from different colonies began to organize their opposition to imperial policies. In New York, merchants organized a boycott of British-made goods in which women as well as men played important roles: the women especially in turning their energies to homespun and other household manufactures so that necessary goods would not have to be purchased. The boycott and other **nonimportation agreements** soon spread North

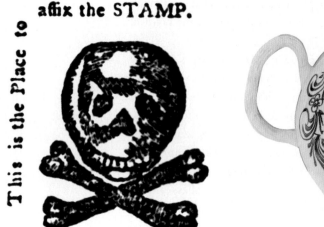

≡ **Early Memes as Popular Protest**   Colonists used formats ranging from newspaper advertisements to teapots to protest the wildly unpopular Stamp Act. The skull and crossbones appeared as a satirical ad in *The Pennsylvania Journal*, symbolizing the death of a free press because of the new tax on paper.

and South. And in October 1765, nine of the colonies sent delegates to a meeting in New York City called the **Stamp Act Congress**. The delegates issued resolutions insisting that the Stamp Act violated the principles of the British constitution, that they were entitled to all the rights of Englishmen, and that taxation without representation was unacceptable.

It is important to remember that delegates at the Stamp Act Congress took the opportunity to express their loyalty to the king. Those who protested or rioted against the Stamp Act did not reject the British monarchy or the institutions of British governance. They had no interest in removing themselves from the empire or in declaring their independence. Indeed, they continuously spoke and wrote of their deep allegiance to the crown and the empire and, instead, blamed Parliament for trampling on the colonists' rights owing to narrow self-interest. If anything, protest leaders and followers believed that the king was on their side and had, perhaps, been unaware of or been overruled by Parliament. By the mere fact of its meeting, however, the Stamp Act Congress advanced the notion of intercolonial political action first suggested by the Albany Congress.

The imperial conflict would soon escalate. Although Parliament, under pressure, repealed the hated Stamp Tax in March 1766, it did not retreat on the larger issue of legislating for the colonies and forcing colonists to pay for the costs of empire. Parliament rejected colonial claims about taxation and representation and proclaimed its power "to bind the colonies and people of America in all cases."

Grenville was sent packing and replaced first by Lord Rockingham, then by William Pitt, then by Augustus Henry Fitzroy, and then by Lord Frederick North.

Serious debates and disagreements took place in Parliament as to how far taxation should go. But there was also little let-up on the British side. First the **Townshend Acts** (1767) imposed new, albeit modest, taxes and provided for clearer means of enforcement. But trade decreased between the colonies and Great Britain under the Townshend Acts, owing in large part to the nonimportation agreements in effect throughout British North America, and in 1770 the Townshend Acts were repealed, except for the tax on tea, a pointed reminder of Parliament's ultimate power. Those colonists who could not abide the symbolism of the tea tax turned to smuggled Dutch tea. Then the **Tea Act** (1773) attempted to undercut the smuggling of tea by colonial merchants and strengthen the hand of the British East India Company, which had the exclusive privilege under the Navigation Acts of shipping tea to the colonies (see Figure 6.1).

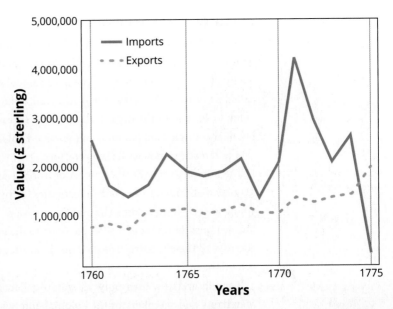

≡ **FIGURE 6.1** **The Economic Impact of Taxation on the Colonies, 1760–1775.**

6.5 Escalation of Protest

||| Explain how changes in British colonial policy generated protest in the colonies.

The colonial response to the Stamp Act in 1765 suggested that North American colonists and the British government had very different perspectives as to how power in the empire should be shared. Should colonists imagine themselves as partners in the British Empire? Or should they be regarded as subjects of crown and parliamentary rule? The colonial response to the Stamp Act also suggested that colonists were ready to push back and had made some efforts to organize themselves across the boundaries of separate colonies.

Boston, Center of Resistance

Much of the resistance centered in New England, especially in Boston, where a large community of merchants and artisans not dependent on imperial favor had emerged. Their leaders, notably the fiery Samuel Adams, founded an organization called the **Sons of Liberty** (1765) to advance the cause of their rights as they had come to see them; the organization would spread to other colonies. They called public meetings, held parades, and harassed colonists who accepted British taxation or refused to side with the protestors.

The Sons also sought the support of laborers and other common folk who had long been excluded from political activities led by more "respectable" elements. A young lawyer, John Adams (he and Samuel were cousins), acknowledged despite his own misgivings that "the People, even to the lowest Ranks, have become more attentive to their Liberties, more inquisitive about them, and more determined to defend them."

It could and did turn ugly, as stamp collector Andrew Oliver had learned. Merchants and members of the colonial elite who were viewed as collaborators with imperial authority were attacked, belittled, and humiliated; their property might be desecrated or destroyed, sometimes as large crowds looked on. "Join, or Die," some demanded, picking up on a slogan Benjamin Franklin had devised at the time of the Albany Congress—and they meant it. Indeed, some of the Sons of Liberty themselves came to worry that things were going too far, that they had unleashed forces beyond their control, insisting as they did that they only wanted "a preservation of the [British] Constitution."

Learning of the growing disorder, Parliament sent two more regiments of troops to Boston in hopes of protecting loyalists and enabling colonial officials to carry out their tasks. But the deployment only made matters worse. On March 5, 1770, as a crowd of mariners, artisans, and laborers gathered to intimidate a number of British troops on Boston's King Street, hurling rocks, snowballs, sticks, and other debris at them, the troops opened fire. Five of those in the crowd would die, one of whom, Crispus Attucks, was a former enslaved man of Native and African ancestry. This **Boston Massacre** was followed by a public funeral organized by the Sons of Liberty that brought 10,000 Bostonians into the streets—the entire population of the city was not much over 15,000. Although British troops were soon removed and some of the perpetrators punished, the episode left a deep imprint on the minds of many colonists.

The struggle had clearly veered in a violent direction, and the violence would only intensify. To some extent protestors drew upon long-standing rituals of meting out community justice to those believed to have transgressed popular norms. Not incarceration (that would come later) but fines and especially corporal punishments were inflicted on offenders, who might be put in the stocks, branded, tarred and feathered (especially brutal), or chased out. Now the wrath of the community was redirected toward the political ends of punishing the British for violating local rights and practices.

What we have come to call the Boston Tea Party is a good example. When the British Parliament passed the Tea Act in 1773, many colonial merchants and their customers were infuriated not because the tax on tea was too high but because, first, it represented taxation without representation and, second, they were forced to deal with the East India Company. Merchants had come to prefer dealing with smugglers who traded on the cheap and were integral to a commercial world of

The Boston Massacre   Silversmith and engraver Paul Revere published this graphic portrayal of the Boston Massacre within days of the event. Revere depicted the British in an organized, military formation, taking deliberate aim at unarmed protestors—even though the actual conflict was much more confusing. Crispus Attucks lies dying in the left foreground as a woman in black with hands clasped, symbolizing sorrow, looks on. This image, widely circulated among the colonies and accompanied by a poem that described the British as "fierce Barbarians grinning o'er their Prey, / Approve the carnage, and enjoy the Day," stoked resentment and resistance against the British.

their own devising. In the fall of 1773, when three East India Company vessels filled with tea sailed into Boston Harbor, the Sons of Liberty decided to act. They mobilized more than 100 members and supporters (some of whom dressed like Mohawks), boarded the ships late at night, and tossed the contents of well over 300 chests of tea into the water. Farther to the south, in New York, Philadelphia, and Charleston, imperial officials responsible for collecting the tax were forced, under threat of violence, to resign.

Why the Native costuming? In part, the Sons of Liberty disguised themselves so they might not be recognized, since their actions plainly were unlawful and likely to be severely punished. Yet, by dressing as Mohawks, they were also making a statement: they were embracing symbols of fierce resistance and guerrilla-style tactics, symbols that rejected the status of British subjecthood and were associated

Gender and Rebellion

≡ A Society of Patriotic Ladies at Edenton in North Carolina

Women in the colonies also participated in protests against British economic policies. But the role of women in society (even wealthy white women) was very different from that of men, and the ways in which women were depicted in popular political cartoons and pamphlets reveal much about their place and how they were perceived. When the Edenton (North Carolina) Ladies' Patriotic Guild met on October 25, 1774 (almost a year after the Boston Tea Party), they pledged to boycott British goods such as tea and cloth. During the meeting, the women voted to drink a local herbal tea rather than the imported "Bohea" tea from England. All fifty-one women further signed their names to a petition published in the *Virginia Gazette*, writing that "we cannot be indifferent on any Occasion that appears nearly to affect the Peace and Happiness of our Country."

The women's efforts were widely satirized in England, as shown in this popular 1775 cartoon. A neglected child drops his dinner while a dog urinates on a tea chest at a woman's feet. By the window, a woman drinks directly from a punch bowl (presumably full of liquor). To the left, women dump English tea from canisters into the hats of waiting men (who are probably going to consume or resell it themselves). At the center, a fashionable lady is distracted from signing the petition by a flirtatious man. As the idea of women taking any political action at all was considered ludicrous, the cartoon underscores not just the condescension of the British toward the wayward colonies but the dismissive treatment of women in politics on either side of the Atlantic.

While the depiction of the Edenton Tea Party mocked real women, stereotypical images of women also appeared in political allegories. "The Female Combatants, or Who Shall," a popular and widely circulated cartoon published in England in 1776, imagines America as an Indigenous woman in traditional garb and Britain as an elaborately and expensively dressed white woman. The idea of two women in a fistfight would have been outrageously funny to most people who saw or purchased this image, but there are deeper political messages as well. The relationship between the two women is depicted as that of a mother (Britain) and her rebellious daughter (America). Britain threatens America, "I'll force you to Obedience, you Rebellious Slut," and America calls out, "Liberty Liberty for ever Mother while I exist." A banner that reads "For Liberty" is at America's feet, while the banner at Britain's feet reads "For Obedience." The shield by America's side, leaning against a flourishing tree, features the French rooster (a nod to the ties between the colonies and France); on Britain's side, the shield includes a compass symbolizing the vast span of the empire.

≡ "The Female Combatants, or Who Shall"

CONSIDER THIS

These two political cartoons rely on stereotypes of Indigenous, colonial, and wealthy white British women to comment on larger political issues. In what ways does political satire in American culture today rely on stereotypes of women, immigrants, or other marginalized groups to capture attention or to make an argument? Irony also plays a role in these images. For example, what do you make of the enslaved African woman bringing a fresh quill and inkpot to the table, so that the Edenton ladies can continue signing a petition about freedom?

with North America rather than with Britain. It was a perspective of what might be called early American "identity," which would continue to flower and then become deeply contested.

Parliament Stokes the Fires

Parliament got the message and reacted accordingly. In 1774, it passed a series of laws that were together known as the **Coercive Acts** (soon called the Intolerable Acts in the colonies). These acts provided for the closing of Boston's port until order was restored and restitution made for the tea; gave colonial officials more latitude to "quarter" (meaning house) British troops; allowed royal officials accused of wrongdoing to be tried in Britain or elsewhere in the empire rather than in North America; and, most stunning, abolished the charter of Massachusetts and brought governance of the colony wholly under imperial control. The final Intolerable Act, the Quebec Act, had little to do with the others (intended to punish Massachusetts for the destruction of the tea), but, ill-timed, it greatly fed the fears of colonists. It confirmed the continuation of French civil law, government form, and Catholicism for Quebec, all an affront to Protestant New Englanders denied their own representative government. The act also gave Quebec control of disputed lands (and hence control of the lucrative fur trade) throughout the Ohio River valley, lands claimed variously by Virginia, Pennsylvania, and Connecticut.

The imposition of imperial control in Massachusetts shocked most colonists there, who had been happy to accept their place within the British Empire so long as they could tend to their own affairs. Now many of them believed it was time to resist. The closing of the port of Boston weakened the Massachusetts economy and threatened farmers with the loss of their land. Imperial governance promised more taxes and elite meddling. Thus, in towns across the countryside, colonists refused to accept the new regime. They drove off imperial officials, continued to select their own, stopped paying taxes into the imperial treasury, and began to arm themselves for possible defense. "In truth, the People here have taken Government into their own hands," one conservative observer wailed.

The Sons of Liberty in Boston and its hinterlands worried that other colonies would not embrace their cause and concerns. They were wrong. News of the Coercive Acts and the Massachusetts resistance spread through word of mouth, public gatherings, and the recently formed (1772–1773) **committees of correspondence**, standing committees established to link the colonies and to share local developments. And it generated sympathy and identification, a sense that the rights of colonists outside of Massachusetts were in similar jeopardy. Some began to think that it was now time for a more unified response.

6.6 Consolidating the Resistance

||| Describe how widely scattered colonial protest brought colonial leaders together.

Unifying the response to parliamentary initiatives would take place quickly, though with a lot of push and pull. After all, the result of the Albany Congress and Plan of Union twenty years earlier seemed to demonstrate that none of the colonies were much interested in joining hands and that perspectives on their place within the British Empire varied a great deal. But under the circumstances, twenty years proved to be a long time, and by the 1770s, acts of colonial protest and networks of communication had begun to transform the political playing field. Through the efforts of the committees of correspondence, the colonies agreed to gather to respond to the crisis.

The First Continental Congress

In September 1774, fifty-six delegates from twelve of Britain's thirteen North American colonies met in the port city of Philadelphia. (Georgia declined to send delegates, as it hoped for British assistance in quelling conflict with Indigenous people on its frontier.) The assemblage was called the **First Continental Congress**, and, in important respects, it built upon the Plan of Union fashioned by the Albany Congress in 1754. Like the Albany Congress, too, goals would not be easy to set— let alone to achieve.

For one thing, few of the delegates were acquainted with one another. They lived far apart, had no special reason to meet earlier for either economic or political purposes, and had little experience working together. There was not much of a basis for trust between them. For another thing, the delegates were seriously divided over how best to respond to the Coercive Acts. The most radical of the delegates, those who were ready to rebel against the authority of Parliament and fashion an entirely new relationship with Britain, were from Massachusetts and Virginia. They included John Adams and Samuel Adams of Massachusetts and Patrick Henry and Richard Henry Lee of Virginia. By contrast, delegates from the Middle Colonies, like Joseph Galloway and John Dickinson of Pennsylvania and John Jay of New York, were more cautious, interested in reforming the empire rather than transforming or breaking it up. Some hoped that the Continental Congress would serve as an American parliament; others saw the Congress as a temporary expedient. Some wished to ready the colonies for warfare against the British; most looked to avoid such preparation for the sake of unity and for fear of bloodshed.

After more than a month, the Congress issued a series of resolutions. They proclaimed that the colonists were entitled to life, liberty, and property, to the protection of the common law, to the rights of assembly and the expression of grievances, and to the freedom of legislating for themselves. They also proclaimed that recent imperial taxes and the Coercive Acts should be repealed "to restore harmony" and that the colonies must not be taxed without their consent. Perhaps most important, the Congress ordered a staggered boycott of trade—imports of British goods prohibited this year, exports the following year, with rice totally exempted, to keep South Carolinians happy. To enforce the boycotts, they created a mechanism called the Continental Association, with chapters in each town. Local chapters, called **committees of safety**, would monitor all commerce and confront suspected violators of the boycotts. Then, before adjourning, delegates to the Continental Congress pledged to reconvene in May 1775 and take the measure of the British response.

Much to the surprise of Parliament and the king, the boycott of British goods, which began December 1, 1774, was remarkably successful in part because committees of safety did their work with very heavy hands. Colonists who did not support the boycotts or the American cause in general could suffer various forms of retribution or persecution; many were terrorized into submitting or fleeing. One Connecticut physician who railed against the Continental Congress was "stripped naked, & hot Pitch was poured upon him, which blistered his Skin. He was then carried to a Hog Sty & rubbed over with Hog's Dung. They threw the Hog's Dung in his Face, & rammed some of it down his Throat." If that was not enough, "his house was attacked, his Windows broke." It was a powerful warning to others with similar views.

Shots of Warfare

Within months, the value of British goods coming into the colonies dropped by 90 percent. At the same time, outside of Boston (where British troops were stationed), committees of safety often began to govern locally, and many colonists began stockpiling weapons, readying themselves for a fight even if their leaders remained reluctant to do so. Those colonists, weary of being British citizens without British rights and eager to rebel against the empire, would be known as Patriots; those who maintained their allegiance to the crown and Parliament would be known as Loyalists or Tories (the name also given to political conservatives in Britain). By mid-April 1775, British officials in Boston learned of what these rebel Patriots were doing, and on April 19 sent several hundred troops west to the town of Concord—where the local weapons were being stored—to arrest the rebel leaders and confiscate the arms. But owing to their communications networks, the rebel Patriots had learned in advance of the British moves, so they removed the weapons and ammunition from Concord and sent a group of militiamen ahead to confront the British soldiers.

They all met at Lexington, a village five miles east of Concord. Shots were fired, and eight members of the Patriot militia fell dead before the rest retreated toward

Concord. There the British troops did some damage before turning back toward Boston. Their retreat was a disaster. Hundreds of armed Patriot militiamen from various parts of Massachusetts had headed toward the area and hidden behind trees, walls, and barns along the soldiers' route, waiting in ambush (a tactic undoubtedly learned from Native warriors). The rebel Patriots were merciless. By the time the British troops made it back to Boston, more than seventy of their number were dead, more than twice as many were wounded, and the Patriot militia had taken the hills surrounding the town, especially those called Bunker and Breed's (see Map 6.5).

Determined to reverse their fortunes and crush the renegade Patriots, the British command led by Major General Thomas Gage, who less than two decades before had fought in the Seven Years' War alongside George Washington, ordered Breed's Hill and Bunker Hill retaken. He ordered a force of nearly 2,500 troops to do the job. It would not be easy. From a strong defensive position, the Patriots turned back two British assaults before being driven off. But it was a costly victory for the British side: well over 200 of their soldiers were killed, and more than 800 were wounded. The imperial government, mortified by what had befallen their troops, replaced Gage with General William Howe, who had recently arrived. John

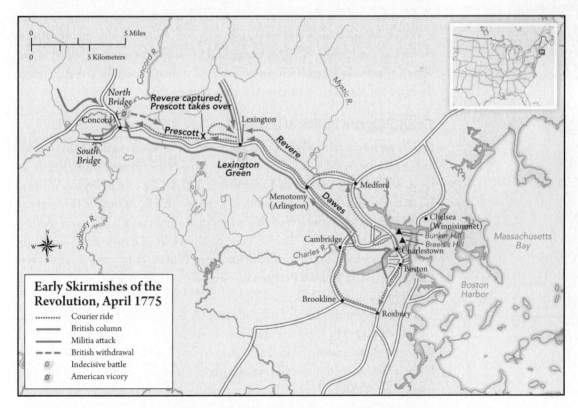

≡ **MAP 6.5   Early Skirmishes of the Revolution, April 1775**

Adams had a different perspective on what had transpired. "The Die was cast, the Rubicon crossed," he concluded. For us, "crossing the Rubicon," an idiom for "passing the point of no return," can be an obscure allusion, harking back as it does to the civil war that beset the ancient Roman Republic. For well-read Patriots like John Adams, though, the meaning was instantly clear.

But had the die in fact been cast? Had the Patriots crossed the "Rubicon" of independence? As we will see, not quite.

6.7   Toward Declaring Independence

Explain how long-standing allegiance to the British crown eventually unraveled and independence was declared.

As promised, the Continental Congress gathered again in Philadelphia in early May 1775 for the **Second Continental Congress**, this time after fighting at Lexington and Concord had already broken out. But the delegates, most of whom had been at the First Continental Congress, were still divided over the proper course to take. One group, mainly from New England, believed the time had come to declare independence and create republics out of the colonies that the British crown had established. Another group, and the largest in number, hoped to find some way to make amends within the imperial system, especially if British troops departed and the hated Coercive Acts were lifted.

Changing the Political Balances

Even if cautious, delegates to the Continental Congress recognized that warfare had begun and, at the very least, they had to provide the colonies with a proper defense. Accordingly, they created a Continental Army, appointed Virginia's George Washington as its commander, resolved to print currency to finance these efforts, and in effect made themselves into something of a governing body over a territory that was still a part of the British Empire. A bold set of moves it was, given the overarching reluctance to "cross the Rubicon." Indeed, in July the Congress sent the king an **Olive Branch Petition** emphasizing continued loyalty and asking for some type of ceasefire.

If at this point the die was not fully cast for the Patriots, it surely was for the crown. Very quickly, King George III rejected the Petition, issued a proclamation declaring the colonies to be in rebellion, and moved to bolster the British army by hiring a mercenary force of German Hessians. He also reshuffled the prime minister's cabinet to include more hard-liners, some of whom sought to restore British "dominion" in the colonies by laying them "waste."

In November 1775 further threats were raised. The royal governor of Virginia, John Murray (also known as Lord Dunmore), issued a proclamation offering freedom to any slave or "indented servant" who would join "His Majesty's Troops" in putting down the Patriot rebellion. It wasn't the first time the British considered emancipating and arming enslaved people who would fight on their behalf. Earlier that spring, abolitionist ideas of various sorts were circulating, so much so that enslaved people in Massachusetts offered their services to the British in exchange for their freedom while others came to believe, in Dunmore's words, that "the Young King" intended to "set the Negroes free." Dunmore's proclamation sparked the flight of more than 800 enslaved people, many belonging to wealthy planters (including George Washington), and suggested that the conflict could well escalate into slave insurrections and widespread civil warfare.

Dunmore may have believed that offering freedom to enslaved Virginians who aligned with the British might be the sort of action that would force the enslavers to see the error of resistance and the benefits of loyalty to the empire. But his move backfired. Many enslavers, now fearing that the British were about to initiate slave emancipation, chose instead to support the rebel Patriots. This was part of a process, clearly under way during the first half of 1776, that shifted the political momentum in the colonies toward independence and plainly demonstrated that the ongoing viability of the slave system would play into the larger question of political allegiance. Nonetheless, the Rubicon had yet to be crossed.

Onto the stage then stepped an unlikely figure. His name was Thomas Paine, an English artisan of modest means, who came to North America in 1774, seeking better prospects for himself after some lean times. He had already mixed in artisan political circles in London, where talk of republicanism and radicalism was rife, and when he arrived in Philadelphia, he had letters of introduction that enabled him to meet those of similar disposition on the western side of the Atlantic and to write for the *Pennsylvania Magazine*. In important ways, Paine and those in his English circles carried on the political traditions of the previous century's Levellers (discussed in Chapter 4) who, though defeated in the English Civil War, imagined an alternative to monarchy or shared rule between the crown

≡ **Laurent Dabos, *Thomas Paine* (c. 1791)** Thomas Paine, whose stirring words in *Common Sense* paved the way for the Declaration of Independence, was not averse to posing for posterity. This is one in a series of full-length portraits of leaders of the French Revolution painted by Dabos—Paine the only non-Frenchman among them.

and parliament: they imagined a republic, a representative form of governance that embodied the sovereignty of "the people."

So, in January 1776, Paine published a pamphlet called *Common Sense*. It was a political tract the likes of which had not been seen in the North American colonies before. In plain and direct prose, Paine not only made the case for American independence but also rejected the British system of monarchy and a mixed constitution involving the Parliament and the crown. In effect, he utterly took down the arguments that had been made on behalf of reforming the empire, which he thought made no sense, and instead insisted that declaring independence and creating a republic with a wide franchise and a unicameral (single-body) legislature was not only advisable: it was "common sense." Indeed, perhaps reflecting the energies of Levellers and other seventeenth-century radicals, Paine spoke not of looking to the past, but of "making the world anew."

No one could have predicted the popularity of Paine's *Common Sense*. Within months, more than 150,000 copies were in circulation (there were only 2.5 million people in the British North American colonies, including the enslaved), and its vision about "making the world anew" persuaded many who were otherwise hesitant to act—including those in the Second Continental Congress.

Choosing Independence

One of them was Thomas Jefferson. Jefferson was just over thirty years old, born to the Virginia gentry, a planter and enslaver who was well educated, had read the classical texts of Greece and Rome, and was familiar with the republican theories being fashioned after the Glorious Revolution in eighteenth-century Britain. He had not participated in the First Continental Congress but had submitted to that body an important tract, *A Summary View of the Rights of British Americans* (1774). In it he articulated the many grievances colonists had against Parliament and the crown, and he boldly suggested that colonists of British North America had the right to govern themselves.

At the time, Jefferson didn't persuade very many of those delegates, and, truth is, *A Summary View* expressed Jefferson's own ambivalence. "It is neither our wish, nor our interest, to separate from [Great Britain]," he wrote in conclusion. But by July 1776, twelve of the thirteen delegations at the Congress (New York was the exception) came out in support of independence, and, with the help of Benjamin Franklin and John Adams, Jefferson drafted a document to back them up. "We hold these truths to be self-evident," the Preamble to the Declaration proclaimed, "that all men are created equal, that they are endowed by their Creator with certain unalienable Rights, that among these are life, liberty, and the pursuit of happiness."

Jefferson went on to justify political revolution against established government, accuse the crown "of repeated injuries and usurpations" that amounted to "tyranny," outline the many offenses the crown had committed, and declare the former colonies to be "Free and Independent States."

The Congress spent several days in intense debate over Jefferson's draft. Delegates merely glanced at the political philosophy, finding nothing exceptional in it; the ideas about natural rights and the consent of the governed were seen as "self-evident truths," just as the document claimed. In itself, this absence of comment showed a remarkable transformation in political thinking since the end of the French and Indian War. The single phrase declaring the natural equality of "all men" was also passed over without comment; no one elaborated on its radical implications.

What the Congress did wrangle over were the specific grievances, especially regarding the issue of slavery. Jefferson had included an impassioned statement blaming the British king for enslaving Africans and "exciting those people to rise in arms among us," which delegates from Georgia and South Carolina struck out. They had no intention of denouncing their labor system as an evil practice. Congress did, however, let stand another of Jefferson's fervent grievances: blaming the king, this time for mobilizing "the merciless Indian savages" into bloody frontier warfare. It was an ill omen for the political future.

On July 4, amendments to Jefferson's text were complete, and the Congress ratified (formerly adopted) the Declaration of Independence. The document was printed and widely distributed, soon gaining the attention of George III and Parliament. Now, it seems, the Rubicon had indeed been crossed.

Conclusion: The Inevitable Fight to Come

But independence, as Jefferson and the Continental Congress well knew, was not simply to be declared. It had to be established, secured, fought for, and won militarily as well as politically and diplomatically. And it had to be won against the most formidable empire on the face of the globe, one that had alliances with other imperial powers as well as with Indigenous people in North America and perhaps, as the response to Dunmore's Proclamation revealed, with enslaved Black people as well. It was one thing to mobilize protest, to resist certain policies of Parliament, and to chase off some imperial officials. It was quite another to defeat the most powerful army and navy in the world now intent on crushing the colonial rebellion and then to create a new political entity in a world of global struggles for power.

MAPPING AMERICA

The Thirteen Colonies on the Eve of Revolution

Just before the Declaration of Independence was signed, Benjamin Franklin reflected on the stakes that were involved. "We must, indeed, all hang together," he said, "or, most assuredly, we must all hang separately." But hanging together was easier said than done. Despite calls to unify the thirteen colonies politically, sharp disparities in wealth among the three distinct regions (New England, the Middle Colonies, and the South) revealed emerging fault lines.

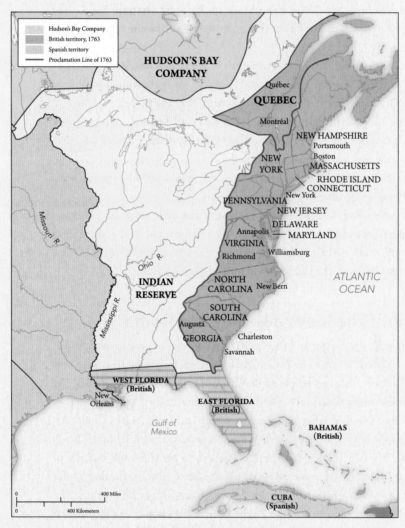

≡ **MAP 1**   A standard view of the thirteen colonies shows a unified swath of territory from Massachusetts to Georgia.

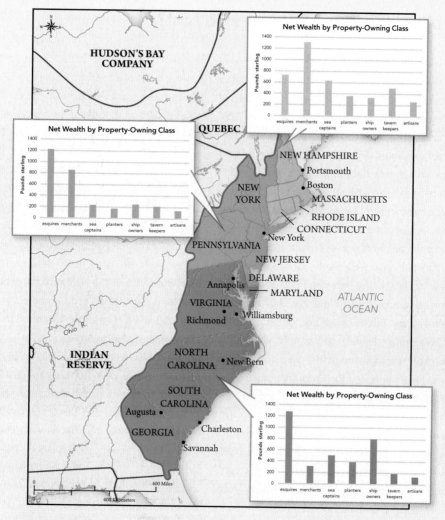

≡ **MAP 2**   Mapping the distribution of wealth reveals sharp regional differences. The South was the most affluent region, with a large portion of its wealth derived from a plantation economy dependent on enslaved labor. Most of this wealth was owned by a small number of white male landowners (esquires), however. New Englanders were less wealthy, but they enjoyed more evenly shared prosperity. In the Middle Colonies the thriving ports of Philadelphia and New York concentrated wealth in a growing merchant class.

Thinking Geographically

1. How might calls like Franklin's for political unity have been received by different economic classes of colonists? Between which groups would common ground have been most difficult to achieve?

2. What future challenges does this emerging economic inequality suggest? What might be one historical outcome of this disparity?

WHAT IF the Rebel Patriots Had Lost?

Just before the Declaration of Independence was signed, Benjamin Franklin reflected on the stakes that were involved and the risks that the members of the Second Continental Congress were taking. "We must, indeed, all hang together," he said, "or, most assuredly, we must all hang separately." By the time independence was declared, that is, the rebellion was turning in a revolutionary direction and the rebels were committing potentially treasonous offenses.

The chances of the rebel Patriots prevailing militarily and politically were not very great, and rebellions turned revolutions have a pretty bad track record in history. Mostly they are defeated or, if not defeated, are forced to accept much less than they demanded. What if the British crown had either accepted the Olive Branch Petition and committed itself to working out an arrangement that was acceptable to most of the Patriots or if the British had quickly defeated the Patriots at Lexington and Concord? The Declaration of Independence either would never have been written or would have been the artifact of failed struggle, perhaps embraced by the radically inclined but never by any country emerging in North America. Consider that Canada—formerly New France—doesn't have such a Declaration.

The Patriot leadership might well have been marginalized or imprisoned and hanged, and the colonial governments would have followed the British model of imperial rule until some sort of independence was eventually agreed to. Indigenous people, who were looking for new allies and were understandably very suspicious of the British colonists, might have benefitted greatly. Their land claims in the trans-Appalachian districts would have been better secured as speculators like the Ohio Company would have been held in better check, and they could have courted British officials diplomatically as counterweights to the colonists.

The enslaved of African descent might have benefitted, too. If the defeat of the rebellion built on moves like that of Lord Dunmore's in Virginia, a new settlement might have loosened the chains of enslavement in North America and at least given the enslaved, like Indigenous people, an ally they never had before and were not likely to have in an independent country presided over, in part by enslavers in the Chesapeake and the Carolinas. The United States as we know it would have a different origin story and a different set of Founders. The Jeffersons, Washingtons, and Franklins might seem foolhardy in retrospect or the symbols for different revolutionaries elsewhere in the world. But would such an alternative have been best for the greatest number of people on the North American continent?

DOCUMENT 6.1:   Dunmore's Proclamation (1775)

In November 1775, the royal governor of Virginia, John Murray (also known as Lord Dunmore), issued a proclamation offering freedom to any slave or "indented servant" who would join "His Majesty's Troops" in putting down the Patriot rebellion.

By his EXCELLENCY, &c.

A PROCLAMATION.

As I have ever entertained hopes that an accommodation might have taken place between *Great-Britain* and this colony, without being compelled, *by my duty*, to this most disagreeable, but now absolutely necessary step, rendered so by a body of armed men, unlawfully assembled, firing on his Majesty's tenders, and the formation of an army, and that army now on their march to attack his Majesty's troops, and destroy the well disposed subjects of this colony: To defeat such treasonable purposes, and that all such traitors, and their abetters, may be brought to justice, and that the peace and good order of this colony may be again restored, which the ordinary course of the civil law is unable to effect, I have thought fit to issue this my proclamation, hereby declaring, that until the aforesaid good purposes can be obtained, I do, in virtue of the power and authority to me given, *by his Majesty*, determine to execute martial law, and cause the same to be executed throughout this colony; and to the end that *peace* and *good order* may the sooner be restored, I do require every person capable of bearing arms to resort to his Majesty's STANDARD, or be looked upon as traitors to his Majesty's crown and government, and thereby become liable to the penalty the law inflicts upon such offences, *such as forfeiture of life, confiscation of lands*, &c. &c. And I do hereby farther declare all *indented servants, Negroes*, or others (appertaining to rebels) *free*, that are able and willing to bear arms, they *joining his Majesty's troops*, as soon as may be, for the more speedily reducing this Colony to a *proper sense* of their duty, to his Majesty's crown and dignity. I do farther order, and require all his Majesty's liege subjects to retain their quitrents, or any other taxes due, or that may become due, in their own custody, till such time as peace may be again restored to this at present most unhappy country, or demanded of them for their former salutary purposes, by officers properly authorized to receive the same.

Given on board the ship William, *off Norfolk, the 7th of* Nov.

Source: John Murray. "Lord Dunmore's Proclamation (1775)" Encyclopedia Virginia. Virginia Humanities, (07 Dec. 2020).

DOCUMENT 6.2: Neolin's Prophecy Explained by Pontiac (1763)

In the early 1760s, the Delaware prophet Neolin preached an explanation for the problems that Indigenous people faced. Robert Navarre, a French colonial resident of Detroit, was one of the few Euro-Americans who claimed to have heard the prophet's message fully expounded—not by Neolin himself but by one of his most fervent disciples, the Ottawa leader Pontiac. Speaking to a council of Ottawas, Potawatomis, and Wyandots in 1763, Pontiac explained that a Delaware man (Navarre said he was of La Nation du Loup, or the Wolf clan) was "eager to make the acquaintance of the Master of Life" and had "resolved to undertake the journey to Paradise, where he knew He resided."

[In a trance, the Delaware prophet] ... imagined that he had only to set out and by dint of traveling would arrive at the celestial dwelling. This he did the next day. Early in the morning he arose and equipped himself for a hunting journey, not forgetting to take provisions and ammunition, and a big kettle. Behold him then setting out like that on his journey to Heaven to see the Master of Life.

After the Indian was seated the Lord said to him: "I am the Master of Life, and since I know what thou desirest to know, and to whom thou wishest to speak, listen well to what I am going to say to thee and to all the Indians:

"I am He who hath created the heavens and the earth, the trees, lakes, rivers, all men, and all that thou seest and hast seen upon the earth. Because I love you, ye must do what I say and love, and not do what I hate. I do not love that ye should drink to the point of madness, as ye do; and I do not like that ye should fight one another. Ye take two wives, or run after the wives of others; ye do not well, and I hate that. Ye ought to have but one wife, and keep her till death. When ye wish to go to war, ye conjure and resort to the medicine dance, believing that ye speak to me; ye are mistaken—it is to Manitou that ye speak, an evil spirit who prompts you to nothing but wrong, and who listens to you out of ignorance of me.

"This land where ye dwell I have made for you and not for others. Whence comes it that ye permit the Whites upon your lands? Can ye not live without them? I know that those whom ye call the children of your Great Father supply your needs, but if ye were not evil, as ye are, ye could surely do without them. Ye could live as ye did live before knowing them—before those whom ye call your brothers had come upon your lands. Did ye not live by the bow and arrow? Ye had no need of gun or powder, or anything else, and nevertheless ye caught animals to live upon and to dress yourselves with their skins. But when I saw that ye were given up to evil, I led the wild animals to the depths of the forest so that ye had to depend upon your brothers to feed and shelter you. Ye have only to become good again and do what I wish, and I will send back the animals for your food. I do not forbid you to permit among you the children of your [French] Father; I love them. They know me and pray to me, and I supply their wants and all they give you. But as to those who come to trouble your lands—drive them out, make war upon them. I do not love them at all; they know me not, and are my enemies, and the enemies of your brothers. Send them back to the lands which I have created for them and let them stay there. Here is a prayer which I give thee in writing to learn by heart and to teach to the Indians and their children."

The Wolf replied that he did not know how to read. He was told that when he should have returned to earth he would have only to give the prayer to the chief of his village who would read it and teach him and all the Indians to know it by heart; and he must say it night and morning without fail, and do what he has just been told to do; and he was to tell all the Indians for and in the name of the Master of Life:

"Do not drink more than once, or at most twice in a day; have only one wife and do not run after the wives of others nor after the girls; do not fight among yourselves; do not 'make medicine,' but pray, because in 'making medicine' one talks with the evil spirit; drive off your lands those dogs clothed in red who will do you nothing but harm. And when ye shall have need of anything address yourselves to me; and as to your brothers, I shall give to you as to them; do not sell to your brothers what I have put on earth for food. In short, become good and ye shall receive your needs. When ye meet one another exchange greeting and proffer the left hand which is nearest the heart.

The Wolf promised to do faithfully what the Master of Life told him, and that he would recommend it well to the Indians, and that the Master of Life would be pleased with them. Then the same man who had led him by the hand came to get him and conducted him to the foot of the mountain where he told him to take his outfit again and return to his village. The Wolf did this, and upon his arrival the members of his tribe and village were greatly surprised, for they did not know what had become of him, and they asked where he had been. As he was enjoined not to speak to anybody before he had talked with the chief of his village, he made a sign with his hand that he had come from on high. Upon entering the village he went straight to the cabin of the chief to whom he gave what had been given to him,—namely, the prayer and the law which the Master of Life had given him.

"In all things I command thee to repeat every morning and night the prayer which I have given."

Source: Collections of the Pioneer Society of the State of Michigan together with Reports of County Pioneer Societies, Volume VIII, Second Edition (Lansing, MI: 1907), 270–271.

Thinking About Contingency

1. How would you assess the relative strengths and weaknesses of the British Empire and the North American British colonies?
2. Where would support for remaining in the British Empire have come from if the British crown and Parliament showed more flexibility?
3. What sort of reforms might have been acceptable even to Patriot leaders before the Declaration of Independence was written and ratified?
4. What might the British have done to gain the upper hand militarily from the outset of the fighting in North America?

REVIEW QUESTIONS

1. Why did hostilities between the British and the French erupt in the Ohio country?

2. How did the small-scale struggles in North America become central to a global war? Who were the major combatants in the Seven Years' War, and what sort of alliances did they make in North America? How were Native Americans involved in what we call the French and Indian War?

3. Why did the religious revivals led in Massachusetts by John Edwards spread to become the First Great Awakening? How were enslaved and free people of African descent involved? What stimulated the spiritual awakening of Indigenous peoples?

4. What did British victory in the Seven Years' War mean for the North American colonies, and how did they attempt to reward their Native allies? How did Native Americans understand the new political situation, now that the French had been defeated?

5. How did British policies after the Seven Years' War serve to antagonize North American colonists? What were their objections to the British imperial system?

6. When did grievances about British imperial policies turn into ideas about American independence, and why?

KEY TERMS

Albany Congress (p. 212)

Boston Massacre (p. 230)

Coercive Acts (p. 234)

committees of correspondence (p. 234)

committees of safety (p. 236)

Covenant Chain (p. 211)

First Continental Congress (p. 235)

First Great Awakening (p. 219)

French and Indian War (p. 216)

League of the Iroquois (p. 211)

nonimportation agreements (p. 227)

Ohio Company (p. 208)

Olive Branch Petition (p. 238)

Pan-Indian identity (p. 222)

Plan for Union (p. 212)

Pontiac's War (p. 222)

Royal Proclamation of 1763 (p. 224)

Second Continental Congress (p. 238)

Seven Years' War (p. 216)

Sons of Liberty (p. 230)

Stamp Act (p. 226)

Tea Act (p. 229)

Townshend Acts (p. 229)

Treaty of Paris (p. 217)

RECOMMENDED READINGS

Danielle Allen, *Our Declaration* (W.W. Norton, 2014).

Daniel Baugh, *The Global Seven Years War, 1754–1763* (Routledge, 2014).

Gregory Evans Dowd, *War Under Heaven: Pontiac, the Indian Nations, and the British Empire* (Johns Hopkins University Press, 2004).

Woody Holton, *Liberty Is Sweet: The Hidden History of the American Revolution* (Simon and Schuster, 2021).

Thomas S. Kidd, *The Great Awakening: A Brief History with Documents* (Bedford St. Martin, 2007).

Gary Nash, *Urban Crucible: Northern Seaports and the Origin of the American Revolution* (Harvard University Press, 1979).

Thomas Paine, *Common Sense* (1776).

Barbara Clark Smith, *The Freedoms We Lost: Consent and Resistance in Revolutionary America* (New Press, 2010).

Alan Taylor, *American Revolutions: A Continental History, 1750–1804* (W.W. Norton, 2016).

Richard White, *The Middle Ground: Indians, Empires, and Republics in the Great Lakes Region, 1650–1815* (Cambridge University Press, 1991).

7

A Political Revolution
1776–1791

Chapter Outline

≡ **Benjamin Franklin** The statesman, diplomat, and scientist in a c. 1777–1778 portrait by French painter Joseph Siffred Duplessis. Duplessis's Benjamin Franklin is on the US hundred-dollar bill.

In September 1787, after four hot and often trying months, Benjamin Franklin rose to address his fellow delegates at the Constitutional Convention in the city of Philadelphia. At the age of eighty-one, Franklin was the oldest of the delegates and one of the few to have participated in most of the key events leading to this remarkable moment. Looking out at his weary colleagues, he acknowledged that there were parts of the new Constitution "which I do not at present approve" but doubted that "any other convention may be able to make a better constitution." "For when you assemble a number of men to have the advantage of their joint wisdom," he continued, "you inevitably assemble with those men all their prejudices, their passions, their errors of opinions, their local interests, and their selfish views." And so, he would "consent to this constitution"—to sign it as he had the Declaration of Independence in 1776 and the Treaty of Paris in 1783—"because I expect no better, and because I am not sure that it is not the best."

Timeline

1776	1777	1778	1779	1780	1781	1782	1783	1784

1776 ›
July Declaration of Independence signed
August British land troops near New York City and soon take control
December Washington crosses Delaware and attacks Trenton and Princeton (January 1777)

1777 ›
September British troops capture Philadelphia; Continental Congress flees to Lancaster, Pennsylvania
October Patriot troops defeat the British at the Battle of Saratoga

1778 ›
February Continental Congress signs Treaty of Alliance with France
December British troops capture Savannah, Georgia

1779 ›
June General Henry Clinton issues Philipsburg Proclamation freeing enslaved peoples of Patriots who sided with the British

1780 ›
March–May British troops capture Charles Town, South Carolina

1781 ›
March Articles of Confederation ratified
October General Cornwallis surrenders at Yorktown

1783 ›
September Treaty of Paris signed, with British recognizing American independence

Franklin's was hardly a ringing endorsement of a founding document, but in this, as in other matters, he was measured, thoughtful, and cognizant of the complex political forces at play. Indeed, shortly after he left the convention, Elizabeth Willing Powel, the wife of Philadelphia's mayor and an important force in her own right, apparently asked Franklin about the convention's deliberations. "Well, doctor," she said, "what have we got, a republic or a monarchy?" "A republic," Franklin famously replied, "if you can keep it."

The Constitutional Convention capped an extraordinary period, just over a decade in length, when some Americans declared independence, fought the British to achieve it, attempted to create a union of states, endured several years of social and political unrest, created another framework of governance, and then struggled over whether or not to live under it. As Franklin suggested in his speech to the Convention, it was

1785	1786	1787	1788	1789	1790	1791	1792	1793

1786 >
Fall– Winter Shays's Rebellion

1787 >
May Constitutional Convention opens in Philadelphia
September Constitutional Convention adopts Constitution and sends it to the states for ratification

1788 >
June Constitution ratified when the ninth of thirteen states agrees to it

1789 >
March First Congress under Constitution meets in New York City
April First US President under Constitution, George Washington, inaugurated in New York City

1791 >
December Bill of Rights adopted

a tumultuous process, a conflict of ideas and ideals, of hopes and fears, that raised serious questions, not only in Franklin's mind, about what the future of independence might bring—even about what to call the series of events that had occurred.

We have come to call the battle for American independence and the creation of an independent political confederation a "revolution." This is, in large measure, because the idea of a revolution—a dramatic break from the past and the making of something new—is a central part of our origin story, of how the United States was forged and would then emerge as a distinctive and "exceptional" country.

Yet, if we look at the period between the mid-1770s and the late 1780s, between the time when the battle for independence began and the Constitution of the United States was written and ratified, all sorts of things were going on simultaneously. The struggle we have come to call a "revolution" was mostly an armed rebellion and civil war before it became a revolution—and a political revolution, in particular. In fact, at certain times it seemed that the British were attempting to be the revolutionaries and the Patriots the conservators of established order.

The objectives of resistance to British rule and rebellion against it united the large numbers of North American colonists known as **Patriots**. But they divided colonists as well, both between the Patriots and the **Loyalists**, who wanted to maintain North America's place in the British Empire, and between those Patriots who differed—sometimes radically—in their views of the political solution that should follow American independence. In the end, a political revolution did take place, though one that established a shaky foundation of American unity.

7.1   Fighting It Out

‖ Describe how the military struggle over American independence unfolded.

When the Second Continental Congress declared American independence in July 1776, Patriot rebels and the British army had been fighting for well over a year. Some of the Patriots had enlisted in the **Continental Army** that the Congress had created; many others fought in militia companies that had been established in different colonies, oftentimes in local towns and counties. Although the British were surprised by the Patriots' tenacity and suffered more casualties and setbacks than they had expected, the Declaration of Independence initially seemed to represent more an abstract hope than a likely reality.

The British Perspective

Yet Patriots had more than a little to show for their rebellion by July 1776. They had forced the British to evacuate military forces from Boston in March 1776, and they had turned back a British attack on Charles Town, South Carolina, in June. That was the good news for them. But Patriot efforts to invade Canada and bolster their position on the North American continent were disastrously defeated that same spring, and as Thomas Jefferson was putting the final touches on the Declaration in early July, a massive British force of over 30,000 troops together with several thousand Hessian soldiers had landed on Staten Island, near New York City, with the intention to crush the Patriots' rebellion. Looking back from our twenty-first-century perspective, the ratification of the Declaration on July 4, 1776, appears as a defining moment of our history; for those on the ground at the time, it may have seemed something of a futile gesture.

British troops in New York served under the command of General William Howe, who had retreated from Boston several months before and was not about to let something like that happen again. He knew very well that the heart of the Patriot rebellion was in New England, so his idea was to secure a base in New York, extend his reach to the south, where loyalism was thought to be more widespread, and effectively isolate New England from the rest of the colonies until he was ready to pounce. It appeared to be a strategy that would do the job.

In August 1776, Howe landed a force of 20,000 British soldiers on Long Island and soon drove Washington's Continental Army across the East River into Manhattan, then north into Westchester County (where they were defeated at White Plains), then into New Jersey, and eventually farther south and west into Pennsylvania. Unlike in Boston, Howe's troops were greeted as liberators by many New York Loyalists, who quickly produced their own "declaration of dependence," signaling their allegiance to the empire and boosting British morale. For his part, Howe, believing he now held the upper hand, summoned members of the Continental Congress to hear his offer of a deal, including pardons, if they gave up their quest for independence. Despite the dispiriting military circumstances, the congressmen—who included John Adams and Benjamin Franklin—refused the deal. "Now nothing remains but to fight it out," Howe's secretary recorded (see Map 7.1).

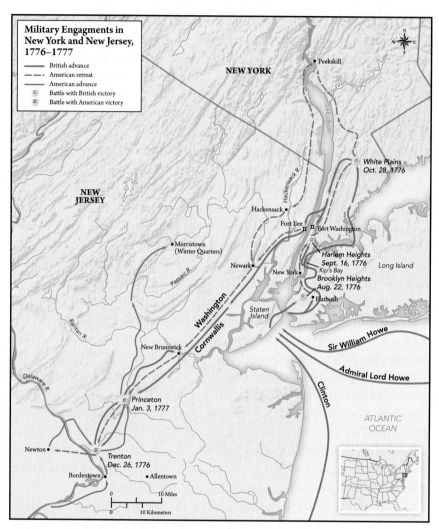

≡ **MAP 7.1**   **Military Engagements in New York and New Jersey, 1776–1777**

Fighting it out, at this point, seemed clearly to favor the British. Indeed, as 1776 drew to a close, the Continental Army was unraveling as weary men deserted or headed home when their terms of enlistment—at first, one year—expired. Many New Jerseyans followed loyalist New Yorkers in either abandoning support for the Patriot side or publicly expressing their support for the empire. "I think the game is pretty near up," Washington confided in a letter to the Congress. Desperate for a victory, Washington led a bold crossing of the Delaware River amid a storm of snow and sleet on the night of December 25 into neighboring New Jersey, where his forces surprised slumbering Hessians the next day at Trenton. He then moved on to nearby Princeton, where his now small army defeated a larger British force before heading off into the New Jersey hills to recoup. The two quick victories renewed Patriot enthusiasm for Washington and his soldiers. But Howe was soon heading out of New York to Philadelphia, both to capture what the Patriots regarded as their capital and, once again, to take on Washington, hoping at last to finish him off. At the prospect, the Continental Congress fled west to the town of Lancaster.

The British had another plan in the works, this one a reflection of Howe's interest in severing the troublesome New Englanders from the rest of the colonists. It was to be a **Three-Pronged Attack** to take control of the New York colony: (1) British General John Burgoyne would move his troops south from Montreal, (2) Colonel Barry St. Leger would move troops east from Lake Ontario, and (3) Howe would move up the Hudson River Valley. All would meet around Albany, defeating Patriot outfits along the way.

But Howe decided to go to Philadelphia instead, and Burgoyne met unexpected resistance from the Patriot side, whose numbers swelled. In October, at Saratoga, rather than securing British dominance in New York, Burgoyne was forced to surrender to Patriot General Horatio Gates, who had cleverly outmaneuvered him in what was a major defeat for the British. Farther to the south, however, Howe's troops were ensconced in Philadelphia, and Washington's Continental Army was about to spend a frigid winter in nearby Valley Forge, Pennsylvania, where about 2,000 of them—almost 20 percent—would die of disease and starvation. Washington's hope had been to wear the British down and convince them to give up the fight and accept American independence. But, by all accounts, it was Washington and his army who were being worn down and maybe worn out.

≡ John Trumbull, *Surrender of General Burgoyne at Saratoga* (1826)
Connecticut-born John Trumbull was an American artist best known for his historical paintings of the American Revolution, of which he was a veteran. This depiction of a pivotal moment in the war, which was painted decades after the events of October 17, 1777, is displayed alongside Trumbull's painting of the signing of the Declaration of Independence in the Rotunda of the Capitol Building in Washington, DC. The American General Horatio Gates (*center*) is shown as a statesman and diplomat as well as a soldier. He refuses to accept the sword offered as a gesture of surrender by the British General John Burgoyne, instead treating Burgoyne as a fellow gentleman.

PERSPECTIVES

Iconography and Myth Making

The crossing of the Delaware River by Washington and his troops on a miserable Christmas night in 1776 is one of the best-known events of the American Revolution as well as a tremendous example of military strategy and daring. There were, of course, no photojournalists or videographers accompanying Washington and his troops. The visual depictions with which we are most familiar were created decades after the Battle of Trenton. They portray Washington as more of an iconic figure than a human soldier or statesman and contribute to a myth of America as a brave and democratic entity for the rest of the world to imitate. Thomas Sully's painting from 1819 is the earliest known depiction of that Christmas night. Here, Washington is on a white horse on the Pennsylvania side of the river, just before he dismounts to join his troops in the crossing to the New Jersey side. To the right of Washington, Generals Henry Knox, Nathanael Greene, and John Sullivan prepare for the crossing. Shown among the generals is Washington's personal valet, William Lee. Lee, an enslaved Black man, wears

≡ Thomas Sully, *The Passage of the Delaware* (1819).

the hat of an officer. Washington relied on Lee throughout the war, but Lee remained enslaved until Washington died and granted Lee freedom in his will.

The immigrant German painter Emanuel Leutze painted *Washington Crossing the Delaware* in 1851, at a time of increasing social and political unrest in the United States. Much about the painting is historically inaccurate. The version of the flag depicted, for example, wasn't adopted until 1777, a year after the crossing. And the actual crossing used much larger boats capable of holding horses and cannons as well as soldiers, not the small frail rowboat imagined by Leutze. The figures in the boat represent many diverse backgrounds working together: a Black man (perhaps William Lee?) is just in front of Washington, along with a man wearing Scottish clothes. At the back of the boat, a man dressed as a Western frontiersman is steering. Leutze was in Germany when he painted this scene, hoping not only to capture a mythical moment in American history but also to inspire political change in Germany.

≡ **Emanuel Leutze,** *Washington Crossing the Delaware* **(1851).**

CONSIDER THIS

With which of these two paintings are you more familiar? Why do you think one painting is more famous than the other, even though neither image—painted decades after the Battle of Trenton—can be considered historically accurate?

Finding Soldiers to Fight

Some of the challenges that the Patriot side faced in this War for Independence were revealed in the small town of Peterborough, New Hampshire, population 549 in 1775. If the local records are accurate, 170 of the town's men performed military service for the Patriots, which means that virtually every eligible man there carried a gun at some point. This would seem to be a remarkable indication of popular support for the Patriot cause. But it also turns out that fewer than one-third of these Peterborough men served for more than one year, and only twenty-four of them served for the entire war. Landowners, artisans, and merchants—those who would seem to have the greatest stake in the fight—tended to give it up quickly. They had property and families and, given the war's duration and uncertain outcome, more often than not returned home when their term of enlistment was up. Those who were best off, from the local elite, often served for only a month or two in locally raised units, mainly to defend their town. By contrast, the hard-bitten twenty-four, those who stuck it out, generally came from the bottom end of the social scale. They were poor, propertyless laboring folk, regularly on the move; at least two of them were Black.

Had this been just a Peterborough story, it would be interesting but not especially meaningful. But it wasn't just a Peterborough story. It was the story of just about every place in the British colonies from which we have information. Well before the Battle of Saratoga and perhaps as early as those of Trenton and Princeton, the Patriot side was facing a serious problem of manpower, of staffing the Continental Army and local militias with enough troops to keep the British at bay and maintain control of territory where the inhabitants supported them. The Patriots clearly needed allies. Where should they look?

Some of the colonies, including Massachusetts, resorted to a draft to fill the ranks of their local units, though for the most part these efforts failed because most towns refused to comply. There was better luck with African Americans, many of whom were enslaved. Massachusetts and Rhode Island, responding to pressure from Black people themselves and hoping to meet quotas established by the Continental Congress, accepted them for military service. Rhode Island went so far as to promise freedom to any enslaved man who would join the Patriot cause, much the same as Lord Dunmore had done for the British side in Virginia (as we saw in Chapter 6—under pressure from enslavers, Rhode Island repealed the law but not before 100 Black men had enlisted). Before too long, Washington and the Continental Army, despite serious reservations (Washington was an enslaver himself), endorsed the recruitment of the enslaved with the promise of freedom—as well as compensation for their enslavers. But farther to the south, the idea gained no traction. South Carolina rejected it and instead attempted to find more white recruits by promising them land and enslaved Black people in return for their military service. Virginia, Washington's home, did something similar.

The Continental Army also confronted the dilemma of enlistment and desertion among those comfortably placed and so looked to recruits who would be willing to join until the war eventually ended. After all, their prospects were already limited, and service in the Continental Army brought with it food, shelter, and at least the promise of pay. The terms of enlistment were extended from one to three years, and, over time, poor white men and Black men, many of whom had been enslaved, made up a substantial portion of the Patriot military forces. Before the war's end, Black people may have made up roughly 10 percent of the Continental Army.

Black Soldiers in the War for Independence The French officer Jean-Baptiste-Antoine de Verger kept a sketchbook of his observations, including this 1781 image of soldiers from the Rhode Island Regiment of the Continental Army. In 1778, Rhode Island offered enslaved Black men (like the soldier depicted here) freedom if they joined the regiment. Historians estimate that as many as 9,000 men of African descent served in the Continental Army and Navy.

Complex Choices in Indigenous America

What of Indigenous people? Could they be lured as allies? In New England and the Middle Colonies, as well as in North Carolina, the Indigenous people who still remained were relatively few in number and living in small villages surrounded by white settlements. They had long before been defeated and then subjected to the authority and demands of whites, so were in no position to do much more than the whites' bidding. Thus some, including the Catawbas in the Carolinas, responded to Patriot appeals and fought with them against the British.

Matters were different farther to the west. From the Great Lakes to the lower Mississippi Valley, Indigenous people had been reconstituting their villages and looking for new trading partners since the French had been driven out after the Seven Years' War (discussed in Chapter 6). Some had begun establishing relations with the victorious British, who had better goods and diplomatic presents to offer. Like the Patriots, at first the British hoped that the Indigenous people would remain neutral. But by 1777 the British knew that they needed help.

It wasn't a difficult decision from the Indigenous perspective. While Indigenous people had their own concerns about British intentions and initially regarded the conflict as a civil war between white colonists and their imperial overseers, they had little doubt about what the Patriots would have in store for them. Patriots and their settler allies would be after Indigenous lands and ready to exterminate those who stood in their way. This the Cherokees learned to their sorrow when, after attacking some white settlements in the early summer of 1776, they faced the wrath of several thousand Patriot militiamen, who burned their villages and forced them into the Appalachian Mountains or the more distant reaches of Georgia.

The Iroquois nations learned much the same. Although the Oneidas leaned to the Patriot side largely because of the influence of a Protestant missionary among them, most of the Iroquois—especially the formidable Mohawks led by war chief Joseph Brant—supported the British and fought with them, especially at the very bloody Battle of Oriskany, part of the 1777 Saratoga campaign. General Washington then decided to settle the score. He ordered Patriot troops into Iroquois country so that their villages "may not be merely overrun but destroyed." More than forty of the villages, chiefly those of the Senecas and Cayugas, were then scorched to the ground, with the result that a great many of the Indigenous people fled west to British lines.

But Indigenous people were not simply being run through by the Patriots. With British encouragement, they launched brutal raids on vulnerable white settlements in western Pennsylvania and western Virginia, well into what was then the county of Kentucky. Shawnees, Delawares, and Seneca-Cayugas laid waste to farms and farmers, killing or capturing many hundreds of them, women and children as well as men. Indeed, as was true during the Seven Years' War and Pontiac's War, the strategic Ohio country became a focus of conflict, a symbol in many ways of the struggle for control of North America east of the Mississippi River.

≣ **Portrait of Power**   The great Mohawk military strategist, leader, and diplomat Joseph Brant, together with his sister Molly, was an important Loyalist ally of the British. This 1797 portrait of Brant by Charles Willson Peale is just one among many by famous artists of the time. Brant, who traveled to London to meet directly with King George III, preferred to wear traditional Mohawk clothing at such occasions.

The Crucial French Alliance

The most important allies the Patriot cause won came not from the North American continent but

from across the Atlantic: from France. It might have seemed an odd development because British colonists had fought against the French during the Seven Years' War and helped defeat and dislodge them from North America. But now that the British Empire itself was being wracked by conflict and warfare, the French looked to gain an advantage and perhaps some serious revenge.

At first, the French King Louis XVI and his foreign minister Charles Gravier (the Comte de Vergennes) agreed to send supplies to the Patriots under a veil of secrecy, largely through the auspices of the Dutch. But three factors combined to cause the French to enter the conflict formally: the influence of Benjamin Franklin, who was in Paris as an American representative; the Patriot victory at Saratoga, which suggested that the Patriots could well prevail; and the rebuilding of the French navy. In early 1778, France and commissioners from the Continental Congress signed a **Treaty of Alliance**, officially recognizing American independence and providing for military and material support. Another political Rubicon had now been crossed.

The alliance reconfigured the entire military and political geography of the conflict. Not surprisingly, the British quickly responded by declaring war on France. A year later, the Spanish joined the French and Americans against the British, and, suddenly, what had begun as a North American struggle—much as was true two decades earlier in the Seven Years' War—became international in scope. Rather than focusing their energies on the Patriots, the British now had to divert resources to a variety of locations around the world. They had to defend their valuable West Indian sugar islands, their strategic posts on Gibraltar and Minorca adjacent to Spain, their East India Company's lucrative footholds in south Asia, and their vital slave trading base in Senegambia, all of which (except for Gibraltar) they had secured at the end of the Seven Years' War. What's more, the prospect of a French-Spanish invasion of Britain itself—widely rumored at the time—required the British to retain much of their navy close to home instead of in the ports and off the coast of North America. It was as if the global warfare of the 1750s and 1760s was being reenacted and, at this point, not to the advantage of Britain.

Recognizing how precarious their situation had become, the British government made one last effort to reach a truce with the rebellious North American colonies, offering a newly balanced imperial relationship that included parliamentary representation for the colonists. The Continental Congress would have none of it. Independence was now the bottom line. And although the British and their loyalist allies then promised "fire and sword," the Patriot rebels, fortified by their European allies, determined to take them on (see Map 7.2).

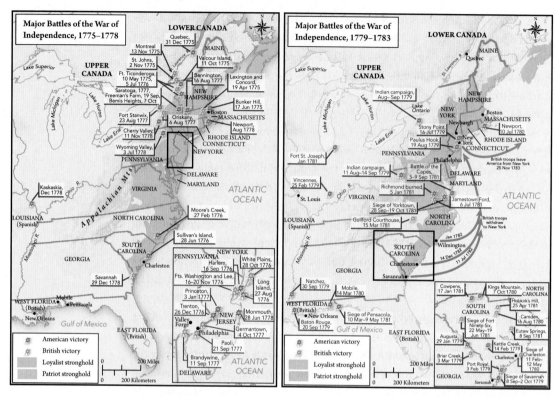

≡ **MAP 7.2**   **Major Battles of the War of Independence**

7.2   Enemies

||| Explain the deep divisions the battle for independence provoked among North American colonists.

We tend to view the American War of Independence as an effectively two-sided conflict: the Patriots on the one side and the British government and army on the other, the first battling for independence and the second attempting to restore the imperial relationship in North America. Yet the actual War of Independence was far more complex and far bloodier. It was, in fact, not only a story of colonial rebellion but also one of civil warfare within the colonies themselves.

Loyalism

John Adams once estimated that about one-third of the colonists supported the Patriots, about one-third supported the British, and about one-third were on the fence. He may have underestimated the Patriot supporters and the fence-sitters and overestimated the Loyalists. But Loyalism was substantial in size and diverse in character. Our best guess is that Loyalists composed somewhere between 15 and 20 percent of the white colonial population (not counting the thousands of enslaved people who fought with the British or the many Indigenous people who allied and fought with them), and that they could be found in every occupation and religious denomination. They were farmers and artisans as well as merchants and lawyers, bakers and laborers as well as ship owners and colonial officials. And they were Methodists, Quakers, and Catholics as well as Anglicans. Indeed, it is likely that when the War for Independence erupted in 1775, every white Patriot knew a Loyalist and probably more than one.

What made the difference in their political leanings? For some Loyalists the choice was obvious. They served the British government in some official capacity, benefitted from the rules of trade that the Navigation Acts established, had great wealth they believed the empire protected, or were culturally attached to the British crown and its aristocratic traditions. Others—Anglicans in Puritan New England, Germans in Quaker Pennsylvania, or the Dutch in Anglo New Jersey— had experienced the hostility of American colonists and thought the empire offered them more tolerance and breathing room. Still others were part of communities who had made their peace with the British system and were prospering despite complaints they might have had.

Many Loyalists did share the colonial grievances of those who would become Patriots. They bridled at the new taxes Parliament imposed, groused about the restrictions imposed by the Proclamation Line of 1763, and disliked the heavy handedness of the Coercive Acts. But they remained devoted to the British crown, to the British constitution, and to the prospect of working out conflicts and disagreements within the imperial system. Many also doubted that the Patriots could defeat the armed might of the empire and looked to side with the winners.

Patriots Versus Loyalists

But the divide between Patriots and Loyalists was not one of polite difference. It was deep and brutally contested. Even before Lexington and Concord, Patriots and their sympathizers harassed the colonists who refused to support their boycotts and the colonial officials required to enforce Parliamentary acts. They imposed fines on those who wouldn't take Patriot oaths and prohibited Loyalists from practicing law, serving as ministers, printing newspapers, or teaching in schools. Loyalists and suspected Loyalists could be jostled on the streets, have their homes desecrated, and suffer physical punishment. Tarring and feathering was widely used both to defile Loyalist bodies and shame them in the eyes of the

A New Method of MACARONY MAKING, as practised
217   at BOSTON in NORTH AMERICA .
Printed for Carington Bowles, N.º 69 in S.ᵗ Pauls Church Yard. London. Published 12 Octᵉʳ 1774.

≡ **Tarring and Feathering**   In this print published
in London in 1774, two American revolutionaries
tar and feather a Loyalist tax collector in Boston.
The caption, "New Method of Macarony Making
as Practiced at Boston," is satirical. To be a
"macarony" (sometimes spelled "macaroni") in
British slang at the time was to be very fancy in
the way you dressed; in the song "Yankee Doodle
Dandy," the line "Stuck a feather in his cap and
called it 'macaroni'" mocks an American simpleton
who thought that a single feather was enough to
make him a dandy.

public. Other Loyalists were subject to whippings, rid-
den on rails (forced to straddle a fence rail held on the
shoulders of two or more bearers, who then paraded the
victim around town), or driven out of their communities entirely. So powerful could these hatreds become
that John Adams insisted he would *hang his own brother*
if he sided with the Loyalists (his brothers didn't side
with the Loyalists).

In some places Loyalists responded by forming their
own associations, with secret military units, though
for the most part they were no match for the mobilizations of the Patriot side. Bullied and terrorized, many
of the Loyalists fled to the relative safety of British
encampments or to towns and cities where they made
up the majority, leaving behind homes and property
that Patriots would confiscate or destroy. For many
Loyalists, there would be no going back.

The violence that exploded between Patriots and
Loyalists was emblematic of a general struggle in
which rules of warfare were barely observed or outright
flouted. Reports of atrocities committed by both sides
spread through the press and by word of mouth, and
although British and Hessian troops were accused
more often than were the Patriots, the ground was dark
and bloody all around. Indeed, some of the worst abuses occurred not between the Continental Army and the
Army of the British but between Patriot and Loyalist
militias conducting their own forms of attack and retribution, well beyond official gaze. Each side took the
opportunity to plunder the farms and communities of
their enemies, rape vulnerable women, and put to death those regarded as the leaders or even mere supporters. In Virginia, Patriot Colonel Charles Lynch was so
quick to hang suspected Loyalists that he not only left a bloody mark on the period but also gave the country a term—lynching—to describe a horrific category of
extralegal execution.

Not surprisingly, those taken prisoner—by the Patriots and the British alike—
often suffered egregious abuse. They were sent to dark and dank confinements,
harassed and beaten, barely fed. Disease ran rampant and mortality rates spiked.
Early on, the British did not generally regard Patriot captives as prisoners of war

since, given the circumstances and the attitude of the crown, they were instead seen as rebels or treasonous subjects. Before long, however, British officials recognized that treating Patriot captives as traitors or rebels courted retaliation against their own troops and so made amends in policy. But this did little to help prisoners, especially those who were not officers, survive a truly perilous ordeal.

The extent to which the Patriot rebellion turned into civil warfare not only showed the serious fractures in the North American colonies but also left wounds that would be difficult to heal. In 1778 it was not at all clear how or when the War for Independence would end, but it was clear that it would be difficult to make allies of these now bloodied enemies and that there would be nasty reckonings well into the future.

7.3   The War Shifts South

Assess why the British changed their military strategy and how it resulted in their defeat.

By 1778, it was also clear that the British had failed to put down the Patriot rebellion either in New England or in the Middle Colonies. A new strategy was necessary. As we have seen, once the British were at war with the French and the Spanish as well as with the Patriots, they could no longer send more troops or naval vessels to North America. They were now busy elsewhere, especially in the West Indies, where British, French, and Spanish plantation colonies were in close proximity and therefore vulnerable to attack. Having looked to the northeast since 1775, the British now would look to the South and hope for better results.

The British Stumble Unexpectedly

The turn of the British government and military command to the southern colonies, in particular to Georgia and South Carolina, reflected a changed perspective on the war. At the outset, the British intended to wage war where support for the Patriots seemed rife and therefore where the rebellion could be stamped out. Now they looked to consolidate their efforts where Loyalism was more widespread and their troops might have an easier time of it. Loyalist allies could be found, they believed, both among wealthy slaveholders with large estates as well as among squatters and hunters in the backcountry who had been harassed by landowners large and small. In the South, too, were Indigenous people—Chickasaws, Choctaws, and remnants of the Cherokees—who had experienced more than their share of bad brushes with white colonists and saw the British as possible allies. In a sense, moving south offered the British a chance to "Americanize" the war: to take important port cities, move through the hinterlands, and, in the process, recruit Loyalists to their fighting force while putting them in control of territory they had reconquered—no need for more British troops or officials on the ground.

At first, the plan seemed to work like a charm. The British, under orders from General Henry Clinton, struck first in December 1778 at Savannah, where despite the support of French troops—including free soldiers of color from the island of Saint Domingue—the Patriots were badly defeated and forced to retreat toward South Carolina. The British then launched an attack on the port city of Charles Town, South Carolina, in March 1780, and after several months of fighting and siege, captured it along with the largest number of Patriot soldiers and supplies of the entire war. As they had been in New York and New Jersey, British troops were welcomed into Charles Town by Loyalists, many of them rich merchants and enslavers, who were happy to be liberated from what they called Patriot tyranny and "rank democracy." It was just what the British had hoped to find in the South, and they followed their victory at Charles Town with one, under the command of Charles (Lord) Cornwallis, at Camden, South Carolina, later that summer. In triumph they then headed into North Carolina. "The Country," a British officer crowed, "is intirely conquered; the People crowd in from all quarters to deliver up their arms."

It seemed that only a mopping-up operation remained before British authority in the southern colonies was secured. But there was unexpected trouble. For one thing, Clinton was heavy-handed in his rule over the territory his troops had occupied and then demanded that eligible Carolinians serve in the Loyalist militia. What's more, Clinton himself had issued a proclamation in June 1779—from Philipsburg, New York, so it's known as the **Philipsburg Proclamation**—that built on Dunmore's Proclamation of 1775 and offered enslaved people owned by Patriots freedom and protection if they joined the British side.

Not surprisingly, word of Clinton's move spread quickly among the dense enslaved populations in Georgia and the Carolinas. "Upon the approach of any detachment of the King's army," British Colonel Banastre Tarleton observed, "all negroes, men, women, and children thought themselves absolved from all respect to their American masters, and entirely released from servitude." So many enslaved people "quitted the plantations and followed the army" (at least 5,000 in Georgia alone) that Clinton was forced to step in and start returning enslaved people who were owned by Loyalists. Now who were the revolutionaries? The fate of the enslaved and the system of enslavement was plainly of issue during the War of Independence (see Table 7.1).

Table 7.1	Black Population in 1770	
New England	Maine	475*
	Massachusetts	4,754*
	New Hampshire	654*
	Vermont	25*
	Connecticut	5,698†
	Rhode Island	3,761†
Mid-Atlantic	New York	19,112†
	New Jersey	8,220†
	Pennsylvania	5,761*
	Delaware	1,836
South	Maryland	63,818‡
	Virginia	187,605‡
	North Carolina	69,600‡
	South Carolina	75,178‡
	Georgia	10,625‡

Black population as percentage of total population, 1770

*less than 3%

†between 3% and 20%

‡between 20% and 38%

All of this sowed doubts in the minds of many white colonists, especially land and slaveholders, who initially were inclined to the British side. Thus, rather than stabilizing the political situation to their benefit, the British reoccupation provoked new rounds of civil warfare, much of it conducted through guerilla means. Patriot irregulars, often led by backcountry planters, began to harass British troops, inflicting significant casualties and making it difficult for them to hold the territory they had marched through. Cornwallis grew frustrated by the guerilla attacks, preferring instead to fight the Patriots on a battlefield with which he was familiar.

Adding to the British woes in the Carolinas was the arrival of Patriot General Nathanael Greene. A favorite of Washington, he took command of demoralized Patriot troops in December 1780 and rallied them to continue harassing and then eluding Cornwallis's troops. After a stunning victory at Cowpens, North Carolina, in January 1781, Greene's men not only became more confident but they also attracted Patriot militias from as far away as Virginia, soon outnumbering Cornwallis's forces. When Cornwallis then took his troops to coastal Wilmington,

North Carolina, in order to regroup and recover, Greene headed into South Carolina.

The Road to Yorktown

What would Cornwallis do now? Rather than pursue Greene to the south and run the risk of more setbacks, he decided to head north into Virginia, where he believed he could fight on his own terms. That he did and, it seemed, to very good effect. Cornwallis gained the upper hand on the battlefields, wrought havoc on Patriot settlements, and even forced Thomas Jefferson—Virginia's wartime governor—and the Virginia assembly to take flight. During the course of the campaign, around 4,000 enslaved people headed to the British, sixteen of whom belonged to Washington and twenty-three to Jefferson. More and more Virginia colonists, including those who had supported the Patriot side, were weary of warfare and the burdens of taxation and coerced enlistment that it brought upon them. By some accounts, the Patriot cause again appeared on the verge of collapse.

Although Cornwallis now wished to return to South Carolina, General Clinton ordered him to remain in Virginia. Cornwallis and his troops therefore set up camp in the village of Yorktown, on the banks of the York River. It proved to be a disastrous mistake. On learning of the British camp, the French fleet in the West Indies, with the assistance of Cuba's Spanish governor, sailed north with 3,000 troops toward Chesapeake Bay in hopes of sealing the Virginia coast off from the British navy. For his part, after learning of Cornwallis's position and the movement of the French fleet, Washington decided to take his troops from the outskirts of New York City and march them nearly 500 miles to the vicinity of Yorktown. By the time Cornwallis knew what was happening, he had been trapped by the French and the Patriots. On October 19, 1781, he surrendered his army.

It was a dramatic turn of events, one made possible by the humble folk who served in the Continental Army, the French and the Spanish who lent the Patriots crucial military and financial support, and the thousands of enslaved people who fled to the British and, in so doing, undermined British hopes of securing the loyalty of many enslavers in the southern colonies. It was also made possible by strategic errors on the part of British military commanders and the tensions that developed among them. There was, of course, no special reason for the British to wholly give up the fight at this point; Cornwallis's army was a small one, and warfare continued in a variety of locations on the North American continent. But Cornwallis's surrender dissipated British morale on both sides of the Atlantic, and it seemed sensible to give up the American colonies for the sake of the empire as a whole.

Winners and Losers

Peace negotiations opened in Paris in April 1782. The Patriot side was represented by Benjamin Franklin (a regular in French circles), John Jay, Henry Laurens, and John Adams. After lengthy discussions, a peace treaty—another **Treaty of Paris**—emerged and was signed in September 1783. The treaty acknowledged the "said United States [the thirteen North American colonies] . . . to be free, sovereign, and independent States" with boundaries stretching from Massachusetts in the north to Georgia in the south, and from the Atlantic in the east to the Mississippi River in the west (with both Britain and the United States granted access to the river). State legislatures were encouraged to restore seized property to those who had been Loyalists and to refrain from engaging in further confiscations. Canada would remain in British hands despite American wishes—in part because the French wanted the British to maintain a presence in North America as a hedge against American power—and the Spanish retained their hold on Florida (see Map 7.3).

   Along with the obvious winners, the War for Independence left many losers and potential losers in North America. Native Americans who supported the British in hopes of limiting the ambitions and onslaughts of American land speculators and farmers now lost an important ally and mediator. Enslaved people who may have imagined that the British would weaken slavery for purposes of political control were now relegated to the control of their American enslavers.

   Loyalists fared particularly badly despite British efforts to protect them. They saw many thousands of acres of their lands confiscated by Patriot governments, and once the war ended, about 60,000 of them (more than 2 percent of all people in the colonies) left the newly independent United States owing to the hostility and persecution they had already suffered. Most went to New Brunswick and Nova Scotia; the remainder scattered to Quebec, Prince Edward Island, and Florida, or, with their enslaved people, to the British West Indies.

   Patriots whose enslaved people had run off to the British during the war expected the American negotiators in Paris to demand their return or some form of compensation for their losses. They got neither. South Carolina's Henry Laurens was the only one at the peace talks who could plead their case, and he failed. Some of the Black Loyalists who had reached British lines during the war were taken to Nova Scotia, Florida, or the West Indies. Others ended up in Britain and eventually in the new British colony of Sierra Leone in West Africa. It was a complex experience for those of African descent who took a chance on the British side. For the most part they gained and kept their freedom but also suffered from various forms of racial discrimination in their new homes. But it was also an unsettling experience for American enslavers who recognized that they could depend only on other enslavers to defend what they viewed as their vital interests.

≡ **MAP 7.3** **North America After the Treaty of Paris**

7.4 Political Reconstructions

||| Identify both the ideas for a political reconstruction of the colonies that Patriots shared and the differences in the first forms of governance that they devised.

Well before the Treaty of Paris—indeed, at a time when the rebellion had just begun and its outcome was in serious question—Britain's North American colonies began to reconstruct themselves politically. Prior to the signing of the

Declaration of Independence, the Second Continental Congress had urged the individual colonies—now regarded as "states"—to write constitutions for their own governance. The idea was for the Patriots to take local power into their own hands and demonstrate to the British and to other colonists that they intended to rule, that independence already had meaning. A bold and possibly foolhardy project it was.

State Constitutions

Leaders in the new states eagerly took up the task and produced documents that broadly resembled one another. For the most part they created bicameral (two-house) legislatures, both houses being popularly elected with different terms and requirements for members; a governor who would be selected by the legislature; and an independent judiciary. Pennsylvania, influenced by radicals in Philadelphia, decided upon a unicameral (one-house) legislature subject to popular election and an elected council that would then choose an executive. Vermont (and very briefly Georgia) embraced a unicameral legislature as well. Everywhere the right to vote and hold office was restricted to whites and depended on the ownership of property and, with the exception of New Jersey, the accident of male birth.

These state constitutions revealed a dramatic shift in political perspective. For years, colonists had protested British policies by invoking their fealty to the British crown, their love of British institutions, and their commitment to the British Empire. What they wanted was reform, the sort of reform that would allow them more self-governance without rearranging the political structure. Now that independence was in the offing, however, they seemed to reject all the fundamentals of the British imperial system: they created governing institutions based on the sovereignty (in other words, the ultimate authority) of the people, representative legislatures, and weak executives. Most commenced with "bills of rights" intended to prevent state governments from limiting freedoms of expression and petition, trial by jury, religious liberty, and due process. What happened to the cheers for monarchy and British subjecthood?

In good part, struggles with the crown and parliament made many white colonists and their leaders wary of any system of government that placed power in relatively few hands. They seemed to have no interest in elevating anyone like a king or royal governor to rule over them. They also took their concerns about representation seriously and, following the precedent of elective colonial assemblies, created legislatures based on popular election.

Making Republics

But of equal importance were the ideas and perspectives that had emerged more than a century earlier, during the English Civil War of the seventeenth century (discussed in Chapter 4)—especially those of the Independents and the Levellers—and found expression in the eighteenth century by a variety of enlightened political theorists who advocated the creation of "republics." To some extent, these theorists drew upon the writings of philosophers from ancient Greece and Rome (who would remain central to elite educations in the Atlantic world), but they also advanced republican thought that dated at least to the Italian Renaissance of the fifteenth and sixteenth centuries and became more robust as monarchical regimes like the English came to be challenged. The theorists held up republics, those based on representative institutions, as the ideal form of governance and tried to determine how republics might best be made. Almost all argued that republics rested on the sovereignty of the people and depended on citizens who were "independent" (free and able to provide for themselves) and "virtuous" (able to know the public good).

But who, in fact, were "the people?" What would "independence" mean? And how could the public good be determined? For the most part, American leaders involved in making the rules for their new republics saw "the people" as those who could achieve and sustain independence, understood independence mainly in economic and legal terms, and believed only independent people could recognize the public good. This meant that "the people" were limited to adult men who were legally free, owned property, and had a stake (such as paying taxes) in the communities in which they lived. Women, children, the enslaved, servants, and the propertyless poor were legally subordinate and dependent on the wills of others; they were to be excluded from formal political participation.

Yet, in the revolutionary environment of the 1770s and 1780s, significant questions were raised about these exclusions and dependencies. When John Adams set off to the Continental Congress in the spring of 1776, even before independence was declared, his wife, Abigail, famously warned him that "in the Code of Laws which I suppose it will be necessary for you to make I desire that you would Remember the Ladies, and be more generous and favorable to them than your ancestors. Do not put such unlimited power into the hands of the Husbands." Abigail Adams was clearly deploying republican worries about the concentration of power to issues republican men did not care to see. But she was not alone.

As we saw in Chapter 6, many women had supported the mobilizations against British imperial rule through their participation in boycotts of British imports and their labor in making food and clothing to offset British goods—activism known as the **homespun movement**. Many others joined crowds harassing Loyalists and British officials and helped construct vital networks of communication.

A few hid their gender and fought in the war itself; more followed the Continental Army and worked as cooks and nurses. Others served as spies for the Patriot side. Some from wealthier backgrounds, like those in the Ladies Association of Philadelphia, helped raise money for the troops.

Much as Abigail Adams, some women who came from middling or more comfortable backgrounds began to suggest that they had a significant role to play in the creation of a republic. As mothers, they had always been crucial to socializing their children to the values of the world in which they lived. If they had more opportunities for education and a larger part in public life, they argued, if they had greater "independence," their roles would be all the more consequential, especially for their sons, the next generation of republican leaders. Indeed, women like Adams insisted on their special moral contributions to republican virtue—historians have come to call this idea **republican motherhood**—and, with that in mind, a few (not Adams) went so far as to call for women's suffrage. Only New Jersey would briefly make this possible at the founding of the United States of America, but a new world of political engagement was clearly being imagined.

Black Americans saw the openings as well. Not only did many of them offer to fight in the Continental Army and state militias, but in New England states like Massachusetts they began to petition the legislatures to abolish slavery and grant them their freedom; in a

☰ **A Revolutionary Model for Marriage?**   The Boston-born society artist John Singleton Copley painted *Portrait of Mr. and Mrs. Thomas Mifflin (Sarah Morris)* in 1773. Although the Mifflins were far wealthier than most Americans, there are clues in this painting that suggest something revolutionary in their politics as well as in their relationship. Sarah's use of a handloom explicitly signals that she would prefer to rely on homespun goods and boycott British wares. It's Sarah who gazes authoritatively at the viewer, while her husband—a successful merchant—pauses from reading aloud from a book they're discussing to gaze at her with admiration.

few cases, they even took their enslavers to court for redress. After all, Jefferson had deemed it "self-evident" in the Declaration of Independence that "all men are created equal, ... endowed by their Creator with certain inalienable rights, that among these are Life, Liberty, and the Pursuit of Happiness." How was their enslavement compatible with ideas such as these? And what place would they have in a republic? In effect, the revolutionary environment enabled African Americans to put emancipation and civil equality on the table of political discussion. Could the reconstruction of American political society go further still?

7.5   Confederation and Its Discontents

‖‖‖ Describe how the Articles of Confederation came to be ratified and why the governing framework it established proved ineffective.

The War of Independence thus raised questions about slavery, race, and gender that would prove impossible to squelch, questions that challenge us to this very day. But the war also, and quickly, raised questions about whether some larger sort of union would join the interests of the thirteen new states. As we saw in Chapter 6, the idea had been broached nearly a quarter century earlier in Benjamin Franklin's Albany Plan of Union, and although it failed to catch hold then, the idea remained in the minds of revolutionary leaders who recognized that independence could neither be achieved nor sustained by thirteen disconnected republics.

Articles of Confederation

The Second Continental Congress, after ratifying the Declaration of Independence, immediately began to draft what it called Articles of Confederation and Perpetual Union—we refer to the document as the **Articles of Confederation**. It was a difficult job because the committee assigned the task had to balance the need for unity and central direction with the fears of concentrated power that went into the making of the colonial rebellion in the first place—and with the local attachments that most Americans held dear. As a result, they proposed a relatively weak union for what they called the "United States of America," which recognized the "sovereignty, freedom, and independence" of each of the states and granted them all powers not "expressly delegated to the United States." The main institution of this confederation would be a Congress in which each of the states would be entitled to between two and seven delegates selected by their legislatures, though each state delegation had only one vote. Congress, that is, would be a direct representative, not of "the people," but of the individual sovereign states. It could also select a president whose powers were not specified—essentially a figurehead.

The Articles made for a "firm league of friendship" between the states, providing mainly for their "common defence" and "mutual and general welfare." The Congress had the authority to conduct foreign affairs, declare war, adjudicate conflicts between states, permit the extradition of fugitives from justice, and ensure the "free citizens of the several states" all the "privileges and immunities of each," along with free movement of persons and goods between them. It also could raise an army and requisition funds for necessary expenditures from the states "in proportion to the value of land" within each of them. But the affairs of the states within their borders (with the possible exception of those involving Indigenous people) or among their citizens and their citizens' dependents were out of the Congress's reach.

The Continental Congress completed work on the Articles and approved them in November 1777. The Articles were then sent to the states for ratification, with the Continental Congress maintaining authority until the process was completed. All states had to sign off before the Articles could go into effect, so ratification took some time. Twelve of the states signed on by February 1779, but Maryland held out until early 1781 owing to a dispute over land claims with Virginia. Indeed, surrendering land claims that were part of original colonial charters and giving some of the new states lands out to the Mississippi River were crucial to ratification as well as to the ability of the United States to raise money through land sales. But on March 1, 1781—months before Cornwallis would surrender at Yorktown—the United States of America was formally proclaimed, with the Articles of Confederation as its operating framework.

Challenges of Union and Governance

It was, in many respects, a remarkable achievement. And there would be some genuine legislative accomplishments, not least the organization of the Northwest Territory in what had long been termed the Ohio Country and the devising of new rules—by the Ordinance of 1784 and the Northwest Ordinance of 1787—through which territorial governance could be established and territories eventually transformed into states. That is, under the Articles, the Congress determined that lands forming the United States, though not initially part of the original thirteen states, were imagined as future states equal to the others in standing rather than permanent colonies or havens for Indigenous people.

Yet the challenges of union and governance, of defense and security, and of stability and social peace in a tumultuous world quickly proved the Articles of Confederation's undoing. An assortment of economic problems was especially pressing. During the war what had been a robust trade in British goods was suspended while American merchants were denied access to the especially lucrative West Indian trade (British colonies there chose to stay in the empire). North American port cities as well as their rural hinterlands began to suffer from shortages of necessary supplies and currency.

At the same time, the enormous costs of fighting the war placed great stress on the Congress, the individual states, and the many communities that had grown up across the country. Weapons and ammunition had to be found, troops had to be clothed and fed, and soldiers had to be paid. The assistance of the French, Spanish, and Dutch was of some help, but there was little alternative to running up debts through the sale of bonds abroad and the extension of what amounted to IOUs, with interest, at home. What's more, the Patriot side lost more than 25,000 soldiers, a higher percentage of the population than any future American war except the Civil War. Many families suffered emotionally while finding it difficult to make ends meet (see Table 7.2).

Before long a major crisis brewed. Unless the debts were repaid, the solvency and viability of the United States would remain in jeopardy. But how would this be done? Since the Congress lacked the power of direct taxation, it had to requisition funds from the states, which themselves owed money to creditors for wartime loans. Thus, the states had to raise taxes, often to unprecedented levels, no small irony given the grievances about British taxation that led up to the War for Independence.

The taxes fell heavily on cash-starved artisans and farmers. And if they failed to pay up, their lands and other property could be seized for nonpayment by the state courts, leaving them unable to provide for themselves and their families. Anger and protests mounted. Some of the aggrieved demanded that the courts be closed down to halt property seizures and sales; elsewhere, voters called upon state legislatures to offer tax relief to debtors and print paper currency to ease the hard economic times. In many cases, the legislators yielded to the popular unrest—much to the dissatisfaction of merchants and creditors—and made it possible for taxes to be lowered or paid in produce and paper currency. But where the state legislatures dug in their heels and continued to favor creditors, anger turned into rebellion.

Table 7.2 Paying the Price for Independence		
	Sterling (£)	**Percentages**
Fiat Currency (Printed/Coined Money)		
States' money	64	39
Congress money	46	28
Total Fiat Currency	**110**	**67**
Borrowed Funds		
States' indebtedness	23	14
Congress debt certificates	16	10
Congress foreign loans	10	6
Congress domestic bonds	6	3
Total Debts	**55**	**33**
Total Cost of [Revolutionary] War	**165**	**100**

Shays's Rebellion

This was the case in Massachusetts, where Boston mercantile interests dominated the state legislature. Beginning in the late summer of 1786, farmers in central Massachusetts rallied to force the courts to close and stop the seizures of tax-delinquent property. They called themselves "regulators," and in the fall their rebellion spread farther west. "We are in a state of Anarchy and Confusion bordering on Civil War," one of John Adams's correspondents despondently told him at the time. The state's governor had trouble finding military support until wealthy merchants helped fund a private militia.

When the regulators, now led by Revolutionary War veteran and indebted farmer Daniel Shays, headed toward an armory in Springfield, a clash of arms was inevitable. It proved to be a one-sided fight. Faced by the 3,000-man militia, the rebellion quickly collapsed, and many of the regulators, including Shays, fled. More than a few members of the Massachusetts political and economic elite, including John Adams, were eager to punish the rebels harshly. But cooler heads prevailed, and although two of the rebels were executed, 4,000 signed confessions in exchange for amnesty and the legislature acted to ease the plight of debtors. Shays himself was pardoned a year later.

The episode is known as **Shays's Rebellion**, and it sent shock waves not only across Massachusetts but also throughout the new confederation, dramatizing both the political weakness of the union and the potential threat of democratically elected legislatures. Indeed, by the time that Shays's Rebellion erupted, growing numbers of American political leaders and their elite supporters had come to believe that the Articles of Confederation provided an inadequate structure of governance for the United States, that a stronger and more centralized government was necessary for the country to survive, its finances stabilized, and democratic excesses prevented. Some wondered whether a monarchy itself would be necessary to solve the problems that a newly independent United States faced. Connecticut's Noah

≡ **Shays's Rebellion** A woodcut from *Bickerstaff's Genuine Boston Almanack for 1787* shows Daniel Shays on the left and regulator Job Shattuck on the right. Shattuck and Shays, both veterans of the Revolutionary War, are depicted wearing the uniform of a Continental Army officer.

Webster who "was once as strong a republican man as any man in America" now preferred "a limited monarchy" as an alternative "to the ignorance and passions of the multitude." Even James Madison, Alexander Hamilton, John Jay, and George Washington wondered privately if a king was needed to protect those of wealth and property, although they still hoped to find "a republican remedy." An agreement was made to meet in convention in Philadelphia in May 1787 to see what could be done.

7.6   A Constitutional Republic

Summarize the circumstances that led to the Constitutional Convention and the compromises that went into the writing of the Constitution.

Initially the idea was to revise the Articles of Confederation so as to meet the challenges posed during the 1780s. That, at least, was the plan as publicly articulated. Under the leadership of Virginia's James Madison, however, the convention moved instead to draft an entirely new framework of governance. The fifty-five delegates representing twelve of the thirteen states generally believed that a stronger and more centralized government was necessary—Rhode Island did not share this view. But the delegates agreed on little else, and the process of constructing a political union that simultaneously gave more power to a central government while insuring the political rights of individual states showed that consensus would be difficult, if not impossible, to find.

Plans and Compromises

The two most significant divisions set the larger states like Virginia, New York, and Massachusetts against smaller ones like Delaware, Maryland, and New Jersey, and the states where enslavement was limited (New England and the Middle Atlantic) against the states where it was the basis of economic and political life (the Chesapeake and the lower South). Recognizing the tensions that were bound to flare, the delegates chose the immensely respected Washington to preside over the deliberations while at the same time lowering a veil of secrecy on the convention. As Madison put it, "no Constitution would ever have been adopted . . . if the debates had been public," though thanks to Madison's notes we have some idea of what went on.

Madison's **Virginia Plan** represented the perspective of those from the larger states who wanted both a strong national government and the initiatives of individual states (as for debtor relief) held in check. The plan proposed three branches of government—executive, judicial, and legislative—with a bicameral legislature, each house organized according to the population and the contributions of each state to the central government. The first house would be subject to popular election; the second would be chosen by the members of the first. Both houses would select the chief executive officer. Equally important, in Madison's view, the central government would be able to veto any state law it found objectionable: a power that struggles like Shays's Rebellion seemed to demand.

An alternative, known as the **New Jersey Plan**, found favor among delegates from the smaller states. Under it, the states would effectively remain sovereign, a one-house legislature in which each state had one vote would remain in place, and the central government would have new power to impose taxes and regulate domestic as well as international trade. Acknowledging the need for an executive, it created a plural presidency to be shared by three men elected by the Congress. Similar as it was to the Articles, the New Jersey Plan stood little chance of passing, but the Virginia Plan also lacked majority support (see Table 7.3).

Delegates to the convention debated in the Philadelphia summer heat for weeks until a plan, originally hatched by Connecticut and then urged forward by an ailing Benjamin Franklin, carried by the barest of margins. It proposed a two-house legislature: one, a House of Representatives, subject to election (with voting qualifications left to the states) and based on population; and one, a Senate, selected by state legislatures, in which each state had two votes (something like the Congress under the Articles). Members of the House would serve two-year terms, and those of the Senate would serve six-year terms. A chief executive or president, with a four-year term, would be chosen by an Electoral College in which each state had the same number of votes as its total congressional delegation. The president, in turn, would select, with the advice and consent of the Senate, a Supreme Court

Table 7.3 The Articles of Confederation, the Virginia Plan, and the New Jersey Plan			
	Articles of Confederation	**Virginia Plan**	**New Jersey Plan**
Executive	Ceremonial position only	Chosen by Congress	Plural; chosen by Congress
Congress	One house; one vote per state	Two houses	One house
Judiciary	None	Yes	Yes
Relation between States and Federal Government	Each state retains sovereignty	Congress can veto state laws	Acts of Congress are the "supreme law of the states"
Powers of Congress	Conduct diplomacy; wage war; cannot levy taxes or raise army	All powers of Articles of Confederation	All powers of Articles of Confederation, plus power to tax states and regulate commerce

and other federal judges who would have lifetime appointments. Madison's hope for federal veto power over state legislation failed, but the convention also determined that states could neither issue paper currency nor do anything else to "impair the obligation of contracts," a major concession to the interests of creditors and merchants.

What of the Enslaved?

Enslavement remained a contentious issue. Delegates from the Chesapeake and lower South depended on the labor of enslaved Black people for their wealth and eyed delegates from states to the North (where some moves toward gradual emancipation were being made) with suspicion. They had watched the Continental Army agree to enlist enslaved men as well as Black men who were free. They were deeply distressed by the failure of American representatives at the Paris peace talks to insist on compensation for the enslaved who had fled to the British. And they recognized that the new United States was vulnerable to the invasion of foreign powers, who, like the British, might offer freedom to their enslaved people in exchange for support. On the one hand, this meant that the southern delegates wanted a central government capable of defending the country from attack and of suppressing a slave rebellion should one erupt; on the other hand, they worried that such a government could intervene in the relationship between the enslavers and the enslaved, perhaps toward the outcome of emancipation, and therefore wanted its powers strictly limited.

An odd and contradictory set of goals it was, but the southern delegates made it clear they would not "confederate" unless they knew that their enslaved people "may not be taken from them." That was the bottom line. And they did remarkably well in part because few northern delegates, at this point, regarded the future of enslavement as an especially significant issue. The convention agreed to count an enslaved person as "three-fifths" of a free white person for the purposes of congressional apportionment: this settlement would be known as the **federal ratio**; the fraction originated in a debate under the Articles about counting enslaved people for the purposes of taxation. Delegates also agreed to require that runaway enslaved people be returned to their owners even if they entered a state where the legality of slavery was in question: this settlement would be known as the **Fugitive Slave Clause**. The convention determined that Congress would not have the authority to tax exports (like tobacco, sugar, or cotton) and potentially weaken the plantation economy. And it agreed, with support from Chesapeake delegates, not to place any restrictions on the Atlantic slave trade for at least twenty years: meaning that the states could continue to import enslaved people from West Africa or elsewhere in the hemisphere until at least 1808.

In short, the convention drafted a Constitution that recognized enslavement and addressed many of the enslavers' concerns—indeed, rewarded enslavers and their allies with more representation than people had in states where enslavement was either illegal or of diminishing importance. Enslavement, that is, was woven into the fabric of the original Constitution.

Yet the convention did all of this without putting the words "slavery," "slaves," or "enslavement" in the Constitution's text. Instead, they used euphemisms, which all the delegates understood but which enabled those who found slavery objectionable and contrary to the spirit of a free republic to hold their noses. These euphemisms included "other persons," "persons bound to service or labor," or "such persons as any of the States . . . shall think proper to admit." The new government created by the Constitution was therefore required to use its resources to protect the institution of enslavement and the enslavers without explicitly owning up to it in the eyes of the United States and those of the world.

It was a problematic set of compromises that left the authority of the new government in some question. Scholars and other students of the Constitution continue to debate what this all really meant for the future of the enslaved and their enslavers. Was enslavement a local institution, subject to the sovereign power of states, or was it a national institution, subject to the power of the branches of the federal government? There was no clear answer, and potential for trouble down the road.

As for Indigenous people who had forged their own political societies over centuries and played no small role in the making of American independence and a constitutional republic, they were denied both rights and representation. They were not to be counted for purposes of taxation or congressional apportionment—"Indians not taxed" was the Constitution's language—and their commercial relations with white Americans were subject to congressional regulation, much as foreign nations and empires would be. In effect, the federal government seized control over treaty-making power (ambiguous under the Articles of Confederation), consigning Indigenous people to a distinctive and, for the most part, subordinate status in the territorial United States.

Neither Indigenous people, Black people, poor people, nor women were invited to the Constitutional Convention that would be shaping their fates: not as observers let alone as delegates. And for all the debates and disagreements that resounded in Philadelphia over the summer of 1787, there was, in the end, enough satisfaction to enable nearly three-quarters of the delegates to affix, some still hesitantly, their names to the new Constitution of the United States on September 17, 1787. Its opening words, "We the People," announced the arrival of a new republic.

7.7   The Challenge of Ratification

Analyze the conflict between Federalists and Anti-Federalists and the contested road to the Constitution's ratification.

All that was left was ratification. Unlike the Articles of Confederation, which required unanimity, only three-quarters of the states—meaning nine of them—had to agree before the Constitution could go into effect and a new structure of governance could get up and running. Special conventions were to be held in each of the states, with delegates to them selected by eligible voters. It was not only the distances between the voters and the states that proved to be the cause of a many-months process. The lengthy debates in the Constitutional Convention and the close votes on the various compromises suggested unease, if not outright opposition, to some of what the convention crafted. Ratification by the states exposed even deeper fault lines.

Federalists and Anti-Federalists

Supporters of ratification, who called themselves **Federalists**, had a good deal going for them. They had strong support among people of wealth, especially in the coastal cities. They had major resources to advance their arguments. And they had the backing of most of the newspapers. They also had important figures who were central to the Constitution's writing making the case, especially Alexander Hamilton and John Jay of New York and James Madison of Virginia, whose essays for the cause, written between October 1787 and May 1788, have together become known as *The Federalist Papers*.

The Federalists argued that the Constitution represented the best framework for the creation of a republic, one that balanced the claims of the states with the enhanced powers of the federal government. They reminded Americans that the Constitution was based on the sovereignty of the people, that it provided the financial stability and means of defense the country needed to survive and prosper, that it established direct representation in the House as well as indirect representation in the Senate, that it enabled the rule of majorities while protecting the rights of minorities, and that it provided for checks and balances on the power of the different federal branches, thereby limiting the dangers of federal tyranny. Madison, in *Federalist Number 10*, made an enormously influential contribution to political thought by arguing that a republic was better suited to a large territory like the United States than a small one, which had been the prevailing view. In a large territory, Madison wrote, there would be so many different factions—organized dissenting groups—spread over such an extensive space that no one faction could rule over the others.

Yet for all of their intellectual heft and political advantages, Federalists faced very substantial opposition. Especially among ordinary rural folk and their leaders, like those who had rallied to Daniel Shays or who had pressured state legislatures to ease their burdens of debt, there was great apprehension about what the Constitution might bring. Called **Anti-Federalists** (by the Federalists), they protested the power the federal government now had (compared to the Articles) at the expense of the states, the distance of the federal government from the day-to-day lives of ordinary Americans, the elitism of the Federalists and the support the Constitution had from the "rich and ambitious" who would exploit "the poor and illiterate," the lack of annual elections for the Congress, and the absence of a bill of rights (most state constitutions had one), which Federalists seemed to believe was either implicit or unnecessary. Even if they agreed that the Articles needed revising, Anti-Federalists hoped to ensure that governance would remain in their hands close to home and what they called their "liberties" would be guarded.

The Federalists used all the advantages they had, including some heavy-handed bullying. They pushed for ratification conventions to meet quickly, organized them so their supporters would have more seats, and played fast and loose with the communications outlets they controlled. "*Bad* measures in a *good* cause," one Federalist conceded. For their part, the Anti-Federalists were often scattered over great distances in the countryside and had difficulties in mobilizing their numbers. Although they had powerful voices like Virginia's Patrick Henry and Massachusetts's Samuel Adams and James Winthrop, they had a tough time turning political argument into convention seats. In many cases, relatively few were able to come out to vote in the elections for delegates.

Passage of the US Constitution

Even so, the Anti-Federalists made their objections felt. After the Delaware, New Jersey, Georgia, and Connecticut conventions ratified the Constitution easily, the opposition built and became heated. Pennsylvania saw bitter debates and rural violence before ratification succeeded. In Massachusetts the legacy of Shays's Rebellion weighed on both sides and required all sorts of maneuvering before ratification squeaked through. South Carolina and Maryland watched Anti-Federalists buckle under the mounting pressure of ratification, and New Hampshire finally became the ninth state to ensure it.

But the crucial states of New York and Virginia remained embattled and required special help. James Madison reminded Virginia enslavers of the support

MAPPING AMERICA

Expulsion and Exile

Two treaties signed in Paris, the first in 1763 and the second in 1783, altered North America's political map in the span of just twenty years. The consequences of these agreements went far beyond the redrawing of political boundaries. Thousands of people were either forcibly removed from their homes or compelled to build new lives in exile.

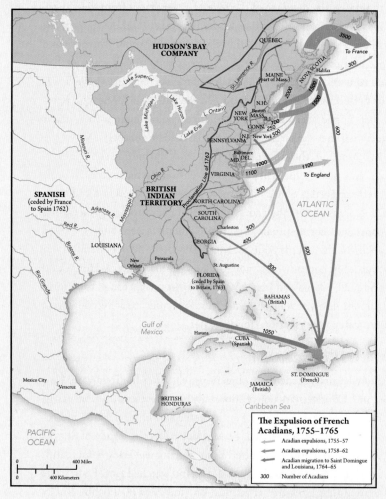

The Expulsion of French Acadians, 1755–1765

⟵ Acadian expulsions, 1755–57
⟵ Acadian expulsions, 1758–62
⟵ Acadian migration to Saint Domingue and Louisiana, 1764–65

300   Number of Acadians

≡ **MAP 1**   France's surrender of Canada after its defeat in the French and Indian War resulted in the expulsion of thousands of Acadians, a Catholic people of French descent who had lived for generations in Nova Scotia. Their homes torched and their fields destroyed, nearly 7,000 Acadians fled to New England, the French colony of Saint Domingue (present-day Haiti), or France. Over the following decades, many resettled in Louisiana, where they began to call themselves Cajuns.

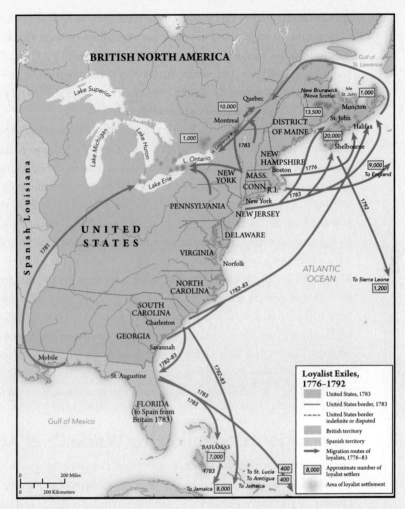

Loyalist Exiles, 1776–1792

- United States, 1783
- United States border, 1783
- United States border indefinite or disputed
- British territory
- Spanish territory
- Migration routes of loyalists, 1776–83
- 8,000 Approximate number of loyalist settlers
- Area of loyalist settlement

≡ **MAP 2**   Somewhere between 60,000 and 100,000 Loyalists left the newly independent United States owing to the hostility and persecution they suffered during the war. Most went to New Brunswick and Nova Scotia; the remainder scattered to Quebec, Prince Edward Island, and Florida or, with their enslaved, to the British West Indies. Hundreds of Loyalist Black men and women settled in Canada or England, seeking opportunities denied to them in the newly formed United States.

Thinking Geographically

1. How are the two maps similar? How are they different? What does each map suggest about the wider relations and connections that went into the forging of America?

2. Maps can show movement, but they cannot reveal the pain and suffering of disrupted lives. Thinking about the expulsion of the Acadians and the exile of the Loyalists, do these experiences change your view of America's founding history?

the Constitution provided them and the New York Federalists, based in New York City, promised to join the new republic regardless of what the Anti-Federalists did. Both states ratified the Constitution by very small margins. Only in North Carolina and Rhode Island did Anti-Federalism prevail at their conventions, though both states came around in 1789 and 1790, respectively. As a result, in June 1788, the Constitution achieved formal ratification.

It was, to say the least, a rocky start to the reconstituted United States, and one that potentially boded ill for the future. George Washington himself wondered whether the republic had been "shipwrecked in sight of the Port." Yet there was at least one especially good outcome to the deliberations. As the price of getting the Constitution ratified in states like Massachusetts and New York, the Federalists promised to add a bill of rights. And energized by James Madison, the first Congress under the Constitution found their way to the goal and crafted the first ten amendments to the Constitution that we would come to know as the **Bill of Rights**. Following many of the states, the amendments provided protection for the rights of speech, religion, the press, assembly, and petitioning; for the right to bear arms; for an assortment of legal rights such as due process, trial by jury, and legal counsel; and for prohibitions on excessive bail and "cruel and unusual punishment." Lastly, the Tenth Amendment "reserved to the States respectively, or to the people" all "powers not delegated to the United States by the Constitution, nor prohibited by it to the States," a clear signal that much would be left to the states.

Conclusion: Beginning the World Over Again?

The Constitution may sensibly be seen as a conservative response to the radical initiatives of the Revolution and the Confederation years, when many Americans of humble origins played a role in the winning of independence and then demanded a voice in the organization and policies of their state governments. Thomas Paine declared in *Common Sense* that Americans could "begin the world over again," and such idealism and boldness stirred the aspirations of thousands who had much to gain just as it worried the minds of those who had much to lose. In the end, the United States of 1789, when the first elections under the Constitution were held, looked quite different from the United States of 1776 or 1781. There was a real central government committed to defending property and keeping the reins of power in the hands of those who owned property and had the resources to rule. But the Constitution also created the first republic in the Western Hemisphere, and the ideals about governance and sovereignty that it embodied, together with those the Declaration of Independence had earlier consecrated, left indelible imprints on the history of the modern world. That's why it represents a political revolution.

WHAT IF the Anti-Federalists Blocked Ratification of the Constitution?

We will never know what proportion of the American voting population preferred adoption or defeat of the Constitution. But there are some reasons to believe that a majority favored the Anti-Federalists and may well have won on a level political playing field. What if they had succeeded in preventing the Constitution that came out of Philadelphia from being implemented?

This is a difficult question because the Constitution is such a central part of the United States origin story that it's hard to imagine the nation without it. And, in fact, there wouldn't have been the United States we have come to know without it. Had the Anti-Federalists defeated the Constitution's ratification, either another convention would have been necessary to make revisions or the Articles of Confederation would have remained in place as the governing framework. Either way, the union would have been a loosely constructed political entity, with a very weak central government to handle collective defense or domestic problems, including disagreements and conflicts between individual states. The states, in turn, would have remained the unquestioned sovereign units, and the state legislatures would have been further empowered to control the full range of their internal affairs. In some states, this would have enabled ordinary Americans to have more of a say in the affairs that most affected their daily lives; in others, this would have allowed elites to seize and wield power as they saw fit, even at the expense of democratic practices.

Over time, had the Constitution not been adopted, it is possible that the states would have gone the way of Spanish colonies in the Western Hemisphere: instead of forming themselves into one large republic, they may well have become a collection of separate—and perhaps competing—republics. Would there have been advantages in such an outcome, if we consider the North American population as a whole: male and female, Native and African American as well as Euro-American? Or was the Constitution and the government it created likely the best result that Americans could have enjoyed?

DOCUMENT 7.1: James Madison, *Federalist Number 10* (1787)

Madison's Federalist Number 10 *was one of the most important explanations of why the Constitution should be ratified and why a republic would fare better in a large territory than a small one. Here is an excerpt.*

The question resulting is, whether small or extensive republics are more favorable to the election of proper guardians of the public weal; and it is clearly decided in favor of the latter by two obvious considerations: In the first place, it is to be remarked that, however small the republic may be, the representatives must be raised to a certain number, in order to guard against the cabals of a few; and that, however large it may be, they must be limited to a certain number, in order to guard against the confusion of a multitude. Hence, the number of representatives in the two cases not being in proportion to that of the two constituents, and being proportionally greater in the small republic, it follows that, if the proportion of fit characters be not less in the large than in the small republic, the former will present a greater option, and consequently a greater probability of a fit choice. In the next place, as each representative will be chosen by a greater number of citizens in the large than in the small republic, it will be more difficult for unworthy candidates to practice with success the vicious arts by which elections are too often carried; and the suffrages of the people being more free, will be more likely to center in men who possess the most attractive merit and the most diffusive and established characters. It must be confessed that in this, as in most other cases, there is a mean, on both sides of which inconveniences will be found to lie. By enlarging too much the number of electors, you render the representatives too little acquainted with all their local circumstances and lesser interests; as by reducing it too much, you render him unduly attached to these, and too little fit to comprehend and pursue great and national objects. The federal Constitution forms a happy combination in this respect; the great and aggregate interests being referred to the national, the local and particular to the State legislatures. The other point of difference is, the greater number of citizens and extent of territory which may be brought within the compass of republican than of democratic government; and it is this circumstance principally which renders factious combinations less to be dreaded in the former than in the latter. The smaller the society, the fewer probably will be the distinct parties and interests composing it; the fewer the distinct parties and interests, the more frequently will a majority be found of the same party; and the smaller the number of individuals composing a majority, and the smaller the compass within which they are placed, the more easily will they concert and execute their plans of oppression. Extend the sphere, and you take in a greater variety of parties and interests; you make it less probable that a majority of the whole will have a common motive to invade the rights of other citizens; or if such a common motive exists, it will be more difficult for all who feel it to discover their own strength, and to act in unison with each other... Hence, it clearly appears, that the same advantage which a republic has over a democracy, in controlling the effects of faction, is enjoyed by a large over a small republic[, is] enjoyed by the Union over the States composing it....

Source: https://guides.loc.gov/federalist-papers/full-text

DOCUMENT 7.2: Brutus, "To the Citizens of New York State" (1788)

Brutus's essay, one of several he wrote, captures some of the reservations that Anti-Federalists had about the Constitution. Brutus was a pen name used by the author, chosen to identify himself with a leader in the conspiracy to assassinate Julius Caesar, whom the original Brutus believed to be intent on replacing the Roman Republic with a dictatorship.

The first question that presents itself on the subject is, whether a confederated government be the best for the United States or not? Or in other words, whether the thirteen United States be reduced to one great republic, governed by one legislature, and under the direction of one executive and judicial; or whether they should continue thirteen confederated republics, under the direction and control of a supreme federal head for certain defined national purposes only? . . . This government is to possess absolute and uncontroulable power, legislative, executive, and judicial, with respect to every object to which it extends. . . . [T]here is no need for any intervention of the state governments . . . to execute any one power vested in the general government, and that the constitution and laws of every state are nullified and declared void, so far as they are or shall be inconsistent with the constitution. . . . It is true . . . some small degree of power is still left to the states, but little attention to the powers vested in the general government, will convince every candid man, that if it is capable of being executed, all that is reserved for the individual states must very soon be annihilated. . . . We shall be constrained to conclude, that a free republic cannot succeed over a country of such immense extent, containing such a number of inhabitants. . . . History furnishes no example of a free republic, anything like the extent of the United States.

Source: Storing, Herbert J., ed. The Complete Anti-Federalist. 7 vols. Chicago: University of Chicago Press, 1981.

Thinking About Contingency

1. What do you think would have been the relationship between the central government and the states if the Anti-Federalists had prevailed? Why?
2. What if the Articles of Confederation had remained as the governing framework? What implications would this have had for domestic affairs? For international affairs?
3. If the states had gone their separate ways, what do you see as the advantages and disadvantages of such an outcome?

REVIEW QUESTIONS

1. What advantages and disadvantages did the Patriot and British sides have in their battles for military victory?

2. What roles did poor white Americans and African Americans play in the outcome of the War for Independence, and which side did their involvements favor?

3. How significant was the civil warfare between Loyalists and Patriots within North American in determining the outcome of the war and the peace?

4. Who were the important allies of the Patriots in their fight, and why did the French enter the war on their side? How important was French participation?

5. Why did the British decide to shift their fight to Georgia and the Carolinas after 1777? What role did enslavement and enslavers play in the outcome?

6. Why did the Second Continental Congress choose to construct such a weak central government under the Articles of Confederation? What was the new central government able to do, and what wasn't it able to do?

7. What type of challenges during the 1780s convinced many Americans that the Articles of Confederation had to be revised, and how much of a revision did the new Constitution represent?

8. What were the arguments of the Federalists and Anti-Federalists in the battle over ratification of the Constitution?

KEY TERMS

Anti-Federalists (p. 285)
Articles of Confederation (p. 276)
Bill of Rights (p. 288)
Continental Army (p. 254)
Federalist Number 10 (p. 284)
Federalists (p. 284)
Federal Ratio (p. 282)

Fugitive Slave Clause (p. 282)
homespun movement (p. 274)
Loyalists (p. 254)
New Jersey Plan (p. 281)
Patriots (p. 254)
Philipsburg Proclamation (p. 268)

republican motherhood (p. 275)
Shays's Rebellion (p. 279)
Three-Pronged Attack (p. 257)
Treaty of Alliance (p. 263)
Treaty of Paris (p. 271)
Virginia Plan (p. 280)

RECOMMENDED READINGS

Carol Berkin, *Revolutionary Mothers: Women in the Struggle for American Independence* (Knopf, 2004).

Colin G. Calloway, *The American Revolution in Indian Country* (Cambridge University Press, 1995).

Saul Cornell, *The Other Founders: Antifederalism and the Dissenting Tradition in America, 1788–1828* (University of North Carolina Press, 1999).

Woody Holton, *Unruly Americans and the Origins of the Constitution* (Hill and Wang, 2008).

Holger Hoock, *Scars of Independence: America's Violent Birth* (Crown, 2017).

Maya Jasanoff, *Liberty's Exiles: American Loyalists in a Revolutionary World* (Vintage, 2012).

Linda Kerber, *Women of the Republic* (University of North Carolina Press, 1997).

Gary Nash, *The Forgotten Fifth: African Americans in the Age of Revolution* (Harvard University Press, 2006).

Stacy Schiff, *The Revolutionary Samuel Adams* (Little, Brown, 2022).

Gordon Wood, *The Creation of the American Republic, 1776–1787* (University of North Carolina Press, 1969).

8

Securing a Republic, Imagining an Empire
1789–1815

Chapter Outline

8.1 A New Republic in a Revolutionary World

||| Outline the process by which the political conflicts that surfaced in the administration of President George Washington led to the formation of the first political parties.

8.2 The Early Republic in Global Context

||| Describe the broad Atlantic conflicts in which the American republic emerged and the importance of the developing slave rebellion in Saint Domingue.

8.3 A Crisis in the Making

||| Connect the foreign policy dilemmas of the 1790s with the deepening political conflicts in the United States of the early nineteenth century.

8.4 A Critical Election: 1800

||| Explain the importance of the election of 1800 to the American political landscape.

8.5 Envisioning and Pursuing an Empire

||| Analyze the vision of empire that emerged among American policymakers, how they hoped to pursue it, and how the Haitian Revolution made possible the purchase of the Louisiana Territory from France.

8.6 Power Struggles on the Seas and the Continent

||| Summarize how the United States became embroiled in the War of 1812 and what was at stake in the conflict.

≡ **Toussaint Louverture**   In 1791, Toussaint Louverture, a free man of color, joined a slave uprising that erupted in Saint Domingue, France's prosperous Caribbean sugar colony. Toussaint, as depicted in this c. 1800 portrait by an unknown artist, possessed strong military skills and soon became the leader of what is known as the Haitian Revolution.

January 1803 found the French emperor Napoleon Bonaparte scowling in the Tuileries Palace in Paris. He had seized power in France four years earlier and looked to establish a massive empire on both sides of the Atlantic. To that end, he had sent thousands of French soldiers in 1802 to the Caribbean islands of Guadeloupe, Martinique, and Saint Domingue—all claimed as colonies by France—to crush rebellions by enslaved people that had erupted over the course of the 1790s and to re-enslave the Black rebels. He was especially interested in Saint Domingue, the richest sugar-producing colony in the world, which he hoped would remain the jewel of the French empire as well as the North American base for his imperial power, which stretched across the midsection and was known as the Louisiana Territory.

Despite Napoleon's great confidence in his troops, the mission turned into a disaster. Tropical disease and a reignited rebellion in Saint Domingue decimated the French

Timeline

1790	1792	1794	1796	1800

1789 › The first government under the US Constitution begins its work in New York City; revolution breaks out in France in July

1791 › A slave rebellion erupts on the French Caribbean island of Saint Domingue; the first Ten Amendments to the US Constitution—the Bill of Rights—are ratified by the states

1792 › George Washington unanimously reelected President of the United States

1794 › The revolutionary government in France abolishes enslavement in its colonies and extends the rights of citizenship to formerly enslaved people; Britain and the United States sign the Jay Treaty, opening trading relations and ending the British occupation of forts in the northwest

1796 › John Adams succeeds George Washington as president after a close election, and Thomas Jefferson, who finished second, becomes vice president

1798 › Congress passes the Alien and Sedition Acts

1799 › Napoleon seizes power in France

1800 › Bitter contest between Federalists and Republicans results in Thomas Jefferson's election as president; Gabriel's slave rebellion fails in Virginia

army, which by the end of 1802 had no option but to flee. Without Saint Domingue, the vast Louisiana Territory, meant to supply Saint Domingue and the other French islands with food while they produced sugar, coffee, and other staple crops, was now little more than a strategic burden. "Damn sugar, damn coffee, damn colonies," Napoleon thundered.

The recently elected US President Thomas Jefferson, who deeply feared the slave rebellions in the French Caribbean but also desperately wanted to secure American control of New Orleans (at the mouth of the Mississippi River), offered to buy the city for as much as $10 million (nearly $250,000,000 in today's dollars). To his astonishment, Napoleon offered up the whole of the Louisiana Territory for a mere $15 million, nearly doubling the size of the United States. Despite an assortment of questions about the sale's legality, it was a deal Jefferson could hardly refuse.

1802	1804	1806	1808	1810	1812	1814

1801 › Napoleon dispatches thousands of French troops to reimpose slavery in Saint Domingue

1803 › The Louisiana Purchase from France nearly doubles the size of the United States

1804 › The new republic of Haiti is proclaimed; the Twelfth Amendment to the Constitution is ratified, changing the rules for voting in presidential elections; Jefferson reelected President; Corps of Discovery led by Meriwether Lewis departs from St. Louis

1807 › The Jefferson administration pushes the Embargo Act through Congress

1808 › James Madison is elected to succeed Jefferson as president

1812 › The US Congress declares war on Britain after seizures of American ships and forced recruitment of American sailors

1814 › Treaty of Ghent ends the War of 1812 between the United States and Britain

What we call the **Louisiana Purchase** of 1803 was perhaps the greatest of several transformations in power that marked the first quarter century of the American republic. A newly ratified Constitution had shifted powers from the states to the central government. New political parties—the Federalists and the Republicans— had organized during the 1790s and battled over the future course of the country. A tumultuous election in 1800 had given Jefferson's Republican Party control of the federal government for the first time, defeating the Federalist Party of George Washington and his presidential successor John Adams. Relations with both France and England frayed and threatened warfare involving the United States. And in 1812, the integrity of American independence was most directly challenged by the British, who sought militarily to regain the power they had lost as a result of the American Revolution.

But the Louisiana Purchase was made possible by one of the most unlikely events in modern history. Enslaved people on the island of Saint Domingue had risen in revolt in 1791, won their freedom, defeated the armies of Spain and Britain, begun to govern themselves, and then fended off the efforts of Napoleon to send them back into enslavement. In doing so, they destabilized the world that enslavers had made and ended France's aspirations for imperial power in the Western Hemisphere. Soon thereafter, on January 1, 1804, they proclaimed the independent republic of **Haiti**, the most revolutionary achievement in a revolutionary age. An entirely new American future was opened up by rebels who threw off the chains of slavery in the Caribbean. There are few more compelling examples of history's most marginal and apparently powerless people setting the world on a new course.

8.1   A New Republic in a Revolutionary World

||| Outline the process by which the political conflicts that surfaced in the administration of President George Washington led to the formation of the first political parties.

The United States began to take shape as a new republic—as a new form of institutional political power—in the 1790s. As we saw in Chapter 7, this came after a lengthy and bloody struggle for independence and after a convulsive political experiment under the Articles of Confederation. But if the revolutionary years of the 1770s and 1780s now seemed in the past, new revolutionary eruptions took place in the Euro-Atlantic world, roiling the political waters that the American republic sought to navigate. It proved to be a turbulent ride, raising questions about whether America's own independence was yet secure and whether America's own dynamic of revolution had run its course.

Directing the Republic

The new American government set out to work in 1789 with a flurry of activity. Meeting in New York City, the temporary capital until a permanent site could be determined, the first Congress created the executive departments of treasury, state, war, and justice and drafted the first Ten Amendments to the Constitution, which were then sent to the states for ratification. Ratification of what we call the Bill of Rights was achieved in 1791. In April of 1789, a reluctant George Washington—the most admired and trusted man in the country—who had been elected unanimously, was inaugurated as the first president. And like Washington, most of the high government officials were members of the economic elite as well as political or military veterans of the American War of Independence. They had come to know one another well over the previous decade and a half. Indeed, Washington's cabinet included Thomas Jefferson at State, Henry Knox at War, and Edmund Randolph as Attorney General. But none would be more forceful or consequential than Treasury Secretary Alexander Hamilton, the cabinet official in charge of devising an economic agenda for the republic.

Hamilton had a remarkable and unexpected life. Born out of wedlock in the British West Indies in the mid-1750s, Hamilton arrived in North America in the early 1770s and, after working as a clerk, began to attend King's College (later Columbia University) in New York City. Along with some classmates, he volunteered for Patriot service once the War of Independence broke out and, before too long, came to the attention of George Washington, who put Hamilton on his staff. Following the war, Hamilton served in the Confederation Congress as a representative from New York while becoming a founder of the Bank of New York. Dissatisfied with the government the Articles of Confederation had established, Hamilton joined the call for a Constitutional Convention, served there as a New York delegate, and then, with James Madison and John Jay, rallied support for the Constitution through essays in *The Federalist* (discussed in Chapter 7).

As secretary of the treasury, Hamilton had clear ideas about the direction he wished to take the new republic. His model was

Alexander Hamilton c. 1790
Hamilton's extraordinary military and political career—and no less complicated personal life—were cut brutally short when a political opponent, Aaron Burr, murdered him in a duel on July 11, 1804.

Great Britain, a formidable urbanizing and industrializing society with a powerful central government and an imperial reach into nearly every continent on the globe. Following Britain's example, he believed, was essential to the defense of the United States, the viability of its political institutions, and the prosperity of its economy.

Hamilton proposed that the new American government begin by paying off its federal and state war debts at their full value (amounting to nearly $80 million, or $2 billion in today's dollars). He also wanted the United States to maintain a permanent national debt to attract creditors and investors and to create a central bank, something like the great Bank of England, to establish a stable currency and promote the economic development of the country. To raise the revenue necessary for debt repayment, the federal government would enact tariffs on imports (which would also aid domestic manufacturers), impose taxes on its citizens, and sell off its lands in the west (see Table 8.1). In the process, it would become an engine of political and economic empowerment. More and more American eyes would then look to the federal government rather than to state and local governments for their needs and interests, solidifying the power shift that the Constitution had initiated. Hamilton submitted these plans to the first Congress in reports on the credit, on manufactures (also with Britain in mind), and on the bank.

Hamilton looked for support from the Virginia Congressman James Madison, with whom he had crafted *The Federalist Papers*. But Madison was far less of a centralizer than Hamilton and, along with Jefferson in the Cabinet, he helped build Congressional opposition to Hamilton's plans. Madison and Jefferson, while

Table 8.1 Sources of Federal Revenue, 1790–1799			
Year(s)	**Tariffs**	**Internal Taxes**	**Other (incl. sale of public lands)**
1790–1791	$4,399,000		$10,000
1792	$3,443,000	$209,000	$17,000
1793	$4,255,000	$338,000	$59,000
1794	$4,801,000	$274,000	$356,000
1795	$5,588,000	$338,000	$188,000
1796	$6,568,000	$475,000	$1,334,000
1797	$7,550,000	$575,000	$563,000
1798	$7,106,000	$644,000	$150,000
1799	$6,610,000	$799,000	$157,000

Source: Curtis P. Nettels, *The Emergence of a National Economy, 1775–1815* (New York: Holt, Rinehart and Winston, 1962), p. 221.

recognizing the need for a stronger federal government than that established under the Articles of Confederation, nonetheless believed that the states and localities should remain the locus of power and authority. As planters, they worried that Hamilton wished to encourage manufacturing and urbanization at the expense of agriculture and the countryside. They also saw themselves as representing the interests of fellow wealthy landowners who depended upon enslaved people to work their plantations. The more powerful the federal government became, the more likely it would be to intervene in their affairs, perhaps toward the end of destabilizing enslavement.

In order to move forward on the federal budget, Hamilton and Madison cut a deal: Madison would rally southern support for Hamilton's plan for the federal government to pay both state and federal war debts; Hamilton would rally northern support for locating the permanent national capital on the Potomac River in the District of Columbia, farther to the south than New York or Philadelphia. Meantime, Philadelphia would serve as the capital until the building was completed.

The First Political Parties

The struggle between Hamilton and Madison became the basis for the first political parties in American history: the **Federalists** and the **Republicans** (also known as the Democratic-Republicans). Those who called themselves Federalists supported Hamilton's vision for the United States, imagining an economically diverse country in which cities and manufacturing would become increasingly important and the federal government increasingly powerful, with political governance remaining securely in the hands of an educated elite. Those who called themselves Republicans shared Madison's vision of an agriculturally based society in which the powers of the federal government would be limited, the important decision-making retained by the states and localities, and access to the instruments of governance more widely available.

What Federalists and Republicans shared was the belief that only "independent" people—those who were free, had full legal standing, and were able to provide for themselves chiefly by means of property ownership (especially land and tools of trade)—could participate in formal politics. Native Americans, enslaved Black people, free people of color, women, and children (all of whom were legally "dependent") would be excluded or assigned subordinate positions. Federalists and Republicans agreed, in sum, that political power would be held by white men even if they disagreed about which white men would rule.

The Federalist and the Republican Parties were not like the political parties of today (and these Republicans were not the forebears of today's Republicans). They were not organizations put together from the government centers as well as from the grassroots. They did not adopt formal platforms. And they did not actively recruit members or candidates for office. They were rather affiliations of like-minded political leaders, brought together mainly for exercising control of the federal government, which had very different views about what the revolution had done and what was left to achieve. And each came to view the other not simply as political opponents but as threats to their ideas of the republic itself. As Federalists and Republicans saw it in the 1790s, the revolution was still very much on the line.

Revolution in France and Saint Domingue

In 1789, just as the first government under the new Constitution was beginning to meet in the United States, a revolution erupted in Paris, France. The revolution was directed against the French crown and royal power more generally and, at least at the start, revolutionaries imagined creating a republican regime much as the American Revolution had previously done. "Liberty, Equality, and Fraternity" was the rallying cry. Ironically, the great costs of supporting the Patriot side in the American Revolution had nearly bankrupted the royal establishment and compelled the crown to burden the French people with higher taxes just to raise the needed revenue.

Very quickly, growing numbers of Parisians rose in protest and demanded change in the ways that power was wielded in the country. They wrote a remarkable treatise, **Declaration of the Rights of Man and the Citizen,** clearly influenced by the ideas of natural rights and universalism in the American Declaration of Independence, which tore down many vestiges of the royal regime, including the power of nobles over peasants on the land. Thomas Paine himself was soon on the scene.

The idealism of the French Revolution proved impossible to contain. It spread from Paris to country towns and villages across France and then, by way of sailors and soldiers, to colonial possessions like **Saint Domingue** in the Caribbean. Occupying the western third of the island of Hispaniola, where Columbus had made landfall three hundred years earlier (the eastern two-thirds, known as Santo Domingo, was controlled by the Spanish), Saint Domingue, as we have seen, had grown to importance for the sugar and coffee that enslaved Africans cultivated on large plantations. By the 1780s, nearly half a million enslaved people labored in the colony, outnumbering French enslavers and their white allies by a ratio of seven to one, and, since at least the middle of the eighteenth century, there were signs of slave unrest and rebelliousness.

Among the first to be roused by word of revolution in France were free people of color (*gens de couleur*): mixed-race people of African descent who had been born free or had been emancipated. Numbering around 30,000 on the island, they hoped the revolution would help end, not enslavement (some were enslavers themselves), but the forms of racial discrimination they suffered in the colony. Soon making their way to Paris, their leaders were disappointed; they learned that the ambitions of the French revolutionaries stopped at the borders of race and colonialism, and their demands for equality with whites were rejected.

Thus, in the fall of 1790, the *gens de couleur* of Saint Domingue took another course. They rose in arms to make their claims by force. And although they met defeat at the hands of local white militias and French soldiers stationed on the island, their efforts shook the colony to the core. News of the *gens de couleur* uprising and of the French Revolution itself, of the ideas of liberty and equality and the struggles for power, emboldened the enslaved to believe that they, too, might have allies in France and could strike on their own account. They seized the time.

On August 22, 1791, enslaved people on the north coast of Saint Domingue made their own rebellion, torching the plantations and recruiting thousands of enslaved men and women to their side. They initially demanded improvements in their conditions—an end to the use of the whip and more free days for themselves—rather than outright freedom, but when the masters responded with contempt and rejected these terms, the enslaved people knew that it was now liberty or death. Led by a former enslaved man named Toussaint Louverture, the rebels went back on the offensive with the new goal of freedom for themselves. The enslaved of Saint Domingue now intended to end their enslavement.

≡ **Insurrection of Enslaved Black People on Saint Domingue, August 22, 1791**   This engraving, from a series of images of the French Revolution published in France between 1791 and 1796, is one of the earliest known representations of the first stirrings of revolt in Saint Domingue (present-day Haiti). Houses and fields are set aflame as Black rebels (dressed in red) rise up against white enslavers (dressed in blue).

It was a desperate and dangerous move. After all, slave rebellions had always ended before in the mass slaughter of enslaved rebels (as in Stono, South Carolina, in 1739). Yet, as fortune would have it, the political winds were soon blowing in more radical directions back in France, and what had been unimaginable in 1791 became revolutionary policy: in 1794, the new French government proclaimed civil and political equality for the *gens de couleur* and freedom and citizenship for the enslaved Black people. A rebellion of the enslaved had turned into a social revolution. Nothing like this had ever happened in the world of Atlantic slavery, and news of it reverberated far and wide. A pillar of white and European power had suddenly been toppled. But the revolution wasn't over.

Ordinarily, white Europeans would be allied in the struggle against enslaved rebels. Britain, Spain, and France were all enslaving empires themselves. But the warfare generated by the French Revolution changed the script. Mindful of European fears of its revolution's spreading influence, the French declared war on Britain and then on Spain in 1793, with fighting on both the continent and the high seas. Now determined to defend its colonies and homeland as well as to export its revolutionary ideals, France was suddenly open to alliances that would have otherwise been inconceivable. Thus, in Saint Domingue French officials invited the rebels to join their military forces with the promise of freedom and citizenship and the now formerly enslaved, led by Toussaint Louverture, rallied to them.

Toussaint had no military training. He grew up enslaved on a sugar plantation, tending to the horses and coaches before he was manumitted, or freed (we don't know the circumstances of his manumission). But Toussaint learned guerrilla tactics from the enslaved rebels he joined in 1791, and he was particularly adept at seizing weapons from his enemies. By the mid-1790s Toussaint had turned himself into a formidable military commander: so formidable that the enslaved and free Black troops under him defeated the armies of Britain and Spain and, at least for a time, secured the slave revolution in what was once the richest sugar colony in the world.

8.2   The Early Republic in Global Context

Describe the broad Atlantic conflicts in which the American republic emerged and the importance of the developing slave rebellion in Saint Domingue.

The outbreak of revolutions in France and Saint Domingue created enormous problems and vulnerabilities for the United States. Caught in an Atlantic world of warfare and social unrest, American leaders had to decide which side to favor and, in the process, had to confront their own political aspirations: their own ideas about what America's revolution and the American republic stood for, what they were forging on the North American continent. In an important sense, the developing conflicts over domestic policies that erupted in Washington's cabinet and in the Congress now spilled onto the international stage.

Debating Foreign Alliances

The political divide that separated Federalists and Republicans was deepened by the French Revolution and its international consequences. Although most Americans cheered the Revolution's outbreak and the values that French revolutionaries claimed to represent, as the Revolution became more radical and bloodier—the king and queen of France were executed in 1793 and the guillotine was used to punish many of the Revolution's enemies—some began to have a change of heart. Republicans mostly remained loyal to France; Federalists became more hesitant. When Britain went to war with France in 1793, the Federalists sided with the British. Now the struggle over the meaning of the American Revolution and the nature of the American republic was going global.

Washington had avoided becoming embroiled in the debates between Federalists and Republicans, but the French and British pressured him to take sides in their fight. The French revolutionary government, invoking the importance of the French alliance to American independence, argued that they were owed American support. The British, who would sign the Jay Treaty (named after John Jay, the American negotiator) with the United States in 1794, offering new trading rights and withdrawing the last of their troops from forts in North America, expected the same. Washington prevailed on his administration and the Congress to maintain neutrality in the conflict, though tensions continued to brew as the French and British alike used strong-arm measures (such as harassing American shipping) to get the Americans involved or to punish neutrality. The bitterness between the Federalists and the Republicans only intensified.

Saint Domingue and the Problem of Slavery

The slave rebellion-turned-revolution in Saint Domingue added to the tensions. As the slave regime in Saint Domingue collapsed and the enslaved and *gens de couleur* gained power, many slave owners fled the colony, often with the people they enslaved. They headed to various parts of the Western Hemisphere, such as in Cuba and South America, but in largest numbers (about 10,000) they came to North America, landing in port cities from New Orleans all the way north to Philadelphia. Word of the slave revolt and of emancipation spread with the migration, ringing in the ears of Black people as well as whites on American shores. So alarmed did enslavers in South Carolina become that they moved to shut down

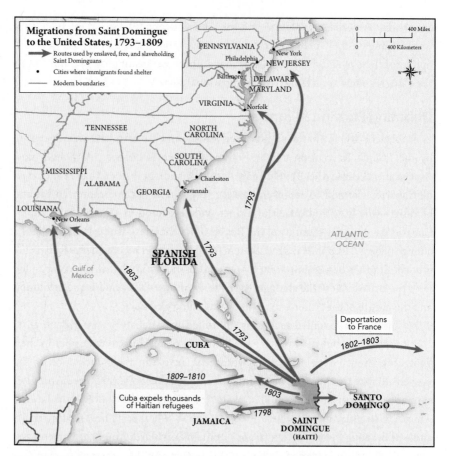

MAP 8.1   Migrations from Saint Domingue to the United States, 1793–1809   As the slave regime in Saint Domingue collapsed, many slave owners fled the colony, often with the people they enslaved. Many fled to North America, landing in port cities from New Orleans all the way north to Philadelphia.

the migration from Saint Domingue along with the African slave trade to the state, assuming that African-born enslaved people were the most rebellious and troublesome (see Map 8.1).

It was no surprise that Federalists were as aghast at the slave rebellion in Saint Domingue as they had become aghast at the Revolution in France. The two, in their minds, went together, the consequences of social hierarchies being shaken by the rabble, white and Black. For them, "democracy" was always a problematic idea, one to be feared rather than fanned, and now the democratic impulses were, so far as they could see, showing their true character.

But what of the Republicans, like Jefferson and Madison, who had spoken of natural rights, liberty, and equality? What were they to say when the enslaved took up the cause for themselves? Some Republicans initially acknowledged that the enslaved, like all people, wished to be free, and they saw justice in what was unfolding in Saint Domingue. But very quickly the temper of Republican opinion changed, and adamant hostility toward the slave rebellion and emancipation prevailed.

None of the Republicans was more consequential in this turn than Thomas Jefferson. Like many Republicans, including Madison, Jefferson was an enslaving planter who nonetheless found it possible both to celebrate human liberty and, for a time, to question the moral and political wisdom of enslavement. In the 1770s, as a young idealist, Jefferson suggested—in both *A Summary View of the Rights of British Americans* (1774) and in a draft of the *Declaration of Independence* (1776)—that abolishing the institution was desirable. In the 1780s, he came up with a vague plan for very slowly ending enslavement in Virginia (perhaps over the course of a century) and wrote in his *Notes on the State of Virginia* (1785) of the dreadful effects that the institution had on enslavers and other whites. "The whole commerce between masters and slaves," Jefferson warned, "is a perpetual exercise of the most boisterous passions, the most unremitting despotism on the one part, and degrading submissions on the other." As a result, Jefferson became recognized internationally as a potential champion of abolitionism, and antislavery advocates encouraged him to play a more public role.

Jefferson's hesitation to advocate forcefully for emancipation was not because he had lost faith in the abstract ideals of freedom and equality. The problem, as he saw it, were the practical realities of outlawing enslavement and creating a world in which Black people were free. For one thing, he learned very quickly that his sentiments were not shared by other enslavers either in Virginia or, especially, farther to the south. Most of them bridled at Jefferson's proposals for undermining their power; his plan for gradual abolition in Virginia was overwhelmingly rejected, and his other gestures in favor of emancipation were largely ignored. The planter class would simply not tolerate such notions, and Jefferson, born to the elite, had no desire to be seen as a renegade.

Even more central to Jefferson's reservations about abolishing slavery was his belief that people of African descent were innately inferior to whites. He presented his racialist views as "speculations" in which he "weighed" pseudoscientific evidence with his own observations about their talents and capacities. Consequently, Jefferson could neither come up with an acceptable plan to end enslavement nor imagine a world in which Black and white people would live together, in peace, as free men and women. As early as the 1780s, Jefferson concluded that emancipation would have to be coupled with the removal of the enslaved population from the land of their captivity to a site outside the United States. He was, that is, the first of those who came to be called **colonizationists.**

What did Jefferson make, then, of the slave rebellion in Saint Domingue? "I tremble for my country when I reflect that God is just; that his justice cannot sleep forever," Jefferson had warned in *Notes on the State of Virginia*, and Saint Domingue suggested that God's justice was now being imposed. Rather than recognizing that

≡ **Sex, Race, and Political Scandal**   Even as Jefferson began his second term as president, the scandalous nature of his relationship with the enslaved woman Sally Hemings was a topic of gossip. This 1804 cartoon by James Akin depicts Jefferson as a proud rooster and Hemings as a devoted chicken. However, despite the obvious pun of the title and the sexual connotations of the image, there's a political message here, too. The proud, strutting rooster had for centuries been a symbol, for France, of the French people. And the quote, just below the title, is from the English play *Cato*: "Tis not a set of features or complexion or tincture of skin that I admire." This play, about Roman resistance to tyranny, was popular in America during the Revolutionary era.

a tipping point had been reached and change was necessary, however, Jefferson dug in his heels and determined to fight against it. Jefferson became an unequivocal foe of Toussaint and his new regime and did all in his power to topple him. As for slavery on his estate of Monticello, Jefferson—despite his hand-wringing—manumitted only 7 of his more than 600 enslaved people, and all were the children or relatives of Sally Hemings, Jefferson's enslaved concubine, whom he never emancipated. After 1791, when the rebellion in Saint Domingue first exploded, Jefferson would never again articulate antislavery sentiments, leaving the problem of enslavement and freedom, by his own reckoning, to the next generation of Americans.

8.3   A Crisis in the Making

‖‖‖ Connect the foreign policy dilemmas of the 1790s with the deepening political conflicts in the United States of the early nineteenth century.

The revolutions in France and Saint Domingue had widespread international repercussions, among them deepening divisions within the political leadership and their constituencies in the American republic. Foreign and domestic issues became increasingly interconnected, and to many it appeared that the struggle to steer the ship of state, which preoccupied the Washington administration, was more and more difficult to contain. Then, in the midst of it all, a major transition in the holding and wielding of executive power took place.

A New Administration for the Republic

George Washington served a second term as president, after again being elected unanimously in 1792. Four years later, in 1796, as another election cycle approached, many Federalists hoped that he would stand for election once again and maintain the reins of presidential power. They would be disappointed. Washington had served his country for more than two decades, militarily as well as politically, and he was clearly exhausted from the work of winning independence and presiding over the organization of the republic. Nearly sixty-five years of age, his health was also failing. He chose to step down.

Washington's decision set a precedent for subsequent presidents—two terms would be regarded as the limit of a presidency despite the absence of any constitutional provisions—and it made for the first contested election for the office since the ratification of the Constitution. Both the Federalists and the Republicans looked to find a successor. The Federalists chose John Adams, who had served as Washington's vice president; the Republicans chose Thomas Jefferson, who had served as Washington's secretary of state. Each had been centrally involved in making the American Revolution and in constructing the framework of the republic. Still, given their developing political differences and party affiliations, they were genuine rivals.

Under the rules of the time, the candidate with the most electoral votes became president while the runner-up became vice president, regardless of their respective party identifications. As it turned out, Adams won in a hotly contested, very close election and was inaugurated president in 1797. Jefferson was a near second and became vice president. It was an odd outcome that encouraged a change in the rules: the **Twelfth Amendment** to the Constitution, ratified in 1804, provided for separate voting for president and vice president.

A Quasi-War and Civil Strife

The new Adams administration stepped into the political storms that had been brewing since 1789 but whose winds kept shifting at home and, especially, abroad. In France, the Revolution had entered a new phase in 1795, overseen by a centralized Directory and focused on France's wars on the European continent and the high seas. As in the Seven Years' War, the British were their main and most formidable enemy. Invoking their treaty of alliance signed in 1778, the French demanded that Americans cease trading with the British and proceeded to seize American merchant ships that carried British goods.

These were moves that Adams, who supported the British, could not tolerate. His administration denounced the French and called upon Congress to make preparations for war, increasing the size of the army and funding the expansion of the navy. At the same time, Adams sent personal envoys to Paris to determine if grounds for negotiation could be found, but agents of France's governing Directory—referred to in diplomatic correspondence as "X, Y, and Z"—made humiliating demands for loans and political favor. As a result of what would be called the **XYZ Affair,** Adams pulled American diplomats from France. All that seemed left was a **Quasi-War** or undeclared war, with France: all treaties between the two countries were dissolved, trade with France was prohibited, and American merchant ships were authorized to resist French vessels that tried to seize them.

Yet the Adams administration and the Federalists saw domestic enemies as well. Many of those enemies were affiliated with the Republicans, who devoted their energies to attacking Federalist policies, often through an expanding press. Others were of foreign origins: French citizens who, the Federalists imagined, were in the country in immense numbers, and Irish immigrants who were fleeing British oppression in their homeland and had little love for pro-British Federalists in the United States.

Since war with France now seemed imminent, Adams and the Federalists in Congress used the circumstance to silence their political adversaries. In June and July 1798, they enacted a **Naturalization Act**, which lengthened the period of time—from five to fourteen years—before an immigrant or "alien" could become an American citizen, required "aliens" to register, and prevented any immigrant who came from a hostile power from becoming a citizen of the United States. They also enacted a Sedition Act, which criminalized "any false, scandalous, or malicious writing or writings against the Government of the United States." Together these pieces of congressional legislation are known as the **Alien and Sedition Acts** of 1798.

The Alien and Sedition Acts raised questions that all governments—including democratically elected governments—may face. What to do about the rights of speech and press in times of war or crisis when organized opposition can appear to threaten the country from the inside? Or how to protect the country from potential antagonists who have recently immigrated or wish to do so? It would not be the only occasion when American society confronted these dilemmas. But in the context of the deep suspicions and hostilities between Federalists and Republicans, the Alien and Sedition Acts proved to be politically explosive.

Republicans were outraged by the actions of the Adams administration. They insisted that the true intentions of the Federalists were to establish a monarchy and aristocratic state, wholly undermining the republic that the Revolution and

Constitution had created. James Madison and Thomas Jefferson were especially important in leading the protest, drafting resolutions in late 1798 that the legislatures of Kentucky and Virginia would enact. Writing the resolutions for Kentucky, Jefferson not only expressed fear for the rights that the Federalists were attacking but went so far as to argue that the American union was merely a diplomatic compact in which the states retained sovereign authority and could reject (Jefferson initially used the term "nullify") any federal law that they believed violated the Constitution. The **Kentucky and Virginia Resolutions** laid the basis for defense of what would come to be called "states' rights" and the "strict construction" of the Constitution.

Adams and Toussaint

Yet, when it came to Saint Domingue, the Adams administration saw opportunities that the Republicans refused. At the heart of the Republican coalition were enslavers from the states of the Chesapeake and Carolinas, who favored the French while hoping to isolate and defeat Toussaint and the formerly enslaved of Saint Domingue. Adams was not a supporter of enslavement, and the Federalists both favored the British over the French and received strong support from merchants deeply involved in the export trade. The slave rebellion clearly frightened them, but the emergence of Toussaint's regime desperately in need of political and economic allies changed the equation.

American export merchants had long looked to the West Indies as a source of trade and enrichment, though the restrictive trade policies of the British and the French relegated them to smuggling. For his part, Toussaint believed that the only way to save the revolution in Saint Domingue and the freedom of the formerly enslaved there was to rebuild the sugar economy and secure the wealth it would generate—not to mention the guns and ammunition he would need.

Toussaint let it be known that he wished to make a deal with the United States, providing trade rights in return for political, economic, and military support. A clear blow to French colonialism, the deal had appeal to Federalists and their mercantile supporters. Through the new Secretary of State Timothy Pickering, the Adams administration began to establish diplomatic relations with Toussaint, and there was serious talk of shipping arms and ammunition and offering monetary assistance to shore up Toussaint's defenses as well as of turning the United States into Saint Domingue's principal trading partner, in effect formalizing activities that had been going on for years. It would have been a remarkable diplomatic feat, joining the first republic in the Western Hemisphere with the first society of formerly enslaved people—and a stunning new constellation of power.

Gabriel's Rebellion

As news of Toussaint's rise to power and rumors of Adams's sympathies circulated in the United States, enslaved and free Black communities pulsed with new senses of expectation. Before 1791, they had been born into a world in which people like them were assumed to be enslaved, with enslavement accepted as part of the order of things. People might escape from or rebel against their enslavers, but they didn't seek to unhinge the institution as a whole. Some might be manumitted by individual enslavers, but this did little to weaken enslavement as a system; and although a few states in the Northeast had enacted gradual emancipation laws (discussed in Chapter 9), these laws were fraught with limits and dangers for African Americans.

Now everything seemed to change. People like them had risen against the most powerful enslaving regime in the Atlantic world, and they appeared to have won. The institution had been abolished in all French colonies. The enslaved had been liberated. And the formerly enslaved themselves were the abolitionists and liberators. Not surprisingly the 1790s saw a great deal of slave unrest in those areas where enslaved people from Saint Domingue had arrived, especially in the lower Mississippi Valley. Slave conspiracies roiled the French and Spanish colony of Louisiana, nearly exploding into a revolt in 1795, not far from New Orleans.

But the most consequential development occurred in Virginia. There, a literate enslaved blacksmith named Gabriel, who had read of the French and Saint Domingue revolutions, organized a revolt in the vicinity of Richmond in the summer of 1800. He may have believed that he had allies in positions of power. Documents indeed suggest that his co-conspirators included two Frenchmen and that Gabriel viewed Quakers, Methodists, and Frenchmen together as "friends of liberty."

As best as we know, Gabriel used his skills as a blacksmith and the mobility they afforded (he could be hired out by his enslaver) to organize among the enslaved in town and countryside alike. He hoped, it seems, to build a small army of enslaved Black people to attack Richmond, seize the arsenal, burn the city's warehouses, take the governor (James Monroe, later a president) hostage, and bargain for their freedom. "Death or liberty," would be their cry. Meaningfully, Gabriel picked August 30, around the anniversary of the slave uprising in Saint Domingue, for his rebellion to begin.

But disaster struck for Gabriel and his followers. A rainstorm washed out the bridges and made the roads impassable on the 30th, and several other enslaved Black people betrayed the rebellion that Gabriel had organized; betrayals were always a danger to slave rebels, a reflection of the enormous personal power that enslavers wielded. White Virginians then rounded up Gabriel and those believed to be his followers, executed him and twenty-five others after brief trials, and began a campaign of brutal repression against enslaved and free Black people that spread into North Carolina. It was a very different ending than in Saint Domingue.

Yet as much as this episode of slave resistance was marked by defeat, the enslavers could hardly take solace. Gabriel met his death before a great crowd in Richmond, and one white observer noted the chilling defiance with which the rebel leader and his comrades mounted the gallows: "The accused have exhibited a spirit, which, if it becomes general, must deluge the Southern country in blood. They manifested a sense of their rights, and contempt of danger, and a thirst for revenge which portend the most unhappy consequences."

8.4   A Critical Election: 1800

Explain the importance of the election of 1800 to the American political landscape.

Gabriel's Rebellion occurred in the midst of one of the most divisive elections in American history: the presidential election of 1800. Gabriel clearly sensed the political divisions that pitted the southern enslavers in his world against their largely Northern opponents, and he may have sensed from their talk about the election that southern political power was threatened. John Adams had served one term as president and was the choice of the Federalists to serve another. The Republicans again picked Thomas Jefferson as their candidate (there were not yet political conventions as we know them), and although neither Adams nor Jefferson himself campaigned—the political standards of the eighteenth century regarded it as inappropriate for a candidate to directly appeal for votes—their supporters in the ranks of Federalists and Republicans made the case in dramatic and often vicious terms.

A Tense Campaign

The advantage in the campaign went to the Republicans because over the course of the 1790s they had made more effective use of print media, especially of newspapers being founded in many of the states, to make their case. In editorials and political cartoons, they painted the Federalists as aristocrats who had nothing but contempt for republics and republican values, who relished elite rule and dreamed of a monarchy modeled on the British example. They attacked John Adams and his supporters for their "corrupt" practices and for their sneering views of the people and popular participation in politics. Republicans depicted Adams and the Federalists as centralizers who sought to extend the power of the federal government over the states and the people, threatening through government policies the independence that ordinary people prized.

Adams and the Federalists were vulnerable. In 1791, in an effort to raise the federal revenue Hamilton had prescribed in his economic plans, the Washington administration persuaded Congress to place a tax on all distilled (alcoholic) spirits produced in the United States. Known as the "whiskey tax," because whiskey was the distilled beverage of choice across the country, the tax angered many back-country farmers who needed the cash that selling homemade grain whiskey would bring. Indeed, in many rural communities whiskey was a crucial item of local trade and could be bartered for services as well.

Hostility to the tax was especially pronounced in western Pennsylvania, where farmers (many veterans of the War of Independence) not only refused to pay but intimidated federal officials who came to collect it. By 1794 a full-scale revolt there against federal authority was looming—we know it as the **Whiskey Rebellion**. Although Washington had earlier led a rebellion against British rule, he would have none of this one. He offered a carrot and stick, sending a commission to negotiate with rebel leaders while calling upon the governors of Pennsylvania and neighboring states to dispatch militia troops—nearly 13,000 of them—in a show of force. Demonstrating his determination, Washington himself rode at the head of one military column. The rebellion quickly collapsed and federal power seemed to be secured, but there was a political price to pay—and in 1800 the Federalists might have to pay it.

The Federalists, of course, had their own repertoire of charges to lodge against the Republicans. They portrayed Republicans as collaborators with the French, who had tried to humiliate the Adams administration diplomatically and wage war on American shipping, and therefore as enemies of the United States. And they vilified Jefferson as an atheist and radical Jacobin (a revolutionary club in France and, more generally, early supporters of overthrowing the French monarchy and turning France into a republic) bent on spilling blood in the streets. George Washington, who died just before the election of 1800 but aligned with the Federalists, had earlier insisted "that you

≡ **Whiskey Rebellion**   Rebels tar, feather, and beat a tax collector during the Whiskey Rebellion in western Pennsylvania in 1794.

could as soon scrub the blackamoor [an African] white, as to change the principles of a professed Democrat [Democratic-Republican]; and that he will leave nothing unattempted to overturn the Government of this Country." The division seemed as deep and the stakes as high as possible.

The election itself added to the tension and confusion. Although Jefferson won a majority of the electoral votes, according to the constitutional rules still in place each elector was to vote for two candidates for president, and as it turned out Jefferson and his running mate, Aaron Burr, received exactly the same number of electoral votes. As a result, the House of Representatives had to pick between them, and the House was still controlled by the Federalists. What's more, Aaron Burr, a Republican, had his own ambitions and was not above cutting deals with Federalists to win their votes.

It required thirty-six ballots in the House—and Alexander Hamilton leaning on Federalists to support Jefferson over Burr, whom he despised—before Jefferson was declared the winner and third president of the United States. Had it not been for the Constitution's federal ratio, which counted an enslaved Black as three-fifths of a free person for the purposes of congressional apportionment, Adams would probably have won a majority of the electoral votes to begin with. And had it not been for Hamilton, Jefferson's longtime enemy in politics, Burr may well have won or the political crisis may have been prolonged. It was one of a number of conflicts between Hamilton and Burr that resulted in a duel between them in 1804, which left Hamilton dead.

Was the Election of 1800 Another Revolution?

To many at the time, Jefferson's victory signaled a sea change in American politics. The Federalists had dominated the government since 1789 and had been in a position to forge their vision of the republic's future. Now the Republicans were in charge, not only of the presidency but of the Congress as well. Thus, when Jefferson was inaugurated in early 1801, he tried to strike a tone of conciliation: "we are all Republicans, we are all Federalists." But some historians, much like the Federalists themselves, have long insisted that a political revolution had been enacted, another in a series that dated back to 1776.

Was this, in fact, the case? If the Federalists had truly hoped to emulate British ideas of aristocracy and monarchy and suppress dissent, it could be said that the Republican victory foiled that plan. But, save for the Alien and Sedition Acts, the Federalists did nothing that could be construed as menacing democratic practices— even though Adams and other Federalists worried deeply about empowering ordinary people—and they certainly accepted the electoral results in 1800, contested as they were. For their part, the Republicans had challenged the authority of the federal government, saw the states as sovereign and capable of blocking federal laws, and, especially in the South, were intent on preserving the local powers of big plantation owners, which included their leadership in political affairs. What's more, the Republican leaders had their own suspicions of democracy and, most everywhere, supported property-holding requirements for voting and office holding at local, state, and national levels.

Rather than a "revolution" in politics, the election of 1800 represented a shift in power and policymaking from the commercial and financial interests based in the Northeast, who anchored the Federalist coalition, to the landed and enslaving interests of the South and West, who led the Republicans. Their representatives would dominate the presidency and the Congress for the next two decades, while the Federalists would become increasingly isolated.

8.5   Envisioning and Pursuing an Empire

Analyze the vision of empire that emerged among American policymakers, how they hoped to pursue it, and how the Haitian Revolution made possible the purchase of the Louisiana Territory from France.

Despite their differences over the amount of power that states should yield to the central government, Federalists and Republicans shared a vision of American empire extending across the continent, all the way to the Pacific. This idea of empire, with an imperial center coordinating the activities of far-flung and often self-regulating outposts, was a political model that Americans inherited from Britain. As colonists, after all, they had rebelled not against the model but rather against the ways in which the British crown and Parliament had abused their power within it.

The idea of an American empire was expressed as early as Thomas Paine's *Common Sense*, which argued that an American republic would usher in a new political world to be shaped well beyond American borders. James Madison, in *Federalist Number 10*, had insisted that a republic itself required a large territory to succeed. Alexander Hamilton spoke of creating a "republican empire" that required significant military strength. For Jefferson it was an "empire of liberty." All knew about the American merchants who were trading in the southern Pacific and Indian Oceans in the third quarter of the eighteenth century and who saw the enormous commercial opportunities that an Asian trade promised.

Making the Louisiana Purchase

No part of the North American continent seemed more crucial to US interests than the lower Mississippi Valley and the port city of New Orleans, widely seen as part of the artery that tapped the continent's vast interior. Together, they connected

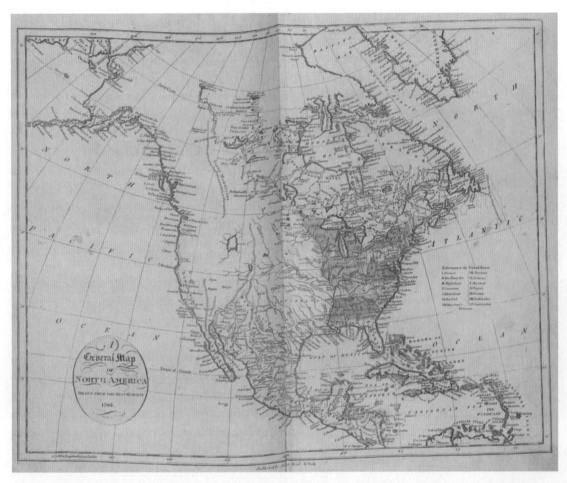

≡ **The Unknown West**   While Federalists and Republicans shared a vision of American empire extending all the way to the Pacific, they had little clear understanding of what the continent looked like west of the Mississippi. Although this map, published in 1796 as part of *The American Atlas*, labels cities, missions, rivers, and state borders, it makes no mention of the Indigenous peoples who inhabited that "empty" territory.

much of the North American continent to the Caribbean basin and then to the larger Atlantic world of politics and commerce. "There is on the globe one single spot," Jefferson observed shortly after becoming president, "the possessor of which is our natural enemy. It is New Orleans."

When Jefferson assumed the presidency in 1801, New Orleans and much of the lower Mississippi Valley—part of what was known as the Louisiana Territory— were in French hands, and the new French leader, Napoleon Bonaparte, who had taken the reins of power in a coup in 1799, imagined creating a great empire of his own in the Americas. The empire's center, as Napoleon saw it, would be in the

Caribbean, organized around the rich sugar-producing colonies of Martinique, Guadeloupe, and Saint Domingue, but Louisiana would serve as the vital periphery, a sprawling storehouse of foodstuffs and livestock for the Caribbean plantations and an extended barrier against the ambitions of the British and the Americans.

Although Saint Domingue and the other French sugar islands had been convulsed for nearly a decade by massive slave rebellions, Napoleon—in pursuit of this empire—determined to reverse the wheels of history. He would send his army to suppress the rebellions, arrest their leaders, restore slavery, and get the sugar estates up and running again. Jefferson could hardly have welcomed the new French project. He warned, "the day that France takes possession of New Orleans . . . we must marry ourselves to the British fleet and nation." Yet, so hostile was he to Toussaint Louverture and the slave revolution in Saint Domingue that Jefferson permitted Napoleon to move ahead, even though Napoleon's success would—by Jefferson's own lights—imperil the future of the United States.

Napoleon assembled a massive military force to overwhelm the rebel leaders and force all the formerly enslaved back onto plantations. In December 1801, twenty thousand troops under the command of Napoleon's brother-in-law, Charles Victor Emmanuel Leclerc, left France for the Caribbean. Within short order, Leclerc and his men appeared to pacify Saint Domingue and arrested Toussaint, who was transported in chains to France. There he would soon die in a frigid jail cell in the French mountains. But when word of French intentions to restore enslavement began to circulate, the officers who had served Toussaint reignited the popular rebellion. They included Jean-Jacques Dessalines and Henri Christophe, who had fought with French troops in Savannah during the American Revolution. Already weakened by tropical diseases, the French forces were soon decimated. Leclerc himself died in November 1802, and his mission utterly collapsed. On January 1, 1804, Jean-Jacques Dessalines proclaimed the independence of the republic of Haiti (Ayiti), named to commemorate the original Native inhabitants rather than the European colonizers.

Before the French defeat in Saint Domingue was at all clear, Jefferson instructed his minister to France, Robert Livingston, to offer as much as $10 million for the city of New Orleans and all or parts of the Floridas east of the Mississippi River. The offer may have seemed far-fetched, though it expressed Jefferson's own interest in establishing at least a toehold at the mouth of the Mississippi. But once Napoleon's army had to retreat and the Haitian Revolution was secured, the American empire Napoleon had dreamed of seemed worthless. And so, to the enormous surprise of Livingston and Jefferson, he offered up the whole of the Louisiana Territory for a mere $15 million (about $320 million in today's dollars). The Louisiana Purchase would nearly double the size of the United States (see Map 8.2).

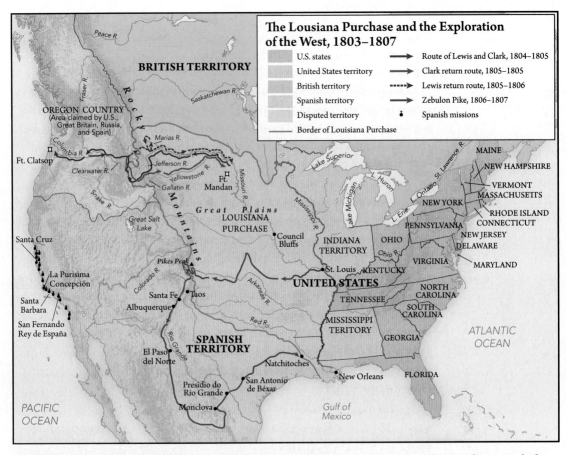

The Lousiana Purchase and the Exploration of the West, 1803–1807

U.S. states	Route of Lewis and Clark, 1804–1805
United States territory	Clark return route, 1805–1805
British territory	Lewis return route, 1805–1806
Spanish territory	Zebulon Pike, 1806–1807
Disputed territory	Spanish missions
Border of Louisiana Purchase	

≡ **MAP 8.2   The Louisiana Purchase**   During the first decade of the nineteenth century, the United States pushed against Spanish and British territory as it sought to expand its holdings.

There were a host of irregularities. It was not at all clear if Napoleon had the authority to sell the territory (he had not consulted with the appropriate political body as French law required) or Jefferson to buy it. At the very least, the purchase required a broad construction of Jefferson's constitutional powers as president, and Jefferson went so far as to write up a constitutional amendment that he ultimately kept in the drawer. Nor was it clear what was ultimately sold. Everyone recognized that the eastern boundary of Louisiana was the Mississippi River, but no one knew just where the river's northern source lay or just how far west the territory extended. And the Spanish, who had controlled Louisiana from 1763 to 1800 and were stunned by Napoleon's actions, insisted on their own claim to a strip of gulf coastal land between Pensacola and the Mississippi River's edge, known as West Florida. These questions and debates would all stir national and international conflicts in the near future.

PERSPECTIVES

Mardi Gras, Tradition, and Rebellion

By the time of the 1803 Louisiana Purchase, the Catholic festival of Mardi Gras had been observed by residents of New Orleans—or, as the French called it, *Nouvelle Orléans*—for nearly a century. Marked by feasting and revelry, Mardi Gras is held the day before Ash Wednesday, which on the Catholic calendar begins the penitential season of Lent. Well into the twentieth century, the Mardi Gras celebrations most familiar to outsiders and tourists were the elaborate balls and parades staged by "krewes," groups made up almost exclusively of white people. But for Black residents of the city, reclaiming the Mardi Gras traditions of their own ancestors has become a way of both preserving non-European forms of costume, dance, and music and recollecting a history of rebellion and survival. The beaded and feathered costumes of the Black Masking Indians (also referred to as the Mardi Gras Indians) call to mind the refuge given by Native Americans to enslaved Black people who escaped their captors. The Black Masking Indians have separate exhibitions on "Super Sunday," just after Mardi Gras. Recently, scholars have suggested that the symbols, dances, and songs unique to each of the more than forty New Orleans Mardi Gras Indian "tribes" can be traced back to the African Kingdom of Kongo, from which many Black enslaved people were descended. Here, the Ninth Ward Comanche Hunters tribe assembles for Super Sunday in 2015.

≡ **The Ninth Ward Comanche Hunters Tribe**

320

A more somber Black Mardi Gras tradition, traced back to 1819, is enacted by the North Side Skull and Bone Gang. Early on Mardi Gras morning, members of the Skull and Bone Gang roam the streets of the historically Black neighborhood of Treme, dancing, drumming, and chanting. The papier-mâché skulls, skeleton suits, and stilt dancing reflect African spirituality and practices of the African diaspora, from voudou in the Caribbean to Day of the Dead observances in Latin America. As the Skull and Bone Gang chants "You next!" or "If you don't live right, the Bone Man is comin' for ya," they remind the community to celebrate resilience while acknowledging mortality. As Skull and Bone Gang leader Big Chief Bruce "Sunpie" Barnes explains, "Having people remember that life is precious and to be able to survive the hard times is nothing to take lightly."

≡ **The North Side Skull and Bone Gang**

CONSIDER THIS

Musician, dancer, performer, and master Black Masking craftsman Chief Shaka Zulu of the Golden Feather Hunters is a recipient of a 2022 National Heritage Fellowship from the National Endowment for the Arts. Chief Zulu observes that until recent decades, "Ash Wednesday came and we burned the suit. Why? The culture started out as resistance, so we didn't want to have evidence of the culture." What are other ways in which marginalized groups in America have used dance, music, poetry, and painting to express resistance to oppression? Is anything lost when those art forms go mainstream?

There were deeper ironies as well. Jefferson, the enslaving plantation owner who saw in the slave rebellion in Saint Domingue his greatest fears come to life, now scored his biggest political and diplomatic coup thanks to the defeat of Napoleon and the victory of the rebellion. Haiti, a republic founded by formerly enslaved Black people, would be the terrorizing image for enslavers throughout the Western Hemisphere. The enslaved people of Saint Domingue, in flexing their power, left a decisive imprint on the course of American history.

Marking an Empire: The Lewis and Clark Expedition

Jefferson had long been fascinated by the North American continent and especially by the vast area west of the Mississippi River. As early as the 1780s, he had spoken of an expedition across the Pacific Northwest and he had read about Captain James Cook's Pacific voyages as well as a French history of Louisiana. As his *Notes on the State of Virginia* reveal, Jefferson's attention was drawn to flora and fauna (plants and animals) as well as to geography and ecology. And much like the European explorers since the fifteenth century, he was also interested in finding "the most direct and practicable water communication across this continent, for the purposes of commerce," thereby turning an expanding empire to economic rewards.

Election to the presidency and especially the Louisiana Purchase provided Jefferson with the opportunity he long sought. With congressional support, he commissioned an expedition—called the **Corps of Discovery**—led by US Army Captain (and his personal secretary) Meriwether Lewis who, in turn, selected William Clark (the brother of revolutionary and Native fighter George Rogers Clark) to join with him. Over time, their names—Lewis and Clark—would become synonymous with the expedition.

To prepare for the journey, Lewis utilized Jefferson's immense library in Monticello to learn what was known about the North American continent. He also went to Philadelphia to be tutored in medicine, astronomy, ethnology (the study of the everyday lives of people), and cartography (mapmaking). Jefferson was clearly interested in the plant and animal life of the continent, in its geologic formations, and its rivers and streams. But he was especially concerned with using the Lewis and Clark expedition to make effective claims to the territory of the Pacific Northwest, where the British, Spanish, and Russians had been active but had not established substantial settlements.

It was a risky operation, not only because of the physical challenges involved but also because Jefferson hoped that Lewis and Clark would traverse land that was not clearly under American control. Indeed, given the uncertainties of the Louisiana Territory's western boundaries, Jefferson wanted the expedition to establish American sovereignty at least over the lands to the headwaters of the Missouri River as well as over the Indigenous people who already occupied them.

The Corps of Discovery gathered near St. Louis and headed off, about forty-five in number, including Meriwether Lewis's enslaved man York, in May 1804. They received vital help—food and scouting—along the way from the **Mandan** people in the northern reaches of the central plains and then from a Shoshone woman among the Mandan named Sacagawea and her French-Canadian husband, who were crucial in enabling translations. They were also spared violent attacks from other Indigenous people, including the Sioux and Nez Perce, whom they encountered on the journey. None of the explorers were prepared for the formidable Rocky Mountains—"the most terrible mountains I ever beheld," one said—and they learned that there was no water passage from the Missouri to the Columbia River. But on November 7, 1805, a year and a half after setting out, William Clark could cry out, "Ocean in view! O! the joy!"

It took another ten months for Lewis and Clark to return to St. Louis, more than two years after they and the Corps had departed. They had separated for a time after re-crossing the Rockies before reuniting in the Mandan villages, where Sacagawea and her family remained when the expedition coursed back down the Missouri. As Jefferson had intended, Lewis and Clark made it to the Pacific, and although they found no water passage through the Northwest, they helped open—with new maps, information, and stories—great expanses of western territory to fur traders and, before long, to colonizing settlers, who by their presence would give some substance to American claims.

Thus was an American empire unfolding over the continent, on lands leading to the Pacific that were claimed in various ways by Indigenous peoples who had been there for millennia: thanks, it seemed, to the remarkable struggles of the enslaved in Saint Domingue, who forced Napoleon and the French to give up on Louisiana but who would have no part of the benefits.

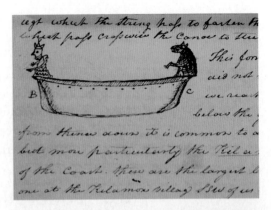

≡ **Observing and Recording**   The Corps of Discovery was charged with recording the cultures they encountered, filling their journals with sketches like this canoe with its intricate carvings at each end, as well as native species like this carefully delineated salmon.

Yet there was more to the imperial vision than the prospect of territorial expansion. Owing to Lewis's training and Jefferson's own scientific dispositions, the Corps of Discovery not only mapped areas of the continent that had scarcely been known to Europeans and Americans but they also identified new species of plants and animals that would frame images and understandings of, and expertise about, the trans-Mississippi West. Knowledge of the flora and fauna as well as of the territory, the assembling and categorizing of the natural world, was a fundamental part of the imperial project (see again Map 8.2).

8.6   Power Struggles on the Seas and the Continent

||| Summarize how the United States became embroiled in the War of 1812 and what was at stake in the conflict.

At the same time that the United States was attempting to expand its power into the trans-Mississippi West, it was reminded of its vulnerabilities as an independent country in a world of empires far larger, more seasoned, and even more aggressive. It was reminded, too, of the determination of Indigenous people west of the Appalachians to stem the tide of white settlement. Warfare in the Euro-Atlantic world, particularly involving the British and French, challenged American sovereignty on the seas while new Indigenous leaders in the Ohio Country attempted to build a confederation of their own, much like Pontiac (discussed in Chapter 6) had attempted earlier. Together, they set the stage and the dynamics for what we call the War of 1812.

Oceans and Embargoes

Napoleon may have suffered an unexpected defeat in the Caribbean, but his armies were extending French power over much of Europe—Switzerland, Italy, the Netherlands, Germany—and the British decided to challenge them. In 1803, the very year Napoleon let Louisiana go, Britain declared war on France and initiated the extremely consequential **Napoleonic Wars** (1803–1815).

Although the fighting raged chiefly on the European continent, both Britain and France warned American merchants not to ship arms or any other military supplies to their enemy. The British were especially wary as well as able to enforce this demand owing to their large navy. They not only began to board and seize American ships but also to "impress" (take into captivity) both suspected British deserters and American sailors. Jefferson and his fellow Republicans were enraged by these actions, but even the pro-British Federalists objected to impressment.

Federalist John Quincy Adams, the second president's son (and future president himself), likened it to "an authorized system of kidnapping on the oceans."

Jefferson responded to British naval actions by convincing Congress to pass the **Embargo Act** of 1807, which prohibited American ships from participating in all international trade. While the Act declared its aims as protecting the "essential resources" of "our merchandise, our vessels and our seamen," the goal was in fact to avoid confrontations with Britain. Not surprisingly, American merchants, who had prospered in traveling to an array of foreign ports, protested the embargo so vehemently that it was repealed. Under the auspices of Jefferson's Republican successor, James Madison (elected in 1808), Congress instead passed the **Non-Intercourse Act** of 1809, directed only against the trade with Britain and France.

Americans feared that their sovereignty and independence were being challenged, that European powers—and Britain most clearly—had accepted the new United States in theory but not in practice: perhaps to the end of seeing the American republic collapse or be recolonized. Indeed, threatening developments were occurring in North America itself, to the north and west of US territory. After the American Revolution, Britain remained on the continent, with colonies in Canada that, since 1783's Treaty of Paris brought an end to the war, were magnets for the roughly 60,000 Loyalists who fled the United States. These colonies—divided into Upper Canada (present-day Ontario) and Lower Canada (present-day Quebec)—also offered potential allies for Indigenous people of the Great Lakes region and Ohio Country, who had mostly aligned with the French and then the British between 1754 and 1783. Indeed, ever since Pontiac's War of the 1760s, a large number of Native groups in the Ohio Country looked to confederate in an effort to block the westward march of European settlers and secure these lands for themselves. For their part, the British continued to occupy forts in the northwest until the **Jay Treaty** was ratified in 1795 (see Map 8.3).

Tecumseh and Tenkswatawa

Pontiac's ambition was taken up in the early nineteenth century by an impressive Shawnee warrior named Tecumseh. With his brother Tenkswatawa, known as the "prophet," who warned fellow Indigenous people against embracing American ways and surrendering their lands, he tried to build a multiethnic confederation in the trans-Appalachian West. In 1808, they established a settlement called Prophetstown at the junction of the Wabash and Tippecanoe Rivers in the Indiana Territory. From there they reached out to as many as fourteen Indigenous tribal groups in making the alliance, though the Shawnee, Delaware, and Potawatomi would be most important. They reached out as well to tribal groups in British Canada.

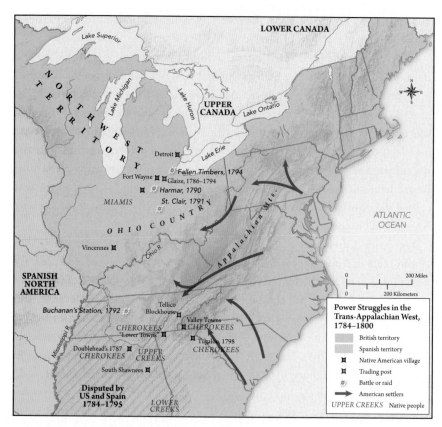

≡ **MAP 8.3**   **Power Struggles in the Trans-Appalachian West, 1784–1800**   At the same time that the United States was attempting to expand its power into the trans-Mississippi West, new Indigenous leaders in the Ohio country sought to stem the tide of white settlement.

Tecumseh's and Tenkswatawa's activities led to increased raiding on white settlers and then to retaliation by Indiana's territorial governor, William Henry Harrison, which left Prophetstown a smoldering ruin. But Tecumseh was not about to leave the scene, and the British were determined to maintain their hold on Canada. Although the British were not looking for war with the United States, they also believed that so long as they had Canada, the American republic might unravel on its own, enabling the British to reassert their power.

British expectations were not entirely misplaced. Although Federalist and Republican leaders protested British naval harassment, the Federalists still looked to Britain as an example and ally while the Republicans thought that Britain meant to threaten what the revolution had achieved. President Madison himself had come to believe that "war is inevitable," and, strengthened by the election of young Republicans known as "War Hawks"—Henry Clay (Kentucky), John C. Calhoun (South Carolina), and Felix Grundy (Tennessee)—he pushed Congress for authorization to wage war.

The War of 1812

After four days of debate, the House voted for a declaration of war against Great Britain; the Senate approved the declaration on June 17, 1812, and Madison signed it into law the following day. It proved to be the closest vote for a war declaration in US history, one that split along party and regional lines. The Republicans and the South and West, despising the British and looking to strengthen trans-Appalachian settlements, voted for war. The Federalists and the Northeast and Middle Atlantic, long aligning with the British and looking to trans-Atlantic commerce, voted against.

The United States hardly seemed prepared to go up against such a great power as Britain. The US Army had fewer than 7,000 troops, and the US Navy had just over twenty vessels, including a collection of gunboats. The British, by contrast, had an army of roughly 250,000 men and over 600 warships ready for service. But Americans had been outnumbered in 1776 as well, and they recognized that Britain's ongoing war with Napoleon in Europe would tie up much of their military. The United States thus set out to defeat the British in Canada and perhaps annex it to expand their North American republic: an imperial move of their own (see Map 8.4).

Conquering Canada proved to be more of a challenge than the Madison administration and its War Hawks had imagined, however. US troops were sent to invade Canada by attacking at three points, beginning with Forts Detroit and Dearborn (near current-day Chicago)

≡ **The Prophet Tenkswatawa (George Catlin, c. 1830)**   In his journals, George Catlin, the Pennsylvania-born artist who was the first to portray Native Americans extensively in their own territories, wrote of his encounter with Tenkswatawa: "he was blind in his right eye, and in his right hand he was holding his 'medicine fire,' and his 'sacred string of beads' in the other. With these mysteries he made his way through most of the North Western tribes, enlisting warriors wherever he went, to assist Tecumseh in effecting his great scheme, of forming a confederacy of all the Indians on the frontier, to drive back the whites and defend the Indians' rights; which he told them could never in any other way be protected."

in the west. But owing to the armed resistance of Tecumseh and the problems the Americans had in raising troops and getting them to fight, they suffered defeats and failures most everywhere. Even a foray across Lake Ontario that enabled American troops to capture and burn the Canadian provincial capital of York (later Toronto) could not obscure the larger fact that retreat was soon the order of the day.

The exception to the military disappointments—and a very consequential one—came on Lake Erie, where a young American naval commander, Oliver Perry, managed to force the surrender of a British fleet and make it possible for US troops to cross into Canada. There they defeated the British and their Native allies at the Battle of the Thames (1813), killing the powerful Tecumseh in the process. It was a massive blow, especially to the Native confederation that Tecumseh had tried to build.

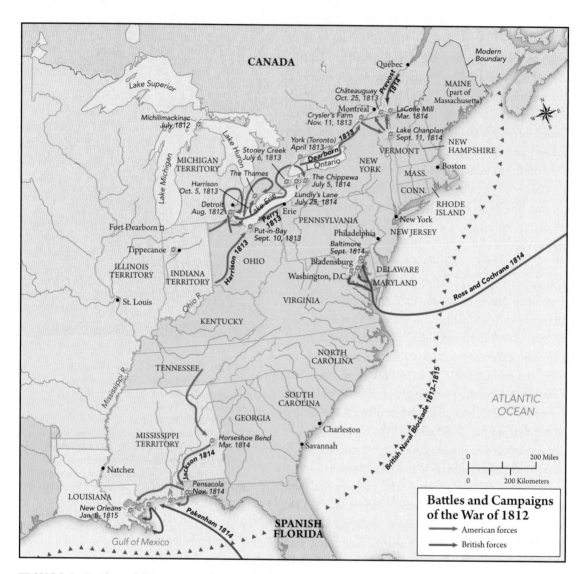

≡ **MAP 8.4**   **Battles and Campaigns of the War of 1812**

Years earlier, Tecumseh had gone south to win the support of Indigenous people there, and the Upper Creeks (also known as the Red Sticks for their body and weapon paint) agreed to form a southern wing of his confederation. They were assisted by the British and Spanish, who sold them weapons, and, after settling scores with enemies among the Creek, launched attacks on white settlements as well as on a number of forts in the Mississippi Territory during the summer of 1813, inflicting serious casualties. Since federal troops were busy with Tecumseh and his British allies, state and territorial officials had to raise militia companies to challenge the Red Sticks. Among the militia commanders who came forward was a Tennessean named Andrew Jackson.

Strains of War

However much it began with plans to protect American sovereignty and hopes to promote territorial expansion, the war with Britain revealed many of the domestic vulnerabilities that plagued a young United States. Indigenous people who had been pushed west across the Appalachians were striking back, determined to limit the reach of American power. In New England, a Federalist stronghold, many men were unwilling to join the army, leaving US forces on the Canadian border weak against British counterattack. As a further sign of internal division, Federalists met in Hartford, Connecticut, in late 1814 to express their grievances about the war and propose constitutional amendments that would prohibit lengthy trade embargoes, require two-thirds Congressional votes for a declaration of war or the admission of new states, and repeal the federal ratio that empowered slaveholders. At this meeting, known as the **Hartford Convention**, there was even talk of secession, of leaving the American Union, the United States.

Tecumseh, c. 1812   This anonymous sketch shows the great leader wearing the epaulettes typical of a British officer's uniform, likely a fanciful addition by the artist.

Then there were the enslaved. In early 1813, the British turned their attention to Chesapeake Bay, where the rich plantations of Virginia and Maryland could be found and large crops of tobacco and wheat were grown. They began by seizing and burning American merchant ships, with the intention of landing troops and establishing a solid foothold. Quickly they found that the enslaved were fleeing to them in hopes of finding freedom. At first, British officers were reluctant to welcome these fugitives into their lines, but by early 1814 they changed their policy and—much as Lord Dunmore had done in 1775 (discussed in Chapter 6)—encouraged enslaved people to escape captivity and come to the British side. Eventually about 3,400 enslaved people took up their offer, striking fear into the hearts of Virginia and Maryland enslavers, who saw an insurrection and abolition in the making.

By the summer of 1814, British troops had marched into the newly created Washington, DC, burned the Capitol Building and the White House (retaliation for the American burning of York), and then headed north to Baltimore, where they were stopped—and where, at Fort McHenry, lawyer and amateur poet Francis Scott Key wrote the words for "The Star-Spangled Banner," the eventual US national anthem. But Britain's readiness to weaken enslavement and enlist the enslaved in their efforts to defeat the Americans suggests how much an outright British victory may have unsettled. Indeed, in late 1814, British ships and troops

MAPPING AMERICA

Comparing Viewpoints

At a single stroke, Thomas Jefferson nearly dou-bled the size of the United States when he acquired Louisiana from France in 1803. While westward expansion is undoubtedly one of the most enduring legacies of Jefferson's presidency, Southern slave-holders were more concerned about the reverbera-tions of the Haitian Revolution (1791–1804) and the newly independent Black republic of Haiti.

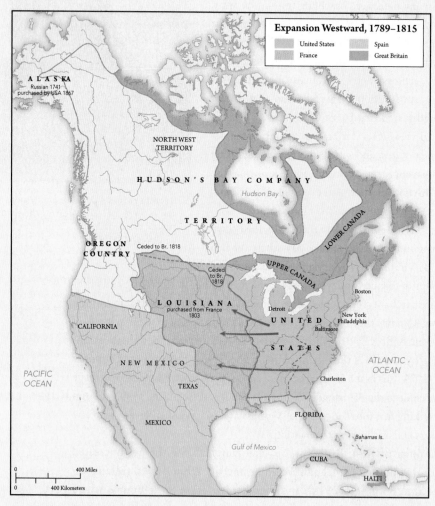

Expansion Westward, 1789–1815

United States	Spain
France	Great Britain

≡ **MAP 1**   A conventional North-South orientation (and including the Louisiana Purchase) shows events in Haiti at the bottom of the map and marginal to US history.

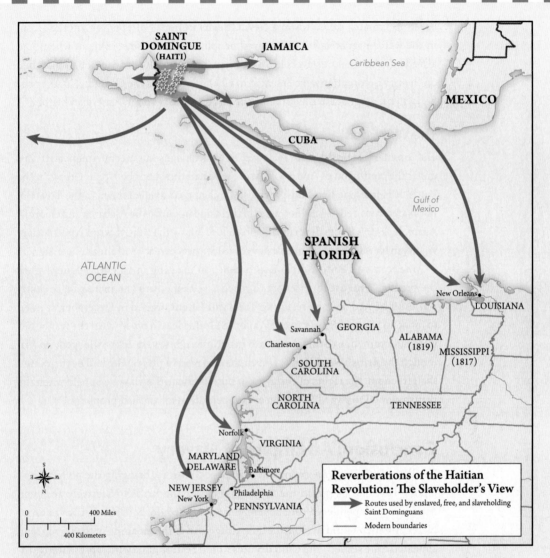

≡ **MAP 2**   A map with an orientation from the Caribbean shows Haiti's proximity to the South, reflecting the perspective of Southern slaveholders.

Thinking Geographically

1. For most readers, the first map will be the more recognizable. Why do you think this is so? What does this say about the way developments discussed in this chapter imprinted themselves on the identity of the nation?

2. Assume the vantage point of a slaveholder from the South. Why does the second map better represent the way this person viewed the world?

based in Jamaica sailed toward New Orleans in hopes of opening another front in the war: in an area full of enslaved people on plantations, some of whom had already defied their enslavers in 1811, when between 200 and 500 rebels marched on the city before they were defeated in what is known as the German Coast or the St. John the Baptist Parish uprising, the largest slave revolt in American history.

The War Ends

The considerable British force that reached New Orleans was met by American troops under the command of Andrew Jackson, who had thrashed the Upper Creeks at the Battle of Horseshoe Bend the previous March and compelled them, in the Treaty of Fort Jackson, to cede 23 million acres of their land in soon to be Alabama and Georgia. Again, Jackson's forces dramatically prevailed. But by the time Jackson could declare victory in New Orleans in the first days of 1815, a peace treaty had already been signed.

American and British diplomats had begun meeting in Ghent, Belgium, since the previous August in an effort to reach a settlement to the increasingly costly war. As it turned out, the resulting **Treaty of Ghent**, signed in December, seemed to mark no winner or loser in the War of 1812. Borders in place when the war began were maintained; existing American maritime rights were acknowledged; and although the British would never return the enslaved fugitives who had been granted their freedom, the rights of enslavers in the American South were upheld when the British agreed to pay $1.2 million as compensation for the lost property.

Conclusion: An Empire of Slavery

The War of 1812 was an important event in US history, bringing the political revolution that had begun in the 1770s to a close. The British effectively accepted American independence and sovereignty—this would be their last invasion of North America—and the four-decade struggle over the meaning of the Revolution appeared to be settled. The United States would be a republic with representative institutions subject to selection, directly or indirectly, by popular vote. Power would be shared between the federal and state governments (though the issue of sovereignty between them and the extent of those powers was still to be determined). And plantation owners not only secured their property but also emerged as the wealthiest and most powerful social group in the country. Over the next decades, southern enslavers and their allies would control the presidency, the Congress, and the Supreme Court; the crops grown by those they enslaved would fill the coffers of merchants and contribute mightily to the country's economic growth; they would direct American foreign policy; and they would pursue an empire continental in scope. Jefferson's imagined empire of liberty would now be tied to an empire of slavery, a knot that would require another revolution to break.

WHAT IF the Slave Rebellion in Saint Domingue Had Been Defeated?

The slave rebellion-turned-revolution was a pivotal event in world history, not only ending enslavement in the world's richest sugar colony but also in reconfiguring the social and political landscape of the Western Hemisphere. But what if the rebellion had gone the way of all slave rebellions before it? What if—as was very nearly the case—it had been defeated brutally within days or weeks?

Undoubtedly the island's planters would have needed to come to terms with what had taken place, but the plantations would soon have been back in operation and revolutionary France would probably have accepted the maintenance of enslavement in its colonies. When Napoleon later claimed power, he would have been in a very strong position to construct an empire revolving around the Caribbean and Louisiana and to reinvigorate a French presence in North America. Jefferson, who saw New Orleans as a place of enormous strategic importance, would have been unable to purchase the city or the Louisiana Territory for any price, and so either the American future would have been bounded in the west by the Mississippi River or the United States would have had to pursue a continental empire through other—perhaps military—means against the French. What's more, Indigenous people from the Great Lakes down toward the Southeast and Gulf Coast would have had a new ally against the aggressive Americans and far better prospects for holding onto their land both east and west of the Mississippi.

The purchase of Louisiana was a turning point of great significance in the history of the United States, enabling the American government and colonizing white settlers to move rapidly into the Gulf states and the trans-Mississippi West and to contest the power of the remaining empires they found there. It would also elevate the struggle over enslavement to the defining issue of the nineteenth century, with wide-ranging implications for the future of all people in the United States. And all of this because of what enslaved people did on a small island in the Caribbean.

DOCUMENT 8.1: Napoleon's Secret Instructions to General Charles Leclerc, October 31, 1801

Napoleon explains to General Leclerc what he wishes his troops to do in Saint Domingue.

In order to understand the instructions, it is necessary to divide the time of the expedition in three periods:

The first will cover the 15 to 20 first days, necessary in order to occupy the places, to organize the national guards, to reassure the well disposed, reunite the ships under escort, to organize the artillery transport, to accustom the mass of the army to the customs and to the physiognomy of the country and take possession of the plains.

The second period is the one when the two armies being separated, one would pursue the rebels to the knife, one would "take them out of the nest," first in the French part, and successively in the Spanish part.

The third period is the one when Toussaint, Moyse and Dessalines will not exist anymore and when 3 to 4000 Blacks, withdrawn in the hillock of the Spanish part will form what is called in the islands the Maroons [communities of fugitive enslaved people] and whom one can succeed in destroying them with time, steadfastness and a well combined system of attack.

The Spaniards, the British and the Americans are equally worried to see a Black Republic. The admiral and the major general will write memorandums to the neighboring establishments in order to let them know the goal of the government, the common advantage for the Europeans to destroy the black rebellion and the hope to be seconded.

If one needs it, one must ask for some supplies in America, in the Spanish islands or even in Jamaica. One must ask at Havana if one needs a thousand or so men, in order to help to occupy the Spanish part of St. Domingue.

Jefferson has promised that as soon as the French army would arrive, all dispositions will be taken in order to starve Toussaint and to help the army.

Toussaint will be subdued only when he will come to the Cap or to Port au Prince, amidst the French army, to pledge fidelity to the Republic. That day, it is necessary, without any scandal, without any insult, but with honor and consideration, to put him on board of a frigate and send him to France. If possible, arrest at the same time Moyse and Dessalines, or pursue them to the bitter end and then, send to France all the white followers of Toussaint, all the blacks having had positions and suspected of malevolence. Declare Moyse and Dessalines traitors to the country and enemies of the French people. The troops will take the field, and take no rest before getting their heads and disperse and disarm all their partisans.

If after the first 15 or 20 days it is impossible to bring back Toussaint, it is necessary, in a proclamation, to declare that if during so many days, he is not coming to take the oath to the Republic, he is declared traitor to the country and, at the end of the delay, one will start war to the knife.

A few thousand blacks, wandering in the hillocks and looking for refuge in these rustic lands, must not prevent the Major general from considering the second period as ended and to arrive quickly to the third one. Then the moment to assure for ever the ownership of the Colony to France had arrived. And the same day, one must on all points of the Colony, arrest all the men in place who would be suspected, whatever their color be, and embark at the same time all black generals whatever their manners, their patriotism, and the services they had rendered, observing meanwhile to let them go with their grades [ ], and with the assurance that they will be well treated in France.

All the whites who served under Toussaint, and who, in the scenes of St. Domingue were covered with crimes, will be sent to Guyana.

All the blacks who behaved, but that their grades don't allow anymore to remain on the island will be sent to Brest [port city in northwestern France].

All the blacks or colored men who misbehaved, whatever their grades will be sent to the Mediterranean sea and dropped in a harbor of the island of Corsica.

If Toussaint, Dessalines or Moyse would be taken bearing arms, they will be within 24 hours judged by a military commission and shot by a firing squad as rebels.

Whatever would happen, one thinks that during the 3rd period, one must disarm all the negroes, whatever the party they will be, and to put them back to cultivation.

After the 3rd period the proclamation which declares at last the island of St. Domingue returned to the Republic, one will give back to all the landholders who are in France, and who never emigrated, their possessions.

Source: Charles Leclerc, *Lettres du Général Leclerc*, ed. Paul Roussier (Paris: Société de l'histoire des colonies françaises, 1937), 263–274.

DOCUMENT 8.2: Letter from Thomas Jefferson to Robert Livingston, April 18, 1802

Jefferson explains to Robert Livingston, his minister to France, how he understands the importance of New Orleans and the larger territory.

The cession of Louisiana and the Floridas by Spain to France works most sorely on the U.S. On this subject the Secretary of State has written to you fully. Yet I cannot forbear recurring to it personally, so deep is the impression it makes in my mind. It compleatly reverses all the political relations of the U. S. and will form a new epoch in our political course. Of all nations of any consideration France is the one which hitherto has offered the fewest points on which we could have any conflict of right, and the most points of a communion of interests. From these causes we have ever looked to her as our *natural friend,* as one with which we never could have an occasion of difference . . . [But] there is on the globe one single spot, the possessor of which is our natural and habitual enemy. It is New Orleans, through which the produce of three-eighths of our territory must pass to market, and from its fertility it will ere long yield more than half of our whole produce and contain more than half our inhabitants. France placing herself in that door assumes to us the attitude of defiance. her . . . The day that France takes possession of N. Orleans . . . . we must marry ourselves to the British fleet and nation. . . . This is not a state of things we seek or desire.

It is one which this measure, if adopted by France, forces on us, as necessarily as any other cause, by the laws of nature, brings on its necessary effect … Will not the amalgamation of a young, thriving, nation continue to that enemy the health and force which are at present so evidently on the decline? And will a few years possession of N. Orleans add equally to the strength of France? She may say she needs Louisiana for the supply of her West Indies. She does not need it in time of peace. And in war she could not depend on them because they would be so easily intercepted …

If France considers Louisiana however as indispensable for her views she might perhaps be willing to look about for arrangements which might reconcile it to our interests. If anything could do this it would be the ceding to us the island of New Orleans and the Floridas. This would certainly in a great degree remove the causes of jarring and irritation between us, and perhaps for such a length of time as might produce other means of making the measure permanently conciliatory to our interests and friendships. It would at any rate relieve us from the necessity of taking immediate measures for countervailing such an operation by arrangements in another quarter. Still we should consider N. Orleans and the Floridas as equivalent for the risk of a quarrel with France produced by her vicinage

Source: Thomas Jefferson to Robert R. Livingston, April 18, 1802, from *The Works of Thomas Jefferson in Twelve Volumes.* Federal edition. Collected and edited by Paul Leicester Ford. http://www.loc.gov/resource/mtj1.026_0131_0134

Thinking About Contingency

1. Do you agree with the assessment of this book's author of how history may have unfolded if the slave rebellion in Saint Domingue had been defeated? Why or why not?
2. Historians emphasize that historical events are not fully predictable but, instead, are "situationally produced"—that is, they are conditioned on previous events that may shape the range of possible outcomes but that do not predetermine any one result. According to this idea, to what extent was the history of the United States in the early nineteenth century situationally produced by events in Saint Domingue?
3. Thinking about the slave rebellion in Saint Domingue and the Louisiana Purchase, how does contingency differ from randomness or chance?

REVIEW QUESTIONS

1. How might the American Revolution have influenced both the outbreak of the French Revolution and the Haitian Revolution?

2. How were the Federalists and Republicans of the 1790s and early nineteenth century related to the Federalists and Anti-Federalists of the 1780s?

3. Why would the Adams administration, which was hostile to revolution and worried about the excesses of democracy, be willing to ally with Toussaint Louverture in Saint Domingue?

4. Did the Republicans, who gained power in 1800, represent better than the Federalists the main currents of the American Revolution?

KEY TERMS

Alien and Sedition Acts (p. 310)

colonizationists (p. 307)

Corps of Discovery (p. 322)

Declaration of the Rights of Man and the Citizen (p. 302)

Embargo Act (p. 325)

Federalists (p. 301)

Haiti (p. 298)

Hartford Convention (p. 329)

Jay Treaty (p. 325)

Kentucky and Virginia Resolutions (p. 311)

Louisiana Purchase (p. 298)

Mandan (p. 323)

Napoleonic Wars (p. 324)

Naturalization Act (p. 310)

Non-Intercourse Act (p. 325)

Quasi-War (p. 310)

Republicans (p. 301)

Saint Domingue (p. 302)

Treaty of Ghent (p. 332)

Twelfth Amendment (p. 309)

Whiskey Rebellion (p. 314)

XYZ Affair (p. 310)

RECOMMENDED READINGS

Carol Berkin, *A Sovereign People: The Crises of the 1790s and the Birth of American Nationalism* (Basic Books, 2017).

Gordon S. Brown, *Toussaint's Clause: The Founding Fathers and the Haitian Revolution* (University of Mississippi Press, 2003).

Ron Chernow, *Alexander Hamilton* (Penguin, 2003).

Gregory Evans Dowd, *A Spirited Resistance: The North American Indian Struggle for Unity, 1745–1815* (Johns Hopkins University Press, 1993).

Laurent Dubois, *Avengers of the New World: The Story of the Haitian Revolution* (Harvard University Press, 2005).

Nicole Eustace, *1812: War and the Passions of Patriotism* (University of Pennsylvania Press, 2015).

John Kukla, *A Wilderness So Immense: The Louisiana Purchase and the Destiny of America* (Anchor, 2003).

Alan Taylor, *The Internal Enemy: Slavery and War in Virginia, 1772–1832* (W.W. Norton, 2014).

Expansion and Its Discontents
1815–1840

Chapter Outline

≡ **The Lowell "Mill Girls" at Work**   Lowell, Massachusetts, was founded in the 1820s as a planned town for the manufacture of textiles. By 1840 the eight mills in Lowell employed more than 6,000 young women, primarily from farming backgrounds.

In 1823, with the inspiration of Francis Cabot Lowell, who had earned his money in the Pacific trade with India and China, the first textile mill opened in the town that took his name, Lowell, Massachusetts. Unlike other early textile mills in New England, those in Lowell planned to employ young women who would operate the machines, spinning cotton and wool into yarn and then yarn into cloth, and live in nearby boardinghouses. One of them was Harriet Hanson Robinson, who was hired in 1834 at the age of ten and continued working in the mill until 1848, when she was twenty-four. Harriet was younger than most of the mill girls when she started—on average, they began work at between fifteen and twenty-five years of age—but she was not alone, and her young age reminds us that child labor was a central part of the American economy and the process of industrialization.

Decades later, Robinson published a memoir, *Loom and Spindle: Or, Life Among the Early Mill Girls* (1898). In it she recalled the opportunities that textile work offered

Timeline

1814	1816	1818	1820	1822	1824	1826

1814 › Treaty of Ghent ends the War of 1812

1817–1825 › Construction of the Erie Canal, the second longest canal in the world

1819 › Adams-Onis Treaty brings Florida under US control

1821 › Mexico achieves independence from Spain; Stephen F. Austin establishes colony in the Mexican province of Tejas

1823 › Textile mills open in Lowell, Massachusetts; Monroe Doctrine asserts independence of Western Hemisphere from European intervention

women, enabling them to gain a measure of independence with the few dollars they earned, though she acknowledged that many were expected to send their wages to family members back home, usually in the countryside. Arrestingly, Robinson also described the difficult conditions that female mill workers endured, whether they could keep their earnings or not. The Lowell "mill girls," as they were known, began their workday at 5:00 in the morning and weren't done until 7:00 in the evening, with short breaks for breakfast and dinner. "Even the doffers [mill girls ten years or younger, who were assigned the job of removing—"doffing"—bobbins from machines and replacing them with new ones] were forced to be on duty fourteen hours a day," she observed. Managers, generally called "overseers," added to the exploitation and surveillance that the mill workers suffered.

But it wasn't just long hours and low pay that were the female mill workers' lot. It was also the new rhythms of work and the great noise of the machinery that were both

1828	1830	1832	1834	1836	1838	1842

1828 ▸ Election of Andrew Jackson, first US president from the trans-Appalachian West; first railroad built in the United States, out of Baltimore

1830 ▸ Indian Removal Act appropriates money to relocate Indigenous tribes west of Mississippi River

1831 ▸ Supreme Court in *Cherokee Nation v. Georgia* rules that it lacks jurisdiction to review claims of a Native American nation within the United States

1832 ▸ Supreme Court in *Worcester v. Georgia* rules that only the federal government, and not the individual states, has power to regulate the Native American nations; Black Hawk War between the United States and Native Americans led by Black Hawk, a Sauk war chief; Jackson vetoes recharter of the Bank of the United States

1834, 1836 ▸ Female mill workers strike in Lowell, Massachusetts

1835–1836 ▸ Texas Revolution and establishment of the Republic of Texas

1835–1842 ▸ Second Seminole War

1837 ▸ Panic of 1837 ushers in major economic depression

1838–1839 ▸ Trail of Tears— Cherokees forced to relocate west

unfamiliar and unsettling. One of the mill girls wrote, "you cannot think how odd everything seemed to me. They set me to threading shuttles and tying weaver's knots, and now I can take care of one loom. I could take care of two if only I had eyes in the back of my head. When I went out at night, the sound of the mill was still in my ears. You know, people learn to live with the thunder of Niagara in their ears."

Very demoralizing it would seem. Yet in 1836, when a tightening economy led the Lowell mill owners to cut the workers' wages, a previously invisible solidarity erupted. "Great indignation was felt," Robinson recalled, "and it was decided to strike or 'turn out' en masse. The mills were shut down, and the girls went . . . in procession to the grove on Chapel Hill and listened to incendiary speeches from early labor reformers." This was, as Robinson proudly declared, "one of the first strikes that ever took place in this country."

The opening of the Lowell mills was an indication of the economic changes sweeping the United States during the first decades of the nineteenth century, as the settlement of the country moved westward, the market economy dramatically expanded, the white and Black populations grew rapidly, and a new mass politics came into being. But the "turn out" in Lowell, led by some of the more unlikely rebels, suggested, too, that the country's expansion brought discontents and challenges along with it. By the late 1830s, as in Lowell, there would be reckonings on numerous fronts as a new political economy was being forged.

9.1   People and Markets

||| Account for the enormous population growth of the United States and the expanded reach of the market economy from 1815 to 1840.

When the Constitution of the United States was ratified in 1788, the new republic was very much an Atlantic and coastal entity. All of the states and the overwhelming majority of the settler population lined the Atlantic coast and its near hinterlands, and trade among them was either intensely local or international. Farmers and artisans mostly exchanged goods and labor in the towns in which, or near which, they lived, while enslaving planters shipped tobacco, rice, indigo, and cotton to European markets. The North American territory farther to the

West remained the homelands of Indigenous people trying to recover from the crushing impacts of disease and violent encounters with the now-American settlers. Then, during the first four decades of the nineteenth century, much of this world was disrupted by a series of dramatic changes that simultaneously reconfigured the dimensions of the United States and laid the groundwork for serious crises.

Demographic and Economic Expansion

The two decades after the War of 1812 saw enormous demographic and economic expansion in the United States. The population grew from about 8.3 million to about 14.7 million, a pace that, if maintained, would have *doubled* the population every twenty-three years (the United States would now have well over 1 billion people instead of its current 331 million). Although immigration, chiefly from Britain and Germany, contributed about a quarter million to the total, it was the remarkable birthrate—and relatively low infant mortality rate—that was most responsible. White women, more than 90 percent of whom lived in the countryside, had, on average, seven children. Enslaved women, nearly all of whom lived on farms and plantations, had between seven and eight. In both cases, limited means of birth control and labor imperatives were key: free rural families depended on the labor of children to run their farms, and enslavers clearly encouraged or coerced enslaved women to reproduce to increase the size of their workforce and the overall value of their property. By 1830, one-third of the population of the United States was under the age of ten (today, one-third of the population is under the age of twenty-six).

American population growth during these two decades sped the settlement of the trans-Appalachian West. Between 1812 and 1836, eight new states entered the Union, all but two of which (Maine, Alabama) could be found west of the Appalachians—Indiana, Mississippi, Illinois, Louisiana, Missouri, and Arkansas—with the latter three west of the Mississippi River in territory purchased from France in 1803. Throughout this area, the population more than tripled from about 1 million in 1810 to more than 3.5 million in 1830 and grew from about 15 percent of the country's total population to nearly 30 percent, a remarkable increase. The exception was among Indigenous people, whose numbers declined from just over half a million in 1810 to about 400,000 in 1830, owing to disease and warfare. Nearly one-quarter of them were still in the trans-Appalachian west, and especially in the new states of the **Deep South**, Alabama and Mississippi most prominently. Most would soon be farther west after being forced to surrender their lands to aggressive white settlers and to the state and federal governments that supported them (see Map 9.1).

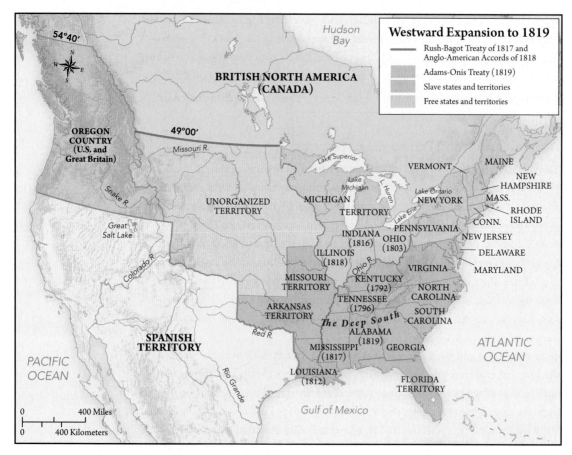

MAP 9.1   Westward Expansion to 1819   American expansion required deliberate action on the part of the federal government. Each stage of the process required diplomatic finesse, military force, and considerable demographic and economic pressure applied by white settlers seeking new lands.

Government's Role in Economic Expansion

The role of governments in facilitating the removal of Indigenous people from desirable areas of white settlement was only one example of the important part that the state, at all levels, played in the economic expansion of the United States—and would continue to play. The nineteenth century is often imagined as a time when the government had little involvement in the American economy, a time of what is called laissez-faire (a French term meaning to let alone) in the economic arena. But this was hardly the case.

On the federal level, the government could and did promote domestic economic activity by placing tariffs on some foreign imports to encourage domestic manufacturing, funding a merchant marine to protect shipping, establishing a central bank as Alexander Hamilton had urged, selling off lands to lure prospective farmers and raise revenue, enabling enslavement to expand geographically, dispossessing Indigenous people, and having US Army troops patrol the edges of western settlement. Even political leaders who wished to limit federal power, including Jefferson and Madison, saw some of these initiatives as crucial to the country's security and prosperity.

On the state and municipal levels, activity was even more robust. States moved against Indigenous populations, supported the interests of enslavers, chartered banks and other new corporations, and, along with municipal governments, invested money in the expensive transportation projects that tied settlers in the rural and urban hinterlands to the port cities of the Atlantic and Gulf coasts.

Turnpikes and canals were especially important in permitting farmers and other producers both to ship their goods to markets more quickly (and at lower costs) and to purchase new commodities that had not previously been available. Turnpikes built upon a tradition of local government support for the maintenance of roads, and by the late eighteenth century they drew upon private sources of investment as well. Toll roads, often run by state-chartered companies, proved particularly significant, and made possible the Philadelphia and Lancaster Turnpike, completed in 1795, which stretched over 60 miles and was the first hard-surfaced (crushed stone), long-distance road in the country.

≡ **The Erie Canal, c. 1829** Bucolic images of the Erie Canal disguise the difficult working conditions for the laborers who had to cut down trees and clear land before they could even begin to dig the canal. Without heavy machinery, all of the rock and soil had to be shoveled out by hand or detonated with unpredictable explosives. Hundreds of Irish immigrant laborers became sick and died from "Genesee fever"—an umbrella term for a variety of maladies likely caused by malaria or typhoid—as they worked in a particularly swampy and mosquito-infested location. As an Irish work song of the time described conditions, "We are digging a ditch through the mire, Through the mud and the slime and the mire, dammit! And the mud is our principal hire; In our pants, down our boots, down our necks, dammit!"

Canals would be more challenging to construct and even more consequential in their impact. The Erie Canal, which linked the Hudson River Valley and, by extension, New York City to the Great Lakes, was one of the most impressive engineering feats of the early

Nature and Technology

For many witnesses in the nineteenth century, industrial technology represented the triumph of imagination over nature. Admirers saw mechanization as romantic, a perspective few people share today. Artists depicted factories in pastoral settings. Composers sought to turn the noises of steam engines into music. Painters of early ironworks attempted to show the sublime in the belching smoke and flame.

George Inness's *Lackawanna Valley* (c. 1856) can be read as an enthusiastic affirmation of technology. The locomotive appears to move through a valley near Scranton, Pennsylvania, in unity with nature. Traditional rural life appears undisturbed, but numerous tree stumps in the foreground lend ambiguity to Inness's painting. Is Inness celebrating technology or lamenting a rapidly vanishing wilderness? *Lackawanna Valley* exemplifies a dilemma that confronted many Americans in the early nineteenth century: expansion inevitably led to the widespread destruction of unspoiled nature, itself a powerful symbol of the nation's greatness. Although it was

≡ *The Lackawanna Valley,* c. 1856

initially commissioned as an homage to the machine, Inness's *Lackawanna Valley* also served as a poignant reminder of a quickly changing landscape.

There is no ambiguity in Thomas Johnson's 1863 photograph of Waymart, a small town in northeastern, Pennsylvania, not far from Scranton. In 1850, the Delaware and Hudson Canal Company built a railroad through Waymart to transport coal. Business briefly boomed, but as Johnson's photo shows, economic success came at a high price. A forest of tree stumps crowd out three men who gaze on the town from a barren hillside. By the end of the century, Waymart and surrounding areas had fallen into decline, bypassed by new rail lines and a rapidly globalizing economy.

≡ *Waymart,* c. 1863

CONSIDER THIS

When looking at a broad historical phenomenon such as the Industrial Revolution, it is important to maintain perspective: the assessment of historical developments at a scale ranging from micro to macro. At what scale do these two images document the dramatic changes brought about by the Industrial Revolution?

nineteenth century—and one of the most costly, well beyond the resources of individual investors. Begun in 1817 with support from the New York State legislature as well as private sources, the canal required the construction of eighty-three locks to negotiate changes in elevation across the land and more than $7 million in cash, a huge amount for the time and equivalent to around $135 million in today's dollars. When completed in 1825, the Erie Canal was, at 363 miles, the second longest in the world after the Grand Canal of China, and it catapulted New York City ahead of Philadelphia (which had benefitted from the turnpike to Lancaster) as the largest and most economically vital city in the United States.

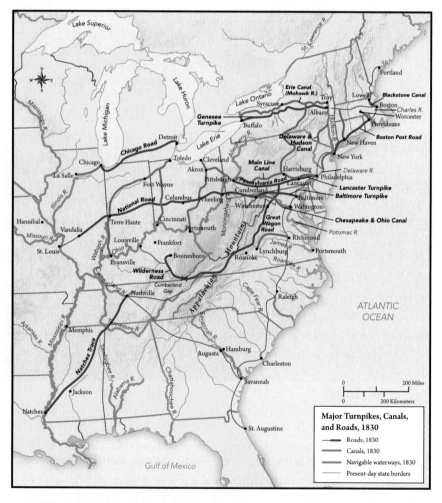

≡ **MAP 9.2   Major Turnpikes, Canals, and Roads, 1830**   By 1830 thousands of miles of roads, tracks, and canals interlaced the United States, especially the Middle Atlantic and New England.

The Erie Canal, which quickly paid off its cost in tolls (an indication of the traffic and a boon to investors), stimulated a burst of canal building, especially in New England, the Middle Atlantic, and the northern sections of the trans-Appalachian west. But the canals were soon rivaled and then surpassed by another and even more significant means of transportation—the railroad—which could traverse any terrain and run even when cold weather froze waterways. First built and tested in Britain in the 1820s, the railroad arrived in the United States by the early 1830s, when small American railroads were constructed out of Baltimore and Charleston with substantial municipal support. A boom then spread up and down the east coast, though especially in the Middle Atlantic states of New York and Pennsylvania. Everywhere, port cities competed to tap the growing trade of their hinterlands and reap the rewards for their merchants, artisans, and shippers. By 1840, the country could boast about 3,000 miles of railroad track, nearly matching canal mileage. Ten years later, railroad tracks covered nearly 9,000 miles, while the canal era was effectively over (see Map 9.2).

≡ **Eli Whitney's Original Patent for the Cotton Gin (1794)** This drawing accompanied Whitney's application for a patent for his cotton gin, a hand-cranked machine that efficiently separated cotton fibers from seeds.

The Cotton Boom

That Charleston built one of the first American railroads, and that Virginia, North Carolina, Georgia, Alabama, Louisiana, and Mississippi quickly followed suggests the great pulse of economic activity spreading across the South, particularly the Deep South. It reflected a surge in the production of cotton. For many years cotton had been grown on farms and plantations in the southern colonies and states mainly for household use. The cotton would be harvested and made into cloth with spinning wheels and looms. Very fine cotton, known as Sea-Island cotton, was also grown along the coast of South Carolina and Georgia, but it was difficult to raise and had a limited consumer market.

What spurred the tremendous expansion of cotton production, called the **cotton boom**, in the early nineteenth century was the developing Industrial Revolution across the North Atlantic world and the invention of a mechanical device known as the cotton gin. Textile manufacturers in Britain, continental Europe, and soon New England needed far more of the crop than ever before, and the gin made it possible to cultivate and market the large quantities necessary to meet their demand.

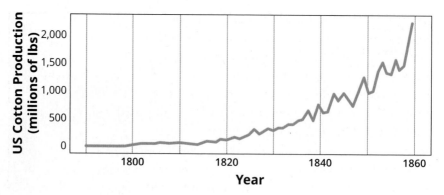

FIGURE 9.1　Cotton Production, 1790–1860.

　　The problem that the gin solved was separating the cotton plant's fleecy fiber (which would be marketed) from the seeds (used to grow more) far more rapidly than could be done by hand. And although numerous gins were in the process of being devised, Eli Whitney, a Yale graduate who headed south to work as a tutor on a Georgia plantation, is generally recognized as the inventor for the gin he built in 1793.

　　The invention of the **cotton gin** meant that "upland" cotton—a tougher, cheaper fiber, more suitable to mass-produced cloth—could be grown in much larger quantities and in many more areas than the Sea-Island variety. As a result, aspiring cotton planters quickly moved into the piedmont of South Carolina and Georgia (the geographic area bounded to the east by the coastal plain and to the west by the southern Appalachian Mountains, featuring rolling hills and rich soil) and then into the fertile areas of Alabama, Mississippi, and Louisiana, pressing state officials to eliminate Indigenous land claims and buying up large tracts of land that they could bring into cultivation. Cotton, that is, became the engine of American economic growth in the first six decades of the nineteenth century (see Figure 9.1).

　　The cotton so important to American economic prosperity was grown mainly by the most exploited portion of the country's population: enslaved Black people. Until the nineteenth century, enslaved people could be found in all the states of the Union but in largest numbers in those of the Chesapeake and farther to the south along the Atlantic coast. There they did the backbreaking work of raising tobacco, wheat, rice, indigo, and Sea-Island cotton. Then the prospects of cotton wealth led to a major geographical shift. Enslavers either moved their laborers south and west to take advantage of the new opportunities or sold them to slave traders in the growing and horrific **domestic slave trade**, often called the "Second Middle Passage." Torn from their families and communities, hundreds of thousands of enslaved people, most of them male, were sent to cut trees, clear land, construct housing, prepare fields, and finally to plant and harvest the cotton crop. In 1820, 144,000 enslaved people could be found in Alabama, Mississippi, and Louisiana; in 1840, the enslaved population of those states had increased more than fourfold to 617,000.

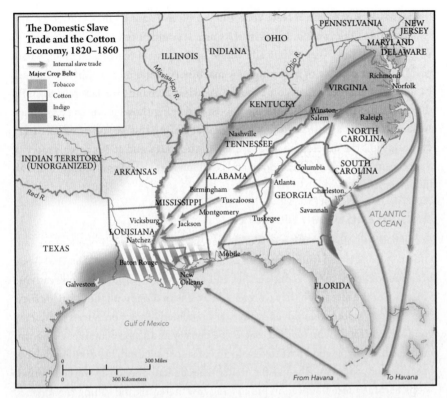

The Domestic Slave
Trade and the Cotton
Economy, 1820–1860

→ Internal slave trade
Major Crop Belts
Tobacco
Cotton
Indigo
Rice

≡ **MAP 9.3** **The Domestic Slave Trade and the Cotton Economy, 1820–1860** By
1860, as many as 700,000 enslaved people had been sold south in the domestic slave trade.
Enslaved labor forged the new cotton economy and the market expansion of the era.

By the 1830s, more and more enslaved people were being sent from the states of
Virginia, Delaware, Maryland, and Kentucky—known as the Upper South—to the
states of Alabama, Mississippi, and Louisiana—known, together with South Carolina
and Georgia, as the Lower or Deep South. By 1860, as many as 700,000 enslaved people had been sold south in this domestic (or interstate) slave trade, leaving their friends
and loved ones behind, to work the fields of cotton planters. Enslaved labor forged the
new cotton economy and the market expansion of the era (see Map 9.3).

9.2 Changing Forms of Urban Labor

Situate the labor systems of the early nineteenth century on a spectrum of
freedoms and unfreedoms.

The pulse of market expansion could be felt even earlier in American cities, particularly those of the eastern seaboard, before it spread to newer cities and towns to

the west—in Rochester in New York, Pittsburgh in Pennsylvania, Cleveland and Cincinnati in Ohio, and St. Louis in Missouri. It could be felt as well in rural areas on or near fall lines (geographically where uplands meet the coastal plain, where rushing water capable of powering new machinery could most readily be found). In all cases, market expansion brought growing demands for laborers to build the infrastructure, manufacture the goods, and bring those goods to consumers. Although we are accustomed to viewing labor during this period as either "free" or "enslaved," the developing labor system of the 1820s and 1830s reveals more of a spectrum of freedom, unfreedom, and coercion that would continue to shape an industrializing world.

Artisans and Urban Workers

Ever since the colonial settlements of the seventeenth century, the work of artisans and master craftsmen (those who had skills and owned the tools of their trade) had been foundational to the economic life and growth of cities, towns, and scattered villages. For the most part, they worked side by side in shops with the aid of journeymen (trained workers employed by master craftsmen) and apprentices, producing goods chiefly for a local clientele. But as the density and scope of market exchanges increased, owing in good part to new forms of transportation, the division of labor became more complex. The master craftsmen who had previously worked in their shops became more involved in purchasing raw materials and selling the finished goods. That is to say, they began acting mainly as merchants. Trusted employees, artisans and journeymen alike, were then left in charge of workshop production. Little by little, as demand continued to grow, the shop might be enlarged, more craft workers hired, and those called **outworkers**—usually women and children who labored in their own homes or tenements—might be brought into the finishing stages.

Nearby, swelling pools of casual and manual laborers, arriving from the American countryside, Canada, or Europe, found their way to the waterfronts, the construction sites, the transportation networks, the mines, and the streets. There, they lifted, hauled, drove, chopped, carried, cut, dug, and dredged, forging America's developing infrastructure and sources of energy. Many had the knowledge and skills that came with life on the land, and most faced the problems of "seasonality," stretches of un- or underemployment due to cycles of weather and trade, which required them to cobble together their subsistence from diverse sources or forced them into the poor houses (known as almshouses) that were growing in number. Market expansion meant hard and challenging times for many laboring people.

These pools of laborers included women, as well as men, who no longer could find places in a rural economy increasingly given over to producing for markets and depending on store-bought supplies. Initially they might seek work in neighboring households. Then they might join brothers who did not inherit farmland and head to cities and towns where they did outwork, found jobs in the garment trades, operated boardinghouses, worked as street vendors, laundresses, or cooks, and, when necessary, entered the sex trade (prostitution). As the market economy extended its reach, the pace of rural-to-urban migration quickened dramatically during the 1820s.

Textile Mills

Women as well as men who began to leave the farms also might find work in the most vivid symbols of a changing market economy: the textile mills of the Northeast that dotted the fall lines from New Hampshire, Massachusetts, Rhode Island, and Connecticut down to Pennsylvania. The first water-powered cotton mill in the United States, built by English immigrant Samuel Slater in Pawtucket, Rhode Island, in the 1790s, featured a mechanical spinning machine that produced thread and yarn. Thanks to large investments by merchants and to technological innovations, some smuggled out of England by entrepreneurs like Slater, that mechanized spinning and weaving, these mills would soon contain within their walls all the steps of the production process. They were among the first **factories** to appear on the economic landscape.

In Lowell, Massachusetts, mill owners embarked on a novel plan: they recruited young, unmarried women who had traditionally done spinning and weaving under the authority of their fathers, to come and live in boardinghouses and turn out yarn and cloth on a scale well beyond anything with which they were familiar. Elsewhere, mills relied on whole families who left declining farms to take up berths in their villages and factories. But even in these family mills, the workforce was composed chiefly of women and children who, the mill owners believed, could be paid less and controlled more easily (see Map 9.4).

Mindful of Britain's "dark Satanic Mills," a phrase from a poem by William Blake that captured the wretched and conflict-ridden road of early industrialization, the owners hoped to construct something of a pastoral alternative. Indeed, reinforcing the connection made by cotton, the mill villages seemed rather like plantations farther to the south, with their residential laborers, supervisors known as "overseers," machine shops, stores, churches, and imposing houses that owners occupied. But the owners quickly learned that the workers would not be so easy to discipline, that they would push back or leave of their own choosing. And the workers quickly discovered, whether they moved or stayed, that they were now in a new world of the marketplace.

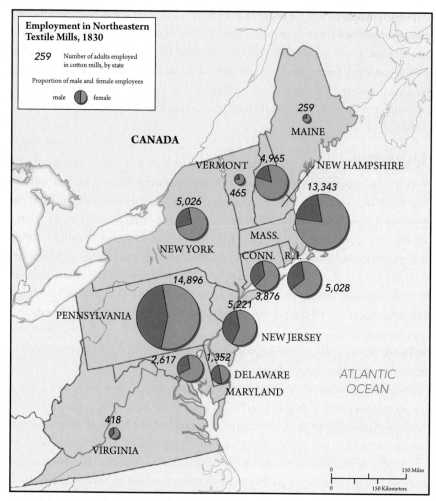

Employment in Northeastern Textile Mills, 1830

259 Number of adults employed in cotton mills, by state

Proportion of male and female employees

male ◑ female

≡ **MAP 9.4** **Employment in Northeastern Textile Mills, 1830** The Northeast experienced the first wave of industrialization. Mill towns like Lowell, Massachusetts, grew quickly into cities.

9.3 Market Evolution or Revolution?

‖‖‖ Describe the character of the economic changes in the early decades of the nineteenth century.

One of the large questions that historians of the early nineteenth century debate is the character of the economic changes that were spreading across the country. Was this a "market revolution," meaning a fundamental transformation in the ways in which people lived and worked? Or was this something less fundamental, more of a continuation or acceleration in the social and economic relations that had prevailed toward the end of the eighteenth century? This argument shapes the ways in which we should view the forging of American economic development during the entire nineteenth century.

Market Intensification

The American economy during the first few decades of the nineteenth century surely saw much that was new in technology, transportation, and the division of labor. But a closer look suggests that there was much more of an expansion and intensification of the ways in which the economy had long operated. The textile mills were, of course, new and a sign of an industrial society in the making. But in their organization and productive capacity they remained the exceptions rather than the rule.

As late as the 1830s, merchants and large landowners were still the dominant actors in American economic life, as they had been among people of European descent since their earliest North American settlement. They still organized the production and distribution of goods that circulated in regional and international markets, and, in the coastal cities, they controlled the wharves, the shipping, and the warehouses. They extended loans and other forms of credit, sold provisions and fineries, employed lawyers, and generally ran the municipal governments. Moreover, very few of the shops and small manufacturing works in the cities and towns had experienced mechanization. When opportune, they expanded production by branching out, incorporating new workers, and beginning to look beyond local horizons.

In the countryside, merchants and large landowners owned the most fertile acres, exploited the labor of men, women, and children in various states of dependency (the enslaved, tenants, servants, farm laborers), offered services to more humble neighbors, and served as magistrates, militia captains, and political patrons generally. Many of the big landowners found their way into mercantile activities. Some invested in the new textile mills. The dynamism of this economy could be seen in the circulation of goods and people, at times over great distances, rather than in major transformations in the ways the goods were produced or in the workforce. Even the cotton plantations of the Deep South followed the models of predecessors along the Atlantic coast in their ways of exploiting enslaved labor and doing business with export merchants and slave traders.

Labor's Coercions

One of the most important ways in which older economic practices persisted was in the legal status of laboring people. Enslavement was the most extreme form of labor exploitation, and although we associate it mainly with the southern states, enslaved workers could be found throughout the United States well into the nineteenth century. The Constitution's Fugitive Slave Clause (discussed in Chapter 7) and subsequent Fugitive Slave Law of 1793, which required that runaways be returned to their owners, put the federal government directly on the side of sustaining enslavement and gave the institution a legal basis in all of the American states and territories.

What about areas where enslaved people were in small numbers compared with the Deep South? Beginning in the 1780s, states in New England and the Middle Atlantic, responding to the pulses of a revolutionary age and to pressure from enslaved and free African Americans, began to enact emancipation statutes. But those statutes did not free *any* enslaved person; they freed only the *children* of enslaved people and only when the children reached adulthood—age twenty-one, twenty-five, or twenty-eight, depending on the state and the gender of the child—in good part to compensate white enslavers for the chattel property they were losing. Emancipation was, therefore, gradual and meant to maintain white control. Even so, there was enough confusion as to who was free and who was still enslaved that most of these states had to pass additional laws in the 1840s and 1850s before enslavement could be pronounced officially dead. Recent research has discovered enslaved people in New Jersey as late as 1860.

Yet, horrific as it was, the enslavement of Black people was by no means the only form of forced labor to be alive and well in the early decades of the nineteenth century. In fact, wherever one looked—at plantations and farms, docks and wharves, shops and garrets, mines and mills, journeymen and apprentices, domestics and outworkers, factory hands and common laborers—various forms of legal and customary dependency and subordination prevailed. They burdened working people with the direct and coercive power of their employers and with an assortment of vulnerabilities that threatened their very survival.

Apprentices, maritime laborers, sailors, servants, and miners faced physical violence if they failed to keep up the pace, punishment if they broke equipment, and even imprisonment if they left the job before the contract under which they were hired had expired. Especially in port cities like Baltimore, Philadelphia, New York, Boston, and Charleston, the jails filled with "runaways" of many sorts and ethnicities, none in greater numbers than seamen. At other work sites, canal diggers, harbor dredgers, building tradesmen, farm laborers, and domestics could be subject to corporal (physical) abuse, pressed into debt, and fired without pay. Across the country, stints in the workhouse or harsh forms of compulsory labor were meted out to vagrants, paupers, and the unemployed, forcing many people into the marketplace whether they liked it or not. In some cases, convicts were leased out to transportation projects; more generally, private manufacturers employed them within prison walls. Either way, the use of convicts undercut the prospects of those in search of work while anticipating the hard labor regimes of the post–Civil War South.

Free Labor

"Free labor" that might be recognizable to us could be found to a notable degree, however. First and foremost, it was a relationship and status characterized by a free exchange: an employee agreed to work for a specified number of hours and days in return for a wage and could quit without fear of penalty. It was also a relationship in which the employer abandoned the use of physical coercion for discipline or control. Free labor was both a political and social relationship: workers had to enter the exchange of their own free will, and employers had to be held accountable for what they did at the workplace.

Generally speaking, free laborers of this period were adult males of European descent who could claim full ownership of their persons and, perhaps, of some productive property like tools of the trade. They were also adult males with some skills, established local residency, and recognized civil and political rights, among them the right to appeal to community standards for justice.

But even those whose working lives came nearest to the ideal of free labor confronted a structure of power that proved unfavorable and difficult to unsettle. That is because American labor relations inherited the tradition of British common law, especially the **law of master and servant**, which required loyalty and obedience on the part of the worker during the term of a contract and imposed serious legal penalties for violations. The law and the courts plainly served the interests, and expressed the power, of employers.

Nonetheless, change was in the air. By the 1820s, some state courts were raising questions about workers who were compelled to stay on the job in order to receive any wages due them and, in the process, casting doubt on the legality of the commonly drawn distinction between "voluntary" and "involuntary" servitude (meaning that "voluntary" servitude could pass muster). Bit by bit, courts recognized the employers' authority in the workplace so long as it did not involve corporal punishment or prohibit employees from leaving. The pressure had come from workers themselves who brought suit or protested on the job. But the emergence of new forms of bargaining that would involve formal organization among working people and recognized rights in the workplace—forms of collective bargaining that would be familiar to us—were still decades in the future.

Redefining Money

One of the things that market expansion brought forth were new forms of exchange involving money. Money as a medium of exchange was still new to many Americans in the late eighteenth and early nineteenth centuries. Alexander Hamilton clearly recognized as much when calling for the establishment of a national bank not just to raise capital, support the public credit, and administer finances but also to lay the "basis of a paper circulation."

The problem, according to Hamilton, was "a deficiency of circulating medium." By this he meant that large numbers of farmers and artisans could do little but engage in barter on the fringes of the market economy. Gold and silver coins did change hands, particularly for official purposes, though in Hamilton's view, these coins (also known as specie) were "dead stock" unless deposited in a bank. Only then could the specie, on the basis of its value, enable the printing of paper money, and only then could regional and national markets expand and draw more and more Americans into its clutches, which Hamilton saw as critical to the country's prosperity.

Hamilton's concerns reflected the workings of local economies. Bank notes and other forms of paper credit, as well as specie, could be found in the 1790s, especially in large urban centers where merchants and small manufacturers depended on them in transactions with distant suppliers. In smaller towns and villages across the United States, however, the very types of barter that worried Hamilton remained robust. Farmers, craftsmen, shopkeepers, blacksmiths, and tenants were short on cash because there was little of it and little need for it. They traded crops for store goods, labor for tools and seeds, skilled services for foodstuffs, and livestock for furniture and clothing; they also "swapped work" when the demands of planting, harvesting, or building were particularly pressing. Although producers and merchants were aware of the value attached to goods in this barter exchange and frequently kept track of their economic activities in account books, they were flexible and informal about the settlement of debts. Store owners often advertised that they would accept "all kinds of country produce" in exchange for their wares.

This was not a subsistence economy or one wholly oriented to local communities. But it was still a world of face-to-face economic relations in which producers and shopkeepers met one another in a marketplace governed by shared understandings of how goods were valued and transactions occurred. For them, money was one of several mediums of exchange and a means of defraying specific obligations, like state taxes, which had to be paid in coin. In Ulster County, New York, a tradesmen could therefore accept payment in "wheat, rye, Indian corn, as well as cash, or, anything good to eat."

As most Americans of the early nineteenth century understood it, money came in the form of gold and silver coins. Some of these coins, since the 1790s, had been made in US mints; many others were of French, Portuguese, and especially Spanish derivation and accepted as legal tender. By the 1830s, silver and the much more valuable gold were coined or valued at a ratio of roughly sixteen to one (meaning 1 ounce of gold was equivalent to 16 ounces of silver), and they circulated most widely in port cities. Paper currencies were also well known. Since the colonial era they were circulated, in limited quantities, either by British authorities or private concerns. Most notoriously, paper currency was printed by the Continental Congress and then by some of the states to finance the great costs of the Revolutionary War. Indeed, so dramatic was the depreciation, or drop in value, of these "continentals" that they encouraged disgust and suspicion of the paper medium more generally.

≡ **William Tolman Carlton, *The Yankee Peddler* (c. 1851)** By the 1830s, thousands of young men crisscrossed rural America with wagons full of goods from the burgeoning manufacturing centers of the East Coast. Writing in 1834, teacher and physician William Alcott noted that young men with a wagon full of "Yankee notions" like clocks, tinware, combs, and even violin strings would sell their stock "rapidly, at large prices and great profits" across the South and West and that "some of them appeared to be getting rich." Because they were itinerant and because they had to purchase the goods themselves directly from the manufacturers, Yankee peddlers had no use for barter—they expected to be paid in cash.

State Banks and Paper Money

Alexander Hamilton had hoped that a national bank would allay those suspicions, but the paper currency flooding American marketplaces by the 1830s was neither being printed nor circulated in the manner he had envisioned. Most of the circulating paper money (or bank notes) of the 1820s and 1830s was the product of privately owned banks chartered by individual state legislatures, much as canal and railroad companies had been. The zeal for bank charters came from commercially minded state residents, often merchants themselves, who wished to speed the expansion of market forces and maintain as much local control as possible. Each of the states had its own rules. For example, states imposed different requirements as to the amount of specie banks had to keep on hand to print notes as well as the ratio of specie to bank notes they had to observe.

It's not hard to predict what happened next. The new state-based paper money system simultaneously accelerated market exchanges and created a sea of monetary chaos. Bank notes printed in one state usually traded at a discount (meaning it was worth less) in the others, and their value ultimately depended on a bank's ability to redeem the paper notes in specie if the note holders came in and presented them, as they were permitted to do. By the early 1830s, over 300 state-chartered banks, responsible for more than $60 million in notes, operated in the United States, though the federal government provided scant oversight of their activities. At most, the **Bank of the United States (BUS)** could collect state bank notes and present them for specie redemption as a way of keeping the state banks accountable. When, as we will see, a major financial panic hit the country in 1837, the effects therefore spread rapidly, and little could be done to limit the consequences.

9.4 Democratization and the Rise of Mass Political Parties

‖‖‖ Determine how the important political reforms of the period helped give rise to the country's first mass political parties.

Of the many expansions that defined the period from 1815 to 1840—market, demographic, territorial—political expansion was equally consequential and related to all the others. Like the economy in the early nineteenth century, politics, too, was either intensely local or national and international. The political horizons of most free Americans were defined mainly by county courthouses and state legislatures. Candidates for office depended on personal patronage rather than political parties. And both voting and office holding usually required ownership of property.

The federal government was very far away, and only the House of Representatives was subject to popular election. Senators and presidents were chosen by state legislatures, the former directly and the latter indirectly through the Electoral College. Here matters of large public policy and foreign relations were debated and determined, and here the early political parties—Federalists and Republicans—took shape. Power relations, therefore, revolved mostly around communities and their local hierarchies and customs and around the large Euro-Atlantic world of commerce, diplomacy, and war-making. Then came a period of change.

Expanding the Male Electorate

Although American politics was still organized in 1815 as it had been when the Constitution was ratified and the Washington administration assembled, the economic and territorial expansions that followed the War of 1812 brought demands for political reform. The demands often came from new groups of merchants, small manufacturers, farmers, and artisans who were interested in advancing their interests and challenging the power of older elites. They called for the elimination of property-owning requirements for voting and office holding and for the increase of political offices subject to election rather than appointment. The rapid white settlement of the trans-Appalachian West gave these demands added force.

One of the initial signs of the changing political system was the presidential election of 1824, in which four candidates—one from the Northeast (John Quincy Adams of Massachusetts), one from the southeast (William Crawford of Georgia), one from the northwest (Henry Clay of Kentucky), and one from the southwest (Andrew Jackson of Tennessee)—vied for the presidency. For the first time the electors were chosen by the popular vote in most states (as they are now—whoever receives the most popular votes then receives the state's electoral votes), and with four candidates in the ring it was impossible for any one of them to get the majority of electoral votes.

As a result, for the second and last time in the country's history (the election of 1800 was the first), the decision on the presidency, according to the prescriptions of the Constitution, was left to the House of Representatives. Only the top three vote getters would remain in the mix (Clay came in fourth and was out), but Clay then threw his support to John Quincy Adams, the son of second president John Adams, who prevailed and was inaugurated (see Map 9.5).

Defeat in presidential elections can be the doom of aspiring political figures, but for Andrew Jackson (whom we met in Chapter 8), 1824 was more of a debut. He was famous for his brutal campaigns against Native Americans and for his victory in the War of 1812 over the British at the Battle of New Orleans. Jackson had also served in the US Congress and as a justice

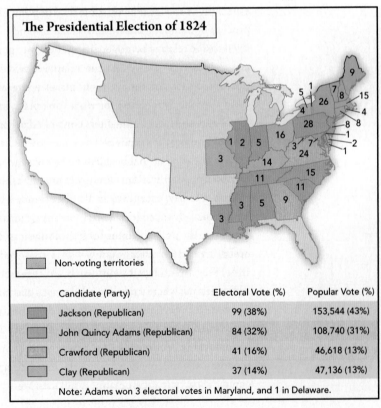

The Presidential Election of 1824

	Candidate (Party)	Electoral Vote (%)	Popular Vote (%)
	Jackson (Republican)	99 (38%)	153,544 (43%)
	John Quincy Adams (Republican)	84 (32%)	108,740 (31%)
	Crawford (Republican)	41 (16%)	46,618 (13%)
	Clay (Republican)	37 (14%)	47,136 (13%)

Non-voting territories

Note: Adams won 3 electoral votes in Maryland, and 1 in Delaware.

≡ **MAP 9.5 The Presidential Election of 1824** The 1824 presidential election was called by the House of Representatives—the last time it has decided the presidency, but not the last time that charges of a stolen election have followed a close contest.

on the Tennessee's Superior Court of Law and Equity (the state's supreme court). In the meantime, Jackson became a wealthy enslaving planter and a favorite of white voters in the West and South.

His defeat in 1824 angered Jackson: he had won more popular votes than anybody else, including Adams. But he was especially aghast at what he called the "corrupt bargain" between Clay and Adams that enabled Adams to secure the presidency and Clay to be appointed secretary of state by Adams. He railed about his popular-vote victory and the "corrupt bargain" for the next four years, and in 1828 Jackson again ran for the presidency. Now in a two-man race against Adams, Jackson won convincingly, sweeping the South, the West, and much of the Middle Atlantic. The trans-Appalachian West had its first president.

During the 1820s, as Adams and Jackson struggled for power and the presidency, more and more states enacted political reforms that did eliminate property-owning requirements for voting and office holding and did make more offices, especially at the local level, subject to popular election. And, to some extent, this process of democratization did shake up and expand the formal political arena. Even so, the relative homogeneity of the white population—most were native-born and Protestant—as well as the relatively wide distribution of property among them, had seen impressive turnouts of white male voters before this time, and clearly set the foundation for what took place in the 1820s and 1830s. Although merchants and large landowners controlled a disproportionate share of wealth and property, many thousands of white men owned some land, or tools of the trade, or a shop: or they reasonably expected to own these things. Those calling for the end to property qualifications rarely met much pushback.

That is to say, except for in Rhode Island, where urbanization and industrialization had advanced further than in any other state and where the struggle to democratize the political arena took the longest and was most conflict-ridden: finally occurring in 1842 after what was known as the Dorr War. The Dorr War (1841–1842) was an attempt by disfranchised residents to force broader democracy in Rhode Island, where a small rural elite was in control of government. Led by lawyer Thomas Dorr, the rebellion was crushed militarily, but it forced the rewriting of the state constitution to expand electoral eligibility. Nowhere, however, did this surge of democratic sentiment bring in new voters who were neither white, Protestant, economically independent, nor male; if anything, the political boundaries that secured the participation of white adult men were pulled tighter still (see Map 9.6).

Advent of Mass Political Parties

A mass base for American politics was coming into being, and with it came new mass political parties. The first of these was called the **Democrats**, who were

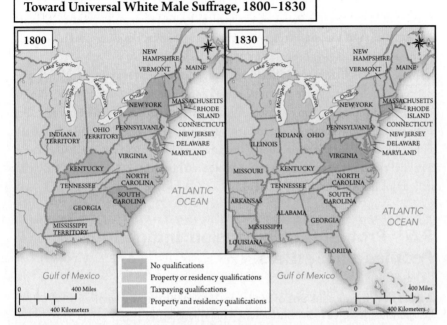

Toward Universal White Male Suffrage, 1800–1830

1800

1830

No qualifications
Property or residency qualifications
Taxpaying qualifications
Property and residency qualifications

≡ **MAP 9.6 Toward Universal Male Suffrage 1800–1830** While more Americans got the vote, the expansion of the franchise did not diversify the political arena.

organized by supporters of Andrew Jackson chiefly from the South and the West. Opponents of Jackson then organized a party of their own, the **Whigs**, named after the British party that had opposed the absolute power of England's crown. For the American Whigs, who were strongest in New England and the Middle Atlantic, their enemy was "King Andrew Jackson." In neither case were these political parties products of conflicts within presidential administrations, as was true for the Federalists and the Republicans. They were established at the grassroots as well as in the upper echelons.

Initially, Democrats and Whigs were defined by strong doses of personal loyalties. Did you like Jackson, or did you hate him? Little by little, however, especially during the 1830s, the parties came to be defined by different policies. The Democrats tended to embrace state rights and local control, support free trade (no protective tariffs), promote geographical expansion even at the expense of conflict with Indigenous people, mobilize Catholics as well as Protestants, and worry about the rapid expansion of the market economy, fearful that it would undermine the economic independence of many Americans. The Whigs tended to see the federal government rather than the states as sovereign, welcomed government activism in the economic arena, supported protective tariffs as a spur to manufacturing, were more cautious about geographical expansion owing to the conflicts it would provoke, cultivated the allegiance of evangelical Protestants, and hoped to advance the expansion of the marketplace by chartering banks, building canals and railroads, and encouraging the printing of paper money.

By 1840, Democrats and Whigs were struggling for power at the local, state, and national levels, giving rise to a new generation of political professionals who focused on winning elections and securing the patronage that went along with it. For their part, eligible voters began to turn out to vote at levels that would define the political culture for the remainder of the nineteenth century: around 80 percent in national elections, far higher than anything we know today. Some historians have called this the **Second Party System**.

9.5   Problems of Expansion: Indigenous Peoples and Settlers

‖‖‖ Assess how the expansions of the period led to the expulsion of Indigenous peoples from lands east of the Mississippi.

The political and economic expansions of the time—vibrant to be sure—caused all sorts of trouble for the country as a whole and for a variety of groups within its presumed borders. The push of white settlers into the trans-Appalachian West not only expanded the boundaries of market activity and energized the impulse for political reform but also provoked further showdowns with the Indigenous people who lived there. The era of market and democratic expansion proved to be an era of intense conflict between American settlers and Indigenous adversaries, and its outcome set worrisome precedents for the character of the republic.

Changing Perspectives and Policies

American colonists and settlers had long viewed Indigenous people in North America as enemies or obstacles in the way of their ambitions. Since the seventeenth century, they pressured Native populations to sell or otherwise surrender their land claims even as they conducted a large and extensive trade with them, and even as they, in some cases, intermarried and came to live among them. What kept settler aggressiveness in check was the complex imperial context of the North American continent. Indigenous people not only battled with each other—as they had always done—but also found allies among the Europeans who competed for power and wealth. They could ally with the British, the French, or the Spanish, and use those alliances to protect their lands, expand their trade, or recoup their losses.

But from the mid-eighteenth century on, the political landscape of North America began to change. As a result of the Seven Years' War (1756–1763), the French were forced to give up their colonies and leave Native allies to their own devices or to the prospects of alliance with the British. After the Revolutionary War, the British, who had tried to keep colonial settlers east of the Appalachians, had to pull up their imperial stakes. After the Haitian Revolution, the French sold off Louisiana to the Jefferson administration. The War of 1812, which didn't bring clear victory to either Britain or the United States, nonetheless forced the British to abandon any hopes of an American reconquest. Indeed, during the war, as we saw in Chapter 8, American troops under Andrew Jackson's command brutally defeated the Red Sticks and doomed the southeastern wing of Tecumseh's Pan-Indian confederation.

If Indigenous people—now increasingly known by the collective term "Indians"—had American allies, they were in the federal government, and they were fair weather allies at that. Federal officials acknowledged Native territorial claims and accepted the treaty as the mechanism to adjust them, though there was little agreement as to how the interests of white settlers and Indigenous people might be aligned. Because of their communal understandings of landed property, their mixing of hunting and horticulture (which required a large territory), and their gendered division of labor in which women did much of the agricultural work, many Native societies were seen—even by sympathetic whites—as backward and barbaric relics that stood in the way of civilization's advance.

From Americanization to Expulsion

Some policymakers, like Henry Knox, George Washington's secretary of war, hoped that Indigenous people could be "civilized": encouraged to abandon hunting and warring, take up farming, live in nuclear families, convert to Christianity, and adopt Euro-American styles of dress. They would then be ready to sell their "surplus" lands and make their peace with American society. Thomas Jefferson occasionally spoke of this sort of Americanization as well. But, especially after the purchase of the Louisiana Territory in 1803, some version of **expulsion**—the coerced exchange of Native lands east of the Mississippi River for something comparable in size to the west—came to be regarded as the best, if not the only, option.

The Cherokees learned the lesson of white intentions very painfully, especially those of them who actually thought that embracing white "civilization" would give them security. Longtime occupants of an extensive area in the southern Appalachians, the Cherokees began to cede portions of their land to aggressive white settlers as early as 1721. Their alliance with the British served them well during and after the Seven Years' War but left them exposed when Britain accepted

SE-QUO-YAH

PUBLISHED BY F. W. GREENOUGH PHILAD.

≡ **Sequoyah (c. 1770–1843)**   The charismatic
leader of the Cherokee people developed a writing
system for the Cherokee in which each of eighty-five
symbols stands for a syllable. In 1839 a Cherokee
assembly used Sequoyah's syllabary to write the
Constitution of the Cherokee Nation. Sequoyah
points to his syllabary in this 1838 portrait.

American independence. By the 1790s, the Cherokees
were under siege. Some of them quickly decided to
move west, across the Mississippi, to what was then
Spanish Louisiana.

But other Cherokees, led mainly by tribal members
who had intermarried with whites, looked to transform their ways. They took up agriculture, purchased
enslaved African Americans, participated in the market economy, embraced Christianity, reformed their
political organization, adopted a written language and
constitution, and laid out a capital at New Echota in
northwestern Georgia. There was, as a result, growing
social differentiation among them, with a small elite
of enslavers and planters at the top and a much larger
peasant and hunter-gatherer class at the bottom. By the
mid-1820s, that is, Cherokee society in the southeast
had come to look very much like the white society that
surrounded it.

The Cherokees were not alone among Indigenous
people east of the Mississippi River in attempting to
adapt to the new conditions. In the Ohio River Valley,
the Algonquian-speaking Shawnees, who already resided in multiethnic villages, divided over whether to
join Tecumseh's Pan-Indian confederation or to pursue new economic activities and the cultural practices
offered by schools and Protestant missionaries. Some
moved beyond the Mississippi, out of the immediate
reach of white settlers. So long as the federal govern-
ment and the president accepted the idea that Indigenous people had, at least, limited claims of sovereignty and that their expulsion (often called "removal," suggesting something less oppressive) must be voluntary, the Shawnees could hold off
their enemies and keep the most divisive of their tribal conflicts in check.

Then the presidential election of 1828 sounded the bell of doom. Elevating
Andrew Jackson to the presidency, the election empowered aggressive white settlers of the West and South and gave them an advocate like none who occupied
the office before. Himself an Indian hater, Jackson rejected the idea of Indian tribal sovereignty, supported the right of states to extend their authority over Indian
lands, and almost immediately put the federal government on the side of an expulsion policy that Indigenous people would be unable to stop.

Dynamics of Expulsion

Despite opposition from some northeastern representatives, Jackson pushed a bill through Congress in 1830 that set aside territory west of the Mississippi for tribal settlement while undermining the legal basis of tribal claims in the east. Known as the **Indian Removal Act**, the bill required the federal government to pay for the improvements Indigenous people had made to their eastern lands, for the costs of relocation, and for annuities (a sum of money paid each year) to the affected tribes. But it also required the Indigenous people to yield. This Jackson saw as a gesture of "humanity and honor" for Indigenous people, who could not deflect the tide of whites "with their arts of civilization."

But many of the Indigenous people saw otherwise and gave Jackson and the federal government a fight. In the Great Lakes region, Black Hawk, the warrior chief of the Sauk, led a band of several hundred of his followers to reclaim land in northwestern Illinois in the early 1830s that had been ceded. When state militia and federal troops were called out to repel this "invasion," the **Black Hawk War** spread across northern Illinois and parts of the Michigan Territory in the summer of 1832 and thinned the ranks of the white soldiers before it was defeated.

The Seminoles of south-central Florida, which the United States had acquired from Spain in 1819 under the auspices of the Adams-Onis Treaty, put up a much more formidable fight. They were, in truth, well out of the path of white "civilization" and could easily have been left alone on that account. But they lived among fugitives from enslavement and their descendants, who had been seeking refuge in Florida since the eighteenth century, and the enslavers of Florida and other parts of the southeast wanted the Seminoles sent west and the Black runaways returned to them.

Seminoles and their Black allies saw what was coming. Beginning in late 1835, they launched attacks on plantations along the St. Johns River and annihilated an army command of 100 men. Indeed, Seminole leaders, with the help of Black advisors, rallied plantation enslaved people and

≡ **The Second Seminole War** An attack by Seminole warriors on a US fort on Florida's Withlacoochee River in December 1835, from a print published in 1837.

dug in. "This is a negro war, not an Indian war," one of the American commanders warned, "and if it not be speedily put down, the south will feel the effects of
it on their slave population." This, the **Second Seminole War**, was not "speedily
put down." It raged until 1842 (one of America's longest wars), and before it was
through and most of the Seminoles (including those of African descent) sent west,
the war claimed the lives of 1,500 American troops and cost the federal government
as much as $40 million (nearly three times the cost of the Louisiana Purchase). A
small group of holdouts remained, withdrawing deep into the recesses of Florida's
Everglades.

The Supreme Court and the Status of Indigenous People

Given US arms and military advantage, Indigenous people sought recourse
through the legal system. In the early 1830s the Cherokees brought suit in federal
court against the state of Georgia that insisted on their tribal sovereignty and the
political resolutions associated with it. The Supreme Court was led by Virginia
Federalist John Marshall (1801–1835 as chief justice), who was determined to
establish the supremacy of the federal government and the status of the court.
In important decisions such as *Marbury v. Madison* (1803) and *McCullough v.
Maryland* (1819), Marshall set out the basis of judicial review (giving the Supreme
Court power to rule an act of Congress unconstitutional) and federal sovereignty
(denying a state the right to tax a federal institution and establishing the principle
that in a conflict between federal and state laws, the federal law must take prece-
dence). Perhaps in this case, Marshall would find for the Cherokees as well.

But, in fact, Marshall's Court offered mixed rulings in *Cherokee Nation v. Georgia*
(1831) and *Worcester v. Georgia* (1832). In the first case, the Court found that while
the Cherokees had a sovereign status of sorts—they and other Indian tribes were
called **domestic dependent nations**—they had no standing as a foreign state and
thus no right to sue Georgia (as Georgia, owing to *McCullough v. Maryland*, had no
right to sue the federal government). Yet, in the second case, the Court did deem
"the Cherokee Nation" a "distinct community, occupying its own territory," over
which Georgia law had no power.

Another president might have taken these decisions as signals to balance the
rights of Indigenous people and those of settlers. Jackson was of a different mind.
He disregarded the Supreme Court and moved to enforce expulsion, bringing
further divisions and new miseries to the Cherokees. In 1838, perhaps 16,000
Cherokees were taken from their homes, imprisoned for many weeks, and then subjected to a forced march across 1,200 rugged miles. At least one-third of them perished along the way, and many more suffered debilitating brutal treatment in what
history would call the **Trail of Tears**. The expelled Cherokees eventually arrived

in what was regarded as **Indian Territory** (or Western Territory), an area roughly between the Platte and Red Rivers, west of the Arkansas and Missouri state lines, where they would reside alongside other expelled Indigenous people to their north as well as to their south (like the Seminoles, Choctaws, and Chickasaws). There the United States promised "forever" to "secure and guarantee" these lands for Native settlement and protect the tribes in their occupancy—without giving them formal title (see Map 9.7).

Yet the political destiny of Indian Territory was left entirely unclear. Ever since the founding of the republic, territories were considered states in the making. At some point they would apply to Congress for statehood and join the other states of

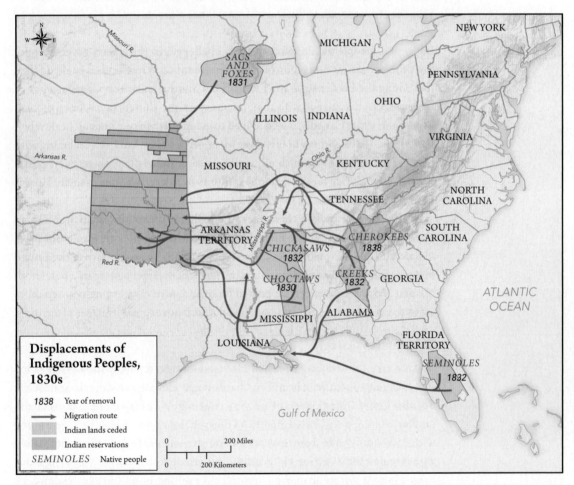

≡ **MAP 9.7   Displacements of Indigenous Peoples, 1830s**   President Andrew Jackson put the federal government on the side of an expulsion policy that Indigenous peoples would be unable to stop.

the Union as equal members. But there was little talk of such a political direction for Indian Territory. The territory would be administered by a commissioner of Indian Affairs and by commandants of military bases and would effectively remain an internal protectorate of the United States marked by impermanent boundaries. It would occupy a status entirely distinct in the United States—set apart and within—eerily foreshadowing the country's imperial future.

9.6 Problems of Expansion: Mexicans and Texans

||| Identify the sources of conflict between American settlers and the Mexican government in the Mexican province of Tejas.

Indigenous people did not offer the only challenges to the federal government of the United States and its vision of continental empire. White settlers could do that, too. Along the border separating the United States and British Canada, some of these settlers, dissatisfied with their prospects in the United States, briefly joined hands with white Canadians who looked to escape British rule in small-scale rebellions of the 1830s. Others in the lower Mississippi Valley had been scheming with potential French and Spanish allies since late in the eighteenth century. Aaron Burr, Jefferson's vice president and Hamilton's murderer, was one of them. He was tried, and acquitted, for treason in 1807.

But the most formidable challenge came farther to the southwest, in the Mexican province of Tejas ("Texas" to English speakers), where a full-scale revolt took place in the mid-1830s. In an important sense, the revolt in Tejas—known in the United States as the **Texas Revolution**—was the result of divergent forces that beset both Mexico and the United States: how to forge and govern sprawling new republics when it was difficult to extend power and authority over great stretches of territory.

The Austin Colony

Mexico, like the United States and Haiti, was a new republic. It had only come into being in 1821, after a brutal and hard-fought eleven-year struggle against the Spanish Empire. Mexico was also a very large republic, with more than twice the landmass of the early United States and the troubles of governance that went along with it. Not only were there leaders in many provinces (Mexico's version of states) who resented the direction of the central government; there were also Indigenous people—none fiercer than the Comanche—pushing in on territory claimed by Mexico from various directions to the north.

One potential solution was to attract settlers into the northern territories and provinces, especially Tejas, who might help to repel the attacks of the Indigenous people or any other hostile political power. And those who lived in the United States seemed very good candidates. Some were already in neighboring Louisiana in the late eighteenth and early nineteenth centuries; many were impressed by the rich soils of eastern Tejas and the prospect of getting hold of large tracts of land. Taking the lead was Connecticut-born Moses Austin, who set up an assortment of mining, banking, and shipping operations in Spanish Louisiana, with the aid of enslaved labor and a large land grant from the Spanish crown. For this, he happily swore allegiance to Spain. American identity at this point was weakly held and easily exchanged.

Once Mexico declared independence, Moses Austin looked to developing a settlement of Anglo-Americans in Tejas, and although he soon died, his ambitious project was taken over by his son Stephen, who convinced the Mexican government to offer generous terms. Each man in the **Austin Colony** would receive a large tract of land for farming and grazing, with even more if family members came along. Although Mexico expected the colonists to become Catholics, little effort was made to see that they did. And although the Mexican government was moving in the direction of outlawing enslavement, Austin managed to offer colonists an extra 80 acres for every enslaved person they brought in.

Austin's colony was therefore especially attractive to active and aspiring enslavers, who either brought their enslaved laborers with them or intended to purchase African Americans once they arrived, eyeing land that was highly suitable for raising cotton. As early as 1825, the Austin Colony had nearly 2,000 occupants, about one-quarter of whom were enslaved, and they had drawn up a slave code. Other Anglo settlements also began to pop up, with similar profiles of settlers and growing numbers of African Americans who were either enslaved or coerced into long-term indentured servitude to please the Mexican government. By the 1830s, Anglo-Texans were laying the foundations of a slave plantation society.

But Anglo-Texans increasingly sensed trouble. Although Stephen Austin attempted to protect the enslavers among them from Mexican officials, by the late 1820s and early 1830s their prospects were rapidly diminishing. The Mexican government under the leadership of Vicente Guerrero, himself of

≡ **Slave Plantation Society**   Watched by a white overseer, enslaved African women pick cotton on a plantation near Columbus, Texas, in the 1850s.

African and mestizo descent, abolished enslavement in 1829. Although Tejas was exempted from the decree, the Mexican government plainly seemed hostile to the Anglo-Texans' long-term interests. Soon, some of them were, as a Mexican official warned, seeking pretexts to "separate from the Republic."

The Anglo-Texans had potential allies in the United States. Andrew Jackson, now president, had long believed that Texas was part of the original Louisiana Purchase (wrongly relinquished) and looked upon the province with a view toward annexation (joining it to the United States) and eventual statehood. Other allies, especially those residing in New Orleans, had been forging a thriving trade in cotton and livestock with the Texans and hoped to expand their activities. Still others in the Deep South states saw the acquisition of Texas by the United States both as an outlet for their economic energies and a necessary buffer for their own system of enslavement. "A population of fanatical abolitionists in Texas," Stephen Austin warned, "would have a very dangerous influence on the overgrown slave population of Louisiana."

Choosing Warfare

By the early 1830s a combustible mix was brewing in Texas, and threats to enslavement formed part of the explosive package of discontent. Although Anglo-Texan leaders were divided over whether to seek greater autonomy within the Mexican Republic (the "peace party") or to strike for independence from Mexico (the "war party"), all of them feared what seemed a rising tide of centralization in Mexico City, as the Mexican government looked to exert more authority over the country's peripheries. In November 1835, led by enslavers, they met in a body called the Consultation, organized an army under a Jackson ally named Sam Houston, and established a provisional government: all without declaring independence.

American supporters in the South and in the lower Mississippi Valley soon rallied to the Anglo-Texans' aid. Organized in paramilitary units, they came to Texas in growing numbers, often through New Orleans, to lend their arms and equipment to the cause. Before too long, most of the soldiers in Texas were recent arrivals from the southern United States, and when word arrived of a large Mexican army heading their way, the split between the "war" and "peace" parties evaporated. In March 1836, a united Anglo-Texan leadership met in convention and formally broke their political ties to Mexico.

The Mexican army of nearly 6,000 men was led by General Antonio Lopez de Santa Anna, who served not only as commander of the troops but also as the president of Mexico. Haughty and temperamental, Santa Anna intended to crush the Texas rebellion and bring the province to heel. He recognized an assortment of Anglo-Texan vulnerabilities, not least the enslaved people, who might see Santa Anna and his forces as liberators and take a hand in supporting them. It therefore would have made sense for Santa Anna to head toward the Texas Gulf Coast, where most of the Anglo-Texans had settled and the enslaved population was concentrated.

But Santa Anna chose otherwise. He and his troops steered straight northward toward San Antonio de Bexar and the **Alamo**, an old Spanish mission in which a small band of Anglos and a few of those they enslaved had taken refuge, and put it under siege. Santa Anna's troops then destroyed the Alamo and killed all the male defenders (except for two enslaved Black people) while other Mexican troops defeated Anglo-Texan rebels at nearby San Patricio and Goliad. On orders from Santa Anna, they also executed those who surrendered.

Santa Anna would pay a high price for the strategy he chose. Although the Alamo is generally seen as a massacre of Anglo-Texans, Santa Anna lost nearly one-quarter of his troops there (three times the number of Anglo-Texans who died inside), and the slaughters he authorized stirred up feelings of vengeance among those left to keep the Texas rebellion alive. Then a fortuitous opportunity for revenge arose. Sam Houston learned from a captured Mexican courier that Santa Anna had divided his army for a multipronged assault, and Houston immediately launched a counterattack with his 900 men. Taken by surprise, Santa Anna's army was routed, and many of those captured were massacred by enraged Texans. Nearly 700 Mexican soldiers died, several hundred more were taken prisoner, and Santa Anna was captured while trying to escape (see Map 9.8).

The Puzzling Aftermath

Although Texas troops demanded Santa Anna's execution, Houston had a different idea. In exchange for his life and safe passage back to Mexico City, Santa Anna would have to accept Texas independence, order his remaining troops south of the Rio Grande, and instruct the Mexican Congress to recognize Texas sovereignty. It was a deal Santa Anna could hardly refuse. On May 14, 1836, he signed the hastily drawn **Treaties of Velasco**. With this, the **Republic of Texas**, with a constitution resembling the American though explicitly supporting enslavement, had apparently come into being.

When Santa Anna returned to Mexico City, however, the Congress would not do as he had promised. It refused to recognize Texas independence and instead regarded Mexico as still at war with the Anglo-Texans. What's more, although many of the Anglo-Texans had expected recognition from the United States, or perhaps even moves toward annexation, the Jackson administration and the administration of Democrat Martin Van Buren that followed (he was Jackson's vice president and was elected president in 1836) remained aloof. The Texas question, tied up as it was with the contentious issue of enslavement's expansion, was clearly too explosive to pursue. It threatened to ignite a war with Mexico while likely dividing the American public. However much the prospect of continental empire appealed to both Jackson and Van Buren, they believed the price, at this point, was too high.

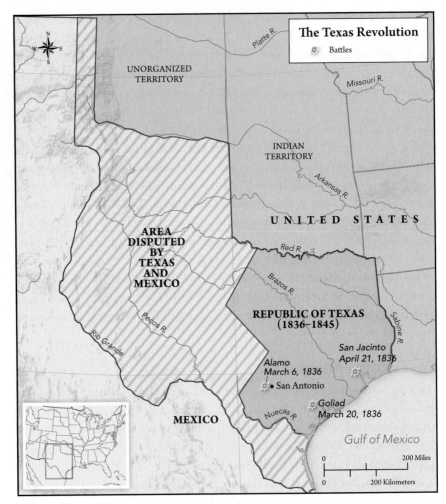

≡ **MAP 9.8   The Texas Revolution**   At first, the Texans appeared to be on the run, but bad decisions and bad luck resulted in a brutal defeat for the Mexican Army at the Battle of San Jacinto and the capture of Santa Anna.

9.7   Problems of Expansion: The Panic of 1837

‖‖‖ Explain the global dimensions of the economic crisis that the United States faced in the late 1830s.

Just as Texas and the Indian Territory to its north were creating political challenges for the government of the United States, a very serious economic challenge erupted. The market boom that had swept the country during the 1820s and 1830s, fueled by the chartering of state banks, the printing of paper money, the widespread use of credit, and the cotton boom, suddenly went bust. Discount (interest) rates shot up and credit dramatically tightened. Debtors ran to convert their paper obligations (whether bank notes or IOUs) into specie (coins). And banks, which had overextended their operations during the good economic times, were caught short. The price of cotton began to tumble, and the large debts secured by the cotton crop became impossible to collect, driving a stake through the businesses of merchants and mercantile houses involved in the cotton trade and eventually through

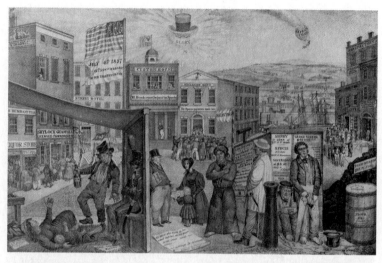

The Panic of 1837 This 1837 political cartoon by Edward Williams Clay depicts the effects of the Panic on New Yorkers. An unhoused family shelters under a tent, the husband with a bottle of gin in his hand; a woman and her child beg from a plump and prosperous landlord; laborers stand about idle while behind them a panicked crowd makes a run on the Merchants Bank.

the institutions that propped them up financially. Banks from New Orleans to New York closed their doors, while a raft of other financial firms in these port cities followed suit. This massive economic crisis is known as the **Panic of 1837**, which left the United States in a deep economic depression.

The Bank War and the Panic of 1837

What happened? And why? Many observers at the time as well as historians since have placed the blame on domestic politics and President Andrew Jackson. And there is much to be said for this perspective. Jackson, who was suspicious of any authority other than his own, had long viewed Nicholas Biddle, the president since 1823 of the Second Bank of the United States (BUS), with deep hostility both because of Biddle's aristocratic airs (he was from a very wealthy Philadelphia family) and because of the power that Biddle and the Bank might wield. It was a view shared by more than a few fellow Democrats.

The Bank had been chartered in 1816 for twenty years—the First Bank's charter had lapsed in 1811—and despite ongoing opposition from those who feared the centralized power that the Bank represented, it had become a major force under Biddle's control. The Bank served as a depository for Treasury funds and federal tax revenues, circulated notes accepted as legal money, sold government securities, made loans, established twenty-five branches in cities around the country,

≡ *General Jackson, Slaying the Many-Headed Monster* (1836) A furious Jackson, swinging a cane labeled "VETO" with such force that he loses his top hat, takes a whack at Nicholas Biddle, the largest of the twenty-four "heads" of this hydra, whose own top hat reminds us of his great wealth. Each head of the hydra represents a state branch of the National Bank. Vice President Martin van Buren holds the head of Jackson's rival John Quincy Adams, representing Massachusetts. Comic relief is provided by the fictional soldier Major Jack Downing, who says in a regional accent, "That's the horrible wiper what wommits wenemous heads I guess, yes Gineral I'll at him agin as soon as I've taken breath, and no mistake."

and, as we noted, could keep state-chartered banks in some check by gathering up their notes and redeeming them for specie.

To Jackson and his supporters, however, the Bank was a "hydra-headed monster" that corrupted "the morals of our people" and "threatened our liberty." They believed that the Bank privileged a small group of "aristocrats" and "moneyed men," at the expense of "producers"; shifted power from the states to the federal government; and potentially threatened local institutions, including enslavement, that depended on access to credit. Thus, as Jackson saw it, the monster bank had to be slain. So when, at Biddle's request, Congress decided to recharter the bank several years earlier than necessary—in 1832 rather than 1836—Jackson seized his opportunity. He vetoed the congressional recharter bill and then proceeded to finish the deed by removing federal deposits from the BUS and redistributing them to state-chartered banks of his choosing (called "pet banks").

The redistribution of federal deposits to state banks, a major blow to the BUS, appeared to stoke the fires of inflation and speculation. It allowed state banks to print more of their own currency and underwrite the purchase of public lands coming on the market. So, too, did a growing federal budget surplus made possible by a rise in tariff rates and the boom in land sales. When the Jackson administration finally tried to rein in the excesses by restricting the circulation of small bank notes and issuing the **Specie Circular** (1836), which required that only gold or silver coin be used for federal land purchases, instead, the bottom fell out quickly and dramatically: like "a tremendous bomb thrown without warning," as one critic put it. Small wonder the affair is known as the **Bank War** (1832–1836).

Global Finance and the Panic of 1837

As disruptive as Jackson's dismantling of the BUS proved to be, it was only partly responsible for the Panic of 1837 and the economic depression that followed. In fact, even more decisive were circuits of investment and exchange that involved four continents, with the City of London, the Bank of England, and several large investment houses operating there (especially Baring Brothers and Brown Brothers) at their center.

Despite suffering defeat at the hands of rebellious American settlers in 1783, Britain emerged from decades of warfare as the world's premier economic and political power. Its empire still stretched across southern Asia, Australia, Canada, and the Caribbean, and London's financial district—known as "The City"—became an engine of domestic and international growth. British investors had bought up large blocks of shares in the Second BUS, and they helped finance many of the costly turnpike, canal, and early railroad projects that undergirded the developing infrastructure of the United States. Britain became the chief market for American goods (cotton most of all), and the United States represented an important market for the British. During the early 1830s, the volume of Anglo-American trade doubled.

Britain's purchases of American securities promoted the flow of specie from east to west, across the Atlantic, and stimulated economic activity in the United States as well as some of the inflationary pressures of the period. But the flow of silver from Mexican mines, well to the southwest, would be even more consequential.

The silver trade was built on the backs of Afro-Mexicans (many of whom had been enslaved) and Indigenous people who labored in the mines of Zacatecas and San Luis Potosí. The silver then moved through the ports of Tampico and Alvarado (later known as Veracruz) to New Orleans and New York. American packet ships brought flour, textiles, carriages, and chairs into Mexico, returning with Mexican coins, often called silver pesos or "dollars Mex," which were accepted as a circulating medium. During the 1820s, $3 to $4 million in silver was imported into the United States from Mexico; during the 1830s, the amount nearly doubled.

Mexican silver was also crucial to a trade developing with China. Initiated in the 1780s, the China trade drew American ships to the port of Guangzhou (it was the only Chinese port open to foreign merchants), in the country's southeast, in search of valuable silks, porcelains, and teas. But because the Chinese lacked interest in American goods, they demanded only silver in payment, all the more so as a trade in the drug opium, which began in the eighteenth century, became extremely robust in the 1820s and 1830s, even though the drug was illegal in China. Linking Bengali poppy (the source of opium) producers and Chinese purchasers

MAPPING AMERICA

Time-Space Convergence

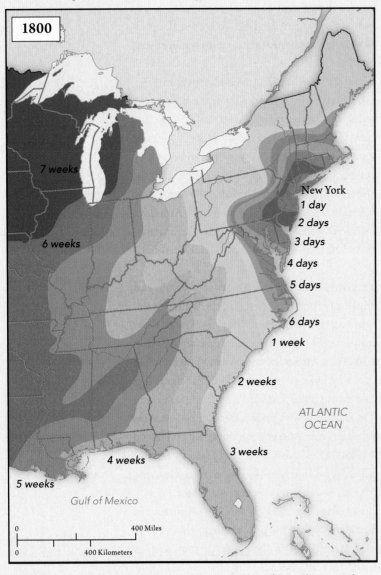

"Time-space convergence" is a term social scientists use to describe the greater interconnection between places that results from improvements in communication. Time-space convergence provides another way of thinking about geography as not just physical space but also of relative distance. While transportation and communication changes do not actually "shrink" the earth, the time and cost of movement decrease, making the earth feel smaller.

≡ **MAP 1   Travel Times in 1800.** In 1800, it took at least five weeks to travel from New York City to the Mississippi River.

Thinking Geographically

1. Thinking about these two maps, how would a traveler's sense of time and space in 1800 compare to a traveler's sense of time and space in 1830?

2. What social, economic, and cultural factors are affected by time-space convergence?

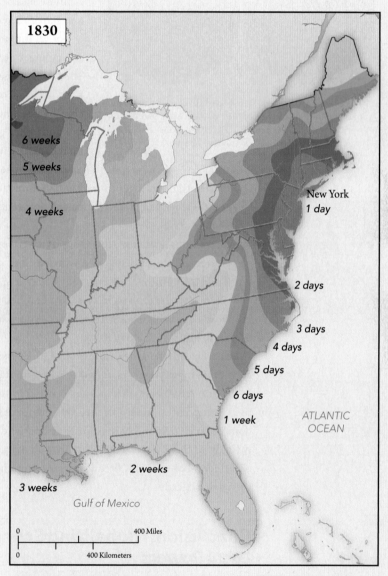

≡ **MAP 2   Travel Times in 1830.** By 1830, travel time between New York and the Mississippi had been cut by about half.

≡ **Forging Global Trade**   This 1840 silver peso shows on one side the coat of arms of Mexico—an eagle perched on a prickly pear cactus devouring a rattlesnake—and on the other side a Phrygian cap, symbol of liberty.

and organized by Britain's East India Company out of Calcutta (known today as Kolkata), the opium trade could be financed by the silver the Chinese had been accumulating from American and European commercial partners.

For all intents and purposes, it was a massive smuggling operation that took a new turn in 1834, when the British government ended the East India Company's mercantile monopoly, thereby opening the India-China trade—in opium and other goods—to all comers. American merchants, with their fast schooners, were among the beneficiaries, now balancing the debit side of their trading ledgers in part with opium rather than silver, which could then be kept in the United States, increasing domestic specie reserves and the decade's inflationary spiral.

China's Qing emperor (the Qing dynasty replaced the Ming dynasty in the early seventeenth century), who worried both about the spike in opium use at home and the outflow of silver, finally decided to crack down on opium smuggling and, in the process, provoked an armed conflict—known as the First Opium War (1839–1842)—with Britain. It would cost the Chinese dearly and extend Britain's empire in the East to Hong Kong.

But even earlier, in the summer of 1836, British bankers, observing a steady decline of their gold reserves, raised the discount rate of the Bank of England from 4 to 5 percent, forcing merchants and other creditors, including those engaged with the United States, to rein in their businesses. As we have seen, the international dominoes fell first and hardest in New York and New Orleans, and they generally followed the lines of the Atlantic cotton market, which was heavily dependent on London-based credit. Broad recovery from the Panic of 1837 would take more than half a decade.

Conclusion: Globalizing Economies, Local Powers

It is likely that the actions of British bankers and investors reflected more than their fears of a gold reserve being drained; it also reflected diminishing confidence in the American economy and the economic agenda of Andrew Jackson. Neither Jackson's Bank War with Nicholas Biddle nor his Specie Circular played well in

London banking circles, and they raised serious questions about where American policy was headed.

Yet it was also clear that in the United States, trade—and particularly foreign trade—was of great importance, that the cotton economy drove American growth and created webs of finance that connected the Atlantic world, and that events in Zacatecas, Guangzhou, Calcutta, and especially London could reverberate powerfully in New York, Philadelphia, Boston, and New Orleans. Market boom and bust were now international events in a globalizing set of imperial economies, and the power of the United States on the world stage as well as the relative power of different social groups at home—enslavers, farmers, bankers, merchants, manufacturers, artisans—hung in the balance.

WHAT IF the Texas Revolution Had Failed?

The Texas Revolution is generally regarded—at least outside of Texas—as one of the lesser events in American history in large part because the Mexican state is usually imagined to be weak and the rebellious Texas settlers assumed to be strong. Indeed, the story of the Alamo has become so iconic precisely because it confirms the sort of expectations we have.

The truth, however, is that the Mexican state was militarily quite formidable. When Spain attempted a reconquest in the late 1820s (as the British had done for the United States in 1812), the Mexican army defeated them. When rebellions occurred in a number of provinces during the 1820s, including far-off Alta California, they were repressed. The Mexican Army, along with the Catholic Church, was one of the basic pillars of the Mexican state; it attracted many members of the elite as officers, and it had an impressive track record when called into service by the central government. At the time of the rebellion in Texas, the Army was also commanded by Mexico's president, Antonio Lopez de Santa Anna.

Santa Anna expected to make quick work of the rebellious Texans, and he was not delusional in thinking so. The Texas settler population was still relatively small and neither well-armed nor well-trained militarily. Many of the troops on the ground were recent arrivals from the United States, especially from the southern states, and they had no battlefield experience. The Mexican Army, by contrast, was 6,000 strong and battle-tested, even though the infantry was drawn heavily from the coerced ranks of the peasantry.

At first, Santa Anna looked like he had the advantage and the Texans appeared to be on the run, fearful of both the Mexican troops and of the slave unrest they were causing. Then came some bad decisions (executing captive Texans) and bad luck (Mexican battle plans falling into Texas hands via a courier). The result was a brutal defeat for the Mexican Army at the Battle of San Jacinto and, most consequentially, the capture of Santa Anna.

It's not difficult to imagine a more likely outcome in which the Mexican Army managed to beat back the Texans and occupy the province. Rebellious Texans would then have been forced either to submit to Mexican authority and abandon any hope of independence, or cut a deal that would have given them greater autonomy within the Mexican state. Either way, Texas would have clearly remained beyond the reach of the United States, and the status of enslavement there would certainly have been weakened, perhaps making possible what Stephen Austin had feared: an abolitionized, potentially hostile country on the border of the United States, particularly the slaveholding states. Enslavers of the Deep South might have mobilized against such a "free soil" Texas, but the Mexicans may also have been able to enlist the support of Europeans, notably the British, to help secure their territory. The future of the North American continent might then have looked very different.

DOCUMENT 9.1:   Views of Mexican General Antonio Lopez de Santa Anna

Santa Anna was the commander of Mexican troops marching north to suppress the rebellion in Texas. These are his questions presuming success in his military objective:

> To the Ministry of War and Marine, 16 February 1836.
>
> The army of operations under my command being already on its march to Bexar, which I expect to occupy before fifteen days [requires] instructions as to the policy I am to observe in dealing with the colonies after order has been restored ... [so that attention be given] to the reorganization of the government of those colonies ... Otherwise we will have gained little by the painful march which our army has undertaken.... As is evident, it was the colonists who unjustly provoked [the campaign] ... What is to be done with the prisoners who are taken either in action or by capitulation? What shall be done with the property of these and that of their families? ... What shall be the fate of those colonists who have not taken an active part in the revolution? ... There is a considerable number of slaves in Texas also [and] who according to our laws should be free. Shall we permit those wretches to moan in chains any longer in a country whose kind laws protect the liberty of man without distinction of cast or color? ... In my judgment those lands have a recognized value both in America and in Europe, and there is no need of giving them to foreigners when we ourselves are capable of settling them. Military colonies such as those established by Russia in Siberia, by England in East India, and even by Spain in this country would be most convenient for Texas.
>
> Source: Carlos Casteneda, *The Mexican Side of the Texas Revolution* (New York, 1976), 64–67.

DOCUMENT 9.2:   Notes from Sam Houston before Battle of San Jacinto

Sam Houston, the commander of the Texas army, wrote the following note before what turned into a decisive battle at San Jacinto suggesting the likelihood of Texan defeat.

> Camp at Harrisburgh
>   19th April 1836
>   This morning we are in preparation to meet Sant Ana [Santa Anna]. It is the only chance of saving Texas. From time to time I have looked for re-inforcements in vain. The Convention adjourning to Harrisburgh struck panic throughout the country. Texas could have started at least 4000 men; we will only have about 700 to march with beside the Camp Guard. We go to conquer. It is wisdom growing out of necessity to meet and fight the enemy now. Every consideration enforces it. No previous occasion would justify it. The troops are in fine spirits, and now is the time for action.

My Adjt Genl Wharton, Inspr Genl Hockley Aid [sic] de Camp Horton

W. H. Patton Collings worth

Volunteer Aid [*sic*] Cerry Perry

Maj. Cook Asst Inspr Genl will be with me.

We will use our best efforts to fight the enemy to such advantage, as will insure [sic] victory, tho' the odds is greatly against us. I leave the result in the hands of a wise God and rely upon his Providence. My country will do justice to those who serve her. The rights for which we fight will be secured, and Texas Free.

Saml Houston

Comr in Chief

Source: Eugene C. Barker, ed. *The Austin Papers* vol. 3 (Austin: University of Texas Press, 1926).

Thinking About Contingency

1. What impact would the defeat of the rebellious Texans have had on the balance of power among the various players in the expanding cotton economy of the United States?
2. How would it have affected the position of the United States on the world stage?

REVIEW QUESTIONS

1. What accounted for the dramatic growth of the American population in the first few decades of the nineteenth century?

2. How important was government aid to the economic expansion of the period?

3. How might the market expansions of the early nineteenth century have worsened conflicts with Indigenous people?

4. What brought settlers and Indigenous people into intense conflict in the early nineteenth century, and what role did the federal government play?

5. How important was the cotton boom in strengthening the system of enslavement in the United States, and how significant was the cotton boom to the economic growth of the country as a whole?

6. Who gained the elective franchise as a result of the democratizations between 1815 and 1840, and who was left out?

7. How did political thinking about Indigenous people compare to political thinking about people of African descent in the United States, and how were the futures of these groups imagined?

8. What did the Texas Revolution suggest about the American identities of the Texans?

9. What international events contributed to the Panic of 1937 and the subsequent economic depression?

KEY TERMS

Alamo (p. 373)

Austin Colony (p. 371)

Bank of the United States (BUS) (p. 360)

Bank War (p. 376)

Black Hawk War (p. 367)

cotton boom (p. 349)

cotton gin (p. 350)

Democrats (p. 362)

Deep South (p. 343)

domestic dependent nations (p. 368)

domestic slave trade (p. 350)

expulsion (p. 365)

factories (p. 353)

Indian Removal Act (p. 367)

Indian Territory (p. 369)

law of master and servant (p. 357)

Panic of 1837 (p. 375)

Republic of Texas (p. 373)

outworkers (p. 352)

Second Party System (p. 364)

Second Seminole War (p. 368)

Specie Circular (p. 376)

Texas Revolution (p. 370)

Trail of Tears (p. 368)

Treaties of Velasco (p. 373)

Whigs (p. 363)

RECOMMENDED READINGS

Jeanne Boydston, *Home and Work: Housework, Wages, and the Ideology of Labor in the Early Republic* (Oxford University Press, 1990).

H. W. Brand, *Lone Star Nation: The Epic Story of the Battle for Texas Independence* (New York: Random House, 2004).

Christopher Clark, *The Roots of Rural Capitalism: Western Massachusetts, 1780–1860* (Cornell, 1990).

Thomas Dublin, *Women at Work: The Transformation of Work and Community in Lowell, Massachusetts, 1826–1860* (Columbia, 1981).

Jessica Lepler, *The Many Panics of 1837: People, Politics, and the Creation of a Transatlantic Financial Crisis* (Cambridge University Press, 2013).

Adam Rothman, *Slave Country: American Expansion and the Origins of the Deep South* (Harvard University Press, 2007).

Claudio Saunt, *Unworthy Republic: The Dispossession of Native Americans and the Road to Indian Territory* (New York, 2020).

Charles Sellers, *The Market Revolution: Jacksonian America, 1815–1846* (Oxford, 1984).

George Rogers Taylor, *The Transportation Revolution, 1815–1860* (Harper and Row, 1951).

10

Social Reform and the New Politics of Slavery

1820–1840

Chapter Outline

10.1 An Era of Social Reform

‖ Analyze how the Second Great Awakening helped give shape to the reform agendas of the
‖ period.

10.2 Building an Abolitionist Movement

‖ Explain how antislavery gradualism became abolitionist immediatism and the roles that
‖ African Americans, free and enslaved, played in the transition.

10.3 The Rough Politics of Enslavement

‖ Describe how politics and violence became interconnected in the 1820s and 1830s,
‖ especially around opposition to abolitionism.

10.4 Class in an Era of Expansion and Reform

‖ Demonstrate how the cultural as well as socioeconomic transformations of the period gave
‖ rise to new social classes in the United States.

≡ **Frontispiece to David Walker's *Appeal to the Coloured Citizens of the World* (1848)** An enslaved African climbs a
mountain toward freedom, reaching toward a scroll in the sky that reads, in Latin, "Libertas Justitia" (Liberty Justice).

By the time David Walker arrived in Boston in the mid-1820s, he had acquired a remarkable education for a free man of color. Born in Wilmington, North Carolina, he had moved for years among densely populated communities of enslaved and free Black people there and then spent some time in Charleston, South Carolina. Along the way, he not only learned to read and write; he also studied history, especially the history of enslavement. Equally important, Walker had become a devout Christian, imbibing the powerful messages of sin and salvation, justice and redemption, preached in early Black Baptist and Methodist churches in towns like Wilmington and Charleston.

It is not clear why Walker chose to migrate to Boston, but once he arrived, he became deeply involved with Black Bostonians and their struggles for freedom and rights. At some point, he also began to write a text attacking the American system of

Timeline

1816	1818	1820	1822	1824	1826	1828

1816 » American Colonization Society founded

1819 » First economic panic in the United States; Missouri's application for statehood leads to a crisis over the expansion of enslavement

1820 » Missouri Compromise admits Missouri as a slave state and Maine as a free state and draws a line through the Louisiana Territory separating land open and closed to slavery

1822 » Denmark Vesey conspiracy in Charleston, South Carolina

1825–1827 » Utopian community of New Harmony, Indiana

1826 » American Society for the Promotion of Temperance founded

enslavement and calling upon people of African descent in America and around the world to join hands and throw off their shackles. He called the text an *Appeal to the Coloured Citizens of the World*, had it published in 1829, and hoped that it would be circulated widely.

The *Appeal* is striking for many things: for its powerful writing, its clarity of argument, its many historical references, and its pan-African vision. It is also infused with a religiosity and biblical erudition that turns the text into something of a thundering sermon. With the many exclamation points that mark the text, the reader can almost hear Walker's passionate language. Walker depicted American enslavement as the cruelest and most brutal form that had ever existed, and he heaped special scorn on Christian enslavers for their sinfulness and moral hypocrisy. God's justice, Walker insisted, would bring a reckoning. Unless, that is, white enslavers saw the error of

1830	1832	1834	1836	1838	1840	1842

1829 > David Walker publishes his *Appeal to the Coloured Citizens of the World* ; Eastern State Penitentiary opens in Philadelphia

1830 > Reverend Charles Grandison Finney leads revivals in Rochester, New York

1831 > William Lloyd Garrison begins publishing *The Liberator* and helps establish the New England Antislavery Society; Nat Turner's slave rebellion in Southampton County, Virginia

1832 > South Carolina nullifies federal tariff laws, provoking a conflict with the Jackson administration

1833 > Great Britain abolishes slavery in its colonial possessions; American Antislavery Society established

1836 > Congress passes the Gag Rule

1837 > Elijah Lovejoy murdered in an anti-abolitionist riot

their ways and chose to repent and change: to treat Black people with humanity and respect. Threaded through his fiery prose, David Walker offered white Americans the possibility of redemption.

Walker embodied and expressed some of the most important changes occurring in American society during the 1820s and 1830s. Along with the economic and political transformations that were creating new forms of empowerment, as we saw in Chapter 9, came intellectual and spiritual changes, anticipated by the Enlightenment and the First Great Awakening (discussed in Chapter 6). For the first time, it was possible to think of humans as rational, self-empowered beings who stood on a plane of equality with one another (think of the Declaration of Independence), might establish a direct relationship with God, and could seek to improve themselves. Indeed, these ideas encouraged people not only to change their own ways (as Walker hoped) but to convince others to do the same. The new spiritual orientations thus became part of a larger age of revolution.

As a result, impulses for reforms burst forth in unprecedented ways. If people had the power to improve themselves, reformers could create circumstances, pressures, and institutions to help them do so. They could think about how children might be socialized or about how men and women who succumbed to poverty, drunkenness, prostitution, or criminality might be put on a better course of life. Some of the reform-minded became especially concerned about forms of power involving violence and personal domination that effectively denied people who were subject to them the opportunity to improve themselves and develop a good character, a stable family life, and a personal relationship with God. And no form of power was more brutal and violent than enslavement, reducing the enslaved to the status of property, of things.

Although individual thinkers, philosophers, and religious leaders had long raised questions about the wisdom and morality of trying to turn human beings into things, not until the late eighteenth and early nineteenth century did a *movement* against enslavement emerge: a product of the same intellectual and spiritual changes that laid the foundation for other reform movements of the time.

The antislavery movement was international in dimension but had a difficult road to travel. The enslaved were valuable property and their enslavers among the richest members of society. The former were Black and of African descent; the latter mostly white and of Anglo descent. Emancipation would thereby pose an assortment of challenges to the free and freed alike. **Gradualism**, that is, a policy of gradual reform rather than sudden change, thus prevailed for several decades, focused initially on the Atlantic slave trade and then on private and state manumission.

By the 1830s, however, a new movement against slavery began to take shape that dramatically raised the stakes. The driving force came from enslaved and free people of color—like David Walker—who had little patience for the gradualism of early anti-slavery advocates and took their moral imperatives further than many were prepared to go. In the process, they also provoked deeper conflicts with enslavers in the United States who did not want to surrender what they viewed as their property or to be regarded as sinners. In the process, in a developing age of social reform, they enshrined new ideas of power in a modernizing world and set the stage for an explosive struggle.

10.1   An Era of Social Reform

Analyze how the Second Great Awakening helped give shape to the reform agendas of the period.

The market expansions and political democratization that occurred after the War of 1812 set the context for a broad and consequential era of social reform. New ideas about personal power and individual responsibility, many owing to the Enlightenment, encouraged questions that had not been raised before about social behavior and society's obligations to promote change. Concerns about poverty, education, the consumption of alcohol, or the punishment of those who violated the law—products of a growing and geographically expansive society—reverberated across the country. They would lead to intellectual debate about a variety of power relations, the emergence of large social movements, and the creation of new institutions. And energizing these transformations was a religious awakening that swept the United States.

The Second Great Awakening

A new spiritual enthusiasm had begun to surface in the very early nineteenth century and, in some ways, built upon the foundations, forms, and practices of the First Great Awakening of the mid-eighteenth century (see Chapter 6). It was advanced by prominent Protestant ministers as well as by their followers, who had small congregations or were mainly itinerants, traveling the land and holding revivals.

CAMP-MEETING

≡ **Camp Meeting**   Camp meetings, such as the one shown in this print from 1832, were a characteristic form of revivalism. Lasting several days, these open-air events involved ecstatic communal prayer; worshippers sometimes traveled great distances to join in the worship.

It emphasized the worth of all human beings regardless of their earthly station and urged the work of benevolence, or the care of the less fortunate. And it brought together the high- and the low-born, the white and the Black, enabling them to rub shoulders in an intense communion of faith. This spiritual phenomenon came to be known as the **Second Great Awakening**.

But the Second Great Awakening was more than a continuation or replay of the First. Although ministers and revivalists embraced some of the Protestant theology that had inspired the faithful in the eighteenth century, they also broke from it in decisive ways. Most important, they rejected the notions of predestination and innate human sinfulness that were central to Calvinism and the American Protestant experience since the establishment of colonial settlements. They rejected the idea that all people were sinners in the eyes of an angry God and that their spiritual destiny was determined before they were born.

Instead, revivalists insisted that human beings were effectively moral free agents, capable of achieving perfection and salvation themselves, capable of determining their own spiritual futures. Men, women, and children could do so by making a choice—by choosing good over evil—and by surrendering themselves in a direct, personal relationship with God. In that relationship, they could be "reborn" (this was the meaning of conversion) as Christians embracing Christ and his teachings. The Reverend Charles Grandison Finney of Connecticut, perhaps the most prominent revivalist of the time, thus preached that "When you come back to God for pardon and salvation, come with all you have to lay at His feet. Come with your body, to offer it as a living sacrifice, upon His altar. Come with your soul and all its powers and yield them in willing consecration to your God and Savior."

Once reborn, once willing disciples of Christ, Christians could then join with their spiritual brethren in a community of believers and go forth to convert the unconverted. In so doing, they became "evangelicals," people who spread the faith and welcomed the newly converted into their spiritual ranks. Only in this way, they believed, could God's kingdom finally come to earth.

Although the revivals of the Second Great Awakening began to move across the country from early in the nineteenth century, they attained their greatest influence during the 1820s and 1830s, especially where market expansions were being most powerfully felt. They erupted in the towns and countryside along the Erie Canal, known as the **burned-over district** for the intensity of its revivalism, into the hinterlands of New England and the Middle Atlantic, where turnpikes, canals, and railroads were being built, and across much of Ohio (called the "Western Reserve"), where many migrants from the Northeast were settling (see Map 10.1).

To be sure, the evangelical message was imbibed by Protestants in many social circumstances, with remarkable cultural impact in a country where most inhabitants who practiced a religion were Protestant. But the message seemed to have a special meaning for those—young and old, female and male—whose futures were most firmly tied to the emerging socioeconomic order and for whom traditional hierarchies and communities had been most destabilized. They were artisans and

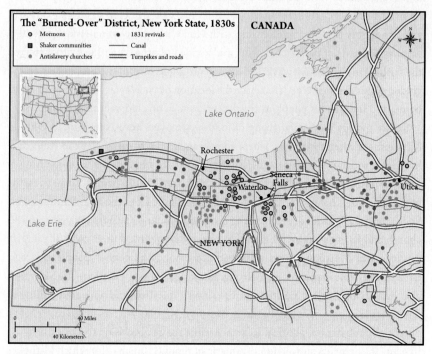

≡ **MAP 10.1   The "Burned-Over" District, New York State**   Itinerant preachers made use of the new network of canals, turnpikes, and railroads to spread their message of a Second Great Awakening.

master craftsmen, clerks and small manufacturers, family farmers and village merchants. And everywhere they were brought to conversion and church membership by women: by mothers, wives, and daughters. The experience of the Second Great Awakening, though inspired by male revivalists, was deeply influenced by gender.

The Mormons

The spiritual fervor of the burned-over district not only led thousands of people to Protestant revivals and a newfound sense of earthly perfectionism; it also spawned religious experiments and denominations led by individuals who claimed to have special prophetic visions. And among the most important—and most enduring—of them was the Church of Jesus Christ of the Latter-Day Saints, better known as the Mormons, who would follow the path set out by Joseph Smith.

Like many who came to reside in the burned-over district, Smith was born in New England (Vermont) around the turn of the nineteenth century and arrived with his family in western New York during the 1910s. There Smith experienced a spiritual awakening whose intensity included a vision in which an angel named Moroni directed him to two buried golden plates that apparently predated the Bible. By 1830, Smith claimed to have translated the writings on the plates and then published them as the *Book of Mormon*. Sharing a millennial vision of God's kingdom on earth and of a highly personal relationship with God with other evangelists, Smith also emphasized a strict patriarchal order and an idea of priestly authority that steered the faithful in distinctive ways. Indeed, according to Smith, the prophecies on the golden plates deemed North America the location of the New Jerusalem or spiritual home, and Indigenous people as the descendants of one of Israel's lost tribes.

Smith and his increasing group of followers moved from New York to Ohio to Missouri and then to Illinois, where they founded the town of Nauvoo (the name has Hebrew origins) along the Mississippi River. There, they set up something of a theocracy. Before long, Nauvoo could count over 12,000 people, surpassing the young town of Chicago in size. But there was trouble from the first. Smith and his flock raised the hackles of neighboring Protestants, many of whom regarded Smith's church and faith as a false religion that rejected or belittled their own. The largely unsuccessful Mormon efforts to missionize among Indigenous people also may have played a role in provoking their aggression against white settlers. The Mormons also had an ambivalent position on the slavery question and appeared willing to convert free people of color. The large Mormon population in Nauvoo gave them a potentially substantial political influence while their submission to a priestly figure like Smith seemed a subversion of American republicanism—for which Catholics had already been harassed. Some even compared Mormonism to Catholicism and Islam, ringing alarm bells of foreign interventions and conspiracies. Rumors began

to circulate, too, about a Mormon practice of plural marriage (polygamy) in which Smith himself
was engaged, effectively mocking the traditional
family structure that was regarded as a foundation of ordered Christian life.

Smith often took his Mormon followers to
new locations just ahead of the sheriffs and lynch
mobs who insisted they had violated local laws
and represented dire threats. A "war" erupted in
Missouri in 1838 that resulted in the slaughter of
seventeen Mormon men, women, and children,
followed by an expulsion order from the state's
governor. "The Mormons must be treated as enemies," the governor proclaimed, "and must be ex-
terminated or driven from the state if necessary
for the public peace."

Nauvoo appeared to offer refuge, and Smith's
flock initially received a welcome from the surrounding communities as well as from the state
government. But there, too, tensions quickly
arose. In 1844, Smith and his brother were jailed

≣ **Mormon Temple**   This plate commemorates the
construction of a temple built in Nauvoo, Illinois, by the
Church of Jesus Christ of Latter Day Saints. The temple
design was based on visions experienced by church leader
Joseph Smith.

in Carthage, Illinois, on charges of treason and rioting. But before any court trial
could take place, a "committee of safety" consisting of at least 250 men broke into
the jail and murdered the Smith brothers. Rather than prosecuting the murderers,
state officials—the Illinois legislature in this case—followed Missouri's example
and repealed Nauvoo's charter, forcing the Mormons out.

Smith's successor, Brigham Young, had also been born in Vermont and migrated
with his family to western New York, where he eventually met Smith and joined the
Church of Latter-Day Saints. Yet, after the disaster at Nauvoo, Young clearly saw
that there was no safe place to go in the United States. Instead, he looked far into the
West, to territory still claimed by Mexico. With his followers, he headed to the dry
and desert-lake Great Basin, land to "be coveted," he assumed, "by no other people." By the time they came through the Wasatch Mountains and began to settle the
Great Salt Lake Valley, however, the US-Mexican War had ended and the land was
now controlled by the United States. More intense struggles lay ahead.

Christian Character and the Temperance Movement

While the central role of women was not distinctive to evangelical Protestantism,
what did prove distinctive was the missionary project with which the faithful were

charged and the new openings for public activism that were consequently made available. Indeed, the church's evangelicalism often became linked to social reforms that brought thousands of women—mostly from middling families—into meetings, organizations, and eventually the streets. Some would find their way into abolitionism and, perhaps, ultimately into feminism. Many others would be drawn to missionary societies, Sunday schools, and groups devoted to the fight against prostitution or the use of tobacco; still others would become involved in the rescue and rehabilitation of the poor, the orphaned, and the fallen, or in organizations aiming at prison and educational reform. All of these were designed to consecrate the idea of Christian character and personal empowerment.

Yet, without question, the greatest number of reform-minded women—and men—rallied to the cause of temperance (abstinence from alcohol), likely because temperance related to both the threats facing a rapidly changing society and the character traits increasingly associated with notions of social respectability. Drinking was, to many evangelicals, a surrender to the baser passions, a sign of lack of self-control, and the cause of poverty and vice. "Intemperance is the sin of our land," the Reverend Lyman Beecher warned, "and if anything shall defeat the hopes of the world, it is that river of fire, which is rolling through the land, destroying the vital air, and extending around an atmosphere of death."

They all had reason for concern. The consumption of alcoholic beverages, particularly distilled alcohol (like whiskey), had not only reached unprecedented levels in the United States; the United States stood out among societies of the Euro-Atlantic world in its apparent addiction to drink. By 1830, per capita consumption of alcohol (yearly consumption per person) reached an astonishing 7.1 gallons, exceeded in the Euro-Atlantic world only by Sweden (today per capita consumption in the United States is about 2.5 gallons). What's more, alcohol-related maladies (such as delirium tremens) were on the rise, catching the attention of observers in town and country alike. Small wonder that evangelical critics considered drinking to be the devil incarnate, and they railed loudly against popular "enslavement" to "demon rum" (see Figure 10.1).

The **temperance movement**, which many called a "crusade," not only attempted to restore the health of families and the body politic but also defined new forms of personal behavior and empowerment organized around the embrace of sobriety. Temperance crusaders touted the virtues of internal power, of self-discipline, self-restraint, self-control, thrift, and industriousness. Some of them hoped for moderation in the consumption of alcohol. More and more pressed for total abstinence. They began with their homes and churches, eliminating alcoholic beverages in the first instance and forcing out members who continued to drink in the second. Then they moved on to their places of work, ending the custom of taking breaks for a "dram" (a drink of hard liquor) or "treating" (buying drinks) after the workday was done,

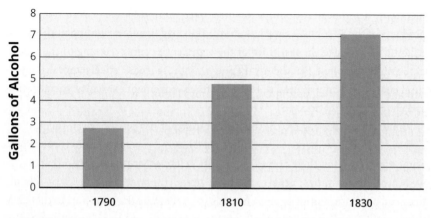

≡ **FIGURE 10.1**   **Per Capita Annual Consumption of Distilled Alcohol.**

and dismissing workers who refused to comply. In 1826, at a meeting in Boston inspired by the Reverend Lyman Beecher, they founded the **American Society for the Promotion of Temperance** (also known as the American Temperance Society), the largest of a growing number of organizations devoted to the cause. Finally, with the help of grassroots politicking, mostly carried forward by women, they succeeded in enacting local and state laws prohibiting the manufacture and sale of alcoholic beverages. By the mid-1850s, most of the Northeast and Midwest were "dry."

Christian Character and Educational Reform

Ideas about character and self-improvement, about the power that an individual had over his or her destiny—as opposed to the power that

≡ **The Temperance Crusade**   In this illustration from a series called "The Bible and Temperance" by the popular printmakers N. Currier & Ives (c. 1835–1836), a man whose drinking has driven his family into poverty finally vows to reform his life. The caption reads: "The words of the sacred volume touch the heart of Brown, who, waiting the departure of the Minister (a feeling of shame for having been seen in his present condition, having passed across his mind), jumps up, & taking the Bible the Minister had left, swears, upon the Book of Salvation, to reform and lead a new life. His wife and children, overpowered by the joyful event, praise Heaven that THE WORD has already borne fruit."

hierarchy, deference, and sinfulness had over the individual—were not simply products of the Second Great Awakening. They had been percolating in the Euro-Atlantic world since the last third of the eighteenth century, owing to the spread of the Enlightenment. But the Awakening gave those ideas a special moral and cultural energy and contributed to further reform movements aimed at socialization and character formation.

Public education was one of the most important of these. Even in the first decades of the nineteenth century, children had limited access to a formal education. Some were taught in their homes by parents, relatives, or tutors depending on the wealth of their families; others may have attended private academies or schools financed by communities or churches. Most—reflecting the expectation that children would simply lead lives similar to their parents' and thus learn the ways of farming, plying a trade, or keeping house—had little or no schooling, perhaps just enough to gain basic literacy, to read and write.

Yet, as a rapidly expanding society raised new questions about social order and a robust Awakening emphasized the possibility of personal improvement, the reform-minded looked to the school as an institution that could mold a respectable and productive character. Leading the way was Horace Mann, from Massachusetts and a prominent member of the Whig Party, who headed up the state's board of education. Mann saw the public school, often referred to as the common school, as an institution that could help children from a variety of backgrounds navigate the changing environment into which they were born. Schools that were state-supported—this was key—could not only teach the rudiments of reading, writing, and arithmetic but could also build the sort of character that a commercializing society demanded, especially if parents were not up to the task. Obedience, punctuality, and

≡ **Educating the Young**   By the end of the nineteenth century, many American children attended public schools influenced by Horace Mann's pedagogical reforms. In this elementary school in Washington, DC, c. 1899, students sit in orderly rows at desks while female teachers present lessons.

steadiness—all manifestations of self-discipline—were among the important lessons to be taught.

Familiarizing himself with the schools in Massachusetts as well as in Europe (Prussia in particular), Mann urged increased funding, the establishment of grade levels, a secular curriculum, and the creation of "normal schools" (from the French *école normale*) to train aspiring teachers. In the process, he would influence educational reformers across the United States and open new employment opportunities, especially for women who were entering the world of the marketplace and were seen as the guardians of culture and morality.

Christian Character and the Penitentiary

But what of those who transgressed community norms, who broke the law and required a different type of discipline? Until the late eighteenth century, criminality was understood as a reflection of innate hierarchies in the human condition (some people were simply destined for trouble) and punishment was assigned to the communities in which crime took place. Lawbreakers would be subjected to fines or to physical discipline and shaming carried out in full public view—whipping, branding, expulsion, relegation to the stocks (both painful and humiliating), or, in the most serious cases, death by hanging. Jails were merely holding pens until the punishment was meted out.

Yet newer views and newer remedies were beginning to emerge. Reflecting Enlightenment ideas of human rationality and potential as well as evangelical notions of moral free agency, reformers called into question assumptions about the rigidity of individual character and the causes of criminality. Benjamin Rush, a physician in Philadelphia who also played important roles in early American politics, was especially concerned, regarding crime as a "moral disease" that required a "house of repentance." And, if crime was a "disease," the afflicted had to be taken out of the community and placed in a context where they could recover. For Rush and other reformers like him, that context was an institution known as a penitentiary.

≡ **The World's First Penitentiary**   Philadelphia's Eastern State Penitentiary operated from 1829 through 1971. Long rows of cells, shown here, housed individual prisoners.

Rather than punish criminals in public, the penitentiary was designed—at least in principle—to isolate them from the influences that led to crime and to allow criminals to put themselves on a path of rehabilitation. By the early 1830s, two models of criminal reform were in place. One, known as the **Pennsylvania system**, pioneered at Philadelphia's Eastern State Penitentiary, placed all inmates in solitary confinement so that they could avoid corrupting influences and proceed—through contemplation—to reform their ways. The other, known as the **Auburn system** (after the New York State prison where it was initially carried out), permitted inmates to labor together in groups (the idea being that steady labor was integral to the process of character reformation) but also required that they remain alone in their cells at night, when a regime of silence was often imposed to encourage reflection and repentance.

The Auburn system became the more widespread as states in the Northeast and Midwest increasingly embraced the penitentiary, in part because it seemed to teach the importance of labor and respect for property (such as the tools the inmates plied), each value highly prized in America's commercializing society. Still, both systems shared a perspective on character and power. Both imagined that the criminally wayward could be rehabilitated, that criminals had to be removed from the environments that bred their evil ways and placed within the confines of special institutions, that self-reformation was the key to rehabilitation, and that criminals would be subjected to the power of prison officials who would enforce obedience to the penitentiary's regime. And both, from the outset, would hold inmates who were disproportionately poor and Black.

Alternative Visions of Society

Although the main direction of social reform in the 1820s and 1830s was toward the ideal of individual self-improvement and the encouragement of a character type compatible with social order in an expanding market economy, there were unexpected developments as well. The evangelical notions of personal salvation and human perfectibility, together with the disruptive effects of expanding markets, led some Americans—especially those in the Northeast and Midwest, who had been most affected—to reject individualism and the intense competitiveness of the marketplace and to imagine a world in which new forms of community and cooperation might be built to replace those that were disintegrating.

Among the largest and most radical of them were the **Shakers**, a group of religious perfectionists (perfectionism being the idea that it is possible for an individual to become free of sin in this life—"perfect"—through religious conversion and will power) in England, who had broken off from the Quakers and were led by a fiery woman preacher named Mother Ann Lee. In 1774, around the time of the

American Revolution, Mother Ann Lee and eight followers migrated to North America, both to spread her gospel and to avoid religious persecution. Their intense religious services involved ecstatic bodily movements that initially had them known as "Shaking Quakers," but there was far more to their spirituality and worldview. Befitting a faith and movement with a female leader, they embraced ideas of equality between the sexes and rejected the traditional marriage relation, with the gendered power it entailed. They also practiced communal ownership of property, cooperative work, and celibacy (as they believed that sexual intercourse was the root of sin), with men and women living in separate dormitories.

≡ **Forging a New Way of Life**   Members of the Mount Lebanon Community of Shakers in New Lebanon Springs, New York, carry their own chairs to dinner. The Shakers were renowned for their craftsmanship, especially evidenced in their simple but elegant furniture. Notice the separate entrances for men and women into the communal dining room.

New converts and children adopted from orphanages increased their numbers so that, by 1840, they had around 6,000 members residing in villages that spread from Maine to Ohio and Kentucky.

The Shakers were an especially robust example of **communitarian (or utopian) experiments** (meaning those organized around communal living) that surfaced in the Northeast and Midwest between the 1820s and 1850s. Some, like the followers of John Humphrey Noyes, a charismatic preacher who first established a community in his native Vermont before moving on to Oneida, New York, combined the spiritual and secular while challenging private property and traditional family life; unlike the Shakers, they encouraged sexuality. Others, like the followers of Robert Dale Owen, were wholly secular and attempted to fashion a cooperative alternative to the budding market society around them.

Owen had been a manufacturer in Britain and, deeply troubled by the social costs of industrialization, built a factory complex in Scotland devoted to the self-improvement of the workers. He then moved across the Atlantic to establish in the mid-1820s a utopian community in Indiana named **New Harmony**. There, like the Shakers and Noyesites, Owens promoted cooperative forms of work together with women's rights; he also looked to educate children to understand and work for the common good. The Shakers and Noyesites fared better, or at least their communities lasted considerably longer, than the few years of New Harmony. But, together, the communitarian experiments, especially the Owenites, would not only stand as alternatives to the world of the marketplace but would also influence labor reformers, socialists, and feminists across the nineteenth century—all of whom imagined new balances in the developing relations of power in American society.

10.2   Building an Abolitionist Movement

Explain how antislavery gradualism became abolitionist immediatism and the roles that African Americans, free and enslaved, played in the transition.

The new ideas circulating in the 1820s and 1830s about personal power and self-improvement, and the evangelical sensibilities that allowed individual salvation and perfectibility through a direct relationship with God, not only inspired reform movements involved with temperance, education, and criminal punishment. They also inspired the movement against enslavement, which many had come to view as America's original sin.

Moral and political concerns about enslavement had, of course, been developing since the latter half of the eighteenth century and especially since the time of the American and Haitian Revolutions. They focused on the personal power and domination that enslavers wielded as well as on the powerlessness and abject submission that the enslaved were forced to accept. And they succeeded in prodding some state legislatures in the Northeast to enact emancipation laws and the US Congress to abolish the Atlantic slave trade in 1808.

But these were all gradualist measures. The emancipation laws freed only the children of enslaved people and only when those children reached adulthood. And Congress cut off the supply of enslaved people only to those areas of the United States where the largest number were concentrated. As a result, they simultaneously accommodated enslaving interests while increasingly enraging those Americans—Black and white—who regarded enslavement as a moral outrage and personal sin. By the late 1820s, owing both to the Second Great Awakening and the work of Black activists, a major turning point was reached and a dramatically new movement took shape.

The Decline of Antislavery Gradualism

Antislavery gradualism had a lengthy history and a slow decline. But some of the process is captured in the relationship between Benjamin Lundy and William Lloyd Garrison. And some of the action took place in Mexico. Born to a family of New Jersey Quakers in 1789, Lundy encountered enslavement firsthand when his family moved to Virginia and, stunned by the violence and degradations he witnessed, committed himself to fighting for enslavement's end.

After marrying and moving to Ohio, Lundy decided to publish a newspaper, *The Genius of Universal Emancipation*, devoted to antislavery's cause. But he moved himself and the paper to Greenville, Tennessee, before settling in Baltimore, Maryland, in the mid-1820s. Along the way, Lundy became interested in establishing a colony for former enslaved Black people and, searching for a suitable site, visited Haiti and Canada before heading out to Mexican Tejas. There, he imagined that the Mexican government, which had some antislavery credentials (having legislated abolition in 1829), might sympathize with his project. Lundy was clearly trying to turn the words of his newspaper into deeds.

However sympathetic the Mexican government might have seemed, Lundy picked a bad time to try to establish a colony of freed people in Tejas. As we saw in Chapter 9, American enslavers had already established colonies of their own there (under the leadership of Stephen Austin) and had a different reaction to the political disposition of the Mexican government: They were intent on securing their property and livelihoods and would not only proclaim their independence but also would write a constitution that protected enslavement. Lundy was forced to retreat.

Nonetheless, Benjamin Lundy had already emerged as one of the leaders of an antislavery campaign that was bubbling in the Northeast, Midwest, and Middle Atlantic, attempting to find a way forward in a country in which the enslavement of African Americans seemed foundational to its economic and political life. Yet Lundy's antislavery politics, like those of most white sympathizers of the time, were decidedly gradualist. Although he—like most Quakers—believed that

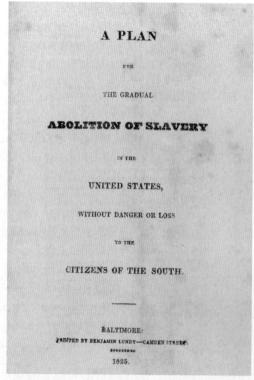

A PLAN

FOR

THE GRADUAL

ABOLITION OF SLAVERY

IN THE

UNITED STATES,

WITHOUT DANGER OR LOSS

TO THE

CITIZENS OF THE SOUTH.

———

BALTIMORE:
PRINTED BY BENJAMIN LUNDY—CAMDEN STREET.
————
1825.

≡ **Gradualism** Benjamin Lundy's 1825 pamphlet, *A Plan for the Gradual Abolition of Slavery in the United States, Without Danger or Loss to the Citizens of the South*, presented a plan for experimental farms worked by enslaved people who would gain their freedom after a certain number of years.

enslaving was a sin, he also thought that any successful plan of emancipation had to unfold slowly and involve the removal of the emancipated Black population from the United States. By journeying to Mexican Tejas, Lundy was planning to enact what had become known as "colonization," and the **colonization movement** grew both as a solution to the problem of emancipation and as an encouragement to slaveholders to emancipate their enslaved workers.

Lundy's ideas were a version of the program unfurled by an organization known as the **American Colonization Society (ACS)**. The ACS was founded in 1816 by elite reformers, including some prominent enslavers, who—like Jefferson (who did not join)—worried about the corrosive effects of enslavement and wanted to imagine a distant future when it would no longer exist in the United States. Some of them had lent their energies to the abolition of the African slave trade, and they believed that promoting the exile of free people of African descent would speed the cause of enslavement's demise. To that end, the ACS established, with support from the federal government, the colony of **Liberia** ("the free land") on the west coast of Africa. By the mid-1820s the first Black migrants began to trickle in and construct settlements in uneasy relation to the Indigenous African population there.

Like Indian removal, colonization reflected the increasing importance of racialist thinking together with a pessimism about the prospects for interracial peace. And it suggested a near consensus among white Americans that the country should continue to be ruled in the interests of white people like them; others would be expelled or required to submit. Benjamin Lundy was critical of the ACS's elitism and its enslaving membership; he would not become a member of the organization. But his gradualism helped form one of the main currents of antislavery sentiment that had begun to emerge during the last third of the eighteenth century: while expressing grave doubts about the wisdom of enslaving, antislavery activists acknowledged

≡ **Membership Certificate for the American Colonization Society**   In 1816, a group of Maryland and Virginia planters formed the ACS to encourage and support the migration of freeborn and emancipated Black people to the continent of Africa.

the enormous financial investments and property holdings enslavement entailed, and they wondered about how well emancipated African Americans were prepared for freedom.

What distinguished Benjamin Lundy from the more complacent and elitist ACS were not only his humble origins and sympathies for enslaved people but also the urgency he felt necessary. Despite the successful campaign against the African slave trade and the gradual emancipation legislation in the Northeast, enslavement seemed to be shifting into an expansionist phase, moving into the new Louisiana Territory and into new states like Louisiana and Missouri, with Texas potentially on the horizon. Thus, along with searching for sites to establish freed Black colonies, Lundy also went on speaking tours to rouse public awareness. On one of them, in 1828, he met a young admirer named William Lloyd Garrison.

Garrison was born to a modest family in the coastal town of Newburyport, Massachusetts, in 1805. He was raised by his mother, a devout Baptist, after his father lost his job and abandoned them. Swept up in the evangelical revivals of the time, he also learned the printing trade and worked at several newspapers. When he met Benjamin Lundy, Garrison had become involved in both the temperance and antislavery movements—temperance advocates were not necessarily supportive of antislavery, but most antislavery activists were sympathetic to temperance—though he embraced the sort of gradualism associated with the ACS. Perhaps impressed by his printing skills and religious zeal, Lundy invited Garrison to Baltimore to help him edit *The Genius of Universal Emancipation.*

Baltimore proved to be an eye-opening and life-changing experience for Garrison. It was the country's second largest city after New York, a thriving seaport, and very much in enslavement's domain, with a substantial population of African descent, nearly half of whom were enslaved. Here Garrison, for the first time (like Lundy in Virginia), encountered a world organized around enslavement: slaveholding, slave hiring, slave punishments, slave sales, and the overall personal power that enslavers could wield. "There is nothing which the curse of slavery has not tainted," he wrote his New England friends.

Perhaps most important, Garrison worked and boarded with free people of color in the city who had a far less gradualist or cautious view of antislavery than he did. He learned that they looked upon the ACS with angry eyes. Garrison read and printed in Lundy's newspaper David Walker's powerful *Appeal to the Coloured Citizens of the World.* By the time he left Baltimore for the more familiar city

≡ **William Lloyd Garrison, ca. 1870** The American crusader published a newspaper, *The Liberator* (1831–1865), and helped lead the abolitionist campaign against enslavement.

of Boston in 1830, Garrison had abandoned gradualism and colonization and was ready to take his antislavery ideas in a new and far more radical direction.

An abolitionist movement usually associated with William Lloyd Garrison alone—Garrisonian abolitionism, it is often called—therefore grew out of a soil already nourished by Black people, enslaved and free, and David Walker helps us understand how this came about. As we have seen, when his *Appeal* was published in 1829, Walker had been in Boston for several years. But he was born a free Black in Wilmington, North Carolina, in the mid-1790s. For most of his life, Walker moved among dense populations of enslaved and free people of color in the environs of Wilmington and Charleston, South Carolina, where various forms of Black unrest had erupted during the 1790s and first three decades of the nineteenth century—including a conspiracy hatched in Charleston in 1822 by another free Black man named Denmark Vesey, which never occurred (other Black people betrayed Vesey) but rocked Charleston nonetheless. Thus, when Walker arrived in Boston, he brought with him the fruits of a remarkable education in the political worlds of slavery and freedom.

In his stunning *Appeal to the Coloured Citizens of the World,* Walker reminded African Americans that their brothers and sisters were enslaved the world over and that freedom was their natural right. He took special aim at Thomas Jefferson's ideas of Black inferiority and advocacy of colonization, and he urged Black people to claim the freedom that was due them. At the same time, Walker offered whites a vision of redemption and social peace in an age when "removal" or expulsion appeared the solution to the "problems" posed by Black people and Native Americans. "Enlighten us and treat us like men," he wrote, "and we will like you more than we now hate you, and tell us no more about colonization, for America is as much our country, as it is yours." Walker died in 1830, likely the result of tuberculosis, leaving behind his riveting and powerful *Appeal.*

The Role of the Enslaved in Antislavery

David Walker wanted his *Appeal* to be widely read and discussed, especially among people of African descent in the South. He therefore stowed copies of his text among Black seamen who traveled to southern port cities in hopes of having it distributed through a variety of contacts. Although Walker recognized that most of the enslaved were illiterate, he also knew that the few who were literate would read the text to the many who were not. And as far as we can judge, his *Appeal* did turn up in Charleston, Wilmington, Savannah, Mobile, and New Orleans, raising great alarm among enslavers and white public officials there.

Walker's interest in circulating his *Appeal* in the South reminds us that the first and most continuous combatants in the fight against enslavement were the enslaved people themselves. Of course, none of the enslaved could wage their struggle in public like their free counterparts. They could not demonstrate, petition the government, sue their enslavers, run for office, or hold political meetings. None of these activities had legal sanction, and all would risk lethal retribution. But there were things they could and did do. They pushed back against the power of their enslavers, built relations and networks across considerable distances, fled their plantations and farms and then constructed fugitive settlements (maroons), exchanged information among themselves, and organized small- and large-scale rebellions. In the process, they weakened the structures of enslavement, won the sympathies of some in the white population, and eventually provoked crises for enslaving regimes.

The movements of enslaved people against enslavement were international in scope. They encompassed the North and South Atlantic as well as the Caribbean basin and increasingly linked the experiences of enslaved Black people and other people of African descent in many different locations and circumstances. The system of enslavement, after all, moved across national boundaries, which the enslaved themselves constantly crossed, taken by enslavers and traders, armies and seaborne vessels, often learning about important political developments along the way.

Still, the struggles of the enslaved against slavery more nearly resembled warfare than recognizable social movements. Indeed, after the Seven Years' War (discussed in Chapter 6) ended in 1763, enslaved people from the Caribbean basin to northerly New England became part of a half-century of increasingly interconnected struggle, which included the British and French Caribbean and Spanish South America as well as the North American mainland. Along with the massive rebellion in Saint Domingue, there was unrest in Louisiana during the 1790s, an aborted rebellion (Gabriel's) in Virginia in 1800, a large-scale rebellion in Louisiana in 1811, a conspiracy of enslaved and free Black people in Charleston in 1822 led by Denmark Vesey, a revolt of the enslaved in Demerara (a British colony on the north coast of South America) in 1823, and then two powerful rebellions in 1831.

One of them, in Southampton County, Virginia, was organized by Nat Turner, an enslaved Black Baptist preacher and prophet, that involved over seventy enslaved rebels and, before it was suppressed, left more than fifty white people dead (the most in US history to that point). The other was a far larger—thousands of enslaved people took part—rebellion, also inspired by an enslaved Baptist preacher and visionary (his name was Samuel Sharpe), that rocked the island of Jamaica during the Christmas season that year and, although defeated, enabled the British antislavery movement to enact emancipation legislation two years later.

Thus, by the time this lengthy era ended, slavery had been abolished in Haiti, in Britain's colonial possessions, and in parts of South America. Too, an emancipation process had been initiated in the United States, pushed as much by enslaved Black people as by white Americans who could not correlate the ideals of their political revolution with enslavement.

The blows that the enslaved landed against enslavement fed off one another as news of them spread across the Atlantic and Caribbean, permitting enslaved and free Black people to discuss and debate the new political possibilities. The revolution in Haiti (discussed in Chapter 8) was especially important, but so, too, was the gradual abolition of slavery in the American Northeast and eventually the abolition of slavery in the British Empire (1833).

The arrival of Haitian refugees and knowledge of growing attacks on the institution of enslavement there and elsewhere came at a crucial moment. The cotton gin (1793) had recently been invented, and, as we saw in Chapter 9, enslavers and the enslaved flooded into the southeastern hinterlands and the states of the Deep South. By 1810, the domestic slave trade—which had not been outlawed—began moving many thousands of the enslaved from the Upper South to the Deep South who, while suffering from exploitation and forced separations, brought with them a range of experiences and expectations and, perhaps, knowledge of the blows that rebel enslaved people were meting out to enslavers.

News of the Haitian Revolution was easier to come by for people of African descent in New England and the Middle Atlantic, where the hold of enslavement had been weakened and the civic culture available to formerly enslaved and free people of color had grown. The late eighteenth and early nineteenth centuries saw the establishment of Black mutual aid societies, Masonic lodges, literary clubs, and churches, including the **African Methodist Episcopal Church (AME)**, the first independent Protestant denomination founded by Black people. Black writers and activists began to circulate reports on Black struggles and also to mobilize among themselves to aid fugitive enslaved people and advance the formal end of enslavement. Their increasing militancy contrasted sharply with the elite and gradualist dispositions of white antislavery societies and set the basis for powerful protests against the program of the ACS.

The protests first erupted in Philadelphia in 1817, and they quickly spread south to Baltimore and north to Boston, where David Walker undoubtedly became involved. Black leaders saw no need to bow to gradualism; they regarded colonization as morally and politically objectionable, a compromise with enslavement and racism. During the 1820s, Black people from New England to the Midwest formed **anti-colonization societies**, and the case against colonization could be heard in Black churches and meetings as well as read in pamphlets and newspapers, like *Freedom's Journal,* established in 1827 in New York City, the first Black-owned and Black-edited newspaper in the United States. David Walker's 1829 *Appeal* was therefore the culmination of a challenge many years in the making.

Immediatism

Soon after returning to Boston from Baltimore, William Lloyd Garrison turned his new ideas about enslavement into action. In January 1831, he began publishing *The Liberator*, a fiery antislavery newspaper, and the next year helped to found the **New England Anti-Slavery Society**. In this, Garrison and his supporters joined a developing international antislavery network bent on undermining the slave systems of the Western Hemisphere. Garrison was well aware of the British movement that would eventually succeed in staring down the powerful West Indian lobby of enslaving planters and enacting a parliamentary emancipation bill in 1833. In the pages of *The Liberator*, he not only denounced colonization and the gradualist stance on antislavery but also proposed an alternative called **immediatism**. By immediatism, Garrison meant, not the immediate emancipation of the enslaved but rather the immediate *recognition* of the sinfulness of enslavement, the immediate *acceptance* of personal responsibility for eradicating such sinfulness, and the immediate personal *commitment* to bringing about enslavement's demise.

Garrison's embrace of immediatism revealed more than the lessons he had learned from history and his experience in Baltimore. It revealed, too, the powerful influence of the Second Great Awakening, in which Garrison himself experienced conversion and which charged antislavery activism with a new moral imperative. This is not to say that evangelical revivals caused immediatism. In fact, in those areas of the United States dominated by enslavement, revivalism and the new ethic of personal responsibility for sin served to buttress the slave regime by encouraging slave owners to convert the enslaved among them to Christianity and, as we will see, by developing a defense of enslavement that drew upon the Bible. Evangelicalism did not have an inherent social or political ideology. But for a generation of young men and women born in New England, the Middle Atlantic, and parts of the West, who grew up in Presbyterian, Congregational, Quaker, or Unitarian households that valued moral responsibility, the revivals offered a vision of perfectibility along with a missionary route of action to bring it about.

Some of the reform-minded, horrified as they were by the violent power of enslavers and the abject powerlessness forced upon the enslaved, thus came to see the institution as a sin and abolition as a major step toward the arrival of God's kingdom. Most of the leading white abolitionists—Elijah Lovejoy, Angelina and Sarah Grimke, and Wendell Phillips, among others, along with Garrison—either experienced conversion during the revivals or were Quakers, who refused to engage in violence or war. And although northern districts given over to evangelicalism did not necessarily favor abolitionism, abolitionists could find welcomes only in places that had been evangelized or had Quaker communities.

Evangelical Protestantism and Quakerism would be enormously important to the politics of abolitionism. Although Garrison never developed a full-blown plan for the abolition of enslavement in the South, he and his followers did see a new way forward. Most would have accepted some version of what the states of New England and the Middle Atlantic already pursued—emancipation immediately embraced but gradually achieved. But since they tended to see state and federal governments as enslavement's allies, the Garrisonians hoped to persuade—they called it "moral suasion"—individual enslavers and their supporters of the sinfulness of their ways and the need to embark on a course of emancipation. They hoped, that is, to make abolition the result of personal Christian redemption.

≡ **Collection Box of the Rhode Island Anti-Slavery Society**   This cardboard coin collection box urges members of the Rhode Island Anti-Slavery Society to honor their weekly financial pledge to sustain the abolitionist campaign. The image of a kneeling, enchained Black man was the movement's iconic image.

A New Antislavery Movement

The Garrisonians mounted an unprecedented campaign, built from the grassroots, to mobilize public opinion around the righteousness and wisdom of abolitionism. Organization was key. The New England Anti-Slavery Society, founded in Boston in 1832 and drawing upon the support of urban reformers, was one step. But with the establishment one year later of the **American Antislavery Society**, a different push was made, one that focused on the hinterlands of the Northeast and Midwest, with their farms and villages, where the majority of Americans lived. Young abolitionists soon fanned out across the countryside calling anti-colonization meetings, circulating newspapers and antislavery tracts, and encouraging the formation of local antislavery societies. Their success was impressive. By late 1833, nearly fifty of these societies had been founded in eight different states and the beat of activity was only quickening. Within five years there may well have been more than 1,000 antislavery societies, together boasting more than 100,000 members.

The people in the hinterlands who were most persuaded by the moral power of the abolitionists had felt the effects of the period's market expansions and had joined evangelical revivals. For the most part, they did not come from the local elites. They were farmers, tradesmen, factory hands, and shopkeepers. They were ordinary white people who earned their bread through manual labor in the shop or in farm fields and owned little property. In all likelihood, their roads to embracing abolitionism showed the influence of parents, kin, and clergy, as well as the new and unsettling demands of the market economy.

The organizational activities of abolitionists were mostly new to the nineteenth century. They involved creating new institutions, meeting regularly, raising funds, distributing printed material, sponsoring lectures, debating divisive issues, boy-cotting slave-made goods, and trying to convert their neighbors to the cause. And, as in the evangelical and Quaker churches to which many of them belonged, the activists were women as well as men. Only the temperance movement of the era was anything like it.

Most characteristic of grassroots abolitionism in the 1830s were the many petition campaigns that antislavery activists launched. Founders of the American Antislavery Society petitioned Congress to abolish slavery in the District of Columbia (which was under the jurisdiction of the federal government), and they urged supporters to petition state legislatures on the slavery question, hoping that lawmakers would take a stand. Most were aware of the great effect that antislavery petitioners in Britain had on popular attitudes and public policy, and they sought to follow in these footsteps. By 1838, nearly 150,000 petitions had been forwarded to Congress, and more than another 400,000 to state houses.

Yet the petition campaign revealed significant changes in its own right. Early on, the petitioners were overwhelmingly male, a measure of the gendered expectations regarding political participation and the male domination of the antislavery movement itself. Women had no official place in antislavery societies—they had to form their own—and were rarely afforded the opportunity to speak in public. But by the mid-1830s, more and more women were signing antislavery petitions, pushing as they did at the boundaries of political

≡ **Angelina Emily Grimké** "Slavery in America reduces a man to a thing," she wrote in 1816, "robs him all of his rights as a human being, fetters both his body and his mind, and protects the master in the most unnatural and unreasonable power."

practice and claiming a new form of power for themselves. They were careful to observe some gender proprieties, submitting petitions only with female signatures or signing collective petitions in columns separate from the men's. Nonetheless, they were stepping out onto new public political terrain and did much of the work that fortified local abolitionism. They also directed special light to what enslaved women endured, recounting the brutalities and violations that they suffered.

Many of the abolitionist women were from families of an emerging middle class of small manufacturers, shopkeepers, clerks, physicians, and ministers, who hoped to turn the cultural attributes of female moral authority to political purpose. Some, though, were mill workers and outworkers in search of more personal independence and sensitive to the perils of inordinate power. The repercussions for the advance of women's rights and the conduct of modern American politics would be enormous.

10.3   The Rough Politics of Enslavement

‖‖‖ Describe how politics and violence became interconnected in the 1820s and 1830s, especially around opposition to abolitionism.

Although Garrisonians focused on grassroots organizing and discouraged participation in formal politics, which they felt would require compromise with enslaving interests, the future of enslavement nonetheless came to roil American politics in ways the republic's founders had hoped to avoid. The acquisition of new territory on the North American continent—the realization of imperial dreams that many of the founders themselves had—raised questions about the status of enslavement there. And the gradual emancipation legislation in the Northeast raised the prospect, both to those who wished to expand enslavement and to those who wished to confine or end it, of using the levers of state power to achieve their ends. As a result, the government, at federal and state levels, became an arena in which struggles for power exploded, challenging the agenda and perspectives of many Garrisonians and their abolitionist allies. Soon, the defenders of enslavement would have their own say.

The Missouri Compromise

In many ways, enslaving planters of the early nineteenth century were in a very strong position in the United States despite their relatively low numbers. Indeed, while they composed only about 3–4 percent of the South's white population, they were the dominant powerholders in a geographical crescent that stretched south and west from the Chesapeake to the Mississippi Valley. They owned the largest tracts of land, exploited the labor of at least twenty enslaved people apiece, produced most of the valuable cotton crop, and served as patrons to smaller landowners and enslavers, who were often related to them. These planters were well represented in county and state legislatures and, because of the federal ratio (which counted an enslaved person as three-fifths of a free one for the purposes of apportionment), they had great influence in all branches of the federal government. People like them—Washington, Jefferson, Madison, Monroe, Jackson—held the presidency almost continuously since the ratification of the Constitution. Some had already moved out to the fertile lands of the Texas Republic; others even looked hungrily at Mexico and Cuba.

But despite their wealth and political power, enslaving planters had reason to worry. As we have seen, an emancipation process had been unfolding in New England and the Middle Atlantic since the 1780s, and by the 1830s it appeared to be part of an international movement. Enslaved Black people had successfully rebelled in Saint Domingue and established the second independent republic in the Western Hemisphere, Haiti, and their counterparts in the British Caribbean helped force London's parliament to accept emancipation there.

At home, the Northwest Ordinance (which prohibited the introduction of enslaved people into the Northwest Territory, now the Midwest) had been enacted in 1787, the African slave trade had been outlawed in 1808, and the American Colonization Society had attracted prominent politicians to its cause. Since the 1790s, slave unrest had been brewing in various parts of the South, and some members of Congress began to raise questions about admitting new slave states to the Union.

The first challenge to the expansion of enslavement came in 1819, when the territory of Missouri—which had been carved out of the Louisiana Territory—applied for statehood with a constitution that gave legal sanction to slavery. This came as no surprise. Enslavers and the enslaved had already settled in the Missouri Territory—there were about 10,000 enslaved people, roughly 15 percent of the population—and Congress had already admitted new states in which enslavement would be legal: Tennessee, Kentucky, Louisiana, and Mississippi.

But now, when Missouri's constitution came before Congress, some members from the Northeastern states raised objections. The leader among them was a representative from New York named James Tallmadge, who proposed that Missouri's admission as a state be contingent on prohibiting any more enslaved people coming within its borders and then beginning to emancipate those who were already there. To the shock of many representatives from the enslaving states, the **Tallmadge Amendment** passed the House and was sent on to the Senate for a vote.

The Senate quickly defeated the Tallmadge Amendment, ensnaring Missouri in a congressional deadlock that put its political status in jeopardy: Would it remain a territory or become a state? And what would be the implications for the future of the country? At this point, the Speaker of the House of Representatives, Henry Clay, who hailed from Kentucky and was an enslaver himself (though he had joined the ACS), deftly crafted a compromise to resolve the crisis. Missouri would be paired with Maine (which had been part of the state of Massachusetts), and both would be admitted to the Union on the basis of the constitutions they submitted. This meant that enslavement would be legal in Missouri and prohibited in Maine. A balance between slave states and free states was therefore maintained.

But what about potential future states? To resolve this question, a line was drawn from Missouri's southern border west through the remaining Louisiana Territory (which was as far west as the country stretched at the time), at latitude 36°30′. All new states organized south of that line would be open to enslavement; all new states organized north of that line would be closed to it. Passed by both houses of Congress and signed by President James Monroe, a Virginia enslaver, in the spring of 1820, this piece of legislation is known as the **Missouri Compromise** (see Map 10.2).

Although some enslavers reluctantly accepted the compromise, many found the conflict over Missouri chilling. In their view, the Constitution plainly left the decision-making power over enslavement to the states, not to the federal government. And if they conceded the principle here, or at any point, what would stop the federal government, if controlled by hostile interests, from extending its power further? In this case, the compromise protected state rights over enslavement: both Missouri and Maine wrote constitutions of their choosing, and the 36°30′ line was in federal territory. But warning flags had most definitely been raised. James Tallmadge had insisted that Congress did have the right to place conditions upon the admission of new states, and he had won strong support from congressional colleagues from the Northeast, where abolitionism would soon become influential.

Nullification and the Gag Rule

Enslavers, especially in the states of the Southeast and Deep South, now prepared a new response. Previously, like Jefferson, some were willing to view enslavement as a "necessary evil" and imagine a very distant day when it might no longer exist. And in states of the Upper South, where there were large numbers of whites who were not enslavers (more than three-quarters of the white families there), they might still be open to discussing some plan of gradual emancipation that would bring labor or monetary compensation to enslavers. But given the changing political circumstances and the moral disapproval the abolitionists heaped upon them, enslavers and their local allies looked to mount a more aggressive defense.

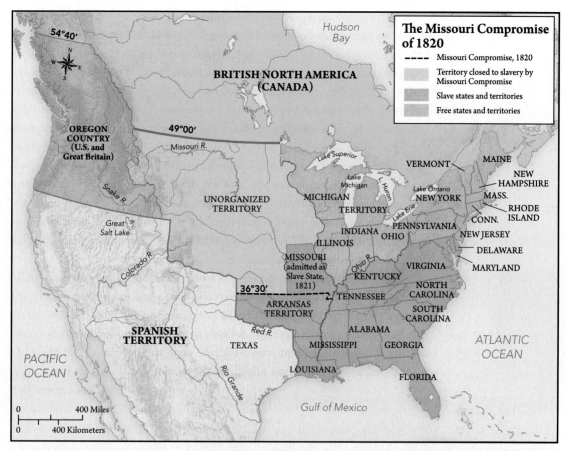

MAP 10.2 The Missouri Compromise of 1820 In the Missouri Compromise, a line was drawn from Missouri's southern border west through the remaining Louisiana Territory, at latitude 36°30′. All new states organized south of that line would be open to enslavement; all new states organized north of that line would be closed to it.

South Carolina, the state most invested in enslavement (enslaved people made up about 60 percent of the population), took the lead, and John C. Calhoun, who held various positions in the federal government, including the vice presidency under Andrew Jackson, led the way. The specific issue of contention was a federal tariff that catered to the interests of northern manufacturers at the potential expense of southern cotton planters, but the larger issue was the power of the federal government and the protection of enslavement.

In 1828, after a new tariff (especially high, it was called the "Tariff of Abominations" by critics) had been passed and signed into law, Calhoun crafted a tract called *South Carolina Exposition and Protest*, in which he railed about the economic consequences of the tariff. Calhoun also insisted that states, not the federal government, were sovereign and therefore had the right to "nullify" or veto a federal law they found to be unconstitutional. (As we saw in Chapter 8, Jefferson had earlier suggested as much in his response to the Alien and Sedition Acts.)

Four years later (1832), following Calhoun's logic, South Carolina political officials refused to enforce the objectionable federal tariff and thereby provoked a crisis with the federal government. Andrew Jackson was still president (Calhoun had resigned the vice presidency when he ran and was elected to a Senate seat that had become vacant); although an enslaving planter, Jackson would not bow to either South Carolina or Calhoun (whom he personally detested). Indeed, Jackson threatened to wage war against the South Carolinians—who insisted they would secede from the Union if coerced—and only backed down after another compromise was engineered by Henry Clay: this one gradually dropping tariff rates in return for South Carolina's repeal of their ordinance of nullification, which the state legislature had passed. This so-called **Nullification Crisis** was a major conflict that raised the prospect of civil warfare.

Part of the reason that the crisis was resolved was that South Carolina "nullifiers" received little support from enslavers elsewhere in the United States, who were not yet ready to embrace nullification or disunion. Still, there were important lessons to be learned. Calhoun was not only interested in raising the issues of constitutional authority and state sovereignty; he was also determined to find a way to keep the matter of enslavement's future out of public debate, where it seemed destined to provoke deep conflict.

The strategy of keeping enslavement out of public debate received some support from the Jackson administration when, in 1836, it backed an effort of congressional enslavers to obstruct the flow of abolitionist petitions to Congress as well as the circulation of abolitionist literature through the US mails. Known as the **Gag Rule**, the law authorized Congress to "table" (or put to the side) any antislavery petitions it received and allowed local postmasters to refuse to deliver abolitionist publications. It was a bold measure, to

≡ **Destroying Abolitionist Literature** "A New Method of Assorting the Mail, as Practiced by Southern Slave-holders," reads the title of this print, published in Boston in 1835. It portrays the nocturnal raid on the Charleston, South Carolina, post office by a mob of proslavery supporters looking for abolitionist literature ready to destroy.

say the least. But what would the Gag Rule mean for freedoms enumerated in the first constitutional amendment listed in the Bill of Rights: freedom of the press and of the right of petition? Defenders of enslavement seemed ready to abandon basic civil liberties to protect what they saw as the foundation of their world.

The Proslavery Argument

For increasingly worried and self-conscious enslavers—including Calhoun—measures like the Gag Rule were insufficient. Nor did they take the sting out of the abolitionist assault. Viewing themselves as modern, cosmopolitan, and devoted Christians, enslavers reeled at the abolitionists' charges that their labor system was a despotism and that they were tyrants and sinners in the eyes of God. Beginning in the 1830s, they mounted an ideological defense of enslavement, calling it, as the governor of South Carolina put it, a "positive good." This was the proslavery argument.

The proslavery argument took account of the racialist thought that had spread around more and more of the Atlantic world, with Jefferson's speculations about Black inferiority taking firmer hold in pseudoscience and popular culture. If people of African descent were destined for little better than a life of menial labor, enslavement was, in the reckoning of these advocates, the best means of maintaining order in a society that depended on their labor. The "negro," one of them wrote in 1835, "is from his intellectual and moral organization incapable of being civilized and enjoying freedom," and, if emancipated, would "corrupt the principles of one half of our population and drag them down." Enslavement, therefore, provided whatever "humanity" enslaved people might attain and permitted them to find their "level."

But racism was not all that defenders of enslavement offered up. Drawing upon traditions of an Atlantic conservatism that had found outlets in Federalism and opposition to the radicalism of the French Revolution (as discussed in Chapter 8), enslavement's defenders began to reject the egalitarianism that the Declaration of Independence had stirringly enshrined. As South Carolina's William Harper put it, all men were not born equal; they were rather born into a state of inequality and "helpless dependency," and enslavement "anticipates the benefits of civilization and retards [its] evils." Unlike Jefferson, who feared that the institution corrupted enslavers as well as the enslaved and ate at the vitals of a republic, they argued that it made a republic possible by excluding those unfit to participate and thereby preventing the emergence of a tyrant who would seek to curry their allegiance. Enslavement alone, they claimed, placed a degraded and dependent labor force under adequate control and allowed poor white people to escape exploitation at the hands of employers.

Using Religion to Justify Slavery

Plantation owner, enslaver, and Baptist preacher Basil Manly (who served as the chaplain to the Confederacy) used the Bible to justify enslavement, preaching that God made holders of enslaved people "their guardians, the conservators of their lives and happiness." The cartoonist E. W. Clay, who published deeply offensive and stereotypical views of Black people, reflects that patriarchal perspective in this c. 1841 print. In his idealized view of the institution, happy enslaved Black people dance while an elderly Black man (seated to the left) addresses the white enslaver as if he were a benevolent father: "God Bless you massa! you feed and clothe us. When we are sick you nurse us, and when too old to work, you provide for us!" The enslaver, his wife in her fashionable bonnet clinging to his elbow, vows piously: "These poor creatures are a sacred legacy from my ancestors and while a dollar is left me, nothing shall be spared to increase their comfort and happiness."

God bless you massa! you feed and clothe us. When we are sick you nurse us, and when too old to work, you provide for us!

These poor creatures are a sacred legacy from my ancestors and while a dollar is left me, nothing shall be spared to increase their comfort and happiness.

≡ America

White women (in both America and England) who dared step outside their roles as good Christian wives and mothers to participate in the abolitionist movement were savagely caricatured in the press on both sides of the Atlantic. The English opponent of enslavement Frances Wright, who was also an early activist for women's suffrage, gave a sensational lecture tour in America in 1829 to argue for the abolition of enslavement. In this caricature by James Akin, Wright is depicted as a silly, bossy goose. The table, lit candles, and pitcher of water, as well as her black dress and long white scarf, suggest that she is attempting to preach. Standing at a respectful distance, a meek man obligingly holds her bonnet.

A DOWNRIGHT GABBLER,
or a goose that deserves to be hissed —

≡ Downright Gabbler, or a Goose That Deserves to Be Hissed

CONSIDER THIS

Anti-abolitionists obviously wanted to continue the institution of enslavement. But what other anxieties might they have had about the abolitionist movement? What do these images suggest, for example, about how the abolitionist movement might change other aspects of society?

None provided more vital aid to the proslavery argument in this era of evangelicalism than did white southern ministers who saw the defense of enslavement as crucial to the building of a Christian community. Embedded in a world of enslavement, these ministers—including the many who welcomed the Second Great Awakening—understood Christianity in the familial terms of hierarchy, patriarchy, and submission. They easily demonstrated the compatibility between enslavement and the Bible: both the Old and New Testaments were filled with enslaved people and injunctions for their obedience. And they delighted in showing their abolitionist critics' "palpable ignorance of divine will."

More effective still was the ministers' likening of enslavement to other household relations, especially marriage, which both naturalized the subordination that enslavement demanded while demonizing emancipation as a dire threat to the foundations of social order. Abolitionism, therefore, promised nothing short of anarchy.

After he left the presidency, Thomas Jefferson himself seemed to recognize the dangers afoot when he responded to those who wanted him to take a public stand against slavery. He insisted that the challenge of abolition was too great for his generation and that a solution to the festering problem of enslavement must be left to the future. In the meantime, he argued, enslavers should acknowledge the duties and obligations that the system imposed on them and do their best to take care of those who could not take care of themselves. As an alternative to abolition, that is, Jefferson offered a notion of paternalism and Christian trusteeship, which proslavery spokesmen of the 1830s held up as the humane alternative to the insecurities of the free labor market.

Anti-Abolitionism

Those who defended enslavement as a "positive good" and tried to strengthen the hands of enslavers in national politics were by no means the only enemies of abolitionism. Many could be found much closer to home. Indeed, for all their moral power and political innovations, abolitionists never won the support of more than a small minority of the white public north of enslavement's heartland. Although they helped to demonize enslavers and what they called the "slave power" (meaning the inordinate power of enslavers) in political life, abolitionists also exposed deep unease about emancipation even in parts of the country where slavery was in retreat. Abolitionists not only denounced colonization and imagined a future that included free Black people in American society, but they also challenged gender norms as well as the very bases of wealth and economic growth in the country. In the eyes of many white Americans, abolitionists appeared ready to install a new and threatening social order.

Opposition to abolition, generally known as anti-abolitionism, took many forms. Abolitionists were denounced in the press and from the pulpit and viciously

lampooned in political broad-
sides and cartoons. They were
called reckless and subversive,
"licentious and incendiary,"
committed to inviting women
to join the men in their crusade
by "turning their sewing parties into abolition clubs." Most
frightening of all, abolitionists
were called "amalgamation-
ists" bent on mixing the races
and "mongrelizing" the population of Anglo-Americans
by adding the blood of Black
inferiors.

No wonder the accusations
sparked violent attacks. During
the mid-1830s, just as abo-

≡ **Anti-Abolitionism in Action**   The printing shop of abolitionist editor Elijah
Lovejoy in Alton, Illinois, was attacked and burned by proslavery rioters on
November 7, 1837. The rioters murdered Lovejoy.

litionist societies spread across the Northeast and the Midwest, angry crowds of
opponents rallied against them. The largest and most destructive clashes came in
New York, Philadelphia, Boston, and Cincinnati, but anti-abolitionist violence also
erupted in smaller cities and country towns. Abolitionist conventions were broken
up, their property and newspaper presses were destroyed, their meeting halls were
burned to the ground, their bodies were tarred and inked, and local Black people
(seen as allies) were beaten and harassed. William Lloyd Garrison was dragged
through the streets of Boston, and in the town of Alton, Illinois, on the Mississippi
River, Presbyterian minister and abolitionist editor Elijah Lovejoy, who had already
fled from threats and harassment in neighboring Missouri, was murdered.

Although it might appear that these eruptions of violence were spontaneous
displays of popular wrath, anti-abolitionists had a social profile and a set of practices. The leaders mainly came from the ranks of merchants, bankers, lawyers, and
public officials whose families dated to the colonial era, belonged to conservative
Protestant denominations, and closely identified with the deeply rooted seaboard
commercial economy. They were the old elite, "gentlemen of property and standing." Many were colonizationists who wanted to stamp out abolitionism either by
the laws of the state or by the "law of [hanging] Judge Lynch."

By contrast, anti-abolitionist followers, the rank and file, were often young and
from the lower reaches of the urban social order. They were journeymen, laborers,
and sailors who were fearful of what abolitionism represented and wished to vent

their own hostilities by attacking the homes and businesses of abolitionists (Black and white), trying to run them out of town and, at times, inflicting enormous damage on local Black communities, some of it lethal. During this period, Black people were far more likely than white to suffer death at the hands of these enemies.

The Violent Tenor of American Politics

One might assume that the violence associated with anti-abolitionism was an exception in American political culture. After all, as we saw in Chapter 9, between 1815 and 1840 many states initiated reforms that enabled most white men (whether or not they owned property) to vote in elections and run for office and that made more and more offices elective rather than appointive. Wouldn't the franchise be enough to express their political views? No, as it turned out. The growing importance of elections in the conduct of popular politics did not mean that the violence and intimidation on display in anti-abolitionism were pushed to the sidelines. If anything, electoral politics incorporated, if it did not thrive on, violence.

When voters went to the polls on Election Day in the early to mid-nineteenth century, especially in urban areas, they were often greeted with a scene that was not for the timid or faint-hearted. Representatives of competing candidates and parties wrestled with one another, shouting insults and swearing, lubricated by the alcohol that was always available, as they tried to mobilize their supporters and terrify the opposition. Scuffling and fighting often broke out, with toughs in attendance to enforce political discipline, while employers might watch as their employees deposited their ballots or announced (in some places *viva voce* voting— publicly announcing one's vote—still prevailed) their choices.

The weeks leading up to an election were often marked by raucous processions and parades—with torches, banners, fifes, and drumbeats—and with militia musters meant to demonstrate the martial basis of political citizenship. Not infrequently, political loyalists took the opportunity to inflict physical punishment on their enemies, especially when antagonisms between different ethnic and religious groups (English and Irish, Protestant and Catholic) were added to the mix.

It was a rough, a rowdy, and very much a male theater of public power: a fierce celebration of the gender exclusions that kept women and other dependents at the margins or on the outside. It showed that the victors in electoral politics needed the muscle as well as the arguments and organizations. And it fed off the rituals of community legitimation and sanction that had governed popular politics well before the vote assumed real importance.

The martial demeanor of electoral politics also reflected the conditions in which substantial populations of the enslaved could be found. State and local politics often revolved around efforts to police enslaved laborers as well as the large stretches of the countryside they might seek to traverse. Militia companies and slave patrols (organized on the county level) were especially important instruments for displaying the power of enslavers, as they galloped the roads on horseback, armed with guns and whips, and drew in the energies of nonenslaving whites, who were required to serve.

Plantations and farms in the slave states were important sites of political combat as authority and submission were contested in overt and covert ways, and networks of communication and alliance were built. Enslavers and enslaved alike relied on webs of kinship and personal loyalty to circulate vital information and defend their own side against attack, issuing warnings and protecting the vulnerable. Politics thereby connected electoral practices among the free, adult male population with mechanisms for controlling the enslaved working class. No wonder that aspiring politicians sought to become militia officers and that the smallest unit of electoral politics was commonly known as the militia district.

The militia companies and urban counterparts like volunteer fire companies played important roles in defining the terrain of local politics and in securing the patron–client relations that remained central to political practice even after democratization took hold. Men from humble rank might now be able to seek office, but they usually needed powerful sponsors both because electioneering could be costly and because public office required them—for the purposes of avoiding fraud or theft—to post thousands of dollars in bonds in order to serve: sums for which only the wealthy could stand.

It was a system of vertical allegiances and reciprocal obligations—"I'll help you out financially in return for your political loyalty"—sometimes mediated by kinship and always open to differing interpretations, not to mention discontent, when one side or the other failed or refused to come through. Instead of truly disrupting patron–client relations, the new electoral politics effectively institutionalized them. Over the course of the nineteenth century, nothing would so trouble those who looked for alternatives to the established order as the patron–client politics that abolitionists encountered in the terrifying crowds called out by "gentlemen of property and standing."

10.4   Class in an Era of Expansion and Reform

Demonstrate how the cultural as well as socioeconomic transformations of the period gave rise to new social classes in the United States.

In these decades of market expansion and social reform, with new forms of antislavery activism and new defenses of enslavement, American society also witnessed the formation and re-formation of social classes.

A Changing Enslaving Class

An enslaving class had begun to emerge in the late seventeenth and early eighteenth centuries as enslaved people flowed to British North America in growing numbers and commodities like tobacco and rice enabled planters to accumulate wealth and power and to codify the relations of enslaver and enslaved. By the last third of the eighteenth century, as we have seen, this enslaving class was sufficiently formidable to lead a challenge to British rule and play a central role in the new republic that independence made possible.

By the 1830s, that class took on a newly aggressive shape. For one thing, its geographical center shifted from east to west: from Virginia and the Carolinas to the Deep South and Mississippi Valley, with New Orleans as one of its hubs. For another thing, the enslaving class saw a transformation in its social composition, combining lineages of the eighteenth-century plantation world with the energies of younger, upwardly mobile members, many of whom had migrated to the Deep South and could imagine an expanding empire to their west and south. The enslavers were, of course, mindful of the abolitionist attacks. Yet, at the same time, they felt a confidence that derived from the thousands of enslaved people who came their way through the domestic slave trade and from the riches that the cotton economy was making possible. The speculator, the labor lord, and the conqueror were integral to their makeup; and the proslavery argument voiced their sense of cultural superiority.

Challenges from the enslaved were significant to the remaking of this slaveholding class. The Haitian Revolution, the conspiracies of Gabriel and Denmark Vesey, and Nat Turner's rebellion in 1831 shook the South's slave regime, as did the tide of emancipation that had moved through New England and the Middle Atlantic. As a result, in an effort to strengthen their social control, many enslavers tried not only to convert their enslaved to Christianity but also to discipline the worst excesses

≡ **Slave Auction**   Members of the new slaveholding class appraise an enslaved child and woman at a New Orleans auction in 1831.

of their fellow enslavers. By the mid-1830s, the strategy appeared to be working. Enslaved people's challenges seemed to have been defeated, and abolitionism had hit a wall in the Chesapeake and the rest of the Upper South. Indeed, there was now more territory open to enslavement in the United States than ever before.

The Emerging Middle Class

But another challenge was already brewing that antislavery itself appeared to embody: the rise of a new class of manufacturers, shopkeepers, and commercial farmers with distinctive economic horizons, cultural practices, moral sensibilities, and political agendas. They had been emerging in port cities, inland towns, and stretches of the Northeastern and Midwestern countryside since the late eighteenth century, but now they were beginning to find one another.

The market expansions of the period provided the necessary openings for this new class. Artisans and craftsmen who availed themselves of growing economic opportunities joined their ranks, as did farm owners, who devoted more of their land to cash crops and sold more of the goods—brooms, palm-leaf hats—that their wives and daughters produced in their households. Merchants began to become involved with regional rather than simply local markets and lost interest in accommodating the bartering practices that once were fixtures of village and small-town life. Together they welcomed internal improvements to facilitate trade, tariff protection for manufacturers, land policies that promoted settlement, and banks that would give them better access to capital and credit.

Politics was therefore a place where members of this new social class could meet one another and learn of their views. Many gravitated to the Whig Party, given its activist stance in relation to domestic economic development. They backed what Henry Clay called the "American System," a package of policies designed to promote internal improvements, manufacturing, and expanded commercial activity across the geographically growing country.

Other meeting places included evangelical churches where they could experience conversion and share new ideas about God's grace, as well as reform organizations where they could address society's ills. In so doing, they could diagnose what set some people on the road to poorhouses, penitentiaries, brothels, and orphanages and what set people like them apart. Invariably, they blamed poverty, crime, prostitution, and other "vices" not on innate sinfulness, low wages, underemployment, or racial discrimination but on idleness, ignorance, drink, gambling, promiscuous sex, recklessness, and family irresponsibility. What was lacking among the poor, unfortunate, and potentially dangerous lower orders were the very character traits that they celebrated and cultivated—and believed that they embodied.

MAPPING AMERICA

Revivals and Utopias

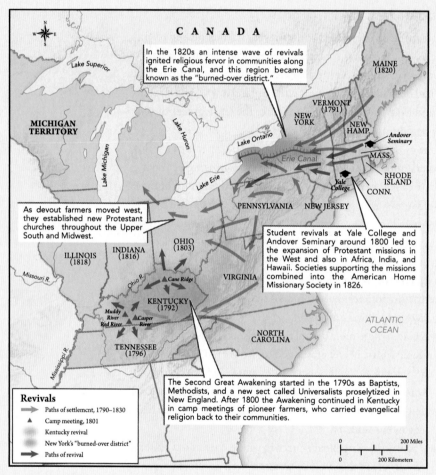

In the 1820s an intense wave of revivals ignited religious fervor in communities along the Erie Canal, and this region became known as the "burned-over district."

As devout farmers moved west, they established new Protestant churches throughout the Upper South and Midwest.

Student revivals at Yale College and Andover Seminary around 1800 led to the expansion of Protestant missions in the West and also in Africa, India, and Hawaii. Societies supporting the missions combined into the American Home Missionary Society in 1826.

The Second Great Awakening started in the 1790s as Baptists, Methodists, and a new sect called Universalists proselytized in New England. After 1800 the Awakening continued in Kentucky in camp meetings of pioneer farmers, who carried evangelical religion back to their communities.

Revivals

→ Paths of settlement, 1790–1830
▲ Camp meeting, 1801
   Kentucky revival
   New York's "burned-over district"
→ Paths of revival

0   200 Miles
0   200 Kilometers

The astonishing variety of religious sects, social reforms, and experiments in relationships between the sexes that it inspired make the Second Great Awakening one of the most important developments in American history. Two distinctive features of the Second Great Awakening were religious revivals and planned communities, or "utopias."

MAP 1 **Revivals** French diplomat and political thinker Alexis de Tocqueville based his work *Democracy in America* on his travels through the United States in the 1830s. He observed that in America religion and freedom "were intimately united, and that they reigned in common over the same country." The Second Great Awakening kindled roaring evangelical revivals across the northern and western parts of the United States. Women played an active role, organizing benevolent activities that accompanied the revivals and participating in the meetings themselves.

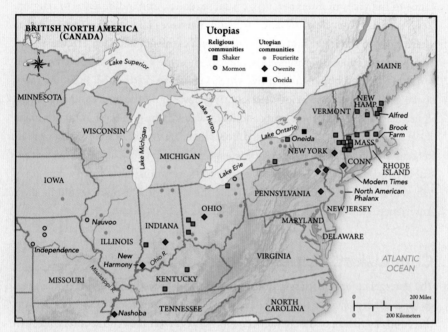

MAP 2   Utopias   The Second Great Awakening prompted national soul-searching over the country's goals and the best means to achieve them. Reformers challenged long-held practices related to the treatment of women, children, and convicts; many founded communities, or "utopias" (from the Greek, "no place"), dedicated to experimenting with new gender roles and family relationships.

Thinking Geographically

1. Compare the two maps. Why do you think the information depicted is strikingly similar?

2. Which region of the country does not appear to have experienced revivals or hosted utopian communities in any significant way? Why do you think this is so?

Female reformers were especially important in developing these new class attitudes because they often had the most direct encounters with the poor and outcast (mostly women) and therefore reflected most deeply on what separated them from the objects of their sympathies. In part, of course, it was the reformers' own resistance to the vices of intemperance, casual sexuality, and indifference to religion. Yet it was also their determination to build marriages and families that served as alternatives to the rough and competitive world of the marketplace. "Domesticity" and "separate spheres," observers would call these new sets of practices and aspirations regarding home and family, which seemed to distinguish their emerging social group from those below (the laboring classes and the poor) and above (the upper class of wealthy merchants and landowners). Thus, in their efforts to make the private home an island of refuge from the cruel and contested world of market relations, to educate their children (especially their sons), and to construct social networks among people like themselves, these women promoted a new set of values and character traits and established the basis for a distinctive middle-class experience.

Conclusion: Opportunities and Divisions

The emergence of new classes in the United States was characteristic of the great changes taking place in the early decades of the nineteenth century. Not only was there the expansion of the market economy and greater interconnections between different parts of the country, but there were also accompanying spiritual and cultural changes that set the groundwork for social reform, the Second Great Awakening being especially important. The reforms, particularly in the Northeast and Middle Atlantic, focused on education, punishment, and temperance, though for growing numbers of Americans they threw the system of enslavement into sharper relief.

For enslavers and their allies, the new spiritual and cultural sensibilities mostly reinforced their commitment to the maintenance of enslavement while emphasizing a paternalistic ethnic for their own self-image; for many others, including enslaved and free Black people, they cast the system of enslavement as brutal and sinful and its abolition as the central goal. Already in the 1820s and 1830s, the future of enslavement was beginning to upend American politics and the very ways in which American democracy was conceived. By the end of this period, it was increasingly clear that the question of enslavement and the forging of American destiny would be difficult to solve short of violent conflict.

WHAT IF Antislavery Gradualism Had Prevailed?

In early 1832, the Virginia state legislature engaged in a remarkable debate. Six months earlier, Nat Turner had led a bloody slave rebellion in Southampton County that roiled Virginia's slave regime, as it did enslavers elsewhere in the South, and it increased tensions between the eastern part of the state, where plantation owners dominated, and the western part of the state, where whites who were not enslavers held power and had long resented how the wealthy planters were able to control the state government.

The debate in the Virginia legislature was mainly about the power that the planters got by counting enslaved as well as free persons for the purpose of legislative apportionment (that's how they controlled the state government), but in due course representatives from western Virginia introduced a proposal to abolish enslavement gradually in the state tied to the idea of colonization and to the possible banishment of free Black people. Virginia's governor was a quiet supporter of the measure, and, in the end, it lost by only a small margin.

But what if, at this point, Virginia—a major slave state—had decided to follow the states of New England and the Middle Atlantic down a lengthy road of emancipation? The American Colonization Society, which was being attacked by Black and white abolitionists, may well have been strengthened, and some of its enslaving members like Kentucky's Henry Clay may have been encouraged to join Virginia and put gradual emancipation on the political table—a gradual emancipation in which enslavers would oversee the process and exert full authority over the freed Black population. After all, in 1833 the British Parliament passed a gradual emancipation bill, signaling that the political tide was turning in that direction.

However much the integrity of gradualism was being challenged by Garrisonian immediatists, it is likely that they would have accepted a gradual emancipation even if it played out over many years. They had no other plan to offer up. Such an outcome may then have resolved the slavery question by peaceful means, as in the Northeast. But what would such a post-emancipation United States have looked like? How long might enslavement and servitude, in some form, have endured? And what would gradualism mean for the civil and political rights of the freed population?

DOCUMENT 10.1: David Walker's *Appeal to the Coloured Citizens of the World*, 1829

In 1829, David Walker, a free man of color who had been born in North Carolina and eventually moved to Massachusetts, published an Appeal to the Coloured Citizens of the World, in which he condemned American slavery and called upon those of African descent to rise up against it.

I appeal to Heaven for my motive in writing—who knows that my object is, if possible, to awaken in the breasts of afflicted, degraded and slumbering brethren, a spirit of inquiry and investigation respecting our misery and wretchedness in this *Republican Land of Liberty!!!!!* . . . we [coloured people of these United States of America] are the *most wretched, degraded and abject* set of beings that *ever lived* since the world began, and that the white Americans having reduced us to the wretched state of *slavery*, treat us in that condition *more cruel* [they being an enlightened and Christian people] than any heathen nation did any people whom it had reduced to our condition. . . . I have been for years troubling the pages of historians, to find out what our fathers have done to *white Christians of America* to merit such condign [fitting and deserved] punishment, as they have inflicted on them, and do continue to inflict on us their children. But I must aver, that my researches have hitherto been to no effect. . . . Men of colour, who are also of sense, for you particularly is my APPEAL designed. Our more ignorant brethren are not able to penetrate its value. I call upon you therefore to cast your eyes upon the wretchedness of your brethren, and to do your utmost to enlighten them. . . . Let the Lord see you doing what you can to rescue them and yourselves from degradation. . . . [Y]our full glory and happiness, as well as all other coloured people under Heaven, shall never be fully consummated but with the *entire emancipation of your enslaved brethren all over the world*. You may therefore, go to work and do what you can to rescue [them] . . . until the Lord shall come upon you all like a thief in the night. For I believe it is the will of the Lord that our greatest happiness shall consist in working for the salvation of our whole body.

Source: David Walker, *Appeal to the Coloured Citizens of the World* (Boston, 1829).

DOCUMENT 10.2: An Act for the Gradual Abolition of Slavery in New York State, 1799

The New York State Assembly in 1799 passed this act providing for the gradual abolition of enslavement in the state. It did not emancipate any enslaved person directly, only the children of enslaved people once they reached a certain age, depending on their gender. It also established rules for those children who were "abandoned" by their enslavers. New York would not pass a final emancipation law until 1827.

Be it enacted by the people of the state of New York represented in Senate and Assembly, That any Child born of a slave within this State after the fourth day of July next, shall be deemed and adjudged to be born free: Provided nevertheless that such Child shall be the servant of the legal proprietor of his or her mother until such servant if a male shall arrive at the age of twenty eight years, and if a female at the age of twenty-five years.

And be it further enacted That such proprietor his, her, or their Heirs or Assigns shall be entitled to the service of such child until he or she shall arrive to the age aforesaid, in the same manner as if such Child had been bound to service by the Overseers of the Poor.

And be it further enacted, That every person being an Inhabitant of this State who shall be entitled to the service of a child born after the four day of July as aforesaid, shall within nine months after the birth of such child, cause to be delivered to the clerk of the city or Town, whereof such person shall be an inhabitant, a certificate in writing containing the name and addition of such master or mistress, and the name age, and sex of every child so born, which certificate shall be, by the said Clerk recorded shall be good and sufficient evidence of the age of such Child, And the Clerk of such City or Town shall receive from said person Twelve cents for every Child so registered, and if any such person neglects to make a return of every such Child as afore said to said Clerk within nine months after the Birth thereof, such person shall forfeit and pay Five Dollars for every such offence, to be sued for and recovered by the Clerk of the City or Town in which such person resides, the one half for his own use and the remainder for the use of the Poor of the said City or Town: Provided nevertheless that it shall be and is hereby made the duty of the Town Clerk to register the certificate of any such child at any time after nine months from its birth and every master or mistress, masters or mistresses of every such Child shall forfeit and pay the sum of One Dollar for every month, he, she, or they shall neglect to deliver such certificate to the Town Clerk.

And be it further enacted that the person entitled to such service may nevertheless within one year after the Birth of such child elect to abandon his or her right to such service by a notification of the same from under his or her hand and lodged with the Clerk of the Town or city where the owner of the mother of any such Child may reside; in which case every child abandoned as aforesaid shall be considered as paupers of the respective Town or City where the proprietor or Owner of the mother of such Child may reside at the time of its birth; and liable to be bound out by the Overseers of the Poor on the same Terms and Conditions that the Children of paupers were subject to before the pafsing [passing] this Act.

And be it further enacted that every Child abandoned as aforesaid shall be supported and maintained till bound out by the Overseers of the Poor as aforesaid at the expense of this State provided however that the said support does not exceed three Dollars and fifty Cents per Month for each child . . . And every owner omitting to give notice in due form as aforesaid shall be answerable for the maintenance of every such child until the arrival of the respective period of servitude specified in the first section of this Act.

And be it further enacted that it shall be lawful for the owner of any slave immediately after the pafsing [passing] of this Act to manumit such slave by a certificate for that purpose under his hand and Seal.

Source: New York State Archives, New York (State). Dept. of State. Bureau of Miscellaneous Records. Enrolled acts of the State Legislature. Series 13036-78, Laws of 1799.

Thinking About Contingency

1. Why do you think gradualism did not prevail? Do you agree that if it had won out, the slavery question may have been resolved peacefully?
2. Considering recent US history, is it reasonable to say gradual emancipation did, in fact, prevail? Why or why not?

REVIEW QUESTIONS

1. What was the relationship between the development of social reform movements and the spiritual revival known as the Second Great Awakening?

2. Why did antislavery gradualism decline and abolitionist immediatism emerge?

3. To what extent was the political violence in the United States of the 1820s and 1830s related to the surge in abolitionist activism, and to what extent was it simply part of the practice of American politics?

4. What were the new and transformed social classes that rose in the years after the War of 1812, and how can we account for their emergence?

KEY TERMS

African Methodist Episcopal Church (AME) (p. 408)

American Antislavery Society (p. 410)

American Colonization Society (ACS) (p. 404)

American Society for the Promotion of Temperance (p. 397)

anti-colonization societies (p. 408)

Auburn system (p. 400)

burned-over district (p. 393)

colonization movement (p. 404)

communitarian (or utopian) experiments (p. 401)

Gag Rule (p. 416)

gradualism (p. 391)

immediatism (p. 409)

Liberia (p. 404)

Missouri Compromise (p. 414)

New England Anti-Slavery Society (p. 409)

New Harmony (p. 402)

Nullification Crisis (p. 416)

Pennsylvania system (p. 400)

Second Great Awakening (p. 392)

Shakers (p. 400)

Tallmadge Amendment (p. 413)

temperance movement (p. 396)

RECOMMENDED READINGS

Drew Faust, *The Ideology of Slavery: Proslavery Thought in the Antebellum South, 1830–1860* (Louisiana State University Press, 1981).

Robert P. Forbes, *The Missouri Compromise and Its Aftermath: Slavery and the Meaning of America* (Chapel Hill, 2009).

Lacy Ford, *Deliver Us from Evil: The Slavery Question in the Old South* (Oxford University Press, 2009).

Peter Hinks, *To Awaken My Afflicted Brethren: David Walker and the Problem of American Slave Resistance* (Penn State University Press, 1996).

Daniel Walker Howe, *What Hath God Wrought: The Transformation of America, 1815–1848* (Oxford University Press, 2009).

Martha Jones, *Birthright Citizens: Race and Rights in Antebellum America* (Cambridge University Press, 2018).

Rebecca MacLennan, *The Crisis of Imprisonment* (Cambridge University Press, 2009).

Manisha Sinha, *The Slave's Cause: A History of Abolition* (Yale University Press, 2016).

Leonard Richards, *"Gentlemen of Property and Standing": Anti-Abolition Mobs in Jacksonian America* (Oxford University Press, 1970).

Christine Stansell, *City of Women: Sex and Class in New York, 1789–1860* (New York, 1986).

Warring for the Pacific
1836–1848

≡ Richard Caton Woodville, *War News from Mexico* (1848)   The "news" to which people in this painting are reacting
is that of the conclusion of the US-Mexican War in 1848, after two years of combat. The characters and composition
of Woodville's painting symbolize political and racial tensions of the time. The "American Hotel" represents America,
the country; the front porch suggests who is welcome within (white, wealthy, well-dressed men) and who is left at the
margins (a Black man and child, in worn and torn clothes).

In the late spring of 1845, President James K. Polk, a Democrat and Tennessee slave-holder who had been elected in 1844, sent 4,000 American troops under the command of General Zachary Taylor down to the Nueces River in south Texas. Taylor had orders to view any attempt by Mexican soldiers to cross the Rio Grande River, only miles away, as an act of war and was poised to fight. Later that fall, Polk sent vessels of the US Pacific Squadron to the coast of California with instructions to seize San Francisco in the event of armed conflict with Mexico, and he advised the US Consul in Monterey to encourage disaffected Californians to rebel against Mexican authorities there. Finally, Polk sent Louisiana congressman James Slidell to Mexico City to explore a negotiated settlement: Slidell would offer $20 million for the acquisition of California, $5 million for New Mexico, and the United States would assume debts owed Americans by the cash-strapped Mexican government in exchange for Mexico's acceptance of the Rio Grande as the southern and western border of Texas.

Timeline

1836	1837	1838	1839	1840	1841	1842	1843	1844

1836 > Republic of Texas proclaimed

1840 > The "Great Peace" among Indigenous peoples established at Bent's Fort on the Arkansas River

1841 > John Tyler becomes president after the death of William Henry Harrison

President Polk's military belligerence toward Mexico seemed audacious to say the least. What was he up to? Ever since the founding of the American republic, there was strong interest, in many quarters, in acquiring new territory and expanding the country's borders. Some sought cheap land for family farms and plantations; some hoped to eliminate magnets for runaway enslaved people (as in Spanish Florida); and some dreamed of extending the culture and politics of the new United States over territories claimed variously by France, Spain, Mexico, and Indigenous people. But policymakers had their eyes riveted first on the Mississippi River, the major artery of interior trade, and then on the Pacific coast, the gateway to the trade of south and east Asia. As we saw in Chapter 8, President Thomas Jefferson not only availed himself of opportunities created by the massive slave rebellion in Saint Domingue to purchase the Louisiana Territory, but he also told explorers Lewis and Clark to find their way to the Pacific "for the purposes of commerce." Three decades later, President Andrew Jackson tried unsuccessfully to obtain the whole of San Francisco Bay from Mexico.

1845	1846	1847	1848	1849	1850	1851	1852	1853

1845 > "Manifest Destiny" of the United States articulated; Texas annexed by the United States and admitted as a state

1846 > US Congress declares war on Mexico; Bear-Flag Republic proclaimed in California; Wilmot Proviso or "White Man's Proviso" fails in the US Senate, but debate over the proposal inflames North-South divisions

1847 > Taos Rebellion in New Mexico; US armed forces launch amphibious (naval and land) attack on Veracruz, Mexico

1848 > Treaty of Guadalupe Hidalgo signed, ending US war against Mexico

A protégé of Jackson's, Polk had an ambitious agenda when he sought the presidency, including the acquisition of the disputed (with Great Britain) Oregon Territory to the northwest. But, like his predecessors, California sat high on his list of priorities. The problem was Mexico and the challenges that Mexico faced, first since throwing off the yoke of Spanish colonialism and declaring independence in 1821, and then once American settlers in the province of Tejas rebelled against the authority of the Mexican government and declared themselves the independent Republic of Texas (as discussed in Chapter 9). With a land mass still roughly twice the size of the United States and thinly populated northern regions subject to raiding by Comanches, Apaches, Utes, and other Indigenous people of the Plains and desert northwest, Mexico remained vulnerable to separatist political intrigues most everywhere. Although Mexican political elites, something like their counterparts during the early American republic, were divided between *centralistas*, who favored a stronger central government, and *federalistas*, who favored a weaker central government and more regional autonomy, they were all committed to defending the territorial integrity of Mexico. How could the goal of a continental or "ocean-bound" US republic be forged, and how high would be the costs militarily and politically?

11.1   The Problem of the Texas Republic

||| Describe how the issue of Texas annexation became so disruptive in the United States and Mexico—and how it sparked conflict over enslavement's future in the United States.

How do we know when a new country comes into being? Is it enough for an interested group of people simply to declare it so? Is it enough for them to write and ratify a constitution and to mark boundaries they are prepared to defend? Must these acts be acknowledged by other countries? The Texan rebels clearly believed they had created a new country and called it the Texas Republic. The Mexican Congress had other ideas. Despite the promises of Santa Anna, his Congress refused to accept Texas independence or recognize the republic. From Mexico's perspective, the war with the insurgents in their province of Tejas was ongoing. And despite the rebels' expectations that the US government would be a strong ally or move toward **annexation** (joining Texas to the United States), the administration of Andrew Jackson, as we saw in Chapter 9, hesitated to get involved. The question of annexing Texas was politically divisive within the United States, and any move toward diplomatic recognition would cause serious conflict with Mexico. It might even threaten war.

To make matters more confusing, the new Texas government defined boundaries that were so immense and disputed—the Sabine River in the east, the Rio Grande River in the south and southwest, and the 42nd parallel in the north—that no sovereign state would accept them (see Map 11.1). Can there be a country if no

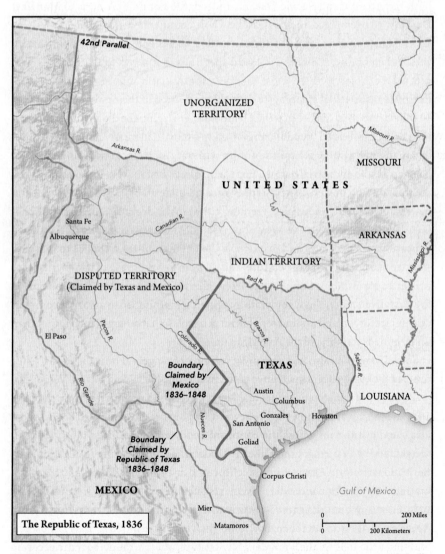

≡ **MAP 11.1   The Republic of Texas, 1836**   The question of annexing Texas was politically divisive within the United States; from Mexico's perspective, the war with the insurgents in their province of Tejas was ongoing.

other country or political power agrees? For all intents and purposes, Texas was little more than an imagined space.

Annexationists

But that imagined space of Texas attracted a great deal of international attention. It would have been difficult to find a political leader in the United States, of any party or region, who did not see their country as a continental power, looking out upon both the Atlantic and Pacific Oceans. Indeed, the notion of America's **Manifest Destiny** "to overspread and possess the whole continent," articulated famously by Jacksonian journalist John O'Sullivan in 1845, was deeply laid in the political culture and embraced across the political spectrum. But it was the Democrats who greeted the project with the most energy and enthusiasm and who saw the acquisition of Texas as a vital steppingstone to the realization of their political goals.

What were these goals? For the Democrats, enlarging the American land mass into an "ocean-bound" republic promised not only to increase US leverage internationally but also to secure the future without resorting to the dangers of urbanization and industrialization. For them, Great Britain was more than a rival and threatening power: Britain represented an undesirable path of development, marked by grinding industries, teeming cities, social degradation, and class conflict. Breathing room in the West thus offered Americans a means of escape, an opportunity to own land and reassemble their communities, a chance to mix subsistence and commercial agriculture, and a way to flee the grasp of banks and other corporate institutions. Some would later call this a "safety valve" for problems in the East. Even more, the Democrats imagined something of an agrarian commercial empire, organized around republican principles, that strengthened rather than undermined the fabric of the American union.

Some Democrats also had a political version of evangelical mission, even as they rejected the evangelical sensibilities of the rival Whigs. Believing themselves unique practitioners of democratic values and culture in a world dominated by monarchies and other forms of tyranny, they believed it was their responsibility to spread these ideals and institutions across the continent and hemisphere. Their most powerful voices could be heard in journals like the *Democratic Review* and in organizations like the National Reform Association, which focused on the land question, and they felt a kinship with popular nationalist movements bubbling at the time in Ireland, Poland, Italy, Germany, and Hungary. They would, in fact, come to call themselves **Young America**, in accord with the many "youth" movements inspired by Italy's Giuseppe Mazzini in the 1830s. "The last order of civilization, which is the democratic, received its first permanent existence in this country," John O'Sullivan proclaimed, "and her example shall smite onto death the tyranny of kings, hierarchies, and oligarchies."

O'Sullivan and Young America provided a language and a set of aspirations that expansionists with less lofty goals could grasp because they generally ignored the "hierarchy" and "tyranny" of enslavement and because their understanding of democratic America was deeply influenced by exclusions of race and gender. The Young American who would transport "democracy" into new territories was recognizably white, male, probably Protestant, and of martial demeanor, ready to conquer a world beset by economic backwardness, ignorance, superstition, Catholicism, and racial mixing. Expansionism would defeat the institutions that bred these conditions and offer

George Caleb Bingham, *The Jolly Flatboatmen* (1846)   Flatboats were used to transport goods, cargo, and people along the waterways of the increasingly occupied Western frontier. As jolly and relaxed as life on this flatboat seems for these white men, new technology—in the form of steam-powered boats, which could move at much greater speed—was already making flatboats obsolete by the time Bingham painted this iconic image.

the benefits of "civilization" for those who wished to seize them. At the very least, it would push those populations and institutions back, weaken them, and allow free and vigorous men (and their families) to find necessary space. How easy it was for the adventurers who set their sights on wealth and power in an "ocean-bound" republic to wrap themselves in the cloaks of democracy and civilization.

Enslavement and Annexation

For many Democrats, especially those from the states of the Deep South, the Texas question had a special urgency. It was not only the lure of more territory, or of another slave state, or of rich cotton land. It was also the threatening alternative to American annexation. With Mexico pressing in on it from the south, Native Americans raiding it from the north and west, and an empty treasury, the Republic of Texas had a dubious future. And it appeared that Britain intended to offer the Texans a deal. Word circulated that, in exchange for abolishing enslavement and refusing annexation to the United States, Texas could expect British financial and military support as well as help in settling hostilities with Mexico.

What might be in it for Great Britain? The British had abolished enslavement in their colonial possessions during the 1830s and intended to pressure their economic and political rivals to follow them down the path of emancipation, leveling the economic playing field. By gaining influence in Texas, Britain could also limit American power in the Gulf of Mexico and, perhaps, in the Western Hemisphere at large. So instead of pushing its borders farther to the west and facilitating the expansion of enslavement, the United States would then face an "abolitionized" state capable of inciting all sorts of turmoil to its southwest.

From his home in Tennessee, former President Andrew Jackson explained, misspellings and all, the frightening logic: "Great Britain enters into an alience with Texas—looking forward to war with us, she sends to Texas 20 or 30,000 organising her army near the Sabine . . . marches through Louisiana and Arkansa, makes a lodgment on the mississippi, excite the negroes to insurrection, the lower country falls and with it Neworleans, and a servile war rages all over the southern and western country." It was not all nightmarish fantasy. The British had done something of the sort during both the American Revolution and the War of 1812, as we saw in Chapters 7 and 8.

Did the British really intend to do this now? Vice President John Tyler of Virginia, who became president when William Henry Harrison died after one month in office in 1841, was sufficiently concerned that he sent newspaper editor Duff Green on a fact-finding mission to London. What Green claimed to have learned was different in detail but no less worrisome in substance. He told of a British plan to use Texas to control the world cotton supply, fasten its hold on the global economy, and destroy American power in the process. Aided by "British capital," one Washington, DC, newspaper predicted, Texas "would soon raise as much cotton as does the United States" and would "either exterminate cotton from our land or limit the market for sale to our own country."

The Annexation and Statehood of Texas

The annexation of Texas consequently held several attractions. It would offer protection against "servile war" and other dangers of potential British encirclement. It would also place "within the limits of our broad confederacy," as some observers reckoned, "all the favored cotton-growing regions of the earth" and with that the "entire control of that great staple, the principal basis of our foreign commerce." As a result, there would be "little to fear from war with European nations." Sam Houston, one of the Anglo-Texan leaders who favored annexation, skillfully played the "British card" to further press the case. By 1843, Tyler had moved into the annexationist corner.

Still, it was a remarkably tough sell in the United States. For all of the enthusiasm that annexation generated among Democrats, particularly those from the slave-holding states, it provoked opposition and outrage among many Whigs, especially those from the nonslaveholding states. This was not because Whigs objected to continental expansionism. Like Democrats, they imagined an "ocean-bound republic" eventually emerging. But they had their own perspectives on the pace and method of achieving that objective, concerns about the political status of newly acquired territories, and fears about the empowerment of some elites—like slave-holders—at the expense of others.

Generally speaking, Whigs hoped to see a more gradual process of expansion that followed the building up of areas already settled. They worried that the population of the United States could be spread too thin, drained from the eastern sections of the country to the western, and they welcomed the urban and industrial development that most Democrats wished to avoid. Many Whigs, showing their racialist attitudes, also doubted whether portions of northern Mexico should become full-fledged states or whether the Catholic, Native American, and mixed-race inhabitants of them should be welcomed to the United States.

Yet, more than anything else, Whigs from the Northeast and Midwest had come to see Texas annexation as a plot hatched by enslavers to extend their reach and power. These Whigs were already convinced that the Texas Rebellion was the work of enslavers in Texas and the United States and were well aware that the Texas Republic had legalized enslavement. They had also heard South Carolina's John C. Calhoun, appointed secretary of state by Tyler, explicitly link the annexation of Texas to the defense and wisdom of Black enslavement. Should Texas be added to the United States, it would clearly strengthen the economic and political leverage of enslavers and breathe added life into the system of enslavement.

President Tyler had his own reasons for pushing ahead with annexation. Although formally a Whig, his politics were much closer to those of the Calhoun Democrats, and, when he became president, he stepped into a political void: cut loose by the Whigs who viewed him as an outsider and regarded with suspicion by the Democrats because he was not officially one of them. Tyler therefore saw Texas annexation as a way of burnishing his political legacy and perhaps of advancing his prospects for election in 1844. His administration negotiated a treaty of annexation during the spring of that year.

The hitch was ratification. The Constitution requires that foreign treaties be approved by a two-thirds vote of the US Senate, and with the Whigs (and a few antislavery Democrats) in opposition, the annexation treaty predictably went down to defeat. To make matters even worse for Tyler, both the Whigs and Democrats nominated other candidates for the presidency in 1844, so his days in office

The Texas Annexation Through Political Cartoons

Cartoonists have been lampooning, satirizing, and caricaturing American politics and political figures since the founding of the Republic. Urban newspapers with large circulations had social, economic, and political clout, and they leveraged their arguments through editorials as well as cartoons. By the 1840s the United States had a thriving and boisterous newspaper culture, and with the invention of the telegraph breaking news could be sent across the country in a matter of days instead of weeks. The Associated Press, a nonprofit news agency, was founded in 1846 by five daily newspapers in New York City to share the expense of covering the US-Mexican War. The pro-Democrat cartoon "Texas Coming In" by James Baillie, makes a forceful argument in support of pro-annexation presidential candidate James Polk. In the upper-right-hand corner, Polk holds an American flag as he cries, "Welcome Texans! Welcome brothers" to Stephen Austin (far left) and Samuel Houston, who are sailing on a boat called "Texas." Austin, in turn, waves the flag of the Lone Star Republic and shouts, "All hail to James K. Polk, the frined [sic] of our Country!" Barely hanging on and about to be swept away in a river, Whig candidate (and anti-annexation campaigner) Henry Clay mutters, "Curse the day that ever

≡ "Texas Coming In"

I got hold of this rope! this is a bad place to let go of it—But I must!" Meanwhile, abolitionist William Lloyd Garrison floats past on a barrel and mocks Clay as a gambler.

Political cartoons also carry subtexts that reveal the passions and prejudices underlying main events. In the 1845 cartoon, "The Danger of Voting Yourself a Farm—The Probability of Getting It in a Horn," an Irish immigrant family is shown leading their four children to a hoped-for farm (and prosperous new life) in Texas. Their Irish accent is crudely reproduced—the father says of the bull, "here's a Great Monsthros Pig wid horns and a beard, that Dish'putes me Title"—and their obvious poverty and physical plight are played for laughs, in keeping with the strong anti-Catholic sentiment of the time.

≡ "The Danger of Voting Yourself a Farm—The Probability of Getting It in a Horn"

CONSIDER THIS

How influential are political cartoons in contemporary American political discourse? In what contexts is humor a particularly effective (and, perhaps, uniquely American) way to make an argument?

were numbered. But neither he nor Calhoun (who was also passed over for the Democratic nomination) were about to give up.

Taking heart when Democrat James K. Polk, an expansionist, won the presidency in November 1844, Tyler decided on a different course. He would press for Texas annexation not as a treaty but, in the last days of his administration, as a joint resolution, which required only majority support in the House and Senate. Lame duck though he was, he now had the votes for this clever political move. In late February 1845, only days before Polk was inaugurated, the resolution passed and went back to Texas for its own ratification process. The outcome was not in doubt. Voting Texans embraced annexation with near unanimity, and in December 1845 the so-called Republic of Texas became America's twenty-eighth state.

11.2   Dynamics of Warfare

‖‖‖ Characterize the roles played by a variety of actors, including Indigenous peoples, in the eruption of war between Mexico and the United States.

When we try to understand the course of events on the national or international stage, we are accustomed to a certain perspective: looking chiefly at a limited group of actors and actions. We observe state leaders and institutions—presidents and prime ministers, congresses and parliaments, diplomats, and formal politicians—and examine what they are thinking and doing. We also focus on the episodes that these actors engage in and regard as important, whether they be wars, treaties, legislative fights, or elections. Yet, in so doing, we can end up with much too limited a view of historical change and ignore the role of actors who may appear to be marginal but often tip the balances in decisive directions. This was surely the case when it comes to explaining the dynamics and outcome of one of the generally overlooked episodes of warfare and conquest in American history: what has come to be called the US-Mexican War. There is a lot to be gained by dramatically widening our perspective.

Indigenous Peoples of the Great Plains

Let's start with the Cheyenne, Kiowas, Arapahos, and Comanches who gathered near Bent's Fort, along the Arkansas River, sometime during the first half of 1840. They hoped to settle conflicts that had erupted between them as their peoples occupied new grounds across the Plains and, with their equestrian-based economies, pursued bison herds for sustenance and exchange. Their battles had been fierce and bloody, and their ranks were further thinned by a smallpox epidemic in the late

1830s. Over two days of ritual gift-giving and serious discussion, they agreed to joint occupancy of much of the Arkansas River Valley, commercial partnerships that included American traders, and, perhaps most important, a political coalition. Called the **Great Peace of 1840**, it ushered in years of cooperation among these formidable peoples.

What made the Great Peace significant for the years to follow was that, while securing an end to hostilities among Indigenous people of the Plains, it turned their attention (especially among the Comanches) southward. Why?

≡ **George Catlin, *Comanche Village, Women Dressing Robes and Drying Meat* (1834–1835)** Traveling to the American West five times during the 1830s, George Catlin wrote about and painted portraits that depicted the life of the Plains Indians. He noted that this particular village included between 600 and 800 tented homes of poles covered with decorated buffalo skins. To the right, women work at preserving buffalo skins, and buffalo meat hangs from poles to dry.

As we saw in Chapter 5, in the late eighteenth century, the Comanches had made peace with the Spanish and organized trade and diplomacy around San Antonio in the east and Santa Fe in the west. They also formed something of a political-military alliance with the Spanish against the Apaches. With Mexican independence in 1821, these relations began to be compromised, in part because of the limited control that the Mexican state could exert over its northern territories and in part because Mexico's treasury was depleted and gift-giving diplomacy proved difficult to maintain at the level the Comanches had come to expect. Comanches therefore stepped up their raiding in Tejas and other northern Mexican states, though continued conflicts with Indigenous people to the north limited their scope and intensity.

The Texas Rebellion and then the declaration of the Texas Republic further complicated the political picture. The Comanches engaged in a mix of military and diplomatic encounters with the Texans to defend their hunting grounds, while the Mexicans lost a territorial platform on which they might reconstruct a peace and a buffer against attack. The Great Peace of 1840 thereby freed up the energies of those who had struggled with the Cheyenne and Arapaho, and directed them not to the heavily armed settlements of east Texas but to the lightly defended ranches and haciendas below the Rio Grande, from which retaliation would be almost impossible to mount. Comanche raids began to push deeper and deeper into Mexico—the civil boundaries that Mexico observed were irrelevant to them—rounding up highly valued horses and mules by the thousands and laying waste to Mexican settlements in ferocious fighting. The question of Texas annexation seems only to have intensified Comanche operations. Farther to the west Apaches, Navajos, and Utes took their own opportunities to strike at the vulnerable Mexicans.

Troubles of the Mexican State

From the perspective of Mexico City, Native raiding in the north was only one of a number of serious political problems in the early to mid-1840s. Ever since independence, the Mexican state had been rocked by turmoil and instability. No social group or faction appeared able to impose its authority, and both the presidency and the governing framework changed often by means of coups rather than elections. Although centralists and federalists were the main opponents, infighting was widespread and usually influenced by powerful institutions that were holdovers from the colonial regime, most notably the army and the Catholic Church. At the very moment that the Plains Indians made their Great Peace of 1840, Mexico City witnessed the most violent coup attempt in its history. The only thing that seemed certain was the presence, in some political guise, of Antonio Lopez de Santa Anna. He would occupy the office of president on eleven separate occasions.

The instability that wracked Mexico City was accompanied by social and political unrest in more distant areas of the country—Alta California, Sonora, Zacatecas, Yucatan, Puebla, Oaxaca—which exacerbated the menace of Texas annexation. Some of the unrest, as in Texas, reflected the interest of local elites in greater autonomy and control over land, labor, and other resources. But equally threatening was growing discontent among the Indigenous peasantry, and especially peasant villagers, who were defending their communal landholdings against the assaults of liberal-minded elites intent on privatizing them. Such assaults were part of a process that had been unfolding in Europe and the Americas for two centuries—it was already driving the dispossession of Native Americans in the United States— and although wrapped in the language of progress and civilization it promised to destroy an entire way of life. In the Cerro Gordo ("fat hill" in Spanish) in Spanish California, the Isthmus of Tehuantepec in southern Mexico, and, most famously, on the Yucatan Peninsula, the rumblings of what would become explosive insurrections were already being felt.

The Mexican army was formidable by the standards of the Americas. It was considerably larger than the army of the United States and battle-tested on numerous occasions, not only in the fight for Tejas but also in the fending off of Spanish and French invasions. It had a proud officer corps and an impressive cavalry. At the same time, the Mexican army was poorly equipped and disciplined. Infantry recruits included peasants, vagrants, and prisoners who had been conscripted or coerced into service. They carried outmoded weapons and artillery, were badly clothed and fed, and, as a result, were prone to desertion. Most troublesome, the army lacked the troop strength and financial resources needed to meet the challenges that a large, decentralized, and territorially threatened social order posed. Settlements in the north of the country begged for more protection against Native raiding, though to little effect. The army, for the most part, remained in central

≡ **Mexican Family** Several generations pose in this daguerreotype photo, taken around 1847. The women's fine dresses, the open book held by the lady on the left, and the coat and tie worn by the boy on the right suggest that the family was literate and well-to-do.

Mexico. As a consequence, provincial governors and political bosses determined to establish their own militias and rural police forces.

Justifying Warfare

American policymakers and, through the press, sections of the American public became increasingly aware both of the political problems of the Mexican government and of the punishing raids inflicted by Plains Indians. Together, they created a picture of Mexico and Mexicans replete with signs of weakness, backwardness, cowardice, ignorance, and ineptitude. Mexicans, from this perspective, seemed unable to create free political institutions, defend their territories and families from barbarous attacks, build a dynamic economy, dispel superstitions, or prepare themselves and their children for the new demands of the nineteenth century. Mexican lands, it seemed, were arid, sparsely populated, and unproductive. Their treasury, it appeared, was fleeced by corruption. Their leaders, by widely accepted accounts, were tyrants who fought among themselves and lorded over submissive followers. And blame was generally placed on the influence of the Catholic Church and, especially, on the impact of race mixing or, as some would say, "mongrelization."

By contrast, as the popular perspectives went, Young Americans and other "Anglo-Saxons" marched to democracy's beat, readily seized economic opportunities, carried the advantages and inclinations of "civilization," and had the drive and skill to make the deserts bloom. When these very different forces engaged in conflict, as they did in Texas during the 1830s—a conflict often depicted in such racialized terms—who could doubt which side would win?

As we have seen, President James K. Polk was far less interested in Mexico's near north, where Indigenous people were stirring havoc, than he was in the far northwest, California and the Oregon Territory. But it is likely that the military successes of the Indigenous people, along with the inability of the Mexicans to defeat or force them into retreat, encouraged him to believe that he could get what he wanted in Mexico's near north without enormous cost and effort. This is why he decided to send American troops to the Nueces River in the spring of 1845, order the Pacific Squadron to the California coast later that fall, and seek a diplomatic settlement that would gain California, New Mexico, and a more generous border between Texas and Mexico for the United States. With $25 million on the table for the cash-hungry Mexican government and American armed forces ready to pounce by land and sea, Polk probably thought he was making the Mexicans an offer they had to accept.

In fact, given the complexities of Mexican politics, Polk's was an offer they had to refuse. The sitting president of Mexico, Jose Joaquin Herrera, was anxious to avoid war and to solve the country's financial problems; reports spread that he might be willing to consider selling California and New Mexico. But even the hint of his willingness to entertain such an option—he did allow Polk's ambassador James Slidell into the country—brought a firestorm of criticism his way. Very quickly Herrera fell victim to a coup led by one of his generals, Mariano Paredes y Arrillaga, an archconservative who nonetheless had support from other political factions. The subsequent movement of Zachary Taylor's troops across the Nueces River to the Rio Grande in early 1846, together with an American ultimatum delivered in March, slammed the door on to a peaceful settlement. Polk and his administration had decided on war, and in the second week of May 1846, after a skirmish on the Rio Grande that resulted in sixteen American casualties, they got what they wanted.

11.3   Bloody Continentalism

||| Assess both the importance of California and New Mexico in the war objectives of American political and military leaders and the cost the American military paid to subdue the Mexicans.

The American war against Mexico, which Congress declared in May 1846, has generally been seen as a minor military episode that brought major territorial rewards. The fighting was over in less than a year and a half. American troops occupied Mexico City far to the south of the Rio Grande. And the United States came away with most of what it had sought through diplomatic means, especially the prize of California.

In truth, however, the US-Mexican War would prove to be one of the costliest, most divisive, and most politically dispiriting episodes in American history. It deserves a long, hard look: from West to East and South to North as well as East to West and North to South. The war involved the full-scale invasion of a foreign country for offensive purposes. It required a major mobilization of military power and federal financial resources. It inflicted pain and atrocities on the Mexican people, motivated in large part by bitter racism and anti-Catholicism among American troops. It resulted in a strikingly high level of American casualties. It raised the possibility that territory and subject populations would be conquered and given a distinctively subordinate status compared to the rest of the United States. It reopened bitter questions about the future of enslavement in the country and encouraged some of the most aggressive political and cultural tendencies in American life. And it would leave a legacy of tension, confusion, violence, and militarism around the newly marked US-Mexican border. In sum, the war with Mexico would pose the most fundamental questions of how and whether to establish a continental empire.

Making War in California and the Southwest

Although President Polk's war message to Congress said nothing about territorial acquisition—he spoke only of a Mexican invasion of *our* territory and the shedding of *American blood*—there was little question that California would be taken at the first opportunity. Even before the US-Mexican War began, Polk and his Secretary of State James Buchanan warned their legal representative in the provincial capital of Monterey of "foreign governments" attempting to "acquire a control" over California and urged him to encourage American settlers in the Sonoma and Napa Valleys to follow the example of the rebels in Texas. Should Americans rise in rebellion, Polk and Buchanan made plain, they would "be received as brethren."

The catalyst of American settler discontent in California was the arrival of explorer and surveyor John C. Frémont, who was well connected to the political establishment in the East. It is not entirely clear why Frémont was in California, what his orders were, or what role he played in the unrest that followed. What we do know is that rebellious Americans in Mexican territory rallied around him and in June 1846 seized the northernmost Mexican outpost in Sonoma. Brazenly—and somewhat like their Texas predecessors—they proclaimed the **Bear-Flag Republic**, looking to Frémont as their leader. Their intention, like that of many of the Texans, was to seek annexation to the United States.

As it turned out, formal annexation was not necessary. Following orders to seize California's ports when "actual hostilities" between the United States and Mexico began, the commander of the United States Pacific Squadron, John D. Sloat, quickly sailed into Monterey Bay, marched his men ashore, and unfurled the American flag without a shot being fired. "Henceforth," Sloat announced July 7, 1846, on his own authority, "California will be a portion of the United States." Another naval squadron soon took Yerba Buena (San Francisco) and sent soldiers to Sonoma, where Sloat's announcement was read again. The Bear-Flag then was lowered and the American flag raised (see Map 11.2). Much the same took place in the Sacramento Valley, where Frémont happened to be at the time.

For the next few weeks, it seemed that Americans would make easy work of extending their occupation over the whole of Alta California and, perhaps, Baja California as well. The Bear-Flag rebels were incorporated into the US Army as

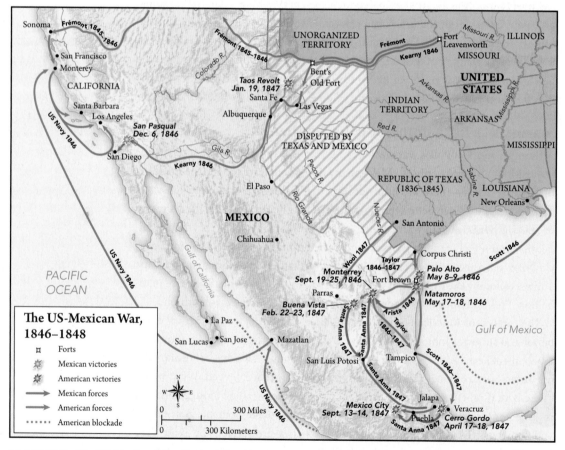

≡ **MAP 11.2   The US-Mexican War, 1846–1848**   The American war against Mexico has generally been seen as a minor military episode, but in fact it was one of the most costly, divisive, and politically dispiriting episodes in American history.

the "California Battalion," and American forces moved south. By the middle of August 1846, facing little resistance from Mexican inhabitants or authorities, they took Santa Barbara, Los Angeles (which had replaced Monterey as the provincial capital), and San Diego. For their part, Mexican troops made a hasty retreat into Sonora and Baja California.

Additional American military power was on its way from the East. Around the time the Bear-Flaggers rose in Sonoma, the Army of the West, under the command of General Stephen Watts Kearney, left Fort Leavenworth, just west of the Mississippi River, and began an 800-mile trek toward Santa Fe. Kearney planned to bring Nuevo Mexico—Polk's second territorial objective—under American control, and with 3,000 troops and wagon loads of supplies the army looked prepared to do it. The Army of the West was such an imposing sight that they traveled through Comanche territory undisturbed and then provoked the Mexican governor of Nuevo Mexico to flee the state without a fight. Like Sloat in California, Kearney raised the flag, proclaimed American occupation, organized a civil government, and declared Nuevo Mexico—now New Mexico—a territory of the United States.

Within a few months, however, the Mexicans unexpectedly struck back. Reorganizing on ranchos outside the coastal towns, **Californios** (Spanish-speaking residents of the state, many of whom owned land) mobilized popular discontent against the Americans and especially against the hard-fisted policies of local commanders. They quickly retook San Diego, Santa Barbara, San Luis Obispo, and Los Angeles. Before long, an insurgency erupted in the Salinas Valley to the north, and then an even more violent one exploded in January 1847 in Taos, New Mexico, which drew upon an alliance of Pueblo Indians and Mexicans and proceeded to murder and scalp the American-appointed governor. It would take another several months of concerted efforts, including some costly battles, before the American conquest of California was finally secured, and the **Taos Rebellion** in New Mexico was crushed.

Crossing the Rio Grande

Popular resentments, especially in New Mexico, were stirred in large part by the despicable behavior of volunteers in the American army. And it would not be the last time that they infuriated Mexican civilians. When President Polk sent General Taylor to the Rio Grande in early 1846, the troops were mostly regular enlisted men. Many had been recruited on the east coast of the United States, and roughly half were immigrants—mainly Irishmen and, to a lesser extent, Germans. They had signed up for five years of service and, as was true in most military institutions of the time, were subject to social isolation and harsh discipline. Officers could use an assortment of physical and humiliating punishments (flogging was still legal) against those who violated orders, and deserters, if caught, could be imprisoned.

With Taylor in command, the regular troops pushed their Mexican counterparts back across the Rio Grande and then occupied the town of Matamoros, where volunteers (who enlisted for only one year) caught up with them. Hailing from states of the South and West and with little formal training, most of the volunteers

≡ **Call to Arms**   Recruitment posters, like this one from Boston, appealed to patriotic ideals and the "Spirit of '76" as they urged men to volunteer to fight in the Mexican War.

arrived by way of New Orleans, the main staging ground for the war, and often after creating serious havoc there. Over the course of the US-Mexican War, they would come to outnumber the regulars in the army by about two to one.

The US regulars did much of the hard fighting, and in Mexico's northeast they were aided in their goals by the raiding of Comanches and Apaches. Potential Mexican manpower had been reduced by years of Native attacks, and communities were reluctant to send men into the Mexican army, leaving themselves even more exposed. "After we have clamored in vain for many years for help in freeing ourselves from the barbarians who have destroyed the wealth of the state," a newspaper in Durango noted, "we have not fielded armies because . . . our brothers have been assassinated by the barbarians, or else fled far away from their fury." Horses and mules needed to equip the Mexican cavalry and help transport supplies had been depleted by the Native raids, and enclaves of Mexican villagers had stopped cooperating with one another.

Would Mexican military resistance have been more formidable were it not for the impact of Native warfare? It is hard to tell. Clearly Taylor and his men would have met a larger and better supported army and experienced more trouble pacifying the countryside and keeping guerilla activity in check. As it was, Mexican

≡ Samuel E. Chamberlain, *Hanging of the San Patricios Following the Battle of Chapultepec*   On the morning of September 13, 1847, dozens of captured members of the San Patricio Battalion were hanged by the American army.

civilians had some cause to look upon the Americans as possible allies against the Comanches and Apaches; they may have reconsidered their own political allegiances were it not for the outrages perpetrated by the American volunteers who were left to police the conquered territory. As one of the American generals put it in 1847, "Our militia & volunteers, if a tenth of what is said be true, have committed atrocities in Mexico sufficient to make Heaven weep." Ill-disciplined and facing weak structures of authority (they could elect their own officers), often young and down on their luck, they ran wild with little consequence. Catholic churches became special targets of their fury, and their desecrations sowed ethnic antagonisms within American ranks. Mexicans were, in fact, able to lure several hundred American deserters (many of them Irish, and most of them Catholic) to their side. The deserters then joined what became known as the **San Patricio Battalion** (Saint Patrick's Battalion) and fought against the United States. The San Patricios were responsible for the toughest battles encountered by the United States in its invasion of Mexico.

11.4   The Political Dilemmas of Conquest

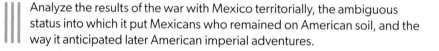

Analyze the results of the war with Mexico territorially, the ambiguous status into which it put Mexicans who remained on American soil, and the way it anticipated later American imperial adventures.

The military occupations of northeastern and northwestern Mexico, together with the aggressive political proclamations issued by American military officers in California and New Mexico, forced the issue of territorial conquest that Polk had initially disclaimed. And, as Polk might have expected, it created a firestorm of controversy in American politics. From the first, the prospect of war had sparked dissent, mainly in the ranks of the Whig Party and among some antislavery Democrats who bridled at Polk's aggression and feared the political and constitutional challenges a war might bring. But most then held their noses and voted for war in Congress, hoping, perhaps, that the territorial problem could be averted. Only a few antislavery Whigs from the Northeast and Midwest remained in steadfast opposition. From their perspective, the war was an imperial move by the "Slave Power."

The Problems of Conquest

Yet, in August 1846, as American troops were taking charge in California and New Mexico, Polk removed all doubt about his intentions. He asked Congress for a $2 million appropriation to pay for any "extraordinary" costs that might be incurred in the war's settlement, which everyone knew to be some sort of territorial acquisition. Would there be any ground rules or political limitations established for these "acquisitions" and the people who resided there? A newly elected Democratic congressman from Pennsylvania, David Wilmot, thought there should be. He was a member of Polk's party and had supported both Texas annexation and the US-Mexican War. But he wanted to make sure that enslavement would not be legal in any land gained from Mexico. He therefore attached a rider to an appropriations bill for the war declaring that "neither slavery nor involuntary servitude shall ever exist in any part of said territory."

Despite the language of the **Wilmot Proviso**, Wilmot was no abolitionist. He was less concerned about the morality of enslavement than about preserving "for free white labor a fair country, a rich inheritance, where the sons of toil of my own race, can live without the disgrace which association with Negro slavery brings upon free labor." Significantly, Wilmot referred to his rider as the "White Man's Proviso," and it nearly succeeded in passing Congress, securing majority approval in the House of Representatives before failing in the Senate. While not becoming law, Wilmot's proviso unmistakably demonstrated that territorial conquest would reignite the question of enslavement's future in a greatly enlarged—possibly continental—United States.

There were other serious questions, too, the resolution of which showed how deeply embedded racialist assumptions were in the vision of continentalism—and how troublesome they would be in the pursuit of American empire. What, after all, was to become of any territory the United States managed to purchase or take from Mexico? Would it assume a territorial status under the jurisdiction of the federal government and, like the Louisiana Territory, gradually be divided into states? Would it forever remain a territory or "possession" under direct federal rule? Or would it be occupied and incorporated, run by federally appointed governors and other officials, as in British India? And what of the people living in the Mexican territories conquered by the United States? Would they all have the opportunity to be treated as other free Americans were, with the same rights and obligations? Would only certain groups have such an opportunity? Or would they all be relegated to some type of permanent subject status? The Constitution offered very little guidance.

☰ **Californio**   Maria Paula Rosalia Vallejo del Leese's assured pose and fine clothes attest to her status as a wealthy Californio. Born into the Vallejo family, a prominent landowning Northern California family in 1811, Maria Paula married American merchant Jacob Leese in 1837. This daguerreotype was probably taken around the time of her marriage.

California seemed to hold the most appealing prospects for incorporation on the Louisiana model, lightly populated as it was with Mexican citizens, and American military officials appeared to be moving in such a direction from the start of the war. General Kearney had already pronounced New Mexico an American territory. But what of the Mexican northeast, or of territories farther toward the center of the United States? Or should the United States try to take charge of the entire Mexican Republic?

How Much to Take?

The possibility of massive territorial conquest developed during the war itself. President Polk's initial intention, after securing California, New Mexico, and the Rio Grande, was to use the northeastern theater of war mainly to demonstrate American military superiority, demoralize the Mexicans, and force them to accept a peace on American terms. But the Mexicans would not play along. Despite a series of military defeats, most notably at Monterrey, Chihuahua, and Buena Vista, the Mexican government simply refused to negotiate with Polk.

Realizing it was time for a new plan, Polk decided to shift the field of operations far to the south, toward Mexico City, the country's capital and seat of government, where a crushing blow would likely do what the campaign in the northeast failed to accomplish: force the Mexicans to give up. The US Army planned to launch an attack by way of the gulf port of Veracruz, reenacting the conquest of Spaniard Hernán Cortés three centuries earlier. Despite serious reservations, Polk chose General Winfield Scott—a Whig with political aspirations—to lead the campaign and potentially to step into the limelight.

Scott proved to be an excellent choice from a strictly military standpoint. After a huge amphibious assault just south of Veracruz in March 1847 (the largest land and naval attack undertaken by Americans before World War II), Scott's troops took control of the town and then headed west toward Mexico City. At times the fighting was fierce, the terrain imposing, and guerilla harassment—some sanctioned by the Mexican government—effective enough to force Scott and his men to cut loose from their supply lines and live off the country. Still, despite the challenges and the unanticipated departure of many volunteers whose terms of enlistment expired along the way, Scott managed to push ahead. In early September, he and his army entered the Mexican capital, completing a campaign that would win Scott enduring military fame. It would also win him, much as Polk had feared, the nomination of the Whig Party for president in 1852.

Scott's military success invigorated American imperial appetites. The occupation of Mexico City not only put the United States in a strong bargaining position; it also increased the opportunity for territorial conquest well beyond anything imagined at the war's outset. Some began to demand the entire country of Mexico as a condition for peace, and a few went so far as to eyeball all of Central America, too. Democrats, as might be expected, led the charge, but advocates also included some abolition-minded Americans who hoped to link emancipation and empire much as the British had done. After all, Mexico had already abolished slavery and was unlikely to restore it, so the acquisition of "4,000,000 square miles" west and south of the slave states could hem them in and "establish Freedom as the fundamental and unchangeable Law of the North American continent."

From the perspective of many enslavers, expansionists

≡ **Carl Nebel, *General Scott's Entrance into Mexico* (1851)**   Painted for an American audience by a German artist and widely distributed through printed reproductions, this image shows an idealized and orderly arrival of the conquering US forces into the Zócalo, the plaza at the center of Mexico City. In the distance, an American flag has been raised over the National Palace. In fact, the battle for Mexico City ended in chaos and bloodshed. General Santa Anna released 30,000 prisoners into the city before he evacuated, and both residents of the city and remaining Mexican soldiers resisted the occupation. Nebel hints at this resistance: to the left, in the foreground, a beggar prepares to throw a stone at Scott's forces; on the rooftop above him, snipers take aim.

among them, that was what made the **All-Mexico** movement dangerous. Perhaps a more measured approach would be best, one that looked to annexing California, New Mexico, and the northeastern tier of Mexico, where settlement was sparse, rather than trying to take areas farther to the south, where the population was denser and the challenges of governance much greater—and, of course, where most of the inhabitants were Native or mixed-race. South Carolina's John C. Calhoun, who had opposed the war to begin with, warned of the cultural and political mire that could await the annexationists, whether greedy or modest in their designs. The United States, Calhoun said on the floor of the Senate, had never "incorporated any but the Caucasian race. To incorporate Mexico would be the first departure of the kind, for more than half its population are pure Indian and by far the larger portion of the residue mixed blood. Ours is a government of white men."

In one form or another, Calhoun's views were widely shared. Northern and southern Whigs, whatever their other differences, alike doubted that American institutions could be adapted to former Mexican territory or that American civil and political society could absorb what they viewed as an uneducated, backward, and superstitious populace. Worries about annexing a land overrun by Catholics and racial "inferiors" found expression even among Whigs of an antislavery bent.

But similar reservations among some Democrats proved especially telling. "We do not want the people of Mexico, either as citizens or subjects," Michigan's influential Senator Lewis Cass told Congress. "All we want is a portion of territory, which they nominally hold, generally uninhabited or . . . sparsely so, and with a population that would soon recede, or identify itself with ours."

Whatever the perspective, military and political options were rapidly narrowing for both sides. The American occupation of Mexico City, as anticipated, struck a devastating blow to the government of Mexico, which was forced to flee to Querétaro, 100 miles to the north. But so, too, did popular unrest—most dramatically in the Yucatán—which showed separatist and anti-elite tendencies. Whatever else might divide them, liberals and conservatives at the helm of the Mexican government could unite in the face of social turmoil from below. By the end of 1847, with a new moderate president in place, they sued for peace.

The signs of defeat in Mexico could have strengthened the position of the aggressive expansionists in the United States. But, to complete their imagined work of conquest, they would have needed more troops and lots more money. And this had become unattainable. Congressional elections in the fall of 1846 gave the Whig Party only narrow control of the House of Representatives, and, even more important, they registered shifting public temper on the war itself. Opposition to annexing Mexican territory south of the Rio Grande was growing in many sections of the country, while the occupying army felt the wrath of Mexican civilians. "The Mexican people generally became hostile to the United States and availed themselves of every opportunity to commit savage excesses on our troops," Polk conceded in December 1847. Without doubt, the time had come to stop fishing and cut bait.

The Treaty of Guadalupe Hidalgo

No one knew this better than Nicholas Trist, the American diplomat whom Polk had sent to Mexico City the previous spring to conclude a treaty of peace. Polk insisted at the time that Mexico cede Alta California and Nuevo Mexico as well as recognize the Rio Grande as the southwest border of Texas. But he also hoped to acquire Baja California together with transit rights across the Gulf of Tehuantepec in the south. And all of this he wanted for $15 to $20 million (about the same amount that Jefferson paid for the Louisiana Purchase). Predictably, Trist got nowhere and Polk, still greedy, called him back to Washington, DC. Trist, however, sensed that the political winds were changing direction in Mexico and the United States, and with moderates coming to power in Mexico, he made a gutsy decision. He ignored Polk's orders to return and began another round of treaty negotiations.

This time Trist made progress. By early February 1848, the **Treaty of Guadalupe Hidalgo** was transmitted to Polk, who was now furious at Trist's insubordination. Still, given the political cross-currents of the moment, he had little choice but to

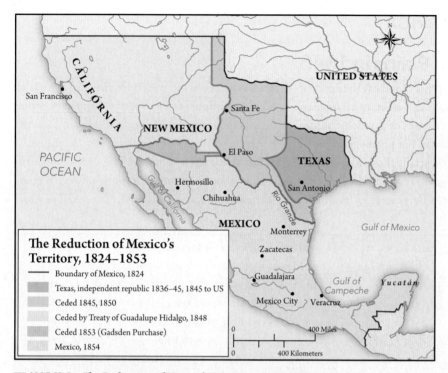

The Reduction of Mexico's Territory, 1824–1853

——— Boundary of Mexico, 1824

Texas, independent republic 1836–45, 1845 to US

Ceded 1845, 1850

Ceded by Treaty of Guadalupe Hidalgo, 1848

Ceded 1853 (Gadsden Purchase)

Mexico, 1854

≡ **MAP 11.3**   **The Reduction of Mexico's Territory, 1824–1853**

send the treaty on to the Senate for ratification. After all, Polk got most of what he wanted and all of what he had demanded. In what is known as the Mexican Cession, the Mexican government gave up Alta California, Nuevo Mexico north of the Gila River, and the disputed land between the Nueces and Rio Grande rivers in Texas to the United States. The American government agreed to pay Mexico $15 million, assume the monetary claims of American citizens against Mexico, and accept responsibility for restraining Native raids from American into Mexican territory—in short, to patrol its new border (see Map 11.3).

More troublesome was the fate of roughly 100,000 Mexicans (including Indigenous people regarded by Mexico as citizens) who lived in the newly conquered territories. The treaty allowed them to stay or leave but required them to choose within a year whether to be Mexican or American citizens. Either way, they were to be protected in the "free enjoyment of their liberty and property and secured in the free exercise of their religion."

Nonetheless, the question of just when those who gave up Mexican citizenship would be able to enjoy "all the rights of citizens of the United States" was left to be determined by Congress in "proper time." Which is to say that whatever the language, Mexicans who remained in what was now the United States occupied a murky and potentially precarious status, and the American government effectively

MAPPING AMERICA

The Southern Plains in 1845

An underlying theme of this chapter is the concept of *borders*. For politicians and military strategists, incursions across and defenses of a nation's border often constitute acts of war. For people who live in or near borderlands—especially those whose livelihoods and families have traversed borders for generations—such wars can be especially traumatic.

And, as we see in our own time, the US border with Mexico continues to be a site of political contention despite the sufferings of people seeking to cross the border to work, to visit family, or to seek asylum.

For cartographers, however, borders tell a specific story about a nation's status and power. In many conventional maps, clearly demarcated lines and

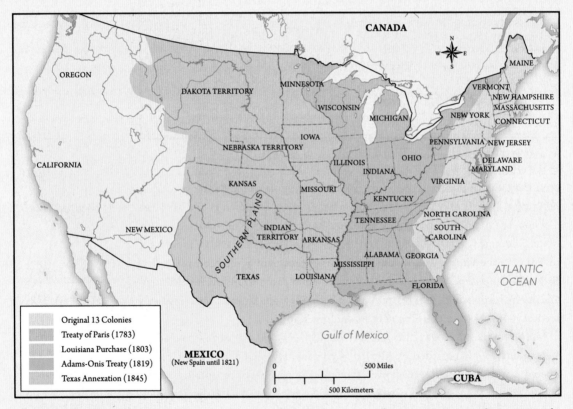

Original 13 Colonies
Treaty of Paris (1783)
Louisiana Purchase (1803)
Adams-Onis Treaty (1819)
Texas Annexation (1845)

≡ **MAP 1   Territorial Expansion of the United States, 1776–1845**   American history presents a steady expansion of the United States westward. In this spatial geometry, the Southern Plains and its peoples are neatly contained within the political borders of the United States by 1845.

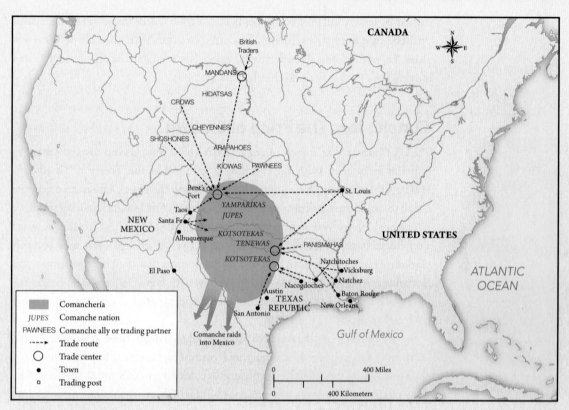

≡ **MAP 2   Comancheria**   A view of the Southern Plains from a Comanche perspective c. 1845 offers a different view of the region. Comanche power and influence extend across hundreds of miles in all directions, disregarding arbitrary political boundaries.

different colors illustrate the Manifest Destiny that drove America westward (Map 1). But what happens when maps are drawn from the perspective of peoples who do not recognize political borders (Map 2)?

Thinking Geographically

1. What sort of spatial geometry is shown in Map 1? How does it represent the aspirations of many white Americans in the 1840s?

2. Examine Map 2. What happens when maps depict spatial geometries of peoples or nations, such as the Comanche, who do not recognize conventional borders? What stories can maps tell once conventional borders have been removed?

turned its new southwest borderlands into a zone where many of the occupants could be seen as fugitives, interlopers, and trespassers with unstable political loyalties. So, while political borders were more clearly established, the borders of belonging remained as fuzzy as they had always been.

Conclusion: The Price of Empire

The US-Mexican War, therefore, suggested both the rewards and costs of America's imperial ambitions. With the ratification in 1848 of the Treaty of Guadalupe Hidalgo, the territory of the United States spanned the North American continent ocean to ocean and the country achieved, as most of its leaders had long sought, a strong position on the Pacific coast. America's apparent Manifest Destiny now had a territorial basis. Texas, with its vast prospective cotton fields, was now securely placed within the American union with the borders that the US government had demanded. And the lower Mississippi Valley, with New Orleans as its headquarters, was emerging as the epicenter of an expanding empire, gazing toward other potential conquests to the south.

Yet the price of empire was also plain for all to reckon. Most Americans could unite over the appeals of an imagined continental empire, but the process of empire-building proved to be deeply divisive. Moving hastily over such enormous space challenged the developmental sensibilities of those who wanted a tighter-knit economy. Waging offensive war for territorial gains offended the diplomatic sensibilities of those who thought that the United States represented an alternative to the war-mongering states of Europe. Rejuvenating the question of enslavement's expansion and enslavers' power outraged the moral and political sensibilities of those who insisted that "empire" be equated with "liberty." Incorporating new populations with complex ancestries confounded the racial and constitutional sensibilities of those devoted to the goal of building a "white man's republic." And establishing new borders while skirting the issue of what residence on American soil meant opened the door to conflicts that the federal state was not even in a position to resolve.

There were human costs, too, that, over time, have been overlooked. US soldiers in the US-Mexican War not only engaged in plunder and atrocities on foreign soil. They also suffered casualties in unexpectedly large numbers. More than 10 percent of those who served in the US Army—as regulars or volunteers—died, overwhelmingly from disease, in fewer than two years, and more than 20 percent were killed, wounded, or otherwise incapacitated. In short, the US-Mexican War, given the short time span of its operations (less than a year and a half), was possibly America's deadliest war. It was a sobering example of what imperial adventurism might bring and the forging of empire could entail.

WHAT IF War with Mexico Had Been Averted?

The course of events that led to the US-Mexican War seemed to build steadily and powerfully for over a decade, suggesting that there were few alternatives to the bloodshed and forcible acquisition of northwestern Mexico. Anglo-Texans, many of them from the United States, had risen in rebellion and succeeded in driving off the Mexican army and proclaiming the Republic of Texas, as we saw in Chapter 9. Annexation sentiment both in Texas and the United States was very strong, particularly among southerners and Democrats, and seemed to await only the right political moment to be achieved. California had been in the sights and imaginations of American political leaders since the birth of the republic, and it lay well outside the orbit of effective Mexican government control. And since the Mexicans refused to recognize either the Republic of Texas or the presumed borders of the new Texas state—and saw annexation as an act of American aggression—hostilities appeared inevitable.

But in truth, there were numerous moments when other outcomes seemed possible. Santa Anna came very near to crushing the Texas rebellion as it was, but had he directed his troops initially to east-central Texas rather than to the Alamo (a strategically worthless target), his chances of succeeding would have been greater still. The Republic of Texas would then have been a mere fantasy, and the United States would have needed to contemplate a full-out war with Mexico to gain any territory west of the Sabine River, without the fiction that it was simply fending off an unprovoked invasion.

Even if the Texas rebellion succeeded and annexation to the United States seemed likely, the move toward war with Mexico could still have been averted.

The presidential election of 1844 set the prominent Whig politician Henry Clay against the little-known Democratic candidate James K. Polk. ("Who is James K. Polk?," Clay partisans asked during the campaign.) Four years earlier, in an election with a high turnout of eligible voters, the Whigs had won the presidency, and despite the death of William Henry Harrison, were fairly well positioned to repeat. Indeed, the 1844 election was extremely close—neither candidate won 50 percent of the popular votes—and had New York State gone to the Whig Party, Clay would have become president.

At most lukewarm about Texas annexation, Clay was in no rush to get into a war with Mexico. With the Whigs triumphant, Tyler may, in fact, have thought better of pushing ahead with annexation by means of joint resolution, and even if he had decided to do so, the mood in Congress may well have been different. For his part, Clay was unlikely to have sent American troops down to the Nueces River with orders about engaging the Mexican army, and the Pacific Squadron would not have been deployed along the coast of California with instructions to move ashore at the first word of hostilities with Mexico.

Perhaps Clay and the Whigs would have looked for a diplomatic solution to the challenge of gaining access to the Pacific coast (though the Whig platform of 1844 said nothing about expansion, the Democrats called for "re-occupying Oregon" and "re-annexing Texas"). But in January 1848, just before the Treaty of Guadalupe Hidalgo was signed, gold was discovered at Sutter's mill in the Sacramento Valley of California, and the Mexicans may have taken a very different view of their northwest. Then what?

DOCUMENT 11.1:   Henry Clay's Speech on the War with Mexico, November 13, 1847

How did we unhappily get involved in this war? It was predicted as the consequence of the annexation of Texas to the United States. If we had not Texas, we should have no war. The people were told that if that event happened, war would ensue. They were told that the war between Texas and Mexico had not been terminated by a treaty of peace; that Mexico still claimed Texas as a revolted province: and that, if we received Texas in our Union, we took along with her, the war existing between her and Mexico. And the Minister of Mexico [Juan N. Almonte] formally announced to the Government at Washington, that his nation would consider the annexation of Texas to the United States as producing a state of war. But all this was denied by the partisans of annexation. They insisted we should have no war, and even imputed to those who foretold it, sinister motives for their groundless prediction.

But, notwithstanding a state of virtual war necessarily resulted from the fact of annexation of one of the belligerents to the United States, actual hostilities might have been probably averted by prudence, moderation and wise statesmanship. If General Taylor had been permitted to remain, where his own good sense prompted him to believe he ought to remain, at the point of Corpus Christi; and, if a negotiation had been opened with Mexico, in a true spirit of amity and conciliation, war possibly might have been prevented. But, instead of this pacific and moderate course, whilst Mr. Slidell was bending his way to Mexico with his diplomatic credentials, General Taylor was ordered to transport his cannon, and to plant them, in a warlike attitude, opposite to Matamoras, on the east bank of the Rio Bravo; within the very disputed territory, the adjustment of which was to be the object of Mr. Slidell's mission. What else could have transpired but a conflict of arms?

Thus the war commenced, and the President after having produced it, appealed to Congress. A bill was proposed to raise 50,000 volunteers, and in order to commit all who should vote for it, a preamble was inserted falsely attributing the commencement of the war to the act of Mexico. I have no doubt of the patriotic motives of those who, after struggling to divest the bill of that flagrant error, found themselves constrained to vote for it. But I must say that no earthly consideration would have ever tempted or provoked me to vote for a bill, with a palpable falsehood stamped on its face. Almost idolizing truth, as I do, I never, never, could have voted for that bill.

How totally variant is the present war! This is no war of defence, but one unnecessary and of offensive aggression. It is Mexico that is defending her fire-sides, her castles and her altars, not we. And how different also is the conduct of the whig party of the present day from that of the major part of the federal party during the war of 1812! Far from interposing any obstacles to the prosecution of the war, if the Whigs in office are reproachable at all, it is for having lent too ready a facility to it, without careful examination into the objects of the war. And, out of office, who have rushed to the prosecution of the war with more ardor and alacrity than the Whigs? Whose hearts have bled more freely than those of the Whigs?—Who have more occasion to mourn the loss of sons, husbands, brothers, fathers, than whig parents, whig wives and whig brothers, in this deadly and unprofitable strife?

I have embodied, Mr. President and fellow-citizens, the sentiments and opinions which I have endeavored to explain and enforce in a series of resolutions which I beg now to submit to your consideration and judgment. They are the following:

1. Resolved, as the opinion of this meeting, that the primary cause of the present unhappy war, existing between the United States of America, and the United States of the Republic of Mexico, was the annexation of Texas to the former; and that the immediate occasion of hostilities between the two republics arose out of the order of the President of the United States for the removal of the army under the command of General Taylor, from its position at Corpus Christi to a point opposite to Matamoras, on the East bank of the Rio Bravo, within territory claimed by both Republics, but then under the jurisdiction of that of Mexico, and inhabited by its citizens; and that the order of the President for the removal of the army to that point, was improvident and unconstitutional, it being without the concurrence of Congress, or even any consultation with it, although it was in session: but that Congress having, by subsequent acts, recognized the war thus brought into existence without its previous authority or consent, the prosecution of it became thereby National.

2. Resolved, That, in the absence of any formal and public declaration by Congress, of the objects for which the war ought to be prosecuted, the President of the United States, as Chief Magistrate, and as Commander in Chief of the Army and Navy of the United States, is left to the guidance of his own judgment to prosecute it for such purposes and objects as he may deem the honor and interest of the nation to require.

3. Resolved, That, by the Constitution of the United States, Congress, being invested with the power to declare war, and grant letters of marque and reprizal, to make rules concerning captures on land and water, to raise and support armies, to provide and maintain a navy, and to make rules for the government of the land and naval forces, has the full and complete war making power of the United States; and, so possessing it, has a right to determine upon the motives, causes and objects of any war, when it commences, or at any time during the progress of its existence.

4. Resolved, as the further opinion of this meeting, that it is the right and duty of Congress to declare, by some authentic act, for what purposes and objects the existing war ought to be further prosecuted; that it is the duty of the President, in his official conduct, to conform to such a declaration of Congress; and that, if, after such declaration, the President should decline or refuse to endeavor, by all the means, civil, diplomatic, and military, in his power, to execute the announced will of Congress, and, in defiance of its authority, should continue to prosecute the war for purposes and objects other than those declared by that body, it would become the right and duty of Congress to adopt the most efficacious measures to arrest the further

progress of the war, taking care to make ample provision for the honor, the safety and security of our armies in Mexico, in every contingency. And, if Mexico should decline or refuse to conclude a treaty with us, stipulating for the purposes and objects so declared by Congress, it would be the duty of the Government to prosecute the war with the utmost vigor, until they were attained by a treaty of peace.

5. Resolved, That we view with serious alarm, and are utterly opposed to any purpose of annexing Mexico to the United States, in any mode, and especially by conquest; that we believe the two nations could not be happily governed by one common authority, owing to their great difference of race, law, language and religion, and the vast extent of their respective territories, and large amount of their respective populations; that such a union, against the consent of the exasperated Mexican people, could only be effected and preserved by large standing armies, and the constant application of military force—in other words, by despotic sway exercised over the Mexican people, in the first instance, but which, there would be just cause to apprehend, might, in process of time, be extended over the people of the United States. That we deprecate, therefore, such a union, as wholly incompatible with the genius of our Government, and with the character of free and liberal institutions; and we anxiously hope that each nation may be left in the undisturbed possession of its own laws, language, cherished religion and territory, to pursue its own happiness, according to what it may deem best for itself.

6. Resolved, That, considering the series of splendid and brilliant victories achieved by our brave armies and their gallant commanders, during the war with Mexico, unattended by a single reverse, The United States, without any danger of their honor suffering the slightest tarnish, can practice the virtues of moderation and magnanimity towards their discomfited foe. We have no desire for the dismemberment of the United States of the Republic of Mexico, but wish only a just and proper fixation of the limits of Texas.

7. Resolved, That we do, positively and emphatically, disclaim and disavow any wish or desire, on our part, to acquire any foreign territory whatever, for the purpose of propagating slavery, or of introducing slaves from the United States, into such foreign territory.

8. Resolved, That we invite our fellow citizens of the United States, who are anxious for the restoration of the blessings of peace, or, if the existing war shall continue to be prosecuted, are desirous that its purpose and objects shall be defined and known; who are anxious to avert present and future perils and dangers, with which it may be fraught; and who are also anxious to produce contentment and satisfaction at home, and to elevate the national character abroad, to assemble together in their respective communities, and to express their views, feelings, and opinions.

Source: Henry Clay's Advice to His Countrymen Relative to the War with Mexico (New York: H. R. Robinson, 1847).

DOCUMENT 11.2:   President James K. Polk's War Message to Congress, May 11, 1846

The existing state of the relations between the United States and Mexico renders it proper that I should bring the subject to the consideration of Congress. In my message at the commencement of your present session the state of these relations, the causes which led to the suspension of diplomatic intercourse between the two countries in March, 1845, and the long-continued and unredressed wrongs and injuries committed by the Mexican Government on citizens of the United States in their persons and property were briefly set forth.

The strong desire to establish peace with Mexico on liberal and honorable terms, and the readiness of this Government to regulate and adjust our boundary and other causes of difference with that power on such fair and equitable principles as would lead to permanent relations of the most friendly nature, induced me in September last to seek the reopening of diplomatic relations between the two countries. The Mexican Government not only refused to receive him or listen to his propositions, but after a long-continued series of menaces have at last invaded our territory and shed the blood of our fellow-citizens on our own soil.

At the commencement of the present session I informed you that upon the earnest appeal both of the Congress and convention of Texas I had ordered an efficient military force to take a position "between the Nueces and the Del Norte." This had become necessary to meet a threatened invasion of Texas by the Mexican forces, for which extensive military preparations had been made. The invasion was threatened solely because Texas had determined, in accordance with a solemn resolution of the Congress of the United States, to annex herself to our Union, and under these circumstances it was plainly our duty to extend our protection over her citizens and soil.

This force was concentrated at Corpus Christi, and remained there until after I had received such information from Mexico as rendered it probable, if not certain, that the Mexican Government would refuse to receive our envoy.

Meantime Texas, by the final action of our Congress, had become an integral part of our Union. The Congress of Texas, by its act of December 19, 1836, had declared the Rio del Norte to be the boundary of that Republic. Its jurisdiction had been extended and exercised beyond the Nueces. The country between that river and the Del Norte had been represented in the Congress and in the convention of Texas, had thus taken part in the act of annexation itself, and is now included within one of our Congressional districts. Our own Congress had, moreover, with great unanimity, by the act approved December 31, 1845, recognized the country beyond the Nueces as a part of our territory by including it within our own revenue system, and a revenue officer to reside within that district has been appointed by and with the advice and consent of the Senate. It became, therefore, of urgent necessity to provide for the defense of that portion of our country. Accordingly, on the 13th of January last instructions were issued to the general in command of these troops to occupy the left bank of the Del Norte. This river, which is the southwestern boundary of the State of Texas, is an exposed frontier. From this quarter invasion was threatened; upon it and in its immediate vicinity, in the judgment of high military experience, are the proper stations for the protecting forces of the Government. In addition to this important consideration, several others occurred to induce this movement. Among these are the facilities afforded by the ports at Brazos Santiago and the mouth of the Del Norte for the reception of supplies by sea, the stronger and more healthful military positions, the convenience for obtaining a ready and a more abundant supply of provisions, water, fuel, and forage, and the advantages which are afforded by the Del Norte in forwarding supplies to such posts as may be established in the interior and upon the Indian frontier.

The movement of the troops to the Del Norte was made by the commanding general under positive instructions to abstain from all aggressive acts toward Mexico or Mexican citizens and to regard the relations between that Republic and the United States as peaceful unless she should declare war or commit acts of hostility indicative of a state of war. He was specially directed to protect private property and respect personal rights.

The Army moved from Corpus Christi on the 11th of March, and on the 28th of that month arrived on the left bank of the Del Norte opposite to Matamoras, where it encamped on a commanding position, which has since been strengthened by the erection of fieldworks. A depot has also been established at Point Isabel, near the Brazos Santiago, 30 miles in rear of the encampment. The selection of his position was necessarily confided to the judgment of the general in command.

The Mexican forces at Matamoras assumed a belligerent attitude, and on the 12th of April General Ampudia, then in command, notified General Taylor to break up his camp within twenty-four hours and to retire beyond the Nueces River, and in the event of his failure to comply with these demands announced that arms, and arms alone, must decide the question. But no open act of hostility was committed until the 24th of April. On that day General Arista, who had succeeded to the command of the Mexican forces, communicated to General Taylor that "he considered hostilities commenced and should prosecute them." A party of dragoons of 63 men and officers were on the same day dispatched from the American camp up the Rio del Norte, on its left bank, to ascertain whether the Mexican troops had crossed or were preparing to cross the river, "became engaged with a large body of these troops, and after a short affair, in which some 16 were killed and wounded, appear to have been surrounded and compelled to surrender."

The grievous wrongs perpetrated by Mexico upon our citizens throughout a long period of years remain unredressed, and solemn treaties pledging her public faith for this redress have been disregarded. A government either unable or unwilling to enforce the execution of such treaties fails to perform one of its plainest duties.

Our commerce with Mexico has been almost annihilated. It was formerly highly beneficial to both nations, but our merchants have been deterred from prosecuting it by the system of outrage and extortion which the Mexican authorities have pursued against them, whilst their appeals through their own Government for indemnity have been made in vain. Our forbearance has gone to such an extreme as to be mistaken in its character. Had we acted with vigor in repelling the insults and redressing the injuries inflicted by Mexico at the commencement, we should doubtless have escaped all the difficulties in which we are now involved.

Instead of this, however, we have been exerting our best efforts to propitiate her good will. Upon the pretext that Texas, a nation as independent as herself, thought proper to unite its destinies with our own she has affected to believe that we have severed her rightful territory, and in official proclamations and manifestoes has repeatedly threatened to make war upon us for the purpose of reconquering Texas. In the meantime we have tried every effort at reconciliation. The cup of forbearance had been exhausted even before the recent information from the frontier of the Del Norte. But now, after reiterated menaces, Mexico has passed the boundary of the United States, has invaded our territory and shed American blood upon the American soil. She has proclaimed that hostilities have commenced, and that the two nations are now at war.

As war exists, and, notwithstanding all our efforts to avoid it, exists by the act of Mexico herself, we are called upon by every consideration of duty and patriotism to vindicate with decision the honor, the rights, and the interests of our country.

Anticipating the possibility of a crisis like that which has arrived, instructions were given in August last, "as a precautionary measure" against invasion or threatened invasion, authorizing General Taylor, if the emergency required, to accept volunteers, not from Texas only, but from the States of Louisiana, Alabama, Mississippi, Tennessee, and Kentucky, and corresponding letters were addressed to the respective governors of those States. These instructions were repeated, and in January last, soon after the incorporation of "Texas into our Union of States," General Taylor was further "authorized by the President to make a requisition upon the executive of that State for such of its militia force as may be needed to repel invasion or to secure the country against apprehended invasion." On the 2d day of March he was again reminded, "in the event of the approach of any considerable Mexican force, promptly and efficiently to use the authority with which he was clothed to call to him such auxiliary force as he might need." War actually existing and our territory having been invaded, General Taylor, pursuant to authority vested in him by my direction, has called on the governor of Texas for four regiments of State troops, two to be mounted and two to serve on foot, and on the governor of Louisiana for four regiments of infantry to be sent to him as soon as practicable.

In further vindication of our rights and defense of our territory, I invoke the prompt action of Congress to recognize the existence of the war, and to place at the disposition of the Executive the means of prosecuting the war with vigor, and thus hastening the restoration of peace. To this end I recommend that authority should be given to call into the public service a large body of volunteers to serve for not less than six or twelve months unless sooner discharged. A volunteer force is beyond question more efficient than any other description of citizen soldiers, and it is not to be doubted that a number far beyond that required would readily rush to the field upon the call of their country. I further recommend that a liberal provision be made for sustaining our entire military force and furnishing it with supplies and munitions of war.

The most energetic and prompt measures and the immediate appearance in arms of a large and overpowering force are recommended to Congress as the most certain and efficient means of bringing the existing collision with Mexico to a speedy and successful termination.

In making these recommendations I deem it proper to declare that it is my anxious desire not only to terminate hostilities speedily, but to bring all matters in dispute between this Government and Mexico to an early and amicable adjustment; and in this view I shall be prepared to renew negotiations whenever Mexico shall be ready to receive propositions or to make propositions of her own.

Source: James K. Polk, Special Message to Congress on Mexican Relations Online https://www.presidency.ucsb.edu/node/200910

Thinking About Contingency

1. People on the losing side of history tend to ask, "What if?," because they like to think that things could have turned out differently. Imagine yourself as a Mexican statesman in 1849. How would you answer the question, "What if war with the United States had been averted?"
2. Consider the other possible outcomes the author of this textbook presents. Do these possibilities help to illuminate that war with Mexico was not inevitable?

REVIEW QUESTIONS

1. What were the motivations for US policymakers in annexing Texas and declaring war on Mexico?

2. Why did the annexation of Texas prove to be a divisive political issue in the United States?

3. What did the United States hope to gain as a result of war with Mexico?

4. What role did Native Americans play in weakening Mexico's ability to mount a strong response to the American invasion?

5. How different was the behavior of regular and volunteer US Army troops, and how did their behavior shape the course of the war?

6. The Treaty of Guadalupe Hidalgo brought the US-Mexican War to an end. What did the United States achieve?

7. What do you think are the short- and long-term legacies of the US-Mexican War?

KEY TERMS

All-Mexico (p. 459)

annexation (p. 438)

Bear-Flag Republic (p. 451)

Californios (p. 453)

Great Peace of 1840 (p. 447)

Manifest Destiny (p. 440)

San Patricio Battalion (p. 456)

Taos Rebellion (p. 453)

Treaty of Guadalupe Hidalgo (p. 460)

Wilmot Proviso (p. 457)

Young America (p. 440)

RECOMMENDED READINGS

Randolph Campbell, *An Empire for Slavery: The Peculiar Institution in Texas, 1821–1865* (LSU Press, 1991).

Brian DeLay, *War of a Thousand Deserts: Indian Raids and the U.S.-Mexican War* (Yale University Press, 2008).

Amy Greenberg, *A Wicked War: Polk, Clay, Lincoln, and the 1846 Invasion of Mexico* (Knopf Doubleday, 2013).

Stephen L. Hardin, *Texas Iliad: A Military History of the Texas Revolution* (University of Texas Press, 1996).

Timothy J. Henderson, *A Glorious Defeat: Mexico and Its War with the United States* (Hill and Wang, 2008).

Andres Tijerina, *Tejanos and Texas under the Mexican Flag, 1821–1836* (Texas A&M Press, 1994).

Coming Apart
1848–1857

≡ *Hauling the Whole Week's Picking* (detail, c. 1842)   Little is known about William Henry Brown, the itinerant artist who created this image while a guest at the Nitta Yuma plantation in Mississippi. Even enslaved children were put to work in the service of a booming cotton economy.

12.7 Kansas Explodes

||| Explain why the issue of enslavement in the territory of Kansas created such division and bloodshed.

12.8 Slavery Everywhere?

||| Summarize how the Supreme Court's decision in *Scott v. Sandford* influenced the crisis over enslavement's future.

In May 1856, four leaders of the "Lafayette Emigration Society" in western Missouri wrote a letter, "To the People of the South," for publication in a New Orleans–based journal called *De Bow's Review*. They wished to inform the people in the "slaveholding states" of the "absolute necessity of immediate action on their part" to carry out the settlement of the Kansas Territory as a slave state. The society's leaders pointed to the great amount of time and money Missourians like them had devoted to the cause of

Timeline

1838	1840	1842	1844	1846	1848	1850

1839 > The *Amistad* uprising

1840 > Liberty Party organized

1841 > Successful slave rebellion on the *Creole*

1845 > Publication of Frederick Douglass's *Narrative of the Life of Frederick Douglass*

1848 > Treaty of Guadalupe Hidalgo ends US-Mexican War; gold discovered in California, initiating the Gold Rush; Women's Rights Convention in Seneca Falls, New York; Free-Soil Party organized

1850 > Congress passes Compromise (or "Armistice") of 1850

enslavement in Kansas over the previous two years, "fighting the battles of the South," but made it clear that they could no longer "stand up single-handed." They needed men and their families—along with the people they enslaved—to flood into Kansas and defeat the fanatical abolitionists, "higher law incendiaries," who sought to make "war upon the institutions of the South." Should Kansas be lost, they warned, it would be the "death knell of our dear Union."

The Missourians chose to communicate through *De Bow's Review* because the journal was in the forefront of enslavers' "rights" and enslavement's expansion, and its Charleston-born editor's perspective on the course of American political events was foreboding. The question of slavery's future had embroiled the country since the founding of the republic, and slave-holders' threats to dissolve the Union if their demands were not met had been made since the 1830s. In each case, compromises had been devised, often by political leaders who were part of America's revolutionary and constitutional generation.

1852	1854	1856	1858	1860	1862	1864

1852 > Publication of Harriet Beecher Stowe's *Uncle Tom's Cabin*

1854 > Congress passes Kansas-Nebraska Act; Ostend Manifesto reflects American designs on Cuba; Republican Party founded

1856 > On May 22, antislavery Senator Charles Sumner nearly beaten to death on the Senate floor

1857 > Lecompton Constitution submitted to Congress; Supreme Court rules in *Scott v. Sandford*

But now, as the aftermath of the US-Mexican War posed new challenges to the destiny and stability of the United States, a new generation of political leaders who came to maturity in the midst of the crisis over enslavement and had no experience with the forging of the Union took their places in state legislatures and the US Congress. Many of them were committed to visions of the future in which slavery thrived, room for compromise was rapidly diminishing, and the resort to violence seemed increasingly acceptable as a means toward their desired ends. The threads holding the Union together appeared to be fraying beyond repair, with the United States on its way to joining other failed republican experiments. And the outcome would be determined, as the Missourians suggested, not in the long-settled states of the East but in the newly acquired and conquered territories of the West. The fate of the Union was in fact a Western story, and those most responsible for hastening the day of reckoning were enslaved people themselves.

12.1   California, Kansas, and the Struggle over Enslavement

||| Explain how the territories of California and Kansas in the trans-Mississippi West reignited the struggle over enslavement's future.

Of all the places one might look to understand how enslavement could break the Union apart, Kansas and California would seem to be among the least likely. Up until 1854, Kansas did not even exist. It was little more than 50 million acres of land in what was then known as the Louisiana Territory, sold to the United States by France in 1803 and, bit by bit, divided into smaller territories and then states. Louisiana, Missouri, and Arkansas had been admitted to the Union in 1812, 1821, and 1836, respectively, but the remainder was barely organized politically. The main occupants were Indigenous people who rode horses, hunted bison, traded with one another as well as with Anglo-American merchants, and commanded a vast landscape that stretched from the Canadian to the Mexican border.

As for California, until 1848 it was a Mexican province, hugging the Pacific, many miles away from the epicenters of struggle over the future of enslavement, having only small populations of Anglos and Californios who had just been fighting one another over their allegiances to Mexico and the United States. What happened showed how much the country was forged from West to East as from East to West.

1850: A Compromise or an Armistice over Enslavement?

There was no good reason for this situation to change, even though the end of the US-Mexican War posed a number of challenging political questions. By virtue of the 1848 Treaty of Guadalupe Hidalgo, the United States formally conquered and gained control of Mexico's northwestern provinces of Alta California and Nuevo Mexico (as we saw in Chapter 11). But, like the Louisiana Territory before it, these provinces encompassed vast tracts of land that would probably be subdivided and then incorporated into the United States as territories and eventually as states. Furthermore, just as with Missouri's contentious admission to the Union (discussed in Chapter 10) and Texas's annexation, the lands conquered from Mexico raised the issue of whether enslavers would be able to migrate there with their human property. Because these new lands were west of the Louisiana Territory, they were not covered by the earlier Missouri Compromise (1820).

American inhabitants of California were first out of the blocks because of an immensely consequential event that occurred just as negotiations over the US-Mexican War were taking place. Gold was discovered in the foothills of the Sierra Nevada mountains in January 1848, and thousands of eager miners from across

Published at the Wide West office, San Francisco.

A ROAD SCENE IN CALIFORNIA.

≡ **Exploitation and Dispossession**   On a California road in the 1850s, displaced Indigenous people along with Chinese and Hawaiian miners move under the watchful gaze of white prospectors on horseback.

the country and around the Pacific world—from east and south Asia, Central and South America, a cultural kaleidoscope of humanity—headed to California, usually through the port of San Francisco, to try their luck in the **California Gold Rush**. Soon boasting the requisite population to qualify for statehood, California's political leaders called a constitutional convention and, instead of organizing as a territory, applied to Congress for admission as a state in 1849. Although the California leadership did include migrants from the slaveholding South, they decided to make the enslavement of Black people unlawful—though not the enslavement of Indigenous people there.

Some of the Californians imagined their state to include all of the land conquered from Mexico, but in their way were Mormon settlers who, led by their prophet Brigham Young, had moved into the valley of the Great Salt Lake in 1847 after being driven out of their settlements east of the Mississippi River. Their population growing rapidly, the Mormon settlers organized a state named **Deseret**, with boundaries stretching from the Pacific coast of southern California in the west to the Rocky Mountains in the east. They then applied to Congress for admission to the United States (see Map 12.1).

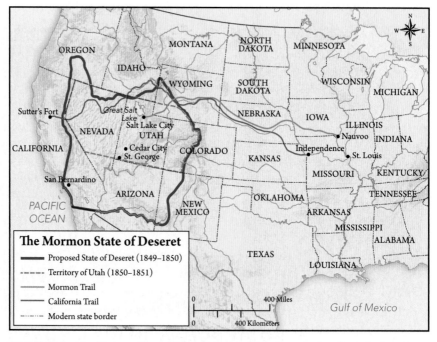

≡ **MAP 12.1   The Mormon State of Deseret**   Stretching from the Pacific coast of southern California in the west to the Rocky Mountains in the east, Deseret complicated questions over the organization of the Mexican conquests.

The questions of statehood for California and Deseret came to a Congress already embroiled in conflict over the organization of the Mexican conquests, conflict that was anticipated in 1846 by David Wilmot's proviso, which, as we saw in Chapter 11, tried—unsuccessfully at the time—to prohibit enslavers and the enslaved from moving into any of these lands. Battle lines were drawn between southern Democrats and Whigs who demanded that the newly conquered territories be open to enslavement; antislavery Whigs and Democrats in the Northeast and Midwest who wanted these territories closed to enslavement; and some moderate, mostly northern, Democrats, who hoped the issues would be resolved not by the US Congress but by the people who would come to live in the territories.

In the past, political compromises—many engineered by Kentucky's Henry Clay—managed to avert a dissolution of the Union. And, as in the past, it was difficult to find enough votes to push a whole compromise package through with a congressional majority. Clay, Daniel Webster, and John C. Calhoun, all making their last speeches on the floor of the US Senate—Calhoun was carried in on a bed—urged their congressional colleagues to join in a compromise, to no avail. Yet, little by little, amid intense debate and failed votes, the floor managers learned that there might be enough votes for each piece of a compromise to be enacted, one at a time. Something of the same sort had been done during the Missouri controversy of 1819 to 1820, as we saw in Chapter 10.

To begin with, far western California was admitted to the Union as a state with the enslavement of Black people prohibited, as California's framers had desired. Deseret was not admitted as a state, but two territories were created—Utah to the north and New Mexico to the south—with the matter of slavery's legality left to the free people there to decide, in a process known as **popular sovereignty**. To further satisfy congressmen holding antislavery beliefs, the slave trade—but not enslavement—was abolished within the boundaries of the District of Columbia, and, in return for enslavers, the **Fugitive Slave Law (1850)** was strengthened to better enable them to recapture runaway enslaved people. Finally, a boundary dispute between Texas and New Mexico was adjudicated much to the annoyance of the Texans (see again Map 12.1).

There were sighs of relief when the last of the bills was passed and signed by President Millard Fillmore in the early fall of 1850. Some in Congress and across the country, in fact, hoped that this would prove to be the "final settlement" of the slavery question and thus the salvation of the Union. Because no majority could be found to support the package of bills as a whole, however, the episode might best be seen as an "armistice" between increasingly warring sides than as a "compromise" (which it is usually called) between politicians sharing a common purpose. A Union that had been forged more than sixty years earlier and maintained despite increasingly sharp differences over the fate of enslavement seemed to be losing its connective threads.

PERSPECTIVES

Mining and the Environment

The nineteenth century saw major mineral finds across the globe (see map). Each discovery generated madcap growth as miners rushed in from all over the world. When gold was discovered near Melbourne, Australia, in 1851, the town's population doubled in a year. In 1871, diamonds were found on a farm in Kimberley, South Africa. By the end of the century, 100,000 miners worked there. After gold was discovered in the foothills of the Sierra Nevada in 1848, newcomers pouring in increased the nonnative population of California from 14,000 in 1848 to nearly 225,000 in 1852.

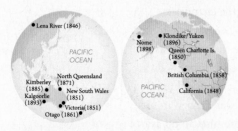

≡ **Major Gold Discoveries of the Pacific Rim, 1846–1898**

After the discovery of gold in California, the first wave of fortune seekers—the "forty-niners"—mostly used pans or shovels to sift the sediment of mountain streams for flakes of the precious metal. However, after 1850 entrepreneurs with capital invested in industrial technology to dislodge the gold more efficiently and in greater amounts. They diverted streams

≡ **Diversion Structures, Water Wheels, and Miners on the Middle Fork of the American River, Northern California, c. 1858**

with dams, flushed gravel through sluices, and blasted hillsides with jets of water. The impact was intense, and the environmental results ruinous. Hydraulic mining generated massive erosion, modifying the flow of rivers downstream, and creating enormous amounts of silt that adversely affected populations of fish and other aquatic organisms. The devastated natural environment was particularly hard on Indigenous people, who were forced to relocate out of riverine valleys, where they were often hunted down or enslaved by white vigilantes. These rare early photographs document the hydraulic mining operations.

≡ **View of Mining Site with Men Working Alongside Large Water Wheels and Elaborate Pumping Equipment, Northern California, c. 1858**

CONSIDER THIS

Reflect on other mineral finds in American or world history. Why does the discovery of precious metals inevitably lead to violence and environmental destruction?

Stephen Douglas and Kansas-Nebraska

No one was more instrumental in seeing this compromise—or armistice—through than Senator Stephen A. Douglas. A Democrat from Illinois, Douglas had risen through the ranks to emerge as one of the party's leading lights, and he took charge of the legislation just when all seemed to be lost. But at the very time Douglas was helping to cobble together the compromise, he was hard at work on a project that was even dearer to his vision of America's future: the construction of the Illinois Central Railroad, planned to link the Gulf of Mexico to the Great Lakes by way of Chicago. Douglas had significant real estate investments in Chicago, which explains part of his enthusiasm for the project; nothing contributed more to rising land values in mid-nineteenth-century America than proximity to a railroad. But at least as important was his sense of how the railroad would promote a growing American empire, organized around the Mississippi Valley and Chicago in particular, that would secure the much vaunted "ocean-bound" republic while extending it southward into the Caribbean. This, he believed, was the best way to preserve the Union and advance the fortunes of his Democratic Party.

Douglas was not only interested in the Illinois Central. Like growing numbers of political leaders, he hoped to see a railroad built to the Pacific coast now that it was part of the United States. "How are we to develop, cherish, and protect our immense interests on the Pacific with a vast wilderness . . . cutting off all direct communication?" he asked. "We must have Rail Roads and Telegraphs from the Atlantic to the Pacific." The problem was that part of the "vast wilderness" west of the Mississippi River was "unorganized territory" (meaning it had no government), and until such a territory was organized no one would put up the money to build a railroad through it. To that end, Douglas helped craft a bill in 1854 that created two territories—Kansas to the south and Nebraska to the north—and explicitly repealed the Missouri Compromise's prohibition of enslavement above the latitude 36°30′. Instead, Douglas left "all questions pertaining to slavery" to "the decision of the people residing therein." In other words, popular sovereignty as the Congress had unveiled in relation to Utah and New Mexico (see Map 12.2).

Douglas did not support the expansion of slavery, even though his wife's family owned land and enslaved people in North Carolina and Mississippi. But he did believe that the Constitution prohibited Congress from interfering with enslavement in either the states or federal territories, and he had no problem with the idea of an American union and empire that contained places where enslavement was legal and places where it was not. That, after all, was how the United States had always been organized and, so far as he could see, the country—and the white people whose destiny with which he was most concerned—were thriving. The organization of the Kansas and Nebraska Territories was thus another step along the

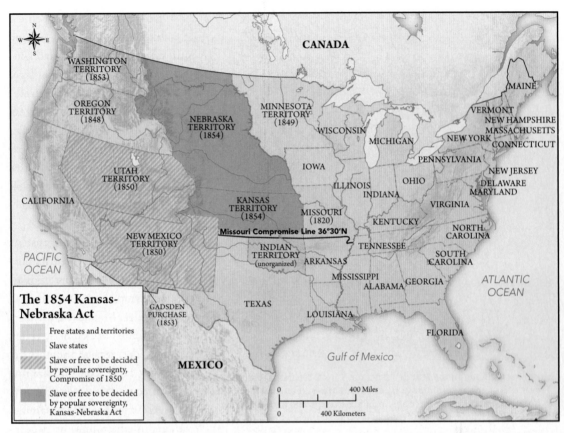

≡ **MAP 12.2   The 1854 Kansas-Nebraska Act**   Following the passage of the Kansas-Nebraska Act, Kansas became the main battleground between proslavery and antislavery forces.

march to greatness, and popular sovereignty exemplified the political ideals that marked the path.

Yet Stephen Douglas was a veteran politician as well as a political visionary, and he had every reason to be worried about the "democratic" practices that popular sovereignty would unleash, especially when the fate of enslavement was at stake. Roughhousing and paramilitarism were the norms for campaigns and elections even when the issues were far less contentious; together with ballots printed by the political parties, revolvers, knives, bull-whips, cudgels, and alcohol were standard equipment at the polls in many parts of the country. It was an explosive mix under any circumstances.

The main battleground, everyone knew, would be Kansas. Nebraska was too far northward and a doubtful host for the staple-crop economy in which enslavement most thrived. Kansas, by contrast, was directly west of slaveholding Missouri, and its eastern parts seemed more promising agriculturally. But it would be an intense scramble. At the time the **Kansas-Nebraska Act** became law (May 1854), Kansas

≡ **Border Ruffians on the March**   After the Kansas-Nebraska Act of 1854, proslavery and anti-abolitionist radicals from Missouri crossed the border into Kansas to interfere with elections, intimidate voters, and harass the Free-Staters who opposed the expansion of enslavement into Kansas.

had only 800 white settlers. Although it was not entirely clear how popular sovereignty would work, a territorial legislature would have to be elected and a delegate sent to Congress. The main project for proslavery and antislavery forces alike therefore became populating Kansas as quickly as possible and gaining the upper hand in the territorial electorate.

By early 1855, the rush to Kansas had increased its population ten-fold, and proslavery sympathizers initially had the edge. Migrants came from a number of southern states, but the largest number of them came from neighboring Missouri. Most were farmers who arrived with their families and, perhaps, one or two enslaved people. Their intention was to establish land claims, defend their labor system, and ward off abolitionists. A more consequential and dangerous contingent, however, was mobilized by Missouri vigilantes—known as "Self-Defensives"—who aimed to protect enslavement in their own state by extending it westward. The people they sent into Kansas, known as **Border Ruffians,** had no intention of settling there. Well-armed, they planned to remain only long enough to allow the proslavery side to win the territorial elections.

By the time Election Day arrived in March 1855, the Border Ruffians loomed large among prospective voters. Despite a proclamation from the territorial governor (a Democrat) that limited voting to those who already lived in Kansas and expected to stay, hundreds of Missourians crossed the Missouri River to participate. Although a census showed only 2,905 eligible voters in Kansas, over 6,000 votes were cast and a legislature favoring enslavement was selected. By that summer the legislators did what they came to do: they enacted a tough slave code for the territory. "It is the duty of the Proslavery Party to know but one issue, Slavery," they resolved, "and that any party making or attempting to make any other is an ally of Abolitionism and Disunionism."

12.2 Kansas and Political Antislavery

Summarize how the controversy over Kansas was provoked in part by the shift in the means and goals of those in the developing antislavery movement.

Whatever advantage proslavery forces may have gained in Kansas was almost immediately contested by those who were just as determined to keep enslavement out of the territory. They had been roused across the Northeast and Midwest by the Kansas-Nebraska Act, which they detested, and especially by the brazen behavior of the Border Ruffians that helped elect the proslavery legislature. Before long, they too were heading to Kansas, where they helped to organize a **Free State Party**, write and ratify a constitution that outlawed enslavement (but excluded free Black people from the territory), and establish a government of their own in the Kansas town of Topeka, only a few miles from Lecompton, the territorial capital where the proslavery legislators were holed up.

Here was popular sovereignty in action. The territory of Kansas now had dual governments, each seeking recognition and admission into the Union—one as a slave state and one as a free state—and each regarding the other as a set of radical impostors. But the proslavery side had an important advantage. President Franklin Pierce, a Democrat and southern sympathizer, quickly weighed in. He termed the Lecompton legislature "legitimate" and the Topeka government "revolutionary" and potentially "treasonable." In fact, Pierce threatened the Free-Staters with the hard fist of military force and asked Congress for funds to move against them. What had begun as an effort to build a railroad to the Pacific was becoming a desperate armed struggle over the future of Kansas and, perhaps, the country as a whole.

From Garrisonian Moral Suasion to Electoral Politics

The deepening crisis in Kansas was only the most vivid example of how the battle over enslavement's destiny was being waged in American political life. During the late 1830s and early 1840s, abolitionists who felt constrained by Garrisonian "moral suasion" or the tactics of legislative petitioning discussed in Chapter 10 began to look to the formal political arena to advance their cause. They rejected Garrison's view that the Constitution was a compact with enslavement and that the federal government and electoral process were irrevocably contaminated by it. Instead, they imagined an entirely different strategy. Acknowledging that the Constitution did protect enslavement in individual states, they nonetheless insisted that federal authority could be deployed to deprive the slave system of support wherever its jurisdiction was recognized. Congress, they believed, could begin to undermine enslavement in Washington, DC, in the federal territories, and at federal military installations, where enslaved labor had been exploited since the birth of the republic. The federal government could block the domestic slave trade, repeal or weaken the Fugitive Slave Law, and, of course, refuse to admit new slave states to the Union. In 1840, these abolitionists organized what they called the **Liberty Party** and began to run candidates for public office, including the presidency.

The Liberty Party is often viewed as a minor act in the great transition from the immediatism of the 1830s to the mass antislavery politics of the 1850s. The party won relatively few votes (though enough in New York to deprive Whig Henry Clay of the presidency in 1844), and its efforts to educate the electorate on slavery's evils and win political favor seemed to fall fairly flat. Yet, from a different perspective and far more important, Liberty Party leaders and intellectuals—Gamaliel Bailey, Thomas Morris, Salmon P. Chase, and Joshua Leavitt—began to lay out a program designed to first curtail and then prohibit the institution of enslavement. Unlike Garrison, they suggested that the Constitution could be interpreted as an antislavery document, turning freedom into a federal institution and leaving enslavement only a local one. Their ideas would find expression in the 1846 Wilmot Proviso (discussed in Chapter 11)

≡ **Free Soil, Free Labor, Free Speech, Free Men**
A Free-Soil Party campaign banner from the election of 1848 features Martin Van Buren and Charles F. Adams as candidates for president and vice president.

and in the fledgling **Free-Soil Party**, organized in 1848 by antislavery Democrats and "conscience" Whigs who lacked the moral fervor of the Liberty Party devotees but embraced their strategy of refusing enslavement's expansion. Rallying to the cry of "free soil, free labor, free speech, and free men," the Free-Soilers demanded, much as Liberty Party supporters had prescribed, that the federal government cut its ties to enslavement where it "possesses the constitutional power to legislate" and prohibit "the extension of slavery." Before long, the "non-extension" of enslavement would emerge as the main alternative to popular sovereignty.

Unlike the Liberty Party, the Free-Soilers were electorally formidable. In 1848, they sent twelve candidates to the House of Representatives, soon to be joined by two senators, and their presidential candidate, a reinvented Martin Van Buren (as president he attempted to soothe the enslavers in his Democratic Party), won more than a quarter of a million popular votes—but no electoral votes. Although the compromise measures of 1850 sapped some of their momentum, Free-Soil ideas gained followings across New England, the Middle Atlantic, and the Midwest, especially among Whigs, who bridled at the enthusiasm their slave state colleagues showed for popular sovereignty and a toughened Fugitive Slave Law. Far more than was true among the Democrats at this point, the question of enslavement fractured the foundation of Whiggery. When the Kansas-Nebraska Act passed in 1854 with the votes of congressional Whigs from the slaveholding states, the party collapsed and with it the whole structure of electoral politics—the Second Party System—that had been constructed in the 1820s and 1830s (see Chapter 9).

Organizing New Political Parties

Even before the Kansas-Nebraska Act became law, what were known as "anti-Nebraska" mobilizations began to take shape. Angered over the ambitions and militance of proslavery Democrats and the willingness of many southern Whigs to go along with them, disenchanted antislavery Whigs together with Free-Soil Democrats from New England to the upper Midwest started to look for a new political home. In the small town of Ripon, Wisconsin, they went so far as to threaten to establish a new "Republican" Party to replace the Whigs and extend the political power of the Free-Soilers.

Yet, just as the Whig Party disintegrated, still another force seemed better placed to step into the political vacuum and form an opposition to the Democratic Party. It attracted former Whigs who feared enslavement's expanding borders but derived even more of its energies from border crossings of a different sort. Drawing on deep traditions of anti-Catholicism and reflecting doubts about political democracy with a growing urban working class, that force was strongly nativist. Members would call themselves the **American or "Know-Nothing" Party**.

12.3   Slaveholder Imperialism

Describe the imperial ambitions of enslavers, especially those in the lower Mississippi Valley.

The paramilitary efforts to claim Kansas for slavery were part of a larger project of what might be called **slaveholder imperialism**, or slavery expansionism, which was based mainly in the lower Mississippi Valley. There the slave regime was most recently established, and the class of enslavers young and aggressive. There, too, the city of New Orleans was a hub of trade in enslaved people and the products, like cotton, that they produced. As we saw in Chapter 11, much of the support for Texas rebels during the mid-1830s and for US military operations against Mexico during the 1840s moved through New Orleans, and the 1850s saw a strong uptick in the beat of slavery expansionism. "I want Cuba, and I know that sooner or later we must have it," Mississippi Senator Albert Gallatin Brown crowed at the time. "I want Tamaulipas, Potosi, and one or two other Mexican states; and I want them all for the same reason—for the planting or spreading of slavery." That is to say, Brown hoped to forge an empire for slaveholders.

Cuba in the Crosshairs

Cuba had been of interest to a variety of Americans from early on in the nineteenth century. By the 1850s, amid a boom that made the island the world's leading sugar producer (once slavery had been toppled in Saint Domingue, as we saw in Chapter 8), investors from New England and the Deep South had put money in railroads, banks, and plantations. Together they made the United States Cuba's most important trading partner next to Spain, the colony's home country, and stimulated calls for acquiring Cuba by diplomatic means (see Figure 12.1). But although annexationist sentiment could be found in many parts of the country, southern slaveholders—and especially southern slaveholding Democrats—were the driving force. As they saw it, the acquisition of Cuba, already a formidable slave plantation society, would strengthen the American position in the Caribbean, enhance the power of enslavers, and orient the political economy of the United States toward the south. "Were Cuba annexed," Louisiana's governor mused, "it would be the nucleus around which would cluster the trade of all the Gulf and many of the South American ports," and Havana "would be a southern city, a slaveholding city."

The annexation of Cuba was a goal of Democratic administrations—Franklin Pierce (1853–1857) and James Buchanan (1857–1861)—throughout the 1850s. Pierce, from the state of New Hampshire but friendly toward enslavers, filled his cabinet and the diplomatic corps with slavery expansionists, requested a $10 million appropriation from Congress to pursue the purchase of Cuba from Spain (the Spanish weren't interested), and then called a meeting of his ministers in Europe to develop a strategy. The result, in the fall of 1854, was called the **Ostend Manifesto** (after its meeting place in Ostend, Belgium), which insisted that "Cuba is as necessary to the North American republic as

≡ **A Cuban Sugar Mill, c. 1857**   Sugar cultivation and harvesting involved backbreaking labor and was devastating to the environment—but idyllic views like this image attracted the interest of wealthy speculators and politicians. This illustration was one of many in a book called *Los Ingenios de la Isla de Cuba* (*Sugar Mills of the Island of Cuba*), which, when it appeared in 1857, was one of the most expensive and beautiful books ever published in Cuba.

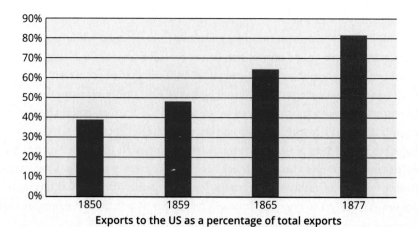

FIGURE 12.1 **Cuban Trade with the United States, 1850–1877.**

any of its present members," and threatened war if Spain refused to sell. When the Manifesto, intended to be confidential, inadvertently became public, opponents of acquisition seized on the threat of war, forcing an embarrassed Pierce to back down. But annexation remained a centerpiece of Democratic policy, and James Buchanan won election to the presidency in 1856 calling for American "ascendancy in the Gulf."

Filibustering

Most of the activity related to the acquisition of Cuba was in fact generated not by formally elected and appointed officials but by privately operated paramilitaries known as **filibusters** (from the French and Spanish terms, *filibustier* and *filibustero*, for freebooter and pirate), who wanted to "liberate" the island by means of armed invasion. (This meaning of "filibuster" has only a vague connection to its contemporary definition, an attempt in the US Senate to delay or block a vote on a piece of legislation or a confirmation.) Filibustering had a history as long as the American union itself and always in complex relation with official power and territorial ambition. At one time or another, filibusters had set their sights on Florida, Louisiana, Canada, Texas, and Mexico as well as Cuba, and often they included men of political or military prominence. Although some believed they were acting with the support of government leaders, most hoped to influence American policy by doing what the government was unable or unwilling to do itself.

The problem for the filibusters was that Congress had passed a **Neutrality Law** in 1818 that prohibited just this sort of thing: initiating or aiding military expeditions against states or territories with which the United States was at peace. Violators could be fined and imprisoned. But as the stakes of slavery expansionism rose to unprecedented heights during the 1850s, the risks of penalty seemed far less worrisome than the rewards of possible success—in any event, juries rarely convicted anyone charged with violating this law. Year after year, some invasion of land in the Caribbean basin was being planned or carried out while eager expansionists in Congress tried unsuccessfully to suspend or repeal the Neutrality Law. The Venezuelan-born Narciso López, aided by a number of prominent southern enslavers, led two separate expeditions against Cuba, involving more than 1,000 filibusters, both of which collapsed in the face of the Spanish colonial army. An organization based mainly in Texas and known as the Knights of the Golden Circle hoped to bring Mexico, Cuba, Central America, and parts of South America into an expanding empire that could yield as many as twenty-five new slave states. And a number of filibustering groups looked greedily to Baja California and Sonora as gateways to the rich Mexican silver mines. It was the sort of empire that Mississippi's Albert Gallatin Brown wished to forge (see Map 12.3).

Easily the boldest, and craziest, of the filibusters was William Walker. Born in Tennessee, he was an adventurer who made his way out to California after an

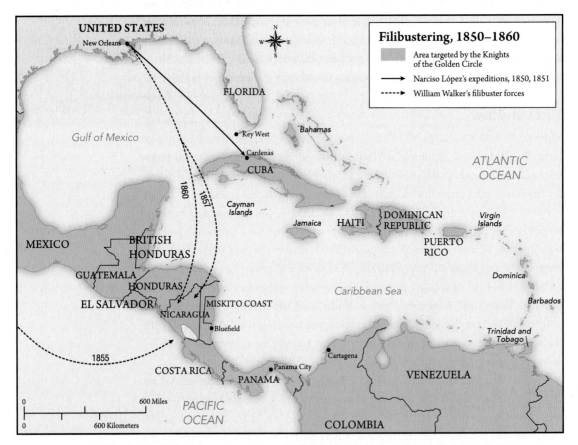

≡ **MAP 12.3   Filibustering Expeditions, 1850–1860**   The filibuster movement peaked in the 1850s. Organizations like the Knights of the Golden Circle hoped to bring Mexico, Cuba, Central America, and parts of South America into an expanding slave empire.

extended stop in New Orleans. There he became involved in Democratic politics and engaged in several duels. Somehow—we're not sure why—he set his sights on establishing a colony first in Mexico and then in Nicaragua, where he took advantage of an internal political struggle to gain a foothold. With a mere fifty-nine men at his side, Walker managed in 1856 to set himself up as president, confiscate landed estates, and reimpose enslavement, probably with an eye toward winning the active support of American slaveholders and their Democratic allies in the United States. And for a time that he did. One New York newspaper even accused Walker of "laying the basis" for a "Southern Slave Empire."

Walker's policies alienated the Nicaraguan factions who had previously been fighting against one another, and together, with the help of Central American neighbors, they soon launched a military campaign against him. Clearly outnumbered, Walker was forced to surrender and then managed to flee to the United States. But in the spring of 1860, after receiving much acclaim from American admirers—especially slaveholders— Walker decided to tempt fate and fight his way back into Nicaragua. This time he never made it out of Honduras. Captured there, Walker was quickly put before a Honduran firing squad and shot dead.

≡ **"Grey-Eyed Man of Destiny"**   Weighing barely over 100 pounds, diminutive in stature, and eyes the color of ash, Walker's motley group of rogue imperialists sought to carve out a slave empire in the tropics.

12.4   New Waves of European Immigrants

Explain the ways in which the influx of Irish Catholic immigrants reshaped American politics in the 1850s.

Large population migrations moving in westerly and northwesterly directions had been a fact of Atlantic life since the late fifteenth century. But while the African slave trade was officially closed in 1808, the volume of free immigration to the United States grew steadily during the 1820s and 1830s, from roughly 10,000 to nearly 90,000 each year (see Figure 12.2). A great many of these migrants were Irish, and although early on they tended to be Protestants from the north of Ireland or Catholics with skills and resources, by the mid-1830s most were poor Catholics from Ireland's rural south

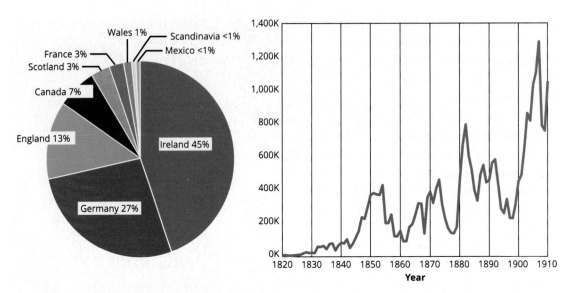

FIGURE 12.2   **Immigration Population by Country of Origin, 1850, and Free Immigration, 1820–1910.**

and west, best described as unskilled laborers. While German immigrants of the time, who were also substantial in number and increasingly Catholic, often headed to Midwestern cities and farming areas, the Irish generally joined the laboring populations of port cities from Boston, New York, Philadelphia, and Baltimore as far south and west as Charleston, Savannah, Mobile, and New Orleans. There they did heavy work on docks, in the harbors, at construction sites, and on city streets, spilling out into the countryside when canals had to be dug, railroad tracks laid, or crops harvested. By the early 1840s, they were the targets of new nativist organizations in cities like Philadelphia and New York, which helped provoke vicious nativist riots as well as aggressors against Black people in their midst.

The Great Famine and Its Impact

But the late 1840s and 1850s saw an influx of immigrants that, to this day, remains unprecedented relative to the size of the American population. Between 1845 and 1854, nearly three million Europeans arrived—roughly 200,000 to 450,000 each year—amounting to about 15 percent of the country's total inhabitants in the mid-1840s. About half came from Ireland, owing to a blight that destroyed the potato crop—the staple of the Irish peasant diet—and eventually claimed a million lives. This **Great Famine** may have reduced Ireland's population by more than 20 percent through starvation and emigration. Not surprisingly, most of those who managed to leave were poor rural people, Catholic in faith, with few goods and no savings.

The impact of this enormous immigration would have been considerable under any circumstances, but it swept into an already simmering cauldron of tension and conflict. The ethnic clashes of the early 1840s were still lodged in popular memory, and to these were added local battles over school funding, Bible reading, and temperance, all of which stoked anti-Catholicism. Even more troubling to native-born and Protestant observers was the question of politics and political power. With loose requirements for voting, many of the new immigrants, especially the Irish Catholics, quickly aligned with the Democratic Party. It made sense for them to do so. The Democrats were neither evangelicals nor interested in waging cultural warfare over drinking, schooling, or forms of entertainment. They were ready to offer jobs and protection in exchange for votes, and they seemed to sympathize with the struggles of working

"Paddy's Ladder to Wealth in a Free Country" An 1852 caricature of an Irish immigrant with offensively stereotyped features. Poor Irish immigrants were frequently compared to apes—less evolved than other white people but strong enough for manual labor—and often depicted with ape-like features. This man is a hod-carrier, a laborer who brings bricks to builders. The caption is cruelly ironic, as such a worker would never become wealthy.

men against both their employers and Black competitors. As a result, the Democrats often grabbed the reins of power in many large cities and, for the most part, dominated the executive and legislative branches of the federal government.

The Rise of the Know-Nothings

In came the oddly named Know-Nothings. Beginning as a secret fraternal organization (whose members were supposed to reply, "I know nothing," to questions about the group), the Know-Nothings wanted to combat what they saw as the growing power of Catholic immigrants and their Democratic patrons. Still, even with all the ethnic tension in the air, they might have remained an obscure local group had it not been for the Kansas-Nebraska Act and the collapse of the Whig Party, which, as we have seen, enabled them to step forward as a major political force. They officially branded themselves the American Party, and found their largest following in the urban Northeast, where Irish immigration was most concentrated. There and elsewhere among America's cities, they tended to attract the support of an emerging middle class that had previously aligned with the Whigs: merchandisers and small manufacturers, clerks and skilled craftsmen, who had

≡ **Nativist and Anti-immigrant Propaganda** An advertisement for the *American Patriot*, a Know-Nothing newspaper published in Boston in the early 1850s. To the left, below a hill labeled "Constitution and Laws," "native" Americans (white people who had been in the United States for some time) hold banners proclaiming "Education, Morality, and Religion" and "None But Americans Shall Rule America." To the right, an unruly crowd of Irish immigrants streams from a ship bearing the Pope's coat of arms. The *American Patriot* explains its mission in part as "protection of American Mechanics against Foreign Pauper Labor" and "Carrying out the laws of the State, as regards sending back Foreign Paupers and Criminals" while opposing "Foreigners holding office" and "being taxed for the support of Foreign paupers millions of dollars yearly."

come of age during the 1840s and early 1850s and had been made uneasy both by the renewed aggressiveness of slaveholders *and* by what they saw as the political corruption pervading urban life.

What did the Know-Nothings aim to do? They did not want to limit the inflow of immigrants, but they did seek to limit the political influence that immigrants could wield by extending naturalization—the process of becoming a citizen—from five to twenty-one years, confining public office-holding to the native-born, and establishing literacy requirements for voting. They clearly touched an appreciative public nerve. As early as the fall elections of 1854, the Know-Nothings swept to power across New England and made impressive gains in Pennsylvania and Indiana. In Massachusetts they took control of the government. With such rapid and remarkable success, they seemed ready to replace the Whigs as the Democrats' main opponents on the country's political stage.

That the Know-Nothings offered a political landing pad for Whigs who disliked (but were not morally outraged by) the Kansas-Nebraska Act and whose antagonism toward Catholic immigrants included their apparent sympathy for enslavers surely limited the party's larger ambitions. While the Know-Nothings' identification with antislavery and temperance, as well as with anti-Catholicism, increased their appeal for rural (and especially evangelical) voters in the Northeast and parts of the Midwest, it offered them little help among former Whigs in the slaveholding states.

So why bother with the Know-Nothings? Because their rise to prominence in sections of the United States should alert us to a developing backlash against the democratic impulses of the 1820s and 1830s as the impact of industrialization was making itself felt and the composition of the urban working class was changing. The Know-Nothings, that is, exemplified a series of efforts to narrow, strengthen, and more closely patrol the boundaries of official political life as the country began to face a political challenge that was already troubling Britain and much of the European continent: whether to admit free but economically dependent adults into the arenas of formal politics. The response, as the Know-Nothings demonstrated, was a disconcerting one for democracy's future.

12.5   **Pushing the Boundaries of Democracy**

Give examples of the efforts of Black men and white women to gain civil and political rights equal to those of white men.

There were, however, new efforts to expand the democracy that had been established during the 1820s and 1830s. And, as is often the case, the pressure for change came from those who had been on the margins or on the outside of the political arena. Formal politics had long been regarded as the preserve of white men, whether or not they owned property. Most free Black people were excluded from the franchise entirely or were required to own a substantial amount of property to qualify to vote or hold office. With the exception of a very brief period in New Jersey (see Chapter 7), women were wholly excluded from participating in politics as electors or office holders. At best, they were deemed spectators for the political rituals of men or as grassroots organizers and petitioners for social and moral reforms. But just as Protestant men were challenging the political rights of Catholic immigrants, Black men and (almost exclusively) white women sought to enlarge the meaning of the democracy in antebellum (pre–Civil War) America.

Black Americans and Antebellum Democracy

Black Americans living in the Northeast and Midwest, who were already organizing against enslavement and the American Colonization Society's efforts to exile them to Liberia, chafed at their exclusion from civil and political society in the states outside northern New England. Many were fugitives from enslavement or the children of enslaved parents; almost all were at the bottom of the economic order, owning little property and working as unskilled, casual, or domestic laborers, very much like the Irish. Worse still, they suffered blatant discrimination in various areas of public life—especially in schools and on public transportation—and in the newer states of the Midwest, so-called Black Laws officially denied them residency. Racial subordination was a fact of the American legal order even where enslavement had been, or was being, abolished.

So, in the 1830s and 1840s, they launched strong protests. Black leaders met in conventions and less formal assemblies, in cities and towns large and small, to express their grievances and mobilize support. They reminded neighboring white people of their American birth and their many contributions to the country's development, and they urged Black people to improve themselves, work diligently, learn to read and write, and look after their families. Most of all, they denounced colonizationists who wanted them removed to Liberia and called for the elective franchise to be extended to them. After all, white men in humble circumstances had already achieved this goal, as we saw in Chapter 9.

But Black demands for the suffrage (the right to vote) fell mostly on deaf or hostile ears. Not only did they fail in their quests for equality and voting rights, but they also often lost what little ground they had previously held. In Pennsylvania, as well as North Carolina and Tennessee, where free Black people had been able to cast ballots, the expansion of the white male franchise was accompanied by the full elimination of the Black franchise. Indeed, together with the strengthened Fugitive Slave Law of 1850 and talk in the slave states of re-enslaving free Black people there, the defeat of free Black people in their efforts to gain the same civil and political standing as free whites showed their increasingly perilous position and prospects: as members of a despised race and degraded section of the working class. Not surprisingly, their alienation from American society and their militancy on the slavery question deepened accordingly.

The Struggle for Women's Rights

White women did not fare much better in their own struggles for equality. They were the largest section of the free adult white population that was both legally dependent and denied participation in electoral politics. As children, they lived under the patriarchal rule of their fathers, and as adults (with rare exception), under that of their husbands. When married, they surrendered claims to property and wages to their husbands, were vulnerable to physical abuse, and had few avenues to seek divorce. And, whether single or married, growing numbers of them worked in the most dynamic sectors of the manufacturing economy as textile operatives, garment workers, outworkers, and domestics. As we saw in Chapter 9, some organized at their workplaces to resist wage cuts and other forms of exploitation, but, for the most part, the question of their civil and political rights was raised and pursued by middle-class women who had the time, education, social connections, and self-confidence to create a women's rights movement.

The road to women's rights invariably passed through the portals of abolitionism. The mobilizations of the 1830s (discussed in Chapter 10) created a cadre of female activists aghast at the consequences of male power and increasingly skilled, despite lacking the vote, in the workings of grassroots politics. Many of the leaders were Quakers and Garrisonians, some of whom had been excluded from the World Anti-Slavery Conference in London in 1840 on account of their sex. Even more were from middling farm families and a range of Protestant denominations who lived in areas that felt the effects of antislavery agitation. They may have begun to petition state legislatures for civil and political equality as early as 1844, but it was Elizabeth Cady Stanton, residing in the upstate New York town of Seneca Falls who, together with Lucretia Mott, sparked the organization of a Women's Rights Convention there in the summer of 1848.

≡ **Cady Stanton** Elizabeth Cady Stanton was thirty-three years old when this portrait of her and her sons, Daniel and Henry, was taken in 1848. Despite the photo's timeworn appearance, a quiet resolve is evident in her facial expression.

It was a heady time across the Atlantic world. Popular revolutions were spreading through continental Europe, the movement known as Chartism was seeking to enlarge the franchise in Britain and won strong working-class support, and, as we have seen, the Free-Soil Party was organizing in the United States. "Thanks to steam navigation and electric wires . . . a revolution cannot be confined . . . but flashes with lightning speed from heart to heart," Frederick Douglass, formerly enslaved but now active in the antislavery movement, observed. Three hundred women and men, including Douglass—all abolitionists—thereby made their way to Seneca Falls, 100 of whom would sign the **Declaration of Sentiments**, named after the founding document of the American Antislavery Society.

WOMAN'S EMANCIPATION.

(Being a Letter addressed to Mr. Punch, with a Drawing, by a strong-minded American Woman.)

≡ **A Fashionable Statement**   The British humor magazine *Punch* featured this caricature of "emancipated" American women in 1851, along with a letter from an imaginary female Boston correspondent named "Theodosia Eudoxia Bang." Bang asserted, "We are emancipating ourselves, among other badges of the slavery of feudalism, from the inconvenient dress of the European female. With men's functions, we have asserted our right to his garb, and especially to that part of it which invests the lower extremities. With this great symbol, we have adopted others—the hat, the cigar, the paletot or round jacket. And it is generally calculated that the dress of the Emancipated American female is quite pretty—as becoming in all points as it is manly and independent."

A remarkable text crafted by Stanton and Quaker Mary Ann M'Clintock, the Declaration proclaimed that "all men and women are created equal" and pressed for civil and political rights without regard to sex, including "the sacred right of the elective franchise."

Yet, for all the political energy of the moment, the quest for women's rights, like the Revolutions of 1848 in Europe, suffered rejection and defeat. Although married women's property legislation began to advance, mainly because it offered cover for the financial woes of men, woman's suffrage was thoroughly repudiated in official circles. Like free Black people and Catholic immigrants, women's rights activists had attempted to redefine the boundaries of formal politics, making them more inclusive and more compatible with the principles of the Declaration of Independence. But they, too, discovered that the boundaries were instead contracting and becoming more and more difficult to cross.

12.6   Testing Slavery's Boundaries

Evaluate how the self-determination and resistance of enslaved people in the United States and the wider Atlantic world deepened the political crisis over enslavement.

The brutal repression that followed Nat Turner's failed rebellion in Southampton County, Virginia, in 1831 (discussed in Chapter 10) seemed to close the slave unrest that had ebbed and flowed for a half century since the early days of the American Revolution. But if enslaved people, recognizing the odds against them, largely ceased to imagine direct rebellions against enslavers, they began to test the boundaries of their enslavement in other consequential ways. On land and sea, mostly as individuals and in small groups, they traversed boundaries of slavery into places where their status was ambiguous and their allies positioned to expose the ambiguities. Did enslavement simply attach to the body, to be carried wherever the enslaved person traveled? What would enslavement mean in a state or foreign country that had declared an end to it? Would fugitives from slavery be entitled to legal recourse or gain substantive protection from abolitionists? Could enslavers remain at peace with people and governments, in the United States and abroad, who threatened or were inattentive to their property and privileges? By moving across sea lanes and borderlands, enslaved people not only marked the limits of their enslavers' authority but also provoked political confrontations that were international in scope. In the process, they forced enslavers to reassess their own place in the American union.

Seeking Freedom by Sea

Among the vehicles of these boundary crossings were the ships used to transport enslaved people from one American market to another. During the 1830s, three of them sailing out of Richmond and Charleston and heading toward New Orleans were swept up by storms and beached in the Bahamas, where enslavement was in the process of being abolished by the British. How would these enslaved people be viewed? Whose perspective would prevail? Despite American protests, British officials boldly freed all the enslaved people on the ships while their government later offered some compensation to American enslavers to avoid a diplomatic crisis. Knowledge of these events may have led an enslaved man, ironically named Madison Washington, to seize control of a ship named the *Creole*, carrying 135 enslaved people to New Orleans for sale in 1841, and steer it toward the British island of Nassau in the Bahamas. There they eventually gained their freedom. It was one of the largest, and certainly the most successful, of American slave rebellions up to that time.

Even more revealing of the Atlantic world of enslavement in its growing complexities was an episode that began in the waters off Cuba and ended in the Supreme Court of the United States. In late June 1839, two Spaniards purchased fifty-three enslaved people in Havana and boarded them on a ship named the *Amistad*, for what they expected to be a short trip to the Cuban plantation district around Puerto Principe. But on the third day out, two of the enslaved, one named Sengbe Pieh or Cinque (Cinquez, too), hijacked the ship, killed the captain, and made the Spanish slave traders their prisoners. Cinque's idea was to sail the *Amistad* to Africa, but with a limited grasp of navigation he was fooled by one of the traders into heading north rather than east. They eventually ran aground on Long Island, New York, and were taken into custody by US naval authorities.

It could have been a relatively simple proceeding since the enslaved rebels were owned by Spanish traders who had reasonable rights of custody, according to nineteenth-century international laws of property. But the rebels had recently been transported from Sierra Leone in West Africa to Cuba in violation of an Anglo-Spanish treaty, and therefore were not only legally free but, in rebelling on the *Amistad*, acting in their own defense. For their part, the slave traders had probably committed a capital offense. Not surprisingly, the case quickly attracted the interest of American abolitionists in the Northeast who began to mount a legal defense as well as a publicity campaign. Whose perspective on the matter would prevail?

Initially, neither the Black rebels nor their abolitionist allies had much cause for optimism. Andrew Jackson's heir, Martin Van Buren, sat in the White House and was facing reelection. He needed the support of slaveholding Democrats, so he just wanted to dispose of the case and have the rebels returned to their owners in Cuba. Too, the federal judge who would hear the case, Andrew T. Judson, was a Jacksonian Democrat with well-known racist dispositions, possibly willing to do President Van Buren's bidding. The abolitionists, therefore, were surprised and relieved when Judson determined that the Black rebels had been transported illegally, that their uprising could not be deemed a crime, and that they were free and should be returned to Africa.

A disgruntled Martin Van Buren quickly had the ruling appealed to the Supreme Court, where he had reason to expect a more favorable outcome. After all, most of the justices came from the slaveholding states, and the new chief justice, Roger B. Taney, was a Democrat and former enslaver from Maryland. For their part, the abolitionists had enlisted the help of former President John Quincy Adams, and they managed to convince the Court to uphold Judson's decision without moving to challenge the legality of enslavement. The decision in *United States v. The Amistad* (1841) would be a defining moment for supporters and opponents of enslavement alike, a resounding clash of politics and perspective.

Fugitive Enslaved People and Militant Abolitionism

The drama of these episodes would be hard to match, but perhaps more consequential to the future of the country were the many small-scale flights of enslaved

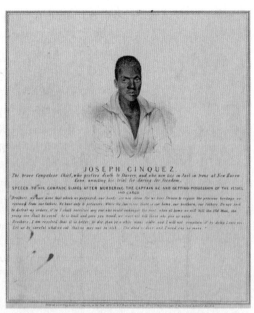

≡ **Joseph Cinque, Leader of the Amistad Revolt**
This portrait of Cinque (or Cinquez), drawn from life, along with an extract from a speech he made to his enslaved comrades was published in the New York *Sun* on August 31, 1839. "I am resolved it is better to die than to be a white man's slave," Cinque said. In 1841, the US Supreme Court ruled in *United States v. The Amistad* that Cinque and his fellow mutineers had been illegally held. They were subsequently freed and allowed to return to Africa.

people from owners in states where slavery remained legal to Black settlements in states where enslavement had been abolished or was in its very last stages of life. No one's story was more riveting or consequential to the fight against slavery than that of Frederick Douglass. Born to an enslaved mother in 1818 on the Eastern Shore of Maryland (the identity of his father has never been confirmed, but he was white and may well have been an enslaver), Douglass experienced many of the traumas of enslaved life. Torn from his family at an early age, he witnessed brutal whippings, was moved about by his enslavers, had a violent showdown with an overseer, and suffered many material deprivations. But when he was hired out to a ship's carpenter in nearby Baltimore, Douglass taught himself to read, learned about the work of abolitionists, and made plans to escape from enslavement. Although his first attempt at flight ended in failure, he was determined to succeed. And, in 1838, traveling by rail and water, Douglass escaped. He arrived in New York City, where he was aided by Black abolitionist David Ruggles, and then quickly moved on to the whaling town of New Bedford, Massachusetts, known as a hub of antislavery sentiment. There Douglass could find work and perhaps some safety from the reach of slave catchers.

Like Frederick Douglass, most fugitives from enslavement fled from border areas where slave and nonslave states (or countries) lay in close proximity (Maryland, Kentucky, Delaware, Missouri, Louisiana, Texas) and had learned of travel routes, safe havens, allies, and sensible destinations that might make for their success. Often referred to as the **Underground Railroad**, as something of a transit line between slavery and freedom, such secretive migrations might better be seen as part of a massive political web, built mainly by enslaved people and free people of color, that was directed toward struggles against enslavement and its poisonous scars (see Map 12.4).

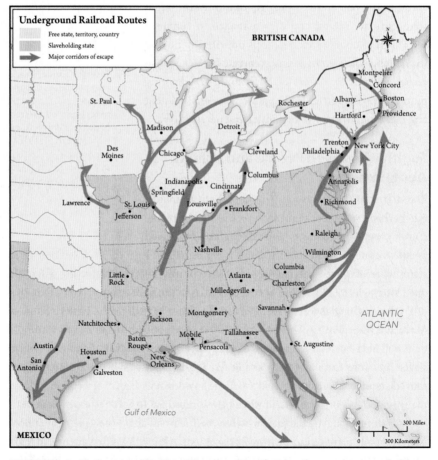

≡ **MAP 12.4 Underground Railroad Routes**   Most fugitives from enslavement fled from border areas where slave and nonslave states lay in close proximity. The overwhelming majority of runaways were captured and returned to their enslavers.

Many of these fugitive enslaved people, much like Frederick Douglass, would align with the abolitionist movement. Indeed, Douglass was recognized early by Black and white abolitionists for his ability to convey the experience of enslavement with powerful words and images. Before long, with the help of abolitionist allies, he crafted a *Narrative of the Life of Frederick Douglass* (1845), which reached a wide audience in the northern states and, to this day, remains a classic of antislavery literature.

Yet, while he initially gravitated to the Garrisonian camp, and would always admire Garrison and his followers, Douglass soon joined other Black fugitives and abolitionists in moving toward greater militancy. More than any other people in the United States, they understood the power and violence that undergirded slavery, the cruel mindset of enslavers and their white supporters, and the need for vigilance and self-defense wherever they might be. They also understood that so long as the overwhelming majority of Black people remained in bondage, the prospects for those who had escaped would be dim. Some publicly celebrated the heroic actions of enslaved rebels; some met in convention and called on "the slave to leave the plantation immediately with his hoe on his shoulder"; and some recommended that David Walker's *Appeal* (which opens Chapter 10) be widely circulated.

≡ **Frederick Douglass**   A towering figure in the struggles against enslavement and oppression, Frederick Douglass (pictured here sometime between 1847 and 1852, shortly after the publication year of his classic *Narrative of the Life of Frederick Douglass*) inspired abolitionists as well as advocates for women's rights.

Douglass himself came to accept the need for the direct "suppression" of slavery, and, especially after the passage in 1850 of the strengthened Fugitive Slave Law, African Americans who remained fugitives or had won their freedom revitalized vigilance committees to assist runaway enslaved people. In some places, they went so far as to form militia units and ready themselves for battle. It was not the first or last time that enslaved and free Black people were out front in recognizing how history was unfolding.

Slave escapes also promoted new types of militancy in states where enslavement had been officially outlawed. Before the 1850s, the work of harboring fugitives and driving off slave catchers fell largely to Black people who patrolled local thoroughfares, surveilled the docks, and tried to protect fugitive enslaved people from being kidnapped and returned to enslavement. During the 1850s, however, they began to receive concerted support from white antislavery activists who were enraged by the tougher Fugitive Slave Law and increasingly willing to join Black people in direct actions. In Boston and New York, Philadelphia and Syracuse, Cincinnati and Milwaukee, Detroit and Sandusky, Ohio, they took to the streets, surrounded jails and federal buildings, and attempted to take fugitives out of federal hands and ferry them to safety.

Sometimes they succeeded; sometimes they failed. But even when they failed, their efforts often made a searing impression on local observers who had not previously been moved by the moral and political dilemmas of slavery. When a Virginia fugitive slave named Anthony Burns was arrested in Boston on a federal warrant in 1854, Black and white abolitionists sprang into action, organizing protest meetings and devising plans of rescue. They also raised money, mobilized legal support, and tried to purchase Burns's freedom. Nothing worked. Yet it still required several corps of US military to clear a path through an estimated 50,000 angry Bostonians and get Burns on a federal ship heading south.

The political work of the enslaved and free people of color in crossing the apparent boundaries of slavery captured public attention and sympathy in new and powerful ways—much as did Harriet Beecher Stowe's blockbuster 1852 novel, *Uncle Tom's Cabin*, which jolted northern readers as to the personal horrors of slavery—and led many white abolitionists to reexamine their perspectives on the necessary road to emancipation. As they watched federal posses join hands with enslavers to capture runaways and watched fugitives and their Black allies battle for their freedom, they increasingly questioned Garrisonian "moral suasion" and accepted violence as a means toward abolitionist ends. At the same time, enslavers saw in the growing militancy of abolitionists and, especially, in their willingness to defy federal law governing fugitive enslaved people a sign of the Union's dangers and limits. If the laws protecting powerful members of one state would not be observed by members of another, what good use would the Union any longer serve?

≡ **A Devastating Scene from *Uncle Tom's Cabin*** Harriet Beecher Stowe's enormously popular novel highlighted the savagery of slavery. In this scene, the enslaved man Scipio, who tried to escape, has been caught by a mob of slave hunters and their vicious dogs. Scipio's enslaver, St. Clare (center), intervenes to save his human property—Scipio would die still enslaved to St. Clare. Chillingly, St. Clare observed that "People, you know, can get up just as much enthusiasm in hunting a man as a deer, if it is only customary."

12.7 Kansas Explodes

||| Explain why the issue of enslavement in the territory of Kansas created such division and bloodshed.

Nowhere did the question of slavery's future in the United States play out more ominously during the 1850s than on the rolling plains of eastern Kansas. It was not because fugitive enslaved people began to flock to Kansas or because big enslavers and committed abolitionists began to arrive in growing numbers. It was because men of relatively modest means in search of land, prospects, and breathing space chose sides in the belief that their destinies were on the line. Few were morally attached or opposed to slavery; fewer still had any interest in the enslaved or in African Americans more generally. But many saw either the slave-state or free-state side as the basis of their security and the opposition as bent on destroying them. They became willing shock troops in a struggle for power that linked the trans-Mississippi West with the highest levels of the American state.

Civil Warfare

The first sign that Kansas was headed in a very bloody direction was not the incursion of Missouri Border Ruffians and their role in the fraudulent election of a territorial legislature in March 1855. That, as we have seen, was only an exaggerated version of politics as usual in the early nineteenth century. Far more worrisome was what that legislature did when it then convened. Not only did the proslavery majority expel the small contingent of Free-Soilers who had won seats, but they outlawed any expression of antislavery sentiments and prohibited Free-Soilers from serving as jurors on any cases that might then be prosecuted. The legislature, one of its leaders crowed, "silenced Abolitionists."

The opposition couldn't be silenced. Viewing the territorial legislature as illegitimate, the Free-Soilers established newspapers, began to form their own government, and applied for statehood. But since Democratic President Franklin Pierce recognized the proslavery legislature and deemed the Free-Soilers revolutionary and treasonous, they understood the dangers they faced. They could not expect any protection from the official authorities and would, instead, have to protect themselves by means of numbers and arms. Any conflict, personal or otherwise, could easily take on political meaning and escalate rapidly into a full-blown confrontation. This is just what happened when a murder case involving a supporter of the proslavery side and a land dispute ended up in May 1856 with armed Missourians sacking the Free-Soil town of Lawrence and burning the house of a Free-Soil leader to the ground (see Map 12.5).

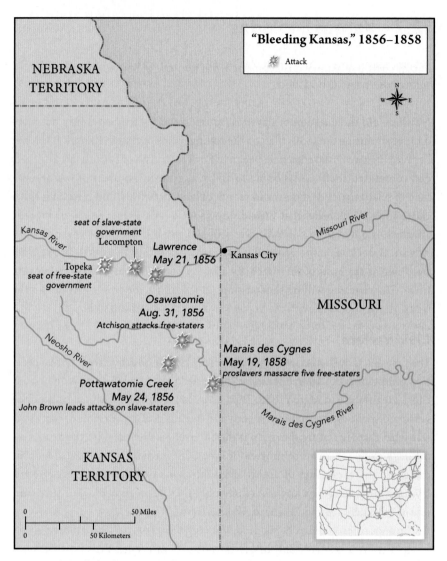

≡ **MAP 12.5** **"Bleeding Kansas,"** **1856–1858** The civil war in Kansas reverberated throughout the country.

The Free-Soil defenders of Lawrence had issued a call for help, and among those responding was a man named John Brown. Already a zealous abolitionist who viewed the struggle over enslavement in biblical terms, Brown had arrived in Kansas several months earlier to join family members at an encampment near the town of Osawatomie and supply them with weapons. Brown's son, John Jr., initially was local leader and had organized a militia company. But the elder Brown soon made his presence felt. Retaliating for what they called a "reign of terror," he and seven others headed to the proslavery settlement on Pottawatomie Creek and brutally murdered five unarmed men. Somehow Brown had hoped that his proslavery enemies would react to the massacre with fear and retreat; instead, the violence and retribution only escalated, and Brown, indicted for the Pottawatomie murders, fled east from Kansas to hatch new and more daring plans.

From Kansas to Congress

The reverberations of the civil war in Kansas spread east ahead of John Brown, roiling the political landscape and, on reaching Washington, DC, shattering all sorts of understandings, alliances, and civilities. Possibly the most shocking episode took place on the floor of the US Senate. There, on May 22, 1856, antislavery Senator Charles Sumner of Massachusetts was beaten within an inch of his life by South Carolina Representative Preston Brooks after Sumner delivered a scathing attack—the speech was called "The Crime Against Kansas"—on the Democratic Party, popular sovereignty, the "thugs" and "assassins" let loose in Kansas, and a number of congressional Democrats, including Brooks's cousin Andrew Butler.

This was neither the first nor the last time that members of Congress would assault one another in their respective chambers, and Brooks did not have a reputation as a hothead. In fact, he had once proposed that his congressional colleagues check their firearms before stepping onto the House floor. But in the context of the bloodshed in Kansas, the attack on Sumner catalyzed moral and political indignation on both sides of the slavery dispute and highlighted the extreme peril that was overtaking the country. Brooks became a hero to ardent defenders of enslavement and a villain to their opponents. "I do not see how a barbarous community and a civilized community can constitute one state," the New England writer and philosopher Ralph Waldo Emerson exclaimed. "I think we must get rid of slavery, or we must get rid of freedom."

The political damage from Kansas did more than deepen the wedge between enslavement's supporters and opponents. It also began to crack the foundations of the Democratic Party. Democrats had been trying mightily to keep slaveholding and nonslaveholding factions together, and they appeared to reach some consensus on popular sovereignty as a formula for the territories of the trans-Mississippi West. No one could feel the cracking more strongly than Stephen Douglas, an architect of popular sovereignty and an aspirant for the presidency, who, as we have seen, had hoped that the promise of an expanding American empire could redirect the battle over slavery's future. After all, whatever happened in Kansas, there was New Mexico and possibly Utah for the enslavers—not to mention lands farther to the south and in the Caribbean—and the northern Plains and northwest for the Free-Soilers.

But popular sovereignty had to seem popular, and the proslavery forces in Kansas, outnumbered in the population, were making a mockery of it. Indeed, despite efforts to maintain something of a truce between the two sides, the proslavery legislature sitting in the territorial capital of Lecompton called for a constitutional convention. With a new document protecting slavery known as the **Lecompton Constitution**, the legislature applied to Congress for statehood in the fall of 1857.

President James Buchanan was ready to have Kansas admitted to the Union as a slave state. His Democratic colleague Stephen Douglas was furious. This, Douglas believed, was a huge mistake. It would jeopardize the party's survival in the nonslaveholding states while damaging his own chances to get the party's nomination for president in the near future. Unsuccessfully urging Buchanan to change course, he then promised to lead the fight against the Lecompton Constitution in Congress. The scrappy Douglas prevailed: Kansas would remain a territory for the time being, and the slavery question would remain in limbo. However, Buchanan, who bridled at Douglas's disloyalty, saw the weak spot in his project. Reflecting on a monumental decision of the Supreme Court the previous March, Buchanan maintained that "slavery exists in Kansas by virtue of the Constitution of the United States" and therefore that "Kansas is as much a slave state as Georgia or South Carolina."

12.8   Slavery Everywhere?

‖‖   Summarize how the Supreme Court's decision in *Scott v. Sandford* influenced the crisis over enslavement's future.

James Buchanan thought he had outflanked Stephen Douglas because he had known of a pending ruling of the Court in a case called **Scott v. Sandford** even before he was inaugurated president on March 4, 1857. That decision was made public two days later, but Buchanan did not anticipate how violently it would rattle the Union: so violently that the reverberations are still being felt today.

What was this all about? The Supreme Court's momentous decision grew out of a lawsuit brought by the most obscure of men and women. They were named Dred and Harriet Scott, an enslaved couple who sought freedom from enslavement through the legal institutions of the state and federal governments. In many respects, this was a contradiction in terms. Enslaved people had no standing in civil or political society, no rights in courts of law, high or low, and, on the surface, at least, little chance of success. But in attempting to thread a legal needle, the Scotts became history makers, and their perspectives—as well as those of their supporters and opponents—became lightning rods in ways they could hardly have imagined.

Dred and Harriet Scott

Dred Scott was born enslaved in Virginia sometime around 1800. His enslaver, Peter Blow, owned a large farm in Southampton County, but in 1818 he decided to move his family and enslaved people to the plantation belt of Alabama, where he hoped to raise cotton for the international market. Twelve years later he moved once again, though this time he abandoned agriculture and the countryside and headed to the city of St. Louis, Missouri, where Blow opened a boarding house named the Jefferson Hotel.

As it turns out, Peter Blow was in poor health, and in 1832 he died, leaving five enslaved people as part of his estate. Although we don't know very much about the disposition of his estate, we do know that by late 1833 one of the enslaved people had been sold to a surgeon in the US Army named John Emerson. That slave was Dred Scott. Emerson was not a typical enslaver. Born in Pennsylvania, he received medical training at the University of Pennsylvania and ended up in St. Louis in the early 1830s after having spent some time in other slaveholding states. There, Emerson won appointment as an army surgeon and was soon on his way, with Dred Scott in tow, to Fort Armstrong in the state of Illinois. That Emerson purchased Scott while already in the Army and with the full expectation of taking him on assignment suggests how deeply implicated the federal government was in the support and protection of Black enslavement.

After two and a half years at Fort Armstrong, Emerson was transferred to Fort Snelling, far up the Mississippi River, in what was then the Wisconsin Territory. Scott again was forced along but this time, while at Snelling, he met an enslaved woman named Harriet Robinson, who was held in bondage by a local Native agent. Scott and Robinson soon married in a civil ceremony—highly unusual for enslaved people, who could not legally marry. When Emerson was

≡ **The Scott Family** Eliza, Lizzie, Dred, and Harriet Scott, as featured in an 1857 newspaper article about Dred and Harriet Scott's family and their case.

reassigned to Jefferson Barracks in St. Louis, Dred and Harriet remained behind, hired out at the Fort.

Eventually the Scotts rejoined Emerson at Fort Jesup in Louisiana, where he had met and married Irene Sandford, also of St. Louis. Emerson continued to move around while the Scotts were left in St. Louis with his wife, who seems to have hired them out while Dred may have renewed his acquaintance with the Blow family, especially Peter Blow's son Taylor, with whom he had apparently been close.

By the early 1840s, Emerson had left the military, was back in St. Louis, and was trying to establish a medical practice. He failed at that, hired out the Scotts, and went off to Davenport, Iowa, where he had previously purchased land. There he began to suffer from what appeared to be late-stage syphilis (contracted many years earlier) and died a short time later. According to his will, Emerson left Dred and Harriet to his wife, Irene, who then hired them out again. Many enslaved people had, of course, been forced to move around with their enslavers, and many—especially if they lived in cities like St. Louis—had a regular experience of being hired out. Yet the Scotts had, in their coerced travels, crossed a remarkable assortment of borders. They not only moved between states and territories but also between areas where slaveholding, supposedly, was and was not legal. In April 1846, before a state circuit court sitting in St. Louis, Dred and Harriet Scott determined to test the meaning of those borders and sue for their freedom.

It is not clear how the Scotts's suit was initiated: whether it was their idea, the idea of friends and sympathizers like the Blow family, or a collaborative effort from the start. We probably will never know for sure. But some things are clear. Although Missouri was a slaveholding state, it was also on the border between slave and nonslave states (like Illinois), and St. Louis was one of two cities in the slave states (Baltimore was the other) where public antislavery activity was possible. Even more important, over the previous two decades growing numbers of enslaved people had filed petitions for their freedom in St. Louis courts on similar grounds (that they had been taken by their owners to some Free-Soil zone before being brought back), and some of them had won. The Scotts may well have heard about these cases and decided to follow in their legal footsteps.

Unfortunately for the Scotts, by the time their suit went forward, the disposition of the courts in Missouri had shifted. They were now far less receptive to freedom suits such as theirs. Although the Scotts won a favorable ruling in a lower court, the high court of Missouri rejected their claims, insisting that even if they had spent time in a state or territory where slavery had been outlawed, the status of enslavement "reattached" to them once they returned to Missouri. Now the Scotts had only one more resort: an appeal to the Supreme Court of the United States.

The *Dred Scott* Decision

There was scant cause for optimism. Five of the nine court justices were from the enslaving states, and the Chief Justice, Roger Taney of Maryland, even though he had previously allowed the *Amistad* rebels to go free, was increasingly upset about what he called "Northern insult and Northern aggression." Although some of the justices were reluctant to insert themselves too deeply into the struggle over enslavement's future, the Scott case did offer them an opportunity to issue a sweeping ruling: all the more so as the conflict in Kansas escalated in violence and lawyers for the Scotts' enslaver raised the issue of the constitutionality of the Missouri Compromise line (see Map 12.6).

≡ **MAP 12.6   The *Dred Scott* Decision, 1857**   Chief Justice Roger B. Taney struck down the 1820 Missouri Compromise ban on slavery north of 36°30′ in one of the worst-ever decisions issued by the Supreme Court.

MAPPING AMERICA

A Nation Dividing

The status of enslavement in the western territories was the flashpoint for the growing divide between northern and southern states in the 1850s. But the conflict between those who sought to expand slaveholding territory and those who sought to limit or eliminate it is not the only way to measure the growing divide. Economic and social data also offer evidence of a nation coming apart.

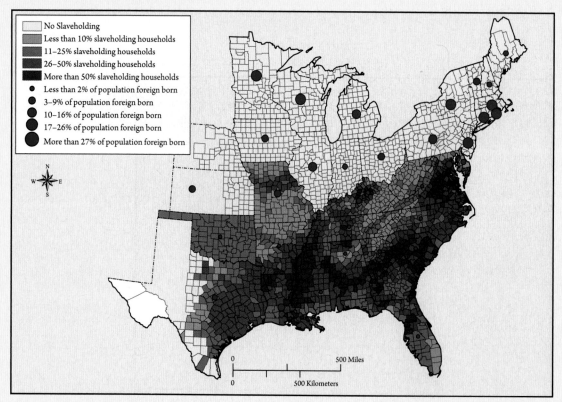

≡ **MAP 1   Slaveholding Households and Foreign-Born Population, 1860**   Demographic data offer clear evidence of a nation diverging. In 1860, the South was far less ethnically diverse than the North. The percentage of the foreign-born population in most southern states did not exceed 10 percent, while in several northern states over a third of their populations were foreign born. Although only 25 percent of southern households owned enslaved persons, the institution permeated all aspects of southern life.

Thinking Geographically

1. Examine Maps 1 and 2. Is there a correlation between those regions which have a high percentage of immigrants and those which have a high percentage of manufacturing establishments? What would such a correlation suggest?

2. Which areas of the South have the highest percentage of slaveholders? What factors do you think account for this?

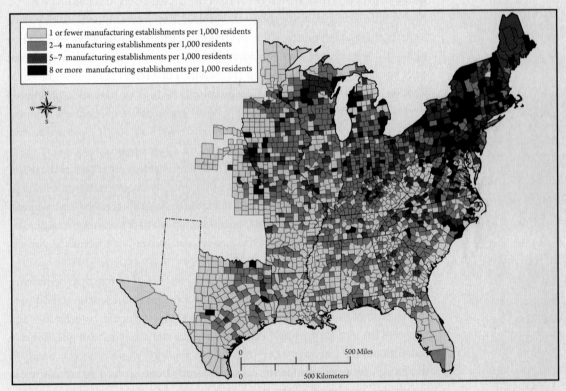

≡ **MAP 2   Manufacturing Establishments in the United States, 1860**   By 1860, North and South sharply differed economically. In 1860, there were as many manufacturing establishments in the North as there were manufacturing workers in the South. The result was dramatically different built environments. Even small towns in the North sported a wide array of shops that carried goods from all over the world. Centered on enslaved people and land, the southern economy was less diversified, though the wealth represented by cotton and enslaved people in 1860 was in the billions of dollars.

What did the court decide? On the most important question for the Scotts, the Supreme Court, by a 7–2 vote in March 1857, rejected their suit and said that they were still enslaved. From the Court majority's perspective, although Dred Scott may have been taken from Missouri to Illinois and the Wisconsin Territory, once he returned, the laws of Missouri again applied to him. He was neither a citizen of Missouri nor of the United States and therefore not entitled to bring suit in either state or federal court. That could easily—and unfortunately for the Scotts—have been the end of it.

But Taney and some of the justices chose to go much further and, in so doing, dramatically advanced the political interests of enslavers in the Union while relegating all people of African descent born in the United States to subordinate status. At the time the US Constitution was ratified, Taney determined, Black people were regarded as inferior to white and therefore, whether enslaved or free, had no rights that white Americans "were bound to respect." Simply put, they could not be or become citizens of the United States. And if that wasn't harsh enough, Taney went on to declare the Missouri Compromise (which, as we have seen, prohibited slavery in parts of the trans-Mississippi West) unconstitutional because it denied enslavers the right to their property (the enslaved) without due process of law, effectively violating the Fifth Amendment of the Constitution.

Although the Court's decision in the Dred Scott case was not far out of the mainstream of American jurisprudence up to that time, it was greeted with shock and outrage in antislavery circles and boded ill for Free-Soil efforts to end enslavement. Not only did the Court insist that Congress was powerless to restrict slaveholders from entering a federal territory; the justices also insisted that territorial governments were similarly powerless.

For enslavers, the *Dred Scott* decision was an enormous boost to their confidence and prospects. It meant that in the vast lands controlled by the federal government in the trans-Mississippi West no boundaries to slavery could be erected—and that even the boundaries imposed by some of the states might be of questionable constitutionality (see Map 12.6). After all, in the legal world of *Scott v. Sandford* (the name of the defendant in the case, technically Irene Sanford Emerson's brother John, was misspelled by the clerk of the Supreme Court), on what basis could a citizen of one state be denied rights to his property if he moved across another state or decided on a brief residency there? But for Stephen Douglas, Taney's decision was a source of great trouble. It challenged the credibility of popular sovereignty, cast doubt on his efforts to join Union and empire, and threatened his standing in the eyes of proslavery and antislavery Democrats alike. And although it would not have been apparent to him, the deed was done not so much by an irascible Chief Justice as—in a tragic irony—by a determined enslaved couple in Missouri and a great many others like them.

Conclusion: A Fraying Republic

The founding of the American republic was made possible by a series of compromises, the most important of which were between the slaveholding and non-slaveholding states. The institution of enslavement was recognized by the new US Constitution, and the power of the new federal government over it and slaveholders was extremely limited. But the terms "slavery" and "slaveholders" were never used in the document—various euphemisms were chosen instead, an implicit acknowledgment of the tensions that enslavement caused in the Union. Over the next decades, the pursuit of a continental empire inevitably led to conflicts between those who sought to expand slaveholding territory and those who sought to limit or outright eliminate it.

A continental empire and an "ocean-bound" republic were goals of most political leaders regardless of their views on enslavement, but perspectives on how that republic should be organized varied dramatically. And those perspectives sharpened in their differences over time, as slavery and antislavery moved to the center of American politics. After 1848, owing to the conquest of Mexican territory, battle lines were more and more clearly drawn, and the struggle moved from the halls of Congress to the lands of Kansas with foreboding results. With the *Dred Scott* decision, it now appeared that control over the federal government and its institutions—rather than just over states and territories—would be crucial to determining how the American destiny would be forged. In a tragic irony, it was the embrace of a continental and Pacific destiny that would threaten more than ever before to break the country apart.

WHAT IF Enslaved People Did Not Take Flight?

Slaveholders often responded to the moral attacks of abolitionists by arguing that enslavement was the best form of social order and governance for people who were culturally backward and racially inferior; that it was something of a "school" that educated Black people in the higher civilization of white people. Many of the slaveholders went further to claim that enslaved people were happy in their circumstances and often contrasted the peaceful climate of their plantations to the social strife that beset much of the "free labor" North.

Had this been true, or had enslaved people determined that attempted escapes were not worth the risk, the problem of fugitive enslaved people would have been limited and its effects on the political culture of the country would have been insignificant. Northern audiences would have learned little about the brutal realities of slavery, and few slave catchers would have traversed state borders to bring runaways back to their enslavers. The difficulties of keeping a Union together with free and slave states would have been diminished, and slaveholders would have felt less vulnerable to the mobilizations of abolitionists. Antislavery politics would have had a tougher time gaining traction, and the struggles in Kansas may well have been easier to contain.

Dred and Harriet Scott, and others like them, would have been brought to various parts of the United States by their enslavers, setting foot on "free" as well as "slave" soil. But it is less likely that such enslaved persons would have been able to sue for their freedom, and so Dred and Harriet Scott would have heard nothing about the suits. At most, their efforts to win their freedom would have been thrown out in the lower courts; there would have been no case of *Scott v. Sandford* and no ruling that explicitly denied Black people citizenship or opened all of the western territories to enslavement. The political prospects of Stephen Douglas would have been enhanced, as would have the possibilities for yet another compromise on the slavery question: one that would have extended enslavement, at least in parts of the United States, indefinitely. It was the fugitive enslaved people, by their courageous actions, who helped bring the conflict to a head.

DOCUMENT 12.1:   Letter to the American Slaves from Those Who Have Fled from American Slavery, August 1850, Cazenovia, New York

At a meeting to protest a harsher fugitive slave law being debated by Congress, which included about fifty fugitives including Frederick Douglass, this letter, likely written by Douglass, was adopted and eventually read aloud in Congress:

Afflicted and beloved Brothers:—The meeting which sends you this letter, is a meeting of runaway slaves. We thought it well that they who had once suffered as you still suffer, that they who had once drank of that bitterest of all bitter cups which you are still compelled to drink of, should come together for the purpose of making a communication to you.

The chief object of this meeting is to tell you what circumstances we find ourselves in—that so you may be able to judge for yourselves whether the prize we have obtained is worth the peril of the attempt to obtain it.

The heartless pirates who compelled us to call them "master" sought to persuade us, as such pirates seek to persuade you, that the condition of those who escape from their clutches is thereby made worse instead of better . . . But owing to the happy change in our circumstances, we are not as ignorant and credulous now as we once were; and if we did not know it before, we know it now, that slaveholders are as great liars as they are great tyrants. . . . When the insurrection of the Southern slaves shall take place, as take place it will unless speedily prevented by voluntary emancipation, the great mass of the colored men of the North, however much to the grief of any of us, will be found by your side, with deep-stored and long-accumulated revenge in their hearts, and with death-dealing weapons in their hands.

We do not forget the industrious efforts which are now making to get new facilities at the hands of Congress for re-enslaving those who have escaped from slavery. But we can assure you that, as to the State of New York and the New England States, such efforts must prove fruitless. Against all such devilism—against all kidnappers—the colored people of these States will "stand for their life"; and, what is more, the white people of these States will not stand against them. A regenerated public sentiment has forever removed these States beyond the limits of the slaveholders' hunting ground.

We cannot forget you, brethren, for we know your sufferings, and we know your sufferings because we know from experience what it is to be an American slave. So galling was our bondage that to escape from it we suffered the loss of all things, and braved every peril and endured every hardship. Some of us left parents, some wives, some children. Some of us were wounded with guns and dogs, as we fled. Some of us, to make good our escape, suffered ourselves to be nailed up in boxes, and to pass for merchandise. Some of us secreted ourselves in the suffocating holds of ships. Nothing was so dreadful to us as slavery; and hence it is almost literally true that we dreaded nothing which could befall us in our attempt to get clear of it . . . Brethren, our last word to you is to bid you be of good cheer and not to despair of your deliverance. Do not abandon yourselves, as have many thousands of American slaves, to the crime of suicide. Live! Live to escape from slavery! Live to serve God! Live till He shall Himself call you into eternity! Be prayerful—be brave—be hopeful. "Lift up your heads, for your redemption draweth nigh."

Source: Nationalhumanitiescenter.org

DOCUMENT 12.2: Excerpt from Albert Taylor Bledsoe's *Liberty and Slavery* (1856)

A professor at the University of Virginia, Albert Bledsoe addressed the Fugitive Slave Law of 1850 in his book, Liberty and Slavery, *arguing why it was necessary and justified:*

> Has Congress the power to pass a Fugitive Slaw Law?
>
> .... [W]e cannot forget that a Fugitive Slave Law was passed by the Congress of 1793, received the signature of George Washington, and, finally, the judicial sanction of the Supreme Court of the United States.
>
> The words of Mr. Madison, who "thought it wrong to admit in the Constitution the idea that there could be property in man," are four or five times quotes in Mr. Sumner's speech [against the Fugitive Slave Law]. As we have already seen, there cannot be, in the strict sense of the terms, "property in man"; for the soul is man, and no one, except God, can own the soul. Hence Mr. Madison acted wisely, we think, in wishing to exclude such an expression from the Constitution, inasmuch as it would have been misunderstood by Northern men, and only shocked their feelings without answering any good purpose.
>
> When we say that slaves are property, we merely mean that their masters have a right to their service or labor. This idea is recognized in the Constitution, and this right is secured. We ask no more.... and if Northern men will, according to the mandate of the Constitution, only deliver up our fugitive servants, we care not whether they restore them as persons or as property. If we may only reclaim them as persons or as property, and regain their service, we are perfectly satisfied.

Source: Albert Bledsoe, *Liberty and Slavery*, 426–430.

Thinking About Contingency

1. Do you agree with the author of this textbook that the difficulties of keeping a Union together with free and slave states would have been diminished, if fewer enslaved people risked escape?
2. What perspective do you gain when you consider the role Dred and Harriet Scott played in helping to bring the conflict over slavery to a head?

REVIEW QUESTIONS

1. Why were California and Kansas so much a part of the deepening conflict over enslavement's future?

2. Why might the congressional settlement of 1850 be regarded as an armistice rather than a compromise?

3. What were the ambitions of slaveholder imperialism, and how did it disrupt American politics in the 1840s and 1850s?

4. How did the very large influx of Irish immigrants in the late 1840s and early 1850s influence American politics and the dominant political parties?

5. What were the implications of the struggle over slavery in the Kansas territory during the 1850s, and how did it intensify political conflict in the country as a whole?

6. How did fugitive enslaved people contribute to the deepening conflict over enslavement during the 1850s?

7. What did the Supreme Court decide in the case of *Scott v. Sandford*, and why was the decision so consequential?

KEY TERMS

American or "Know-Nothing" Party (p. 489)

Amistad (p. 502)

Border Ruffians (p. 486)

California Gold Rush (p. 480)

Creole (p. 502)

Declaration of Sentiments (p. 500)

Deseret (p. 480)

filibusters (p. 491)

Free-Soil Party (p. 488)

Free State Party (p. 487)

Fugitive Slave Law (1850) (p. 481)

Great Famine (p. 494)

Kansas-Nebraska Act (p. 485)

Lecompton Constitution (p. 510)

Liberty Party (p. 488)

Neutrality Law (1818) (p. 491)

Ostend Manifesto (p. 490)

popular sovereignty (p. 481)

Scott v. Sandford (p. 510)

slaveholder imperialism (p. 489)

Underground Railroad (p. 504)

RECOMMENDED READINGS

Tyler Anbinder, *Nativism and Slavery: The Northern Know Nothings and the Politics of the 1850s* (Oxford University Press, 1992).

Nicole Etcheson, *Bleeding Kansas: Contested Liberty in the Civil War Era* (University of Kansas Press, 2004).

Don Fehrenbacher, *The Dred Scott Case: Its Significance in American Law and Politics* (Oxford University Press, 1978).

Eric Foner, *Free Soil, Free Labor, Free Men: The Ideology of the Republican Party Before the Civil War* (Oxford University Press, 1970).

Kellie Carter Jackson, *Force and Freedom: Black Abolitionists and the Politics of Violence* (University of Pennsylvania Press, 2020).

Martha Jones, *Birthright Citizens: A History of Race and Rights in Antebellum America* (Johns Hopkins University Press, 2018).

Matthew Karp, *This Vast Southern Empire: Slaveholders at the Helm of Foreign Policy* (Harvard University Press, 2018).

Kelly Kennington, *In the Shadow of Dred Scott: St. Louis Freedom Suits and the Legal Culture in Antebellum America* (University of Georgia Press, 2019).

Kate Masur, *Until Justice Be Done: America's First Civil Rights Movement from the Revolution to Reconstruction* (W.W. Norton, 2021).

Judith Wellman, *The Road to Seneca Falls: Elizabeth Cady Stanton and the First Women's Rights Convention* (University of Illinois Press, 2004).

13

A Slaveholders' Rebellion
1856–1861

Chapter Outline

≡ **Opening Shots** Confederate troops inspect damage to Fort Sumter in Charleston, South Carolina, on April 14, 1861. Union troops, exhausted by the Confederate bombardment of the fort two days earlier, had surrendered and evacuated. The Civil War was the first American conflict to be extensively documented by photographers.

Shortly after he took the oath of office on March 4, 1861, to become the sixteenth president of the United States, Abraham Lincoln called an urgent meeting of his cabinet.
Seven states in the Deep South had already seceded from the Union and then formed
what they called the Confederate States of America, a newly independent country
as they saw it. Claiming political sovereignty over the territory within their borders,
they also began laying claim to a number of federal forts in Florida and along the Gulf
Coast. The previous Democratic administration of President James Buchanan had
done nothing to stop them, but now Lincoln learned that a newly constructed—in
fact, still unfinished—fort in the harbor of Charleston, South Carolina, with a small
garrison of US troops, was running out of supplies. According to a report from its
commanding officer, General Robert Anderson, the fort—known as Fort Sumter—
either had to be resupplied or surrendered to the Confederates, who had demanded its
evacuation.

Timeline

1855	1856	1857	1858	1859

1856 > Republican Party nominates John C. Frémont for president

1857 > Supreme Court's *Dred Scott* decision

1858 > Lincoln-Douglas debates in Illinois

1859 >
John Brown's
Raid on
Harpers
Ferry,
Virginia

Lincoln understood what was at stake. If he resupplied the fort, the Confederates would regard it as an act of war and commence hostilities. And if he bowed to Confederate demands for evacuation, he would, in essence, be recognizing the legitimacy of the Confederacy—which he saw as the product of a slaveholders' rebellion—for the sake of continued peace. Lincoln asked the cabinet members for their advice, and they were divided. Secretary of State William Seward, a former rival for the Republican presidential nomination and perhaps the most prominent member of the Republican Party, along with General-in-Chief of the Army Winfield Scott urged him to evacuate, maintain the loyalty of the eight slave states in the Upper South, and preserve the Union in hopes that secessionist sentiment would soon run its course and the Deep South states would return. Democrat Stephen Douglas, one of his opponents in the recent presidential election (though not a cabinet member) agreed, and he implored Lincoln to put politics aside, pull the troops out of Fort Sumter, and keep

1860	1861	1862	1863	1864

1860 >
June Republican Party nominates Abraham Lincoln (IL) for president; Democratic Party divides and nominates both Stephen Douglas (IL) and John Breckinridge (KY) for president; Constitutional Union Party nominates John Bell (TN) for president
November In a four-way contest, Lincoln wins a majority of the electoral votes and becomes president
December South Carolina becomes the first state to secede from the Union

1861 >
February Representatives from states of the Deep South form the Confederacy
March Lincoln inaugurated president of the United States
April Confederates fire on federal Fort Sumter; Lincoln calls for troops to suppress the rebellion

the peace. Many Republican members of Congress, newly empowered by the election, also hoped for some sort of compromise to avert warfare.

But there were others in the cabinet, Secretary of the Treasury Salmon P. Chase chief among them, who insisted that Fort Sumter be resupplied because surrendering the fort to the Confederates would be disastrous for the party and the country. Opinion in the Northeast, Midwest, and Far West was divided as well, with strong advocates on both sides of the question. As a relatively unknown political figure—he had only served one term in Congress in the late 1840s—Lincoln could well have determined to back down, avoid conflict, bide his time, and hope that some peaceful solution to the secession crisis would be found. After all, previous crises over the question of slavery's future in the United States had resulted in compromises, most famously the Missouri Compromise enacted in 1820 and the Compromise of 1850 (discussed in Chapters 10 and 12).

But Lincoln was clear about two things. The first was his firm belief in Republican Party demands to prevent slavery from expanding into the territories of the trans-Mississippi West. Second, he believed that the Constitution made the people (not the states) sovereign and that secession and the formation of the Confederacy was nothing less than an act of rebellion organized by radical slaveholders. So, instead of backing down, Lincoln loaded ships with only nonmilitary provisions, informed the Confederates in South Carolina of this fact, and had the ships sail to Fort Sumter. As he may have expected, the Confederates were in no mood to bargain. On April 12, even before the ships arrived, they began to bombard the fort, forcing its surrender. So began, in ways that would have been impossible to imagine at the time, the bloodiest war in American history.

13.1   The Republican Challenge

‖‖‖ Identify the ideas and policies that enabled the Republican Party to build a winning political coalition.

In 1858 Senator Stephen Douglas was preparing himself for a reelection campaign he had every reason to believe would be successful. He had been a member of Congress for nearly twenty years, had become an important Democratic dealmaker and legislator in the Senate, and his home state of Illinois had been reliably

Democratic. The Whigs never carried the state in a presidential election, and the Democrats controlled the state legislature (which selected their US Senators) and governor's office during the 1840s and 1850s. Given his political prominence and efforts to make Illinois a vital hub in an expanding American empire, Douglas expected to hold his Senate seat and then use it as a launching pad for the Democratic Party's nomination for the presidency in 1860.

But Douglas could also sense that a new and radically different political party was stirring. As we saw in Chapter 12, ever since Douglas orchestrated the passage of the Kansas-Nebraska Act in 1854, the American political system had become unhinged. Antislavery Whigs in the Northeast and Midwest could no longer work with fellow Whigs from the slaveholding states who had supported Douglas's legislation and were intent on protecting the rights of enslavers. The Whig Party had no future, and in short order it collapsed. Those Whigs from the southern slave states were cut adrift, unwilling to join the Democrats and unable to find a suitable political home. Those from the northern states had better options. At first, a good many gravitated toward the nativist Know-Nothing Party, concerned as it was with the power of immigrants and enslavers. But before too long they shifted direction yet again and began to join an organization called the Republican Party.

The Republican Appeal

First established in the upper Midwest as part of the protests against the Kansas-Nebraska Act, the **Republicans** continued to attract support and build a political coalition. Much like the Whigs before them, the Republicans were concerned with domestic economic development and believed that the federal government should play an active role toward that end. They favored protective tariffs to bolster American manufactures, the rapid advance of transportation and communication networks, and the encouragement of commercial banking, with the paper money that the banks printed. Although many Republicans had imperial eyes, they imagined a more slowly unfolding and densely interconnected empire than did the Democrats. For the most part, they also sympathized with the Protestant-based social reform impulses of the time—temperance, education, penitentiaries—in hopes of fashioning a respectable American character. And many continued to carry the prejudices of anti-Catholicism even though they may have abandoned the Know-Nothings. Like Free-Soil Democrats with whom they would now coalesce, Republicans favored land policies meant to speed the settlement of the trans-Mississippi West by farmers who did not enslave people. Toward that end, they came to support "homestead" legislation intended to make cheap land available to farming households.

Yet the most powerful force that drew them together and would continue to define their main objectives was opposition to enslavement. Some came to the

☰ **California Power Couple**   Presidential candidate John C. Frémont's wife, Jessie Benton Frémont, was the daughter of the powerful US Senator Thomas Hart Benton, who represented Missouri for thirty years. An outspoken opponent of enslavement as well as a talented writer, Jessie Benton Frémont (shown here with her husband) publicized her husband's explorations of the American West and became very active in California politics. In recognition of her vigorous participation in her husband's 1856 campaign for president, one campaign slogan read, "Frémont and Jessie too."

Republicans by way of political abolitionism and the Liberty Party; others from the Free-Soil Party or the antislavery, "conscience," Whigs. Nearly all were concerned with the aggressiveness of what they called the "Slave Power" and its designs on the American Union: the tough Fugitive Slave Law of 1850; the Kansas-Nebraska Act, which repealed the Missouri Compromise; and the *Dred Scott* decision of the Supreme Court, which showed the hold of enslavement on all the branches of the federal government and threatened to secure much of the American West for enslavers. By 1856, the Republicans were formidable enough to take aim at the presidency, and they nominated the western explorer and former Senator from California, John C. Frémont, as their candidate.

The Rise of Lincoln

For a brand-new political party, the Republicans made a surprisingly good showing in 1856, winning about one-third of the popular vote and more than 100 electoral votes (see Map 13.1). Although Republicans failed to carry Illinois, the Democratic margin there was now very small, and, even more impressively, the Republicans managed to win the governor's office from the Democrats. By 1858, the Illinois Republicans were eager to challenge Stephen Douglas with a candidate who had spent little time in elective office but who had become one of the party notables largely because of his attacks on Douglas and popular sovereignty. His name was Abraham Lincoln.

Lincoln didn't find his way to the Republican Party by way of the Liberty or Free-Soil Parties. He had been a staunch member of the Whig Party and in fact viewed organized antislavery with mistrust. Born in the slave state of Kentucky before moving with his family, first to Indiana and then to Illinois, Lincoln's political hero was Henry Clay (the chief architect of the Missouri Compromise and himself an enslaver) and his main concern the protective tariff. He served briefly in the Illinois state legislature and one term (1847–1849) in the United States House of Representatives, all the while attending to his law practice in Springfield, which focused on debts, land titles, domestic disputes, and, especially, the defense of railroad companies. Even out of office, Lincoln remained active in Illinois Whig politics, but the public notice he would win came as a result of his increasing outspokenness on the issue of slavery.

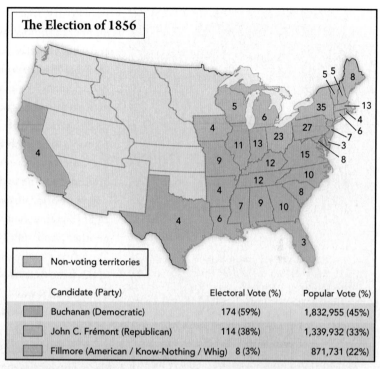

The origins of Lincoln's unease with enslavement are not entirely clear—his Baptist parents had an aversion to human bondage though some of his relatives were enslavers—and he certainly lived most of his life on slavery's borders without much trouble. The hiring of enslaved people from Kentucky or Missouri was not unknown in southern Illinois, and racist exclusions were state policy. Lincoln himself could deploy racist language and images, and he had a hard time imagining a future in which white and free Black people would live together in peace. But for a self-educated man, Lincoln was well read

The Election of 1856

Candidate (Party)	Electoral Vote (%)	Popular Vote (%)
Buchanan (Democratic)	174 (59%)	1,832,955 (45%)
John C. Frémont (Republican)	114 (38%)	1,339,932 (33%)
Fillmore (American / Know-Nothing / Whig) 8 (3%)		871,731 (22%)

Non-voting territories

☰ **MAP 13.1   The Election of 1856**   By 1856, the Republicans had emerged as a formidable political party. In the presidential election, only losses in lower North states of Pennsylvania, Indiana, and Illinois prevented John C. Frémont from winning.

in political economy, the study of how economic and political systems are linked. He had been influenced by antislavery Whigs while in Congress, and, when there, he did present a bill that would have gradually abolished slavery in the District of Columbia (it failed to pass).

By the early 1850s, Lincoln seemed to share the perspective of moderate Free-Soilers. He acknowledged that the Constitution protected enslavement in states where it had been deemed legal while objecting to its expansion into the territories of the trans-Mississippi West. Although Lincoln had no idea how enslavement might be abolished where it lawfully existed, he seemed to believe that any plan of abolition would be gradual (as in the northern states), involve compensation of some sort to the enslavers, and be followed by the voluntary exile of the freed population, better known to Whigs and then Republicans as "colonization" (see Chapter 10).

But it was in the fall of 1854, in response to the Kansas-Nebraska Act, that Lincoln came to be seen as a powerful speaker. After studying for weeks in the

≡ **Foreteller of a "House Divided"**   The young trial lawyer Abraham Lincoln in May 1858, just a few weeks before his prophetic "house divided" speech, in which he accepted the nomination of the Illinois Republican Party for senator.

state library, Lincoln went before large audiences in a number of Illinois towns and took on Senator Douglas and what he had orchestrated. Although dismissing the idea that Black people could be "politically and socially our equals," he condemned the constitutional logic of popular sovereignty, told of moves the founders had made against enslavement, and warned of the system's probable expansion into Kansas and other territories. Yet Lincoln also could shift to higher, international ground, pointing to the rise of "liberal parties throughout the world," insisting that "there can be no moral right in connection with one man's making a slave of another," and suggesting the American hypocrisy of "fostering Human slavery and proclaiming ourselves, at the same time, the sole friends of Human Freedom." Strong stuff it was.

Soon Lincoln would be actively involved in building the Illinois Republican Party and making a name for himself in party circles. He denounced the *Dred Scott* decision and the Supreme Court under Roger Taney, and, in June 1858, was selected by the Republican state convention as the party's candidate for the US Senate seat held by Stephen Douglas. In accepting the nomination, Lincoln continued to condemn *Dred Scott*, but he also warned, drawing upon a biblical metaphor, of a "house divided against itself." "The government cannot endure permanently half *slave* and half *free*," he said. "Either the *opponents* of slavery will arrest the further spread of it, and place it ... in the course of ultimate extinction; or its *advocates* will push it forward, till it shall become alike lawful in *all* the States, *old* as well as *new*—*North* as well as *South*."

The Lincoln-Douglas Debates

These ideas framed seven debates between Lincoln and Douglas in the summer and early fall of 1858. Douglas—also known as the "Little Giant"—would have been the betting favorite, given his experience in Congress and the political temper of the state's voters. He aggressively attempted to portray Lincoln as an antislavery radical and racial egalitarian, arguing that Lincoln not only opposed the Fugitive Slave Act and the admission to the Union of any more slave states but also wished to make African Americans citizens of the United States. Such accusations would land among audiences whose politics combined antislavery with white supremacy.

For his part, Lincoln accused Douglas of betraying the intentions of the republic's founders and the spirit of the Declaration of Independence, and he pressed Douglas on the implications of the *Dred Scott* decision for the viability of popular sovereignty. If the Supreme Court had determined, as the law of the land, that enslavers could not be excluded from the western territories, Lincoln asked him, how was it possible for a territory to prohibit slavery at all? Was Douglas's formula of popular sovereignty now effectively nullified?

Taking place in the state of Illinois, the debates between Lincoln and Douglas nonetheless exposed deeply conflicting perspectives about the country's development as a whole. Douglas, a Democrat, mocked Lincoln's view that a "house divided against itself cannot stand." After all, this was the way the United States had been organized from its first days, "divided into free and slave states," and, as Douglas crowed, the result has been a growing, expanding, and prosperous Union. "We have risen from a weak and feeble power," he proclaimed, "to become the terror and admiration of the civilized world. Our Government was formed on the principle of diversity in local institutions and laws, and not on that of uniformity."

Lincoln denied that he was calling for "uniformity," but along with growing numbers of Republicans he rejected the constitutional basis of Douglas's "diversity." Although the Constitution did offer protections for slavery where it existed, Lincoln and his party insisted the founders believed that freedom and equality were the natural conditions of humankind and that enslavement was no more than a temporary and unsavory institution. They pointed out that the words "slave" and "slavery" never appeared in the Constitution's text and that the framers' euphemisms—"other persons" or "persons bound to labor and service"—testified to their unease. Equally important, they maintained that the Constitution and federal government were made by the "people" and not by the "states," and it was the people in whom sovereignty resided. Freedom was "national"; slavery was only "local."

In essence, Douglas and Lincoln each had a strong case. There was room for enslavement and an assortment of separate sovereignties—for "diversity"—in the continental and, perhaps, hemispheric empire or union such as Douglas imagined. But there was no such room in the political union that Lincoln and the Republicans envisioned: a *nation* or *nation-state* with recognized borders and sets of principles, with common ideas of belonging and institutions over which the federal government ruled directly without the interventions of those claiming their own sovereign rights, as slaveholders did over the people they enslaved. These perspectives were deeply at odds and seemed impossible to reconcile.

PERSPECTIVES

The Lincoln-Douglas Debates in American Memory

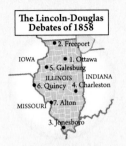

The Lincoln-Douglas Debates of 1858

≡ **Lincoln-Douglas Debates**

It is considered an integral part of the process. However, before 1858 joint debates did not occur in American elections. All of this changed over the course of two months, in the late summer and early fall of 1858, when Abraham Lincoln and Stephen Douglas traded blows on the thorniest issues of the day. The Lincoln-Douglas debates are thus more than legendary pieces of political theater: they transformed the way Americans approached elections and thought about candidates.

Their impact was immediate. From the first debate in Ottawa, Illinois, attendees sensed the historic nature of the event. The crowd gathered close around Honest Abe and the Little Giant, eager to soak up the action. Although there were no photographers, the nation hung on every word, thanks in part to a pool of stenographers and a recently formed telegraphic news service, the Associated Press. A little over a year later, Lincoln published *Political*

ꟼ ꟼ ꟼ ꟼ ꟼ ꟼ ꟼ ꟼ ꟼ

Last Great Discussion.

Let all take notice, that on Friday next, Hon. S. A. Douglas and Hon. A. Lincoln, will hold the seventh and closing joint debate of the canvass at this place. We hope the country will turn out, to a man, to hear these gentlemen.

The following programme for the discussion has been decided upon by the Joint Committee appointed by the People's Party Club and the Democratic Club for that purpose.

Arrangements for the 15th inst.

The two Committees—one from each party—heretofore appointed to make arrangements for the public speaking on the 15th inst., met in joint Comnittee, and the following programme of proceedings was adopted, viz:

1st. The place for said speaking shall be on the east side of City Hall.

2d. The time shall be 1½ o'clock, P. M. on said day.

3d. That Messrs. C. Stickman and W. T. Miller be a Committee to erect a platform; also, seats to accommodate ladies.

4th. That Messrs. B. F. Barry and William Post superintend music and salutes.

5th. Messrs. H. G. McPike and W. C. Quigley be a committee having charge of the platform, and reception of ladies, and have power to appoint assistants.

6th. That the reception of Messrs. Douglas and Lincoln shall be a quiet one, and no public display.

7th. That no banner or motto, except national colors, shall be allowed on the speakers' stand.

On motion, a committee, consisting of Messrs. W. C. Quigley and H. G. McPike, be appointed to publish this programme of proceedings.   W. C. QUIGLEY,
                                    H. G. McPIKE.

Alton, Oct. 13, 1858.

To the above it should be added that the C. A. & St. Louis Railroad, will, on Friday, carry passengers to and from this city at half its usual rates. Persons can come in on the 10:40 A. M. train, and go out at 6:20 in the evening.

≡ **Lincoln-Douglas Debate**   Notice in an Illinois newspaper announcing the final debate between Abraham Lincoln and Stephen A. Douglas, October 15, 1858.

≡ **Anniversary of the Lincoln-Douglas Debate**   Flanked by busts of Lincoln and Douglas, President William McKinley addresses a crowd in Galesburg, Illinois, on October 5, 1898, to commemorate the fortieth anniversary of the debates.

Debates Between Honourable Abraham Lincoln and Honourable Stephen A. Douglas.
It became an instant bestseller and helped solidify Lincoln's stature ahead of the
Republican national convention in May 1860. The slim volume also ensured that
the debates would forever enjoy an honored place in American memory.

≡ **Lincoln-Douglas Debates (1958)** Postage stamp
from 1958 commemorating the 100th anniversary of the
debates.

≡ **Lincoln-Douglas Debate, Du Page County
Centennial** Works Progress Administration
poster from 1939 announcing a reenactment of a
Lincoln-Douglas debate to be held at the centennial
celebration of DuPage County, Illinois, showing
profiles of Lincoln and Douglas.

CONSIDER THIS

The newspaper notice from October 15, 1858, describes the debate between
Lincoln and Douglas as a "great discussion." How does this compare with political
debates today? Would you characterize them as discussions?

13.2   The Growth of Secessionism

||| Assess the nature of secessionist sentiment and how it grew out of state rights and sectionalism.

By the time Abraham Lincoln debated with Stephen Douglas, very different perspectives had gained traction in the states where enslavement was legal. Ever since the 1820s, when the admission of Missouri to the American Union provoked conflict, enslavers worried about their prospects in the United States. They saw that some congressional representatives from the Northeastern and Middle Atlantic states were hostile to enslavement and that the powers of the federal government might be used against them. Although those in the antislavery movement complained about the expansive designs of the "slave power," many enslavers began to see themselves as an embattled minority seeking political safety and protection for their valuable property. Thus, between the 1820s and the mid-1850s, a new language of conflict over enslavement was forged around some bracing ideas.

The Ideas of Sectionalism and State Rights

Most widely circulated was the idea of a region, of a "section," an idea of a "South" that had an identity, a set of economic and political interests, and a feeling of cultural distinctiveness. Although the framers of the Constitution could speak of a South and of "southern" concerns and leaders of the early republic could invoke regional and sectional issues, it was only in the 1830s that **sectionalism** became central to the political vocabulary of the United States.

Abolitionists and other antislavery advocates played an important role here, especially as they mounted a critique of slave labor and contrasted what could be found where enslavement did and did not exist. Some would refer to a "North" above the Mason-Dixon line and Ohio River, where slavery had been eradicated and free labor thrived, and to a "South" below marked by aristocratic hierarchies, social degradation, and cultural backwardness. Indeed, the political language of antislavery effectively erased the long history the Northeast and Midwest had with enslavement and emancipation, and instead fashioned a perspective that marked a sharp divide between evolving sectional worlds.

Proslavery political leaders and intellectuals joined the fray. Theirs was a response in part to new questions about the wisdom and morality of slaveholding and in part to a perception of shifting balances of power. At the time of the ratification of the Constitution, Americans widely believed that the country's population was moving in a southwesterly direction, strengthening the position of those who lived where enslavement held sway. But by the 1830s, it was apparent that states where slavery had been abolished or was under attack were growing even faster and that, in an international age of emancipation, slavery's destiny might be in serious jeopardy (see Figure 13.1).

The political idea of the "South" developed alongside theories of power that focused on states and households. As we saw in Chapter 10, South Carolina's John C. Calhoun most famously combined a defense of slavery and local rights in his writings on state sovereignty and nullification (when Congress overstepped its powers, states had the right to nullify congressional acts), but his was only the most sophisticated argument. **State rights** became the political mantra for en-slavers, their representatives, and Democrats more generally; though far more than their colleagues in the North, southern Democrats believed that the states

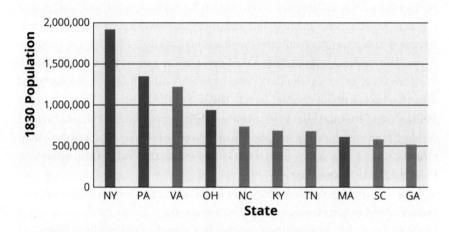

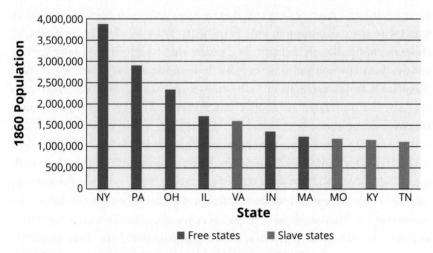

≡ **FIGURE 13.1   Ten Most Populous States in 1830 and 1860.**

had created the Union *and* retained their sovereignty. This reflected the perspectives of slaveholding and patriarchy. Indeed, for enslavers large and small, state rights derived meaning not from some abstract notion of political institutions and balances but chiefly in relation to the personal power they could exercise, power over the people they enslaved certainly but also over other household dependents: their wives, children, and others who might live under their command. Abolitionism, they declared, represented a world they knew turned upside down, a world that set enslaved people loose and, more generally, undermined their patriarchal household authority.

The Threat of Secession

For all of his efforts to promote the idea of state rights, Calhoun remained a unionist. He viewed the nullification doctrine that he devised in the early 1830s as a means to preserve the United States and protect slaveholding interests within it. But fellow South Carolina nullifiers did threaten **secession**—leaving the Union— if President Andrew Jackson determined to wage war against them, and although few if any of the other slaveholding states were yet ready to go along, secession was thereafter on the political table. During the rest of the 1830s and for most of the 1840s, there it sat, quietly, as slaveholders and their representatives battled over the building of an American empire, the annexation of Texas and Cuba, and the extent of conquest in Mexico, all while cotton became king and enslavement seemed to be on the march once again.

Yet, as the country decided what to do with the territory it had conquered from Mexico, slaveholders saw increasingly worrisome signs. Some northerners called for excluding slavery from all these new lands; California was quickly admitted as a "free state"; and it seemed the best they could hope for was popular sovereignty working to their advantage in only parts of the trans-Mississippi West. Taking their cue from Calhoun, militant slaveholders who imagined the Union turning against them now looked to defend their way of life. Some, increasingly called **Fire-eaters**, embraced secession as the only sensible means for protecting slavery; others hoped to consider the "South's" options and unify the political leadership of the slaveholding states.

It was a slow process. But secessionism had clearly reared its head, and secessionists from the Deep South and Virginia began to create something of a political network. They recognized that what seemed obvious to them—the need to leave the Union—would require a concerted campaign if secession were to win significant public support. They would have to use speeches, the newspapers, political clubs, and civic associations to spread their ideas and explain their logic. They would also have to fill state and local offices with secessionist advocates and sympathizers, who could shape opinion and prepare constituents for action. And they would have to realize that a unified movement might not at first be possible, that one state might have to take the lead.

By the mid-1850s, secessionists were in a strong position in the Deep South. Little by little, they elected their candidates to local and state office and gained influence as editors on Democratic newspapers, all the more so after the Whig Party unraveled. Their message may not yet have

≡ **New Orleans in 1858**   Its strategic position made New Orleans the link that connected the expanding cotton hinterland with overseas markets.

been accepted in all quarters, but its impact could easily be seen. Even unionists and moderate opponents of secessionism in the South increasingly conceded that secession was a legitimate course of action if the interests and vulnerabilities of the slave states were ignored. As the political crisis of the Union deepened, secessionists were beginning to steer the slaveholders' ship. But what really energized secessionism and gave it momentum was a perspective that looked abroad and recognized international political currents that may have started to flow the slave South's way.

How was that? Whatever the gains of abolitionism, Deep South enslavers, in particular, could believe that on a world stage antislavery may have run its course and slaveholders may have weathered the storm. The politically liberal revolutions of 1848 in continental Europe had been defeated. The emancipations that already occurred in the Caribbean and Latin America seemed to have produced so much conflict and disorder that even former champions of abolitionism expressed disenchantment. Haiti, the first mass emancipation in the Atlantic, had quickly been cordoned into isolation by Europe and the United States and was stagnating under the burdens of rural poverty and political authoritarianism. All the while, an accelerating Industrial Revolution was creating what seemed a limitless market for the cotton that American enslavers nearly alone supplied.

So long as their representatives wielded power in the federal government, enslavers might be able to pursue their future within the Union; if the government passed into hostile hands, all bets were off.

MAPPING AMERICA

The Course of Empire

In November 1862, as the slaveholders' rebellion deepened into hard warfare, a large mural was installed in the Capitol. Painted by German-American Emanuel Leutze, *Westward the Course of Empire Takes Its Way* celebrates the western expansion of the United States. Explorers and pioneers trek across the seemingly empty wilderness, as if no Native Americans lived in these lands. But if secessionists had been able to view Leutze's painting, they would have disagreed with his perspective. For many of them, American destiny led not just across to the Pacific but also to the Caribbean, Mexico, and Central America.

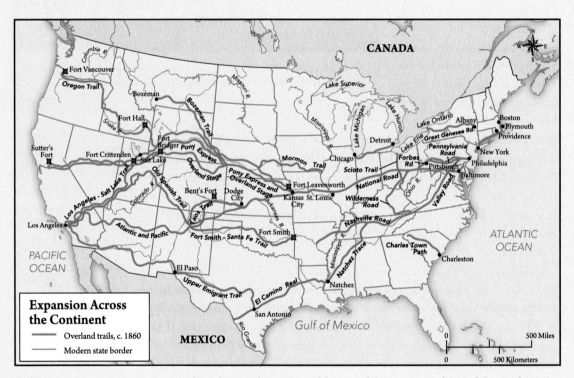

Expansion Across the Continent

——— Overland trails, c. 1860

------ Modern state border

≡ **MAP 1**   Most Americans, North and South, viewed expansion of the United States westward toward the Pacific Ocean as destined and justified.

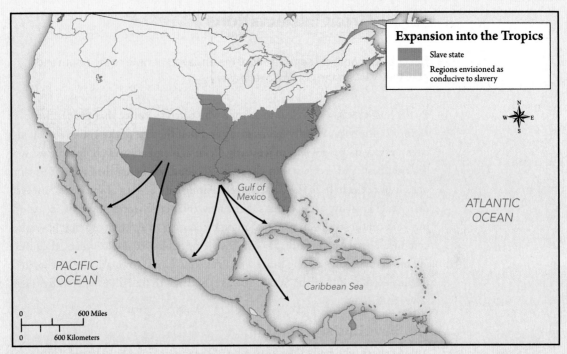

Expansion into the Tropics

- Slave state
- Regions envisioned as conducive to slavery

Gulf of Mexico

ATLANTIC OCEAN

PACIFIC OCEAN

Caribbean Sea

0   600 Miles

0   600 Kilometers

≡ **MAP 2**   Many young, upwardly mobile slaveholders also imagined a prosperous future for themselves in the tropics, so long as slave property could be secured. They cast hungry eyes on Cuba, and even supported the reopening of the African slave trade.

Thinking Geographically

1. Examine Maps 1 and 2. What is the relative place of the Pacific Ocean in each map? The Gulf of Mexico?

2. In Map 2, enslavers would have transported the enslaved across sea lanes and borderlands. In this scenario, how would the limits of the enslavers' authority come into question? What type of political confrontations would have been provoked?

13.3 Great Expectations

‖‖‖ Describe the political sensibilities of the enslaved people of the South and how they viewed the conflict over slavery.

By the mid-1850s, it was clear to anyone who cared to notice that the conflict over slavery's future was rapidly intensifying and that the fate of the Union forged just over sixty years before was in jeopardy. Prior agreements and compromises were shaky at best, and, as we saw in Chapter 12, blood was being shed from the plains of Kansas to the halls of the US Congress. Along with concerns and fears, however, many held growing expectations that a new and better world might be in the offing, that centuries of enslavement might be coming to an end, and that liberation could well be at hand. And although these hopes buoyed abolitionists, they were felt most powerfully among those who lives would most dramatically be changed: the enslaved people of the South. It was their time to find allies and ready themselves to strike.

The Slave Underground

Among those who had taken keen note of the intensifying battle over slavery was the enslaved man William Webb. Although formally excluded from the arenas of electoral politics, he had a special interest in the battle's course and outcome. Born in Georgia in the mid-1830s, Webb was taken out to Mississippi by his enslaver and then moved several times between Mississippi and Kentucky owing to the changing fortunes of his enslaver's family. Along the way, he found God, sought God's graces, and assumed a prophetic stance. But around 1856, when John C. Frémont was running as the first Republican presidential candidate, Webb became involved in political debates and discussions in the slave quarters. Posting guards to warn of slave patrols and taking oaths to maintain secrecy, Webb and his enslaved followers "held great meetings" and "put all their trust in Frémont to deliver them from bondage."

Frémont lost the election, and his defeat proved disheartening to Webb and his comrades. But the news was not debilitating. They made more "speeches among themselves" and argued about "what steps they would take." Some, Webb remembered, "would speak about rebelling and killing, and some would say, 'wait for the next four years,'" imagining that the "next President would set the colored people free." Equally important, they created a network of communication so that enslaved people in the vicinity and across far greater distances could be informed and coordinate their understandings and activities. In Webb's view, "Frémont was a small light, and it would keep burning till it was spread over the whole world."

Within a short time, he claimed that he had "friends all over the country" and "was receiving news from a great many states."

William Webb's account demonstrates that enslaved people had knowledge of both the substance and cycles of American politics. He and the enslaved people he lived among had plainly heard about John C. Frémont, recognized him as a potential ally in the fight against slavery, and knew something about when elections would take place. But Webb also opens our eyes to more than a particular group of the enslaved; he opens our eyes to a world of "underground" politics that allowed enslaved people to feel the pulse of change, register their expectations, and play a part in the struggle for power in the United States. Keen to signs of conflict among whites, they attempted to gather intelligence, assess its meanings, and secretly spread the word across southern towns and rural districts.

Enslaved people obtained political information in a variety of ways. They could get it from white politicians they overheard making speeches, from newspapers and tracts (like David Walker's *Appeal*, discussed in Chapter 10) smuggled for the few of them who were literate, from forced migrants like William Webb who arrived from other states and localities, from enslavers who expressed their fears and concerns within earshot, and from fugitives who might return to ferry more of the enslaved to Black settlements in the North. Most often, they learned about politics from other enslaved people who had mobility, worked in the plantation house, were hired out in towns and on docks, were coachmen or boatmen, and who then brought news back to the slave quarters. In the process, the enslaved in many parts of the South constructed stories and expectations about their friends and enemies, their prospects for freedom, and what freedom would bring them. In whatever way they imagined the coming of emancipation—whether it would be brought forth by the work of God or by one of God's earthly agents—they readied themselves to assist in the task once the day of judgment arrived.

John Brown: An Ally in the Fight?

Among slavery's enemies who counted on the political expectations of the enslaved and their willingness to act upon them was John Brown, the fiery abolitionist we met in Chapter 12. After fleeing from Kansas, Brown began to focus on a far more ambitious project. He planned to strike a massive blow against the slave regime by encouraging enslaved people to escape their captivity and form a hostile state in the heart of slaveholding country. The idea was audacious in the extreme, but it reflected a growing perspective among abolitionists that enslavement was organized violence and warfare, that formal campaigns against it were ineffective, and that emancipation would probably require force of arms. "There was a time when slavery could have been ended by political action," abolitionist Gerrit Smith declared.

≡ **John Brown** The zealous abolitionist viewed the struggle over enslavement in biblical terms. This daguerreotype was taken in Kansas in 1856.

"But that time has gone by. There was not enough virtue in the American people to bring slavery to a bloodless termination, and all that remains for them is to bring it to a bloody one."

Brown had been imagining such a slave rebellion since about 1857, when he was still raising arms and money for the ongoing struggle in Kansas. He met and won a sympathetic hearing from some of white abolitionism's most important activists with means—Franklin Sanborn, George L. Stearns, Thomas Wentworth Higginson, Samuel Gridley Howe, Theodore Parker, and Gerrit Smith, together known as the **Secret Six**—who would provide him with financial support. He also attracted the interest of Black abolitionists Frederick Douglass and Martin Delany, whose disenchantment with the course of antislavery and the plight of Black people in the United States had deepened. Brown was, after all, a proven fighter in the developing war against enslavement, and unlike other militant abolitionists, he appeared to have a blueprint for success.

What was the plan? It might best be described as a type of maroon warfare that fugitives from enslavement who had settled in remote areas waged against attacking enslavers. Brown would gather a large fighting force, arm it, and, from bases in the Appalachian Mountains, raid slaveholding farms and plantations and rally the enslaved there to join him. As the Appalachian hideouts swelled in size, they would form governing bodies while continuing to weaken the stability of enslavement from Virginia to Alabama by means of armed attack and slave flight. To that end, Brown drew up a "Provisional Constitution," which pledged "protection" to the "oppressed races of the United States," made all property equal and communal, required labor from everyone, and encouraged those who came among him to "carry arms openly." Some who read their constitution noticed a resemblance to the politically formidable maroons of Jamaica and the Guianas, and Brown was careful to note that he had no interest in "the overthrow of any State Government of the United States" or the "dissolution of the Union." His interest was rather in forcing slavery's abolition.

Brown did not assume that enslaved people would spontaneously join his war once they learned of it. He knew it would be necessary to lay the groundwork, which is what drew him to Harpers Ferry, Virginia. For although Harpers Ferry was best known as the site of a federal arsenal—and thus a source of weapons—it was also a gateway into the Appalachians and very much on a long-established route of fugitive slave escapes. Nearby areas of Virginia, Maryland, and Pennsylvania had scattered populations of enslaved people as well as communities of free people of color, and Brown began to build a network that included local free Black leaders, recognizing that the involvement of African Americans was crucial to the undertaking. By the summer of 1859, a good many Black people, enslaved and free, in the Harpers Ferry perimeter probably knew something of John Brown's intentions.

Soon thereafter, in the fall, Brown decided to commence his war with an attack on Harpers Ferry instead of heading there after raids on slave plantations and farms had begun, as he initially had planned. This may have been because his efforts at recruiting brought him a smaller fighting force than he had anticipated. Still, with a growing sense of urgency and just over twenty men—only five of whom were Black—Brown set out for Harpers Ferry on the night of October 16, dispatching a small party to round up slaveholders and liberate enslaved people nearby.

Although the raid went smoothly at first, an eastbound train was let through and quickly alerted authorities about a "Negro insurrection" in progress. Before long, local militias and angry town residents had Brown's raiders surrounded, and US troops under the command of Robert E. Lee and J. E. B. Stuart were on the way. On the morning of October 18, Lee demanded Brown's unconditional surrender and, when Brown refused, ordered the soldiers in. When the smoke finally cleared, ten of Brown's men, including two of his sons, and as many as seventeen of the Black people who had taken up arms with them lay dead or mortally wounded. Five of the raiders managed to escape, and seven, including Brown himself, who had sustained head and shoulder injuries, were taken into custody. Less than two months later, after brief trials, they were hanged.

Under the best of circumstances, there was only so much that John Brown could have expected from the enslaved people in the surroundings of Harpers Ferry. The white population there outnumbered the Black by four to one, and the enslaved generally lived on farms, rather than plantations, with at most only a few peers. Communications among them would have been difficult, and the task of organizing a militarily formidable number nearly impossible. Although some of the enslaved and free Black people eagerly took up the arms provided them by Brown and fought tenaciously, most others either stayed put or fled back to the relative safety of their cabins. Had Brown and his men managed to collect weapons and escape into the mountains, they might have served as a beacon for fugitives and been able to stage attacks on slaveholdings in adjacent valleys. As it was, Brown chose to hole up in the armory and the battle ended quickly.

If anything, in the months before Brown's raid, the free Black and enslaved people who heard of the project likely puzzled over its character and prospects for success. Brown's was not a familiar name among them. He was not the leader of a political party or visible to them in the antislavery cause. Enslavers and their political representatives probably didn't mention him, nor was the fall of 1859 a season of electioneering when tensions over slavery's future would daily be in evidence. Many of the African Americans, enslaved and free, may have found the plan wanting or destined for disaster. Others may have decided to wait and see how events unfolded before they decided to act. None would have been surprised by the brutal suppression of the raid, the public executions of the captured participants, or the role of the federal government in defending the interests of slaveholders. Although they recognized that the raid testified to the growth of antislavery sentiment and sensed the panic among their enslavers in its aftermath, they would require a more politically powerful confluence of events before seizing the time.

13.4   Battling to Control the Federal Government

||| Contrast the efforts of slaveholders and antislavery forces to win control of the federal government as the conflict over enslavement intensified.

When John Brown went to the gallows on December 2, 1859, he predicted that "the crimes of this *guilty land: will* never be purged *away*; but with Blood," and it was easy to imagine that his failed raid was either the opening salvo of a wider and more deadly conflagration or the next occasion for the shedding of blood after Kansas, in which Brown also played a part. Yet the immediate danger to the Union came less from abolitionist-inspired slave insurrection or the general militarization of the slavery question than from a new struggle at the heart of the system of American politics, a struggle that weaponized formal electoral politics.

The Sectionalization of Parties

Into the early 1850s, the political system of the United States was dominated by two parties—the Whigs and the Democrats—with very different outlooks and policies but also with constituencies in every part of the country. As we have seen, the Whigs were more favorably disposed to the exercise of federal power in pursuit of economic development, though they won support from some planters and commercial interests in the slave states. The Democrats stood for the supremacy of state and local authority and were especially organized among southern enslavers, but they also attracted support from farmers and urban workers in the northern and midwestern states.

By the late 1850s, however, a very different sort of contest was brewing, with potentially devastating consequences for the future of the Union. On the one hand, the collapse of the Whigs and the rise of the Republicans elevated a party organized almost entirely in the nonslaveholding states that was intent upon destroying the "Slave Power" and advancing the interests of social groups in America least dependent on the slave plantation system. On the other hand, the Democrats, still organized throughout the country, were increasingly divided by the implications of popular sovereignty. The Taney Court held in the 1857 *Dred Scott* case that the Constitution protected the rights of slaveholders in the federal territories, whether or not settlers in them approved. Stephen Douglas, for his part, tried to save popular sovereignty by suggesting that enslavement could be kept out of a territory if the settlers' representatives refused, through "unfriendly legislation," to enact a slave code and thus placed slaveholding at risk.

Needless to say, slaveholding Democrats were not amused by Douglas's gambit and began to contemplate remedies that required—ironically for devotees of state rights—a firm hold on federal power. In the view of Mississippi's Democratic Senator Jefferson Davis, it was "the duty of the Federal Government to afford needful protection" to slavery if a territorial government did not. This meant that the federal government would have to craft a slave code to cover all the territories under its jurisdiction. Thus, as the election of 1860 approached, the battle for control of the central government was reaching a new and unprecedented intensity, with alarming prospects for the winners and losers alike.

Four Candidates for the Presidency

Had incumbent President James Buchanan decided to seek a second term, a crisis in the Democratic Party may have been averted. Buchanan, from Pennsylvania, was popular among Democrats in the South and the North, and he had voiced his support for the *Dred Scott* decision. But Buchanan chose not to run and thereby made the party find another candidate. Ordinarily, Stephen Douglas would have been the logical pick. He had eyed the presidency for a long time, had cultivated a following in both the slave and free states, and was one of the leading advocates of American imperial expansion into the Caribbean and beyond. But Douglas's defense of popular sovereignty alienated many southern Democrats and encouraged them to look elsewhere. When the party met to nominate a standard-bearer in April 1860, the southerners wanted to reject Douglas and force the Democrats to demand a federal slave code in their platform. They quickly failed and just as quickly walked out, determined to run their own candidate and craft their own platform. The result was two Democratic tickets: one headed by Douglas and asking the Supreme Court to rule once again on the slavery question and one headed by the sitting vice president, John C. Breckinridge of Kentucky, and backing a federal slave code.

The challenge for the Republicans was finding a presidential candidate who satisfied the delegates on the slavery question but could also win the election. The front runners were Senator William Seward of New York and Governor Salmon P. Chase of Ohio, longtime devotees of antislavery politics who nonetheless were likely to have trouble prevailing in the states of Pennsylvania and the lower Midwest, which the Democrats had won in 1856. Edward Bates of Missouri, a former Whig leader who briefly joined the Know-Nothing Party before turning to the Republicans, was more appealing to conservative and nativist Republicans but put off many of the party faithful. Thus, the door opened for what one Republican described as "the second choice of everybody," Abraham Lincoln of Illinois. Lincoln had stepped into the national spotlight during his debates with Stephen Douglas and saw to it that he never stepped out. He won the nomination on the convention's third ballot and would run on a platform that denounced the *Dred Scott* decision and demanded that enslavement be kept out of the western territories (Republicans called it the "non-extension of slavery").

Finally, and almost desperately, former Whigs from the border states stretching from Virginia through Kentucky, tried to throw a "hail Mary" pass to save the Union. They formed the **Constitutional Union Party**, recognized "no principle other than the Constitution," and nominated former Whig and Tennessee enslaver John Bell as their presidential candidate. Not since 1824 had there been four different candidates for the presidency, and that election (discussed in Chapter 9) had to be decided, as the Constitution stipulates when no one wins a majority of the electoral votes, in the House of Representatives.

The Election of 1860

The election that followed was easily the most unusual and consequential the country had ever witnessed. The Republicans had strong organizations in the nonslaveholding states but little more than outposts in the border states of Kentucky, Missouri, Maryland, and Delaware. Further South, Lincoln wasn't even on the ballot. The Breckinridge Democrats had some clout in Connecticut and Pennsylvania (owing to connections with Buchanan) and especially in Oregon and California, where Democrats who sympathized with the South could be found in large numbers and Breckinridge's vice presidential partner, Joseph Lane, resided (in Oregon). Douglas campaigned tirelessly across much of the country and gained some traction in the slaveholding states of Kentucky, Missouri, Louisiana, Arkansas, and Georgia—almost all in the Mississippi Valley. But his bases of support were definitely in the nonslaveholding states, especially those outside New England. As for the Constitutional Unionists, their strength was in the slaveholding states of the border.

In some respects, it seemed to be two elections rather than one: Lincoln against Douglas in the free states (where they won over 90 percent of the votes), and Breckinridge against Bell in the slave states (where they won well over 80 percent of the votes). But, in truth, the Republicans and the Breckinridge Democrats best succeeded in mobilizing the electorate around the slavery question and the American future: only they managed to win half of the votes in any of the states, and they were the clear front runners when the electoral votes were counted.

Had Lincoln faced a united Democratic Party, perhaps a different result would have unfolded. At the very least, he would have lost California and Oregon, where he squeaked out pluralities. Yet he duplicated Frémont's successes of 1856 in New England, New York, and the upper Midwest, and, as the party had hoped, managed to peel off enough voters to win small majorities in Indiana and Illinois (51 percent each) and a larger one in Pennsylvania (56 percent). The American political calculus had turned in his favor. Although he received just under 40 percent of the total popular vote, Lincoln won a decisive majority (59 percent) of the electoral vote and hence the presidency of the United States—no need for deliberation in the Congress. Coupled with sweeps of most state legislatures and governorships in the nonslaveholding states and more seats in the US House of Representatives, the Republicans were poised to claim the reins of federal power. No one charged that the election was "rigged" or attempted to intervene in the peaceful transfer of presidential power. Everyone acknowledged who won; the angry enslavers prepared not a coup but a secessionist rebellion (see Map 13.2).

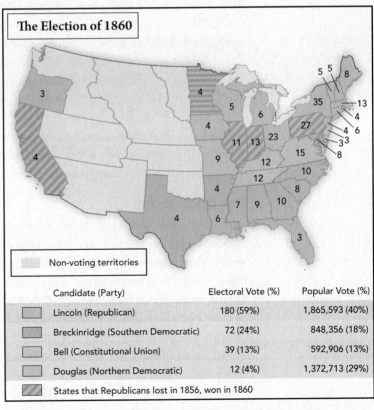

The Election of 1860

Candidate (Party)	Electoral Vote (%)	Popular Vote (%)
Lincoln (Republican)	180 (59%)	1,865,593 (40%)
Breckinridge (Southern Democratic)	72 (24%)	848,356 (18%)
Bell (Constitutional Union)	39 (13%)	592,906 (13%)
Douglas (Northern Democratic)	12 (4%)	1,372,713 (29%)
States that Republicans lost in 1856, won in 1860		

Non-voting territories

≡ **MAP 13.2 The Election of 1860** By 1860, a united North could elect Lincoln without any southern support. In response, enslavers prepared a rebellion.

13.5   The Enslavers Rebel

‖‖‖ Explain why Lincoln's election led to the secession of the states of the Deep South.

From its very founding, the United States witnessed a variety of forms of secessionism, or disunionist sentiment. It flared most prominently in the backcountries of the original states (expressed in Anti-Federalism), in New England during the War of 1812, and in the lower Mississippi Valley of the early republic (see Chapters 7 and 8). Some abolitionists themselves, who viewed the Constitution as a compact with enslavement, believed political withdrawal from the Union an appropriate goal, and the conquest of the Mexican Cession brought with it a host of challengers from the Mormons in Deseret to Bear-Flaggers and Mexican sympathizers in California (see Chapters 11 and 12).

White southerners who adopted secessionism at some point before the election of 1860 thereby took their place alongside what were (and would continue to be) formidable opponents of state centralization. They often compared themselves to the revolutionaries of the American independence movement. They had made concerted efforts to convince other white southerners, especially in the slaveholding leadership, of the dangers that inaction or compromise posed, and they helped orchestrate circumstances that increased the probability of the very political outcome they were warning against: the Republican assumption of federal power. As the election of 1860 neared, more and more of them publicly stated that a Lincoln victory would require disunion, and when the day of reckoning arrived, they were well placed to carry out their plans.

The Deep South

All along, the secessionist impulse was strongest in the states of the Deep South, from South Carolina out west to Texas. There, most enslaved persons lived on plantations, most of the country's cotton was grown, and most of the richest slaveholders resided. There, too, the dynamic of political and economic life, as well as visions of the future, turned not toward the North but toward the Caribbean, Mexico, and the new southwest. With some exception, the Deep South was home to the Fire-eaters and to the newspapers and journals that regularly lobbied for secession, such as *De Bow's Review* (which opens Chapter 12). The movement had a substantial popular base together with political support to move it ahead. The only question was how best to proceed.

Secessionists had done so good a job over the years that the main issue on the political table in the Deep South was not whether to secede, but whether individual states should go it alone as an expression of their sovereignty or wait to do so collectively. Supporters of the former were known as **immediate secessionists** and those of the latter as **cooperationists**. The immediate secessionists were the more energized element of the slaveholding leadership, and they worked hard to keep their momentum going. "I do not believe that the common people understand it," one supporter said of secession, "but whoever waited for the common people when a great movement was to be made?"

As many expected, South Carolina seized the moment, quickly holding a secession convention and enacting an ordinance (a declaration or decree) of secession on December 20, 1860. By that time, six other states of the Deep South had set the wheels of secessionism in motion, calling for their own conventions, but South Carolina's boldness surely gave them a jolt. They seem to have needed it. Although immediate secessionists appeared focused and cooperationists in disarray, the resistance to immediate secession was not insignificant. In Mississippi, Florida, and Alabama, cooperationists won the support of between 35 and 45 percent of the vote in elections for convention delegates, and in Georgia and Louisiana they won nearly 50 percent. Out in Texas, the cooperationists had the support of Governor Sam Houston, of Texas Revolution fame (discussed in Chapter 11), and nearly prevented the holding of a secession convention entirely.

Even so, immediate secessionists claimed the majority of delegates at the conventions, and one by one the other Deep South states followed South Carolina out of the Union. It was a stunning victory, waged with patience and firmness by radical enslavers and those who spoke for them. They had organized a rebellion against the authority of the new Republican administration and thus against the federal government of the United States more generally, convincing enough of the doubters and enough of the nonslaveholders to accept the outcome. All that the cooperationists could salvage was an agreement to meet with the immediate secessionists in Montgomery, Alabama, in February 1861, to establish a union among themselves (see Map 13.3).

Forming the Confederacy

Representatives from the seven seceded states met and moved quickly to establish what they called in their founding document a "permanent federal government." They had, of course, a document and structure of governance with which to work—the Constitution of the United States—that their forebears had played a leading role in constructing. Much has been made of the similarities between the two, in language and logic. But, in truth, the Montgomery convention marked the beginning of a very different journey. Unlike the US Constitution, this new one, bringing into being what the drafters called the **Confederate States of America**, expressed the wills, not of "the people," but of the individual states in

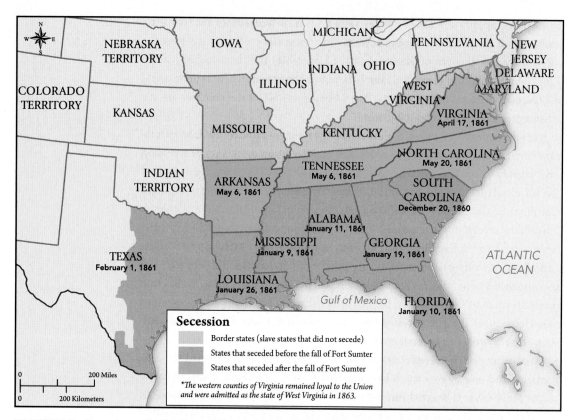

≡ **MAP 13.3   Secession**   The South seceded from the Union between December 1860 and May 1861. The lower South seceded first. The Upper South—Virginia, Tennessee, North Carolina, and Arkansas—seceded next. The border slave states of Kentucky, Missouri, Maryland, and Delaware never left the Union.

their "sovereign and independent character." Even more arrestingly, they clearly and boldly inscribed the words "slavery" and "slaves" into the heart of the text (discarding the euphemisms in the US Constitution), reserved to their new "federal government" the right to determine the qualifications of eligible voters, and required any new state or territory wishing to join their Confederacy—they had their own imperial aspirations—to make slaveholding legal and allow slaveholders and their human property to pass through them. These were powers well beyond anything the US Constitution granted to its federal government, which made plain whose interests were front and center. The representatives in Montgomery, that is, created a government of the enslavers, by the enslavers, and for the enslavers with *no explicit right of secession from it.*

Unlike the US Constitution, too, the framers of the Confederacy made no provision to submit their constitution for popular approval, and, given the heat of the moment, they decided to continue sitting as a "provisional" congress until elections could be held in November. They also chose a president and vice president for their new central government who would, as well, stand for election in the late fall: for president, Jefferson Davis of Mississippi, and for vice president, Alexander Stephens of Georgia. Both had formidable political and, in the case of Davis, military careers, though they were studies in contrast with little chemistry between them. Davis had been an immediate secessionist and was a wealthy planter and enslaver in the lower Mississippi Valley; Stephens was a lawyer and enslaver in Georgia who opposed immediate secession. What they shared was an abiding belief that slavery was the "cornerstone" of their rebellion.

13.6   Showdown

Summarize how the Lincoln administration and Confederate rebels ended up at war with each other.

Although secessionist leaders in the Deep South acted quickly and resolutely, with secession ordinances passed in each of their states within the span of three months, they trained nervous eyes on the slaveholding states to their north, what is generally known as the Upper South. Fire-eaters could be found there but only as a distinct minority, and while the states of the Deep South embraced secession, those of the Upper South balked. In one state after another the movement for secession was defeated: either by rejecting secession at state conventions (Virginia and Arkansas), rejecting calls for a secession convention (Tennessee and North Carolina), or refusing even to begin a deliberative process (Delaware, Missouri, and Kentucky). It was not because enslavers in the Upper South lacked political power or commitment to the institution of slavery; it was because the character of their societies and their geographical locations gave them a perspective on secession and the unfolding crisis that differed in important ways from their counterparts in the Deep South, even after the Confederacy was established.

Hesitation and Efforts at Compromise

What was different about the system of enslavement in the Upper South? Crucially, enslavement there was organized on a smaller scale than in the Deep South (more farms and fewer plantations), was much less oriented to staple crops like cotton, and was more given over to seasonal labor demands and the hiring out of enslaved people. For the most part, the Black population in the Upper South was smaller (though in absolute numbers Virginia always had more enslaved people than any other state) and the nonslaveholding white population larger. And unlike Deep South slaveholders who looked to the South and West, those in the Upper South looked North and East, with stronger economic and cultural ties to the lower Midwest and Middle Atlantic. In the election of 1860, John Bell and the Constitutional Union Party won most of their votes in these states, and ballots were also cast for the Republican Lincoln. Even with Lincoln's victory—the trigger for Deep South secession—hesitation over disunion widely prevailed.

In part, hesitation in the Upper South reflected efforts at compromise and reconciliation that President James Buchanan and Congress had advanced hastily. In his last message before Congress in December 1860, Buchanan proposed a constitutional convention to address the issues breaking the Union apart, and in one form or another, the passage of constitutional amendments was the instrument of choice for those seeking to pull back from the precipice of secessionism. Kentucky's Senator John J. Crittenden, Henry Clay's successor, offered a slew of amendments and resolutions, all designed to protect enslavement and enable its expansion into at least some portion of the trans-Mississippi West. The centerpiece of Crittenden's plan was extending the old Missouri Compromise line (latitude 36°30′) all the way to the Pacific, permitting enslavement to the south of it and prohibiting it to the north.

For all this maneuvering, there was not much in the so-called Crittenden Compromise for those in the antislavery movement who had spent years mobilizing to defeat the "Slave Power." Even as president-elect, Abraham Lincoln had no intention of cutting the heart out of Republicanism to appease the slaveholders. Crittenden's proposals, Lincoln insisted, "would lose us everything we have gained by the election and put us again on the high road to slave empire. If we surrender, it will be the end of us." To be sure, Lincoln conceded that slavery in the states remained constitutionally beyond the reach of the federal government, and he was open to endorsing a constitutional amendment, passed by the Congress in February, that would have prohibited the federal government from abolishing or interfering with slavery there (it would have been the Thirteenth Amendment if ratified; it wasn't). But "on the territorial question," he was "inflexible." "The tug has to come," Lincoln recognized, "and better now than any time hereafter."

From Lincoln's perspective, secession was politically impossible. The Union, he insisted, was created by "the people" and was therefore "perpetual" or indestructible. "No government proper," Lincoln observed in his inaugural address on March 4, 1861, "ever had a provision in its organic law for its own termination, [and] no State . . . can lawfully get out of the Union." This meant that secessionists could not be enacting the sovereign rights of states, as they claimed; they were, instead, engaging in rebellion against the United States. As Lincoln saw it, "the central idea of secession is the essence of anarchy" and a mockery of the "majority principle." The organization of the Confederacy was not an act of state-building. It was an act of treason.

Who Blinks?

Even so, there was good reason for Lincoln to act with restraint. More slave states initially rejected secession than embraced it (8 to 7), and if the fists of federal coercion were unleashed on the rebellious states, the other eight might reconsider and join the Confederacy. Lincoln hoped profoundly that unionist sentiment remained close to the surface of public opinion, even in the Deep South, and, given time and calm, might well reassert itself. The key was to avoid conflict or provocations. But this was easier said than done, especially since the states of the new Confederacy took control of US property—arsenals, customs houses, forts— within their presumed borders. Although Lincoln promised to hold this property and enforce "the laws of the Union," for the time being discretion seemed to be the better part of valor, and he seemed comfortable holding back.

Fort Sumter was another matter. Newly constructed and still unfinished, Sumter sat in the middle of South Carolina's Charleston Harbor with a small federal force inside. The good news was that the fort was very difficult to attack and occupy; Confederates could not take it as easily as they could other federal property within their domain. The bad news was that Sumter was also difficult to maintain, and as supplies began to dwindle, the Lincoln administration would either have to send ships to provision the fort or, as the Confederates demanded, pick up and evacuate.

This was the crisis and decision Lincoln faced as soon as he took the reins of the presidency. As we saw at the start of this chapter, advice was coming from all sides, and most of it from inside his administration urged him to retreat. But outside the administration a different political dynamic was already in play. Rumors of a possible surrender of Fort Sumter provoked outcries in the Northeast and Midwest, not only among Republicans but also among some loyalist Democrats. They seemed to recognize that whatever their specific perspectives on the future of slavery, the fate of the Union was now at stake. "If Fort Sumter is evacuated, the new administration is done forever," one correspondent predicted, while the influential journalist and advisor Francis Blair warned Lincoln that giving up the fort would be "virtually a surrender of the Union" and might itself constitute a treasonable offense.

By the end of March, Lincoln decided to act. The ground was shifting in his cabinet, and although his Secretary of State William Seward, in a last-ditch attempt at delay, urged Lincoln to start a war with Spain or France, in hope of unifying all Americans, North and South, against a foreign foe, Lincoln rejected Seward's proposal. Instead, he chose to risk hostilities with the rebellious Confederates and send the troops in Sumter the supplies they desperately needed. Cleverly shipping only food and clothing, he ordered an expedition to proceed to Sumter and, on the same day, notified the governor of South Carolina of his peaceful intentions. Lincoln had no way of knowing how his efforts to provide "food for hungry men" would be greeted in the North or the Upper South, but by his action he put the ball in the court of the Confederacy.

Jefferson Davis and his newly assembled cabinet were in much the same position as Lincoln and his. Neither wanted to be seen as the aggressor, while both eyed the border states between them with great anticipation. Those states were now the political battleground, either isolating or strengthening the slaveholders' rebellion. And like Lincoln's, the Davis administration came under growing pressure to take action appropriate to its apparent status as an independent republic. Thus, when he learned about Lincoln's move to provision Fort Sumter, Davis convened his cabinet on April 9 and ordered his commander in Charleston, General P. G. T. Beauregard, to "reduce" (that is, destroy) the fort before the provisioning expedition arrived. Beauregard then demanded that the troops under the command of Kentuckian Major Robert Anderson surrender, and when Anderson refused, he opened fire in the early morning hours of April 12. Nearly a day and a half later, with the fort ablaze and all his troops exhausted but alive, Anderson gave up Fort Sumter. The last great symbol of United States authority in their midst had now fallen to the Confederates.

Lincoln responded immediately. Invoking the obstruction of the laws of the United States in the Deep South states "by combinations too powerful to be suppressed by the ordinary course of judicial proceedings, or by the power vested in the Marshals," he called upon "the militia of the several states of the Union" (including those in the Upper South) to provide 75,000 men

The Fall of Fort Sumter "South Carolina is Independent!" blares a Charleston newspaper on April 13, 1861. The American Union, which had been forged less than eighty years before, seemed to have entered its death throes.

for ninety days service. They were to march into the South and put down the rebellion. It made sense for a Republican like Lincoln to do this. After all, the United States was a sprawling Union that covered an entire continent still not well knit together. And from California to the Atlantic Coast, especially in New York and the textile towns of New England, which depended on southern-grown cotton, there were political forces, chiefly within the Democratic Party, who sympathized with the slaveholders and resisted a more centralized federal government. Had Lincoln hesitated once shots were fired, the American Union could have begun a process of disintegrating, not just between North and South but in several pieces from West to East.

But for the states of the Upper South, Lincoln had gone much too far. Not one of these slaveholding states agreed to send troops, and most replied to Lincoln with contempt. Kentucky's governor seemed to express the ire of the others. He refused to "furnish a single man for the wicked purpose of subduing her sister Southern States." Worse still for Lincoln, four of these states quickly revisited the question of secession and now decided to support it. By early June 1861, North Carolina, Arkansas, Tennessee, and Virginia had severed their connection with the United States and joined the nascent Confederacy. The American Union, which had been forged less than eighty years before and spread its empire across the continent by military and diplomatic means, seemed to have entered its death throes with few prospects of rehabilitation.

Conclusion: A House Divided

The United States was not a unified republic to begin with. A substantial portion of the colonial population sided with the British during the Revolution and, after independence, divided over the type of government that should be created. A great many either rejected the Constitution when it was up for ratification or called for significant changes. From there, the forces of decentralization were powerful, fortified by enslavers who regarded themselves as sovereign actors and the federal government as a potential threat. But the commitment to maintaining the Union remained strong, especially among those of the revolutionary generation who had brought it into being. Many of them shared an imperial perspective about American destiny: that the United States would be a continental, "ocean bound" republic, stretching from the Atlantic to the Pacific, conquered if necessary, and that the fruits of this empire would be the glue to hold the expanding country together.

Yet the pursuit of empire always posed challenges of organization and governance, and, if anything, it intensified rather than resolved the struggle over slavery.

By the 1850s, a new generation of political leaders, all too young to have played a role in the country's founding, had come to the fore with dueling perspectives. On the one side were those who regarded the slave system as the essential basis of social and political order, without which all was chaos. On the other side were those who regarded enslavement as a cancer on the body politic, whose growth ate at the vitals of the republic. Even the embrace of white supremacy on both sides was insufficient to mend the rift. By 1861 it seemed that the American political system lacked the capacity to enact another of the compromises that had previously allowed the country to push on.

WHAT IF Lincoln Hadn't Won in 1860 or, as President, Had Hesitated on Fort Sumter?

We usually tell the story of the coming of secession and the outbreak of the Civil War as if all the forces pointed in those directions and that by the mid- to late 1850s they proved unstoppable. But for all the drama of these events, there were a number of alternative possibilities up to the very end. Two are particularly worthy of considering, and one involves the sitting President James Buchanan. A Democrat from the state of Pennsylvania, Buchanan was highly regarded among Democratic enslavers because he supported the *Dred Scott* decision and was sensitive to their interests. He could have run for a second term (as most American presidents had chosen to do up to that time), helped craft a platform that was acceptable to all sides, and run a far more formidable campaign than the divided efforts of Douglas and Breckinridge in the general election. It is true, of course, that while Lincoln won only a plurality of the popular vote, he did win a majority of the electoral votes, and only in California and Oregon would a unified Democratic ticket have shifted their electoral votes from the Republican to the Democratic column: not enough to have changed the outcome. Yet a Buchanan candidacy would surely have changed the dynamic of the election and possibly turned a state in the lower Midwest—say Illinois or Indiana—where Lincoln won very slim majorities to the Democrats. Had Lincoln not won the election of 1860 or had the electoral vote been remarkably close, the radical secessionists may have been stopped on the road to disunion.

A second, more likely, alternative involves decision-making over Fort Sumter. Lincoln clearly wavered, and, at one point, Secretary of State William Seward was so confident that Lincoln would choose to abandon the fort that he leaked word to Confederates of this likely decision. There was some reason for Seward's confidence. Other federal forts in territory claimed by the Confederates had already been abandoned, and Lincoln wished to avoid an escalation of the conflict in hopes that, given time, the secessionists would be overthrown by those who still wanted to preserve the Union.

Had Lincoln been persuaded by his Secretary of State to avoid a showdown over Fort Sumter, it is conceivable that the Upper South would have remained in the Union for the time being and the winds of secessionism would have abated. But it is equally likely that Lincoln's caution would have raised questions about his and the Republican Party's ability to rule the country—Lincoln was a relatively unknown and untested politician, and his was a new, sectional party—and perhaps he would have given the green light to separatist forces in many places outside the Deep South, particularly on the West Coast, where a substantial number of southern sympathizers could be found. Rather than splitting in two, the United States might then have unraveled from many directions and left the North American continent awash in potentially rivalrous states and confederacies. Could our history have been any more different?

DOCUMENT 13.1: Seward's Advice to Lincoln on Fort Sumter

President Lincoln called a cabinet meeting for March 15, 1861, and asked each of the members for their advice about the situation in Charleston Harbor. This is the reply of Secretary of State William Seward.

DEPARTMENT OF STATE, WASHINGTON, 15th March, 1861.

The President submits to me the following question—namely: "Assuming it to be possible to now provision Fort Sumter, under all the circumstances is it wise to attempt it?"

If it were possible to peacefully provision Fort Sumter, of course I should answer that it would be both unwise and inhuman not to attempt it. But the facts of the case are known to be that the attempt must be made with the employment of military and marine force, which would provoke combat, and probably initiate a civil war, which the government of the United States would be committed to maintain through all changes to some definite conclusion.

Next to disunion itself, I regard civil war as the most disastrous and deplorable of national calamities, and as the most uncertain and fearful of all remedies for political disorders. I have, therefore, made it the study and labor of the hour, how to save the Union from dismemberment by peaceful policy and without civil war.

Influenced by these sentiments, I have felt that it is exceedingly fortunate that, to a great extent, the Federal Government occupies, thus far, not an aggressive attitude, but practically a defensive one, while the necessity for action, if civil war is to be initiated, falls on those who seek to dismember and subvert this Union.

I have believed firmly that everywhere, even in South Carolina, devotion to the Union is a profound and permanent national sentiment, which, although it may be suppressed and silenced by terror for a time, could, if encouraged, be ultimately relied upon to rally the people of the seceding States to reverse, upon due deliberation, all the popular acts of [*legislatures and conventions by which they were hastily and violently committed to*] disunion. The policy of the time, therefore, has seemed to me to consist in conciliation, which should deny to disunionists any new provocation or apparent offense, while it would enable the unionists in the slave States to maintain, with truth and with effect, that the claims and apprehensions put forth by the disunionists are groundless and false.

I may be asked whether I would in no case, and at no time, advise force—whether I propose to give up everything? I reply, no. I would not initiate war to regain a useless and unnecessary position on the soil of the seceding States. I would not provoke war in any way now. I would resort to force to protect the collection of the revenue, because this is a necessary as well as a legitimate minor object. Even then it should be only a naval force that I would employ for that necessary purpose, while I would defer military action on land until a case should arise when we would hold the defense. In that case we should have the spirit of the country and the approval of mankind on our side. In the other, we should imperil peace and union, because we had not the courage to practise prudence and moderation at the cost of temporary misapprehension.

WILLIAM H. SEWARD

Source: William Seward to Abraham Lincoln, in Nocolay and Hay, eds., *Lincoln Works*, Vol. 6, 192–201.

DOCUMENT 13.2:   Montgomery Blair's Advice to Lincoln on Fort Sumter

Montgomery Blair had been appointed Postmaster General. This is his reply to Lincoln's call for advice from members of the Cabinet on March 15.

Post Office Department

The ambitious leaders of the late Democratic Party have availed themselves of the disappointment attendant upon defeat in the late presidential election to found a military government in the seceding States. To the connivance of the late administration it is due alone that this rebellion has been enabled to attain its present proportions. It has grown by this complicity into the form of an organized government in seven States, and up to this moment nothing has been done to check its progress or prevent its being regarded either at home or abroad as a successful revolution. Every hour of acquiescence in this condition of things, and especially every new conquest made by the rebels, strengthens their hands at home and their claims to recognition as an independent people abroad. It has been from the beginning, and still is, treated practically as a lawful proceeding, and the honest and Union loving people in those States must by a continuance of this policy become reconciled to the new government, and, though founded in wrong, come to regard it as a rightful government.

I, in common with all my associates in your council, agree that we must look to the people in these States for the overthrow of this rebellion, and that it is proper to exercise the powers of the Federal Government only so far as to maintain its authority to collect the revenue and maintain possession of the public property in the States, and that this should be done with as little bloodshed as possible. How is this to be carried into effect? That it is by measures that will inspire respect for the power of the government, and the firmness of those who administer it, does not admit of debate.

In 1860 the rebels were encouraged by the contempt they felt for the incumbent of the presidency [James Buchanan].

But it was not alone upon Mr. Buchanan's weakness the rebels relied for success. They for the most part believe that the Northern men are deficient in the courage necessary to maintain the government. It is this prevalent error in the South which induces so large a portion of the people there to suspect the good faith of the people of the North, and enables the demagogues so successfully to inculcate the notion that the object of the Northern people is to abolish slavery, and make the negroes the equals of the whites. Doubting the manhood of Northern men, they discredit their disclaimers of this purpose to humiliate and injure them.

Nothing would so surely gain credit for such disclaimers as the manifestation of resolution on the part of the President to maintain the lawful authority of the nation. No men or people have so many difficulties as those whose firmness is doubted.

The evacuation of Fort Sumter, when it is known that it can be provisioned and manned, will convince the rebels that the administration lacks firmness, and will, therefore, tend more than any event that has happened to embolden them; and so far from tending to prevent collision, will insure it unless all the other forts are evacuated, and all attempts are given up to maintain the authority of the United States.

Mr. Buchanan's policy has, I think, rendered collision almost inevitable, and a continuance of that policy will not only bring it about, but will go far to produce a permanent division of the Union.

This is manifestly the public judgment, which is much more to be relied on than that of any individual. I believe Fort Sumter may be provisioned and relieved by Captain Fox with little risk; and General Scott's opinion, that with its war complement there is no force in South Carolina which can take it, renders it almost certain that it will not then be attempted. This would completely demoralize the rebellion. The impotent rage of the rebels, and the outburst of patriotic feeling which would follow this achievement, would initiate a reactionary movement throughout the South which would speedily overwhelm; the traitors. No expense or care should, therefore, be spared to achieve this success.

MONTGOMERY BLAIR

Source: Montgomery Blair to Lincoln, in Nicolay and Hay, eds., *Lincoln Works*, Vol. 6, 214–217.

Thinking About Contingency

1. Does reconsidering the possible outcomes of the election of 1860 change the way you think about the coming of secession and the Civil War?
2. Do you agree with the author that "the United States might then have unraveled from many directions and left the North American continent awash in potentially rivalrous states and confederacies" if Lincoln had avoided a showdown at Fort Sumter? Do you think Lincoln was aware of these possibilities?

REVIEW QUESTIONS

1. Why was the presidential election of 1860 important, and why were there so many candidates?

2. What policy on enslavement held most Republicans together, and how did Lincoln view it?

3. What was the meaning of Lincoln's "house divided" speech, and how did Stephen Douglas argue against it?

4. What role did enslaved people play in the developing crisis over slavery and the Union?

5. What was the relationship between state rights and secessionism, and where was secessionist sentiment strongest?

6. How did Lincoln understand the secession of the slave states, and how did this understanding shape his response to the crisis when he assumed office?

KEY TERMS

Confederate States of America (p. 549)

Constitutional Union Party (p. 546)

cooperationists (p. 549)

Fire-eaters (p. 536)

Fort Sumter (p. 553)

immediate secessionists (p. 549)

Republicans (p. 527)

secession (p. 536)

Secret Six (p. 542)

sectionalism (p. 534)

state rights (p. 535)

RECOMMENDED READINGS

Shearer Davis Bowman, *At the Precipice: Americans North and South During the Secession Crisis* (University of North Carolina Press, 2010).

William Freehling, *The Road to Disunion: The Secessionists Triumphant, 1854–1861* (Oxford University Press, 2007).

Tony Horwitz, *Midnight Rising: John Brown and the Raid That Sparked the Civil War* (Henry Holt & Co., 2012).

Keri Leigh Merritt, *Masterless Men: Poor Whites and Slavery in the Antebellum South* (Cambridge University Press, 2017).

David Potter, *The Impending Crisis, 1848–1861* (Harper & Row, 1975).

Manisha Sinha, *The Counterrevolution of Slavery* (University of North Carolina Press, 2000).

Kevin Waite, *West of Slavery: The Southern Dream of a Transcontinental Empire* (University of North Carolina Press, 2007).

William Webb, *A History of William Webb, Composed by Himself* (Detroit, 1874).

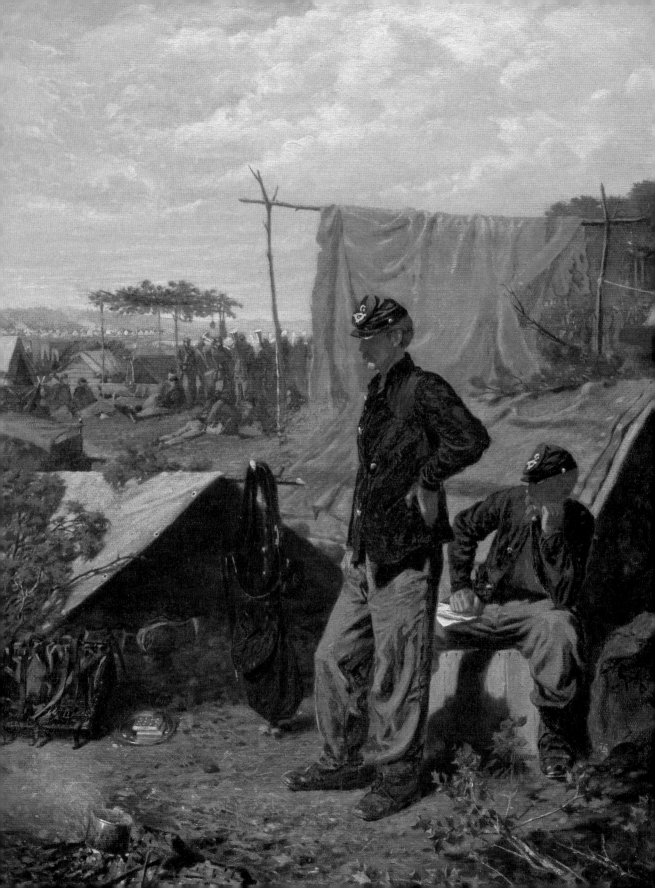

The War of the Rebellion
1861–1863

Chapter Outline

≣ *Home, Sweet Home*   In this 1863 painting by Winslow Homer, two Union infantrymen listen as the regimental band plays "Home, Sweet Home."

Soon after fighting began in the spring of 1861 between the forces of the US federal government and the Confederate rebels, an African American named Harry Jarvis arrived at Fortress Monroe, a US Army encampment at the tip of the Virginia peninsula. Jarvis's journey to the fortress had been a perilous one. Born enslaved in Virginia's Northampton County around 1830, Jarvis had been laboring for an enslaver he described as "the meanest man on all the Eastern shore" of Chesapeake Bay who became even more brutal "after the war come." Living in terror, Jarvis fled into the woods and managed to survive for three weeks thanks to "friends who kept me informed how things were going on and brought me food." Then, having learned that his enslaver was throwing himself a big birthday party and "they'd all be drinking and carousing night and day," Jarvis slipped down to the shore, "got a canoe and sail, and started for Fort Monroe" about "thirty-five miles across the bay."

Timeline

1861 APR	JUL	OCT	1862 JAN	APR	JUL	OCT

1861 >

April Confederates fire on federal Fort Sumter; Lincoln calls for 75,000 troops

July Confederates defeat US Army forces at Bull Run (Manassas)

August Congress passes First Confiscation Act

1862 >

January Confederacy officially incorporates the Arizona Territory

February–March Confederates defeat US forces in New Mexico campaign

April US naval forces take control of New Orleans

May Confederates defeat US Army forces in the Peninsula campaign; Congress passes Homestead Act

June Congress passes Pacific Railway Act

August Confederates defeat US Army forces at the Second Battle of Bull Run; Congress passes Second Confiscation Act; Sioux uprising in Minnesota

September Lincoln issues Preliminary Emancipation Proclamation

Fortress Monroe, although occupied by the US Army, was not a safe place. At the time of Jarvis's arrival, the federal government had no policy about enslavement or enslaved people beyond the Fugitive Slave Law, which required that enslaved runaways be returned to their enslavers. Jarvis took his chances anyhow. He found General Benjamin Butler, the commander of the post, "and asked him to let me enlist." Baffled, Butler refused him, replying that "*it wasn't a black man's war.*" But Jarvis stood his ground. "I told him it *would* be a black man's war before they got through."

Butler didn't force Jarvis out of the fortress or return him to his enslaver, though Butler claimed to be "in the utmost doubt what to do with this species of property." For the time being, he set Jarvis to work on the fortifications, tasks that Jarvis readily performed until one day he saw "a [Black] man given up to his master that come for

1863 JAN	APR	JUL	OCT	1864 JAN	APR	JUL

December Federal government executes thirty-eight Sioux in Minnesota

1863 ›
January Lincoln issues Final Emancipation Proclamation

July Confederate forces defeated at Gettysburg and Vicksburg

November Lincoln delivers Gettysburg Address

him." Concluding that Fortress Monroe "was not the place for me," Jarvis slipped away once more, "hired on a ship going to Cuba and then one a going to Africa." He would be gone for two years until, landing in Boston, Jarvis learned "that it had got to be a black man's war," as he predicted. Days later, Jarvis managed to do what General Butler wouldn't allow. On December 21, 1863, he enlisted in the famed Fifty-fifth Massachusetts Regiment and joined the now-bloody effort to defeat the Confederate rebels.

Jarvis's perspective and experiences exemplify what was more widely true as the American civil warfare erupted. Whatever political leaders on each side might say about saving the Union or defending state rights, enslaved people—the most subordinated social group in the country, having no accepted standing in civil or political life—recognized from the first that what Lincoln termed the "War of the Rebellion" was a life-and-death struggle over the future of enslavement in the United States. And, like Harry Jarvis, they not only understood that this would be a "black man's war" but also determined that they would act. Rarely in all of history has an exploited and repressed people brought their perspectives into reality and utterly transformed the meaning of a great historical event.

14.1   The Balances of Warfare

||| Evaluate the military strengths and weaknesses of the federal government and the Confederate rebels when the Civil War began.

The shelling of Fort Sumter by Confederate rebels and President Lincoln's call for 75,000 troops to put it down suggested that the many violent encounters over enslavement during the 1850s were prologues to a final showdown. Proslavery and antislavery forces in Kansas during the mid-1850s had been ready for such a fight. John Brown and his followers, in their attack on Harpers Ferry, had been ready for such a fight. Confederate forces in Charleston that fired on Fort Sumter seemed to be ready for such a fight. But was the United States as a whole ready to mobilize militarily to suppress the Confederate rebellion? And were the Confederate rebels ready to resist and defend what they claimed was a new country? The answer is a resounding "no." Both sides had a great deal of work to do if they had any hope of succeeding.

Military Strength of the United States

On the face of it, the United States (usually known as the "Union" side) seemed to have significant advantages in a fight against the Confederate rebels. The population of the states that remained loyal was around 22,000,000, or about 70 percent of the population of the United States as a whole, and if we consider only the "military population"—that is, free men between the ages of eighteen and forty-five—the United States boasted 80 percent. Owing to the market expansions and early industrialization during the first six decades of the nineteenth century, the United States could also claim about three-quarters of the manufacturing capacity generally and even more in textiles, iron, and armaments, all of which would be crucial for clothing and arming their troops. Between the 1820s and the late 1850s, the country experienced a remarkable railroad boom, but two-thirds of the track mileage laid ran through the states that still aligned with the federal government. The US treasury and most of the banks, moreover, remained in the loyal states, as did about three-quarters of all the country's wealth (see Figure 14.1).

Numbers such as these would appear to be daunting, but numbers don't necessarily translate into troops on the ground, ships on the rivers and seas, and commanders devising strategies and tactics. From the founding of the republic, most Americans opposed a large standing army, for them a symbol of centralized power and authority most readily associated with European monarchies. As a result, when Confederates fired on Fort Sumter, the army of the United States had only about 16,000 men, most of whom were scattered on small posts in the trans-Mississippi West, defending boundaries and settlers from Indian attacks. They included ten infantry regiments (about 1,000 men each), four artillery regiments, and five cavalry regiments—not exactly formidable. Much of the elite officer corps had been in military service since the War of 1812, and the army's current general-in-chief, Winfield Scott, was seventy-four years old and in poor health, not to mention inclined toward appeasement, as we saw at the start of Chapter 13 in his recommendations to Lincoln on the Fort Sumter crisis. For its part, the US Navy was very small, its ships mostly in foreign waters, with only three available for immediate service.

By and large, the military arms of the United States were to be found in the militias of individual states, many of which were poorly organized and supplied, infrequently drilled, and sometimes under the authority of state governors who may not have shared Lincoln's determination to act forcibly against other Americans, even if they were enslavers. Indeed, for a time after Lincoln issued his order for 75,000 troops for ninety days' service (optimistically), few showed up and he had to wonder whether he would be able to suppress the rebellion at all.

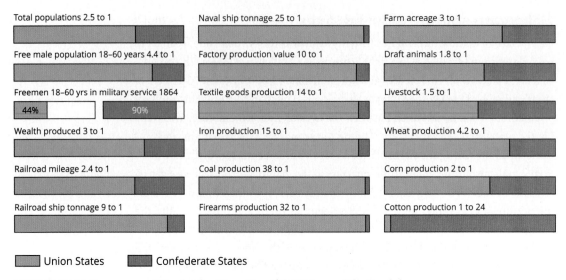

Total populations 2.5 to 1

Free male population 18–60 years 4.4 to 1

Freemen 18–60 yrs in military service 1864
44%   90%

Wealth produced 3 to 1

Railroad mileage 2.4 to 1

Railroad ship tonnage 9 to 1

Naval ship tonnage 25 to 1

Factory production value 10 to 1

Textile goods production 14 to 1

Iron production 15 to 1

Coal production 38 to 1

Firearms production 32 to 1

Farm acreage 3 to 1

Draft animals 1.8 to 1

Livestock 1.5 to 1

Wheat production 4.2 to 1

Corn production 2 to 1

Cotton production 1 to 24

☐ Union States   ☐ Confederate States

≡ **FIGURE 14.1** Resources and Productive Capacities of the Union and the Confederacy.

Could Confederate Rebels Stand Up?

According to the numbers, Confederate rebels would have been in poor shape. They had neither a standing army nor navy, no treasury or gold supply to support their mobilization for war, relatively few banks to issue currency or sources of credit not dependent on banking houses in the Northeast, and very little manufacturing that would be of use in wartime. Textile and clothing production was concentrated along the East Coast from Massachusetts and New Hampshire to Pennsylvania. Coal mines were to be found chiefly in Pennsylvania. And iron manufacturing mostly took place in the Middle Atlantic and Midwest. As for potential manpower, the rebel states not only had a relatively small military population but also had a large and potentially dangerous enslaved population to police. Seemingly, the Confederates had a mountain to climb if they wished to avoid quick defeat.

Strategically, however, the balances were more complex and, in some cases, favored the Confederate rebels. Because whatever its advantages, the United States also had the more formidable goal to accomplish. It had to invade rebel territory, crush the rebellion, compel the rebels to surrender, and then dismantle rebel forces. This would not be easy to do. The Confederate states encompassed about 750,000 square miles of territory, some of which would be very difficult to penetrate, as John Brown himself understood when he planned his assault against slavery. What's more, the Confederates did not have to conquer the United States: their goal was to establish their independence and win recognition as a country. To that end, they only had to fight a defensive war, fending off the federal invasion, protecting their families and homes, and inflicting enough damage to force the US Army and the Republican-controlled federal government to give up the fight.

Further advantages for the Confederate rebels could come from the international and trans-Atlantic arena. The United States counted on its wealth and standing as well as political power to discourage unwanted foreign interference. But the Confederates believed they had a special card to play: the cotton crop. By the time of the war's outbreak, the states of the Deep South—now under the control of the Confederate rebels—had been the major suppliers of cotton on the international market, a crucial raw material for the textile industries in Britain and France (as well as in the United States) and a massive source of wealth for the United States as a whole. With thousands of men, women, and children laboring in their textile factories, could Britain and France afford to ignore Confederate demands for political recognition and the military equipment it would bring them? What neither side counted on or even considered was the role that enslaved people like Harry Jarvis would play in defining the meaning and outcome of the struggle (see Map 14.1).

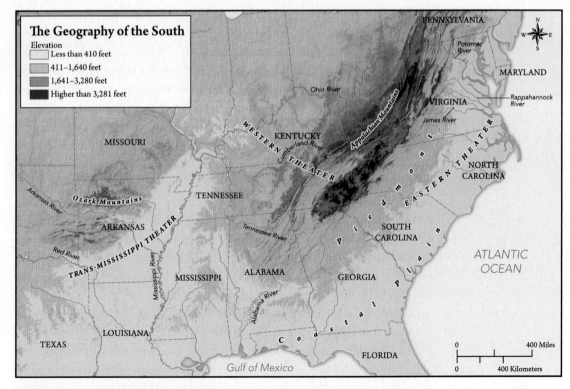

≡ **MAP 14.1   The Physical Geography of the South**   Geography played a crucial role in shaping the war, with the Confederacy enjoying an advantage. Its sheer size—larger than continental Europe—ensured that the war would be fought in distinct theaters.

14.2   Confederates Look West

||| Assess Confederate interests in the territories of the trans-Mississippi West and northern Mexico.

Most treatments of America's Civil War begin with the Eastern Theater, especially the state of Virginia and its environs. That was where United States and Confederate troops were massed, where the capitals of the United States (Washington, DC, just across the Potomac) and the Confederacy (Richmond) were located, and where some of the early consequential battles occurred. That was where the eyes of the country and the Euro-Atlantic world were focused. But the reach of warfare and wartime politics was vast, encompassing much of the trans-Mississippi West as well as the East. And for that, the Confederate rebels played a large part.

The Lure of the West

There was good reason for the Confederate rebels to look West as well as North and East. The political battles that resulted in secession and the formation of the Confederacy had, after all, been over the future of the sprawling trans-Mississippi West, and the Confederate constitution made explicit provision for the incorporation of new territories and states, as long as enslavement was legal and the rights of enslavers respected. Although most of the trans-Mississippi West still belonged to the United States, the Lincoln administration could not assume that its inhabitants would remain loyal. California and Oregon veered strongly Democratic in politics (Lincoln won a plurality of the popular vote in 1860 but, combined, the two Democratic candidates won the majority), had many Confederate sympathizers, and were toying with the idea of forming an independent Pacific Coast republic. Mormon Utah had been in a state of rebellion against the federal government in the late 1850s and now faced a Republican regime that officially regarded polygamy (practiced among Mormons in Utah) along with enslavement as the "twin relics of barbarism." The territory of New Mexico, established on the basis of popular sovereignty, had enacted a slave code in 1859 and had southerners sitting in the governor's chair and on the territorial supreme court.

    Confederate officials first looked to the Indian Territory that bordered Texas, Arkansas, and Kansas, particularly to the "Five Civilized Tribes" (the US term for the Cherokee, Creek, Choctaw, Chickasaw, and Seminole nations) who had been forcibly exiled there in the 1830s. Although southern white men had exerted much of the military and political pressure that resulted in the expulsion of most Indigenous people from the country's southeast, some of the powerful tribal members shared an interest in Black slaveholding with the Confederates. They were also embittered by their experiences with the US government and had reason to hear the appeals of any emissaries who came calling. As it turned out, the rebellious Confederates, not the federal government, first decided to pay a call.

The Confederate government sent an Arkansas lawyer named Albert Pike, authorized to spend up to $100,000, to secure political and military alliances with the tribes and to offer better terms than they currently enjoyed under the federal government. Pike offered them sovereignty within their territorial borders, representation in the new Confederate congress, and guarantees of future annuity payments. Although bitter divisions among the Creeks, Seminoles, and especially the Cherokees complicated Pike's work, by the end of October 1861 he had reached agreements with at least factions of all the tribes, including for provision of troops to the rebel armies. He then convinced Tonkawas, Caddos, Wacos, Senecas, Osages, Shawnees, and some Comanches farther to the west to put themselves under the Confederacy's protection. Stand Watie, leader of the Cherokee mixed-blood faction, became a colonel (and later a general) in the Confederate army, and Pike was given command of the newly established Confederate Department of Indian Territory. In effect, the Confederates moved into a space that had been abandoned by the Lincoln administration. Once the war started, Lincoln withdrew federal troops from Indian Territory, cut off tribal annuities, and, unlike the Confederates, refused to enlist Indigenous people as soldiers.

Expanding Southwest

Confederate rebels looked to the southwest as well. As secretary of war under Franklin Pierce, Confederate president Jefferson Davis had been interested in securing a southern route for a transcontinental railroad, and to that end he helped bring about the Gadsden Purchase in 1853 on the borderlands of Mexico and New Mexico. With secession and the organization of the Confederacy, Davis then tried to establish friendly relations with the Mexican government of Benito Juarez and to extend Confederate influence into the border regions of northern Mexico, which, he feared, might be invaded by the United States from the Pacific. The Juarez regime turned a cold shoulder, but some of the Mexican provincial governors in the north seemed more encouraging and helped stoke the vision of slave empire that had taken hold in previous decades (as we saw in Chapter 11). "We must have Sonora and Chihuahua," one of Davis's agents in Mexico declared. "With Sonora and Chihuahua we gain lower California, and by railroad to Guaymas render our state of Texas the great highway of nations."

But that vision was tempered with caution. As soon as warfare commenced, the US Navy blockaded the south Atlantic and Gulf Coasts, cutting off both exports and imports and potentially squeezing the economic life out of the rebellion;

that is, unless Confederate rebels could gain international recognition so that the blockade could be broken. Although many of the rebels were confident that their power in the cotton market dealt them a strong diplomatic hand—it became known as **King Cotton diplomacy**—they also knew that aggressive advances in Mexico and the Caribbean might court hostility from the countries they needed most: France, Belgium, Russia, Spain, and, most of all, Great Britain. Confederate secretary of state Robert Toombs of Georgia took special care to assure Europeans about Cuba, which had long been eyed by slaveholding imperialists. "It is the policy of the Government of the Confederate States that Cuba will continue to be a colonial possession of Spain."

Both the British and the French felt certain that the United States was coming apart and that the federal government would be unable to subdue the Confederates. At the same time, both also knew that any move to offer the Confederacy diplomatic recognition would bring retaliation from the Lincoln administration. They therefore chose the course of neutrality, though the British did assign Confederates **belligerent status** (legitimately engaged in war), enabling international credibility in trading goods and borrowing money. The Europeans would simply wait and see, hope to bring about negotiations designed to end the fighting, and perhaps reassert their influence in North America.

Still, there was the American southwest and the possibility of extending Confederate reach in that direction. Davis saw New Mexico, with its slave code and Confederate supporters, as a gateway to California and the Pacific. He thought southern Utah suitable for cotton growing and the mineral wealth of gold and silver mining regions a boon for the Confederate treasury. But the greatest enthusiasm for a southwestern campaign came from Confederate Texans who had reluctantly given up claims to sections of New Mexico in 1850. In July 1861 they quickly took control of federal forts in the western section of their state and forced the surrender of US troops outside the secessionist New Mexican town of Mesilla. One month later, they proclaimed the Confederate territory of Arizona that the Confederacy would officially incorporate in January 1862.

An even more ambitious plan was hatched by Louisiana-born Henry Sibley, commander of Texas troops in San Antonio, who had resigned from the US Army to join the Confederates. He envisioned an expedition not only to seize control of New Mexico and Arizona but also to occupy the gold mining districts of Colorado and California. Davis gave him the green light, and by the fall of 1861 Sibley had attracted over 3,000 Texas volunteers. In February 1862, Sibley marched them into the Rio Grande Valley of New Mexico. Within days, he defeated a federal force at Valverde, and by mid-March his troops had taken Albuquerque, hoisted the Confederate flag over Santa Fe, and looked north toward mineral-rich Colorado (see Map 14.2).

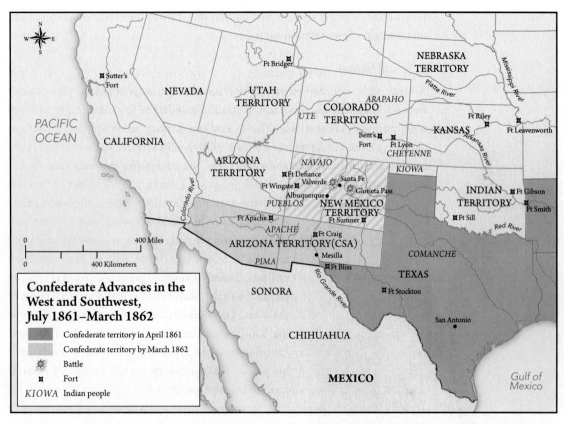

≡ **MAP 14.2   Confederate Advances in the West and Southwest, July 1861–March 1862**   Confederate leaders looked to the American Southwest and the possibility of extending their reach in that direction.

14.3   Growing the Federal Government

||| Describe how the demands of suppressing the Confederate rebellion led the federal government to expand its powers.

As the election of 1860 approached, secessionists had warned fellow white southerners that Abraham Lincoln and the Republican Party intended to create a massive central state that not only would turn its power against enslavement and enslavers but also would intervene in many other areas of public and private life. These "Black Republicans," as some secessionists called them, would turn the world they knew upside down, setting enslaved against enslaver, wife against husband, nonslaveholder against slaveholder, and Black against white. It was a chilling and compelling picture, but in November 1860 the reality was a far cry from what secessionists warned against. Ironically, it was the war the secessionists provoked that brought some of their fears to life.

A Small State

In truth, although their party platform imagined an activist federal government, Republicans and the Lincoln administration initially had few such desires and relatively little with which to work. The federal bureaucracy had fewer than 37,000 employees and the US Army fewer than 17,000 men in service. There was no central bank and, aside from gold and silver coins, the circulating currency consisted of notes printed by more than 1,500 different state banks. Capital accumulation and investment were carried on by private firms and banks as well as by state and local governments, which sold interest-bearing bonds. European investors remained a vital source of capital, especially for transportation projects. Federal revenue came mainly from tariffs and public land sales. Taxation was minimal at all levels of the state. Democrats across the country, not only in the South, were strong supporters of state rights, and Lincoln was often at pains to admit what was beyond his power: first and foremost, the system of enslavement in the states where it was legal.

In fact, Lincoln behaved as anything but a tyrant or central state-builder in the making. Although he called for 75,000 troops to put down the rebellion, he asked only for ninety-day volunteers. Although he nearly as quickly suspended the writ of habeas corpus (a right in the Constitution that protects against arrest and detention without formal charge) in the Washington-to-Philadelphia corridor and imposed martial law in Baltimore, he did so only in the face of secessionist activity and after US troops were attacked and the District of Columbia made vulnerable. Washington, DC, was surrounded on three sides by the slave state of Maryland, which was teetering on the edge of joining the Confederacy.

But by the time Congress reassembled in July 1861 (it was out of session when he took the oath of office), Lincoln had a sobering sense of what he was up against and what success might require. Disavowing

≡ **In Defense of the Union** When Congress authorized a million-man army to put down the Southern insurrection, Northern men enthusiastically responded to its call for volunteers. This print depicts two Union soldiers and one sailor gesturing upward toward an enormous American flag.

any intention to "interfere with slavery in the States where it exists," he asked the congressmen and senators for "at least four hundred thousand men [they would authorize a million] and four hundred millions of dollars." Before too long, owing to the demands of an increasingly destructive and protracted war, the Lincoln administration would take major steps in a variety of areas with lasting impact for the United States. They would promote the development of a massive standing army, a growing manufacturing sector, a new structure of finance and banking, a system of labor in the rebellious states based on contract rather than enslavement, and an ambitious set of projects in the trans-Mississippi West.

Funding the War

An immediate challenge facing the Lincoln administration was raising money to wage war. Treasury Secretary Salmon P. Chase decided to follow a path that the federal government had previously staked out when it needed extra funds: selling securities, mostly interest-bearing bonds. Ordinarily those securities would be sold to European investors, but once the fighting broke out, the Europeans pretty much disappeared; the United States now seemed a very risky investment. So, Chase turned to private bankers and investors in Philadelphia, Boston, and especially New York City, effectively the financial centers of the country, pursuing the sort of alliance between private creditors and the central state that Alexander Hamilton had hoped for in the 1790s (discussed in Chapter 9).

When that came up short, too, Chase imaginatively devised a plan to sell government bonds to a wider public in denominations as low as $50 while seeking help to bring the bigger investors on board. For the latter, he called upon the son of a prominent Ohio family named Jay Cooke, who had recently opened a banking house in Philadelphia and was able to make use of his own financial networks. It worked. Cooke marketed bonds both to northeastern bankers and to regular folks in bond drives accompanied by patriotic advertising. By the time the war ended, the United States had raised about two-thirds of its revenue through the sale of bonds and other securities.

But even this was not enough to cover the enormous costs of the war. Further moves had to be made. In 1861, Congress placed a modest tax on incomes over $800, and the next year it passed a **Legal Tender Act**, which authorized the circulation of what would become $450,000,000 in treasury notes called **greenbacks** (the bills were green, as they still are). Treasury Secretary Chase then moved toward constructing a new banking system, in which private banks could get national charters and print paper currency if they met a number of requirements, none more important than the purchase of government securities. Legislated in 1863, the **National Bank Act** thus established a stable market for federal bonds and discouraged state bankers from printing money at will (they were taxed if they did). In all these ways, the Lincoln administration was able to pay for the war while promoting the emergence of a new class of finance capitalists who, like Jay Cooke, had come to the aid of the country and stood to benefit personally if the country survived the war.

New Networks of Power

Bankers and private investors were not the only beneficiaries of war-related federal initiatives. Federal contracts brought windfalls to a variety of sectors of the US economy that could supply and transport the troops. The 1850s had seen a spike in railroad building, especially in the Mid-Atlantic and lower Midwest, and these railroads would prove crucial to military operations. Although Lincoln could have used his authority as commander-in-chief to seize control of the railroads, he not only decided to leave them in private hands but appointed Thomas Scott, head of the Pennsylvania Railroad, as assistant secretary in charge of government transportation. Similar partnerships boosted the fortunes and encouraged the concentration of ownership in meat packing, iron and steel making, ready-made clothing manufacture, coal mining, gun and ordnance production, and blacksmithing along a belt stretching from southern New England through New York and Pennsylvania and out to Chicago. This economic belt would be the foundation of Republican political power for many years to come.

Equally, if not more, significant were policies oriented to the trans-Mississippi West. Ever since the 1840s, congressional leaders across the political spectrum showed interest in promoting white settlement in the new western territories and encouraging the construction of railroad lines to the Pacific. Although the question of enslavement's expansion doomed these efforts, both Democrats and Republicans called for a transcontinental railroad in their 1860 platforms, and the departure of most southern Democrats owing to secession left Republicans with the votes to pursue western development as they saw fit. The **Homestead Act** of 1862 made 160 acres of land available to individuals or family heads who would farm them for five years and then pay a small fee. The **Pacific Railway Act**, also passed in 1862, chartered the Union Pacific Railroad Company and offered enormous incentives in land and financial assistance to build between Omaha, Nebraska; and Sacramento, California. The beneficiaries were mostly men of considerable wealth, an indication of the priorities Republican officials would continue to set.

A transcontinental railroad made little economic sense at the time. Most of the interior west was populated by Indigenous people who raised neither crops nor livestock for sale. But railroad and homestead legislation was more political than economic in intent and must be understood as part of a Republican project to bring the west under control. Well aware—as were the Confederates—of the gold-mining strikes in Colorado in the late 1850s, of gold and silver mines in southern New Mexico and the Sierra Nevada, of the California gateways to the Pacific trade, of secessionist activities across the trans-Mississippi West, and, soon, of Confederate advances into New Mexico, the Lincoln administration moved to extend its reach.

For similar reasons, the Republican Congress created the Dakota (1861), Nevada (1861), Arizona (1863), Idaho (1863), and Montana (1864) Territories and the patronage appointments that went with their governance. Congress finally admitted Kansas as a free state in 1861 after refusing to accept the proslavery Lecompton Constitution in 1857 (discussed in Chapter 12), and it encouraged Colorado and Nevada to apply for statehood in 1864. It reorganized military districts to raise more volunteers and keep disloyalty in check. And it ordered the US Army to reclaim Indian Territory, subdue Native Americans across the plains, and crush pro-Confederate guerillas in Missouri. The future of the trans-Mississippi West, Lincoln and other Republicans recognized, would be determined as the war unfolded.

14.4   An Indigenous Rebellion

Explain why Indigenous peoples of the Great Plains took the opportunity of the Civil War to launch their own rebellion.

In the late summer of 1862, out in the state of Minnesota, many miles from the main theaters of warfare or from the seats of government, the eastern division of the Sioux, about 6,500 in all, rose up in rebellion. Theirs was a product of at least two decades of mounting tensions that turned what had been relatively friendly exchange relations with British, French, and American traders into hard-bitten conflicts with federal officials and white settlers who eyed the fertile and game-rich lands that the Sioux occupied. Under pressure, the Indigenous people had given up millions of acres of land, which included ancestral grounds, in return for a strip of reservation land along the Minnesota River, annuity payments, and supplies for sustenance. But stinginess in the halls of Congress combined with corrupt practices among Indian agents on the scene to stretch a series of treaties to the breaking point; some of the Sioux bands faced starvation.

As the Sioux debated how best to proceed, the federal government's determination to wage war against the Confederate rebellion caught their attention. Southern sympathizers in their orbit told of federal defeats, and some Sioux leaders imagined "that the South was getting the best of the fight, and the North would be whipped." One of the chiefs, Big Eagle, concluded "now would be a good time to go to war with the whites and get our lands back." In mid-August, under the leadership of Little Crow (Taoyateduta), a column of Sioux warriors overran an agency outpost and killed a white agent there. Other Sioux war parties quickly spread across the Minnesota countryside and then farther west into the Dakota Territory, inflicting lethal vengeance. Alarms were raised to the south in Iowa and Nebraska, and rumors about the number of Sioux warriors further fanned white fears. Before long, the governors of the respective states and territories were wiring Lincoln and his Secretary of War Edwin Stanton for help in the form of men, arms, and horses (see Map 14.3).

Federal Defeats in Virginia

The last thing the Lincoln administration needed in the late summer of 1862 was a western Native uprising with which to contend. It was now well over a year since Lincoln had called for volunteers to put down the rebellion in

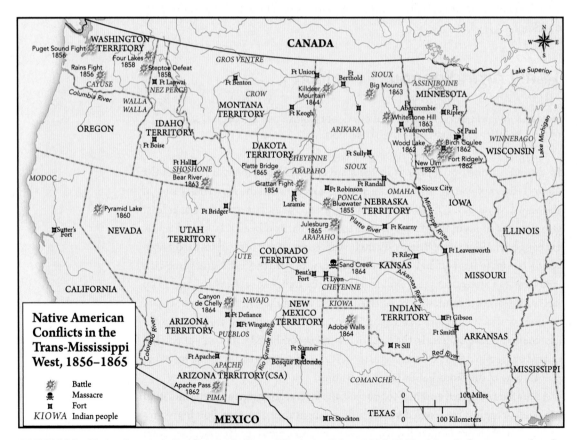

≡ **MAP 14.3   Native American Conflicts in the Trans-Mississippi West, 1856–1865**   Many Indigenous peoples of the Great Plains took the opportunity of the Civil War to launch their own rebellions.

the southern states, and, as the British and French had predicted, there was very little to show for it. Although state governors and their male constituents in the Northeast and Midwest eventually responded enthusiastically to Lincoln's summons, many of the army's commanding officers, especially in the Eastern Theater, seemed reluctant to lead the new soldiers into battle. First Irvin McDowell and then George B. McClellan complained endlessly of their troops' inexperience and need for more men before they could move out and fight the Confederates.

They stalled and stalled and stalled, much to Lincoln's alarm and anger. And when they did finally act, the results were disastrous. McDowell, heading out of Washington in July 1861 in hopes of capturing the Confederate capital of Richmond, suffered a devastating defeat that nearly ended in the Confederate capture of Washington, DC, the US capital. Northerners named this first major land battle of the Civil War **Bull Run** after a stream running through the battle-field, whereas Confederates called it **Manassas** (sometimes Manassas Junction) after the closest town. Some months later, in the spring of 1862, McClellan made another attempt at taking Richmond, this time from the southeast, by way of the Virginia peninsula, but while he outnumbered the rebels and came within ear-shot of Richmond's church bells, he and his army were forced to retreat, mainly because of the clever maneuvering of rebel commanders Robert E. Lee, Thomas "Stonewall" Jackson, and J. E. B. Stuart.

Out in the Western Theater, the federal army was doing better. Control of the Mississippi River was the great prize, and federal troops attacked from the north and the south. They first pushed into Tennessee and Missouri, and then later sailed up from the Gulf of Mexico and took the crown jewel of New Orleans in April 1862. That same month, at the bloody **Battle of Shiloh** (also known as the Battle of Pittsburgh Landing, since the battlefield was located between a church named Shiloh and Pittsburgh Landing) on the Tennessee River, federal troops managed to maintain military momentum despite being nearly overrun by a surprise Confederate assault. Among the officers who helped drive rebels out of Missouri and establish a federal hold on the Mississippi River as far south as Memphis was West Point graduate and US-Mexican War veteran John Pope. So impressive was Pope's record in the west that Lincoln, desperate for better results in the east, ordered him back to command the newly formed Army of Virginia, with 50,000 men, assembled north of Richmond.

Yet another march on Richmond was planned, and Pope believed he was just the man to carry it off. "I come to you out of the West, where we have always seen the backs of our enemies," Pope crowed to his troops. "Success and glory are in the advance, disaster and shame lurk in the rear." That was about the last of his boasts.

After skirmishing for several weeks with portions of Lee's army, Pope engaged the Confederates in full-scale battle near Manassas Junction, site of the first and dispiriting **Battle of Bull Run**. This time—a second Battle of Bull Run—the results were no better. After losing 16,000 men, it was Pope whose back was visible to the enemy. Like McDowell before him, Pope was forced to retreat toward Washington, DC (see Map 14.4).

But Pope wasn't there for long. McClellan, still the head of military forces in the east and seeking a fall guy, blamed Pope for the debacle at Bull Run, and although Lincoln had clashed from the start with McClellan, he could not afford to reprimand the commander, who was very popular with the troops even though he didn't lead them to any victories. Instead, Lincoln sent Pope packing, out to Minnesota to take command of the new Military Department of the Northwest and deal with the Sioux.

Taking on the Sioux

General Pope felt humiliated by his apparent banishment to the West, but he also intended to make quick work of the rebellious Indigenous people. "It is my purpose," he announced, "utterly to exterminate the Sioux if I have the power to do

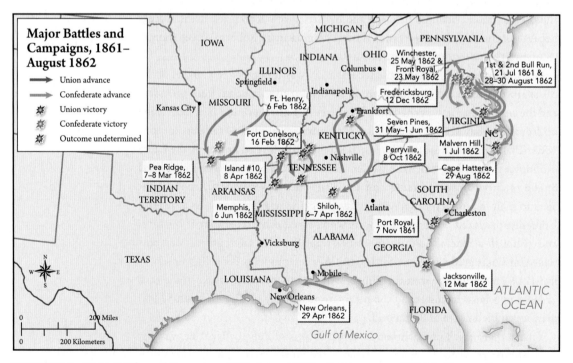

≡ **MAP 14.4   Major Battles and Campaigns, 1861–August 1862**   By late summer 1862 it had been well over a year since Lincoln had called for volunteers to put down the rebellion, but there was very little to show for it in the East. In the Western Theater, however, federal forces had pushed into Tennessee and Missouri and had taken New Orleans.

so and even if it requires a campaign lasting the whole of next year." Aided by the 3rd Minnesota Infantry, which had surrendered to Confederates in Tennessee and been sent home, Pope began to round up the Sioux and treat them as prisoners of war. Within a month, nearly 2,200 Sioux had been brought under federal control and Pope, along with his second in command, determined to exact "a final settlement with all these Indians." Setting up a five-man commission, they had the captives tried "for being connected in the late horrible outrages." They then sentenced 303 of them to be hanged. Learning of the impending executions, Lincoln had serious misgivings and, on reviewing the trial transcripts, was shocked at the lack of evidence and the bitter contempt of the commissioners. Although Minnesotans demanded revenge, Lincoln agreed to the execution of only thirty-eight of the Sioux, offering pardons and reprieves to the others. As it was, when the hangings took place on December 26, 1862, they would form—and remain—the largest official mass execution in the history of the United States.

Yet, in some ways, the federal Congress, with Lincoln's assent, dealt the Sioux more devastating blows. In early 1863, Congress voided all treaties with the eastern Sioux, effectively stripping them of their reservation lands, ending annuity payments, and forcing them out onto the open plains. There they would be joined by 2,000 Winnebagos (also known as Ho-Chunks) suspected of participating in the Sioux rebellion and, like the Sioux, pushed out of Minnesota by congressional action.

If Pope had his way, he would have hastily departed for the East and the thick of the war against the Confederates, a suitable reward, in his mind, for completing his assignment with flying colors. Instead, he was left in the West and so decided to launch a new campaign, beginning in the spring of 1863, against the Sioux in the Dakota Territory. By early July, Pope had the upper hand and more than a little blood to show for it: Little Crow was dead, his scalp brought back for display at the Minnesota Historical Society, and the federal war against the Indigenous people of the trans-Mississippi West that would last for more than another two decades had begun.

≡ **Mass Execution** This colored print from 1865 depicts the execution of thirty-eight Sioux at Mankato, Minnesota, on December 26, 1862. Cordoned off by soldiers, spectators gather to watch the grisly proceedings.

14.5   The Rebellion of the Enslaved

||| Demonstrate how enslaved people of the South rebelled against their Confederate enslavers and changed the goals of the Civil War relating to the future of slavery.

At the time he decided to send John Pope out west to subdue the Sioux rebellion, President Lincoln was preparing a momentous executive order on the slavery question in the United States. We don't know when, precisely, he had the idea for such an order, but we do know that he presented it to his cabinet in July 1862 and waited for a federal military victory before making it public. Issued in his capacity as President of the United States and Commander-in-Chief of the Army and Navy, Lincoln's order gave the rebellious states until January 1, 1863, to lay down their arms. Otherwise, all their enslaved would be "thenceforth, and forever, free." Excluded from the order would be slave states "not then in rebellion against the United States," where Lincoln offered federal assistance for the "immediate or gradual abolishment of slavery" and for the colonization of "persons of African descent." Announced on September 22, 1862, shortly after the **Battle of Antietam** in Maryland (as we will see, something less than a clear Union victory though one of the bloodiest engagements of the war), it is known as the **Preliminary Emancipation Proclamation**. But Lincoln did not come to this moment on his own or without significant struggle.

Lincoln's Indecision

Lincoln had long been committed to keeping enslavement out of the federal territories of the trans-Mississippi West, but he was equally committed to keeping federal hands off of the system in the slave states and, as best as feasible, out of the war against the Confederate rebellion. Despite appeals from abolitionists and the efforts of Britain and France to negotiate an armistice, Lincoln was reluctant to strike a death blow against the Confederacy's very being. If anything, Lincoln appeared to bend over backwards to appease loyal enslavers in the border states of Missouri, Kentucky, Maryland, and Delaware, offering them many incentives to support the United States or embrace emancipation while talking tough to abolitionists. When abolitionists called for action, he balked. When they proposed recruiting Black soldiers for the Army, he scoffed. When antislavery officers took initiatives in the field, he reprimanded or dismissed them.

Lincoln was especially direct with a Black delegation with whom he met in August 1862. "You and we are different races and you are yet far removed from being placed on an equality with the white race," he bluntly stated. "But for your race among us there could not be war." Even as he began to contemplate an emancipation, Lincoln imagined it as very gradual (extending over thirty-five years) and involving colonization. Thus, only a few short weeks before issuing the Preliminary Emancipation Proclamation he could write, "My paramount object in this struggle *is* to save the Union, and is *not* either to save or destroy slavery. If I could save the Union without freeing *any* slave I would do it, and if I could save it by freeing *all* the slaves I would do that. What I do about slavery, and the colored race, I do because I believe it helps to save the Union."

The Enslaved People's Perspectives

But enslaved people had other ideas about the meaning of the struggle. Although Lincoln would not have been able to imagine them as political actors, the enslaved had been imagining Lincoln as a political leader for quite some time. Ever since the presidential election campaign of 1860, reports circulated across the southern states of political attentiveness and restlessness among the enslaved. Observers noted the attraction of enslaved people to "every political speech," their inclination "to linger around" the courthouse square "and hear what the orators say," and, as if to confirm William Webb's account of his activities in 1856 (discussed in Chapter 13), their interest in collecting information and deciphering its meaning. Yet, more significantly, as the story of Harry Jarvis at the start of this chapter reveals, Lincoln's campaign seemed to promote expectations among the enslaved that he intended "to set them all free."

Information about the political conflict rupturing the country was not difficult for the enslaved to come by. There were railroad depots and river docks, market days and militia musters, church services and electioneering events, where enslaved people could always be found with their enslavers, on hire, or on an errand with a pass. Most of all, they could overhear the worries of their enslavers, sometimes expressed with dire predictions of what Lincoln's presidency would bring: abolition, the destruction of the plantations, racial "amalgamation," in short, the end of the world as they knew it. Lincoln, it appeared, was the mortal enemy of their mortal enemies, and therefore perhaps a friend and political ally.

Indeed, once Lincoln assumed office and determined to crush the secessionists' rebellion, the expectations of the enslaved inspired actions. There were reports of enslaved people marching off plantations, making preparations to aid Lincoln and the Union, declaring themselves to be "as free as [their] masters." "During the campaign when Lincoln was first a candidate for the Presidency," African American leader Booker T. Washington later remembered, "the slaves on our far-off plantation knew what the issues involved were [and] when the war was begun every slave on our plantation knew that the primal [issue] was that of slavery."

The Lincoln administration had no interest in encouraging rebellious behavior among the enslaved in the Confederacy. If anything, the possibility of a war-induced slave rebellion haunted the Union side as much as the Confederate, and federal army commanders were directed to leave enslavement undisturbed and to "suppress" any slave "insurrections" that might break out. Yet the enslaved found ways to enact their own form of rebellion, not by rising up violently against their enslavers but, like Harry Jarvis, by taking flight from the plantations and farms on which they were held in captivity and heading to federal army encampments where they thought freedom might beckon.

The Enslaved Force Change

These were not spontaneous actions of enslaved individuals. They were the products of collective discussion and organization among enslaved people as to the meaning of the war, the intentions of the federal government, the location of the federal army and of Confederate patrols, and the relation between the departure of individuals and small groups and the fate of those they left behind. In an important sense, it was just the sort of engagement that John Brown had hoped to see from the enslaved in the vicinity of Harpers Ferry, Virginia. The enslaved rebelled against the demands and authority of their enslavers, who warned them to stay put (often with double-barreled shotguns), and effectively presented themselves to federal army commanders as allies in what they believed to be a battle against slavery.

It was a risky undertaking for the enslaved rebels, not only because their enslavers had guns and were quite prepared to shoot but also because they might discover that such an alliance was rejected by federal army officers. When Harry Jarvis fled to Fortress Monroe in the spring of 1861 and sought out commanding General Benjamin Butler, he was among the first enslaved people to force an issue the Lincoln administration would have preferred to avoid. As we have seen, Jarvis's actions placed Butler in a quandary, with only the Fugitive Slave Law as a guide. But when Butler learned that Confederates nearby were exploiting slave labor to construct fortifications, he took a different view of the enslaved seeking refuge within his lines. He declared them to be **contrabands of war** (enemy property that fell into Union hands and would not be returned) and set the able-bodied among them—like Jarvis—to work on federal fortifications. In doing this, Butler didn't challenge the property basis of enslavement. He offered neither freedom nor a blanket policy to cover the enslaved regardless of their enslavers' politics. Yet his contraband policy was something of an invitation to the enslaved who contemplated flight and had their own ideas of what being received into federal lines signified. And this was only the beginning. As federal armies pushed farther south, first to the coast of South Carolina (November 1861) and then to the lower Mississippi

Valley (April 1862), where some of the largest plantations were to be found, the enslaved began to appear in the tens and hundreds, increasingly making a mockery of the absolute power their owners claimed to enjoy.

The rebellious flight of the enslaved forced federal troops and then the Lincoln administration to deal directly with the slavery question, and it began to shift the balances of power for the enslaved people who remained on the plantations and farms of their enslavement. The US Congress quickly ratified Butler's contraband policy with the **First Confiscation Act** in August 1861, and, as the war dragged on, Radical Republicans—the faction of the Republican Party known for their strong opposition to enslavement—and Lincoln took several steps to undermine the system where they believed they had the authority to proceed. They outlawed enslavement in the Western territories (upending part of the *Dred Scott* decision), abolished enslavement in the District of Columbia (with monetary compensation to slaveholders), prohibited federal soldiers from returning enslaved runaways to their enslavers (rejecting the Fugitive Slave Law), and offered financial support to any state that would pursue gradual, compensated (compensation to enslavers) emancipation.

At the same time, enslaved people who remained in captivity often seized the moment to renegotiate the relations and demands that governed their lives. They pressed for more time in their provision grounds, for more control over the working of the farm or plantation, and even for small wages or shares of the growing crop. In at least one case, they threatened to hang their enslaver if he refused to yield. By the summer of 1862, slavery was in the process of unraveling through official and unofficial means, though, in all cases, as a consequence of the blows that rebellious enslaved people themselves determined to land.

But the relation of emancipation—in whatever form—to the war and the future of the United States had still to be decided. Would the slave system continue to be destroyed piecemeal? Would the power

≡ **Flight to Freedom**   The German-born painter Theodore Kaufmann served as a Union soldier where he may have seen Confederate troops retreating with enslaved men, leaving behind women and children. Here he portrays a group of fleeing figures navigating their route to freedom.

and responsibility for pursuing emancipation continue to be left to the states or to individual enslavers? What would happen if the federal government failed to suppress the Confederate rebellion and an armistice was reached? Not even radical abolitionists had a clear vision of either how slavery should end or who should take the lead in ending it. The only models were Haiti on the one side, where slavery was destroyed in the midst of violent revolution (as we saw in Chapter 8), or gradualism on the other, which attended to the concerns of enslavers. Lincoln's desire to have the border states take the lead and move down the road of gradualism was utterly refused, even by tiny Delaware.

Arming the Enslaved

Whenever Lincoln decided to chart a new path on the slavery question, he did so in a context that demanded a re-envisioning of the war's goals and methods and of the country that might emerge from it. Much of the policy initiative came from Radical Republicans in Congress who, in July 1862, enacted two important pieces of legislation. One, the **Second Confiscation Act**, officially declared the slave-holders' rebellion to be "treason" and made "forever free" any enslaved persons owned by rebel enslavers who came within army lines. This was the first law to commit the US government to a policy of general emancipation. On the same day, Congress also passed a **Militia Act** that authorized Lincoln to receive "for military service . . . persons of African descent," a measure that finally overrode the exclusion of African Americans, since the founding of the republic, from the US Army and Navy.

Although Lincoln's Preliminary Emancipation Proclamation said nothing about arming the enslaved or other Black people, the final **Emancipation Proclamation**, which Lincoln issued on January 1, 1863—the Confederate states not having laid down their arms—did. While several slave states and counties within them were exempted from the Proclamation's reach because they remained loyal to the United States or were under federal army occupation, all references to gradual emancipation or colonization were now gone, and explicit provision was made to begin enlisting previously enslaved men as soldiers. Thus, while the Proclamation still justified emancipation on the grounds of "military necessity" and was silent on the position of formerly enslaved people in American society, it did advance the radical remedies of abolition without compensation to enslavers and the arming of enslaved and free Black men to defeat them in battle.

The impact was enormous. Although talk of British mediation did not suddenly cease, the Emancipation Proclamation swelled support for the federal side in British cities and especially in the manufacturing districts, where King Cotton diplomacy had predicted it would crumble amid a cotton famine. Among the strongest supporters were textile workers, some of whom saw a relation between the political struggles of the enslaved and their own. "When the slave ceases to be, and becomes enfranchised free men," one of them could reckon, "then the British workingman's claim may be listened to."

The abolitionist Frederick Douglass had an even broader grasp of what had happened. Mixing the language of the secular and the sacred, Douglas saw in the Emancipation Proclamation not only the hand of God but also the mark of a new stage in the history of the United States, when a nation seemed to emerge, one in which "the cause of the slave and the cause of the country" had finally been linked. He made a powerful point. Since the late eighteenth century, nation-states across the Atlantic world had risen from the ashes of enslavement and servitude, propelled by their determination to dismantle the petty sovereignties of enslavers and lords and to claim the military service of freedmen and peasants within their borders. In the United States, the rebellion of the enslaved transformed the objectives of America's civil warfare and made possible the forging of a nation.

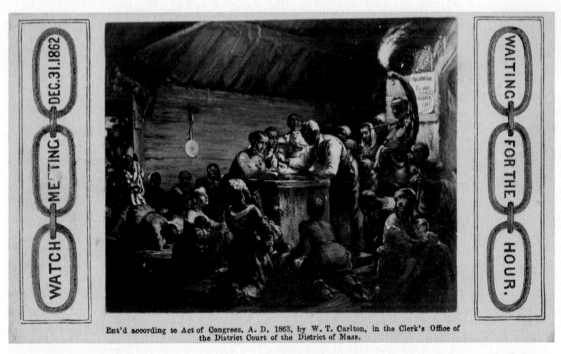

Ent'd according to Act of Congress, A. D. 1863, by W. T. Carlton, in the Clerk's Office of
the District Court of the District of Mass.

≣ **Anticipating Emancipation**   This image memorializes the moment the Emancipation Proclamation took effect, just after midnight on January 1, 1863. The original painting was given by abolitionists to Abraham Lincoln as a token of gratitude and a reminder of the human dimension of the proclamation.

14.6   Trouble Behind the Lines

‖‖‖   Describe the nature and extent of opposition to the Lincoln administration even in the states that remained loyal to the federal government.

From the time of his inauguration, Abraham Lincoln and his administration faced an assortment of rebellions that threatened to sever the American union along a number of deeply laid political and social fault lines. The slaveholders' rebellion was the most massive and dangerous of them, but from the first it also raised the prospect of political rebellions in the West, Midwest, and parts of the urban East that could have fractured the country beyond recognition. Indigenous rebellion in the upper Plains and in Indian Territory looked to take advantage of an apparently weakened federal government to recover ground that had been lost. And enslaved people who had followed the prolonged battles over the future of slavery in the United States and elsewhere rebelled against their enslavers' authority once their imagined allies in the federal government struck the first blow. But as time went on, Lincoln had still another rebellion on his hands, this time within the ranks of those who had remained loyal to the United States and on whom Lincoln had to rely to fight the Confederates to a successful conclusion.

The Fire in the Rear

These rebels were northern Democrats who mobilized to challenge Republican initiatives on the economy and the expansion of government powers, and, especially, on new war aims involving the end of enslavement. Although most had rallied to the defense of the federal government when the war broke out and condemned the Confederates, it didn't take very long for some to have a change of heart. The early defeats that the federal government sustained on the battlefields raised questions about the war's outcome and the political consequences of fighting it. After all, the Lincoln administration had suspended the constitutional writ of habeas corpus, enacted legislation that favored banks, manufacturers, and cities, and attacked Confederate property, particularly their right to human property.

Where would it end? These Democrats saw a Republican state greatly overreaching its authority and threatening the country with "tyranny" and racial "amalgamation." They combined a populist opposition to new concentrations of wealth and power with racism and localism. They could be found in largest numbers in the lower Midwest as well as in the urban Northeast, and their slogan came to be, "The Constitution as it is; the Union as it was; the negroes where they are." Republicans knew them as **copperheads,** as venomous snakes; Lincoln called their rebellion a "fire in the rear." Led by Ohio Congressman Clement L. Vallandigham, they would harass the Lincoln administration for the remainder of the war.

Vallandigham and other copperheads charged that the Republican government had violated constitutional liberties and that "King Lincoln" should be removed from office. But the fists of the Lincoln administration were by no means iron. Arbitrary civilian arrests mostly took place in Confederate territory or near the border, and they generally took in those suspected of espionage or smuggling. Few Americans on either side of the conflict were jailed for dissenting beliefs, and Lincoln ignored newspapers in the loyal states that regularly howled at his policies.

Conscription and Conflict

A far more significant cause of trouble in the rear was military conscription and its relation to emancipation. Although at the outset of hostilities enlistment—in the United States and the Confederacy—was organized through volunteering at the local level, it was not long before the demands of warfare exposed the limits of such a decentralized system. Within the first year of fighting most of the sources of volunteering had been tapped, and pressures from the home front in what were still overwhelmingly rural and agricultural communities mounted. Since its population of eligible soldiers (free, white men) was roughly one-fifth the size of the US population and many of its volunteers had enrolled for a limited amount of time, the Confederacy faced a manpower crisis as early as the winter of 1861–1862. The options for finding new ways of stimulating re-enlistments were limited. While the Louisiana Native Guards, a unit of free people of color from New Orleans, had been mustered into service in the spring of 1861 (well before the Union made comparable moves), no one initially contemplated using enslaved people (about 40 percent of the Confederate population) for anything other than military or civilian labor. As a consequence, the Confederate congress was forced to enact a draft law that April.

Even though the Confederate draft law asked state governors to meet quotas and included numerous exemptions, it provoked immediate conflict and controversy. Governors like Joseph Brown in Georgia and Zebulon Vance in North Carolina found the law an example of the very "despotism" they had embraced secession to avoid

≡ **Confederate Volunteers**   Young southern men pose for a Richmond photographer before the first Battle of Bull Run in 1861.

MAPPING AMERICA

The Call to Arms

At the beginning of the conflict, enlistment in the United States and the Confederacy was organized through volunteering at the local level, but it was not long before the demands of warfare exposed the limits of such a decentralized system. By 1863 both the United States and the Confederacy had enacted draft laws that sometimes sparked violent opposition, as the riots in New York City in July 1863 demonstrate. But even in places that did not experience riots, enlistment rates varied widely, in both the Union and the Confederacy.

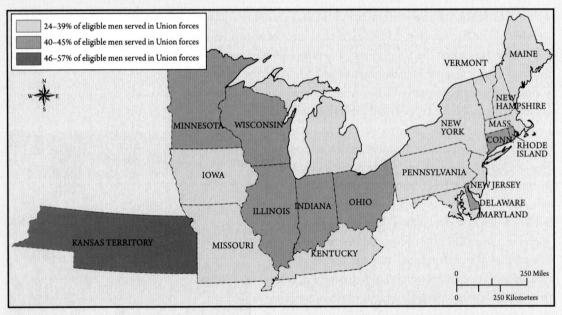

≡ **MAP 1**   Since it waged an offensive war, the North required more soldiers than the Confederacy, and because of the population advantage it enjoyed, it was able to enlist more men with less pressure on individual communities. On average, northern counties sent 35 percent of their military-aged men to fight, with the highest percentages coming from the tightly knit communities of the Midwest.

Thinking Geographically

1. Compare the different enlistment rates across the North and South. What reasons would explain why the rate of enlistment was lower in Missouri and Kentucky than in Minnesota and Wisconsin?

2. What would explain the relatively low rate in South Carolina, even though it was the first state to secede?

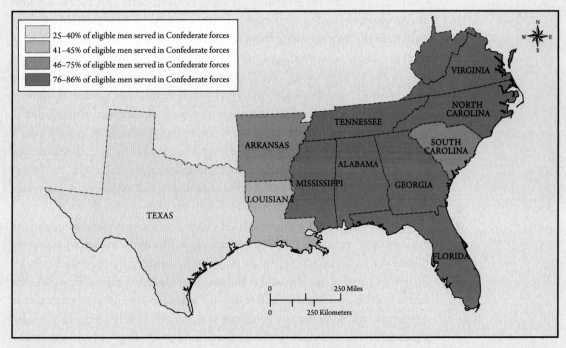

≡ **MAP 2**   The South had fewer men it could enlist, but its search for volunteers was organized and energetic, and by the end of the war, it had expanded eligibility so that men as young as seventeen and as old as fifty-five could sign up to fight. On average, southern counties sent twice the percentage of men to fight as northern counties.

and said they wouldn't cooperate. Closer to the ground, soldiers in the ranks often bridled at the Confederacy's demands and, especially if they were humble nonslaveholders, felt that the burdens of warfare had been shifted to their shoulders. Legislation passed several months later that permitted owners or managers of plantations with twenty or more enslaved people to stay out of the military only reinforced that sense. It was, some complained, "a rich man's war and a poor man's fight." Resistance to the draft began to fester, particularly in districts filled with yeoman and poor white families. Desertion from Confederate ranks became a gnawing problem.

The prospect of rebellions from within (other than of the enslaved) thus started to haunt the Confederate leadership. It flared among self-interested slaveholders, who refused to allow the government to claim the labor of the men they enslaved or discourage them from growing cotton. It flared among common soldiers, who took leave from the fighting to aid their struggling families at home. It flared among renegades in the hills or valleys, who fended off the conscription and impressment officers and, in some cases, joined up with the federal army. And it flared among soldiers' wives, who demanded relief and support from the Confederate government and eventually showed their anger in a wave of food riots. Attempting to build a state on the foundation of slaveholding was an enormous gamble even if Confederates thought that the winds of history might be blowing in their direction and that slave labor and bountiful cotton might be sources of strength. By the end of 1863, a few of them began to think the unthinkable and envision a path of emancipation organized around the military enlistment of the enslaved.

State-building had its own perils for the federal government, and the resistance could be more explosive still. The policies of the Lincoln administration and the Republican Congress not only drew power to the center from the peripheries but also favored certain social groups at the potential expense of others. Bond sales enriched a new class of bankers and financiers, who then joined forces with railroad developers favored by massive government incentives. Federal contracts provided windfalls for manufacturers in the clothing, food-processing, and armaments sectors. Tariffs and banking legislation favored cities and industry at the expense of the countryside and agriculture. And the inflation that came with printing greenbacks cut into the living standards of workers, many of whom were immigrants traditionally aligned with the Democrats.

Social and political tensions were therefore on low simmer in the Union when the Lincoln administration inflamed them by enacting a draft that also permitted the hiring of a substitute or the payment of a $300 exemption fee. It came a year later than the Confederacy's, in the spring of 1863, in good part because the federal pool of manpower was larger and the initial terms of service longer.

And it was greeted with much the same language of opposition—despotism, favoritism, tyranny—as was true in the South. But the federal draft also came in the immediate aftermath of the Emancipation Proclamation and the decision to enlist large numbers of African Americans, enslaved and free, in the armed forces and therefore appeared part of a massive government effort to expand its authority and reorganize the war.

Opposition to the federal draft law erupted in Democratic strongholds across the northern states, with special intensity in enclaves of working-class immigrants, especially among Irish Catholics, who had long been struggling with their employers. Indeed, the draft could become a vehicle of mobilization for workers and employers alike, allowing the former to depict conscription as an example of the tyranny and unfairness of the wartime social order and the latter to call in the troops to break strikes.

It was in New York City that the tensions burst forth in an immensely destructive rebellion and deadly racial brutality. For three days beginning on July 13, 1863, what has come to be known as the **New York City Draft Riots** swept over the city in what remains the second largest domestic insurrection in US history, after the Civil War, of which it was a part. Offices of Republican newspapers and political officials were attacked, the homes of prominent Republicans were ransacked, the Colored Orphanage was torched, and Black men and boys suffered random attacks. Pitched battles occurred in the streets and factories, and one vicious mob cried, "Vengeance on every n—r in New York" (Black people were only 2 percent of the population). By the time the riots were suppressed by several regiments of troops redeployed from the blood-soaked fields of Gettysburg, Pennsylvania, the city of New York smoldered, at least eleven Black men had been murdered, and hundreds of Black men, women, and children were fleeing the city. Within a few days, the city's draft office reopened and names were quietly pulled.

14.7 Envisioning a Nation

Summarize how the unfolding of the Civil War led the Lincoln administration to envision a new form of federal governance.

On November 18, 1863, three months after the draft had resumed in New York City, President Lincoln departed Washington, DC, on a five-hour train trip to Gettysburg, Pennsylvania. It was not the sort of thing Lincoln often did. Since his inauguration in 1861, Lincoln had rarely left the capital city. But this was

Executive Mansion,

Washington,   *, 186 .*

Four score and seven years ago our fathers brought forth, upon this continent, a new nation, conceived in liberty, and dedicated to the proposition that "all men are created equal"

Now we are engaged in a great civil war, testing whether that nation, or any nation so conceived, and so dedicated, can long endure. We are met

≡ **The Gettysburg Address**   There are five known drafts of the Gettysburg Address in Lincoln's hand, but only two were written before he delivered the address. The one presented here belonged to Lincoln's secretary, John G. Nicolay. Although Nicolay believed that this was the copy Lincoln held in his hand and appeared to read, what Lincoln actually said differed significantly from the text of this document.

a special, if somber, occasion. A cemetery was to be dedicated in Gettysburg where, the previous July, a massive Union army had turned back an equally massive and ambitious Confederate advance in one of the war's great bloodbaths. Over the course of three days, several thousand Union soldiers had been killed and then hastily buried. Now they were being reinterred and honored for their heroic deeds. Four train cars carried Lincoln, a few members of his cabinet, and other federal officials who would be joining governors from several of the loyal states together with local dignitaries and citizens as they assembled the following day to hear the main address by famed orator and conservative Massachusetts Republican Edward Everett. Lincoln had agreed to make only "a few appropriate remarks."

Although he seemed to be an add-on, Lincoln took his assignment very seriously. For several months he had been thinking about a speech that would explain the meaning of this long and awful war to a public that had suffered grievous losses and needed perspective on what they had endured and where they were headed. Now he had that opportunity, and despite later myths that he jotted the speech on the train at the last minute, he was well prepared and saw fit to make several handwritten copies. What he managed to do was offer a deep history of a "nation" that in fact was being born almost as he spoke. And he did it in fewer than 300 words. They are known as the **Gettysburg Address**.

Blood-Soaked Stalemate

It required impressive leaps of faith for Lincoln to envision "a new birth of freedom" as he stood on the speaker's platform, overlooking markers of death rather than life and of near calamity for the country he had pledged to protect. The war against the slaveholders' rebellion was more than two and a half years old, and for the most part the story seemed one of collapse instead of creation. Despite Lincoln's oft-proclaimed goal of "saving the Union," the results on the battlefields offered few signs that this could happen anytime soon, and with an assortment of rebellions on his hands, it was increasingly doubtful that there would be much left to save.

Militarily, the best the Lincoln administration could show at this point in the war was stalemate. The most encouraging results were in the West. The Confederate offensive in the far southwest, which had established the new territory of Arizona, had taken Albuquerque and Santa Fe in New Mexico, and had Colorado and possibly California in its sights, eventually stumbled into trouble in late March 1862. Initially the US War Department planned to send a contingent of California volunteers across the southwestern deserts to challenge the rebel soldiers, but the deployment was delayed by problems with secessionists and Confederate sympathizers in southern California itself. By the time the Californians were ready to move, the Confederates were already in northern New Mexico. Instead, Colorado's territorial governor was ordered "to send all available forces," and after a long and difficult march, Colorado volunteers surprised the Confederates at Glorieta Pass. Although the casualties were relatively light, the rebels were driven into a lengthy retreat from northern New Mexico back to Texas. With that, the Californians were left to occupy Tucson, establish federal authority in Arizona and western New Mexico, and stare down any further Confederate adventures there. For the remainder of the war their main engagements were with bands of Chiricahua Apaches under their powerful chiefs Mangas Coloradas and Cochise, a sign of things to come.

Federal military successes were also achieved in the vital Mississippi Valley. Only days after Glorieta Pass, the federal army and navy reclaimed New Orleans and began fanning out into the surrounding sugar plantation parishes, where unionism had a toehold among Whiggish planters and where the enslaved flocked to their lines. To the north, federal forces had been pressing in from Tennessee, Missouri, and Arkansas, taking Forts Henry and Donelson in Tennessee, sending the rebels packing at Pea Ridge in Arkansas, surviving another bloodbath at Shiloh, and then taking Memphis. The objective was control of the Mississippi River, but it would not be easy. Vicksburg, strategically overlooking the river, remained a Confederate stronghold, and with the rebels dug in and the streams and bayous difficult to cross, the varied offensives of Generals Ulysses S. Grant and William T. Sherman were stymied for months on end.

Moving eastward, the military picture grew bleaker for the Union side. The Army of the Cumberland had failed to make much headway in middle Tennessee, and in the fall of 1862 had to fight off a bold Confederate invasion of Kentucky that came within a stone's throw of Cincinnati (on the Ohio-Kentucky border) and nearly inaugurated a state government in Frankfort. But the situation in Virginia was nothing short of drastic. Every effort the US Army made to take Richmond had been decisively turned back, and after the second defeat at Bull Run in August 1862, rebel troops under Robert E. Lee went on the offensive. Their hope was to move into federal territory, attract some support in the slaveholding state of Maryland, win a military victory, further demoralize the northern public, embolden the copperheads, convince Europeans that the cause of the United States was lost, and perhaps force Lincoln to seek an armistice. It made sense even while involving serious risk. Northern morale was at low ebb, state and congressional elections were to take place in November, and McClellan (who, according to Lincoln, had "the slows") was still in charge of federal forces.

Lee and his 55,000 men crossed the Potomac River in early September 1862 and marched into Maryland. Their first surprise was the silence that greeted their arrival; sympathetic Marylanders did not come forward. Their second surprise was that, owing to sheer luck (the discovery of Lee's plans, carelessly discarded), the federal army was ready for them (though, as usual, McClellan hesitated). The subsequent battle at Antietam involved over 100,000 men, nearly one-quarter of whom would be killed or wounded. And although there was not a clear winner, Lee retreated back into Virginia (Map 14.5).

But the setback did not cause Lee to reassess the strategy. In the spring of 1863 he again looked north, to Maryland and Pennsylvania, this time bolstered by a victory that May at Chancellorsville, Virginia, over federal troops who outnumbered him. In the meantime, Alexander Stephens, the Confederacy's vice president, proposed a meeting with Lincoln, under a flag of truce, to discuss prisoner exchanges and a possible peace: on terms dictated by the Confederates.

Gettysburg and Vicksburg

Then, during the first two weeks of July, the dynamics of war and political authority clearly swung toward the federal government. In early June, Lee's army began moving north through the Shenandoah Valley of Virginia before crossing into Maryland and Pennsylvania. All the while, he was being shadowed by federal forces, initially under General Joseph Hooker and later under General George Meade, who positioned themselves between the rebels and Washington, DC,

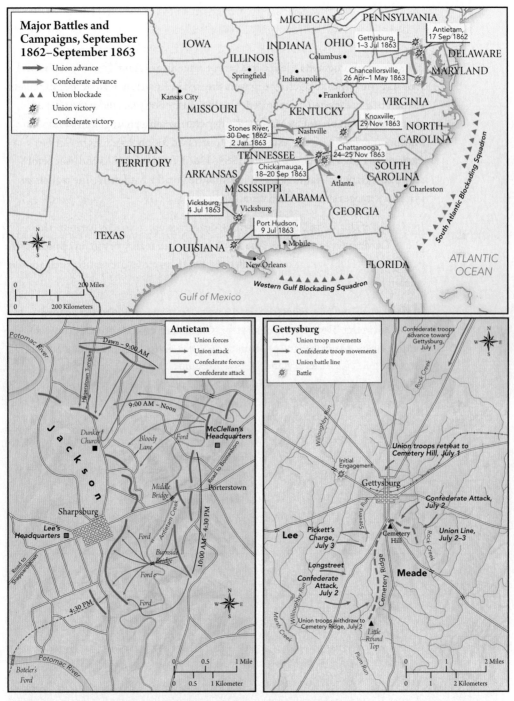

Major Battles and Campaigns, September 1862–September 1863

- → Union advance
- → Confederate advance
- ▲▲▲ Union blockade
- ✷ Union victory
- ✷ Confederate victory

Antietam
- → Union forces
- → Union attack
- → Confederate forces
- → Confederate attack

Gettysburg
- → Union troop movements
- → Confederate troop movements
- --- Union battle line
- ✷ Battle

≡ **MAP 14.5 Major Battles and Campaigns, September 1862–September 1863** Antietam was the bloodiest single day of the war, and it was an important turning point for the North. The Union's repulse of Robert E. Lee's army in July 1863 at Gettysburg inspired jubilation, but successes in the West were even more striking. The Union reclaimed all of Tennessee, and it took full control of the Mississippi River.

PERSPECTIVES

Photographing the Fallen

The seventy photographs Alexander Gardner and his assistant Timothy H. Sullivan took just two days after Gettysburg were the first in American history to show fallen soldiers before they had been buried. Gardner, forty-one years old at the time of the battle, was employed by Mathew Brady, who owned a photography studio in Washington, DC. After the war, Gardner published his photographs in *Gardner's Photographic Sketch Book of the War* (1865–1866). Few Americans had ever before seen photographs of slain soldiers lying unburied on the battlefield. The realism of Gardner's images shocked the nation.

In *Harvest of Death*, six Union soldiers lie dead, face up, stomachs bloated. The photo, Gardner writes, conveys "the blank horror and reality of war, in opposition to its pageantry. Here are the dreadful details! Let them aid in preventing such another calamity falling upon the nation."

In *Home of a Rebel Sharpshooter* a dead Confederate sharpshooter lies against a stone wall in the "Devil's Den," a strategic Confederate fortification during the battle. Gardner describes the photo as showing "a sharpshooter who had evidently

≡ *Harvest of Death*

been wounded in the head by a fragment of shell which had exploded over him, and had laid down upon his blanket to await death. There was no means of judging how long he had lived after receiving his wound, but the disordered clothing shows that his sufferings must have been intense. Was he delirious with agony, or did death come slowly to his relief, while memories of home grew dearer as the field of carnage faded before him?" In fact, historians who have studied the photograph conclude that in order to make the shot more dramatic, Gardener or Sullivan moved the dead soldier approximately 40 yards, placed him next to the stone wall, put a backpack under his head, and propped a rifle near him.

≡ *Home of a Rebel Sharpshooter*

CONSIDER THIS

How do you think Gardner's photographs changed the way Americans viewed war? Knowing that in at least one instance a dead soldier had been moved to make the image more dramatic, does it change the way you view the image? Does it change the way you think about the way the dead should be remembered?

to prevent a direct attack on the capital. Lee's troops fed off the rich fields of south-east Pennsylvania, taking the opportunity to ransack Radical Republican Thaddeus Stevens's ironworks along the way, and eyeing the state capital of Harrisburg. But on July 1, while looking for shoes in the small town of Gettysburg, they encountered the federal cavalry and commenced what turned into three horrific days of battle. This time there was no doubt about the outcome. On July 3, Lee, having lost one-third of his army, recognized defeat and painfully headed back across the Potomac into Confederate Virginia. Alexander Stephens's mission now seemed pointless; Lincoln, an old friend of his, refused him safe passage through federal lines.

The next day was July 4, and there was more good and important news. Hundreds of miles to the south and west, another large rebel force, this one under siege for weeks at Vicksburg, finally surrendered to General Grant, giving the federals full control of the Mississippi River and effectively cutting the Confederacy in two. Lee had hoped that military success in Pennsylvania might relieve the pressure on the rebels in Vicksburg as well as energize copperheads in the North. The draft riots in New York City suggested the explosive charges that might be bubbling below the surface of the federal union had further weakness been exposed. The rebel defeats at Gettysburg and Vicksburg, together with the suppression of the riots, thus constituted staggering, though not necessarily fatal, blows, and encouraged a growing feeling, both in the United States and Europe, that the federal union would likely survive.

A New Birth of Freedom for Whom?

But what sort of union might it be? Since the establishment of American independence and the founding of the republic this was the question with which Americans, at all levels, intensely struggled. Was it a loose confederation of relatively sovereign states? A country in which power was shared between federal and state governments? An empire with many different component parts held together by a weak center with an effervescent idea of destiny? Had the war brought about a major transformation in the very nature of the union itself? Lincoln and other antislavery Republicans had begun to answer these questions well before secession and the war by envisioning not just a confederation or a union or an empire but a "nation": a distinctive form of political organization and state, with specific sorts of territorial reach, economies, sets of social relations, and cultural ambitions.

The vision had been conjured, the ideas developed, the arguments made, but when Lincoln began to speak that November afternoon at Gettysburg's cemetery of the fallen federal soldiers, he seemed to be announcing a nation's presence. Indeed, he gave the nation a deep historical pedigree, lent it a clear political character, and explained the War of the Rebellion not as the moment of the nation's emergence but as the measure of its very survival. "Four score and seven years ago, our fathers brought forth on this continent, a *new nation*, conceived in *Liberty*, and dedicated to the proposition that *all men are created equal*. Now we are engaged in a great civil war, *testing* whether that *nation*, or any *nation* so conceived and so dedicated, can long *endure*." He saw the cemetery as "a great battle-field of that war" which had become the final resting place for those who gave their lives "that the *nation* might live," and insisted that the "brave men, living and dead, who struggled here, have consecrated it, far above our power to add or detract." Still, it was left to "us the living" to carry on the "unfinished work" which they "so nobly advanced," and the "cause" to which "they gave the last full measure of their devotion" was described by Lincoln with a pithy and riveting eloquence: "that this *nation* shall have a new birth of freedom—and that government of the people, by the people, and for the people, shall not perish from the earth."

At no point in the address did Lincoln speak explicitly of emancipation or political democracy, but in describing the "cause" of the war, he clearly suggested that, in his view, both would be foundational to the very meaning of the "nation." Yet there were other things left unspoken and unacknowledged that would have a great deal to do with the sort of "nation" this would be. Lincoln said nothing about the Sioux rebellion, its suppression, the execution of alleged participants, the fate of other Indigenous allies and enemies, or the offensive federal troops were in the midst of carrying out against many of them. Nor did he mention battlefields where newly recruited Black troops had fallen in large numbers—especially at Battery Wagner, South Carolina, only days after Gettysburg—and what place those troops and their communities might have in the "nation" experiencing "a new birth of freedom." Those matters, large, consequential, and contradictory, were still left to be decided.

Conclusion: From a War for Union to a War for Emancipation

After several decades of struggling with the question of slavery's future in the United States, the election in 1860 of Republican President Abraham Lincoln provoked a rebellion among enslavers in many southern states, the organization of the breakaway "Confederate States of America," and, as the Lincoln administration sought to suppress the rebellion, the start of America's civil warfare. Most people on both sides imagined the war would be brief and that their favored side would win; few could imagine the bloody duration of what Lincoln termed the "War of the Rebellion." And few could have seen how the goals of warfare would change over the years from one focused on restoring the tattered Union to one intent on destroying the system of enslavement. The change would be shaped by a series of rebellions against the authority of the Republican-controlled federal government: of Indigenous people on the Plains, of disgruntled Democrats in northern cities and towns, and of Irish immigrants who fumed at the prospect of a political alliance between the Republicans and liberated Black men. But most of all, the change would be influenced by a rebellion of enslaved people in the Confederate states who understood better than anyone else where the winds of history were blowing and, with great courage and fortitude, seized the moment. The war, however, was still to be won.

WHAT IF   Enslaved People Had Stayed Put?

In the fall of 1859, John Brown organized an attack on the federal armory at Harpers Ferry in hope that the enslaved people in the vicinity would rise in rebellion, come join him, and begin the process of destroying slavery in the United States. But the enslaved people, for the most part, didn't show up. What if the enslaved people had responded in much the same way to the federal invasion of the rebellious South? The Lincoln administration very much wanted them to stay out of the way. It was, in the view of the US government and the Confederacy, a white man's war over the future of the country. The enslaved could well have kept to themselves, suspicious of the federals and Confederates alike, or fearful of what concerted action might bring, and left the enemies to fight it out between themselves.

Had enslaved people mostly stayed out of the Civil War, the Lincoln administration, at best, could have defeated the Confederacy, kept slavery out of the territories of the trans-Mississippi West, and perhaps prodded the defeated Confederate states to enact some form of gradual emancipation—with compensation to enslavers and federal support for some type of colonization of free Black people. This, after all, had been Lincoln's vision of enslavement's end even after the Civil War began. Slavery therefore would have continued to exist, and enslavers, even in military defeat, would have remained a force in American life. What might this have meant for the post-war history of the United States?

DOCUMENT 14.1

On December 26, 1861, President Lincoln drafted two bills for the Delaware legislature concerning the end of enslavement. The bills represent his thinking at the time about how an emancipation plan might look. Neither bill was ever introduced for fear of its rejection by the state legislature.

Drafts of a Bill for Compensated Emancipation in Delaware

[No. 1]

Be it enacted by the State of Delaware, that on condition the United States of America will, at the present session of Congress, engage by law to pay, and thereafter faithfully pay to the said State of Delaware, in the six per cent bonds of said United States, the sum of seven hundred and nineteen thousand and two hundred dollars, in five equal annual instalments, there shall be neither slavery nor involuntary servitude, at any time after the first day of January in the year of our Lord one thousand, eight hundred and sixtyseven, within the said State of Delaware, except in the punishment of crime, whereof the party shall have been duly convicted: *Provided*, that said State shall, in good faith prevent, so far as possible, the carrying of any person out of said State, into involuntary servitude, beyond the limits of said State, at any time after the passage of this act; and shall also provide for one fifth of the adult slaves becoming free at the middle of the year one thousand eight hundred an[d] sixtytwo; one fourth of the remainder of said adults, at the middle of the year one thousand eight hundred and sixtythree; one third of the remainder of said adults, at the middle of the year one thousand eight hundred and sixtyfour; one half the remainder of said adults at the middle of the year one thousand eight hundred and sixtyfive; and the entire remainder of adults, together with all minors, at the beginning of the year one thousand eight hundred and sixtyseven, as hereinbefore indicated. And provided also that said State may make provision of apprenticeship, not to extend beyond the age of twenty-one years for males, nor eighteen for females, for all minors whose mothers were not free, at the respective births of such minors.

[No. 2]

Be it enacted by the State of Delaware that on condition the United States of America will, at the present session of Congress, engage by law to pay, and thereafter faithfully pay to the said State of Delaware, in the six per cent bonds of said United States, the sum of seven hundred and nineteen thousand, and two hundred dollars, in thirty one equal annual instalments, there shall be neither slavery nor involuntary servitude, at any time after the first day of January in the year of our Lord one thousand eight hundred and ninety three, within the said State of Delaware, except in the punishment of crime, whereof the party shall have been duly convicted; nor, except in the punishment of crime as aforesaid, shall any person who shall be born after the passage of this act, nor any person above the age of thirty five years, be held in slavery, or to involuntary servitude, within said State of Delaware, at any time after the passage of this act.

And be it further enacted that said State shall, in good faith prevent, so far as possible, the carrying of any person out of said state, into involuntary servitude, beyond the limits of said State, at any time after the passage of this act.

And be it further enacted that said State may make provision of apprenticeship, not to extend beyond the age of twentyone years for males, nor eighteen for females, for all minors whose mothers were not free at the respective births of such minors.

DOCUMENT 14.2

On March 6, 1862, President Abraham Lincoln asked Congress to pass a Joint Resolution on a plan to have the states move forward with the abolition of slavery. The plan involved gradual emancipation together with federally supported compensation to slaveholders.

Fellow-citizens of the Senate and House of Representatives:

I recommend the adoption of a joint resolution by your honorable bodies, which shall be substantially as follows:

"*Resolved*, That the United States ought to co-operate with any State which may adopt gradual abolishment of slavery, giving to such State pecuniary aid, to be used by such State in its discretion, to compensate for the inconveniences, public and private, produced by such change of system."

If the proposition contained in the resolution does not meet the approval of Congress and the country, there is the end; but if it does command such approval, I deem it of importance that the States and people immediately interested should be at once distinctly notified of the fact, so that they may begin to consider whether to accept or reject it. The federal government would find its highest interest in such a measure, as one of the most efficient means of self-preservation. The leaders of the existing insurrection entertain the hope that this government will ultimately be forced to acknowledge the independence of some part of the disaffected region, and that all the slave States north of such part will then say, "the Union for which we have struggled being already gone, we now choose to go with the southern section." To deprive them of this hope substantially ends the rebellion; and the initiation of emancipation completely deprives them of it as to all the States initiating it. The point is not that *all* the States tolerating slavery would very soon, if at all, initiate emancipation, but that while the offer is equally made to all, the more northern shall, but such initiation, make it certain to the more southern that in no event will the former ever join the latter in their proposed confederacy. I say "initiation," because in my judgment gradual, and not sudden, emancipation is better for all. In the mere financial or pecuniary view, any member of Congress, with the census tables and treasury reports before him, can readily see for himself how very soon the current expenditures of this war would purchase, at fair valuation, all the slaves in any named State. Such a proposition on the part of the general government sets up no claim of a right by federal authority to interfere with slavery within State limits, referring as it does the absolute control of the subject in each case to the State and its people immediately interested. It is proposed as a matter of perfectly free choice with them.

Thinking About Contingency

1. Delaware rejected Lincoln's offer for gradual emancipation of enslaved persons and compensation for slaveholders. But what if Delaware had accepted it? Would the other border states have followed Delaware's example? How would this have affected the course of the war?

2. Congress and the general public expressed widespread support for Lincoln's March 1862 message of "gradual, and not sudden, emancipation." What if this vision for the ending of slavery had been implemented, and not the one expressed in the Emancipation Proclamation? What would this have meant for the post-war history of the United States?

REVIEW QUESTIONS

1. What advantages and disadvantages did the federal government and the Confederate rebels have, militarily, when the Civil War began? Which side had the better chance to succeed, and why?

2. What plans did the Confederacy have for the trans-Mississippi West, and what did Confederates do to execute those plans? How did these plans fit into the Confederate vision of their state-in-the-making?

3. In what ways did the federal government expand its powers to mobilize against the Confederate rebellion? Who were the greatest beneficiaries of expanding federal power?

4. What part did Native Americans play in the Civil War, and how was it significant?

5. What part did enslaved people play in the policies of the federal government toward slavery, and why did they choose to rebel against their enslavers and support the federal government's side?

6. How much opposition was there in the North to the Lincoln administration and its policies about the war, and what was its nature? Was there similar opposition within the Confederate states to the policies of the Confederate government?

7. What vision of an American future did Lincoln convey in his Gettysburg Address? How much of a change did it represent from the ways in which the United States was organized since the founding of the republic?

KEY TERMS

Battle of Antietam (p. 582)

Battle of Bull Run (Manassas Junction) (p. 580)

Battle of Shiloh (p. 579)

belligerent status (p. 572)

contrabands of war (p. 584)

copperheads (p. 588)

Emancipation Proclamation (p. 586)

First Confiscation Act (p. 585)

Gettysburg Address (p. 594)

greenbacks (p. 575)

Homestead Act (p. 576)

King Cotton diplomacy (p. 572)

Legal Tender Act (p. 575)

Militia Act (p. 586)

National Bank Act (p. 575)

New York City Draft Riots (p. 593)

Pacific Railway Act (p. 576)

Preliminary Emancipation Proclamation (p. 582)

Second Battle of Bull Run (Second Manassas) (p. 579)

Second Confiscation Act (p. 586)

RECOMMENDED READINGS

Gary Clayton Anderson, *Massacre in Minnesota: The Dakota War of 1862* (University of Oklahoma Press, 2019).

Ira Berlin, et al., eds, *Free At Last: A Documentary History of Slavery, Freedom, and the Civil War* (New Press, 1992).

Iver Bernstein, *The New York City Draft Riots* (Oxford University Press, 1991).

Drew Gilpin Faust, *Mothers of Invention: Women of the Slaveholding South in the American Civil War* (University of North Carolina Press, 2004).

Eric Foner, *The Fiery Trial: Abraham Lincoln and Slavery* (W.W. Norton, 2010).

Thavolia Glymph, *The Women's Fight: The Civil War Battles for Home, Freedom, and Nation* (University of North Carolina Press, 2022).

James M. McPherson, *Battle Cry of Freedom: The Civil War Era* (Oxford University Press, 1988).

Megan Kate Nelson, *The Three-Cornered War: The Union, The Confederacy, and Native Peoples in the Fight for the West* (Scribner, 2019).

Armstead Robinson, *Bitter Fruits of Bondage: The Demise of Slavery and the Collapse of the Confederacy* (University of Virginia Press, 2004).

Amy Murrell Taylor, *Embattled Freedom: Journeys Through the Civil War's Slave Refugee Camps* (University of North Carolina Press, 2020).

Ending the Rebellion and (Re)constructing the Nation

1863–1865

Chapter Outline

15.1 The Problem of Confederate Territory

⫿ Explain the challenges of reunification once the Civil War ended.

15.2 The Future of the Formerly Enslaved

⫿ Identify the issues that emancipation raised for the future of Black people.

15.3 Indigenous People and the Future of the West

⫿ Describe how the war between the federal government and the Confederates came to involve Indigenous peoples in the West.

15.4 Making Freedom

⫿ Summarize what did and didn't change in the status and experiences of formerly enslaved people.

15.5 When Did the War End?

⫿ Analyze the complexities of bringing the Civil War to a conclusion.

15.6 Reunification According to Andrew Johnson

⫿ Explain the emerging clash between President Andrew Johnson and congressional Republicans over Reconstruction policy.

≡ **"Bread or Blood!"**   With a threat of famine hanging like a dark cloud over the Confederacy, a large crowd of women ransack bakeries and dry goods stores in Richmond on April 2, 1863.

On April 2, 1863, a crowd of more than 200 women, mostly the wives of Confederate soldiers and local iron workers, marched on the Virginia governor's mansion in Richmond, then the Confederate capital. Led by Mary Jackson and Minerva Meredith, the latter described as "tall, daring, and Amazonian looking," they had met the day before amid growing hardship that food shortages, Confederate policies, and spiraling inflation had brought upon them and their families. Their plan was to meet with the governor and demand action. But when the time came, the governor refused to see them, and so the women—soon joined by many hundreds more, some carrying knives, axes, and other weapons—took to the streets shouting, "We celebrate our right to live! We are starving!" and, more ominously, "Bread or Blood!" Quickly, they turned their wrath on the symbols of their plight, on the government warehouses and the dry goods stores that were hoarding supplies and asking highly inflated prices

Timeline

1863 OCT		1864 JAN	APR	JUL	OCT
		1863 › **December** Lincoln issues Proclamation of Amnesty and Reconstruction			
				1864 › **July** Republican Congress passes Wade-Davis Bill regarding Reconstruction, which Lincoln refuses to sign	
				September Atlanta falls to federal forces under General William Sherman	

for their sale. The women sacked them, seizing food, clothing, and other necessities. It was a classic food riot of the sort that exploded in many societies when starvation loomed and some profited off the miseries of most others.

Arriving on the scene, Richmond's mayor demanded that the women withdraw, but to no avail. The governor finally appeared, to little effect. And then came Jefferson Davis, the Confederacy's president and commander in chief. Climbing on a wagon, Davis begged the women to disperse, emptied his pockets of coins, and tossed them their way. He then warned that an artillery unit would arrive and fire upon them if they persisted. Slowly, the women moved off; their food riot was at an end.

Richmond was not alone. Food riots led by women occurred in other parts of the Confederacy in March and April 1863, and they testified to the internal crises that

	1865 JAN	APR	JUL	OCT	1866 JAN

November Lincoln reelected president; Sand Creek Massacre

1865 >
January General William Sherman issues Special Field Orders No. 15 reserving land for Black settlement

March Congress establishes the Freedmen's Bureau

April Generals Robert E. Lee and Joseph Johnston surrender their troops in Virginia and North Carolina; President Lincoln is assassinated and Democratic Vice President Andrew Johnson becomes president

May President Johnson issues Proclamation of Amnesty

afflicted the Confederacy as its troops struggled to hold their lines on the battlefields. The War of the Rebellion, as would be true of other modern wars, wreaked havoc on civilian as well as military populations. Both the federal government and the Confederate rebels needed to contain social tensions and conflicts within their own sides. How these conflicts were managed would play an important role in the outcome of the war and in ways in which the peace might be imagined.

15.1   The Problem of Confederate Territory

▎▎▎   Explain the challenges of reunification once the Civil War ended.

Even before federal armies marched into the rebellious slaveholding states in 1861, new Republican policymakers began to think about how and in what form the country might be reunified. The rebels had met in special conventions, broken their ties with the United States, formed what they called the Confederate States of America, and vowed to resist federal coercion in a fight for their independence. But what did this really mean in political and constitutional terms, and what powers did the federal government have to act? How was the rebellion to be interpreted, and how would the interpretation shape a process of reconstruction? And which branches of government—the president, Congress, or the courts—had the authority to make the rules?

Republican Perspectives

At the outset, the prevailing view of Lincoln and fellow Republicans was that secession was constitutionally impossible. There was simply no basis in the Constitution to permit a state to leave the union of states. As a result, secession and the Confederacy—Lincoln always referred to it as the "so-called Confederacy"— were regarded as nothing more than the work of rebels who had taken control of their respective states and determined to wage war against the federal government to achieve their ends. The Confederacy could not be diplomatically recognized because it had no legal existence and, as it turned out, no other country in Europe or the Western Hemisphere lent the Confederacy formal recognition. The Republicans optimistically imagined that the Confederate rebels composed only a minority of the population and that loyalty to the United States remained widespread though temporarily pushed below the surface of public opinion. Therefore, from the perspective of the Lincoln administration, the task was to suppress the rebellion, find people loyal to the United States, and return control of the affected states to them. Under these circumstances, the position of the states in the Union would not have changed and their laws and institutions—as well as the status of their citizens who had not engaged in rebellion—would still be in place.

This perspective, of course, was based on the expectation that the rebellion would be defeated quickly and unionism again would rise to the surface of political life. "The States have their *status* in the Union," Lincoln told Congress in July 1861, "and they have no other *legal status.*" Yet, as it became clear that the rebellion would not be rapidly subdued and that Republicans couldn't count on much of a base of loyalty among whites in the rebellious states, such thinking appeared misguided. New thinking was necessary.

Republicans, mainly from the radical wing of the party, began to devise a very different argument and perspective. They did not deny that the United States was perpetual or that secession was constitutionally impossible. What they did deny was that nothing fundamental had happened. Radical Republican leaders claimed that the "treasonably civil organization" created in those states effectively forfeited "*their* powers and rights as States," and Massachusetts Senator Charles Sumner went so far as to insist that by the act of secession the states had committed constitutional "suicide." They had ceased to exist. Many of Sumner's colleagues, though rejecting his specific analogy, nonetheless came to a similar conclusion: that the rebel states had been returned to the condition of territories subject to the jurisdiction of the federal government.

This argument was called **territorialization**, though it didn't bring with it any specific plan for reorganizing those states politically. As Congress began to debate the question in early 1862, all sorts of ideas and approaches were offered, some involving the very heavy hand of the Republican-dominated government and a lengthy road to reunification. Lincoln was more hesitant and was not among those Radical Republicans who embraced the concept of territorialization. In principle, he remained committed both to the notion that secession was constitutionally impossible and that loyal state governments should be established as soon as feasible. Even so, his thinking had evolved. More than a year into the war and with little prospect of an end to the rebellion, he could hardly have expected those states to rejoin the United States on their own. Instead, the federal government through its military arm would have to step in and take charge, providing for elections and identifying eligible voters. And, as the Lincoln administration and Congress committed the war to emancipation, the issue of abolition as a prerequisite to any reunification now defined the process.

In this context, Lincoln, shortly after his address at Gettysburg, issued in December 1863 a **Proclamation of Amnesty and Reconstruction**. More of a

THE WAR IN THE SOUTHWEST. ADJUTANT GENERAL THOMAS ADDRESSING THE NEGROES IN LOUISIANA ON THE DUTIES OF FREEDOM.—[SKETCHED BY MR. HAMILTON.]

≡ **Freed African Americans** A large crowd of African American men, women, and children, some wearing federal military uniforms, listen to General Lorenzo Thomas speak "on the duties and responsibilities of freedom," in Louisiana in 1863.

framework than a clear-cut plan and designed to end the war as soon as feasible, the proclamation set out guidelines for the establishment of new state governments in those parts of the South occupied by federal troops. Offering pardons to all rebels who would now pledge allegiance to the United States, with the exception of top Confederate leaders, Lincoln determined that when such loyalists made up at least one-tenth of all those who voted in the 1860 presidential election, they could adopt a new state constitution and seek representation in Congress. Since the proclamation began by declaring that "treason" had been committed by "many persons" in those states, Lincoln's terms were remarkably generous; that is, save for enslavement.

Lincoln's pardon would carry the "restoration of all rights of property, *except as to slaves*," and he expected the new state governments to provide for the "permanent freedom" of enslaved people. Nothing at all was said about the civil or political status of the formerly enslaved, and Lincoln accepted the likelihood of arrangements "consistent with their present condition as a laboring, landless, and homeless class." Thus, as the problem of enslavement moved toward resolution, the problem of freedom for the formerly enslaved increasingly reared its head. Still, Lincoln had embarked on a course that he had once considered unconstitutional. He asserted the supremacy of the federal government over the states and required them to abolish slavery as a condition for regaining their place in the Union.

The proclamation has become known as Lincoln's "ten-percent plan," and it initially enjoyed support among most Republicans because of its insistence on emancipation. Then, much of that support evaporated as the policy played out in Louisiana, where the federal army had gained a significant foothold in 1862 and loyalist factions—wealthy sugar planters among them—were jockeying for advantage. Some of those who took oaths of allegiance still hoped to be compensated for the chattel property that had been taken from them and to resume their familiar stations in civil and political life. As the Boston-born radical reformer Wendell Phillips saw it, Lincoln's policy "leaves the large landed proprietors of the South still to domineer . . . and makes the negro's freedom a mere sham." Those pardoned under the ten-percent plan, men like Phillips feared, could be of dubious loyalty and, if quickly readmitted to Congress, threaten Republican power.

Clashing Perspectives and Policies

Republicans in Congress increasingly embraced two perspectives that brought them into conflict with Lincoln. One was that Lincoln's plan was too hasty and lenient, and something much tougher was needed. After all, by Lincoln's own telling, the Confederate rebels had committed treason. The other perspective was that, in their view, the Constitution gave Congress, not the president, the power to determine whether a state had an appropriate form of government.

By the early summer of 1864, congressional Republicans put together an alternative policy that reflected their views. It was called the **Wade-Davis Bill** (for co-sponsors Ohio Senator Benjamin Wade and Maryland Representative Henry Winter Davis), and although it made no move in the direction of Black citizenship or suffrage, it did demand that a majority of "white male citizens" (not 10 percent of 1860 voters) pledge their loyalty to the United States before any reorganization of state governments could go forward. Then, only those who never held military or political office under the Confederacy or never "voluntarily" took up "arms against the United States" could participate in the process. They would, furthermore, have to abolish slavery, disfranchise top Confederate leaders, and extend to "all persons," including the formerly enslaved, the right to justice before the law. Until these conditions were met—and they would not be easy to meet—the states would remain under the control of a provisional governor appointed by the president with the consent of the Senate.

Passed with overwhelming support in Congress, the Wade-Davis Bill went to Lincoln's desk for his signature. There it sat. Lincoln didn't fundamentally oppose the bill's requirements and had no problem if any rebellious state chose, of its own accord, to follow them. But he feared that if the bill became law, it would derail the process already underway as a result of his ten-percent plan (in Arkansas, Tennessee, and Virginia, as well as Louisiana) and perhaps lengthen the war. Consequently, he refused to sign the bill (an action known as a "pocket veto") and deeply angered his Republican colleagues. It was the first of many struggles that would play out for another decade between the executive and legislative branches of the federal government over basic questions of constitutional power and between warring elements of the Republican Party over the pace and extent of Reconstruction policy. But a momentous shift nonetheless was taking place. After seven decades of confusion, struggle, and compromise over the question of political sovereignty—over whether the states or the central government was ultimately in charge—the War of the Rebellion enabled the Republicans to begin defining the character of a new and different entity: not a union but a nation.

15.2   The Future of the Formerly Enslaved

‖‖‖ Identify the issues that emancipation raised for the future of Black people.

For all of their sweep and political drama, the laws and decrees abolishing slavery said nothing about the civil or political rights of those men, women, and children who had been enslaved. Nothing about citizenship, nothing about the right to vote, nothing about the ability to sue or testify in court or to sit in judgment of those who allegedly violated the law. As a result, enslaved people who had been liberated would enter a world still governed by the Supreme Court's *Dred Scott* decision of 1857 and the racially discriminatory practices widespread at the state and local levels. This was a world in which people of African descent had "no rights that whites were bound to respect" and could not be citizens of the United States. At best, policymakers imagined them, much like Lincoln did, as laboring people who would now work for wages. This was true of most abolitionists as well, even the full-throated William Lloyd Garrison.

Limits of Change

The assumption that freedmen and women would continue to endure a life of labor, chiefly on the agricultural lands of the southern states, had a powerful logic. No one could deny that the cotton plant had fueled the engine of antebellum (prewar) economic growth, and most political leaders in the United States envisioned a revitalized cotton economy as crucial to the future prosperity of the country. Some saw the opportunity to demonstrate the superior efficiency and productivity of free, as opposed to enslaved, labor. Others were eager to cash in on the high prices cotton fetched on the international market. In all cases, the availability of Black labor was seen as critical to ending the war and shaping the peace.

The federal government embarked upon or encouraged a series of initiatives during the war itself that paved the road to such an end. Through the auspices of the military, it first introduced, in parts of the occupied South, what was called the "**contract labor system**." Enslaved people who had fled to federal army lines—becoming contrabands—and were not needed by the military could be hired out to southern landowners who had taken the loyalty oath or to the thousands of northerners who had leased or purchased agricultural lands in the South. They would receive small monthly wages and basic subsistence while being subject to close supervision and limited mobility. At the same time, organizations like the American Missionary Association, which had been involved in the antislavery movement since the late 1840s, mobilized missionaries and teachers to go into areas occupied by the federal troops both to lend aid to the contrabands and to prepare them for the new world of freedom. Worried that the formerly enslaved might not yet be "ready" for freedom, they hoped to tutor them in freedom's demands and responsibilities. They instructed them in literacy, sexual propriety, the values of thrift and industry, the proper roles for men and women, and the nature of Christian worship.

The Lincoln administration took its own measures of the condition of the freedpeople in 1863 by appointing the **American Freedmen's Inquiry Commission**. The Commission toured the occupied South and interviewed military officials, former slaveholders, and missionaries as well as the previously enslaved and free people of color to learn about the conditions and prospects for African Americans in a post-emancipation South. When they completed their work, the commissioners recommended the creation of a federal organization to supervise the transition out of enslavement, provide for education and the administration of justice, and ensure that the now freedpeople received wages for their work. In March 1865, the Congress implemented the recommendation when it established the **Freedmen's Bureau** (formally known as the Bureau of Refugees, Freedmen, and Abandoned Lands) for one year, hoping that contract rather than coercion would organize new labor relations and that avenues to redress grievances would be made available for Black laborers and white employers alike.

Aspirations of the Freedpeople

For all of the paternalistic concerns about whether the once enslaved were "ready" for freedom, African American men and women demonstrated, in a variety of settings across the South, that they were indeed prepared for freedom and had well-developed perspectives as to what their freedom might entail. Along the coast of South Carolina and Georgia and in southwestern Mississippi, where plantation owners and enslavers had fled in the face of federal troops, they continued to cultivate lands they had tended as enslaved people and established their own forms of self-governance, including constitutions, elected officials, and local courts. In the Mississippi Valley, some groups pooled their meager resources to rent plots of land either from the federal government or from northern lessees and made an

≡ **Teachers and Relief Workers**   Ten teachers, all women, from the American Missionary Association of New York pose in front of their mission house in Port Royal, South Carolina, in 1862. Two African American children stand at left, hiding their faces with their caps.

impressive go of it. In occupied portions of North Carolina and Virginia, the formerly enslaved gradually turned contraband camps and the immediately surrounding countryside into what one federal official could call "African villages," constructing their own shelters, farming for themselves, building churches and schools, and running stores. Where territory was still controlled by Confederate rebels, those still enslaved attempted to renegotiate the rhythms and rules of their captivity, demanding small wages and greater leverage over their working conditions.

As Black people struggled to make their aspirations known and to pursue them as best as they could, they showed that the transition from enslavement to freedom would be deeply contested. They also showed that they could win allies among the federal officials, teachers, and missionaries they encountered in contraband camps, leased plantations, and army units, some of whom came to discover that, even as enslaved people, African Americans held complex "notions of liberty," were often familiar with the Bible, were "shrewd" and understood "compensation received for work," and, more than anything else, wished "to possess land, if it only be a few acres." It seemed, in short, for those willing to see, that Black people had constructed relations and expectations as to family, work, and community that had a lot in common with those of whites but did not easily accord with the type of nation-building many Republican leaders wished to pursue.

15.3   Indigenous People and the Future of the West

‖‖‖ Describe how the war between the federal government and the Confederates came to involve Indigenous peoples in the West.

The eyes of the developing American nation looked West as well as South and on Indigenous people as well as newly emancipated Black people. The threads of a policy toward Indigenous people had, as we have seen, been in place since the founding of the republic, mixing the carrot of assimilation with the stick of expulsion and confinement on reservations. Reformers who viewed Native Americans, much as they viewed African Americans, as culturally backward though potentially redeemable urged that efforts be made to promote "civilization." They imagined that white teachers could encourage literacy, missionaries could spread Christianity, Indigenous men could turn from hunting to agriculture, and communal forms of property could be discarded.

Treaties and Reservations

But the reformers offered little to challenge the designs of white settlers and their political allies, who hungered for the land that Indigenous people claimed and had no interest in the goal of assimilating them. In general, the settlers saw Indigenous people as barbaric obstacles in the way of "progress" who had to be reduced and pushed out of the way. Even those like the mixed-blood faction of the Cherokees, who tried to reorganize their lives and politics in the ways of the whites (as we saw in Chapter 9), learned that the stick of retribution was unavoidable. Since the reformers mostly accepted the settlers' distinction between "progress" and "barbarism" and wished to advance the former at the expense of the latter, they could only limit the worst effects of a process whose objectives—economic development and evangelicalism—they largely shared. This is what scholars now term **settler colonialism** to suggest the goals and power involved in the process.

As a result, the reservation became the means to resolve the tensions between coercion and civilization. Indigenous people would agree to give up lands that white settlers desired, move to tracts of land set aside for them by the government, and there, with the help of federal Indian agents, annuities, and missionaries, embrace the ways of the whites. On reservations, as white officials saw it, the "wild energies" and "haughty pride" of the Indigenous people could be "subdued" and they could be "trained in the pursuits of civilized life." Beginning with a series of arrangements covering 139 small tribes in California in the early 1850s, such reservations soon became the policy orientation of choice among those in the federal government charged with supervising "Indian affairs."

The centerpiece of this process was, as it had previously been, the treaty, very much a reflection of the multiple forms of sovereignty that defined the American union and empire before the War of the Rebellion erupted. As we saw in Chapter 9, in the 1830s the Supreme Court had ruled that Native Americans were members of "domestic dependent nations," something less than full-fledged sovereigns but distinctive political entities neither to be counted for purposes of congressional apportionment nor subject to taxation. But treaty-making almost invariably created divisions among the Native Americans who entered into it, and the onset of civil warfare in 1861 unhinged the relations and understandings that supported the treaties.

Civil Warfare and Indigenous Warfare

Almost immediately, the Five Civilized Tribes in Indian Territory made formal alliances with the Confederacy that simultaneously recognized their sovereignty and encouraged their political and military participation in the Confederate rebellion (as discussed in Chapter 14). By mid-May 1861, Chickasaws and Choctaws were sending troops and, before long, pro-Confederate Cherokees were driving pro-Union Cherokees, Creeks, and Seminoles into neighboring Kansas. By November 1861, the Confederacy defined Indian Territory as one of its military departments, and Cherokee leaders gained commissions in the Confederate Army—one chief, Stand Watie, even achieved the rank of general. For his part, Lincoln stopped annuity payments and withdrew all federal troops from the area, and Congress soon permitted him to terminate treaties with any tribe "in actual hostility to the United States."

Then Lincoln thought better of abandoning Indian Territory and determined to reoccupy it. A decisive federal victory at Pea Ridge in northwestern Arkansas in March 1862 against a combined Confederate-Indigenous force opened the way and symbolized the militarization of federal Indigenous policy. The ball was now in the court of federal army commanders who had little patience for diplomacy and more interest in dealing with Indigenous people through force. In Minnesota, General John Pope, sent to suppress the Sioux rebellion of that summer (discussed in Chapter 14), scorned treaty-making and the entire "Indian system" more generally. He wanted authority over Indigenous matters shifted from the Interior to the War Department and sizeable military posts established that would control tribes once they had been defeated and confined to reservations.

Out in the territory of New Mexico, federal Brigadier General James Carlton, who had marched his troops from California to intercept Confederate advances in the Southwest, took a similar view after encounters with Navajos and Apaches. Acknowledging the objective of getting the Indigenous people onto a reservation where they could acquire "new habits" and "modes

≡ **Indigenous Fighters at the Battle of Pea Ridge**   Confederate cavalry and infantry, assisted by mounted Cherokee and Chickasaw warriors, attack a line of Union cannon and infantry at Pea Ridge.

of life," he nonetheless insisted that the "application of force" could never be "relaxed." Like Pope, he scoffed at signing treaties and instead believed that hostile Indigenous people had to be pursued without mercy and beaten into submission. Mangas Coloradas, one of the powerful Apache leaders, felt the lethal brunt of this policy. Lured into a trap by soldiers waving a flag of truce, Coloradas was brutally tortured and shot to death. His body was then decapitated and his large head sent east to the Smithsonian Institution in Washington, DC, where it found a place among a growing collection of Indigenous bones and artifacts: museum pieces testifying to the superior culture of white Americans.

The aggressiveness of Carlton and Pope in the apparent service of "civilization" and the United States was indicative of an increasingly iron-fisted and violence-ridden politics that spread across the Plains beginning in 1862 (see Map 15.1). Carlton

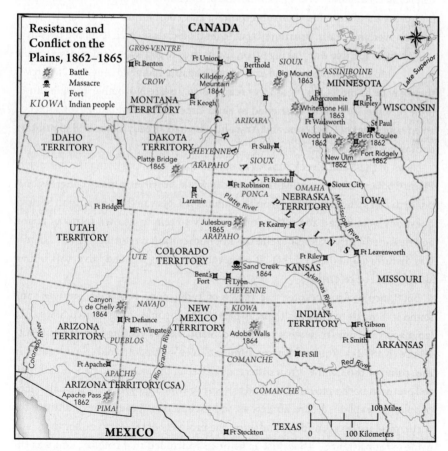

≡ **MAP 15.1 Resistance and Conflict on the Plains, 1862–1865**   In response to increasing belligerence from the United States, Cheyennes, Arapahos, Kiowas, Comanches, and Sioux began a general uprising across the Plains.

not only put several thousand Apaches and Navajos (themselves enemies) onto the small reservation of Bosque Redondo in eastern New Mexico but ruled them in a dictatorial fashion. An equally autocratic regime took shape in the Colorado Territory under Governor John Evans, a railroad promoter originally from Illinois (where he was one of the founders of Northwestern University, located in the town renamed for him, Evanston). Less concerned about Confederate sympathizers than about the hunting and raiding of the Cheyenne and Arapaho, Evans believed that suppressing Indigenous resistance was the key to attracting a transcontinental railroad through Denver, a potential financial windfall. In John Chivington, who commanded a regiment of Colorado volunteers, he found a kindred spirit.

But if Evans and Chivington assumed that the Indigenous people could easily be forced into submission, they miscalculated. Indeed, by the summer of 1864, Cheyennes, Arapahos, Kiowas, Comanches, and Sioux had begun a general uprising across the Plains and interrupted traffic and communication along the Santa Fe and Overland Trails. Frustrated that federal officials seemed to ignore his warnings about a "terrible war" taking place, Evans then urged white Coloradans to take matters into their own hands and exterminate hostile Indigenous people "wherever they may be found." Chivington was ready to go. In late November 1864, he and a force of some 700 soldiers marched to Sand Creek, southeast of Denver, attacked an encampment of Cheyenne and Arapaho who had already submitted to military authorities, and massacred them.

News of the **Sand Creek Massacre** spread quickly, intensifying the outrage of Plains Indians who expanded their attacks while horrifying many congressional policymakers who saw Chivington's actions as savagery in their own right. Serious questions were raised about the army's ability to rein in its own forms of terror, and new credibility was lent to the ways of humanitarian reformers. Even Lincoln was disturbed and pledged that "if we get through this war and I live, this Indian system shall be reformed."

But Lincoln also accepted the image of Indigenous people as "savages" and found it difficult to envision them as part of the "people of the United States." In language very similar to what he offered Black leaders visiting him at the White House in 1862—"You and we are different races"—Lincoln told tribal leaders in the spring of 1863 of the "great difference between the pale-faced people and their red brethren both as to numbers and the way in which they lived." "The pale-faced people," he explained, "are numerous and prosperous because they cultivate the earth, produce bread, and depend upon the products of the earth rather than wild game for subsistence." Thus, just as he once concluded that colonization was the proper solution to the dilemmas of white and Black, so he regarded "the plan of concentrating Indians and confining them to reservations" as the "fixed policy of the government."

Reinforcing this "fixed policy" was Lincoln's perspective on the relation of the civil warfare to the development of the trans-Mississippi West. Noting the "steady expansion of the population," the "great enterprise" of connecting the Atlantic and Pacific by rail and telegraph, and the discovery of gold and silver mines, he hoped to provide a "proper government of the Indians" to make the West "secure for the advancing settler." "That portion of the earth's surface which is owned and inhabited by the people of the United States is well adapted to be the home of one national family,"

≡ **Delegation of Plains Indians at the White House** This March 1863 photograph shows a delegation of leaders from the Kiowa and Cheyenne nations during a visit to the White House. Eighteen months after this photo was taken all four men in the front row were dead, including two who were killed at Sand Creek. The woman in the back row on the far right has been identified as Mary Todd Lincoln.

Lincoln observed, "and it is not well-adapted for two or more." It was a strange and ominous twist on the concept of the "house divided."

15.4 Making Freedom

||| Summarize what did and didn't change in the status and experiences of formerly enslaved people.

The question of who the "people of the United States" were, of how membership in the "national family" would be determined, was not only raised by Indigenous people reluctant to live like whites. It was also raised by people of African descent already in rebellion against their enslavers and enslavement. Ever since the 1820s and 1830s, fugitives from enslavement together with free Black allies had been pressing state and federal authorities to end their cooperation with slaveholders and reject the markers of subordinate status that African Americans were forced to bear. Increasingly they demanded civil equality, access to education and other public institutions, and the right to vote on the same basis as whites. But it was the arming of enslaved men to aid in crushing the Confederacy that shifted the nature of discussion and the horizon of possibility.

Black Men in Blue

The military recruitment of African Americans—enslaved and free—came in the face of deep traditions of exclusion and then wartime rebuffs from federal officials despite their need for thousands of volunteers. Indeed, it was the enslaved who accomplished what free Black leaders like Frederick Douglass failed to do by fleeing the sites of their captivity in numbers never anticipated by the federal government and flooding into contraband camps and other military sites. A chaplain in the Army of the Tennessee could compare the volume of enslaved people who had abandoned neighboring cotton plantations and headed to federal lines to an "army in themselves." Contract labor and other leasing arrangements offered one means of alleviating the pressure, but as manpower shortages challenged the goals of the Lincoln administration, Black recruitment emerged as an option that could no longer be ignored. In July 1862, Congress passed a Militia Act and soon thereafter the War Department permitted the establishment of the **First South Carolina Volunteers**, a regiment made up of formerly enslaved men from the state that had led the secession process.

But full-scale mobilization had to await the Emancipation Proclamation of January 1, 1863. Only then did the Lincoln administration allow northern governors to begin enrolling Black men living in their states (many were fugitives from enslavement and their children). Nearly three-quarters of those between the ages of eighteen and forty-five came forward (about 33,000), a much higher proportion than was true among eligible white men. By far the greatest number, however, were recruited in the slave states, especially those of the Confederacy. Totaling over 140,000, they would come to compose over 10 percent of the US Army and, in some departments, nearly half of it. Emancipation, therefore, not only came as a war measure but was directly tied to the military recruitment of Black men who gained freedom for themselves as well as for their mothers, wives, and children. It thereby embedded a gender hierarchy—the men were the prime political movers and liberators—that was central to the political and cultural vision of the developing nation.

Initially federal officials imagined that Black troops would serve mainly behind the lines as laborers, enabling more of the white troops to do the fighting. But before long African Americans could be found armed and in the heat of battle. Behind their own lines, however, Black soldiers faced an assortment of challenges. Their units were segregated from those of white troops and, with a few exceptions, they were denied the opportunity to become commissioned officers (sergeant was the highest rank they could attain). They were put to work doing the most degrading work in camp and, as a consequence of their presumed status, paid less than one-half of their white soldiering counterparts. Many of the white officers and enlistees treated them with derision and contempt, believing that Black bodies were more expendable than white ones.

But these were only some of the special liabilities that defined the Black experience of military service. Although many Black men who had been enslaved relished the opportunity to help defeat the Confederacy and the system of enslavement on which it rested, they were vulnerable to a retribution not shared by white soldiers. Simply put, the Confederacy regarded them as slaves "in flagrant rebellion." According to the Confederates, they were not to be recognized as soldiers "subject to the rules of war" but rather as "slaves in armed insurrection," meriting, by order of Jefferson Davis, the punishment of re-enslavement

THE GALLANT CHARGE OF THE FIFTY FOURTH MASSACHUSETTS (COLORED) REGIMENT.
On the Rebel works at Fort Wagner, Morris Island near Charleston, July 18th 1863, and death of Colonel Robt G. Shaw.

Storming Fort Wagner The print dramatizes the 54th Massachusetts' assault on the parapets of Fort Wagner. Colonel Robert Gould Shaw, the regiment's white leader, clutches his chest as he is mortally struck by a bullet. The soldier holding the American flag is William Harvey Carney, who was awarded the Congressional Medal of Honor for his gallantry in guarding the regimental colors.

or execution. "It was understood among us," a Confederate soldier wrote in 1864, "that we take no negro prisoners." Small wonder that Black people fought with a special ferocity. "There is death to the rebel in every black man's eyes," one northerner reported.

That ferocity and determination had significant effect. Black people steadily dispelled doubts among federal policymakers that enslavement had rendered them too cowardly and undisciplined to fight. In major engagements at Milliken's Bend and Port Hudson in the lower Mississippi Valley and at Fort Wagner in South Carolina—all during the spring and summer of 1863—they faced down enemy fire and performed valiantly. They would soon appear in most theaters of warfare, especially in Virginia, as the army commanded by General Ulysses S. Grant battled to defeat rebel forces under Robert E. Lee. The arming of African American men came at a time of military stalemate and low morale in much of the North. Thus, their participation proved to be a tipping point in the war, fortifying the United States and weakening the Confederacy, while challenging the racial attitudes of many white northerners.

The Political Significance of Black Soldiering

The political significance of Black soldiering may have been as great as the military. Contraband camps and army units drew African Americans together in numbers that dwarfed the size of plantations and farms. Here they met enslaved and free

Black people from near and far as well as white officers who had spent years in the antislavery movement or had fled as political refugees from failed midcentury (1848) republican revolutions in Europe. Here they could also follow the progress of the war, learn of federal policies, discover forms of authority and loyalty other than those prescribed by their enslavers or small communities, and achieve basic literacy. "The general aim and probable consequences of this war," Thomas Wentworth Higginson, an abolitionist who commanded Black troops, observed, "are better understood in my regiment than in any white regiment."

The political consciousness that so impressed Higginson could be seen on a number of fronts. Within the army, Black soldiers soon mobilized to protest discrimination in combat status, pay, and promotion, eventually forcing the Congress to equalize pay scales. In a series of important assemblies in the Northeast, Midwest, and occupied South, they demanded not only the "immediate and unconditional" abolition of slavery everywhere in the United States but, citing their military role in the service of the country, the "full measure of citizenship." "If we are called on to do military duty against the rebel armies in the field," one group of them asked, "why should we be denied the privilege of voting?" Now the world defined by *Scott v. Sandford* (1857), which denied citizenship or rights to Black people, was under direct attack by those who were its intended victims.

But the repercussions could go even further. In January 1865, after marching his troops from Atlanta to Savannah, Georgia, federal army General William T. Sherman organized a meeting of local Black ministers, many of whom had been enslaved, to take the temperature of Black aspirations. He learned that the ministers understood slavery as "receiving by *irresistible power* the work of another man" and freedom as "placing us where we could reap the fruit of our labor, [and] take care of ourselves." He learned, too, that they believed "the way we can best take care of ourselves is to have land, and to turn it by our own labor." Sherman was no revolutionary, but he despised the Confederate rebels and had been getting bad press back at home for his treatment of the enslaved people who left their plantations and followed in his wake across Georgia. So, to meet what he termed "the

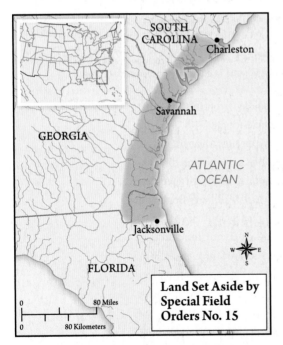

≡ **MAP 15.2 Land Set Aside by Special Field Orders No. 15** Special Field Order No. 15 confiscated as federal property a strip of coastal land extending about 30 miles inland from the Atlantic and stretching from Charleston, South Carolina, to Jacksonville, Florida. The order gave most of the roughly 400,000 acres to newly emancipated Black people in 40-acre plots along with access to surplus army mules.

pressing necessities of the case," he stepped into the radical role that only such a war made possible. On January 16, 1865, Sherman issued **Special Field Orders No. 15**, which set apart, for exclusive Black settlement, the islands and coastal rice fields south from Charleston to the St. John's River in Florida, to be subdivided into 40-acre plots. It was 400,000 acres of the richest plantation land in the southern states, effectively destroying the haughty coastal ruling class and possibly laying the foundation of a new social order. Black people in the United States would long commemorate this event by speaking of the reward of "forty acres and a mule" that the federal government had provided for their forced captivity and military service to the country (see Map 15.2).

15.5 When Did the War End?

||| Analyze the complexities of bringing the Civil War to a conclusion.

As revolutionary as Special Field Orders No. 15 was, Sherman would not have been able to issue it if he did not have the rebels on the run and their defeat in sight. It was a dramatic shift in the course of events. Before the summer of 1863, the military outcome of the war seemed in serious doubt. Robert E. Lee and his troops, fresh from stunning victories at Fredericksburg and Chancellorsville in Virginia, readied themselves for another offensive across the Potomac and into Maryland and Pennsylvania. A military triumph on northern soil might deflate Union morale beyond repair, release pressure on besieged Confederates at Vicksburg, and force Lincoln to seek a truce that would place the sweeping Emancipation Proclamation in jeopardy. Then, in fairly quick succession, Lee suffered a devastating defeat at Gettysburg, exhausted Confederates surrendered to Grant at Vicksburg, and Sherman pushed rebel troops out of Tennessee and into northwest Georgia. What would this mean for the objectives of the Lincoln administration?

Confederates on the Defensive

An important change in the dynamics of warfare accompanied all of this. The arming of enslaved African Americans indicated a new resolve to defeat the Confederate rebellion and destroy its base of enslavement. At the same time, the resources available to the Lincoln administration in railroad transportation, armaments manufacture, and manpower slowly made their significance felt. The federal armed forces would be able to mobilize twice as many men as their Confederate counterparts, and they would be able to feed, clothe, and provision troops in ways that the rebels simply could not. Eventually, men of foreign birth and African descent would

≡ **Lincoln's Generals**   In Grant (*left*) and Sherman (*right*) Lincoln finally found military leaders who shared his vision of how the war needed to be fought, and they battled relentlessly to crush the rebel armies.

compose more than half of the federal army. Equally important, Lincoln finally found in Grant and Sherman military leaders who shared his vision of how the war needed to be fought, and they battled relentlessly to crush the rebel armies.

Yet it was one thing to put the Confederate rebellion on the defensive and quite another to fully end the rebellion in ways that both sides recognized. Lincoln sought "unconditional surrender," but of whom and to what effect? Clearly, he wanted Confederate troops to lay down their arms and the Confederate government to be disbanded, but since he never acknowledged the Confederacy and insisted that the rebellion was one of individuals in the states, what would have to happen before the rebellion could be regarded as over and the authority of the federal government accepted?

There was no getting around the fact that the Confederates were in deep trouble. By 1864 they were under enormous strain on the home front as well as on the battlefield. Desperate for soldiers, supplies, and workers behind the lines, they had enacted a draft, imposed a tax-in-kind on agricultural produce (seeking goods rather than money), and authorized provision officers to take (impress) needed supplies from private citizens. No one in the Confederate states was unaffected, but it was the nonslaveholders and their families who suffered most grievously. With adult men and even teenage boys off in the army, women, children, and the elderly were left to bring in the crops and provide for themselves. Growing numbers experienced deprivation and, given rampant inflation (by this time the Confederate government was pretty much just printing money), were unable to purchase necessities in town. Some women, like those organized by Mary Jackson and Minerva Meredith in Richmond, rioted against merchants and planters who hoarded supplies, but many others wrote to their husbands and sons about their plight and encouraged them to desert. By early 1864 somewhere between one-third and one-half of the Confederate troops may have been absent from their units: many had deserted, taking the advice of their wives and mothers, and others had granted themselves leave from the fighting to aid their families.

The prospect of defeat could lead even those who remained loyal to the rebel cause in opposing directions. Patrick Cleburne from Arkansas, who had supported secession and risen to the rank of major general, came to the conclusion that the only way Confederates could hope to prevail was by recruiting the enslaved to fight with a promise of freedom for those who remained loyal. Enlist the enslaved and abolish slavery to salvage the Confederate rebellion? The initial response from Cleburne's superiors was nothing short of outrage, though over time the idea did win a small following—including Lee and Davis—but not enough of one to initiate a genuine policy. All that rebels were left to do was assume a defensive posture, drag out the war for as long as possible, and hope that the political winds might shift in a more favorable direction.

Military and Political Turning Points

There was still some reason for Confederate hopefulness. In the fall of 1864, the United States would hold regular elections for the presidency and the Congress, and Lincoln was in trouble. Radical members of the Republican Party had been angered by his moderation, and one of them, Secretary of the Treasury Salmon P. Chase, contemplated challenging him for the nomination; he soon thought better of it when Lincoln called both for a "complete suppression of the rebellion" and a constitutional amendment abolishing slavery. In an unprecedented move, Lincoln, the Republican, also took Tennessee Democrat, Andrew Johnson, as his vice president on what was now called a Union ticket. Johnson was widely lauded for his stance against secession and the rebels, and Lincoln expected that such a ticket would find more votes among soldiers in the field and Democrats at home than a Republican one.

He seemed to need all the votes he could get. Lincoln faced a formidable opponent in the election who pledged to follow a very different set of political goals. For the Democrats nominated the popular federal General George B. McClellan, whom Lincoln had sent into retirement months before, and they approved a platform that

MAPPING AMERICA

Contrabands and Refugees

All wars displace civilian populations. After World War II, millions of refugees moved across the borders of Eastern Europe as ethnic groups fled or were expelled from their homes. Since Russia's invasion in February 2022, over thirteen million people in Ukraine have been displaced. Though the

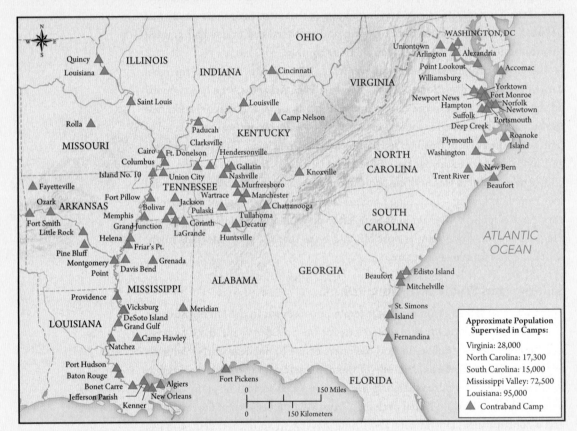

Approximate Population Supervised in Camps:

Virginia: 28,000
North Carolina: 17,300
South Carolina: 15,000
Mississippi Valley: 72,500
Louisiana: 95,000

▲ Contraband Camp

≡ **MAP 1**   More than 500,000 enslaved African Americans escaped to Union lines during the war. Known as "contrabands," about a third of the escapees lived for varying amounts of time in camps. For many freedpeople, the camps were the first step in the transition to freedom.

condemned Lincoln's "usurpation" of power. Instead, despite federal advances on the battlefield and the Emancipation Proclamation, they called for an immediate armistice with no mention of enslavement or abolition. In other words, the Democrats appeared ready to abandon the goal of ending slavery if they could reach an agreement

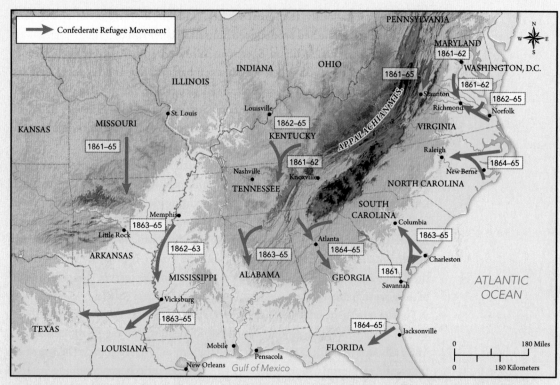

≡ **MAP 2**   Beginning with the wealthy planters of the South Carolina Sea Islands who fled their plantations when Union ships captured Port Royal in November 1861, thousands of white Confederates fled before advancing Union armies. Some relocated to secondary homes not far from the places they were fleeing. Others traveled greater distances, bringing their enslaved workers with them in the hopes of maintaining their old way of life in a different setting. Most poor white people, however, simply stayed where they were and hoped for the best.

magnitude of the displacements caused by the War of Rebellion was not as great as these other conflicts, the effect they had on free and unfree civilian populations was just as profound.

Thinking Geographically

1. Examine the two maps. Is there a correlation between the locations of contraband camps and the movements of Confederate refugees? If so, what is the likely reason for this correlation?

2. Which geographical features influenced the movements of contrabands and refugees?

to stop the war. So convinced was Lincoln that the contest was lost that he pledged to work with McClellan to "save the Union between the election and the inauguration" because it would be impossible to "save it afterward." "I am a beaten man," Lincoln concluded in late August, "unless we can have some great victory."

Almost miraculously, the "great victory" Lincoln looked for did come—and only two days after he had pronounced himself a "beaten man." The miracle maker was none other than William Sherman. While Grant's Army of the Potomac was mired in the blood-soaked Virginia soil battling Lee and his rebel soldiers, Sherman and his troops, after a protracted struggle in north Georgia, marched into the strategic rail center of Atlanta on September 3, 1864. The city had been torched by retreating Confederates, but Sherman stood triumphant while the rebels were in disarray.

The political effect was nothing short of electric. By the time voters cast their ballots in early November, the electoral landscape had been transformed, and Lincoln and the Republicans won an overwhelming victory: 55 percent of the popular vote and every state in the Union except Kentucky, Delaware, and New Jersey. Especially gratifying for Lincoln was the soldier vote, which went for him by nearly 80 percent despite McClellan's standing with the troops. Especially consequential, the Republicans would also control three-quarters of the seats in Congress and all of the governorships and legislatures in the states Lincoln carried.

For the rebels, the effect of Sherman's "great victory" was nothing short of disastrous. "Since Atlanta I have felt as if it were all dead within me," South Carolina's Mary Chesnut, an ardent rebel from the first, wrote. "We are going to be wiped off the earth." In Virginia, morale among Lee's besieged units began to sink so fast that hundreds of his men were deserting each week. By late January 1865 Lee was suggesting to Davis that his army could not hold out very much longer (see Map 15.3).

Confederates Begin to Surrender

Davis was determined to fight on, even at the price of arming enslaved men on the Confederacy's behalf and accepting some plan of gradual emancipation. Perhaps this would bring English and French recognition and the economic and military aid bound to come with it. Perhaps, too, Davis could negotiate a peace based on an implicit recognition of the integrity and independence of the Confederacy. But in this Davis seems to have taken the wrong message from a conciliatory meeting Lincoln had held with a small Confederate delegation at Hampton Roads, Virginia, in early February 1865. Whatever olive branches were extended, he had no intention of recognizing the Confederacy and would only accept an "unconditional surrender." Much of the rebel political leadership, both within Davis's cabinet and among the war governors, saw the options more clearly than Davis did, and they were ready to admit defeat. Their main interest was no longer in sustaining the rebellion militarily but in cutting a deal that would allow them to hold onto power in their states and localities, maintain their political rights, protect their property from confiscation, and avoid prosecution for secession- and war-related offenses,

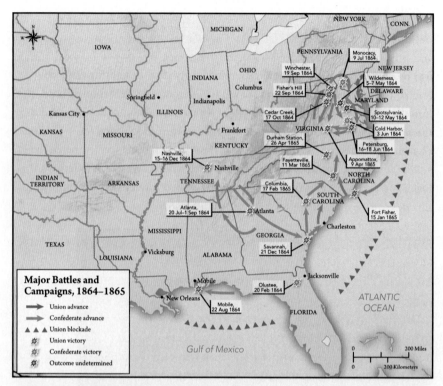

≡ **MAP 15.3   Major Battles and Campaigns, 1864–1865**   Sherman's capture of Atlanta and his ensuing "march to the sea" demonstrated the ability of Union forces to cut straight through the center of the Confederacy. His army then moved north to join Ulysses S. Grant in trapping the two remaining Confederate armies.

particularly for treason. After four years of fighting and hundreds of thousands of casualties, it was a lot to ask.

Lee had also foreseen defeat, and although some of the rebels—including Davis—hoped he might disperse his own forces to fight on in guerilla fashion, Lee decided otherwise. To that end, Lee agreed to meet with Grant on April 9, 1865, at Appomattox Court House in Virginia, and, as painful as it might have been for him to give up, he could not have hoped for better terms. Rebel officers and their men would be paroled (not taken as war prisoners), their arms stacked and turned over to Grant, and they would all be permitted to return home with their sidearms and horses, not to be "disturbed by United States authority so long as they observe their paroles and the laws in force where they reside." No one was taken into custody—not Lee or anyone else—and nothing was said of arrests, charges of treason, or punishments of any sort.

Sherman, the bane of the rebel armies, unaccountably offered even more generous terms to Joseph Johnston and his rebel troops in North Carolina. They would

Martyrdom and Defeat

The memorialization of the war began immediately after the fighting ended, but the North and South remembered the war in different ways. A Memorial Day speech Frederick Douglass gave in 1878, in which he paid homage to "the heroic deeds of and virtues of the brave men who volunteered, fought, and fell in the cause of Union and freedom" is representative of the way northerners remembered the war. In contrast, a Lost Cause ideology took hold among defeated southerners, idealizing the slave system and righteous martyrs overwhelmed by the ruthless

≡ **George Washington, Abraham Lincoln, and a Choir of Angels**

Yankee war machine. In the popular poem, "The Conquered Banner," published right after Appomattox, the Confederate flag is sacralized: "yet 'tis wreathed around with glory, / And 'twill live in song and story / though its folds are in the dust!" The South occupied the moral high ground and had no cause for shame.

After Lincoln's death, northerners gathered to hear sermons preached to their martyred president. An estimated seven million people—one in every four Americans—watched his funeral train over the course of its thirteen-day trip to Springfield, Illinois; and more than one million paid respects to his remains as he lay in state in the cities the train passed through. In this 1866 engraving, we see George Washington and a choir of angels welcoming the victorious martyr to paradise.

The Lost Cause was constructed quite sometime after the war ended, in the late 1870s and 1880s, when women played a prominent role. Believers in the Lost Cause had their own martyr: Robert E. Lee. While Lee was not felled by an assassin's bullet, Confederate armies had been mercilessly crushed by heartless Union armies. Despite overwhelming odds, Confederate generals like Lee fought valiantly to the end. They were righteous and blameless. This undated print casts a warm glow on Lee's Farewell Address to his troops. Set amid scenes of his life, the Address extols Confederate "valor and devotion" that ultimately was "compelled to yield to overwhelming numbers and resources." For many white southerners, Lee's Farewell Address held layers of meaning.

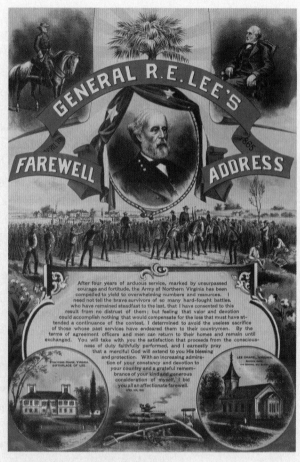

≡ **Robert E. Lee's Farewell Address**

CONSIDER THIS

In the different ways the North and South remembered the war, which side viewed America's best days in the past? Is this viewpoint still prevalent in American society today?

have to disband militarily rather than formally surrender and would be permitted to take their arms home, supposedly to be deposited in their state arsenals. Their existing governments would be recognized as soon as elected officials took oaths of loyalty to the United States, and inhabitants of the rebellious states would be guaranteed their civil, political, and property rights as long as they abstained from acts of armed hostility. It was a far cry from Special Field Orders No. 15 and far more lenient than the Lincoln administration ever had in mind. Grant immediately stepped in. He traveled to North Carolina and insisted that Johnston accept the same terms presented to Lee at Appomattox.

Both Lee and Johnston seemed to think that their surrenders amounted to the end of the Confederacy. But was this, in fact, the end of the slaveholders' rebellion? Jefferson Davis and his cabinet had fled Richmond in early April and headed south with the intent of reestablishing their government. Even when Davis learned of the surrenders, he still believed that Confederate troops could be rallied and looked to the trans-Mississippi West, where he might link up with forces there under General Edmund Kirby Smith, who hadn't yet laid down their arms. Davis could then seek an alliance with the Mexican state, now in the hands of French-imposed monarch Maximilian. Perhaps there was still life to the rebellion.

The Assassination of Lincoln

In the meantime, the federal government sustained a tragic and unprecedented blow at the hands of a Confederate sympathizer and conspirator. On the night of April 14, 1865, four years to the day after federal troops at Fort Sumter had themselves surrendered, Abraham Lincoln was assassinated by actor John Wilkes Booth at Ford's Theater in Washington, DC. Maryland-born and the son of a famed theatrical actor, Booth regarded Black enslavement as "one of the great blessings that God ever bestowed" and detested Lincoln as a tyrant, particularly when he heard Lincoln suggest that political rights might be conferred on some of the previously enslaved men. Indeed, like Davis, Booth thought that the fortunes of the Confederacy might be turned around by "something decisive and great," and so he plotted with a small group to murder Vice President Andrew Johnson and Secretary of State William Seward as well. The plot very nearly succeeded. Although Johnson escaped unharmed, Seward was brutally assaulted and, for a time, lingered near death. Never before had a president of the United States fallen victim to an assassin.

And never before or since, had a president from one political party served with a vice president from another. Initially, the problems that this might pose were not apparent. From a humble background, Johnson was also an experienced politician in the tradition of Jacksonian Democrats, who saw themselves representing the interests of small landholders and laboring people. He seemed to have a special animosity for the southern planter class, remained loyal to the United States, and promised to make treason "odious" and have "traitors punished."

Jefferson Davis blanched when he heard of Lincoln's assassination. Knowing of Johnson's temperament and sensibilities, he thought the results would be "disastrous for our people." That fear was widely shared. Would the federal government now move to arrest and punish the rebel leaders and wreak vengeance on the rebellious South? For their part, some Radical Republicans seemed heartened by the turn of events. Whereas Lincoln had spoken a language of generosity and reconciliation, Johnson spoke one of punishment and retribution. "I believe that the Almighty continued Mr. Lincoln in office as long as he was useful," one of the radicals explained, "and then substituted a man better suited to finish the work."

Although some Confederates were still holding out, Johnson could have lowered the boom. He could have imposed martial law, arrested the rebel leadership (Davis was captured in Georgia in early May), set strict terms, such as the Wade-Davis Bill did, for the restoration of the states, allowed the Freedmen's Bureau to subdivide confiscated and abandoned land, and extended civil equality to people of African descent and the franchise to at least some of them. With that, the Confederate rebellion would have been at an end.

15.6 Reunification According to Andrew Johnson

Explain the emerging clash between President Andrew Johnson and congressional Republicans over Reconstruction policy.

Andrew Johnson was in no hurry to remove federal troops from the rebellious South or to declare the rebellion officially over. But when he did become president after Lincoln's death, he suddenly had a great deal of power at his disposal. The Congress was out of session until December, so he stepped onto the contested ground that Lincoln had earlier occupied. Who was tasked with the authority to set the terms of reunification? Was it Johnson, the president, or was it Congress, the federal legislature? Or was the authority to be shared? Johnson could have called Congress into emergency session, as Lincoln did in the summer of 1861, and worked with both houses to craft the necessary legislation. But he didn't. Instead, he seemed to follow Lincoln's earlier lead and issued orders and proclamations of his own devising. It was the beginning of a major political struggle with the outcome of the War and the fate of the nation in the balance.

Presidential Reconstruction

In late May 1865, when President Johnson issued proclamations outlining his policy, the tone and requirements were very different from what radicals and rebels had expected. He granted blanket amnesty and pardons to all but an elite cut of Confederates—restoration of their property, excluding enslaved people, and their civil and political rights—once they took an oath of loyalty to the United States. He went on to appoint a provisional governor for each of the states from the ranks of the population who did not actively support secession, and they, in turn, would oversee the rewriting of state constitutions that had been the political foundations of slave societies. All that Johnson required was that the states acknowledge the abolition of slavery, renounce secession, and void all state debts contracted to aid the rebellion. He also only hinted that he would look favorably on a limited enfranchisement of Black men. No African Americans either voted for delegates to constitutional conventions or took part in the rewriting of the constitutions under what is generally called Johnson's **Presidential Reconstruction**.

What happened? Had Johnson lost his nerve? Did radicals and rebels alike misunderstand him? It's easy to exaggerate what appears to have happened, at least from Johnson's point of view. On the one hand, Johnson's policy was not much different from what Lincoln had suggested before his death: establishing the authority of the federal government and the illegitimacy of secession, securing the end of enslavement, offering most former rebels the opportunity to demonstrate their loyalty and responsibility, and enabling the rebellious states to rejoin the Union quickly. On the other hand, Johnson singled out the rebel leadership for possible punishment to a far greater extent than Lincoln ever had. His refusal to grant blanket pardons to those Confederates who owned $20,000 or more of property—they had to apply to him for special pardons—threatened a potential political earthquake, weakening the wealthy planter class and strengthening smaller landowners who were less beholden to enslavers and the rebellion.

Johnson, in short, could have used his power to work a political transformation in the rebel South. But Democrat that he was (he couldn't count on Republican support for the presidential nomination in 1868), he chose instead to seek powerful allies there. Although Jefferson Davis and Alexander Stephens, the president and vice president of the Confederacy, were in custody, Johnson decided not to press a legal case against them for treason. As individual applications for pardon swamped his desk—mostly from rich planters—he granted almost all of them. Furthermore, Johnson moved to restore landed property that had been abandoned or confiscated to its original owners, even if the formerly enslaved had already begun cultivating it as under Sherman's Special Field Orders No. 15. And when Freedmen's Bureau officials sympathetic to the formerly enslaved tried to drag their feet in carrying out his orders, Johnson pressured them to obey.

Confederate Defiance and a Reset

Needless to say, Confederates were relieved to hear of Johnson's moves. Some had been predicting a world turned upside down of the sort they imagined when Lincoln was elected president in 1860. But instead of breathing a sigh of relief and showing a measure of gratitude and compliance, they turned brazen and defiant. Now it seemed that they could turn the clock back rather than suffer as victims of defeat.

Their response was quite remarkable given their surrenders only weeks before. When delegates of the rebellious states met to rewrite their constitutions, they often thumbed their noses at the Johnson administration. Mississippi and Alabama would only acknowledge that enslavement had been abolished. Mississippi, Georgia, and Florida refused to nullify (invalidate) their secession ordinances. The state legislatures elected under Johnson's policy included large numbers of active rebels, and they quickly began to pass laws that would limit the new freedom of the previously enslaved. Known as **Black Codes**, these included vagrancy laws that required gainful employment by a certain date at the risk of arrest; game and fence laws that prohibited customary hunting and fishing on unenclosed land; laws narrowing the rights of freedpeople to gain justice in the courts, especially the right to testify against white people; and laws restricting their ability to rent or purchase land. In localities where the plantation order had prevailed, planters and their clients resumed their places as sheriffs, treasurers, and magistrates. And although most of the congressional representatives chosen by the states had opposed secession even if they then supported the rebellion, the Georgia legislature sent none other than Alexander Stephens, former Confederate vice president, to take a seat in the US Senate.

≣ **Slavery Is Dead?**   Perhaps not. Cartoonist Thomas Nast juxtaposes the sale of enslaved people (on the left) with the whipping of freedpeople (on the right) after the war, suggesting that conditions had not really changed all that much for African Americans in the South.

When the duly elected members of Congress returned to Washington, DC, in December 1865, they were in no mood to offer welcomes to their recent enemies. Many were shocked at the results of Johnson's policies and the chaos it produced in the states of the former Confederacy. They were especially aghast at how the freedpeople, many of whom supported their efforts to defeat the Confederates, were being treated by their one-time enslavers. They could reasonably ask whether the rebellion had truly been suppressed or whether it had taken new form. But now they had the opportunity to set reunification terms of their own.

Conclusion: How to Secure the Peace?

From the start of the War, the Lincoln administration faced two massive challenges: how to defeat the Confederate rebellion militarily and how to reunify the country as a whole. Both posed great problems, though in effect they were interconnected. Not long after ordering an invasion of the South, Republicans had to determine what secession really meant in constitutional terms and how that meaning would shape policy. They also had to determine who held the power—Congress or the president—to make policy. In the process, they not only embraced emancipation and the arming of Black men; they also had to decide the terms on which Indigenous people in the trans-Mississippi West would have a place in a reunified country, the signs marking the defeat of the Confederate rebellion, and the future status—and possible punishment—of the rebels themselves.

For a time, it was unclear whether the Lincoln administration would accomplish either of its major goals. The war dragged on, with little end in sight. As it did, great strains were placed on civilian populations across the country, especially in the rebellious states, and Confederates faced explosions of violent resistance to their policies, particularly from the ranks of nonslaveholders and their families. Eventually the combination of federal military and economic power—greatly strengthened by Black soldiers—and social tensions within the Confederate rebellion itself enabled federal forces to prevail on the battlefield and to move forward with plans for peace. Setting the terms of peace would not, however, be easy, not only because differences between Congress and the president had already erupted in the midst of civil warfare but also because Lincoln was felled by an assassin's bullet and Andrew Johnson became president. The issue that hovered had yet to be resolved. How would the Union be restored or reconstructed? Out of the ashes of civil warfare would a new nation be forged?

WHAT IF Lincoln Hadn't Been Assassinated?

No counterfactual question is more commonly asked of this period than what might have happened if Lincoln escaped assassination and served out his second term. The question is a good one. It reflects the very high regard in which Lincoln is held and a somber sense about what his death meant for the future of the country. Since Lincoln commanded the struggle that saved the Union and eventually abolished enslavement and since his words still speak powerfully to us, it's not surprising that many Americans feel that he would have continued to guide the United States along a righteous path. Perhaps so. But what we know of the policies he was developing toward the end of his presidency and of his perspectives on a postwar South raise some cause for doubt. Lincoln was clearly committed to upholding the abolition of enslavement and strongly supported a Thirteenth Amendment to the Constitution that would make abolition nearly impossible to overturn. Yet he was less clear about the status that the formerly enslaved would occupy in the post-emancipation South, about whether they would become full citizens or claim the political rights that free white people enjoyed. And although he regarded the slaveholders' rebellion as an act of treason—and called it that

by name—he seemed more interested in healing wounds than in punishing traitors. He had already clashed with more radical members of his own party over Reconstruction policy, and he would likely clash again now that the war was ending and more policies had to be implemented.

To be sure, unlike Johnson, Lincoln was a Republican and not in search of renomination. He might have developed a closer working relationship with the congressional Republicans and avoided antagonizing them as Johnson would do. During the war itself, Lincoln had shown a capacity for growth on the questions of enslavement and emancipation, and there is evidence that he was extremely impressed by and grateful for the heroism of Black soldiers. At the same time, Lincoln may well have formed an alliance with more moderate Republicans, and either the position of the formerly enslaved could have been weakened or Lincoln could have struggled and lost the political fight with the radicals in his party, in which case the position of the formerly enslaved might have been placed on a firmer social and political footing.

Had Lincoln lived to oversee postwar Reconstruction until his term ran out, would we have come to think less or more of him?

DOCUMENT 15.1: Lincoln's Second Inaugural Address

On March 4, 1865, only forty-one days before his assassination, Lincoln was sworn in for a second term and gave the following address to the nation. What does it portend for the character of Reconstruction on his watch and for the policies of his second term more generally?

Fellow countrymen: at this second appearing to take the oath of the presidential office there is less occasion for an extended address than there was at the first. Then a statement somewhat in detail of a course to be pursued seemed fitting and proper. Now, at the expiration of four years during which public declarations have been constantly called forth on every point and phase of the great contest which still absorbs the attention and engrosses the energies of the nation little that is new could be presented. The progress of our arms, upon which all else chiefly depends is as well known to the public as to myself and it is I trust reasonably satisfactory and encouraging to all. With high hope for the future no prediction in regard to it is ventured.

On the occasion corresponding to this four years ago all thoughts were anxiously directed to an impending civil war. All dreaded it—all sought to avert it. While the inaugural address was being delivered from this place devoted altogether to saving the Union without war insurgent agents were in the city seeking to destroy it without war—seeking to dissolve the Union and divide effects by negotiation. Both parties deprecated war but one of them would make war rather than let the nation survive, and the other would accept war rather than let it perish. And the war came.

One eighth of the whole population were colored slaves not distributed generally over the union but localized in the southern part of it. These slaves constituted a peculiar and powerful interest. All knew that this interest was somehow the cause of the war. To strengthen perpetuate and extend this interest was the object for which the insurgents would rend the Union even by war while the government claimed no right to do more than to restrict the territorial enlargement of it. Neither party expected for the war the magnitude or the duration which it has already attained. Neither anticipated that the cause of the conflict might cease with or even before the conflict itself should cease. Each looked for an easier triumph and a result less fundamental and astounding. Both read the same Bible and pray to the same God and each invokes His aid against the other. It may seem strange that any men should dare to ask a just God's assistance in wringing their bread from the sweat of other men's faces but let us judge not that we be not judged. The prayers of both could not be answered—that of neither has been answered fully. The Almighty has His own purposes. "Woe unto the world because of offenses for it must needs be that offenses come but woe to that man by whom the offense cometh." If we shall suppose that American slavery is one of those offenses which in the providence of God must needs come but which having continued through His appointed time He now wills to remove and that He gives to both North and South this terrible war as the woe due to those by whom the offense came shall we discern therein any departure from those divine attributes which the believers in a living God always ascribe to Him. Fondly do we hope—fervently do we pray—that this mighty scourge of war may speedily pass away. Yet, if God wills that it continue until all the wealth piled by the bondsman's two hundred and fifty years of unrequited toil shall be sunk and until every drop of blood drawn with the lash shall be paid by another drawn with the sword as was said three thousand years ago so still it must be said "the judgments of the Lord are true and righteous altogether."

With malice toward none with charity for all with firmness in the right as God gives us to see the right let us strive on to finish the work we are in to bind up the nation's wounds, to care for him who shall have borne the battle and for his widow and his orphan—to do all which may achieve and cherish a just and lasting peace among ourselves and with all nations.

Source: Library of Congress.

DOCUMENT 15.2: President Andrew Johnson's Proclamation of Amnesty

On May 29, 1865, the new president, Andrew Johnson, issued his own Proclamation of Amnesty to set the stage for his Reconstruction policies. How different are his views from those expressed in Lincoln's second inaugural address?

To the end, therefore, that the authority of the government of the United States may be restored, and that peace, order, and freedom may be established, I, ANDREW JOHNSON, President of the United States, do proclaim and declare that I hereby grant to all persons who have, directly or indirectly, participated in the existing rebellion, except as hereinafter excepted, amnesty and pardon, with restoration of all rights of property, except as to slaves, and except in cases where legal proceedings, under the laws of the United States providing for the confiscation of property of persons engaged in rebellion, have been instituted; but upon the condition, nevertheless, that every such person shall take and subscribe the following oath, (or affirmation,) and thenceforward keep and maintain said oath inviolate; and which oath shall be registered for permanent preservation, and shall be of the tenor and effect following, to wit:

I, _____ _____, do solemnly swear, (or affirm,) in presence of Almighty God, that I will henceforth faithfully support, protect, and defend the Constitution of the United States, and the union of the States thereunder; and that I will, in like manner, abide by, and faithfully support all laws and proclamations which have been made during the existing rebellion with reference to the emancipation of slaves. So help me God.

The following classes of persons are excepted from the benefits of this proclamation: 1st, all who are or shall have been pretended civil or diplomatic officers or otherwise domestic or foreign agents of the pretended Confederate government; 2nd, all who left judicial stations under the United States to aid the rebellion; 3d, all who shall have been military or naval officers of said pretended Confederate government above the rank of colonel in the army or lieutenant in the navy; 4th, all who left seats in the Congress of the United States to aid the rebellion;

5th, all who resigned or tendered resignations of their commissions in the army or navy of the United States to evade duty in resisting the rebellion; 6th, all who have engaged in any way in treating otherwise than lawfully as prisoners of war persons found in the United States service, as officers, soldiers, seamen, or in other capacities; 7th, all persons who have been, or are absentees from the United States for the purpose of aiding the rebellion; 8th, all military and naval officers in the rebel service, who were educated by the government in the Military Academy at West Point or the United States Naval Academy; 9th, all persons who held the pretended offices of governors of States in insurrection against the United States; 10th, all persons who left their homes within the jurisdiction and protection of the United States, and passed beyond the Federal military lines into the pretended Confederate States for the purpose of aiding the rebellion; 11th, all persons who have been engaged in the destruction of the commerce of the United States upon the high seas, and all persons who have made raids into the United States from Canada, or been engaged in destroying the commerce of the United States upon the lakes and rivers that separate the British Provinces from the United States; 12th, all persons who, at the time when they seek to obtain the benefits hereof by taking the oath herein prescribed, are in military, naval, or civil confinement, or custody, or under bonds of the civil, military, or naval authorities, or agents of the United States as prisoners of war, or persons detained for offenses of any kind, either before or after conviction; 13th, all persons who have voluntarily participated in said rebellion, and the estimated value of whose taxable property is over twenty thousand dollars; 14th, all persons who have taken the oath of amnesty as prescribed in the President's proclamation of December 8th, AD 1863, or an oath of allegiance to the government of the United States since the date of said proclamation, and who have not thenceforward kept and maintained the same inviolate.

Provided, That special application may be made to the President for pardon by any person belonging to the excepted classes; and such clemency will be liberally extended as may be consistent with the facts of the case and the peace and dignity of the United States.

Source: U.S. Congress, *United States Statutes at Large* (Washington, DC: U.S. G.P.O., 1937), vol. 13, pp. 758–760.

Thinking About Contingency

1. What does Lincoln's Second Inaugural portend for the character of Reconstruction on his watch and for the policies of his second term more generally?
2. How different are Johnson's views from those expressed in Lincoln's second inaugural address?

REVIEW QUESTIONS

1. How did Republicans understand the nature of secession and the Confederate rebellion, and how did this understanding shape their wartime approaches to reunifying the country?

2. Why did Lincoln and the Republican-dominated Congress struggle over Reconstruction policy?

3. How did the Civil War shape relations between the federal government and Indigenous people as well as between the Confederates and Indigenous people?

4. What sort of future did Republican policymakers imagine for previously enslaved people and for Native Americans?

5. In what ways were Black people, previously enslaved and free, politicized during the war, and how did their developing political consciousness give shape to the war and its meaning?

6. How could the Confederate rebellion be ended, and what would be the fate of those who carried on the rebellion?

7. What did Confederates expect from President Andrew Johnson?

8. Should we accept the label of "Civil War" to capture the brutal conflagration that erupted between 1861 and 1865, or should we speak of it as a "War of the Rebellion"?

KEY TERMS

American Freedmen's Inquiry Commission (p. 617)

Black Codes (p. 639)

contract labor system (p. 616)

First South Carolina Volunteers (p. 624)

Freedmen's Bureau (p. 617)

Presidential Reconstruction (p. 638)

Proclamation of Amnesty and Reconstruction (p. 613)

Sand Creek Massacre (p. 622)

settler colonialism (p. 619)

Special Field Orders No. 15 (p. 627)

territorialization (p. 613)

Wade-Davis Bill (p. 615)

RECOMMENDED READINGS

Ira Berlin, et al., eds., *Freedom: A Documentary History of Emancipation: The Black Military Experience* (Cambridge University Press, 1982).

Eric Foner, *Reconstruction: America's Unfinished Revolution, 1863–1877* (Harper and Row, 1988).

Thavolia Glymph, *The Women's Fight: The Civil War Battles for Home, Freedom, and Nation* (University of North Carolina Press, 2020).

Steven Hahn, *A Nation under Our Feet: Black Political Struggles in the Rural South from Slavery to the Great Migration* (Harvard University Press, 2003).

Chandra Manning, *What This Cruel War Was Over: Soldiers, Slavery, and the Civil War* (Vintage 2008).

David A. Nichols, *Lincoln and the Indians: Civil War Policy and Politics* (Minnesota Historical Society Press, 2012).

Michael Perman, *Reunion Without Compromise: The South and Reconstruction, 1865–1868* (Cambridge University Press, 1973).

Lawrence N. Powell, *New Masters: Northern Planters During the Civil War and Reconstruction* (Yale University Press, 1980).

Joseph P. Reidy, *Illusions of Emancipation: The Pursuit of Freedom and Equality in the Twilight of Slavery* (University of North Carolina Press, 2020).

Willie Lee Rose, *Rehearsal for Reconstruction: The Port Royal Experiment* (Bobbs Merrill, 1964).

16

The Promise and Limits of Reconstruction

1865–1877

Chapter Outline

≡ **Suffragists**   By 1870, when this photo was taken, Elizabeth Cady Stanton and Susan B. Anthony were household names. The two women are seated around a circular desk similar to the ones where Stanton penned the 1848 "Declaration of Sentiments." Contrary to popular belief, Anthony was not present at the famous gathering of women at Seneca Falls in 1848.

In the late summer of 1865, both Elizabeth Cady Stanton and Susan B. Anthony, antislavery and woman suffrage activists, were deeply disturbed by the news that was leaking out of Congress. Concerned about the status of the formerly enslaved people in the South and by President Andrew Johnson's conciliatory policies toward the former Confederate rebels, Republicans were drafting a Fourteenth Amendment to the Constitution, which would grant citizenship to African Americans, effectively overturning the *Dred Scott* decision of 1857. Further, it would encourage the states of the former Confederacy to grant African American men the franchise (right to vote) by taking congressional representation from them if they failed to do so.

Stanton and Anthony had collected thousands of names on a petition to Congress in 1864 calling for a Constitutional Amendment to abolish enslavement, hoping, too, that as part of this remarkable—indeed, revolutionary—era, emancipation would be linked to the enfranchisement of women as well as Black men. But what they learned

Timeline

1865	1866	1867	1868	1869	1870	1871	1872	1873

1865 >
January Congress passes Thirteenth Amendment abolishing enslavement
May President Johnson issues Proclamation of Amnesty
December Congress returns to session and rejects new members from former Confederate states; states ratify Thirteenth Amendment

1866 >
March Civil Rights Act and Freedmen's Bureau Act passed by Congress over President Johnson's vetoes
June Congress passes Fourteenth Amendment granting birthright citizenship
November Republicans increase congressional majorities in fall elections

1867 >
March Military Reconstruction Acts imposing federal military rule on the South passed by Congress over President Johnson's vetoes

1868 >
March House of Representatives passes Articles of Impeachment against President Andrew Johnson
May President Johnson acquitted by the Senate
July Fourteenth Amendment ratified by the states

1869 > Congress passes Fifteenth Amendment prohibiting discrimination on account of race, color, or previous condition of servitude for the right to vote

1870 > Fifteenth Amendment ratified by the states

1870–1871 > Congress passes Enforcement Acts to combat attacks on the voting rights of African Americans from state officials or paramilitary groups like the Ku Klux Klan was that the Fourteenth Amendment would require universal adult "male" suffrage, for the first time marking a distinction in constitutional rights based on gender. Stanton sensibly worried that, "if the word 'male' be inserted it will take a century at least to get it out." And so, she and Anthony sent another petition directly to Congress arguing that, "as you are now amending the Constitution [and] placing new safeguards round the individual rights of four million of emancipated ex-slaves, we ask that you extend the right of Suffrage to Women and thus fulfill your constitutional obligation 'to guarantee to every State in the Union a Republican form of Government.'"

They made a powerful argument, using broad rights language with a basis in the Constitution. Yet male abolitionists had already indicated that woman suffrage would have to take a back seat to the civil and political rights of freed*men*. The Republicans were deeply concerned about holding on to power and safeguarding their achievements, and they recognized that Black male suffrage, alone, was bound to provoke

1874	1875	1876	1877	1878	1879	1880	1881	1882

1874 ▸ Democrats take control of House of Representatives

1876 ▸ Contested presidential election between Rutherford B. Hayes (Republican) and Samuel Tilden (Democrat)

1877 ▸ Compromise of 1877 gives Hayes the presidency with concessions to the Democrats that effectively end Reconstruction; Hayes withdraws last US troops from the South

opposition in the North as well as in the South. Nonetheless, they viewed Black suffrage as essential to their success in building up their party in the rebellious states and in maintaining their hold on Congress and the presidency. As Radical Republican Wendell Phillips saw it, "in time" he hoped he could be bold enough to demand suffrage for women as well as men, but "this hour belongs to the Negro."

Stanton responded bitterly, asking Phillips if he "believe[d] the African race is composed entirely of males?" There was, however, little that she or her suffrage movement could do since women did not have the right to vote and could not sit in Congress debating legislation and amendments. When Congress subsequently drafted the **Fifteenth Amendment**, in 1869, they again chose not to add "sex" to "race, color, or previous condition of servitude" as unlawful exclusions from voting rights. Thus, seeing that their antebellum (pre–Civil War) alliances were now at an end, Stanton and Anthony turned their attention to building a new, independent woman suffrage movement. They were, it appeared, on their own.

The defeat of woman suffrage and the victory of Black male suffrage reveal much about American Reconstruction. Before the War of the Rebellion, there were few places where even free people of African descent could vote and little interracial support for Black voting rights. Now, a majority of Republicans in Congress, through the Military Reconstruction Acts (1867) and the Fifteenth Amendment (1870), supported the enfranchisement of Black men. It was a remarkable and controversial move. But the failure of woman suffrage suggested the limits to the changes that Reconstruction would usher in. In understanding both the promise and limits of Reconstruction, we might begin by asking why it was so much more difficult for Republicans—even the Radicals among them—to end gender discrimination in political rights than it was to end discrimination based on "race or previous condition of servitude."

16.1 The Black Struggle for Rights and Independence

‖‖‖ Describe the aspirations of the formerly enslaved and free people of color in their struggles during Reconstruction.

The unexpected course of President Andrew Johnson's Reconstruction policies was contested from the first by African Americans across the rebellious states. Stepping into the public light in the occupied South and owing to enlistment in the federal armed forces, they advanced a very different perspective on a post-emancipation world than either Lincoln or Johnson had offered. In meetings and processions, they called for civil rights, full citizenship, the right to vote, land to cultivate, and community independence. In the process, they brought on intense conflict with their former enslavers and recently disbanded Confederate soldiers in what would prove to be the final battles of the rebellion. As a result, they paved the way for a new settlement and political order.

Opening Forays

The earliest mobilizations of African Americans came in southern cities and in adjacent districts where federal troops had arrived before Confederate forces began to surrender. They occurred in New Orleans; Memphis; Mobile, Alabama; Norfolk, Virginia; and the coastal districts south of Charleston, South Carolina. Political organizations connected with the Republican Party, such as the Union League, became vehicles of a new political presence. They organized meetings, introduced leaders from near and far, and celebrated the role of Black troops in destroying enslavement and defeating the enslavers. They also protested discriminatory treatment by federal officials and Confederates alike, framed aspirations and grievances, taught thousands of Black people about the workings of the government, and pressed for entrance into civil and political society.

Nothing better exemplified the alternatives to Johnson's Reconstruction policies devised by African Americans than the **freedmen's conventions** held in most of the rebellious states in the summer and fall of 1865. Led mainly by free people of color from the North and South, they met in the states' capitols or largest cities and insisted that "we are part of the American republic." Often anticipating or coinciding with the whites-only constitutional conventions held under Johnson's plan, they effectively cast doubt on the legitimacy of Presidential Reconstruction. In the resolutions that virtually all of the freedmen's conventions passed, they emphasized their desire for education, loyalty to the United States, courage in the country's "darkest hour," and "right to carry their ballot to the ballot box." "Any attempt to reconstruct the states without giving to American citizens of African descent all the rights and immunities accorded to white citizens," the Virginia freedmen's convention declared, "is an act of gross injustice." In an important sense, these conventions followed the precedents of those that took place in the North before the war erupted (discussed in Chapter 12).

The Land Question

Things were different in the rural areas where the freedpeople still overwhelmingly resided. There, what circulated at the very time the freedmen's conventions were demanding "equal rights" were rumors of a massive redistribution of land accomplished either by the federal government or by armed Black insurrection. A powerful logic was at play, at least for the freedpeople. The idea of land reform reflected both their sense of what a just and meaningful emancipation would involve and their expectations of what the federal government would do. Much like their emancipated counterparts in other slave-plantation societies of the Western Hemisphere, they associated land with subsistence, independence, and community stability. As formerly enslaved people, they were well aware that their labor had given the lands their value and the slaveholders their prosperity. Some even recognized their contributions to the economic growth of the entire country. "Didn't we clear the land and raise the crops? And then didn't them large cities in the North grow up on the cotton and the sugars and the rice that we made?" a Virginia freedman asked, insisting, "we have a right to [that] land."

Such ideas about a "right to land" were reinforced by the actions of the federal government. Owing to the Confiscation Acts of 1861 and 1862 as well as Sherman's Field Orders No. 15, the government controlled more than 900,000 acres of rebel land with authority to divide it into 40-acre tracts for distribution among the freedpeople. Land reform appeared to loom as a real possibility, and even President Johnson's efforts to restore confiscated land to white owners failed to dim the fires of expectation. As a result, starting in the summer of 1865, talk of a general, government-sponsored property division began to spread among the freedpeople, especially in areas where they could be found in largest numbers. One Freedmen's Bureau official stationed in the lower Mississippi Valley reported that "a majority of the colored population positively believe that the government would take the plantations, cut them up into forty acres parcels and give them to the colored people." Although some imagined that the great day might arrive at any time, more and more looked to the Christmas season, especially to Christmas or New Year's Day: the time when gifts were customarily exchanged and the slaveholders' paternalism was most fully on display.

Yet the very prospect of land reform and the Black power it would promote sparked reorganizations of disbanded rebel troops. Planters and white landowning supporters just home from the battlefields told one another of "extravagant ideas of freedom" that the formerly enslaved entertained and of plans devised by the freedpeople to stage an "insurrection" to take the land by force if the federal government refused to act. Much of the blame, they insisted, could be placed on the shoulders of African American troops in the army of occupation, who "emboldened" the freedpeople politically and "demoralized" them at their work.

Here the fatal weaknesses of Johnson's policies became apparent. Alarmed white landowners brought their concerns to the attention of the state provisional governors selected under Presidential Reconstruction. Although the governors may have opposed secession and kept a low profile during the war, they usually sympathized with the fears of fellow property owners. The provisional governors in turn contacted federal officials and, if necessary, Johnson himself to tell of the alleged insurrectionary activities and demand both the removal of Black troops and the authority to mobilize militia companies to maintain order. Johnson and the Freedmen's Bureau commissioner then sent Bureau agents into the rural districts to "disabuse" the freedpeople of the "false impression" they had about land redistribution and urge them to make labor contracts. At the same time, Johnson gave the governors the green light to reorganize the militias, which were little more than disbanded Confederate units and slave patrols.

Why did Johnson do this? Why did he allow defeated Confederates to rearm and threaten the lives of the formerly enslaved? Johnson despised the antebellum southern elite, the big plantation owners, but he had no love either for the enslaved or the freedpeople. He imagined—much like Lincoln—that the post-emancipation

≡ **Power Conflicts**   In this allegorical representation of the Freedmen's Bureau from 1868, a Union soldier keeps the peace between unruly groups of Black people and white men.

MAPPING AMERICA

The Changing Landscape of the South

The War of the Rebellion rearranged human relations in the South—between white people and Black people, and between men and women—and it also transformed the built environment. The environmental costs of four years of war were staggering. Sherman's march through Georgia and the Carolinas was particularly devastating, with tens of thousands of horses, mules, and livestock killed, and millions of pounds of corn, grain, and other foodstuffs destroyed. On a smaller scale, the war also rearranged the way people lived in the places they called home. We can see this change by looking at the Barrow Plantation in central Georgia before and after the war.

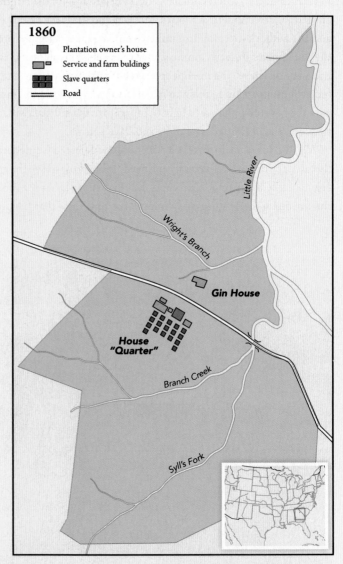

1860

- ■ Plantation owner's house
- ▭ Service and farm buldings
- ▦ Slave quarters
- ═ Road

Little River

Wright's Branch

Gin House

House "Quarter"

Branch Creek

Syll's Fork

≡ **MAP 1**   In 1860, the ninety-four enslaved workers on the Barrow Plantation lived in quarters near the owner's house. They were subject to strict control, but they also could build a tightly knit community.

Thinking Geographically

1. How would you describe the built environment of the Barrow Plantation in 1860? How does this landscape reflect the cultural values of the people who lived there?

2. How would you describe the built environment of the Barrow Plantation in 1881? How does this new landscape reflect the economic priorities and cultural values of the people who lived there? What patterns of continuity and change do you see when you compare the two maps?

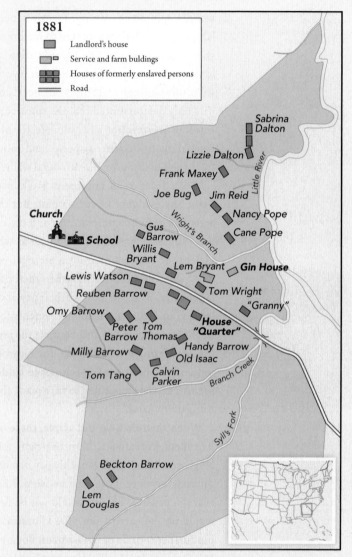

1881

- Landlord's house
- Service and farm buldings
- Houses of formerly enslaved persons
- Road

Sabrina Dalton

Lizzie Dalton

Frank Maxey

Joe Bug   Jim Reid

Little River

Nancy Pope

Wright's Branch

Cane Pope

Church

Gus Barrow

School

Willis Bryant

Lem Bryant   **Gin House**

Lewis Watson

Reuben Barrow

Tom Wright

"Granny"

Omy Barrow

Peter Barrow   Tom Thomas

House "Quarter"

Milly Barrow

Handy Barrow

Old Isaac

Tom Tang

Calvin Parker

Branch Creek

Syll's Fork

Beckton Barrow

Lem Douglas

≡ **MAP 2**   Twenty-one years later, the estate had been divided into small plots worked by the formerly enslaved people as sharecroppers. The croppers had also constructed a church where they could worship and a school where their children could learn to read and write. Only the gin house, where picked cotton was cleaned, remained in the same position as before the war, evidence of the crop's continuing economic importance.

world would be run by and for white people with Black people as a subordinate laboring class. He also wanted to restore self-government rapidly in the rebellious states through policies that would allow one-time rebels to show their newfound loyalty and demonstrate to the country that the rebellion was truly at an end. But Johnson's willingness to allow former Confederates to police their states and localities only demonstrated that the spirit of rebellion was very much alive. Using the threat of insurrection as a rationale, the planters and their allies brazenly launched campaigns to disarm, disperse, and intimidate rural Black people. When away from their posts, even Black federal soldiers fell victim to vigilante violence.

White fears of an imminent Black insurrection were unwarranted; there was never any evidence of such a plot. But the fears did spotlight the early political activities of freed communities and the contests for power that developed in the wake of emancipation. Indeed, just as white landowners spread rumors of Black violence to reassert their local prerogatives, so did the freedpeople use rumors of land redistribution to strengthen their own bargaining positions. Wrestling with landowners over the terms of their pay or over claims to the land, some freedpeople refused to enter into labor agreements for 1866, not only out of worry that they might be coercive but also because the prospect of land would provide the opportunity to farm for themselves. "The Negroes are not inclined to make any contracts until after Christmas," a Tennessee landowner complained that October. "They seem to expect something to take place about that time, a division of land or something of the kind."

When the new year did arrive, these Tennessee freedpeople and many others like them were able to sign contracts for better terms than they had originally been accorded: higher monthly pay or larger shares of the crop, access to provision grounds, lower rents on their housing. But in signing contracts, they acknowledged that the promise of land would not be fulfilled and the threat of an insurrection would not be carried out. The Christmas season brought them not land reform but further rounds of harassment, floggings, and late-night searches by white militias and vigilantes. Black people had learned the hard lesson that the promise of sweeping change that granted them freedom and independence could be painfully limited and even withdrawn.

The Collapse of Presidential Reconstruction

For their part, rebels who had briefly been humbled by the official surrender of their armies and the prospects of being punished as traitors reorganized their resistance to federal authority and started to carve out a post-emancipation order that was favorable to them. Johnson granted most of them amnesty and the return of their property that had fallen into federal hands. Federal army commanders agreed to planters' demands to remove Black soldiers from trouble spots in rural areas.

Freedmen's Bureau agents tried to convince the formerly enslaved that land would not be distributed and they had to sign labor contracts. And southern legislatures elected under Johnson's plans—with no African Americans in them—quickly enacted Black Codes, which, as we saw in Chapter 15, restricted Black opportunities for either economic independence or civil equality, enforced labor contracts, and punished those deemed "vagrants." These were the first official signs of the coercive measures that former enslavers would deploy against the formerly enslaved.

Presidential Reconstruction was clearly in tatters, and the support Johnson once received from Republicans in Congress was collapsing. The Radicals in the party had been worried that Johnson's pardons to individual rebels and his conditions for the readmission of rebel states were too lenient. But nothing angered more northerners or pushed more moderate and conservative Republicans toward disenchantment with, if not outright opposition to, his policies than the epidemic of violence against Black people and white loyalists that exploded amid rumors of federal land reform. Together they seemed to threaten the results of the war and to rupture the boundaries of northern tolerance. "The most favorable opportunity was afforded to the southern people," a Cincinnati newspaper editorialized in December 1865, "but the spirit in which this was responded to was a rebellious one."

Congress agreed. When the House and Senate reconvened the first week of December 1865, their members acted with dispatch. They refused to seat the representatives elected by the rebellious states; they formed the Joint Committee on Reconstruction to investigate conditions in the South; and they began to challenge Johnson's policies and authority. Recognizing that rebels who had been defeated militarily might claim victory on terrain of their own choosing, the Republican Congress determined to seize the initiative and bring the rebellion to a different sort of end.

16.2   Toward Radical Nationhood

||| Explain the political vision of the Reconstruction Republicans and how they understood the nation they were trying to forge.

Even while Lincoln was alive, the federal government, through its executive and legislative branches, had assumed powers and envisioned a reconstructed government that moved well beyond the boundaries established by the original Constitution. In good part, this was the result of fighting a war on a scale that could not have been imagined in 1861. But it also grew out of the challenges that Republicans faced once the shooting stopped. Many worried that the results of the bloody war might be undermined or reversed and that the party itself might be driven from power once the rebellious states had been readmitted to the Union. Andrew Johnson's behavior was a warning sign, and Republicans determined that having won the war they would not lose the peace. In the process a new nation was forged.

The Thirteenth Amendment

Congress took a dramatic step in asserting its authority and extending the reach of federal power, though much of the initiative came from outside its walls. Pressure had been building among abolitionists and other antislavery activists to secure an emancipation that was universal and permanent. As early as the spring of 1863 the **Women's Loyal National League** led by Elizabeth Cady Stanton and Susan B. Anthony launched the massive petition drive noted at the start of this chapter; they would collect about 400,000 signatures. By the end of that year, congressional Republicans and a small number of Democratic colleagues were ready to act. They saw the limits of the Emancipation Proclamation, which did not abolish slavery in all of the states, only in those that had rebelled against the federal government. Further, its reach was dependent on the arrival of the federal army both to announce the Proclamation and to enforce its authority. In east Texas, the ending of slavery was not officially decreed until June 19, 1865, when US General Gordon Granger arrived in Galveston with his troops and publicly read the Emancipation Proclamation. This important event has since been commemorated as **Juneteenth**, now observed as a national holiday.

Abolitionists, congressional Republicans, and antislavery Democrats also feared that, as a war measure, the Emancipation Proclamation might be overturned by hostile courts once the war had ended. Although they first considered the idea of passing a statutory law to end enslavement in the United States, they ultimately decided to craft an abolition amendment to the Constitution—the "Supreme Law of the Land" and therefore preeminent over all other federal laws, not contained in the Constitution.

A constitutional amendment did, however, raise a great many questions. What should such an amendment include, and how far should it go? Should the amendment's language be confined to the abolition of enslavement within the borders of the United States, or should it also address the civil status of those who had been emancipated? Influenced by what had happened in France in 1794 as a result of the Haitian Revolution, Radical Republican Charles Sumner of Massachusetts proposed that the amendment not only abolish enslavement but also stipulate that "all people are equal before the law," a move in the direction of citizenship that the French had pioneered. But Sumner couldn't get enough support for his proposal, and the result was an amendment that adopted the language of the Northwest

Ordinance of 1787 (discussed in Chapter 7) and said nothing about equality or citizenship: "Neither slavery nor involuntary servitude except as a punishment for crime whereof the party shall be duly convicted, shall exist within the United States, or any place subject to their jurisdiction." The amendment did thereby prohibit enslavement in any future territory of the United States (quite the opposite of the Confederate constitution), and it granted Congress the "power to enforce [it] by appropriate legislation."

Although the congressional power of enforcement might appear to be a bureaucratic add-on, it worried most northern Democrats as well as former enslavers, and for good reason. It gave the federal government sovereign power beyond anything previously enjoyed under the Constitution and opened the door for an assortment of initiatives as to the civil and political status of the freedpeople. If enslavement and involuntary labor were prohibited, what type of legislation would be necessary "to enforce" the prohibition? Would the Black Codes invite federal intervention, and would the Republican majority use the enforcement power to press the matters of African American citizenship and voting rights? More than a few southern legislators feared that it would. But with the Republicans in control of all branches of the federal government and of most legislatures in the North and West, the **Thirteenth Amendment** was passed by Congress in January 1865 and ratified by the requisite number (three-fourths) of states by the following December.

☰ **The Black Codes in Action** The services of a freedman, unable to pay a fine, are sold to the highest bidder in Monticello, Florida, in 1867. The scene does not look all that different from a prewar slave auction.

Civil Rights and the Fourteenth Amendment

The fears of white southerners were justified. While President Johnson, Secretary of State William Seward, and loyal Democrats were quick to argue that the Thirteenth Amendment would end rather than spark conflicts over Black rights, most Republicans did see the opportunity to demonstrate that freedom meant more than, in the words of Ohio congressman and future president James A. Garfield, "the bare privilege of not being chained." Citing the enforcement clause, Republicans moved quickly to give freedom substance. In early 1866 they drafted and passed bills extending the life of the Freedmen's Bureau—and authorizing agents to protect freedpeople in the "civil rights belonging to white people"—and prescribing that "all persons born in the United States and not subject to any foreign power, excluding Indians not taxed, are hereby declared to be citizens of the United States." The latter is known as the **Civil Rights Act of 1866**. Their passage reflected Republicans' insistence that slavery's end required a new civil status for the formerly enslaved, that citizenship would be defined and granted by the federal government, and that *Dred Scott* was no longer the law of the land. It also suggested that Indigenous people would continue to be excluded even in this radical redefinition of rights.

President Johnson vetoed both bills. He called them "strides toward centralization," and he appeared interested in isolating Radical Republicans and building support for himself among Democrats and Republican conservatives. If this was his motivation, however, he blundered again. His vetoes served only to unify Republicans in an effort to defend their own power and remove Johnson's hands from their policy objectives. It would mean another constitutional amendment, but this time they were following the lead of African Americans who had struggled to put Black political rights on the table for decades and now were making strong arguments about the relation of soldiering and political citizenship. A growing number of Republicans, for reasons of principle as well as opportunism, came to embrace their cause. After all, the Republican Party was barely organized in the former slave states, and the end of enslavement meant that the federal ratio, which counted an enslaved person as three-fifths of a free person for apportioning congressional seats and electoral votes, would no longer prevail. Now freedpeople would count five-fifths, and their former enslavers would have even more power regardless of the civil and political status of Black people. It was a recipe for Republican defeat.

But if Republicans were to push forward with a political revolution, how far should it go? What would citizenship mean in the new nation that was under construction? Woman suffrage activists, with deep ties to abolitionism, had fought spirited but losing battles for the vote for years and then put aside their aspirations to support the federal government and the emancipation of the enslaved. Now a moment for extending the revolution seemed to have arrived, a moment, as Elizabeth Cady Stanton put it, "to bury the woman and the negro in the citizen."

As Cady Stanton indicated, woman suffrage advocates hoped to maintain and strengthen, not break, their alliance with the formerly enslaved. But the case that African American men made to support their enfranchisement demonstrated the vulnerability of women's position. By arguing that military service had revealed their courage and manhood, they embraced the gendered political culture of the nineteenth century that masculinized claims for citizenship and political rights. Republicans, who mostly aligned with the culture of evangelical Protestantism, saw male-headed households as the basis of social stability, with "separate spheres" (for women in the home and men in the outside world, as discussed in Chapter 10) the organizing principle of public and private life. As slavery collapsed during the war, they looked for assurances that the formerly enslaved were acquainted with middle-class values, could respond to market incentives, and would construct their family relations in a morally acceptable hierarchy. Thus, while Radical Republican Wendell Phillips hoped that "in time" the franchise could be extended to women, for him "this hour belongs to the negro."

The **Fourteenth Amendment** that came out of Congress in June 1866 showed both the reach and limits of this revolutionary moment. Building on the Civil Rights Act of 1866, it established a **birthright citizenship** ("All persons born or naturalized in the United States") that offered the same "privileges and immunities" and the "equal protection of the laws" wherever citizens resided in the United States. A more direct and ringing rejection of the world of *Dred Scott* could hardly be found. The amendment also disfranchised any political or military office holder who had joined the Confederate rebellion after taking an oath of allegiance to the Constitution, though Congress could remove this disqualification by a two-thirds vote.

But the second section of the amendment revealed the barriers that were still in place. Congress could have taken up the franchise question by establishing a broad principle of political citizenship that did not allow state tampering and that held open the door for more expansive political participation. Instead, Congress took the indirect route on federal authority and the direct route on the matter of gender. It would now count five-fifths of all persons for apportionment and penalize any state that denied voting rights to any of its "inhabitants" over twenty-one years of age by reducing congressional representation proportionally; thus, if Black people were not enfranchised and composed 40 percent of the population, the state would lose 40 percent of its congressional seats. Yet, in a move that put a dagger into the heart of women's suffrage, the amendment also designated those "inhabitants" as "male," making explicit the exclusion of women. So ended an alliance that had helped defeat the Confederate rebellion and drive the revolution of emancipation.

16.3   Political Revolution and Its Limits

‖‖‖ Assess the extent of political change that occurred in the Reconstruction South as well as in the nation as a whole.

It was one thing for Congress to pass the Fourteenth Amendment; it was another to get the requisite three-fourths of states to ratify it. Ratification was now the requirement for readmission to the United States, yet all but one of the rebellious states—Tennessee, Johnson's home state, being the ironic exception—refused to ratify the Fourteenth Amendment during the fall and early winter of 1866–1867, citing both the threat of Black suffrage and the exclusion of former Confederates. For Radical Republicans the lesson was obvious. The rebellious states could not be left to their own devices; they had to be subject to federal authority.

Advent of Military Reconstruction

The Radical Republicans saw an important opening. Congressional elections would take place in the fall of 1866, and Radicals turned them into a referendum on the Fourteenth Amendment. They were aided in this effort by Andrew Johnson himself, who set out on an extended speaking tour to mobilize Democratic opposition but behaved so erratically—often haranguing Republican adversaries in the most bitter and demeaning terms and occasionally appearing intoxicated—that even potentially sympathetic voters abandoned him and his party in droves. When the ballots were counted, the Republicans won handily. They increased their control of Congress to more than two-thirds of the seats (making it veto-proof). Johnson was now the one who appeared isolated.

The radicalism that emerged from what one newspaper called "the fiery ordeal of a mighty revolution" was now at the height of its influence and would meet the last phase of the Confederate rebellion with terms far different from those considered by Lincoln, Johnson, or moderate Republicans. In the **Military Reconstruction Acts**, passed overwhelmingly in March 1867, Congress decisively rejected Johnson's approach of encouraging rebels to show their loyalty and permitting them to rebuild their political institutions as they saw fit. Instead, the rebellious states were now divided into five military districts, each under the command of a US Army general, who would supervise still another reorganization of state constitutions. Constitutional conventions would again be held, popular ratifications of their work would occur, and elections for local, state, and national offices would take place. But this time Black men, most of whom had been enslaved, would participate as voters and delegates. And this time the constitutional conventions would have to enfranchise African Americans on the same basis as whites and ratify the Fourteenth Amendment as a condition of readmission.

Over the following months, the US Army carried out the first voter registration in American history. Although a daunting undertaking, it proved a remarkable success. By the fall of 1867, the rolls of eligible voters had been compiled, and they included an astonishingly high proportion of eligible Black men: over 90 percent everywhere except Mississippi, where 83 percent had registered. Even more consequentially, Black voters now made up a substantial portion, if not a majority, of the total electorate in the rebellious states, especially in the localities where slaveholding planters had long ruled.

The rebellion now appeared to be at an end, with the elements of a new political order in the South seemingly in place. The federal government proclaimed its sovereign authority over the territorial United States. The leading rebels, though avoiding arrest and punishment, were penalized politically, and a once-powerful southern bloc in Congress and national political life was subdued. A national citizenship had been established, and universal manhood suffrage advanced as a principle of American political culture. The formerly enslaved and other people of African descent won access to power where they resided in largest numbers. And Radical Republicans were in a position to shape the country's future. What had begun as a battle to quell a rebellion of slaveholders had turned into a social and political revolution that gave rise to a new nation (see Table 16.1). Nowhere else in the world of Atlantic enslavement, not even in Haiti, did emancipation lead to such potential empowerment for the formerly enslaved who, just a few short years earlier, cultivated acres of crops under threat of the lash and had no rights that whites needed to respect. For all of these reasons, the War of the Rebellion and the Reconstruction that followed may be considered one of the greatest and most sweeping revolutions in all of modern history.

Indigenous People in a New Nation

Still, the full meaning of that revolution had yet to be determined. Land reform in the South and woman's suffrage in the nation at large had tested the limits of change and been repelled. Questions about money, banking, tariffs, and railroads hovered over Congress, asking whose interests the great transformations of war and emancipation would serve. But the signs of the future may have been revealing themselves most consequentially in the trans-Mississippi West. With the slaveholders' rebellion defeated, the federal government was more determined than ever to suppress Indigenous rebellions that continued to erupt across the Plains, the Southwest, and the Northwest. Only a few months after the last Confederate armies surrendered, the tribes in Indian Territory were made to pay for their

		Table 16.1	Reconstruction Amendments, 1865–1870
Amendment	**Main Provisions**	**Congressional Passage (two-thirds majority in each house required)**	**Ratification Process (three-quarters of all states including ex-Confederate states required)**
Thirteenth	Slavery and involuntary servitude prohibited in the United States	January 1865	December 1865 (twenty-seven states, including eight southern states)
Fourteenth	1. Birthright citizenship for anyone born or naturalized in the United States	June 1866	Rejected by twelve southern and border states, February 1867
	2. State representation in Congress reduced proportionally to number of male voters disfranchised		Radicals make readmission of southern states hinge on ratification
	3. Former high-ranking Confederates denied right to hold office until Congress removes disabilities		Ratified July 1868
	4. Confederate debt repudiated; validity of US public debt not to be questioned		
Fifteenth	Denial of franchise because of race, color, or previous condition of servitude explicitly prohibited	February 1869	Ratification required for readmission of Virginia, Texas, Mississippi, and Georgia; ratified March 1870

alliances with the rebels. They would have to forfeit all annuity payments, make new treaties, set aside lands for tribes that had been friendly to the United States, and grant railroads rights-of-way through their lands. They would also have to accept the emancipation of all the enslaved Black people they held as well as the inclusion of those formerly enslaved into their tribes "on an equal footing with original members."

Earlier that summer of 1865, Secretary of the Interior James Harlan instructed his agents to impress upon the Indigenous people, "in the most forcible terms," that white settlement would be spreading rapidly, that the government had no intention of slowing it down, and that Indigenous people would be well advised to "abandon [their] wandering life" and settle upon reservation lands. Nearly three years later, as the first elections under Military Reconstruction were taking place, General William Tecumseh Sherman—he who had practiced "total warfare" against the Confederate rebels and issued Field Orders No. 15 to confiscate and redistribute their lands—traveled out to Wyoming with an Indian Peace Commission to negotiate an agreement with the previously rebellious Sioux and their allies. Known as the Treaty of Fort Laramie and drafted in the spring of 1868, it defined the boundaries of their reservation and demanded that they no longer resist the construction of railroads then being built on the Plains (see Map 16.1).

Not all the Sioux signed the treaty, and some of the most militant, led by Lakota chief Sitting Bull, continued to raid federal forts along the upper Missouri River. Elsewhere on the Plains and in the Southwest and Northwest, the summer months of 1868 saw Kiowas, Comanches, Cheyenne, Apaches, and Paiutes engage in warfare against the flood of white settlement. By October, the Indian Commission was ready to take further stock of the situation and urge a dramatic shift in federal policy. The Commissioners recommended that Native American tribes no longer be recognized by the federal government as "domestic dependent nations" and instead be held subject to the laws of the United States. Three years later, Congress

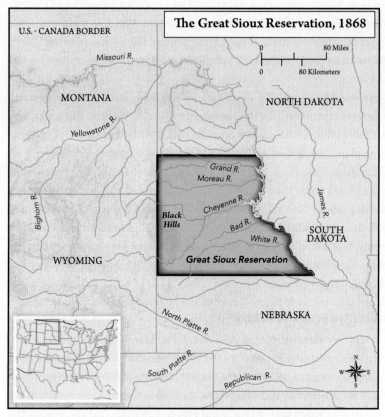

≡ **MAP 16.1   The Great Sioux Reservation, 1868**   The Great Sioux Reservation defined by the Treaty of Fort Laramie encompassed more than 48,000 square miles of land between the Missouri River and the Black Hills.

made official what a new nation would demand of those who resided within its borders: "hereafter no Indian nation or tribe . . . shall be acknowledged or recognized as an independent nation, tribe, or power with whom the United States may contract by treaty." The Reconstruction of the South and the Reconstruction of the West thereby formed part of a sweeping national project.

16.4   Building a Republican Base in the South

||| Summarize how Republicans tried to build bases of political support in the formerly rebellious states of the South.

The Military Reconstruction Acts showed the determination of Radical Republicans to win the peace as well as the war, to make sure that the Confederate rebellion was defeated and a new nation based on expanded freedom and citizenship came in its place. But the Military Reconstruction Acts also highlighted the politically precarious situation that Republicans found themselves in as the War of the Rebellion ended and the formerly rebellious states were being restored to the American Union.

When the war broke out, the Republican Party had little basis in the states where enslavement remained legal. Outside Maryland, Delaware, Kentucky, and Missouri, Lincoln didn't even make it onto the ballot. Although Lincoln's wartime "ten-percent plan" (discussed in Chapter 15) created openings for the party in Virginia, Arkansas, Tennessee, and Louisiana, had the rebellious states been readmitted to the Union under Johnson's policies—before freedmen gained the vote—the Democrats would have taken full control of them. The Republicans would have had their congressional initiatives, including the Fourteenth and Fifteenth Amendments, blocked, if they were not driven from national power entirely. The destiny of the Republican Party and the new nation they intended to forge teetered in the balance.

The Challenge and the Allies

When the Military Reconstruction Acts passed in March 1867, General Philip H. Sheridan was appointed governor of the newly created Fifth Military District, encompassing Louisiana and Texas (see Map 16.2). One of five army generals selected to impose martial law and oversee the reconstruction and restoration of the rebellious states, he was a particularly good choice. Sheridan had run roughshod over Confederates in the Shenandoah Valley of Virginia, and he was just as tough minded now that hostilities had ceased. He insisted on establishing the authority

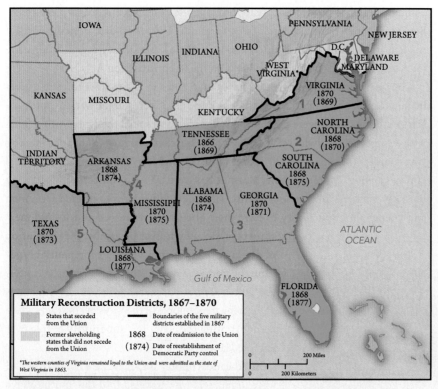

≡ **MAP 16.2 Military Reconstruction Districts, 1867–1870** The Military Reconstruction Acts divided the South into five districts commanded by a military governor, usually, as in the case of Philip H. Sheridan, a former Union army general.

of the federal government, had no interest in appeasing defeated rebels and their collaborators, and believed that the freedom of the formerly enslaved had to be placed on a secure basis. He knew what he was up against. Witnessing rampant "lawlessness" in his district and finding "more disloyalty now than in '61," Sheridan removed officials who had been empowered under Johnson's policies—including the governors of both states—and conducted a massive registration of newly enfranchised Black voters.

Neither Sheridan nor any of the other military governors had great resources at their disposals. The Army of Occupation had been dwindling in size since the spring of 1865; roughly 20,000 soldiers were left to enforce the Military Reconstruction Acts, most of whom were stationed in or near the larger towns and only scattered about across the countryside. The Freedmen's Bureau, authorized to take charge of abandoned rebel lands and supervise the implementation of a free labor system, was already having its operations curtailed. And despite hopes that there would be supportive people in the southern white population, few such allies could be found. Indeed, hostility to the Republican reconstruction project and to Black suffrage in particular continued to simmer if not boil over in many parts of the South. It assumed deadly incarnation in white paramilitary organizations like the Ku Klux Klan, which came to life with the Reconstruction Acts.

Congressional Republicans did have some allies in their effort to turn the rebellious South and its new Black citizens into components of the nation-state they were building. Many were northern missionaries and social reformers, often filled with evangelical zeal, who set up schools and churches designed to advance literacy, Christianity, the values of thrift and industry, and the formation of patriarchal families among the freedpeople. Many others were US Army officers, often serving in the Freedmen's Bureau and locally based detachments, who offered freedmen and women an opportunity to have their grievances redressed and to find measures of justice and protection against the retribution of defeated rebels. Some were entrepreneurial types from the northern states, still fired by antislavery fervor, who leased or purchased plantations with hopes of tutoring freedpeople in the ways of contracts while demonstrating the economic superiority of free over enslaved labor.

≡ **"The First Vote"**   In this sympathetic portrayal of Black men casting their first vote in 1867, the artist has represented individuals who symbolize respectable, responsible citizens worthy of the vote, including an artisan (note the tools in his pocket) and a Union soldier.

But the most important allies the Republicans had were organizers who traveled into the South to give the party its first real footing along with the Black constituents they mobilized to turn that footing into political power. And no organization was more important to the undertaking than the **Union League**.

Emerging in 1862 and 1863 to rally public support for the Lincoln administration and the war, the League followed the federal army into the occupied South and, once the fighting formally ended, did political work mainly among white Unionists who resided in the hill and mountain districts, outside the plantation belt. But once the Reconstruction Acts provided for a Black male franchise and voter registration, League organizers fanned out into the countryside, particularly into the plantation counties, where African Americans lived in greatest numbers. Associated with the national Republican Party, the League attracted a diverse lot of activists. Some were northern Republicans with experience in the military and Freedmen's Bureau, and some were southern white Unionists who had already helped establish Leagues in white-majority counties. But more and more important were African Americans who had served in the federal army, attended freedmen's conventions, or preached the gospel, especially ministers of the African Methodist Episcopal (AME) Church. The work of these Union League organizers was especially difficult and dangerous. Intent on mobilizing freedpeople, they often fell victim to swift and deadly retaliation at the hands of white landowners and vigilantes. Secrecy and armed self-defense were crucial.

The success of Union League organizers could hardly have been predicted. Although more than a few Republicans worried that new Black voters might be manipulated by their employers, freedmen confounded these fears. Building on communications networks and spiritual communities they had forged while enslaved, they not only registered to vote in overwhelming numbers; they also resisted the threats of white Democrats, marched to the polls in legions, participated in the writing of new state constitutions, and, with few exceptions, gave their support to the Republican Party. Without question, at a very critical moment, they enabled the Republicans to consolidate their regime.

Black People and Republicans: A Complex Alliance

The developing alliance between Republicans in Washington, DC, and the formerly enslaved, mediated at the grassroots by the Union League and party activists, was logical, necessary, and deeply problematic. Beyond question, they had a shared interest in emancipation, the military defeat of the enslavers, birthright citizenship, Black male suffrage, and the establishment of the Republican Party in the South. Without Black votes, the Republicans had little chance to move forward with their projects of nation building: very few southern whites were willing to join them, and most saw the Black vote and the political mobilizations it made possible as an illegitimate outrage. And without Republican support, the freedpeople would have faced much difficulty in exercising their new rights or adequately protecting themselves from vigilante violence.

But the alliance was as tense as it was extraordinary. Although they may have shared a commitment to free labor, civic equality, and political democracy, Republican leaders and freedpeople occupied very different social stations. Republicans had put together a complex coalition, but their policymaking heart increasingly beat for the interests of manufacturers, financiers, and other propertied producers; they were concerned mainly with advancing industrialization, stabilizing money and credit, reviving the cotton economy, and drawing more and more of the United States into the capitalist marketplace. The freedpeople, by contrast, were overwhelmingly working people who owned very little property and had to labor for employers in the fields as well as on docks, on railroads, in mines, in forests, and in towns and cities. Their aspiration was to escape economic dependency and provide for themselves. Short of that, they struggled to limit their exploitation, improve their material conditions, rebuild their communities, and use the political process to improve their prospects. Never before or since has a section of the American working class been as closely aligned with a political party as freedmen were with the Republicans. But it was not "their" party.

Black Power in the South

For a time, especially in the early phases of Military Reconstruction, the alliance not only held but offered participants political rewards well beyond what any of them anticipated. African American activism was the key. Despite dangers and direct threats, they organized their communities, rallied to the Republican banner, and turned out to vote in stunning numbers (80 to 90 percent of those eligible), drawing as they often did on forms of communication and self-defense that they had fashioned when enslaved. Indeed, politics was for African Americans very much a collective undertaking and one in which lines of age and gender could become blurred. It is true, of course, that the franchise was extended only to Black men, and without doubt it tipped the balances of community power and authority further in their direction at a time when all sorts of social relations were being renegotiated. But participation and important forms of decision-making were more widely dispersed, connecting the electoral sphere with other arenas of social and political life. Black women not only attended rallies and meetings and registered their views; they became so deeply involved with the expression of party loyalties that the vote itself could be seen as something of a family property. Some of them gathered and transmitted necessary information (as did children); some taught in rural schools; and some helped defend public assemblies from attack. Where possible, Black women accompanied voting-age men to the ballot box, providing added cover and steeling men's nerves.

Black electoral support allowed the Republican Party to strengthen its hold on the national government and to extend its reach into the South. In 1868, Black ballots gave Republican presidential candidate Ulysses S. Grant the majority of popular votes cast—he won only a minority of the white vote—and, owing to African American turnout in the rebellious states, a comfortable margin in the electoral college as well. Grant won six of them (see Map 16.3). As these states began to hold elections under their new constitutions, which enfranchised Black men and disfranchised some of the rebels, the Republicans then won control of the governorships and legislatures most everywhere (Virginia was the exception) and took charge of county and municipal governments in many places, especially in the plantation districts. It was a political revolution of the sort that few modern societies have ever witnessed, displacing a wealthy and formidable elite that had claimed local sovereignty with far more humble officials directly tied to the newly proclaimed sovereignty of the nation.

In no way was the political revolution more striking or consequential than in the election of African Americans, most of whom had recently

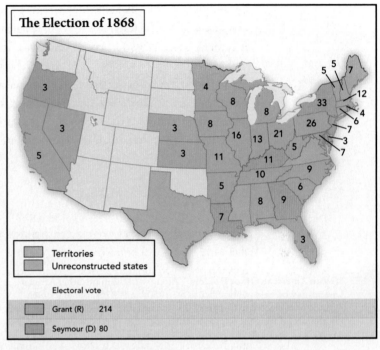

≡ **MAP 16.3   The Election of 1868**

been enslaved, to office. Two Black men—Hiram R. Revels and Blanche K. Bruce, both from Mississippi—were elevated to the US Senate. Sixteen Black men, many from the secessionist stronghold of South Carolina, would sit in the House of Representatives. But as dramatic as election to Congress was, Black officeholding in the states and localities counted for even more. Nearly 300 Black people served in constitutional conventions called under Military Reconstruction, where they helped move state governments in far more inclusive and democratic directions. More than 100 won election or appointment to posts having jurisdiction over entire states, including one as lieutenant governor of Louisiana—P. B. S. Pinchback, who would briefly serve as governor when the sitting governor was impeached. And nearly 800 took seats in state legislatures, in some cases forming majorities (South Carolina and Mississippi) or near majorities (Louisiana), where they battled to create new post-emancipation societies. One northern journalist, observing the changes in the South Carolina statehouse, saw "the spectacle of a society turned bottomside up."

Yet such a "spectacle" was most evident in the rural counties, where freedpeople composed the majority of the population. There, in the one-time realm of enslavers, Black men—maybe as many as 1,400 or 1,500 of them—now held

≡ **African American Office Holders**   Along with the many other African Americans who held public office in the 1860s and 1870s, the Black men pictured were elected to Congress, disproving critics who charged that Black officeholding during the Reconstruction era led to irresponsible government.

the levers of power: as jurors, magistrates, county commissioners, tax assessors, school superintendents, coroners, constables, and even as sheriffs. It was an unprecedented political transformation that directly threatened the social order that southern whites had known. As Georgia's Black Republican leader Henry McNeal Turner explained, white Democrats "do not care so much about Congress admitting negroes to their halls but they don't want negroes over them at home."

Republican Rule

It surely was a world "turned bottomside up." Aghast, white Democrats howled about the onset of "Negro rule." In point of fact, however, it was whites, not Black people, who predominated among Republican leaders and officeholders during this period, especially among those who took the most visible and formidable seats of power. National offices, like senators and congressmen, as well as statewide offices, were filled overwhelmingly by white men. Governorships (except for Pinchback's brief reign) were filled exclusively by white men, and outside of South Carolina, Mississippi, and Louisiana, Republican legislative delegations were majority white. Even on the local level, most of the offices—especially those with police or taxing power—were held by whites. It was, more accurately, "Republican rule," in which the predominant base of support was Black.

So, why the alarm? What the idea of "Negro rule" did capture was the significant shift in political power that Military Reconstruction made possible: from the former slaveholding elite toward a number of groups who had previously been outsiders to southern politics. In addition to the freedmen, they included white northerners, known derisively as **carpetbaggers**, who had served in the US Army and Freedmen's Bureau, had taken up planting or merchandising, or had engaged in teaching and missionary work; white southerners, known even more derisively as **scalawags**, who had been Unionists or unenthusiastic rebels, had been non-slaveholders or small slaveholders, or who had lived beyond the immediate orbit of the planter class; Black northerners, some having escaped enslavement, who had been educated and had come South with the army or the church; and some Black southerners who had been free before the war. Together they were substantially less wealthy, less experienced politically, and less committed to perpetuating the old plantation order than the antebellum elite while, for the most part, owing their positions to Black votes.

Although their programs and achievements varied some from place to place, the Republican regimes that took charge of the rebellious states in 1868 began to carry out sweeping reforms and innovations. They rebuilt the region's infrastructure, reorganized its political life, adjusted the balances of local power, and tied the fortunes of its new governments closely to the national state. Republicans were responsible for creating the first systems of public education in the South (serving white as well as Black people, though in a segregated fashion) while establishing or significantly increasing the resources of public institutions such as hospitals, asylums, orphanages, and penitentiaries. They raised taxes and shifted the burden from individuals (head taxes) to landed and personal property owners, in some cases forcing plantation land onto the market for nonpayment. In alliance with railroad developers, they repaired lines destroyed during the war and constructed new ones that reached into areas previously on the edge of the market economy and linked the South more directly to the Northeast and Midwest.

Republicans generally centralized the power of political appointments, putting it in the hands of the governors, blocked planter attempts to enforce the dependency of Black laborers, outlawed corporal punishment, and reduced both the number of capital offenses and the penalties for minor crimes. They liberalized women's ability to get a divorce, granted new property rights to women who were married, and enabled African Americans to sue and testify in court as well as sit on juries. It was a far cry from the old order, when enslavers ruled over their sovereign domains, rail and river transportation mainly connected the plantation belt with southern ports, and the public sector was scarcely more than a shell.

Paramilitary Counterrevolution

Not surprisingly, this Republican political revolution provoked turmoil. Former enslavers, most of whom supported the Democratic Party, recognized that power and authority were changing hands and that their ability to enforce the submission of Black workers was seriously compromised. And when their efforts to convince freedpeople to follow their leads came to little, they turned very quickly to methods of battle that had long maintained order under slavery: paramilitarism and vigilante

≡ **"Worse Than Slavery"**   Some imagined that the harassment and violence that many African Americans suffered in the Reconstruction was less tolerable than slavery, as shown in this 1874 illustration by Thomas Nast.

violence. Paramilitary organizations like the local units known as the **Ku Klux Klan** were generally composed of rebel officers and other young war veterans who had been paroled or allowed to desert without surrendering their arms, ammunition, and horses. They began to police the countryside— much as slave patrols had once done—harassing and punishing freedpeople who took advantage of their freedom, showed signs of economic independence, or behaved in ways regarded as insubordinate.

But more than anything else, the paramilitaries moved against local Black leaders and their allies: Union League organizers, Black grassroots activists and candidates for office, sympathetic teachers and ministers, and African Americans determined to vote for the Republican Party. Many Black leaders were assassinated or driven away, families and communities were terrorized, and schools and churches were torched. So fierce and successful could the paramilitaries be that in 1868 they enabled the Democrats to carry the presidential electoral votes of Georgia and Virginia.

The big question was whether the federal government together with the loyal state governments in the South would use the political and military means at their disposal to protect Republican voters and officeholders and secure the power of their regimes. For a time, the answer was "yes." The Grant administration dispatched federal troops to quell serious disturbances and suppress the most outrageous examples of vigilantism. Congress, in turn, launched an investigation of the Klan that resulted in legislation known as the **Enforcement Acts** of 1870 and 1871, which outlawed "conspiracies" that deprived Black people of their civil and political rights. Closer to the ground, some of the Republican governors reorganized state militias—sometimes with Black troops heavily represented—and put them to good use in Klan-infested areas.

16.5 The Weakening of the Radicals and the Ending of Reconstruction

||| Explain how and why the Reconstruction experiment came undone.

But the political temper of the times was shifting away from the Radical faction of the Republican Party and toward the more numerous Moderates, thereby favoring a retraction of federal involvement in southern affairs. In part, it was the empowerment of the formerly enslaved and in part the impeachment of President Andrew Johnson by the House of Representatives for violations of federal laws that provoked a backlash against the Radicals. It was also the growing influence of financial and industrial interests in Republican policymaking circles. What would a Radical agenda in the South mean for the governance and economy of the nation? Reconstruction was first hobbled by those who were supervising it, and then it was overthrown by those who had once been Confederate rebels.

The Impeachment of Andrew Johnson

The Constitution of the United States allows for the **impeachment**, conviction, and removal of a sitting president for "treason, bribery, or other high crimes and misdemeanors" (Article II, Section 4), but as of 1868, no sitting president had ever been so charged. There was a high bar for removal. The House of Representatives first had to impeach—effectively indict—the offending president by a majority vote, and then the Senate—effectively sitting as a jury—had to convict by a vote of at least two-thirds of its members. Once removed from office, according to the Constitution, the convicted president could never again run for public office.

But after several years of fighting with Andrew Johnson, the Republicans were fed up. He was continually tampering with their Reconstruction policies and, even though Congress overrode his vetoes, he retained the power to replace officials acceptable to the Republicans with those Johnson believed were more loyal to him and might sabotage the Republican projects. Finally, they determined to act and brought articles of impeachment against Johnson for doing just this sort of thing—specifically for violating the recently passed **Tenure of Office Act**, which required Senate approval for the filling of certain federal posts.

The House of Representatives quickly supported the articles and voted to impeach Johnson. The case then went to the Senate, where the Republicans were in the majority but divided between Radical and Moderate factions. And although the Radicals and some of the Moderates were ready to convict, other Moderates had serious doubts. Should Johnson be removed, he would be replaced, not by a sitting vice president—there was none, Johnson having been Lincoln's vice president—but by the president pro tempore of the Senate, Ohio's Benjamin Wade. Wade was a prominent leader of the Radical faction at a time when the winds were shifting away from the Radicals in the Republican Party. He strongly supported Military Reconstruction in the South as well as policies more favorable to labor and small producers than the industrialists and financial interests who were becoming more and more powerful in the Party and the nation.

A President Wade was too much for the Moderates to allow, and so, after receiving assurances from Johnson that he would no longer trouble them, they helped find the votes to prevent his conviction and removal. Johnson survived, the first and last president to suffer impeachment (or threat of impeachment) for another century, and the Radicals sustained a blow from which they would never really recover.

Economic and Political Turbulence

The hobbling of Reconstruction was accompanied and influenced by the painful impact of an economic panic in 1873 (discussed in Chapter 17) and by the widespread retrenchments it ushered in. Not only were the financial and manufacturing sectors of the Republican coalition hard hit, but the labor unrest that quickly erupted shook their confidence. Hundreds of textile, railroad, and mine workers went out on strike to oppose the wage cuts their employers imposed, and many thousands were thrown out of work in the deepening economic depression that followed. Together these workers took part in massive demonstrations in industrializing cities of the Northeast and Midwest that called upon state and municipal governments to help mitigate their suffering, perhaps by initiating public works projects to provide needed employment.

As a result of the social unrest spreading around them, northern employers and financiers felt a growing sympathy for southern planters who had been complaining about the insolence and political insubordination of their Black laborers. Further, the Grant administration had less and less enthusiasm for coming to the aid of embattled Republicans at any level in the South. When, in such an atmosphere, the Democratic Party reclaimed control of the House of Representatives in 1874, the arms of the Republican state were further weakened and their ability to guide a variety of ambitious projects hatched during the War of the Rebellion was placed in jeopardy.

While the Panic and its aftermath aggravated tensions between Republican leaders at the national level and Black constituents in the South, they also aggravated tensions among Republicans within the South. Well before the economic panic, Black Republicans were feeling ill at ease with the leadership that white Republicans were willing to provide. They feared their status as junior partners to the whites was too deeply etched, their aspirations and concerns poorly understood or ignored, their claim to a fair share of offices rejected, and their vulnerabilities to violence insufficiently addressed. One Black South Carolinian bitterly complained about white Republicans who made "loud and big promises to the freedmen till they got elected to office, then did not do one single thing," who refused to support the nomination of "a colored man" for major office, who "removed a number of black trial justices," and who "disarmed a number of black militia companies." "The first duty of any race," he insisted, "is to see to their own interests specially."

Black discontent soon forced white Republican officeholders, especially governors, to make a critical choice. They could attend more fully to the interests of their Black supporters and risk alienating white ones, or they could curry the favor of moderate Democrats by cutting taxes and spending, decrying "corruption," championing "reform," and offering Democrats a share of the patronage and offices. Most chose the latter, but even that was to little avail. Democrats had no inclination to join hands with white Republicans. They preferred to rally southern whites against the threat of "Negro rule" and rely on paramilitaries to achieve what ballots might fail to do: drive the Republicans and their Black supporters from political power.

Redemption

The Ku Klux Klan may have been targeted by the federal government, but its place was soon taken by a variety of rifle clubs known as the White Leagues or Red Shirts—closely tied to the Democratic Party and fixed upon dismantling and destroying the opposition. Using networks of kinship, patronage, and military service that crossed county lines, they brought a reign of terror into the plantation districts and

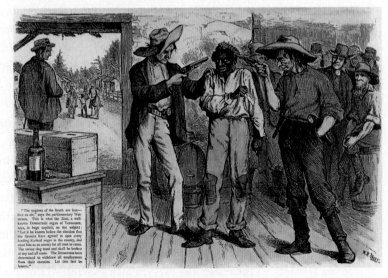

≡ **Voter Intimidation**   In 1875 and 1876, paramilitary units connected with the Democratic Party helped topple the last Republican governments in Mississippi, Louisiana, and South Carolina.

eventually to the doors of the state legislatures. Rifle club members (who, unlike Klansmen, did not bother with disguises and therefore did not technically violate the Enforcement Acts) attacked Republican meetings and incited riots that claimed the lives of many Black people in attendance. They beat and murdered local Black and white Republican leaders, threatened prospective voters, and then menaced them at the polls. Even if Republicans managed to win elections, the rifle clubs tried to prevent successful candidates from taking office or to drive them off once they did.

More and more counties were redeemed in this way, undermining Republican state and local regimes or isolating them in a rising sea of paramilitarism. In Louisiana, while several thousand White Leaguers brazenly attempted to oust the Republican governor and legislature in 1874 (failing only because of the last-minute intervention of federal troops), their rural counterparts did them better. They crippled or overthrew Republican officials in at least eight parishes in a wave of bloody violence. Red River Parish was particularly gruesome. There, in August, the duly elected sheriff, tax collector, and justice of the peace together with a registrar, a Republican attorney, and several Black supporters were summarily slaughtered near the county seat of Coushatta.

Remarkably, African Americans maintained their loyalty to the Republican Party, and as white Republicanism shrank in the face of paramilitarism and Black assertiveness, they became the mainstays of the party. Their support in states like South Carolina, Mississippi, Louisiana, and Florida enabled Republican regimes to hold on. Black officeholding in the South grew during the early 1870s. It may have peaked around 1874 and, in some localities, Black militants effectively stared the rifle clubs down. For all of their saber-rattling, night-riding, and terrorism, the Democrats, without massive electoral fraud, would have remained on the losing end, out of power, especially in the Deep South, where Black political strength was greatest.

The Contested Election of 1876

Yet the reach of the Republican state would extend only so far. Republicans had crushed the slaveholders' rebellion, abolished enslavement, fortified the power of the federal government, established a national citizenship, and organized the party in the rebellious states with a social base that had previously been enslaved. They had imposed martial law and prescribed a raft of political and social conditions that had to be met before those states could regain their status in what was now a nation. And they also succeeded, to the benefit of Black men both inside and outside of the rebellious states, in enacting the last of the Reconstruction Amendments, the Fifteenth (1870), which guaranteed that the "right to vote," would not be denied on account of "race, color, or previous condition of servitude" (though not on account of "sex" as woman suffrage activists had demanded).

This was the political and social revolution that had been made, and for that revolution to continue or to be fully preserved the force of federal arms would have to be flexed for some time to come. But the long-term interests of the Republican Party were increasingly aligned with property and capital, not with the Black laborers who had made the revolution possible and whose lives and rights were most in jeopardy. As a result, little by little, in the halls of Congress and on the ground in the South, the revolution was being rolled back, pushing the Radicals to the margins nationally and leaving Republican Party supporters in jeopardy in the former rebellious states. How would this end? And who would the winners be?

The die was finally cast in 1876. That year a presidential election set Republican Rutherford B. Hayes of Ohio against Democrat Samuel J. Tilden of New York, and when all the ballots were counted, no winner could be declared. Tilden, it seemed, had bucked the trend of the previous four election cycles. He won the popular vote and was within one vote of having a majority in the electoral college. But the returns of South Carolina, Florida, and Louisiana were in dispute, owing to charges of fraud and harassment at the polling places (see Map 16.4). For a time, tempers were so frayed that it appeared hostilities might again erupt. At the very least it was unclear whether a victor could be determined by inauguration day, then March 4, making for an unprecedented political and constitutional crisis. In the meantime, the disputed vote also brought dual state governments in South Carolina and Louisiana, one Democratic and one Republican, each claiming to be the rightful authority. In this tense atmosphere, Democratic rifle clubs made the first move. They surrounded the Republican governors and legislators in the state capitals and demanded that they surrender their offices.

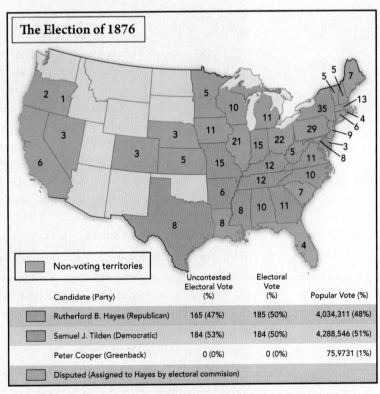

		Uncontested Electoral Vote (%)	Electoral Vote (%)	Popular Vote (%)
	Rutherford B. Hayes (Republican)	165 (47%)	185 (50%)	4,034,311 (48%)
	Samuel J. Tilden (Democratic)	184 (53%)	184 (50%)	4,288,546 (51%)
	Peter Cooper (Greenback)	0 (0%)	0 (0%)	75,9731 (1%)
	Disputed (Assigned to Hayes by electoral commision)			

≡ **MAP 16.4 The Election of 1876** The election was marred by white violence and vote-rigging, and Congress deadlocked on choosing a victor. An Electoral Commission eventually determined that Rutherford B. Hayes would be sworn in. As a bow to Democrats, Hayes then withdrew the last federal troops from the South.

PERSPECTIVES

Contrasting Views of Reconstruction

Reconstruction is widely regarded as comprising a revolution in American society and politics, but revolutions often have their limits as well as promises. On the one hand, Reconstruction fundamentally changed the South. The Thirteenth, Fourteenth, and Fifteenth Amendments established limited economic and political equality, the Freedmen's Bureau protected African Americans, and, perhaps most obviously, the federal government divided the defeated Confederacy into military districts under direct army supervision. As a result, hundreds of Black people served in state legislatures, and sixteen served in Congress. Therefore, the postwar South showed the beneficial effects of Congressional Reconstruction.

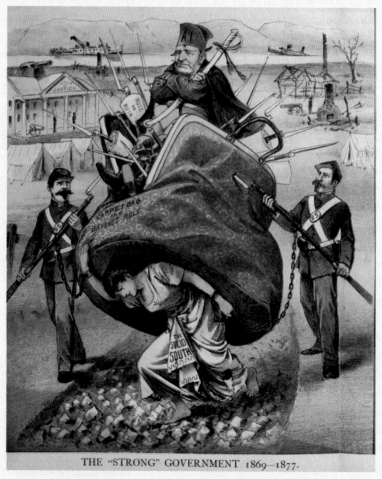

THE "STRONG" GOVERNMENT 1869–1877.

≡ Political Cartoon (Part 1): "Strong" Government.

On the other hand, although the federal government made limited attempts to expand equality for freedpeople, it was unable to achieve real equality. Relatively few African Americans won federal elections, tenants and sharecroppers enjoyed few rights, and vigilantes terrorized free Black people and their supporters (see Chapter 17). As a result, **Redeemers** quickly retook control over southern Democrats, ensuring an end to Reconstruction.

This two-part cartoon from 1890 shows how many southerners viewed Reconstruction. In the first image, "The Solid South" is seen struggling under the "Carpet Bag and Bayonet Rule" of the "Strong" US government, led by President Ulysses S. Grant, who is seen riding among bayonets with an escort of two federal soldiers. In the background, we see a destroyed and occupied South.

We see a different picture in the second image. Under the presidency of Rutherford B. Hayes, the "Carpet Bag and Bayonet Rule" is being plowed under by the president's "Let'em Alone Policy." Under this "Weak" government, the South flourishes amid factories and fertile fields. A white man, presumably a landowner, gives orders to an African American tenant farmer.

THE "WEAK" GOVERNMENT 1877–1881.

≡ Political Cartoon (Part 2): "Weak" Government.

CONSIDER THIS

According to the cartoonist, why did southern states desire a "weak" government? How would an African American living in the South in 1890 have viewed these two time periods?

Seeking to find a settlement and defuse the crisis, Congress appointed an independent electoral commission and, with a thin majority of Republican members, the commission determined that all the disputed electoral votes would go to Rutherford Hayes, giving him the presidency. In the process, however, Hayes made a devil's bargain of his own, known as the **Compromise of 1877**. To appease the Democrats, he agreed to give them some important posts in his cabinet and, far more important, he ordered the remaining US Army troops in the rebellious states to return to their barracks rather than aid the besieged Republicans of South Carolina and Louisiana. As a result, just as Hayes took his oath of office the last of the Republican governments fell. The Reconstruction experiment was over.

Conclusion: The Limits of Revolution

The War of the Rebellion and Reconstruction are widely regarded as comprising a revolution in American society and politics: a second American revolution, some have called it. And, indeed, it was revolutionary in the nineteenth-century world to abolish slavery without any compensation to enslavers and on the backs of their military defeat. Along with this, the political power of the former enslavers and of the big southern landowners was dramatically curtailed in national politics while the civil and political rights of the people they had enslaved were established. No one, in any part of the United States at the beginning of 1861, would have imagined such a country four years later. Only the Haitian Revolution (1791–1804, discussed in Chapter 8) is comparable in its reach and reverberations, and even it did not go so far in shifting political power to the formerly enslaved.

But revolutions often have their limits as well as promises, and this one did on the matters of private property, economic growth, race, and gender. Only a small group of Radical Republicans dared suggest that Confederate rebels be punished for treason, have their lands confiscated and redistributed to Black people and white yeoman farmers, and subject the rebellious South to a lengthy period of federal supervision. The Republican Party, more generally, was too committed to private property to confiscate and redistribute land, even the land of traitors to the republic. It was too committed to the country's economic growth to risk the future of the cotton economy of the South by enabling Black laborers to become landowners. It was too committed to developing the trans-Mississippi West into a commodity-producing region to permit Indigenous people to be incorporated into the country on a basis of citizenship and maintain their ways of life and culture. And it was too committed to patriarchy and the nuclear family to disrupt the gender hierarchy of households and the country at large by awarding women the right to vote. We still live with the consequences of what they did and didn't do.

WHAT IF the Confederate Rebels Had Been Punished as Traitors?

In many respects, the leniency of the federal government toward the Confederate rebels was astonishing. During the American Revolution, loyalists were driven off and sometimes killed by the patriots, and once the Revolution ended, many were forced into exile and had their property confiscated. They were regarded as traitors, and nothing was more damning in political life.

President Lincoln, moderate though he was, nonetheless called the Confederates traitors and their rebellion treasonous. Some Radical Republicans thought that, in order to prevent another such rebellion, the leadership should be severely punished and the basis of their wealth and power destroyed by confiscating their lands and redistributing them to the formerly enslaved and to humble white people who did not support the Confederacy. They were not alone. Many people in the northern states, especially those whose husbands and sons fought and died in the bloody war, worried that without an iron hand crushing down on the rebels the war would have been fought in vain.

What if, upon the surrender of Confederate armies, the top political and military leaders of the rebellion—Jefferson Davis, Alexander Stephens, Robert E. Lee, the war governors, members of the Confederate congress, the secessionist delegates who precipitated the war—were taken into custody, charged with treason, and made to stand trial? Most would have been convicted and sentenced either to long prison terms or execution, the usual punishment for treason. What if the richest slaveholding planters were sent into exile—a version of colonization, as Frederick Douglass once suggested to Lincoln—and their allies disfranchised for at least a decade? What if the plantations owned by people who had participated in the rebellion were confiscated by the federal government and—in the manner of Sherman's Field Orders No. 15—redistributed to formerly enslaved families in 40-acre plots, enough for them to grow not only subsistence but some market crops? And what if the federal government chose to protect white family farmers, too, and used its resources to enable them, as well as freed farmers, to get necessary credit at low rates of interest, so that they would not fall into debt and lose their land?

These are not pipe dreams. In one form or another they were all proposed at the time either by political leaders or ordinary citizens. What would the postwar United States have looked like if there was "malice" toward some and "charity" for those who were loyal to and helped save the country from the Confederate rebellion?

Document 16.1: Committee of Freedmen on Edisto Island, South Carolina, to the Freedmen's Bureau Commissioner, October 20 or 21, 1865

In the fall of 1865, under orders of President Johnson, land that had been confiscated and distributed for exclusive Black settlement along the South Carolina coast and its Sea Islands (in accordance with Sherman's Field Orders No. 15) was returned to its former owners. A committee of freedmen then wrote to the commissioner of the Freedmen's Bureau, General Oliver Howard, to protest the president's decision.

[Edisto Island, S.C., October 20 or 21, 1865]

General   It Is with painfull Hearts that we the committe address you, we Have thorougholy considered the order which you wished us to Sighn, we wish we could do so but cannot feel our rights Safe If we do so,

General we want Homestead's; we were promised Homestead's by the government, If It does not carry out the promises Its agents made to us, If the government Haveing concluded to be-friend Its late enemies and to neglect to observe the principles of common faith between Its self and us Its allies In the war you said was over, now takes away from them all right to the soil they stand upon save such as they can get by again working for *your* late and thier *all time ememies.*–If the government does so we are left In a more unpleasant condition than our former

we are at the mercy of those who are combined to prevent us from getting land enough to lay our Fathers bones upon. We Have property In Horses, cattle, carriages, & articles of furniture, but we are landless and Homeless, from the Homes we Have lived In In the past we can only do one of three things   Step Into the public *road or the sea* or remain on them working as In former time and subject to thire will as then. We can not resist It In any way without being driven out Homeless upon the road.

You will see this Is not the condition of really freemen

You ask us to forgive the land owners of our Island, *You* only lost your right arm. In war and might forgive them. The man who tied me to a tree & gave me 39 lashes & who stripped and flogged my mother & my sister & who will not let me stay In His empty Hut except I will do His planting & be Satisfied with His price & who combines with others to keep away land from me well knowing I would not Have any thing to do with Him If I Had land of my own.–that man, I cannot well forgive. Does It look as If He Has forgiven me, seeing How He tries to keep me In a condition of Helplessness

General, we cannot remain Here In such condition and If the government permits them to come back we ask It to Help us to reach land where we shall not be slaves nor compelled to work for those who would treat us as such

we Have not been treacherous, we Have not for selfish motives allied to us those who suf-fered like us from a common enemy & then Haveing gained *our* purpose left our allies In thier Hands   There Is no rights secured to us   there Is no law likely to be made which our Hands can reach. The state will make laws that we shall not be able to Hold land even If we pay for It   Landless, Homeless. Voteless. we can only pray to god & Hope for *His Help, your Infuence & assistance*   With consideration of esteem your Obt Servts In behalf of the people

	Henry Bram
Committe	Ishmael Moultrie
	yates Sampson

Source: Henry Bram et al. to Major General O. O. Howard, [October 20 or 21, 1865], B 53 1865, Letters Received, ser. 15, Washington Hdqrs., RG 105.

Document 16.2: Speech of Representative Thaddeus Stevens (PA) to Congress, March 1867

This speech was delivered by Radical Republican Thaddeus Stevens of Pennsylvania in March 1867 in support of legislation that would punish Confederate rebels and offer necessary rewards to Black and white loyalists in the South.

The fifth section [of the 1862 Confiscation Act] enacts that—"To insure the speedy termination of the present rebellion, it shall be the duty of the President of the United States to cause the seizure of all the estates and property, money, stocks, credits, and effects of the persons hereinafter named in this section, and apply and use the same and the proceeds thereof for the support of the Army of the United States."

The cause of the war was slavery. We have liberated the slaves. It is our duty to protect them, and provide for them while they are unable to provide for themselves. Have we not a right ... "to do ourselves justice respecting the object which has caused the war," by taking lands for homesteads [for] these "objects" of the war?

Have we not a right, if we chose to go to that extent, to indemnify [compensate] ourselves for the expenses and damages caused by the war? ...

We could be further justified in inflicting severe penalties upon this whole hostile people as "a fierce and savage people," as an "obstinate enemy," whom it is a duty to tame and punish. Our future safety requires stern justice. ...

I must earnestly pray that [the provision granting land to freedmen] may not be defeated. On its success, in my judgment, depends not only the happiness and respectability of the colored race, but their very existence. Homesteads to them are far more valuable than the immediate right of suffrage, though both are their due.

Four million of persons have just been freed from a condition of dependence, wholly unacquainted with business transactions, kept systematically in ignorance of all their rights and of the common elements of education, without which none of any race are competent to earn an honest living, to guard against the frauds which will always be practiced on the ignorant. ... Make them independent of their old masters, so that they may not be compelled to work for them upon unfair terms, which can only be done by giving them a small tract of land to cultivate for themselves, and you remove all this danger. You also elevate the character of the freedman. Nothing is so likely to make a man a good citizen as to make him a freeholder. Nothing will so multiply the productions of the South as to divide it into small farms. Nothing will make men so industrious and moral as to let them feel that they are above want and are the owners of the soil which they till. It will also be of service to the white inhabitants. They will have constantly among them industrious laborers, anxious to work for fair wages. How is it possible for them to cultivate their lands if these people were expelled? If Moses should lead or drive them into exile, or carry out the absurd idea of colonizing them, the South would become a barren waste.

Source: Speech of Hon. T. Stevens, of Pennsylvania, delivered in the House of Representatives, March 19, 1867: on the bill (H.R. no. 20) relative to damages to loyal men, and for other purposes.

Thinking About Contingency

1. How did the Edisto Island freedmen justify their right to the land?
2. Besides the formerly enslaved people themselves, who might have supported an alternative Reconstruction plan such as the one proposed by Stevens?
3. What were the challenges to the plan to severely punish Confederate leaders and to turn a plantation-based society into one based on small yeoman farms?
4. To what extent would this plan have changed the socioeconomic and political history of the United States or shaped relations between Black and white Americans?

REVIEW QUESTIONS

1. What visions did the formerly enslaved and free Black people have for a post-emancipation South, and why did those visions stir fears among many white southerners?

2. Why was President Johnson so strongly opposed to Republican Reconstruction plans, and how far were Republicans prepared to go to transform the South?

3. Why did the Republican-controlled Congress extend voting rights to Black men but refuse to do so for any women?

4. How did the Republican Party build a base of support in the southern states, and how much political power did formerly enslaved people gain in the process?

5. What did Republican Reconstruction governments try to accomplish in the southern states, and how were they driven from power?

6. How much of a revolution did Republican Reconstruction carry through?

KEY TERMS

birthright citizenship (p. 661)

carpetbaggers (p. 672)

Civil Rights Act of 1866 (p. 660)

Compromise of 1877 (p. 682)

Enforcement Acts (p. 674)

Fifteenth Amendment (p. 650)

Fourteenth Amendment (p. 661)

freedmen's conventions (p. 651)

impeachment (p. 675)

Juneteenth (p. 658)

Ku Klux Klan (p. 674)

Military Reconstruction Acts (p. 662)

Redeemers (p. 681)

scalawags (p. 673)

Tenure of Office Act (p. 675)

Thirteenth Amendment (p. 659)

Union League (p. 668)

Women's Loyal National League (p. 658)

RECOMMENDED READINGS

Justin Behrend, *Reconstructing Democracy: Grassroots Politics in the Deep South After the Civil War* (University of Georgia Press, 2017).

Gregory Downs, *After Appomattox: Military Occupation and the Ends of War* (Harvard University Press, 2019).

W. E. B. Du Bois, *Black Reconstruction in America, 1860–1880* (1936; Free Press, 1998).

Ellen Dubois, *Feminism and Suffrage: The Emergence of an Independent Women's Movement in America, 1848–1869* (Cornell University Press, 1978).

Carole Emberton, *Beyond Redemption, Race, Violence, and the American South After the Civil War* (University of Chicago, 2015).

Eric Foner, *Reconstruction: America's Unfinished Revolution, 1863–1877* (Harper and Row, 1988).

Eric Foner, *The Second Founding* (W.W. Norton, 2020).

Steven Hahn, *A Nation Under Our Feet: Black Political Struggles in the Rural South from Slavery to the Great Migration* (Harvard University Press, 2003).

Edward Magdol, *A Right to the Land: Essays on the Freedman's Community* (Praeger, 1977).

Alaina Roberts, *I've Been Here All the While: Black Freedom on Native Land* (University of Pennsylvania Press, 2021).

Julie Saville, *The Work of Reconstruction* (Cambridge University Press, 1994).

Appendix A
Historical Documents

The Declaration of Independence (1776)

When in the course of human events, it becomes necessary for one people to dissolve the political bands which have connected them with another, and to assume, among the powers of the earth, the separate and equal station to which the Laws of Nature and of Nature's God entitle them, a decent respect to the opinions of mankind requires that they should declare the causes which impel them to the separation.

We hold these truths to be self-evident, that all men are created equal, that they are endowed by their Creator with certain unalienable Rights, that among these are life, liberty and the pursuit of happiness. That to secure these rights, governments are instituted among men, deriving their just powers from the consent of the governed; that whenever any form of government becomes destructive of these ends, it is the right of the people to alter or to abolish it, and to institute new Government, laying its foundation on such principles and organizing its powers in such form, as to them shall seem most likely to effect their safety and happiness. Prudence, indeed, will dictate that Governments long established should not be changed for light and transient causes; and, accordingly, all experience hath shown, that mankind are more disposed to suffer, while evils are sufferable, than to right themselves by abolishing the forms to which they are accustomed. But when a long train of abuses and usurpations, pursuing invariably the same object evinces a design to reduce them under absolute despotism, it is their right, it is their duty, to throw off such government, and to provide new guards for their future security. Such has been the patient sufferance of these colonies; and such is now the necessity which constrains them to alter their former systems of government. The history of the present King of Great Britain is a history of repeated injuries and usurpations, all having in direct object the establishment of an absolute tyranny over these States. To prove this, let facts be submitted to a candid world:

He has refused his assent to laws, the most wholesome and necessary for the public good.

He has forbidden his governors to pass laws of immediate and pressing importance, unless suspended in their operation till his assent should be obtained; and, when so suspended, he has utterly neglected to attend to them.

He has refused to pass other laws for the accommodation of large districts of people, unless those people would relinquish the right of representation in the legislature, a right inestimable to them and formidable to tyrants only.

He has called together legislative bodies at places unusual, uncomfortable, and distant from the depository of their public records, for the sole purpose of fatiguing them into compliance with his measures.

He has dissolved representative houses repeatedly, for opposing with manly firmness his invasions on the rights of the people.

He has refused for a long time, after such dissolutions, to cause others to be elected; whereby the legislative powers, incapable of annihilation, have returned to the People at large for their exercise; the State remaining in the mean time exposed to all the dangers of invasion from without, and convulsions within.

He has endeavored to prevent the population of these States; for that purpose obstructing the laws for naturalization of foreigners; refusing to pass others to encourage their migrations hither, and raising the conditions of new appropriations of lands.

He has obstructed the administration of justice, by refusing his assent to laws for establishing judiciary powers.

He has made judges dependent on his will alone, for the tenure of their offices, and the amount and payment of their salaries.

He has erected a multitude of new offices, and sent hither swarms of officers to harass our people, and eat out their substance.

He has kept among us, in times of peace, standing armies without the consent of our legislatures.

He has affected to render the Military independent of, and superior to, the civil power.

He has combined with others to subject us to a jurisdiction foreign to our constitution and unacknowledged by our laws; giving his assent to their acts of pretended legislation:

For quartering large bodies of armed troops among us;

For protecting them, by a mock trial, from punishment for any murders which they should commit on the inhabitants of these States;

For cutting off our trade with all parts of the world;

For imposing taxes on us without our Consent;

For depriving us, in many cases, of the benefits of Trial by Jury;

For transporting us beyond Seas to be tried for pretended offences;

For abolishing the free System of English Laws in a neighbouring Province, establishing therein an Arbitrary government, and enlarging its Boundaries so as to render it at once an example and fit instrument for introducing the same absolute rule into these colonies;

For taking away our charters, abolishing our most valuable laws, and altering fundamentally the forms of our governments;

For suspending our own legislatures, and declaring themselves invested with power to legislate for us in all cases whatsoever.

He has abdicated government here, by declaring us out of his protection and waging war against us.

He has plundered our seas, ravaged our coasts, burnt our towns, and destroyed the lives of our people.

He is at this time transporting large armies of foreign mercenaries to complete the works of death, desolation and tyranny, already begun with circumstances of cruelty and perfidy scarcely paralleled in the most barbarous ages, and totally unworthy the head of a civilized nation.

He has constrained our fellow citizens taken captive on the high seas to bear arms against their country, to become the executioners of their friends and brethren, or to fall themselves by their hands.

He has excited domestic insurrections amongst us, and has endeavored to bring on the inhabitants of our frontiers, the merciless Indian savages, whose known rule of warfare, is an undistinguished destruction of all ages, sexes and conditions.

In every stage of these oppressions we have petitioned for redress in the most humble terms; our repeated petitions have been answered only by repeated injury. A prince whose character is thus marked by every act which may define a tyrant, is unfit to be the ruler of a free people.

Nor have we been wanting in attentions to our British brethren. We have warned them from time to time of attempts by their legislature to extend an unwarrantable jurisdiction over us. We have reminded them of the circumstances of our emigration and settlement here. We have appealed to their native justice and magnanimity, and we have conjured them by the ties of our common kindred to disavow these usurpations, which, would inevitably interrupt our connections and correspondence. They, too, have been deaf to the voice of justice and of consanguinity. We must, therefore, acquiesce in the necessity, which denounces our separation, and hold them, as we hold the rest of mankind, enemies in war, in peace friends.

We, therefore, the representatives of the United States of America, in general Congress, assembled, appealing to the Supreme Judge of the world for the rectitude of our intentions, do, in the name, and by the authority of the good people of these colonies, solemnly publish and declare, that these united colonies are, and of right ought to be free and independent states; that they are absolved from all allegiance to the British Crown, and that all political connection between them and the state of Great Britain, is and ought to be totally dissolved; and that, as free and independent states, they have full power to levy war, conclude peace, contract alliances, establish commerce, and to do all other acts and things which independent states may of right do. And for the support of this declaration, with a firm reliance on the protection of Divine Providence, we mutually pledge to each other our lives, our fortunes and our sacred honor.

The Constitution of the United States of America (Ratified 1788)

We the People of the United States, in Order to form a more perfect Union, establish Justice, insure domestic Tranquility, provide for the common defence, promote the general Welfare, and secure the Blessings of Liberty to ourselves and our Posterity, do ordain and establish this Constitution for the United States of America.

Article I

SECTION 1

All legislative Powers herein granted shall be vested in a Congress of the United States, which shall consist of a Senate and House of Representatives.

SECTION 2

The House of Representatives shall be composed of Members chosen every second Year by the People of the several States, and the Electors in each State shall have the Qualifications requisite for Electors of the most numerous Branch of the State Legislature.

No Person shall be a Representative who shall not have attained to the Age of twenty five Years, and been seven Years a Citizen of the United States, and who shall not, when elected, be an Inhabitant of that State in which he shall be chosen.

Representatives and direct Taxes shall be apportioned among the several States which may be included within this Union, according to their respective Numbers, which shall be determined by adding to the whole Number of free Persons, including those bound to Service for a Term of Years, and excluding Indians not taxed, three fifths of all other Persons. The actual Enumeration shall be made within three Years after the first Meeting of the Congress of the United States, and within every subsequent Term of ten Years, in such Manner as they shall by Law direct. The Number of Representatives shall not exceed one for every thirty Thousand, but each State shall have at Least one Representative; and until such enumeration shall be made, the State of New Hampshire shall be entitled to choose three, Massachusetts eight, Rhode-Island and Providence Plantations one, Connecticut five, New York six, New Jersey four, Pennsylvania eight, Delaware one, Maryland six, Virginia ten, North Carolina five, South Carolina five, and Georgia three.

When vacancies happen in the Representation from any State, the Executive Authority thereof shall issue Writs of Election to fill such Vacancies.

The House of Representatives shall choose their Speaker and other Officers; and shall have the sole Power of Impeachment.

SECTION 3

The Senate of the United States shall be composed of two Senators from each State, chosen by the Legislature thereof for six Years; and each Senator shall have one Vote.

Immediately after they shall be assembled in Consequence of the first Election, they shall be divided as equally as may be into three Classes. The Seats of the Senators of the first Class shall be vacated at the Expiration of the second Year, of the second Class at the Expiration of the fourth Year, and of the third Class at the Expiration of the sixth Year, so that one third may be chosen every second Year; and if Vacancies happen by Resignation, or otherwise, during the Recess of the Legislature of any State, the Executive thereof may make temporary Appointments until the next Meeting of the Legislature, which shall then fill such Vacancies.

No Person shall be a Senator who shall not have attained to the Age of thirty Years, and been nine Years a Citizen of the United States, and who shall not, when elected, be an Inhabitant of that State for which he shall be chosen.

The Vice President of the United States shall be President of the Senate, but shall have no Vote, unless they be equally divided.

The Senate shall choose their other Officers, and also a President pro tempore, in the Absence of the Vice President, or when he shall exercise the Office of President of the United States.

The Senate shall have the sole Power to try all Impeachments. When sitting for that Purpose, they shall be on Oath or Affirmation. When the President of the United States is tried, the Chief Justice shall preside: And no Person shall be convicted without the Concurrence of two thirds of the Members present.

Judgment in Cases of Impeachment shall not extend further than to removal from Office, and disqualification to hold and enjoy any Office of honor, Trust or Profit under the United States: but the Party convicted shall nevertheless be liable and subject to Indictment, Trial, Judgment and Punishment, according to Law.

SECTION 4

The Times, Places and Manner of holding Elections for Senators and Representatives, shall be prescribed in each State by the Legislature thereof; but the Congress may at any time by Law make or alter such Regulations, except as to the Places of chusing Senators.

The Congress shall assemble at least once in every Year, and such Meeting shall be on the first Monday in December, unless they shall by Law appoint a different Day.

SECTION 5

Each House shall be the Judge of the Elections, Returns and Qualifications of its own Members, and a Majority of each shall constitute a Quorum to do Business; but a smaller Number may adjourn from day to day, and may be authorized to compel the Attendance of absent Members, in such Manner, and under such Penalties as each House may provide.

Each House may determine the Rules of its Proceedings, punish its Members for disorderly Behaviour, and, with the Concurrence of two thirds, expel a Member.

Each House shall keep a Journal of its Proceedings, and from time to time publish the same, excepting such Parts as may in their Judgment require Secrecy; and the Yeas and Nays of the Members of either House on any question shall, at the Desire of one fifth of those Present, be entered on the Journal.

Neither House, during the Session of Congress, shall, without the Consent of the other, adjourn for more than three days, nor to any other Place than that in which the two Houses shall be sitting.

SECTION 6

The Senators and Representatives shall receive a Compensation for their Services, to be ascertained by Law, and paid out of the Treasury of the United States. They shall in all Cases, except Treason, Felony and Breach of the Peace, be privileged from Arrest during their Attendance at the Session of their respective Houses, and in going to and returning from the same; and for any Speech or Debate in either House, they shall not be questioned in any other Place.

No Senator or Representative shall, during the Time for which he was elected, be appointed to any civil Office under the Authority of the United States, which shall have been created, or the Emoluments whereof shall have been increased during such time; and no Person holding any Office under the United States, shall be a Member of either House during his Continuance in Office.

SECTION 7

All Bills for raising Revenue shall originate in the House of Representatives; but the Senate may propose or concur with Amendments as on other Bills.

Every Bill which shall have passed the House of Representatives and the Senate, shall, before it become a Law, be presented to the President of the United States: If he approve he shall sign it, but if not he shall return it, with his Objections to that

House in which it shall have originated, who shall enter the Objections at large on their Journal, and proceed to reconsider it. If after such Reconsideration two thirds of that House shall agree to pass the Bill, it shall be sent, together with the Objections, to the other House, by which it shall likewise be reconsidered, and if approved by two thirds of that House, it shall become a Law. But in all such Cases the Votes of both Houses shall be determined by yeas and Nays, and the Names of the Persons voting for and against the Bill shall be entered on the Journal of each House respectively. If any Bill shall not be returned by the President within ten Days (Sundays excepted) after it shall have been presented to him, the Same shall be a Law, in like Manner as if he had signed it, unless the Congress by their Adjournment prevent its Return, in which Case it shall not be a Law.

Every Order, Resolution, or Vote to which the Concurrence of the Senate and House of Representatives may be necessary (except on a question of Adjournment) shall be presented to the President of the United States; and before the Same shall take Effect, shall be approved by him, or being disapproved by him, shall be re-passed by two thirds of the Senate and House of Representatives, according to the Rules and Limitations prescribed in the Case of a Bill.

SECTION 8

The Congress shall have Power

To lay and collect Taxes, Duties, Imposts and Excises, to pay the Debts and provide for the common Defence and general Welfare of the United States; but all Duties, Imposts and Excises shall be uniform throughout the United States;

To borrow Money on the credit of the United States;

To regulate Commerce with foreign Nations, and among the several States, and with the Indian Tribes;

To establish an uniform Rule of Naturalization, and uniform Laws on the subject of Bankruptcies throughout the United States;

To coin Money, regulate the Value thereof, and of foreign Coin, and fix the Standard of Weights and Measures;

To provide for the Punishment of counterfeiting the Securities and current Coin of the United States;

To establish Post Offices and post Roads;

To promote the Progress of Science and useful Arts, by securing for limited Times to Authors and Inventors the exclusive Right to their respective Writings and Discoveries;

To constitute Tribunals inferior to the supreme Court;

To define and punish Piracies and Felonies committed on the high Seas, and Offences against the Law of Nations;

To declare War, grant Letters of Marque and Reprisal, and make Rules concerning Captures on Land and Water;

To raise and support Armies, but no Appropriation of Money to that Use shall be for a longer Term than two Years;

To provide and maintain a Navy;

To make Rules for the Government and Regulation of the land and naval Forces;

To provide for calling forth the Militia to execute the Laws of the Union, suppress Insurrections and repel Invasions;

To provide for organizing, arming, and disciplining the Militia, and for governing such Part of them as may be employed in the Service of the United States, reserving to the States respectively, the Appointment of the Officers, and the Authority of training the Militia according to the discipline prescribed by Congress;

To exercise exclusive Legislation in all Cases whatsoever, over such District (not exceeding ten Miles square) as may, by Cession of particular States, and the Acceptance of Congress, become the Seat of the Government of the United States, and to exercise like Authority over all Places purchased by the Consent of the Legislature of the State in which the Same shall be, for the Erection of Forts, Magazines, Arsenals, dock-Yards, and other needful Buildings;—And

To make all Laws which shall be necessary and proper for carrying into Execution the foregoing Powers, and all other Powers vested by this Constitution in the Government of the United States, or in any Department or Officer thereof.

SECTION 9

The Migration or Importation of such Persons as any of the States now existing shall think proper to admit, shall not be prohibited by the Congress prior to the Year one thousand eight hundred and eight, but a Tax or duty may be imposed on such Importation, not exceeding ten dollars for each Person.

The Privilege of the Writ of Habeas Corpus shall not be suspended, unless when in Cases of Rebellion or Invasion the public Safety may require it.

No Bill of Attainder or ex post facto Law shall be passed.

No Capitation, or other direct, Tax shall be laid, unless in Proportion to the Census or enumeration herein before directed to be taken.

No Tax or Duty shall be laid on Articles exported from any State.

No Preference shall be given by any Regulation of Commerce or Revenue to the Ports of one State over those of another; nor shall Vessels bound to, or from, one State, be obliged to enter, clear, or pay Duties in another.

No Money shall be drawn from the Treasury, but in Consequence of Appropriations made by Law; and a regular Statement and Account of the Receipts and Expenditures of all public Money shall be published from time to time.

No Title of Nobility shall be granted by the United States: And no Person holding any Office of Profit or Trust under them, shall, without the Consent of the Congress, accept of any present, Emolument, Office, or Title, of any kind whatever, from any King, Prince, or foreign State.

SECTION 10

No State shall enter into any Treaty, Alliance, or Confederation; grant Letters of Marque and Reprisal; coin Money; emit Bills of Credit; make any Thing but gold and silver Coin a Tender in Payment of Debts; pass any Bill of Attainder, ex post facto Law, or Law impairing the Obligation of Contracts, or grant any Title of Nobility.

No State shall, without the Consent of the Congress, lay any Imposts or Duties on Imports or Exports, except what may be absolutely necessary for executing it's inspection Laws: and the net Produce of all Duties and Imposts, laid by any State on Imports or Exports, shall be for the Use of the Treasury of the United States; and all such Laws shall be subject to the Revision and Control of the Congress.

No State shall, without the Consent of Congress, lay any Duty of Tonnage, keep Troops, or Ships of War in time of Peace, enter into any Agreement or Compact with another State, or with a foreign Power, or engage in War, unless actually invaded, or in such imminent Danger as will not admit of delay.

Article II

SECTION 1

The executive Power shall be vested in a President of the United States of America. He shall hold his Office during the Term of four Years, and, together with the Vice President, chosen for the same Term, be elected, as follows:

Each State shall appoint, in such Manner as the Legislature thereof may direct, a Number of Electors, equal to the whole Number of Senators and Representatives to which the State may be entitled in the Congress: but no Senator or Representative, or Person holding an Office of Trust or Profit under the United States, shall be appointed an Elector.

The Electors shall meet in their respective States, and vote by Ballot for two Persons, of whom one at least shall not be an Inhabitant of the same State with themselves. And they shall make a List of all the Persons voted for, and of the Number of Votes for each; which List they shall sign and certify, and transmit sealed to the Seat of the Government of the United States, directed to the President of the Senate. The President of the Senate shall, in the Presence of the Senate and House of Representatives, open all the Certificates, and the Votes shall then be counted. The Person having the greatest Number of Votes shall be the President, if such Number be a Majority of the whole Number of Electors appointed; and if there be more than one who have such Majority, and have an equal Number of Votes, then the House of Representatives shall immediately choose by Ballot one of them for President; and if no Person have a Majority, then from the five highest on the List the said House shall in like Manner choose the President. But in choosing the President, the Votes shall be taken by States, the Representation from each State having one Vote; A quorum for this purpose shall consist of a Member or Members from two thirds of the States, and a Majority of all the States shall be necessary to a Choice. In every Case, after the Choice of the President, the Person having the greatest Number of Votes of the Electors shall be the Vice President. But if there should remain two or more who have equal Votes, the Senate shall choose from them by Ballot the Vice President.

The Congress may determine the Time of choosing the Electors, and the Day on which they shall give their Votes; which Day shall be the same throughout the United States.

No Person except a natural born Citizen, or a Citizen of the United States, at the time of the Adoption of this Constitution, shall be eligible to the Office of President; neither shall any Person be eligible to that Office who shall not have attained to the Age of thirty five Years, and been fourteen Years a Resident within the United States.

In Case of the Removal of the President from Office, or of his Death, Resignation, or Inability to discharge the Powers and Duties of the said Office, the Same shall devolve on the Vice President, and the Congress may by Law provide for the Case of Removal, Death, Resignation or Inability, both of the President and Vice President, declaring what Officer shall then act as President, and such Officer shall act accordingly, until the Disability be removed, or a President shall be elected.

The President shall, at stated Times, receive for his Services, a Compensation, which shall neither be increased nor diminished during the Period for which he shall have been elected, and he shall not receive within that Period any other Emolument from the United States, or any of them.

Before he enter on the Execution of his Office, he shall take the following Oath or Affirmation:—"I do solemnly swear (or affirm) that I will faithfully execute the Office of President of the United States, and will to the best of my Ability, preserve, protect and defend the Constitution of the United States."

SECTION 2

The President shall be Commander in Chief of the Army and Navy of the United States, and of the Militia of the several States, when called into the actual Service of the United States; he may require the Opinion, in writing, of the principal Officer in each of the executive Departments, upon any Subject relating to the Duties of their respective Offices, and he shall have Power to grant Reprieves and Pardons for Offences against the United States, except in Cases of Impeachment.

He shall have Power, by and with the Advice and Consent of the Senate, to make Treaties, provided two thirds of the Senators present concur; and he shall nominate, and by and with the Advice and Consent of the Senate, shall appoint Ambassadors, other public Ministers and Consuls, Judges of the supreme Court, and all other Officers of the United States, whose Appointments are not herein otherwise provided for, and which shall be established by Law: but the Congress may by Law vest the Appointment of such inferior Officers, as they think proper, in the President alone, in the Courts of Law, or in the Heads of Departments.

The President shall have Power to fill up all Vacancies that may happen during the Recess of the Senate, by granting Commissions which shall expire at the End of their next Session.

SECTION 3

He shall from time to time give to the Congress Information of the State of the Union, and recommend to their Consideration such Measures as he shall judge necessary and expedient; he may, on extraordinary Occasions, convene both Houses, or either of them, and in Case of Disagreement between them, with Respect to the Time of Adjournment, he may adjourn them to such Time as he shall think proper; he shall receive Ambassadors and other public Ministers; he shall take Care that the Laws be faithfully executed, and shall Commission all the Officers of the United States.

SECTION 4

The President, Vice President and all civil Officers of the United States, shall be removed from Office on Impeachment for, and Conviction of, Treason, Bribery, or other high Crimes and Misdemeanors.

Article III

SECTION 1

The judicial Power of the United States shall be vested in one supreme Court, and in such inferior Courts as the Congress may from time to time ordain and establish. The Judges, both of the supreme and inferior Courts, shall hold their Offices during good Behaviour, and shall, at stated Times, receive for their Services a Compensation, which shall not be diminished during their Continuance in Office.

SECTION 2

The judicial Power shall extend to all Cases, in Law and Equity, arising under this Constitution, the Laws of the United States, and Treaties made, or which shall be made, under their Authority;—to all Cases affecting Ambassadors, other public Ministers and Consuls;—to all Cases of admiralty and maritime Jurisdiction;—to Controversies to which the United States shall be a Party;—to Controversies between two or more States;—between a State and Citizens of another State;—between Citizens of different States;—between Citizens of the same State claiming Lands under Grants of different States, and between a State, or the Citizens thereof, and foreign States, Citizens or Subjects.

In all Cases affecting Ambassadors, other public Ministers and Consuls, and those in which a State shall be Party, the supreme Court shall have original Jurisdiction. In all the other Cases before mentioned, the supreme Court shall have appellate Jurisdiction, both as to Law and Fact, with such Exceptions, and under such Regulations as the Congress shall make.

The Trial of all Crimes, except in Cases of Impeachment, shall be by Jury; and such Trial shall be held in the State where the said Crimes shall have been committed; but when not committed within any State, the Trial shall be at such Place or Places as the Congress may by Law have directed.

SECTION 3

Treason against the United States, shall consist only in levying War against them, or in adhering to their Enemies, giving them Aid and Comfort. No Person shall be convicted of Treason unless on the Testimony of two Witnesses to the same overt Act, or on Confession in open Court.

The Congress shall have Power to declare the Punishment of Treason, but no Attainder of Treason shall work Corruption of Blood, or Forfeiture except during the Life of the Person attainted.

Article IV

SECTION 1

Full Faith and Credit shall be given in each State to the public Acts, Records, and judicial Proceedings of every other State. And the Congress may by general Laws prescribe the Manner in which such Acts, Records and Proceedings shall be proved, and the Effect thereof.

SECTION 2

The Citizens of each State shall be entitled to all Privileges and Immunities of Citizens in the several States.

A Person charged in any State with Treason, Felony, or other Crime, who shall flee from Justice, and be found in another State, shall on Demand of the executive Authority of the State from which he fled, be delivered up, to be removed to the State having Jurisdiction of the Crime.

No Person held to Service or Labour in one State, under the Laws thereof, escaping into another, shall, in Consequence of any Law or Regulation therein, be discharged from such Service or Labour, but shall be delivered up on Claim of the Party to whom such Service or Labour may be due.

SECTION 3

New States may be admitted by the Congress into this Union; but no new State shall be formed or erected within the Jurisdiction of any other State; nor any State be formed by the Junction of two or more States, or Parts of States, without the Consent of the Legislatures of the States concerned as well as of the Congress.

The Congress shall have Power to dispose of and make all needful Rules and Regulations respecting the Territory or other Property belonging to the United States; and nothing in this Constitution shall be so construed as to Prejudice any Claims of the United States, or of any particular State.

SECTION 4

The United States shall guarantee to every State in this Union a Republican Form of Government, and shall protect each of them against Invasion; and on Application of the Legislature, or of the Executive (when the Legislature cannot be convened), against domestic Violence.

Article V

The Congress, whenever two thirds of both Houses shall deem it necessary, shall propose Amendments to this Constitution, or, on the Application of the Legislatures of two thirds of the several States, shall call a Convention for proposing Amendments, which, in either Case, shall be valid to all Intents and Purposes, as Part of this Constitution, when ratified by the Legislatures of three fourths of the several States, or by Conventions in three fourths thereof, as the one or the other Mode of Ratification may be proposed by the Congress; Provided that no Amendment which may be made prior to the Year One thousand eight hundred and eight shall in any Manner affect the first and fourth Clauses in the Ninth

Section of the first Article; and that no State, without its Consent, shall be deprived of its equal Suffrage in the Senate.

Article VI

All Debts contracted and Engagements entered into, before the Adoption of this Constitution, shall be as valid against the United States under this Constitution, as under the Confederation.

This Constitution, and the Laws of the United States which shall be made in Pursuance thereof; and all Treaties made, or which shall be made, under the Authority of the United States, shall be the supreme Law of the Land; and the Judges in every State shall be bound thereby, any Thing in the Constitution or Laws of any State to the Contrary notwithstanding.

The Senators and Representatives before mentioned, and the Members of the several State Legislatures, and all executive and judicial Officers, both of the United States and of the several States, shall be bound by Oath or Affirmation, to support this Constitution; but no religious Test shall ever be required as a Qualification to any Office or public Trust under the United States.

Article VII

The Ratification of the Conventions of nine States, shall be sufficient for the Establishment of this Constitution between the States so ratifying the Same.

The Word, "the," being interlined between the seventh and eighth Lines of the first Page, the Word "Thirty" being partly written on an Erazure in the fifteenth Line of the first Page, The Words "is tried" being interlined between the thirty second and thirty third Lines of the first Page and the Word "the" being interlined between the forty third and forty fourth Lines of the second Page.

Attest William Jackson Secretary

Done in Convention by the Unanimous Consent of the States present the Seventeenth Day of September in the Year of our Lord one thousand seven hundred and Eighty seven and of the Independence of the United States of America the Twelfth In witness whereof We have hereunto subscribed our Names,

G°. Washington
Presidt and deputy from Virginia

Delaware
Geo: Read
Gunning Bedford jun
John Dickinson
Richard Bassett
Jaco: Broom

Maryland
James McHenry
Dan of St Thos. Jenifer
Danl. Carroll

Virginia
John Blair
James Madison Jr.

North Carolina
Wm. Blount
Richd. Dobbs Spaight
Hu Williamson

South Carolina
J. Rutledge
Charles Cotesworth Pinckney
Charles Pinckney
Pierce Butler

Georgia
William Few
Abr Baldwin

New Hampshire
John Langdon
Nicholas Gilman

Massachusetts
Nathaniel Gorham
Rufus King

Connecticut
Wm. Saml. Johnson
Roger Sherman

New York
Alexander Hamilton

New Jersey
Wil: Livingston
David Brearley
Wm. Paterson
Jona: Dayton

Pennsylvania
B Franklin
Thomas Mifflin
Robt. Morris
Geo. Clymer
Thos. FitzSimons
Jared Ingersoll
James Wilson
Gouv Morris

Articles

In addition to, and Amendment of the Constitution of the United States of America, proposed by Congress, and ratified by the Legislatures of the several States, pursuant to the fifth Article of the original Constitution.

(The first ten amendments to the U.S. Constitution were ratified December 15, 1791, and form what is known as the "Bill of Rights.")

AMENDMENT I

Congress shall make no law respecting an establishment of religion, or prohibiting the free exercise thereof; or abridging the freedom of speech, or of the press; or the right of the people peaceably to assemble, and to petition the Government for a redress of grievances.

AMENDMENT II

A well regulated Militia, being necessary to the security of a free State, the right of the people to keep and bear Arms, shall not be infringed.

AMENDMENT III

No Soldier shall, in time of peace be quartered in any house, without the consent of the Owner, nor in time of war, but in a manner to be prescribed by law.

AMENDMENT IV

The right of the people to be secure in their persons, houses, papers, and effects, against unreasonable searches and seizures, shall not be violated, and no Warrants shall issue, but upon probable cause, supported by Oath or affirmation, and particularly describing the place to be searched, and the persons or things to be seized.

AMENDMENT V

No person shall be held to answer for a capital, or otherwise infamous crime, unless on a presentment or indictment of a Grand Jury, except in cases arising in the land or naval forces, or in the Militia, when in actual service in time of War or public danger; nor shall any person be subject for the same offence to be twice put in jeopardy of life or limb; nor shall be compelled in any criminal case to be a witness against himself, nor be deprived of life, liberty, or property, without due process of law; nor shall private property be taken for public use, without just compensation.

AMENDMENT VI

In all criminal prosecutions, the accused shall enjoy the right to a speedy and public trial, by an impartial jury of the State and district wherein the crime shall have been committed, which district shall have been previously ascertained by law, and to be informed of the nature and cause of the accusation; to be confronted with the witnesses against him; to have compulsory process for obtaining witnesses in his favor, and to have the Assistance of Counsel for his defence.

AMENDMENT VII

In Suits at common law, where the value in controversy shall exceed twenty dollars, the right of trial by jury shall be preserved, and no fact tried by a jury, shall be otherwise re-examined in any Court of the United States, than according to the rules of the common law.

AMENDMENT VIII

Excessive bail shall not be required, nor excessive fines imposed, nor cruel and unusual punishments inflicted.

AMENDMENT IX

The enumeration in the Constitution, of certain rights, shall not be construed to deny or disparage others retained by the people.

AMENDMENT X

The powers not delegated to the United States by the Constitution, nor prohibited by it to the States, are reserved to the States respectively, or to the people.

AMENDMENT XI

Passed by Congress March 4, 1794. Ratified February 7, 1795.
Note: Article III, Section 2, of the Constitution was modified by Amendment XI.
The Judicial power of the United States shall not be construed to extend to any suit in law or equity, commenced or prosecuted against one of the United States by Citizens of another State, or by Citizens or Subjects of any Foreign State.

AMENDMENT XII

Passed by Congress December 9, 1803. Ratified June 15, 1804.

Note: A portion of Article II, Section 1, of the Constitution was superseded by the Twelfth Amendment.

The Electors shall meet in their respective states and vote by ballot for President and Vice-President, one of whom, at least, shall not be an inhabitant of the same state with themselves; they shall name in their ballots the person voted for as President, and in distinct ballots the person voted for as Vice-President, and they shall make distinct lists of all persons voted for as President, and of all persons voted for as Vice-President, and of the number of votes for each, which lists they shall sign and certify, and transmit sealed to the seat of the government of the United States, directed to the President of the Senate;—the President of the Senate shall, in the presence of the Senate and House of Representatives, open all the certificates and the votes shall then be counted;—The person having the greatest number of votes for President, shall be the President, if such number be a majority of the whole number of Electors appointed; and if no person have such majority, then from the persons having the highest numbers not exceeding three on the list of those voted for as President, the House of Representatives shall choose immediately, by ballot, the President. But in choosing the President, the votes shall be taken by states, the representation from each state having one vote; a quorum for this purpose shall consist of a member or members from two-thirds of the states, and a majority of all the states shall be necessary to a choice. [And if the House of Representatives shall not choose a President whenever the right of choice shall devolve upon them, before the fourth day of March next following, then the Vice-President shall act as President, as in case of the death or other constitutional disability of the President.—]* The person having the greatest number of votes as Vice-President, shall be the Vice-President, if such number be a majority of the whole number of Electors appointed, and if no person have a majority, then from the two highest numbers on the list, the Senate shall choose the Vice-President; a quorum for the purpose shall consist of two-thirds of the whole number of Senators, and a majority of the whole number shall be necessary to a choice. But no person constitutionally ineligible to the office of President shall be eligible to that of Vice-President of the United States.

AMENDMENT XIII

Passed by Congress January 31, 1865. Ratified December 6, 1865.

Note: A portion of Article IV, Section 2, of the Constitution was superseded by the Thirteenth Amendment.

*Superseded by Section 3 of the Twentieth Amendment.

Section 1

Neither slavery nor involuntary servitude, except as a punishment for crime where-of the party shall have been duly convicted, shall exist within the United States, or any place subject to their jurisdiction.

Section 2

Congress shall have power to enforce this article by appropriate legislation.

AMENDMENT XIV

Passed by Congress June 13, 1866. Ratified July 9, 1868.

Note: Article I, Section 2, of the Constitution was modified by Section 2 of the Fourteenth Amendment.

Section 1

All persons born or naturalized in the United States, and subject to the jurisdiction thereof, are citizens of the United States and of the State wherein they reside. No State shall make or enforce any law which shall abridge the privileges or immuni-ties of citizens of the United States; nor shall any State deprive any person of life, liberty, or property, without due process of law; nor deny to any person within its jurisdiction the equal protection of the laws.

Section 2

Representatives shall be apportioned among the several States according to their respective numbers, counting the whole number of persons in each State, excluding Indians not taxed. But when the right to vote at any election for the choice of electors for President and Vice-President of the United States, Representatives in Congress, the Executive and Judicial officers of a State, or the members of the Legislature thereof, is denied to any of the male inhabitants of such State, being twenty-one years of age,* and citizens of the United States, or in any way abridged, except for participation in rebellion, or other crime, the basis of representation therein shall be reduced in the proportion which the number of such male citizens shall bear to the whole number of male citizens twenty-one years of age in such State.

Section 3

No person shall be a Senator or Representative in Congress, or elector of President and Vice-President, or hold any office, civil or military, under the United States, or under any State, who, having previously taken an oath, as a member of Congress, or as an officer of the United States, or as a member of any State legislature, or as an executive or judicial officer of any State, to support the Constitution of the United

*Changed by Section 1 of the Twenty-sixth Amendment.

States, shall have engaged in insurrection or rebellion against the same, or given aid or comfort to the enemies thereof. But Congress may by a vote of two-thirds of each House, remove such disability.

Section 4
The validity of the public debt of the United States, authorized by law, including debts incurred for payment of pensions and bounties for services in suppressing insurrection or rebellion, shall not be questioned. But neither the United States nor any State shall assume or pay any debt or obligation incurred in aid of insurrection or rebellion against the United States, or any claim for the loss or emancipation of any slave; but all such debts, obligations and claims shall be held illegal and void.

Section 5
The Congress shall have the power to enforce, by appropriate legislation, the provisions of this article.

AMENDMENT XV
Passed by Congress February 26, 1869. Ratified February 3, 1870.

Section 1
The right of citizens of the United States to vote shall not be denied or abridged by the United States or by any State on account of race, color, or previous condition of servitude.

Section 2
The Congress shall have the power to enforce this article by appropriate legislation.

AMENDMENT XVI
Passed by Congress July 2, 1909. Ratified February 3, 1913.
Note: Article I, Section 9, of the Constitution was modified by Amendment XVI.
The Congress shall have power to lay and collect taxes on incomes, from whatever source derived, without apportionment among the several States, and without regard to any census or enumeration.

AMENDMENT XVII
Passed by Congress May 13, 1912. Ratified April 8, 1913.
Note: Article I, Section 3, of the Constitution was modified by the Seventeenth Amendment.
The Senate of the United States shall be composed of two Senators from each State, elected by the people thereof, for six years; and each Senator shall have one vote.

The electors in each State shall have the qualifications requisite for electors of the most numerous branch of the State legislatures.

When vacancies happen in the representation of any State in the Senate, the executive authority of such State shall issue writs of election to fill such vacancies: Provided, That the legislature of any State may empower the executive thereof to make temporary appointments until the people fill the vacancies by election as the legislature may direct.

This amendment shall not be so construed as to affect the election or term of any Senator chosen before it becomes valid as part of the Constitution.

AMENDMENT XVIII

Passed by Congress December 18, 1917. Ratified January 16, 1919. Repealed by Amendment XXI.

Section 1

After one year from the ratification of this article the manufacture, sale, or transportation of intoxicating liquors within, the importation thereof into, or the exportation thereof from the United States and all territory subject to the jurisdiction thereof for beverage purposes is hereby prohibited.

Section 2

The Congress and the several States shall have concurrent power to enforce this article by appropriate legislation.

Section 3

This article shall be inoperative unless it shall have been ratified as an amendment to the Constitution by the legislatures of the several States, as provided in the Constitution, within seven years from the date of the submission hereof to the States by the Congress.

AMENDMENT XIX

Passed by Congress June 4, 1919. Ratified August 18, 1920.

The right of citizens of the United States to vote shall not be denied or abridged by the United States or by any State on account of sex.

Congress shall have power to enforce this article by appropriate legislation.

AMENDMENT XX

Passed by Congress March 2, 1932. Ratified January 23, 1933.

Note: Article I, Section 4, of the Constitution was modified by Section 2 of this amendment. In addition, a portion of the Twelfth Amendment was superseded by Section 3.

Section 1

The terms of the President and the Vice President shall end at noon on the 20th day of January, and the terms of Senators and Representatives at noon on the 3d day of January, of the years in which such terms would have ended if this article had not been ratified; and the terms of their successors shall then begin.

Section 2

The Congress shall assemble at least once in every year, and such meeting shall begin at noon on the 3d day of January, unless they shall by law appoint a different day.

Section 3

If, at the time fixed for the beginning of the term of the President, the President elect shall have died, the Vice President elect shall become President. If a President shall not have been chosen before the time fixed for the beginning of his term, or if the President elect shall have failed to qualify, then the Vice President elect shall act as President until a President shall have qualified; and the Congress may by law provide for the case wherein neither a President elect nor a Vice President shall have qualified, declaring who shall then act as President, or the manner in which one who is to act shall be selected, and such person shall act accordingly until a President or Vice President shall have qualified.

Section 4

The Congress may by law provide for the case of the death of any of the persons from whom the House of Representatives may choose a President whenever the right of choice shall have devolved upon them, and for the case of the death of any of the persons from whom the Senate may choose a Vice President whenever the right of choice shall have devolved upon them.

Section 5

Sections 1 and 2 shall take effect on the 15th day of October following the ratification of this article.

Section 6

This article shall be inoperative unless it shall have been ratified as an amendment to the Constitution by the legislatures of three-fourths of the several States within seven years from the date of its submission.

AMENDMENT XXI

Passed by Congress February 20, 1933. Ratified December 5, 1933.

Section 1
The eighteenth article of amendment to the Constitution of the United States is hereby repealed.

Section 2
The transportation or importation into any State, Territory, or Possession of the United States for delivery or use therein of intoxicating liquors, in violation of the laws thereof, is hereby prohibited.

Section 3
This article shall be inoperative unless it shall have been ratified as an amendment to the Constitution by conventions in the several States, as provided in the Constitution, within seven years from the date of the submission hereof to the States by the Congress.

AMENDMENT XXII
Passed by Congress March 21, 1947. Ratified February 27, 1951.

Section 1
No person shall be elected to the office of the President more than twice, and no person who has held the office of President, or acted as President, for more than two years of a term to which some other person was elected President shall be elected to the office of President more than once. But this Article shall not apply to any person holding the office of President when this Article was proposed by Congress, and shall not prevent any person who may be holding the office of President, or acting as President, during the term within which this Article becomes operative from holding the office of President or acting as President during the remainder of such term.

Section 2
This article shall be inoperative unless it shall have been ratified as an amendment to the Constitution by the legislatures of three-fourths of the several States within seven years from the date of its submission to the States by the Congress.

AMENDMENT XXIII
Passed by Congress June 16, 1960. Ratified March 29, 1961.

Section 1
The District constituting the seat of Government of the United States shall appoint in such manner as Congress may direct:

A number of electors of President and Vice President equal to the whole number of Senators and Representatives in Congress to which the District would be entitled if it were a State, but in no event more than the least populous State; they shall be in addition to those appointed by the States, but they shall be considered, for the purposes of the election of President and Vice President, to be electors appointed by a State; and they shall meet in the District and perform such duties as provided by the twelfth article of amendment.

Section 2
The Congress shall have power to enforce this article by appropriate legislation.

AMENDMENT XXIV
Passed by Congress August 27, 1962. Ratified January 23, 1964.

Section 1
The right of citizens of the United States to vote in any primary or other election for President or Vice President, for electors for President or Vice President, or for Senator or Representative in Congress, shall not be denied or abridged by the United States or any State by reason of failure to pay poll tax or other tax.

Section 2
The Congress shall have power to enforce this article by appropriate legislation.

AMENDMENT XXV
Passed by Congress July 6, 1965. Ratified February 10, 1967.
Note: Article II, Section 1, of the Constitution was affected by the Twenty-fifth Amendment.

Section 1
In case of the removal of the President from office or of his death or resignation, the Vice President shall become President.

Section 2
Whenever there is a vacancy in the office of the Vice President, the President shall nominate a Vice President who shall take office upon confirmation by a majority vote of both Houses of Congress.

Section 3
Whenever the President transmits to the President pro tempore of the Senate and the Speaker of the House of Representatives his written declaration that he

is unable to discharge the powers and duties of his office, and until he transmits to them a written declaration to the contrary, such powers and duties shall be discharged by the Vice President as Acting President.

Section 4

Whenever the Vice President and a majority of either the principal officers of the executive departments or of such other body as Congress may by law provide, transmit to the President pro tempore of the Senate and the Speaker of the House of Representatives their written declaration that the President is unable to discharge the powers and duties of his office, the Vice President shall immediately assume the powers and duties of the office as Acting President.

Thereafter, when the President transmits to the President pro tempore of the Senate and the Speaker of the House of Representatives his written declaration that no inability exists, he shall resume the powers and duties of his office unless the Vice President and a majority of either the principal officers of the executive department or of such other body as Congress may by law provide, transmit within four days to the President pro tempore of the Senate and the Speaker of the House of Representatives their written declaration that the President is unable to discharge the powers and duties of his office. Thereupon Congress shall decide the issue, assembling within forty-eight hours for that purpose if not in session. If the Congress, within twenty-one days after receipt of the latter written declaration, or, if Congress is not in session, within twenty-one days after Congress is required to assemble, determines by two-thirds vote of both Houses that the President is unable to discharge the powers and duties of his office, the Vice President shall continue to discharge the same as Acting President; otherwise, the President shall resume the powers and duties of his office.

AMENDMENT XXVI

Passed by Congress March 23, 1971. Ratified July 1, 1971.

Note: Amendment XIV, Section 2, of the Constitution was modified by Section 1 of the Twenty-sixth Amendment.

Section 1

The right of citizens of the United States, who are eighteen years of age or older, to vote shall not be denied or abridged by the United States or by any State on account of age.

Section 2

The Congress shall have power to enforce this article by appropriate legislation.

AMENDMENT XXVII
Originally proposed Sept. 25, 1789. Ratified May 7, 1992.

No law, varying the compensation for the services of the Senators and Representatives, shall take effect, until an election of representatives shall have intervened.

Lincoln's Gettysburg Address (1863)

Four score and seven years ago our fathers brought forth on this continent, a new nation, conceived in Liberty, and dedicated to the proposition that all men are created equal.

Now we are engaged in a great civil war, testing whether that nation, or any nation so conceived and so dedicated, can long endure. We are met on a great battle-field of that war. We have come to dedicate a portion of that field, as a final resting place for those who here gave their lives that that nation might live. It is altogether fitting and proper that we should do this.

But, in a larger sense, we can not dedicate—we can not consecrate—we can not hallow—this ground. The brave men, living and dead, who struggled here, have consecrated it, far above our poor power to add or detract. The world will little note, nor long remember what we say here, but it can never forget what they did here. It is for us the living, rather, to be dedicated here to the unfinished work which they who fought here have thus far so nobly advanced. It is rather for us to be here dedicated to the great task remaining before us—that from these honored dead we take increased devotion to that cause for which they gave the last full measure of devotion—that we here highly resolve that these dead shall not have died in vain—that this nation, under God, shall have a new birth of freedom—and that government of the people, by the people, for the people, shall not perish from the earth.

Appendix B
Historical Facts and Data

US Presidents and Vice Presidents

	President	Vice President	Political Party	Term
	Table App B-1 Presidents and Vice Presidents			
1	George Washington	John Adams	No party designation	1789–1797
2	John Adams	Thomas Jefferson	Federalist	1797–1801
3	Thomas Jefferson	Aaron Burr George Clinton	Democratic (Pres.) Republican (VP)	1801–1809
4	James Madison	George Clinton Elbridge Gerry	Democratic (Pres.) Republican (VP)	1809–1817
5	James Monroe	Daniel D. Tompkins	Democratic (Pres.) Republican (VP)	1817–1825
6	John Quincy Adams	John C. Calhoun	National Republican (Pres.) Republican (VP)	1825–1829
7	Andrew Jackson	John C. Calhoun (1829–1832) Martin Van Buren (1833–1837)	Democratic	1829–1837
8	Martin Van Buren	Richard M. Johnson	Democratic	1837–1841
9	William Henry Harrison	John Tyler	Whig	1841
10	John Tyler	None	Whig	1841–1845
11	James Knox Polk	George M. Dallas	Democratic	1845–1849
12	Zachary Taylor	Millard Fillmore	Whig	1849–1850
13	Millard Fillmore	None	Whig	1850–1853
14	Franklin Pierce	William R. King	Democratic	1853–1857
15	James Buchanan	John C. Breckinridge	Democratic	1857–1861
16	Abraham Lincoln	Hannibal Hamlin Andrew Johnson	Republican Democratic	1861–1865
17	Andrew Johnson	None	Democratic	1865–1869

	President	Vice President	Political Party	Term
18	Ulysses Simpson Grant	Schuyler Colfax Henry Wilson	Republican	1869–1877
19	Rutherford Birchard Hayes	William A. Wheeler	Republican	1877–1881
20	James Abram Garfield	Chester Alan Arthur	Republican	1881
21	Chester Alan Arthur	None	Republican	1881–1885
22	Stephen Grover Cleveland	Thomas Hendricks	Democratic	1885–1889
23	Benjamin Harrison	Levi P. Morton	Republican	1889–1893
24	Stephen Grover Cleveland	Adlai E. Stevenson	Democratic	1893–1897
25	William McKinley	Garret A. Hobart Theodore Roosevelt	Republican	1897–1901
26	Theodore Roosevelt	Charles W. Fairbanks (no VP 1901–1905)	Republican	1901–1909
27	William Howard Taft	James S. Sherman	Republican	1909–1913
28	Woodrow Wilson	Thomas R. Marshall	Democratic	1913–1921
29	Warren Gamaliel Harding	Calvin Coolidge	Republican	1921–1923
30	Calvin Coolidge	Charles G. Dawes	Republican	1923–1929
31	Herbert Clark Hoover	Charles Curtis	Republican	1929–1933
32	Franklin Delano Roosevelt	John Nance Garner Henry A. Wallace Harry S. Truman	Democratic	1933–1945
33	Harry S. Truman	Alben W. Barkley (1949–1953)	Democratic	1945–1953
34	Dwight David Eisenhower	Richard Milhous Nixon	Republican	1953–1961
35	John Fitzgerald Kennedy	Lyndon Baines Johnson	Democratic	1961–1963
36	Lyndon Baines Johnson	Hubert Horatio Humphrey (1965–1968)	Democratic	1963–1969
37	Richard Milhous Nixon	Spiro T. Agnew Gerald Rudolph Ford	Republican	1969–1974
38	Gerald Rudolph Ford	Nelson Rockefeller	Republican	1974–1977
39	James Earl Carter Jr.	Walter Mondale	Democratic	1977–1981
40	Ronald Wilson Reagan	George Herbert Walker Bush	Republican	1981–1989
41	George Herbert Walker Bush	J. Danforth Quayle	Republican	1989–1993
42	William Jefferson Clinton	Albert Gore Jr.	Democratic	1993–2001
43	George Walker Bush	Richard Cheney	Republican	2001–2009
44	Barack Hussein Obama	Joseph R. Biden Jr.	Democratic	2009–2017
45	Donald J. Trump	Michael R. Pence	Republican	2017–2021
46	Joseph R. Biden Jr.	Kamala D. Harris	Democratic	2021–

Admission of States into the Union

	Table App B-2	Admission of States into the Union
	State	**Date of Admission**
1	Delaware	December 7, 1787
2	Pennsylvania	December 12, 1787
3	New Jersey	December 18, 1787
4	Georgia	January 2, 1788
5	Connecticut	January 9, 1788
6	Massachusetts	February 6, 1788
7	Maryland	April 28, 1788
8	South Carolina	May 23, 1788
9	New Hampshire	June 21, 1788
10	Virginia	June 25, 1788
11	New York	July 26, 1788
12	North Carolina	November 21, 1789
13	Rhode Island	May 29, 1790
14	Vermont	March 4, 1791
15	Kentucky	June 1, 1792
16	Tennessee	June 1, 1796
17	Ohio	March 1, 1803
18	Louisiana	April 30, 1812
19	Indiana	December 11, 1816
20	Mississippi	December 10, 1817
21	Illinois	December 3, 1818
22	Alabama	December 14, 1819
23	Maine	March 15, 1820
24	Missouri	August 10, 1821
25	Arkansas	June 15, 1836
26	Michigan	January 26, 1837
27	Florida	March 3, 1845
28	Texas	December 29, 1845
29	Iowa	December 28, 1846
30	Wisconsin	May 29, 1848

	State	Date of Admission
31	California	September 9, 1850
32	Minnesota	May 11, 1858
33	Oregon	February 14, 1859
34	Kansas	January 29, 1861
35	West Virginia	June 20, 1863
36	Nevada	October 31, 1864
37	Nebraska	March 1, 1867
38	Colorado	August 1, 1876
39	North Dakota	November 2, 1889
40	South Dakota	November 2, 1889
41	Montana	November 8, 1889
42	Washington	November 11, 1889
43	Idaho	July 3, 1890
44	Wyoming	July 10, 1890
45	Utah	January 4, 1896
46	Oklahoma	November 16, 1907
47	New Mexico	January 6, 1912
48	Arizona	February 14, 1912
49	Alaska	January 3, 1959
50	Hawaii	August 21, 1959

Credits

Image Credits

Cover and p. iii *(left)*, Magite Historic / Alamy Stock Photo; Cover and p. iii *(right)*, Art Collection 2 / Alamy Stock Photo; p. xxxi, Digital Image © The Museum of Modern Art/Licensed by SCALA / Art Resource, NY

Chapter 1

P. 2, A240915-0, Department of Anthropology, Photo by Lucia RM Martino, Smithsonian Institution; p. 7, A: Manuel Cohen / Art Resource, NY, B: HIP / Art Resource, NY; p. 12, Kimon Berlin, user: Gribeco modified from Image: 1500 map by Juan de la Cosa / Wikipedia /public domain; p. 18, Image courtesy of the Newberry Library; p. 19, Kent Raney / Shutterstock; p. 22, travelpixpro / iStockPhoto; p. 24, Werner Forman / Art Resource, NY; p. 27, JORDI CAMÍ / Alamy Stock Photo; p. 30, Bridgeman Images; p. 30, Bridgeman Images; p. 31, Tibbut Archive / Alamy Stock Photo; p. 36, HIP / Art Resource, NY; p. 38, Courtesy of the Library of Congress; p. 39, Top Image: RooM the Agency / Alamy Stock Photo, Bottom Image: Heritage Image Partnership Ltd / Alamy Stock Photo

Chapter 2

P. 42, Heritage Image Partnership Ltd / Alamy Stock Photo; p. 49, Rob Fenenga / Alamy Stock Photo; p. 51, Zip Lexing / Alamy Stock Photo; p. 54, GRANGER; p. 57, Jimlop collection / Alamy Stock Photo; p. 60, WHPics / Depositphotos; p. 60, Unknown, see page for license, via Wikimedia Commons; p. 62, Lienzo de Tlaxcala, Ex-Stendahl Collection, Benson Latin American Collection, LLILAS Benson Latin American Studies and Collections, The University of Texas at Austin; p. 63, Art Collection 4 / Alamy Stock Photo; p. 69, Peter K Burian / Wikipedia / CC BY-SA 4.0;

p. 70, Rapp Halour / Alamy Stock Photo; p. 72, Historic Images / Alamy Stock Photo

Chapter 3

P. 84, State Archives of Florida / Florida Memory / Alamy Stock Photo; p. 91, ErickTErick / Wikipedia / public domain; p. 94, Efrain Padro / Alamy Stock Photo; p. 95, CC BY 4.0 / BIBLIOTECA DIGITAL HISPÁNICA BIBLIOTECA NACIONAL DE ESPAÑA; p. 101, © The Trustees of the British Museum; p. 102, © The Trustees of the British Museum; p. 102, bpk Bildagentur / Kunstbibliothek/ Staatliche Museen/Berlin/Germany / Art Resource, NY; p. 103, © The Trustees of the British Museum; p. 103, pk Bildagentur / Kunstbibliothek/Staatliche Museen/Berlin/Germany / Art Resource, NY; p. 104, Niday Picture Library / Alamy Stock Photo; p. 105, National Portrait Gallery, Smithsonian Institution; transfer from the National Gallery of Art; gift of the A.W. Mellon Educational and Charitable Trust, 1942; p. 107, The National Library of Medicine believes this item to be in the public domain; p. 108, Courtesy of the Library of Congress; p. 114, Michael Carter / Wikipedia / CC BY-SA 2.0; p. 117, Courtesy of the Library of Congress; p. 120, Courtesy of the John Carter Brown Library; p. 123, National Museum of the American Indian, Smithsonian Institution (00/1855)

Chapter 4

P. 126, The History Collection / Alamy Stock Photo; p. 132, public domain; p. 134, Universal History Archive / Contributor; p. 135, The Picture Art Collection / Alamy Stock Photo; p. 143, A: Courtesy Historic St. Mary's City, B: Courtesy of the Maryland Center for

History and Culture Object ID 1960.108.1.2.33; p. 147, Courtesy of the Museum of Indian Arts and Culture/Laboratory of Anthropology; p. 150, Smithsonian American Art Museum, Gift of Genevieve Wisel in memory of Dan Wisel; p. 151, Yale Center for British Art, Public domain, via Wikimedia Commons; p. 153, Wellcome Collection. Attribution 4.0 International (CC BY 4.0)

Chapter 5

P. 160, Pictures Now / Alamy Stock Photo; p. 169, Album / British Library / Alamy Stock Photo; p. 170, public domain; p. 172, The History Collection / Alamy Stock Photo; p. 175, Courtesy of the State Archives of North Carolina; p. 176, Chronicle / Alamy Stock Photo; p. 176, Courtesy, Georgia Archives, Vanishing Georgia Collection, sap093; p. 177, GRANGER; p. 177, Black Rice: Rice winnowing with a fanner basket, South Carolina. Courtesy of The Charleston Museum, Charleston, S.C.; p. 180, Courtesy of the Library of Congress; p. 183, The Picture Art Collection / Alamy Stock Photo; p. 187, public domain / Wikipedia; p. 188, Courtesy of UC Berkeley, Bancroft Library; p. 197, Smithsonian American Art Museum. Gift of Mrs. Joseph Harrison, Jr.

Chapter 6

P. 204, GRANGER - Historical Picture Archive / Alamy Stock Photo; p. 211, Birmingham, Ala. Public Library Archives; p. 212, public domain / Wikipedia; p. 215 Album / Alamy Stock Photo; p. 216, public domain / Wikipedia; p. 217, public domain / Wikipedia; p. 218, 53.3, Collection of the Newport Historical Society; p. 219, © National Portrait Gallery, London; p. 221, From The New York Public Library; p. 228, A: Science History Images / Alamy Stock Photo, B: Division of Cultural and Community Life, National Museum of American History, Smithsonian Institution; p. 231, The Metropolitan Museum of Art, New York; p. 232,

Courtesy of the Library of Congress; p. 233, Yale University Library; p. 239, © National Portrait Gallery, London

Chapter 7

P. 250, National Portrait Gallery, Smithsonian Institution; gift of the Morris and Gwendolyn Cafritz Foundation; p. 258, Gift of the Owners of the old Boston Museum; p. 259, The Metropolitan Museum of Art, New York; p. 257, Architect of the Capitol / public domain; p. 261, Alpha Stock / Alamy Stock Photo; p. 262, Zuri Swimmer / Alamy Stock Photo; p. 266, public domain / Wikipedia; p. 275, public domain / Wikipedia; p. 279, National Portrait Gallery, Smithsonian Institution

Chapter 8

P. 294, Heritage Image Partnership Ltd / Alamy Stock Photo; p. 299, public domain / Wikipedia; p. 303, Carnavalet Museum, History of Paris; p. 308, Courtesy, American Antiquarian Society; p. 314, Glasshouse Images/Shutterstock; p. 317, Courtesy, the Winterthur Library: Printed Book and Periodical Collection; p. 320, Image Courtesy of Pableaux Johnson; p. 321, Brynn Anderson/AP/Shutterstock; p. 323, A: The Picture Art Collection / Alamy Stock Photo. Missouri Historical Society, St. Louis., B: Missouri Historical Society, St. Louis; p. 327, public domain / Wikipedia; p. 329, Historic Collection / Alamy Stock Photo

Chapter 9

P. 338, North Wind Picture Archives / Alamy Stock Photo; p. 345, Everett Collection / Shutterstock; p. 346, Gift of Mrs. Huttleston Rogers; p. 347, Gift of Mary and Dan Solomon; p. 349, Courtesy of National Archives, photo no. 102278457; p. 359, Harvard Art Museums / Fogg Museum, Bequest of Mrs. William Hayes Fogg. Photo © President and Fellows of Harvard College; p. 366, Courtesy of the Library of Congress; p. 367, Wikipedia / public domain; p. 371, From the Collection of The Bryan Museum. Galveston, Texas;

p. 375, Courtesy of the Library of Congress; p. 376, Harry T. Peters "America on Stone" Lithography Collection; p. 380, Windrain / Wikipedia

Chapter 10

P. 386, Courtesy of the Library of Congress; p. 392, Harry T. Peters "America on Stone" Lithography Collection; p. 395, Division of Cultural and Community Life, National Museum of American History, Smithsonian Institution; p. 397, Courtesy of the Library of Congress; p. 398, Library of Congress / Contributor; p. 399, Cory Seamer / Shutterstock; p. 401, HIP / Art Resource, NY; p. 403, Courtesy of the Library of Congress; p. 404, Wikipedia / public domain; p. 405, Courtesy of the Library of Congress; p. 410, Collection of the Smithsonian National Museum of African American History and Culture, Gift of the Garrison Family in memory of George Thompson Garrison; p. 411, Courtesy of the Library of Congress; p. 416, Courtesy, American Antiquarian Society; p. 418, Courtesy of the Library of Congress; p. 419, Courtesy of the Library of Congress; p. 421, North Wind Picture Archives / Alamy Stock Photo; p. 424, The Historic New Orleans Collection

Chapter 11

P. 434, Wikipedia / public domain; p. 441, Courtesy of National Gallery of Art, Washington; p. 444, Courtesy of the Library of Congress; p. 445, Heritage Auctions, HA.com; p. 447, Smithsonian American Art Museum. Gift of Mrs. Joseph Harrison, Jr.; p. 449, Amon Carter Museum of American Art, Fort Worth, Texas; p. 454, Division of Cultural and Community Life, National Museum of American History, Smithsonian Institution; p. 455, Art Collection 3 / Alamy Stock Photo; p. 457, public domain / California Historical Society; p. 459, incamerastock / Alamy Stock Photo

Chapter 12

P. 474, © Historic New Orleans Collection / Bridgeman Images; p. 479, A road scene in California, before 1856 February 16; California lettersheet collection,

Kemble Spec Col 09; California Historical Society; p. 482, BANC PIC 1958.024:10--ffALB, from the collection Photographs of the Middle Fork of the American River and Forest Hill, the Yosemite Valley and Mariposa Big Trees, Coloma and Placerville, The Bancroft Library, University of California, Berkeley; p. 483, BANC PIC 1905.16242:095—CASE, from the collection Zelda Mackay collection of daguerreian era photography in California, The Bancroft Library, University of California, Berkeley; p. 486, GRANGER ACADEMIC; p. 488, Heritage Auctions, HA.com; p. 490, © British Library Board / Robana / Art Resource, NY; p. 493, Courtesy of the Library of Congress; p. 495, GRANGER; p. 496, Courtesy of the Library of Congress; p. 499, Courtesy of the Library of Congress; p. 500, Look and Learn / George Collection / Bridgeman Images; p. 503, Courtesy of the Library of Congress; p. 505, Wikipedia / public domain; p. 506, Sarin Images / GRANGER; p. 511, Courtesy of the Library of Congress

Chapter 13

P. 522, Courtesy of the Library of Congress; p. 528, SAN FRANCISCO HISTORY CENTER, SAN FRANCISCO PUBLIC LIBRARY; p. 530, public domain / Wikipedia; p. 532, GRANGER; p. 532, Courtesy of the Library of Congress; p. 533, Courtesy of the Library of Congress; p. 533, U.S. Post Office. Hi-res scan of postage stamp by Gwillhickers / Wikipedia; p. 537, The Picture Art Collection / Alamy Stock Photo; p. 542, Boston Athenæum; p. 554, Division of Cultural and Community Life, National Museum of American History, Smithsonian Institution

Chapter 14

P. 562, Patrons' Permanent Fund; p. 574, Harry T. Peters "America on Stone" Lithography Collection; p. 581, Harry T. Peters "America on Stone" Lithography Collection; p. 585, Gift of Erving and Joyce Wolf, in memory of Diane R. Wolf, 1982; p. 587, Collection of the Smithsonian National Museum of African

American History and Culture; p. 589, GRANGER; p. 594, Courtesy of the Library of Congress; p. 598, Division of Cultural and Community Life, National Museum of American History, Smithsonian Institution; p. 599, Division of Cultural and Community Life, National Museum of American History, Smithsonian Institution

Chapter 15

P. 608, Courtesy of the Library of Congress; p. 614, Courtesy of the Library of Congress; p. 618, Courtesy of the Library of Congress; p. 620, Courtesy of the Library of Congress; p. 623, Courtesy of the Library of Congress; p. 625, Division of Cultural and Community Life, National Museum of American History, Smithsonian Institution; p. 628, A: National Portrait Gallery, Smithsonian Institution, in memory of Kenneth G. Murphy, B: William T. Sherman Mathew Brady Studio. Glass plate collodion negative. National Portrait Gallery, Smithsonian Institution; Frederick Hill Meserve Collection; p. 634, Courtesy of the Library of Congress; p. 635, Courtesy of the Library of Congress; p. 639, Courtesy of the Library of Congress

Chapter 16

P. 646, National Portrait Gallery, Smithsonian Institution; p. 653, Sarin Images / GRANGER; p. 659, Sarin Images / GRANGER; p. 668, Division of Political and Military History, National Museum of American History, Smithsonian Institution; p. 672, National Portrait Gallery, Smithsonian Institution; p. 674, Sarin Images / GRANGER; p. 677, Sarin Images / GRANGER; p. 680, GRANGER; p. 681, GRANGER

Text Credits

Chapter 2

P. 79, from The History of the Conquest of New Spain by Bernal Díaz del Castillo, edited by Davíd Carrasco. Copyright © 2008 University of New Mexico Press

Chapter 8

P. 335, Library of Congress, Manuscript Division

Chapter 12

P. 518, Nationalhumanitiescenter.org

Chapter 13

P. 558, William Seward to Abraham Lincoln, Nocolay and Hay, eds., Lincoln Works, Vol 6, 192–201; p. 559, Montgomery Blair to Lincoln, Works, eds. Nicolay and Hay, 6: 214–217

Chapter 14

P. 603, The ALA herewith grants to OUP the full right and permission to print the words of the document as you read them in the published (1953) Collected Works of Abraham Lincoln, ed. by Roy P. Basler et al., in 9 volumes, which the ALA caused to be published by the Rutgers Univ. Press; p. 604, Courtesy of the Library of Congress

Chapter 15

P. 641, Courtesy of the Library of Congress; p. 643, Courtesy of the Library of Congress

Index

Note: Tables and figures are indicated by an italic *t* and *f* following the page number.